PLAZAS
Lugar de encuentro para la hispanidad

Robert Hershberger
DePauw University

◆◆◆

Michael Fast
University of Massachusetts

◆◆◆

Guadalupe López-Cox
Austin Community College

◆◆◆

Susan Navey-Davis
North Carolina State University

◆◆◆

Lisa Nalbone
University of Central Florida

THOMSON
™
HEINLE

UNITED STATES • AUSTRALIA • CANADA • MEXICO • SINGAPORE • SPAIN • UNITED KINGDOM

PLAZAS
Lugar de encuentro para la hispanidad
Robert Hershberger, et al.

Publisher: Wendy Nelson
Marketing Managers: Stephen Frail & Jill Garrett
Senior Production & Development Editor Supervisor: Esther Marshall
Developmental Editor: Helen Alejandra Richardson
Associate Marketing Manager: Kristen Murphy-LoJacono
Senior Manufacturing Coordinator: Mary Beth Hennebury
Project Manager: Susan Lake
Photo Researcher: Billie Porter
Interior Designers: Susan Gerould & Ha Nguyen
Illustrator: Dave Sullivan
Cover Designer: Ha Nguyen
Compositor: Pre-Press Company, Inc.
Printer: R.R. Donnelley & Sons

Printed in the United States of America
4 5 6 7 8 05 04 03

For more information contact Heinle, 25 Thomson Place, Boston,
Massachusetts 02210 USA, or you can visit our Internet site at
http://www.heinle.com

For permission to use material from this text or product contact us by
Tel   1-800-730-2214
Fax   1-800-730-2215
Web   www.thomsonrights.com

Library of Congress Cataloging-in-Publication Data
Plazas : Lugar de encuentro para la hispanidad / Robert Hershberger ... [et al.].
          p. cm.
  Includes index.
  ISBN **0-8384-1111-8** (Student Text)—ISBN 0-8384-1180-0 (IAE)
1. Spanish language—Textbooks for foreign speakers—English. I. Hershberger,
Robert.

PC4129.E5 P63 2000
438.2'421-dc21
00-058045

	CAPÍTULO Preliminar ¡Mucho gusto! 1	CAPÍTULO 1 En una clase de español: Los Estados Unidos 20	CAPÍTULO 2 En una reunión de familia: México 46	CAPÍTULO 3 El tiempo libre: Colombia 72
VOCABULARY	Hellos and good-byes Numbers 0 to 30 Question words The Spanish alphabet	The classroom Colors Foreign languages and other majors Places and buildings on campus Telling time and days of the week	The family Descriptive adjectives Nationalities Numbers 31 to 100	Sports and pastimes Places in town Months and seasons Weather expressions
FUNCTIONS	Greeting others Introductions Farewells Saying where one is from Exchanging addresses and telephone numbers Asking questions and making negative statements Telling age	Identifying people and things in the classroom Indicating relationships and specifying colors Describing everyday activities Talking about academic courses and university buildings Indicating likes and dislikes Telling time	Defining and asking about family relationships Indicating ownership and possession Describing people and things Indicating nationality Describing daily activities at home or at school	Describing leisure-time activities Expressing likes and dislikes Expressing plans and intentions Describing basic actions and places and activities in town Talking about seasons, the weather, and months of the year
GRAMMAR	Subject pronouns Present tense of the verb **ser** Sentence negation The verb form **hay** Question words and inflection The verb **tener**	Definite and indefinite articles Gender and plural of nouns The preposition **en** Present tense of regular **-ar** verbs **Me gusta** + infinitive Recycling of **hay**	The use of the verb **ser** Possessive adjectives Possession with **de(l)** Agreement with descriptive adjectives Present tense of regular **-er** and **-ir** verbs Present tense of **tener** and certain idioms	The verb **gustar** + infinitive and **gustar** + noun The contraction **al (a + el)** and **ir + a(l)** Present tense of irregular **yo** verbs **Saber** versus **conocer** The personal **a** **Tener + que** and **tener frío/calor**
CULTURE	Meeting and greeting others Spanish speakers in the United States La Paz, Bolivia Addressing others: **tú** and **usted** The telephone The Spanish-speaking world	Mérida, México Latinos in the United States Education in Latin America and Spain Telling time in the Spanish-speaking world	Hispanic names Families in the Spanish-speaking world Gestures	Sports in the Spanish-speaking world Patacones Shakira El café Fernando Botero Vallenato

	CAPÍTULO 10	**CAPÍTULO 11**	**CAPÍTULO 12**	**PLAZAS 4** 355
CHAPTER	Las relaciones sentimentales: Honduras y Nicaragua 277	El mundo del trabajo: Panamá 300	El medio ambiente: Costa Rica 330	
VOCABULARY	Personal relationships Weddings and receptions	Professions The office, work, and the job hunt Personal finances	Rural and urban geography Conservation and exploitation of the environment Animals and the wildlife preserve	
FUNCTIONS	Talking about relationships and courtship Describing recent actions, events, and conditions Describing reciprocal actions Talking about receptions and banquets Using adverbs to qualify actions Using the Spanish equivalents of *who, whom, that, and which*	Talking about professions, the office, and work-related activities Making statements about motives, intentions, and periods of time Describing the job hunt, benefits, and personal finances Making informal requests Expressing desires and intentions	Talking about rural and urban locales and associated activities and problems Using the subjunctive to express emotion and make impersonal statements Talking about the conservation and exploitation of natural resources Using the subjunctive to state uncertain, doubtful, or hypothetical situations Talking about a nature preserve, animals, and endangered species	
GRAMMAR	The present perfect tense The reciprocal **se** Adverbs Relative pronouns	The prepositions **por** and **para** Negative **tú** commands Formation of the present subjunctive The subjunctive mood and volition	The present subjunctive with emotion, impersonal expressions, and **ojalá** The present subjunctive following verbs and expressions of doubt and uncertainty The present subjunctive in adjective clauses	
CULTURE	Francisco Morazán Dating in the Spanish-speaking world Las Islas Bahías, Honduras Rubén Darío Marriage in the Spanish-speaking world	The Panama canal *La Prensa* Business protocol in the Spanish-speaking world The Balboa The Panamerican Highway Colón Free Trade Zone	Golfito, Costa Rica San José, Costa Rica Urban migration Ecology in Costa Rica Monteverde and Tortuguero Parks Piedras Blancas Park Wildlife in Costa Rica	

Acknowledgments

We would like to thank Wendy Nelson, Publisher, at Heinle and Heinle for her inspiration and confidence in us which were instrumental in both the inception and completion of this project, and to Helen Richardson, Developmental Editor, our muse and constant editorial collaborator, for her unfaltering hard work and dedication. Our gratitude and special thanks for her hard and meticulous work reflected throughout the book goes to Esther Marshall, Senior Production and Developmental Editor Supervisor. Many thanks to David Sullivan for the beautiful artwork he created for this program, Sue Gerould for her spectacular design of the *Plazas* sections, the copyeditor Susan Lake, the native reader Ana Ras, the proofreader and indexer Camilla Ayers, and the proofreaders Peggy Hines, Sharla Volkersz, Luz Galante.

We are deeply indebted to our colleagues who invigorated our thinking with their exemplary teaching and scholarship, and granted us the time to complete this project. We also owe special thanks to our Teaching Assistant Consultants: Michelle Evers (University of Kansas) and Travis Bradley and Jason Duncan (The Pennsylvania State University) who brought to this project incredible insight and perspective, and to Dr. Joel Rini of the University of Virginia who reviewed every page of the manuscript and provided much valuable overall guidance. Finally, we owe our deepest gratitude to Jim Hendrickson, whose legacy of publishing excellence lives on in the pages of this program.

Plazas Reviewers

We are grateful for the comments and suggestions made by our colleagues who reviewed this work during all stages of development. Your contribution to this project makes it truly a community effort and your expertise and experience are reflected on every page.

Ellen Abrams, Northern Essex Community College

María Álvarez, Stetson University

Diana Álvarez-Amell, Seton Hall University

Eileen Angelini, Philadelphia University

Marta Antón, Indiana University-Purdue University at Indianapolis

Frank Attoun, College of the Desert

Miriam Ayres, New York University

Helga Barkemeyer, Montclair State University

Keith Brower, Salisbury State University

Suzanne M. Buck, Duke University

Karina Collentine, Yavapai College

Richard K. Curry, Texas A&M University

John Deveny, Oklahoma State University

Doug Duno, Chaffey College

Ray Elliott, University of Texas at Arlington

José Antonio Fabres, Saint John's University

Anna Gemrich, University of Wisconsin-Madison

Ana Hnat, Houston Community College

Lina Lee, University of New Hampshire

Roxana Levin, St. Petersburg Junior College

Hilda López Laval, Chadron State College

Ernest Norden, Baylor University

Gabriela Pozzi, Grand Valley State University

Jim Rambo, DePauw University

Kay Raymond, Sam Houston State University

Steve Richman, Mercer County College

Joel Rini, University of Virginia

Mirna Rosende, County College of Morris

Vanisa Sellers, Ohio University

Julie Stephens, Central Missouri State University

Brian Stiegler, Salisbury State University

Jason Summers, University of Arkansas Fayetteville

Bruce Williams, William Patterson University

Elizabeth Willingham, Baylor University

Diane Wright, Grand Valley State University

Daniel Zalacaín, Seton Hall University

To the Student

Dear Student,

Spanish is quickly becoming a major second language of the United States. Although southern and coastal states have seen dramatic increases in Spanish-speaking populations for years, the presence of Latino communities in every large city throughout the nation is now a reality. Spanish radio and television stations are multiplying and playing to huge audiences. Latino entertainers are soaring to the top of the charts with smash hits, and Spanish can be seen on road signs, menus, and product literature. In the entertainment, leisure, and travel industries, Spanish is more prevalent than ever before. Business people, teachers, civil servants, store clerks, and especially emergency and hospital personnel are scrambling to keep up with an increasingly Spanish-speaking client base. Real-world incentives to learn Spanish are all around you. *Plazas* welcomes you to join a community of Spanish speakers not only in your class, but also in your neighborhood, work environment or travel destination. *Plazas* is based on the Five Cs of Communication, Communities, Connections, Comparisons, and Culture to ensure that your interaction with the Spanish-speaking world is dynamic and profound. In *Plazas* we not only introduce you to a language, but also to the people—their history, traditions and culture—who speak the language.

Learning Spanish successfully requires determination, good study habits, and patience. You must commit yourself to learning the language every day. Mastery is the result of daily study and practice. Everything you learn relies, to a certain extent, on previous material. If you invest the time now, what you learn later will not appear to be so daunting and foreign.

We wish you the very best in your introduction to Spanish and welcome you to the community of *Plazas.*

Bob Hershberger

Mike Fast

Guadalupe López-Cox

Susan Navey-Davis

Lisa Nalbone

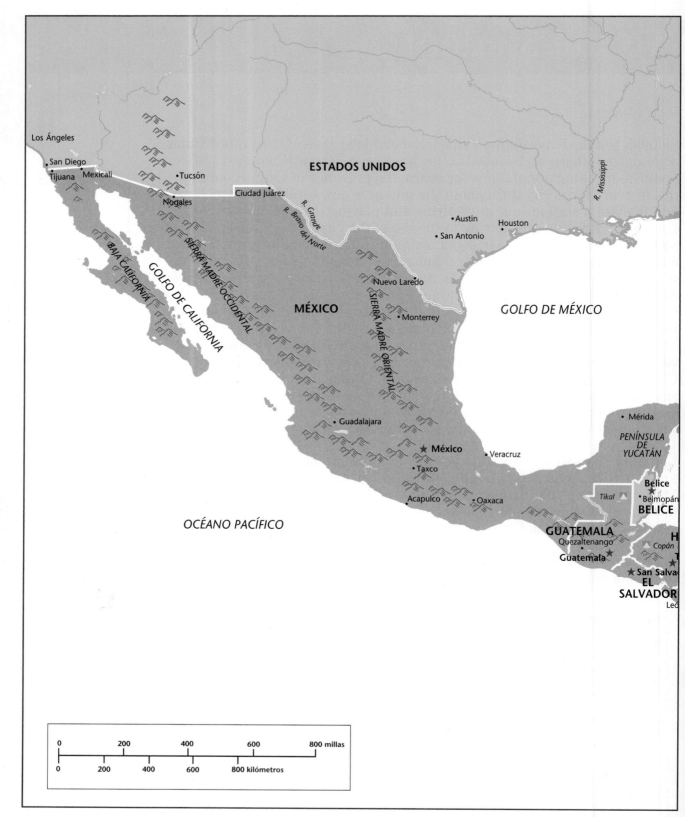

Los Ángeles

San Diego
Tijuana
Mexicali • Tucsón

ESTADOS UNIDOS

Nogales

Ciudad Juárez

R. Grande

R. Bravo del Norte

• Austin

Houston

• San Antonio

R. Mississippi

BAJA CALIFORNIA

GOLFO DE CALIFORNIA

SIERRA MADRE OCCIDENTAL

Nuevo Laredo

MÉXICO

SIERRA MADRE ORIENTAL

• Monterrey

GOLFO DE MÉXICO

• Guadalajara

★ México • Veracruz

• Taxco

Acapulco • Oaxaca

OCÉANO PACÍFICO

• Mérida

PENÍNSULA
DE
YUCATÁN

Tikal

Belice
★
• Belmopán
BELICE

GUATEMALA
Quezaltenango
★
Guatemala

Copán

H

T

★ San Salva
EL
SALVADOR

Leó

0   200   400   600   800 millas

0   200   400   600   800 kilómetros

[Note: The map of Spain is in the back of the book.]

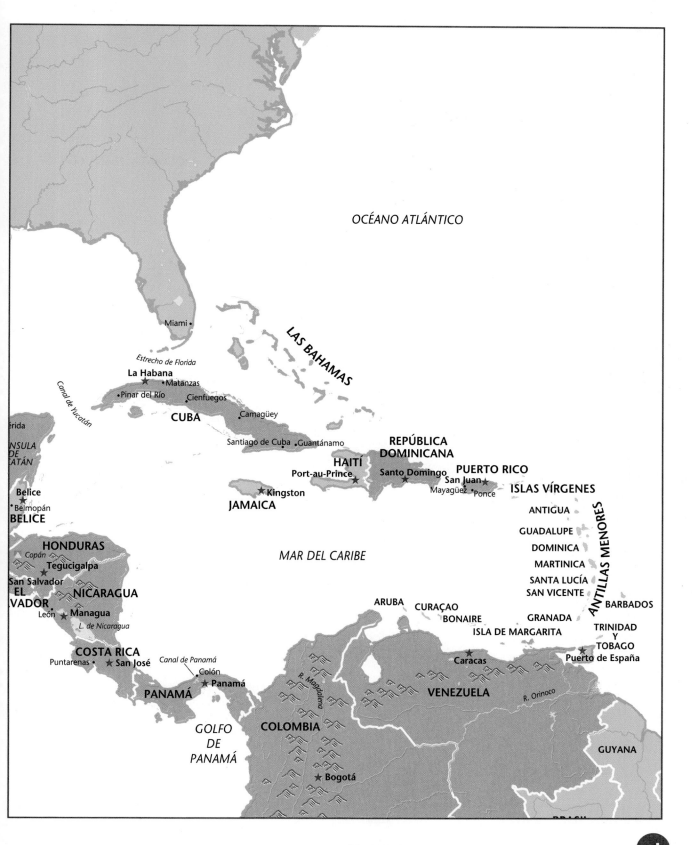

OCÉANO ATLÁNTICO

LAS BAHAMAS

Miami

Estrecho de Florida

Canal de Yucatán

La Habana
Matanzas
Pinar del Río
Cienfuegos
CUBA
Camagüey
Santiago de Cuba
Guantánamo

REPÚBLICA
DOMINICANA

HAITÍ
Port-au-Prince
Santo Domingo
PUERTO RICO
San Juan
Mayagüez
Ponce
ISLAS VÍRGENES

Kingston
JAMAICA

érida

NSULA
DE
ATÁN

Belice
Belmopán
BELICE

HONDURAS
Copán
Tegucigalpa

San Salvador
EL
VADOR
León
NICARAGUA
Managua
L. de Nicaragua

COSTA RICA
Puntarenas
San José

PANAMÁ

Canal de Panamá
Colón
Panamá

GOLFO
DE
PANAMÁ

MAR DEL CARIBE

ANTIGUA

GUADALUPE

DOMINICA

MARTINICA

SANTA LUCÍA
SAN VICENTE

ANTILLAS MENORES

BARBADOS

ARUBA
CURAÇAO
BONAIRE
GRANADA
ISLA DE MARGARITA

TRINIDAD
Y
TOBAGO
Puerto de España

Caracas

VENEZUELA
R. Orinoco

R. Magdalena

COLOMBIA

Bogotá

GUYANA

BRASIL

MAR CARIBE

Barranquilla
Cartagena
Maracaibo
Caracas
R. Orinoco
VENEZUELA
Medellín
Manizales
Bogotá
Cali
COLOMBIA

Port of Spain
TRINIDAD Y TOBAGO

Georgetown
GUYANA
Paramaribo
SURINAM
Cayenne
GUAYANA FRANCESA

OCÉANO ATLÁNTICO

Quito
ECUADOR
Quayaquil
ECUADOR
Iquitos
PERÚ
Cajamarca
Machu Picchu
Lima
Ayacucho
Cuzco
Arequipa
L.Titicaca
BOLIVIA
La Paz
Sucre
Arica
Potosí
Iquique

R. Amazo
R. Madeira
Manaus
Belem
R. Amazo
BRASIL
Recife
Brasilia
Salvador
Belo Horizonte
São Paulo
Río de Janeiro
Santos

OCÉANO PACÍFICO
Antofagasta
PARAGUAY
Salta
Asunción
CHILE
Tucumán
Porto Alegre
R. Paraná
R. Uruguay
Córdoba
URUGUAY
Valparaíso
Mendoza
Rosario
Buenos Aires
Montevideo
Santiago
La Plata
Río de la Plata
Concepción
ARGENTINA
Bahía Blanca

TRÓPICO DE CAPRICORNIO

Puerto Montt

CORDILLERA DE LOS ANDES

ISLAS MALVINAS

| 0 | 200 | 400 | 600 | 800 millas |
| 0 | 200 | 400 | 600 | 800 kilómetros |

Punta Arenas
TIERRA DEL FUEGO
Cabo de Hornos
Estrecho de Magallanes

¡Mucho gusto!

Communicative goals

In this chapter you will learn how to . . .

- Greet others
- Introduce yourself
- Say good-bye
- Say where you are from
- Exchange addresses and telephone numbers
- Ask questions and make negative statements
- Tell your age

Grammar

- Subject pronouns
- Present tense of the verb **ser**
- Sentence negation
- The verb form **hay**
- Question words and inflection
- The verb **tener**
- The Spanish alphabet

Cultural information

- Addressing others: **tú** and **usted**
- Meeting and greeting others
- The Spanish-speaking world

Vista desde una ventana de la Plaza Vieja en La Habana, Cuba

A SALUDAR Y A CONOCER A LA GENTE *(Greeting and meeting people)* In this section you will learn how to greet and say good-bye to people in Spanish while distinguishing between formal and informal situations.

UNA SITUACIÓN FORMAL: ENTRE UN PROFESOR Y UNA ESTUDIANTE[1]

UNA SITUACIÓN INFORMAL: COMPAÑEROS DE CLASE[2]

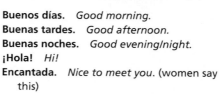

Buenos días. *Good morning.*	**Encantado.** *Nice to meet you.* (men say this)
Buenas tardes. *Good afternoon.*	**Mucho gusto.** *Nice to meet you.* (men and women say this)
Buenas noches. *Good evening/night.*	
¡Hola! *Hi!*	**El gusto es mío.** *The pleasure is mine.* (men and women say this)
Encantada. *Nice to meet you.* (women say this)	

---

[1] A Formal Situation: Between a Professor and a Student
[2] An Informal Situation: Classmates

Preguntas formales[1]   *Formal questions*

¿De dónde es usted?   *Where are you from?*
¿Cómo está usted?   *How are you?*
¿Cómo se llama usted?   *What is your name?*
¿Y usted?   *And you?*

Preguntas informales[2]   *Informal questions*

¿Cómo estás?   *How are you?*
¿Cómo te llamas?   *What's your name?*
¿Y tú?   *And you?*
¿De dónde eres?   *Where are you from?*
¿Qué hay?   *What's new?*
¿Qué tal?   *What's up?*

Respuestas   *Answers*

Así así.   *So-so.*
Bastante bien.   *Rather well.*
Bien, gracias.   *Fine, thanks.*
Más o menos.   *So-so.*
(Muy) Bien.   *(Very) Well.*
Yo soy de...   *I am (from) . . .*
Me llamo...   *My name is . . .*

Despedidas   *Farewells*

Adiós.   *Good-bye.*
Buenas noches.   *Good night.*
Chau.   *Bye. (informal)*
Hasta luego.   *See you later.*
Hasta mañana.   *See you tomorrow.*
Hasta pronto.   *See you soon.*
Nos vemos.   *See you later.*

¿NOS ENTENDEMOS?

When you ask questions in Spanish, the voice rises on the last syllable of the last word in the question and falls on the last syllable of the last word in a statement, for example:

¿Cómo está usted?

No hay más dinero.

Palabras útiles

con permiso   *pardon me, excuse me* (to ask permission to pass through)
disculpe   *pardon me* (to ask formally for someone's forgiveness or to get someone's attention)
perdón   *pardon me, excuse me* (to ask for someone's forgiveness)
por favor   *please*

¿NOS ENTENDEMOS?

The expressions **nos vemos** and **chau** are used in informal situations with the expectation that you will see the other person(s) in the near future.

➡ *Palabras útiles* are for recognition only—you will not be tested on these words. These words are provided to help you interact in Spanish.

Títulos personales   The following personal titles and their abbreviations are used in formal interactions between people. There is no standard Spanish equivalent for *Ms.;* use **señorita** or **señora,** as appropriate.

señor (Sr.)   *Mr., sir*   señora (Sra.)   *Mrs., ma'am*   señorita (Srta.)   *Miss*

¡A practicar!   *(Let's practice!)*

A.   ¿CÓMO RESPONDES? *(How do you respond?)* Answer the following questions or respond to the following statements with a logical statement. Pay attention to whether you are being addressed formally or informally.

MODELO: ¿De dónde eres tú?
    Yo soy de Houston, Texas.

1. Mucho gusto.
2. ¿Cómo se llama usted?
3. Hasta mañana.
4. ¡Hola!
5. Y tú, ¿qué tal?
6. Encantada.

B.   ¿QUÉ DICES? *(What do you say?)* Match the situations on the left with an appropriate expression from the list on the right. Remember to distinguish between formal and informal situations.

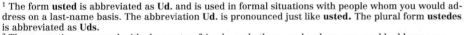

---

[1] The form **usted** is abbreviated as **Ud.** and is used in formal situations with people whom you would address on a last-name basis. The abbreviation **Ud.** is pronounced just like **usted.** The plural form **ustedes** is abbreviated as **Uds.**
[2] These questions are used with classmates, friends, and other people whom you would address on a first-name basis.

1. You're introduced to Sra. Fuertes. _____ *c*

   a. ¡Hola!
2. You're asking a child where he or she is from._____ *b*
   b. ¿De dónde eres?
3. You're greeting a stranger on the way to class at 8:00 A.M._____ *e*
   c. Mucho gusto, señora.
4. You're saying good-bye to a friend going on vacation._____ *f*
   d. ¿Cómo está usted?
5. You're asking your mother's friend how she's doing._____ *d*
   e. ¡Buenos días!
6. You're saying hello to a friend._____ *a*
   f. ¡Adiós!
7. You're leaving a party at a friend's house at 2:00 A.M._____ *g*
   g. ¡Chau!
8. You're asking an old man in the park what his name is._____ *h*
   h. ¿Cómo se llama usted?
9. You're walking to an afternoon class and you see your TA._____ *i*
   i. ¡Buenas tardes!
   j. ¡Buenas noches!

En voz alta (Out loud)

C. ¿DE DÓNDE ERES? Use the following dialog as a model to learn about another student in your class. Replace the italicized words to describe yourselves. Then change roles.

E1: ¿De dónde eres?
E2: Soy de *Milwaukee.*
E1: ¿Eres estudiante?
E2: Sí, soy estudiante.
E1: ¿Qué estudias?[1]
E2: Estudio *español.*
E1: ¿Cómo se llama el (la) profesor(a)?
E2: *La profesora* se llama *Echavarría.*
E1: ¿Cómo estás?
E2: *¡Muy bien, gracias! (Así así.)*

D. ¡MUCHO GUSTO, PROFESOR(A)! In pairs, role-play the following dialog between and instructor and a student. Follow the model.

MODELO: —Buenas tardes. Soy Tulia Gómez. ¿Cómo se llama usted?
         —Me llamo Jason Phillips.
         —Encantada.
         —Mucho gusto, profesora.
         —El gusto es mío. ¿De dónde eres, Jason?
         —Soy de Chicago.
         —¿Cómo estás?
         —Muy bien, gracias. ¿Y usted?
         —Bien, gracias.

Profesor(a):   Buenos(as) _____ . Soy _____ . ¿ _____ ?
Estudiante: Me llamo _____ .
Profesor(a):   _____ .
Estudiante: Mucho _____ , profesor(a).
Profesor(a):   _____ . ¿De dónde _____ ?

---

[1] E1: **¿Qué estudias?** *What do you study?*
E2: **Estudio español.** *I study Spanish.*

Estudiante:	Soy de _____ .
Profesor(a):	¿Cómo estás?
Estudiante:	_____ . ¿Y usted?
Profesor(a):	_____ , gracias.

ENCUENTRO *cultural*

Meeting and Greeting Others

Being warm, friendly, and affectionate are common traits in Spanish-speaking cultures. In social situations, Spanish speakers usually exchange physical hellos and good-byes; for example, Hispanic men and women often shake hands when greeting each other and when saying good-bye. A nod of the head, a wave of the hand, or saying ¡**Mucho gusto!** are not enough. In fact, if you do not shake hands when introduced to a Spanish speaker, he or she may think you are unfriendly or ill-mannered. Simple handshakes, however, may not convey enough warmth among relatives and close friends. Men who know each other well often follow a handshake with a hug and several pats on the back.

Often, when close male friends have not seen each other for a long time, they give one another a hearty embrace accompanied by several slaps on the back. Spanish-speaking teenage girls, adult women, and males and females who are good friends often greet one another by placing their cheeks lightly together and kissing the air. In Spain the kiss is given on both cheeks, whereas in Latin America and the United States, it is generally on one cheek.

E. PREGUNTAS *(Questions)* Answer the following questions based on the reading.

1. How would you greet your aunt at a family reunion?
2. How would you greet your cousin at your uncle's house?
3. Are there differences between the way you greet people and the way Spanish speakers greet one another?

EN CONTEXTO *(In context)*

The following dialog describes the Ortega family's first meeting with Raquel, the new babysitter, at their home in Miami. Notice how Mr. Ortega and Raquel use the formal form of **usted** to address one another. However, when Raquel meets Mr. Ortega's daughter, María José, she talks to the child using the informal **tú** form, appropriate when addressing someone younger than the speaker. ►►

RAQUEL:	¡Buenas noches, señor!
SR. ORTEGA:	¡Buenas noches! ¿Es usted la señorita Gandía?
RAQUEL:	Sí, soy yo. *(Yes, I am.)* Me llamo Raquel.
SR. ORTEGA:	Mucho gusto, Raquel. Yo soy Ricardo Ortega.
RAQUEL:	Encantada, señor Ortega.
SR. ORTEGA:	¿De dónde es usted?
RAQUEL:	Yo soy de aquí *(here)*... de Miami.[1] ¿Y usted?
SR. ORTEGA:	Nosotros somos de La Paz, Bolivia.[2] Llevamos un año aquí. *(We have been here for a year.)* ¿Y cómo es que usted habla tan bien *(you speak so well)* el español?
RAQUEL:	Mi madre es de Puerto Rico, y en mi barrio *(neighborhood)* hay *(there are)* mucha gente *(a lot of people)* de allí *(from there)*, de Cuba y de la República Dominicana.
SR. ORTEGA:	Raquel, quiero presentarle a *(I want to introduce you to)* nuestra hija *(our daughter)*, María José.
MARÍA JOSÉ:	¡Hola!
RAQUEL:	¡Hola, María José! ¿Cómo estás?
MARÍA JOSÉ:	Bien, gracias, ¿y usted?
RAQUEL:	Muy bien, gracias. ¿Y cuántos años tienes tú *(how old are you)*, nena?
MARÍA JOSÉ:	Yo tengo nueve años *(I am nine years old)*.
RAQUEL:	¡Dios mío! *(Oh my gosh!)* ¿Sólo *(Only)* nueve años? Pareces mayor. *(You look older.)*

¿NOS ENTENDEMOS?

Nena or **nene**, particularly in Puerto Rico, is used when an adult wants to gently get a young person's attention.

F. ¿COMPRENDISTE? *(Did you understand?)*

Decide whether the following statements are **cierto** *(true)* or **falso** *(false)*. If the statement is false, change it to a true statement. The easiest way to do this is to negate the sentence by placing the word **no** in front of the verb. If the sentence is already negated, remove the **no** before the verb.

MODELO: Raquel es la madre de María José. *(Raquel is María José's mother.)*
          Falso. Raquel no es la madre de María José.

1. El señor Ortega es boliviano.
2. Raquel es de Miami.
3. Raquel no habla bien el español.
4. La madre de Raquel es de Cuba.
5. No hay muchas personas hispánicas en la Florida.
6. María José tiene nueve años.

---

[1] Miami, Florida, has a large Spanish-speaking population as a result of large-scale immigration, especially from Cuba, Puerto Rico, and the Dominican Republic. Millions of Hispanic Americans also live in San Diego, Los Angeles, San Antonio, Chicago, and New York City.
[2] La Paz, the capital city of Bolivia, is located at 12,001 feet above sea level in the Altiplano (a high plateau region). It is the world's highest capital city and is nestled in a canyon. The center of the city's cultural life is the Plaza Murillo.

Addressing Others: *tú* and *usted*

When Spanish speakers address one person, they express the word *you* in one of two ways: **tú** or **usted**. The following guidelines should be helpful to you:

- **Tú** is an informal form of address. In general, use **tú** with someone with whom you are on a first-name basis. For example, Spanish speakers use **tú** when addressing a relative, a close friend, a person of the same age or social position, a classmate, a small child, or a pet.

- In general, use **usted** when speaking or writing to a person with a title such as **señorita, doctor, profesora,** and so forth. Spanish speakers use **usted** when addressing a stranger, a casual acquaintance other than a child, a person much older than themselves, or a person in a formal position or in a position of authority such as a supervisor, a store clerk, or a police officer. When you are unsure about whether to use **tú** or **usted,** it is wiser to use **usted.**

G. ¿TÚ O USTED? How would you address the following people? Write either **tú** or **usted** after each of the following phrases.

1. your Spanish teacher
2. a pen pal from Guatemala
3. Mirta Ramírez, an eight-year-old girl
4. Doctor Ramírez, Mirta's father
5. a waiter in a restaurant
6. an exchange student from Ecuador
7. your mom
8. your best friend
9. a classmate you just met
10. a distant relative you just met

GRAMÁTICA I: *Subject pronouns and present tense of the verb ser*

A verb is a word that expresses action (run, jump, etc.) or indicates a state of being (is, seems, etc.). The subject of the verb is either a noun or a pronoun that identifies who does the action of a verb. Subjects that are nouns include names, such as *Mary, Fred, Jerome,* and so forth. Subjects that are pronouns include words such as *you, I,* or *we.* Study the Spanish subject pronouns along with the present-tense forms of the verb **ser.**

ser *(to be)*

Singular			Plural		
yo	soy	*I am*	nosotros(as)	somos	*we are*
tú	eres	*you (informal) are*	vosotros(as)	sois	*you (informal) are*
usted (Ud.) }	es	*you (formal) are;*	ustedes (Uds.) }	son	*you (formal) are;*
él, ella		*he/she is*	ellos(as)		*they are*

vosotras	*you are* ⎤		Alicia y Regina, **vosotras sois** muy sinceras.
		sois	*Alicia and Regina, **you are** very sincere.*
vosotros	*you are* ⎦		David y María, **vosotros sois** mis amigos.
			*David and María, **you are** my friends.*

In Latin America, **ustedes** is the plural form for both **tú** and **usted**.

¡A practicar!

H. **¿QUIÉNES SOMOS? ¿QUIÉNES SON?** *(Who are we? Who are they?)* Complete the following sentences with the correct form of the verb **ser.**

MODELO: Mike Myers *es* un cómico famoso.

1. Nosotros _____ estudiantes de español.
2. Tú _____ mi compañero(a) de clase.
3. Clint Eastwood y John Wayne _____ dos actores famosos.
4. Dave Matthews _____ un músico famoso.
5. Vosotros _____ de España.
6. Ustedes _____ de Costa Rica.
7. Ella _____ muy inteligente.
8. Salma Hayek _____ mexicana.
9. Yo _____…

¿NOS ENTENDEMOS?

In most of Spain, the plural form of **tú** is **vosotros** (referring to males only or to a mixed group of males and females) and **vosotras** (referring to females only).

En voz alta

I.   **¿SÍ O NO?** Say whether you agree (**sí**) or disagree (**no**) with the following statements.

MODELOS: Whoopi Goldberg es actriz.
Sí. Whoopi Goldberg es actriz.

Whoopi Goldberg es profesora.
No. Whoopi Goldberg no es profesora.

1. Sandra Bullock es actriz.
2. Michael Jordan no es atlético.
3. Mis profesores son cómicos.
4. Robin Williams es estudiante.
5. Mis amigas son independientes.
6. Mi papá es profesor.
7. Mi mamá es bailarina.
8. Yo soy sentimental.

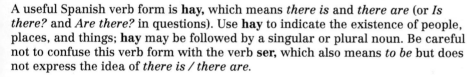

ASÍ SE DICE: *How to say there is and there are*

A useful Spanish verb form is **hay,** which means *there is* and *there are* (or *Is there?* and *Are there?* in questions). Use **hay** to indicate the existence of people, places, and things; **hay** may be followed by a singular or plural noun. Be careful not to confuse this verb form with the verb **ser,** which also means *to be* but does not express the idea of *there is / there are.*

—¿Cuántas personas **hay** en tu clase de español?

*How many persons **are there** in your Spanish class?*

—**Hay** una profesora y veintisiete estudiantes.

***There is** a teacher and twenty-seven students.*

VOCABULARIO: *Los números del 0 al 30*

0	cero	11	once	22	veintidós
1	uno	12	doce	23	veintitrés
2	dos	13	trece	24	veinticuatro
3	tres	14	catorce	25	veinticinco
4	cuatro	15	quince	26	veintiséis
5	cinco	16	dieciséis	27	veintisiete
6	seis	17	diecisiete	28	veintiocho
7	siete	18	dieciocho	29	veintinueve
8	ocho	19	diecinueve	30	treinta
9	nueve	20	veinte		
10	diez	21	veintiuno		

Uno has three different forms.

1. When counting, the form **uno** is used.
    Uno, dos, tres...   *One, two, three . . .*
2. When preceding a singular, masculine noun, the **-o** is dropped to form **un** (**un señor, un chico**).
    Hay **un** profesor en la clase.   *There is **one** professor in the class.*
3. Before a singular, feminine noun, **una** is used (**una señora, una chica**).
    Hay **una** cafetería buena en esta universidad.   *There is **one** good cafeteria in this university.*

The number **veintiuno** changes to **veintiún** before a plural masculine noun.
    Hay **veintiún** estudiantes.   *There are **twenty-one** students.*

The numbers 16 to 19 and 21 to 29 can be written either as one word (e.g., **dieciséis**) or as three words (e.g., **diez y seis**). In most Spanish-speaking countries, people prefer to use the single word.

¡A practicar!

J. **¿CUÁNTOS HAY?** *(How many are there?)* State how many units there are of the following items.

MODELO: 18 trombones
          Hay dieciocho trombones.

1. 11 naranjas *(oranges)*
2. 1 perro *(dog)*
3. 5 libros *(books)*
4. 3 mochilas *(backpacks)*

5. 1 señora *(woman)*
6. 13 pájaros *(birds)*
7. 27 globos *(balloons)*

K.   PROBLEMAS DE MATEMÁTICAS Do the following math problems with another student.

MODELOS: 2 + 2 = ?
          E1: *¿Cuántos son dos más dos?*
          E2: *Dos más dos son cuatro.*

          3 − 1 = ?
          E1: *¿Cuántos son tres menos uno?*
          E2: *Tres menos uno son dos.*

1. 3 + 3 = ?
2. 8 − 3 = ?
3. 11 + 4 = ?
4. 16 + 10 = ?

5. 6 − 2 = ?
6. 7 + 3 = ?
7. 14 + 5 = ?
8. 25 − 11 = ?

9. 4 + 2 = ?
10. 9 − 1 = ?
11. 15 − 4 = ?
12. 22 + 7 = ?

13. 6 + 1 = ?
14. 7 − 4 = ?
15. 16 − 3 = ?
16. 30 − 9 = ?

En voz alta

L.   ¿CUÁNTOS ESTUDIANTES HAY? In pairs, answer these questions about your class. Follow the model. Then switch roles.

MODELO: E1: ¿Cuántos chicos / muchachos / hombres *(boys / men)* hay en la clase?
          E2: *Hay doce chicos.*

1. ¿Cuántas chicas / muchachas / mujeres hay en la clase?
2. ¿Cuántos hombres y mujeres hay en la clase?
3. ¿Cuántos profesores hay en la clase?
4. ¿Cuántos(as)... ?
5. ¿Cuántos(as)... ?

VOCABULARIO: *Palabras interrogativas*

¿Cómo? *How?*	**¿Dónde?** *Where?*
¿Cuál(es)? *Which?*	**¿Por qué?** *Why?*
¿Cuándo? *When?*	**¿Qué?** *What?*
¿Cuántos(as)? *How many?*	**¿Quién(es)?** *Who?*
¿De dónde? *From where?*	

As an English speaker, there are a few basic linguistic points to keep in mind when using Spanish question words.

¿Cuál? *(Which?)* is used far more frequently in Spanish than in English. It has the same meaning as *What?* when someone's name, address, or telephone number is being asked. When it refers to a plural noun, it becomes **¿Cuáles?**

¿Cuál es tu nombre? ***What's*** *your name?*
¿Cuál es tu número de teléfono? ***What's*** *your telephone number?*
¿Cuál es tu dirección? ***What's*** *your address?*
¿Cuáles son tus amigos? ***Which ones*** *are your friends?*

¿Quién?, like **¿Cuál?**, must be made plural when referring to a plural group of people.

¿Quiénes son tus padres? ***Who*** *are your parents?*

¿Cuántos(as)? must agree in gender (masculine or feminine) with the noun it describes.

¿Cuántos hombres hay en la clase? ***How many*** *men are in the class?*
¿Cuántas personas hay en tu familia? ***How many*** *people are in your family?*

Notice that all question words carry accents. The accent indicates that the word is being used as an interrogative. For example, **que** without an accent means *that*. The word only means *What?* when it appears as **¿Qué?**

¡A practicar!

M. PREGUNTAS A friend of yours is doing a survey in a Spanish-speaking neighborhood. Help him fill in the missing question words. Are the survey questions addressed formally or informally?

MODELO: *¿Cómo se llama usted?*

1. ¿De _____ es usted?
2. ¿_____ es su dirección?[1]
3. ¿_____ personas hay en su familia?

---

[1] The words **su** and **sus** are formal possessive adjectives that mean *your*. You will be learning more about possessive adjectives in *Capítulo 2*.

4. ¿_____ son sus padres?
5. ¿_____ es su número de teléfono?
6. ¿_____ es la fiesta *(party)*?
7. ¿_____ es Juan tan *(so)* curioso?

En voz alta

N. INFORMACIÓN PERSONAL Circulate around your classroom to obtain the phone numbers and addresses for at least three different people. Be sure to use the appropriate mode of address (informal or formal).

MODELOS: Kyle: ¿Cuál es tu número de teléfono?
Cindy: Es el dos, tres, nueve..., cuatro, nueve, siete, uno (239-4971). ¿Y el tuyo? *(And yours?)*

Kyle: ¿Cuál es tu dirección?
Cindy: Camino Linda Vista, número tres, cinco, cuatro, siete (3547); apartamento número once (11).

O. ¿QUÉ? ¿CUÁNTOS? ¿CÓMO? Create questions in Spanish in order to find out personal information about two classmates. You want to get the following information: where they come from, their names, the names of their friends, their parents' names, their best friend's name, and so on. Take turns asking each other the questions you come up with.

ENCUENTRO *cultural*

El teléfono

In the Spanish-speaking world there is more than one way to answer the phone. For example, in Spain you can say **Diga, Dígame,** or **Sí,** whereas in Mexico it is very common to say **Bueno.** In Argentina **Hola, Aló, Sí,** and **Hable** are used, and in some parts of Colombia people answer by saying **A la orden.**

Generally, telephone numbers have seven digits, although in small cities telephone numbers may have only five or six digits. To tell someone your telephone number, you would say, for example, **cuatro, veinticuatro, trece, quince** for the number 4-24-13-15. For those countries that use only five digits, such as Bolivia, you would say, for example, **dos, dieciséis, treinta** for the number 2-1630. The verb **marcar** means *to dial the telephone.*

The numbers that precede the actual telephone number (e.g., area code, country code, city code) have different names in some countries. For example, in Spain it is **prefijo,** and in Mexico it is **clave lada** (**lada** is an abbreviation for **larga distancia** or long distance).

1. Give three ways to answer the phone in Spanish-speaking countries.
2. Based on what you've read, say these phone numbers out loud:
   a. 2-0229
   b. 12-25-15
   c. 409-1920

GRAMÁTICA II: *The verb tener*

One of the uses of the verb **tener** *(to have)* is to express age in Spanish. Spanish speakers say they *have* _____ *years* rather than they *are* _____ *years old.*
Tener is conjugated as follows:

tener *(to have)*

Singular			Plural		
yo	**tengo**	*I have*	nosotros(as)	**tenemos**	*we have*
tú	**tienes**	*you (informal) have*	vosotros(as)	**tenéis**	*you (informal) have*
Ud.		*you (formal) have*	Uds.		*you (formal) have*
él, ella }	**tiene**	*he/she has*	ellos(as) }	**tienen**	*they have*

¡A practicar!

Q. **EDADES** *(Ages)* Indicate the age of the following people using the verb **tener**.

MODELO: El profesor (30)
El profesor tiene treinta años.

1. Susana (25)
2. Lourdes (1)
3. Jorge y Héctor (19)

4. Yo (__)
5. Mi amigo(a) _____ (__)
6. Mi amigo(a) _____ y yo (__)

En voz alta

R. **¿CUÁNTOS AÑOS TIENES?** Ask a classmate how old he or she is based on the model below.

MODELO: E1: *¿Cuántos años tienes?*
E2: *Tengo* _____ . *¿Y tú?*
E1: _____ .

ENCUENTRO *cultural*

El mundo hispánico

Spanish is a Romance language spoken in Spain, Latin America (except Brazil, Belize, and the Guyanas), parts of the Caribbean, the United States, and some parts of Africa. There are over 400 million Spanish speakers in the world.

Spanish developed from Latin with influences from other languages such as German, Greek, Basque, and Arabic. It was also influenced by American languages such as Nahuatl in Mexico. In addition, diverse historical influences produced regional differences in spelling, pronunciation, and vocabulary of Spanish. These differences occur not only among the various Spanish-speaking countries, but also within those countries. For example, in most Spanish-speaking countries the words **carro, coche,** and **automóvil** all mean the same thing: *car.* On the other hand, if one wants to say *bus* in Spain one says **autobús**; in Mexico, **camión**; in Cuba and Puerto Rico, **guagua**; and in some Spanish-speaking portions of the United States, **bus.**

The fact that Spanish, like English, is still spoken and is always changing defines it as a living language, unlike Latin or Classical Greek. Spanish varies from country to country and region to region because it is a living language. Even though these differences exist, it is very rare that Spanish speakers from different places do not understand one another.

S. PREGUNTAS Answer the following questions based on the reading.

1. What is the difference between a living language and a dead language? Elaborate.
2. How do different Spanish-speaking countries use different words to express the same thing?
3. In which Latin American countries is Spanish not the principal language?

The symbol of the new Latin American era is the creation of free-trade agreements such as NAFTA and MERCOSUR. With at least 152 million consumers (46% of Hispanics worldwide), South America holds the greatest potential for the Hispanic common market, and someday hopes to rival the economic powerhouse that the European Union is forecast to become.

T. PREGUNTAS

1. Identify three countries in South America.
2. What are the populations of Venezuela and Chile?
3. What are the capitals of Argentina, Peru, and Colombia?
4. Why would the economic integration of South America rival the European Union?

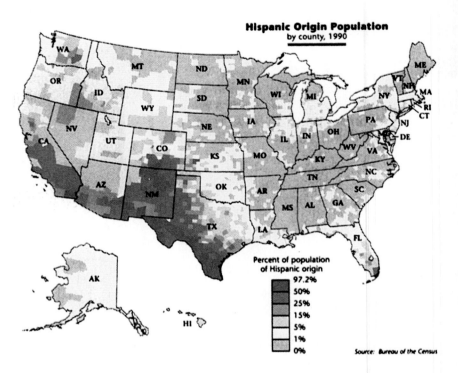

Hispanic Origin Population
by county, 1990

Percent of population
of Hispanic origin

97.2%
50%
25%
15%
5%
1%
0%

Source: Bureau of the Census

There are more than 20 million Hispanics in the United States. Hispanics are the fastest growing minority group in the nation, with the largest concentrations in California, Arizona, New Mexico, Texas, Colorado, Illinois, New York, and Florida.

U. PREGUNTAS

1. Where is Spanish spoken in the United States?
2. What states have you visited where Spanish is spoken?

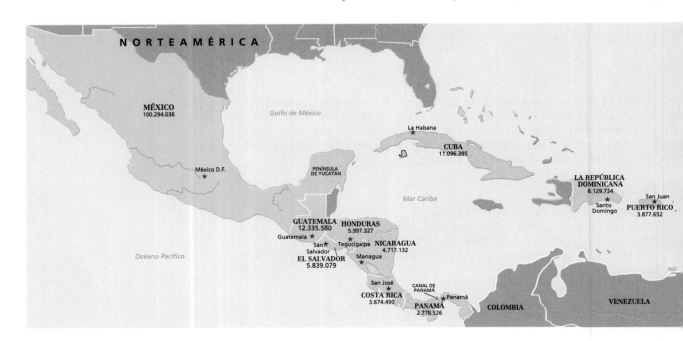

NORTEAMÉRICA

MÉXICO
100.294.036

Golfo de México

La Habana ★

CUBA
11.096.395

México D.F.
★

PENÍNSULA
DE YUCATÁN

LA REPÚBLICA
DOMINICANA
8.129.734

San Juan
★
PUERTO RICO
3.877.652

Santo
Domingo
★

Mar Caribe

GUATEMALA
12.335.580

HONDURAS
5.997.327

Guatemala ★

San ★
Salvador

Tegucigalpa ★

NICARAGUA
4.717.132

EL SALVADOR
5.839.079

Managua
★

Océano Pacífico

San José
★
COSTA RICA
3.674.490

CANAL DE
PANAMÁ

★ Panamá

PANAMÁ
2.778.526

COLOMBIA

VENEZUELA

Mexico City, the capital of Mexico, has more than 23 million inhabitants in the greater metropolitan area, making it the world's largest city. The Yucatan Peninsula in Mexico is popular for its beaches and famous Mayan ruins. Cuba, Puerto Rico, and the Dominican Republic are three Caribbean islands that have a history of both cooperation and confrontation with the United States. Costa Rica's major industry is ecotourism because of its many national parks and natural resources.

V. PREGUNTAS

1. Where is Cuba located? Is Cuba an island or a peninsula? What is the capital of Cuba?
2. Is Yucatan an island or a peninsula?
3. Where is the Panama Canal?
4. What part of the United States is in the Caribbean?

Although Spain occupies an important place in Hispanic culture, Spain's population represents only 12% of Hispanics worldwide. Spain makes up the largest part of the Iberian Peninsula; Madrid, Spain's capital, is located in the center of the country. Lisbon is the capital of Portugal, where, of course, Portuguese is spoken.

W. PREGUNTAS Indicate the correct answers.

1. España está en _____ _____.
   a. la Península Ibérica   c. Madrid
   b. Portugal   d. el centro de la península
2. La capital de España es _____ _____.
   a. Lisboa   c. Portugal
   b. Madrid   d. Europa

El alfabeto en español (The Spanish Alphabet)

The Spanish alphabet contains thirty letters:[1]

a	a	América Central
b	be	Buenos Aires
c	ce	Costa Rica
ch	che	Chile
d	de	Durango
e	e	Ecuador
f	efe	Santa Fe
g	ge	Guatemala, Gibraltar
h	hache	Honduras
i	i (i latina)	isla
j	jota	Juárez
k	ka	kilo
l	ele	León
ll	elle	Manzanillo
m	eme	México
n	ene	Nicaragua
ñ	eñe	España
o	o	océano
p	pe	Paraguay
q	cu	Quito
r	ere	Río Grande
rr	erre	Tierra del Fuego
s	ese	San José
t	te	Tegucigalpa
u	u	Uruguay
v	ve (ve chica, ve corta, uve)	Venezuela
w	doble ve (doble uve)	Washington
x	equis	Extremadura
y	i griega	Yucatán
z	zeta	Zaragoza

- All letters in the alphabet are feminine: **la a, la be, la ce,** etc.

- As opposed to the English alphabet, there are four more letters in the Spanish alphabet: **ch, ll, ñ,** and **rr.** In all dictionaries published prior to 1995, you will find separate sections for words beginning with **ch** and **ll** (**ñ** has always had its own section; **rr** is never found at the beginning of a word). Most dictionaries published after 1995, however, do not treat **ch** and **ll** separately.

- The letters **k** and **w** are not common in Spanish, and appear only in words of foreign origin, such as **karate** and **whiski.**

---

[1] The alphabet is presented here for your information only. Pronunciation is practiced extensively in the Lab Manual and CD-ROM. Some Spanish speakers argue that there are only 28 letters, no longer considering **ch** and **ll** to be part of the alphabet.

Cómo saludar *How to greet*

Buenos días. *Good morning.*
Buenas tardes. *Good afternoon.*
Buenas noches. *Good evening (night).*

¡Hola! *Hi!* (informal)
¿Qué tal? *What's up?* (informal)
¿Qué hay? *What's new?* (informal)

¿Cómo estás? *How are you?* (informal)
¿Cómo está usted? *How are you?* (formal)

Cómo contestar *How to answer*

Bastante bien. *Rather well.*
Bien, gracias. *Fine, thanks.*

Más o menos. *So-so.*
(Muy) Bien. *(Very) Well.*
Así así. *So-so.*

¿Y tú? *And you?* (informal)
¿Y usted? *And you?* (formal)

Presentaciones *Introductions*

¿Cómo se llama usted? *What's your name?* (formal)
¿Cómo te llamas? *What's your name?* (informal)

¿Cuál es tu nombre? *What's your name?* (informal)
Me llamo... *My name is . . .*
El gusto es mío. *The pleasure is mine.*

Encantado(a). *Nice to meet you.*
Mucho gusto. *Nice to meet you.*
Soy... *I am . . .*
Yo soy de... *I'm from . . .*

Cómo despedirse *How to say good-bye*

Adiós. *Good-bye.*
Buenas noches. *Good night.*
Chau. *Bye.* (informal)

Hasta luego. *See you later.*
Hasta mañana. *See you tomorrow.*
Hasta pronto. *See you soon.*

Nos vemos. *See you later.*

Los números *Numbers*

cero *zero*
uno *one*
dos *two*
tres *three*
cuatro *four*
cinco *five*
seis *six*
siete *seven*

ocho *eight*
nueve *nine*
diez *ten*
once *eleven*
doce *twelve*
trece *thirteen*
catorce *fourteen*
quince *fifteen*

dieciséis *sixteen*
diecisiete *seventeen*
dieciocho *eighteen*
diecinueve *nineteen*
veinte *twenty*
veintiuno *twenty-one*
veintidós *twenty-two*
veintitrés *twenty-three*

veinticuatro *twenty-four*
veinticinco *twenty-five*
veintiséis *twenty-six*
veintisiete *twenty-seven*
veintiocho *twenty-eight*
veintinueve *twenty-nine*
treinta *thirty*

Palabras interrogativas *Question words*

¿Cómo? *How?*
¿Cuál(es)? *Which?*
¿Cuándo? *When?*

¿Cuántos(as)? *How many?*
¿De dónde? *From where?*
¿Dónde? *Where?*

¿Por qué? *Why?*
¿Qué? *What?*
¿Quién(es)? *Who?*

Cómo pedir información *How to ask for information*

¿Cuál es tu dirección? *What's your address?* (informal)
¿Cuál es tu número de teléfono? *What's your telephone number?* (informal)

¿De dónde es usted? *Where are you from?* (formal)

¿De dónde eres tú? *Where are you from?* (informal)

Verbos *Verbs*

hay *there is, there are*
ser *to be*
tener *to have*

Pronombres *Pronouns*

él *he*
ella *she*
ellas *they*
ellos *they*

nosotros(as) *we*
tú *you* (informal)
usted (Ud.) *you* (formal)

ustedes (Uds.) *you* (formal plural in Spain; formal and informal plural in Latin Amer.)

vosotros(as) *you* (informal plural in parts of Spain)
yo *I*

Expresión idiomática *Idiomatic expression*

¡Qué casualidad! *What a coincidence!*

En una clase de español: Los Estados Unidos

Communicative goals

In this chapter you will learn how to . . .

- Identify people and things in the classroom
- Indicate relationships and specify colors
- Describe everyday activities
- Talk about academic courses and university buildings
- Indicate likes and dislikes
- Tell time

Grammar

- Definite and indefinite articles
- Gender and plural of nouns
- The preposition **en**
- Present tense of regular **-ar** verbs
- **Me gusta** + infinitive
- Recycling of **hay**

Cultural information

- Latinos in the United States
- Education in Latin America and Spain
- Telling time in the Spanish-speaking world

La Plaza de Rockefeller, Nueva York, Estados Unidos

EN LA SALA DE CLASE DE LA PROFESORA MUÑOZ *(In Professor Muñoz's class)*
In this section you will practice identifying people and things in the classroom.
How does Professor Muñoz's class compare to your own?

Otras cosas	*Other things*	Otras personas	*Other people*
el dinero	*money*	el (la) amigo(a)	*friend*
el examen	*exam*	el (la) compañero(a)	
la lección	*lesson*	de cuarto (de clase)	*roommate (classmate)*
la palabra	*word*	el hombre	*man*
la tarea	*homework*	la mujer	*woman*
		el (la) novio(a)	*boyfriend, girlfriend*

¿NOS ENTENDEMOS?

In Latin America, *computer* is either **la computadora** or **el computador**. In Spain it is generally called **el ordenador**.

Palabras útiles

el (la) bibliotecario(a)   *librarian*
el (la) consejero(a)   *adviser*
el (la) decano(a)   *dean*
el (la) presidente de la universidad   *president of the university*
el (la) secretario(a)   *secretary*

➡ *Palabras útiles* are for recognition only; you will not be tested on these words. These words are provided to help you describe your university better.

¡A practicar!

A. **¿CIERTO O FALSO?** Study the drawing of Professor Muñoz's classroom above and then decide whether the following statements are true (**cierto**) or false (**falso**). If the statement is false, correct it to make a true statement.

MODELO: Hay doce mujeres en la clase.
Falso. Hay diez mujeres en la clase.

1.   Hoy es martes.
2.   La señorita Muñoz es profesora de francés.

3. Todos los estudiantes son hombres.
4. Dos estudiantes tienen mochila.
5. Todos los estudiantes tienen el libro de texto.
6. Es una clase de matemáticas.
7. Hay una pluma en el escritorio de la profesora.
8. Un hombre escribe con bolígrafo.

B. **¿CUÁNTOS HAY EN LA CLASE?** Based on the drawing on page 21, state the number of each of the items listed below. Remember that **uno** changes to **una** before a singular feminine noun and changes to **un** before a singular masculine noun.

MODELO: Hay _____ estudiante(s) en la clase.
Hay quince estudiantes en la clase.

1. Hay _____ tiza(s) en la clase.
2. Hay _____ mujer(es) en la clase.
3. Hay _____ hombre(s) en la clase.
4. Hay _____ luz (luces) en la clase.
5. Hay _____ mapa(s) en la clase.
6. Hay _____ cosas *(things)* en la pared *(wall)*. Son: el reloj,
   _____, _____, _____.

En voz alta

C. **¿CUÁNTOS... HAY?** Working with two of your classmates, take turns asking about the quantities of the items listed below for your classroom. Remember to use **¿Cuántos... ?** for plural masculine nouns and **¿Cuántas... ?** for plural feminine nouns.

MODELO: estudiantes
E1: *¿Cuántos estudiantes hay en la clase?*
E2: *Hay quince estudiantes en la clase.*

1. cuadernos	6. mujeres
2. lápices	7. profesores(as)
3. bolígrafos	8. tizas
4. diccionarios	9. borradores
5. hombres	10. estudiantes inteligentes

D. **LA CLASE IDEAL** Working with a partner, design the ideal classroom. One student describes the room to the other who draws it. The student who draws the classroom should then describe the drawing to the class.

MODELO: *En la clase ideal, hay muchos amigos, pero no hay un profesor.*

E. **¿ESTÁS DE ACUERDO?** *(Do you agree?)* Below is a list of ideal characteristics for people you know in and outside of class. If you agree with a statement, give an example of someone you know. If you disagree, indicate the characteristic that makes the statement true for you.

MODELO: El profesor ideal es generoso.
Sí, para mí (for me), *el profesor ideal es generoso. El profesor Jones es muy generoso.*
o: *No, para mí, el profesor ideal no es generoso. El profesor ideal es inteligente.*

1. El amigo ideal es paciente.
2. La novia ideal es independiente.
3. El novio ideal es romántico.
4. El compañero de cuarto ideal es interesante.
5. La compañera de clase ideal es inteligente.
6. El estudiante ideal es honesto.

VOCABULARIO: *Los colores*

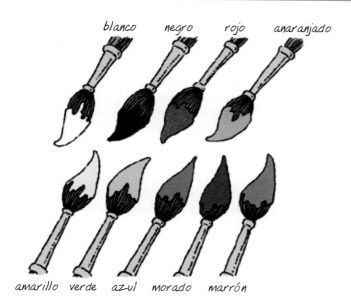

blanco   negro   rojo   anaranjado

amarillo   verde   azul   morado   marrón

Colors, like other adjectives, must agree in gender and number with the noun they describe.

El papel es roj**o**.   *The paper is **red**.*
La mochila es roj**a**.   *The backpack is **red**.*
Las plumas son roj**as**.   *The pens are **red**.*

The colors **verde** and **azul** do not change when used with a feminine singular noun.

La pizarra es **verde**.   *The blackboard is **green**.*
La mochila es **azul**.   *The backpack is **blue**.*

¿NOS ENTENDEMOS?

The color brown has more than one name in Spanish. It can be **color café, castaño, moreno,** or **color pardo. Color café** tends to refer to the color of eyes, while **castaño** and **moreno** refer to hair color.

¡A practicar!

F. **¿DE QUÉ COLOR ES... ?** Match the following to the colors most generally associated with them.

1. _____ EE.UU. (los Estados Unidos de América)   a. rojo
2. _____ Sierra Club, Greenpeace   b. rojo, azul y blanco
3. _____ los Bulls de Chicago   c. rojo y negro
4. _____ Coca-Cola   d. marrón
5. _____ chocolate   e. verde

En voz alta

G. MUCHOS COLORES Using the colors you have learned, describe the colors of the following items to a partner.

MODELO: tu *(your)* bolígrafo
Mi bolígrafo es anaranjado.

1. tu mochila
2. la pizarra
3. tu bolígrafo

4. los ojos *(eyes)* del (de la) profesor(a)
5. los escritorios
6. tu casa

EN CONTEXTO

Ana Guadalupe Camacho Ortega, a prospective student at the University of Chicago whose family plans to move to Illinois from Puerto Rico next year, is talking to Claudio Fuentes, a teaching assistant for Professor Muñoz. Ana is telling Claudio about her studies at the Universidad de San Juan.

CLAUDIO: ¡Hola! Soy Claudio Fuentes. ¿Cómo te llamas?

ANA: Ana Camacho. Mucho gusto.

CLAUDIO: El gusto es mío. ¿De dónde eres, Ana?

ANA: Soy de Puerto Rico. Ahora *(Right now)* estudio *(I study)* en la Universidad de San Juan. ¿Y tú?

CLAUDIO: Este... Originalmente soy de Mérida, Yucatán.[1] Pero estudio *(I have been studying)* en esta universidad hace dos años. ¿Qué estudias allí *(there)*, Ana?

ANA: Sicología, geografía, francés, alemán e inglés.[2]

CLAUDIO: Ah, eres estudiante de lenguas, ¿verdad?

ANA: Sí. Deseo ser intérprete. Y tú, ¿qué estudias aquí?

CLAUDIO: Yo estudio literatura y cultura latinoamericana.

ANA: ¡Genial! ¿Hay muchos hispanohablantes *(native speakers)* en tus clases?

CLAUDIO: Sí, hay varios *(several)*. Algunos de ellos tienen dos especialidades. Ahora hay estudiantes que combinan el español con el inglés, la computación, la administración de empresas, con las ciencias...

ANA: ¡Parece que *(It appears that)* el español es muy popular!

CLAUDIO: ¡Sí! Pues, la verdad es que *(the truth is that)* ahora hay muchas personas en los Estados Unidos que hablan *(that speak)* español. Los estudiantes que toman *(take)* clases de español aquí frecuentemente lo usan después *(use it later)* cuando trabajan *(they work)* en ciudades como *(like, such as)* Miami, Nueva York, Chicago y Los Ángeles.

¿NOS ENTENDEMOS?

In the same way that English speakers say *umm* . . . to indicate a pause in their train of thought, Spanish speakers use words such as **pues** *(well . . .)* and **este.**

---

[1] Merida is the capital of the Mexican state of Yucatan, located 955 miles southeast of Mexico City in the Yucatan Peninsula. Merida's Plaza Mayor, also called Plaza de la Constitución, was built from rocks that were once used in Mayan temples.

[2] The word **y** *(and)* becomes **e** before a word beginning with **i** or **hi.** The conjunction **o** *(or)* becomes **u** before a word beginning with **o** or **ho.** Both of these changes occur for pronunciation reasons. Note examples: **Hablo español e inglés. El padre e hijo son amables. ¿Te llamas Omar u Oscar? ¿Estudiamos mañana u hoy?**

H. ¿COMPRENDISTE? *(Did you understand?)* Indicate whether the following statements are true (**cierto**) or false (**falso**). If a statement is false, correct it to make a true statement.

1. Ana is a student at the University of Chicago.
2. Ana is from the Yucatan Peninsula.
3. Claudio studies Spanish history.
4. Ana studies science.
5. In the department, there are only a few students who are native speakers.
6. Many students combine Spanish with other majors.
7. Many former students use their Spanish when working abroad.

ENCUENTRO *cultural*

El español en los Estados Unidos

Éstas son unas palabras nuevas para la lectura:

la mayoría *majority*
desde *from*
algunos *some*
emigraron *emigrated*
el estado libre asociado *free associated state*
llegaron *arrived*
ha aumentado *has grown*
dado que *since, due to*

Entre los grupos hispanos en los Estados Unidos, el de los mexicanos es el más grande porque representa un 60% (sesenta por ciento) del total de esta población. **La mayoría** de los hispanos de origen mexicano vive en los estados de Tejas, Nuevo México y California; muchos viven en los estados de Arizona e Illinois también. Muchas familias mexicanas están aquí **desde** la colonización española de las Américas. **Algunos** mexicanos **emigraron** después de la declaración de la independencia de Tejas en 1836. La Revolución Mexicana de 1910 causó otro movimiento migratorio a los Estados Unidos.

Los puertorriqueños son ciudadanos de los Estados Unidos porque Puerto Rico es un **estado libre asociado** de los Estados Unidos. La mayoría de los puertorriqueños que no vive en la isla vive en Nueva York y habla español e inglés.

Otro grupo importante de hispanos es el de los cubanos que viven en su mayoría en Miami y que **llegaron** a este territorio después de la Revolución Cubana. Ellos hablan tanto inglés como español. En los últimos años la población de hispanos que llega de Centroamérica y Sudamérica **ha aumentado**. **Dado que** hay diferencias culturales dentro de la población hispana de este país, hay mucha variedad en el español que habla cada grupo, en la pronunciación y también en el vocabulario.

Para pensar: ¿De dónde es tu familia originalmente? ¿Sabes algo de ese país? ¿Tiene tu familia algunas costumbres de otros países?

PREGUNTAS Answer the following questions based on what you read.

1. The largest Spanish-speaking population living in the United States is:
   a. Cuban   **b.** Mexican American   **c.** Puerto Rican
2. Select one of the Spanish-speaking groups that has lived in the United States since the Spanish colonization.
   a. Mexican Americans   **b.** Puerto Ricans   **c.** Cubans
3. Choose the country that is associated with the United States and whose citizens are U.S. citizens.
   a. Puerto Rico   **b.** Cuba   **c.** Mexico

GRAMÁTICA I: *Definite and indefinite articles and how to make nouns plural*

A noun names a person (**Ana, estudiante**), a place (**Mérida, ciudad**), a thing (**libro, computadora**), or a concept (**clase, español**). In Spanish, all nouns are classified as having a gender—either masculine or feminine. A noun is often preceded by a definite article—**el, la, los, las** *(the)*—or by an indefinite article—**un, una** *(a, an)*, **unos, unas** *(some)*. The words **un** and **una** can mean *a* or *an* as well as *one*, depending on the context.

How to determine gender of nouns

1. In Spanish, nouns referring to males and most nouns ending in **-o** are masculine. Nouns referring to females and most nouns ending in **-a** are feminine. Definite and indefinite articles must match the gender (masculine or feminine) and number of the nouns they modify.

el/un amig**o**	**la/una** amig**a**
el/un escritori**o**	**la/una** bibliotec**a**

2. Most nouns ending in **-l** or **-r** are masculine, and most nouns ending in **-d** or **-ión** are feminine.

el/un pape**l**	**la/una** universida**d**
el/un borrado**r**	**la/una** lecci**ón**

3. Some nouns do not conform to the rules stated here. One way to remember the gender of these nouns is to learn the definite articles and the nouns together, for example, **la clase**, **el día** *(day)*, **el mapa**, and **la mano** *(hand)*.

How to make nouns plural

In Spanish, all nouns are either singular or plural. Definite articles (**el, la, los, las**) and indefinite articles (**un, una, unos, unas**) must match the number (singular or plural) of the nouns they modify.

To make Spanish nouns plural, add **-s** to nouns ending in a vowel, and add **-es** to nouns ending in a consonant.

Singular	**Plural**
el amig**o**	**los** amigo**s**
la amig**a**	**las** amiga**s**
una clas**e**	**unas** clase**s**
un profeso**r**	**unos** profesore**s**
una universida**d**	**unas** universidade**s**

Here are two additional rules for making nouns plural:

1. For nouns ending in **-án, -és,** or **-ión,** drop the accent mark before adding **-es.**

el/un alem**án**	**los/unos** alem**anes**
el/un japon**és**	**los/unos** japon**eses**
la/una lec**ción**	**las/unas** lec**ciones**

2. For nouns ending in **-z,** drop the **-z,** then add **-ces.**

el/un lápi**z**	**los/unos** lápi**ces**

Spanish speakers do not consider nouns as being male or female (except when referring to people or animals). Therefore, the terms *masculine* and *feminine* are simply labels for classifying nouns.

¡A practicar!

J. *¿EL, LA, LOS O LAS?* Give the correct definite article for each of the nouns below.

MODELO: *las* mochilas

1. _____ mapa
2. _____ universidad
3. _____ exámenes
4. _____ tarea
5. _____ bolígrafo
6. _____ lecciones
7. _____ compañero de clase
8. _____ salas de clase

K. ¿QUÉ ES? Identify the following objects using the indefinite articles **un, una, unos,** or **unas.**

MODELO: calendario
Es un calendario.

1.

2.

3.

4.

5.

L. ¿HAY UNA PROFESORA EN LA CLASE? Use indefinite and definite articles together to complete the following statements.

MODELO: Hay *un* libro en *el* escritorio.

1. Hay _____ mujer en _____ silla.
2. Hay _____ diccionario en _____ clase.
3. Hay _____ plumas en _____ mochila.
4. Hay _____ cuadernos en _____ escritorio.

ASÍ SE DICE: *The preposition en*

The preposition **en,** as shown in the last activity, is used in Spanish to mean *on* or *in*. Consider the following examples:

Hay un cuaderno **en** el escritorio. *There is a notebook **on** the desk.*
Hay una pluma **en** la mochila. *There is a pen **in** the backpack.*
En la clase, hablamos **en** español. *In class, we speak **in** Spanish.*

¡A practicar!

M. ¿EN O EN? Make sentences with the following words using the preposition **en.** Use the appropriate indefinite and definite articles.

MODELO: hay / calculadora / escritorio
Hay una calculadora en el escritorio.

1. hay / palabra / pizarra
2. hay / libros / silla
3. hay / estudiante / sala de clase
4. hay / diccionario / mochila
5. hay / libro de texto de español / escritorio

En voz alta

N. CUESTIONARIO: ¿CUÁNTOS TIENES? Form the plural of each noun in the questionnaire, and then ask two of your classmates how many he/she has of each.

MODELO: libro
libros
E1: *¿Cuántos libros tienes en la mochila?*
E2: *Yo tengo tres libros de texto en la mochila.*

CUESTIONARIO

En esta clase

1. compañero de clase_____

2. amigo(a) _____

Este semestre

3. compañero(a) de cuarto _____

4. profesor(a) _____

5. clase _____

En la mochila

6. cuaderno _____

7. bolígrafo _____

En el cuarto

8. computadora _____

9. silla _____

10. televisor_____

VOCABULARIO: *Lenguas extranjeras y otras materias*

In this section you will learn how to talk about foreign languages and other academic courses and majors in Spanish.

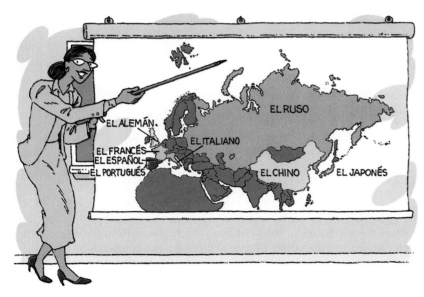

EL ALEMÁN
EL FRANCÉS
EL ESPAÑOL
EL PORTUGUÉS
EL ITALIANO
EL RUSO
EL CHINO
EL JAPONÉS

¿NOS ENTENDEMOS?

In some Spanish-speaking countries, like Argentina and Spain, **el español** is interchangeably referred to as **el castellano,** or Castillian Spanish. **El castellano** originated from the language spoken in the Spanish region of **Castilla.**

Cursos y especializaciones   *Courses and majors*

la administración de
  empresas   *business
  administration*
el arte   *art*
la biología   *biology*
las ciencias   *science*
la computación   *computer
  science*
el derecho   *law*
la economía   *economics*

la educación   *education*
la filosofía   *philosophy*
la física   *physics*
la geografía   *geography*
la historia   *history*
la ingeniería   *engineering*
el inglés   *English*
la literatura   *literature*
las matemáticas   *math*
la medicina   *medicine*

la música   *music*
los negocios   *business*
el periodismo   *journalism*
la pintura   *painting*
la química   *chemistry*
la sicología   *psychology*
la sociología   *sociology*
el teatro   *theater*

Palabras útiles

la arquitectura   *architecture*
el baile/la danza   *dance*
la contabilidad   *accounting*

la ecología   *ecology*
la geología   *geology*
las humanidades   *humanities*

el turismo   *tourism*
la zoología   *zoology*

¡A practicar!

O.   ¿HABLAS ALEMÁN? *(Do you speak German?)* Match the greetings on the left with the language on the right.

1. _____ Bonjour!
2. _____ Bom día, Pele!
3. _____ ¿Qué tal?
4. _____ Molto bene!
5. _____ Ni ho ma?
6. _____ Sprechen sie Deutsch?
7. _____ Kak diela?
8. _____ Kon' nichiwa

a. el alemán
b. el español
c. el francés
d. el ruso
e. el chino
f. el japonés
g. el italiano
h. el portugués

P.   ¿QUÉ LENGUA HABLA? *(What language does he/she speak?)* State where each person is from and the native language he/she speaks (**habla**). Do you speak any other languages besides English and Spanish?

MODELO: Antonio Banderas / España
          Es de España y habla español.

1. Gerhard Schröder / Alemania
2. Marcel Marceau / Francia
3. Sun Wen / China
4. Masao Miyoshi / Japón
5. Fernanda Montenegro / Brasil
6. Boris Yeltsin / Rusia
7. Giorgio Armani / Italia
8. Yo soy _____ y hablo *(I speak)* _____, _____,...
9. Mi amigo(a) _____ es de _____ y habla _____, _____,...
10. Mis padres son de _____ y hablan *(they speak)* _____, _____,...

En voz alta

Q.   ¡UN DESASTRE EN LA LIBRERÍA! *(A disaster in the bookstore!)* An earthquake has left all of the textbooks in the bookstore on the floor. Help put them back on the shelf by indicating the subject for which each book is intended.

MODELO: *Beginning Calculus*
          Es para una clase de matemáticas.

1. *Introduction to Shakespeare*
2. *The Life and Works of Pablo Picasso*
3. *Voilà!*
4. *Fresh-Water Ecosystems*
5. *The Criminal Mind*
6. *Designing the User Interface*
7. *Using Statistics in Today's Markets*
8. *Principles of Organic Chemistry*
9. *Copyrights and You*
10. *Strategies of Classroom Management*
11. *Interpretations of the Mexican Revolution*

R. MIS ESTUDIOS Y MIS LIBROS Create sentences that state what books you use for the following classes.

MODELO: español
*Mi libro de español se llama **Plazas**.*

1. matemáticas   2. inglés   3. geografía   4–6. ¿ ?

ENCUENTRO *cultural*

La educación en Latinoamérica y España

Éstas son unas palabras nuevas para la lectura:

dura *lasts*
el cognado falso *false cognate*
el politécnico *technical school*
gratis *free*
la carrera *major, field of study*
las pensiones *boarding houses*

la oposición *competitive examination for entrance into a school or job*
la matrícula *tuition*

Para pensar: ¿Cómo son las escuelas en tu país? Describe las etapas *(stages)* diferentes y compáralas al sistema del mundo hispano.

En el mundo hispánico, la escuela primaria tiene varios nombres. A veces se llama escuela básica, escuela primaria, o simplemente escuela o primaria. **Dura** seis o siete años. La escuela secundaria también tiene muchos nombres: liceo, bachillerato, instituto, escuela superior, o secundaria, y dura cinco o seis años. El colegio es generalmente una escuela particular para niños de menos de 17 años. La palabra colegio es **un cognado falso** inglés; la palabra college es universidad.

Después de terminar la primaria, los latinoamericanos y los españoles van a un **politécnico** o estudian varios años más en la secundaria. Hay muy pocos *junior* o *community colleges* en el mundo hispánico. Después de terminar la secundaria, algunos estudiantes van a la universidad.

La oposición o examen de ingreso para entrar en una universidad pública es difícil. **La matrícula** es **gratis** en muchas universidades públicas. Por eso, los estudiantes que desean ir a la universidad tienen que tomar exámenes de ingreso muy rigurosos. Una vez aceptados en la universidad, los estudiantes **siguen** una **carrera** en un programa muy estructurado.

Pocas universidades tienen residencias estudiantiles como en los Estados Unidos y en Canadá. Los estudiantes generalmente viven en sus casas con sus padres, en **pensiones** o en casas particulares.

S. **PREGUNTAS** Answer the following questions based on the reading.

1. Give a name for each of the following schools where you live.
   a. escuela primaria   **b.** secundaria   **c.** colegio
2. How do your living arrangements (while a student) compare to a student's living arrangements in a Spanish-speaking country?

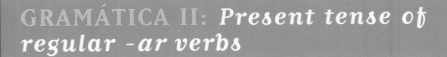

GRAMÁTICA II: *Present tense of regular -ar verbs*

An infinitive is a nonpersonal (unconjugated) verb form, such as **hablar.** Spanish infinitives end in either **-ar, -er,** or **-ir.** All Spanish infinitives have two parts: a stem (**habl-**) and an ending (**-ar**). To form the present tense of Spanish infinitives ending in **-ar,** drop the infinitive ending from the verb and add a personal ending to the stem.

How to form the present tense

hablar *(to speak, to talk)*

yo	habl**o**	*I speak*
tú	habl**as**	*you* (informal) *speak*
Ud., él, ella	habl**a**	*you* (formal) *speak; he/she speaks*
nosotros(as)	habl**amos**	*we speak*
vosotros(as)	habl**áis**	*you* (informal) *speak*
Uds., ellos(as)	habl**an**	*you* (formal) *speak; they speak*

How to use the present tense

Spanish speakers use the present tense to express (1) what people do over a period of time, (2) what they do habitually, and (3) what they intend to do at a later time. In this sense the present tense in Spanish is more flexible than in English.

1. Anita estudia lenguas.
   Anita is studying languages.

2. Ella estudia mucho por la noche.
   She studies a lot in the evening.

3. Mañana estudia con Laura.
   Tomorrow she's studying with Laura.

In this chapter, you have already seen some **-ar** verbs in the **En contexto** section on page 24. Now study the following verbs with useful example phrases:

descansar por una hora	*to rest for an hour*
escuchar música	*to listen to music*
estudiar en la biblioteca	*to study in the library*
llegar a clase	*to arrive at class*
mandar cartas	*to send letters*
regresar a casa	*to return home*
tomar clases/exámenes	*to take classes/tests*
trabajar por la noche	*to work at night*

Here are some common **-ar** verbs:

ayudar	*to help*	**mirar**	*to watch*
bailar	*to dance*	**necesitar**	*to need*
buscar	*to look for*	**pagar**	*to pay*
caminar	*to walk*	**pasar**	*to spend (time); to pass*
cantar	*to sing*	**practicar**	*to practice*
comprar	*to buy*	**preguntar**	*to ask (a question)*
contestar	*to answer*	**terminar**	*to finish*
desear	*to want, to wish*	**tocar**	*to touch; to play an*
dibujar	*to draw*		*instrument*
enseñar	*to teach*	**usar**	*to use*
entrar	*to enter*	**viajar**	*to travel*
esperar	*to hope; to wait*	**visitar**	*to visit*
llamar	*to call, to phone*		

¡A practicar!

T. **¡JUAN TIENE UNA VIDA LOCA!** Conjugate the verbs in parentheses to agree with the subjects in the following paragraph.

Yo _____ (**ser**) Juan y yo _____ (**tener**) una vida loca. Mi compañero de cuarto, Miguel, y yo _____ (**tomar**) seis clases este se-mestre. Miguel también _____ (**trabajar**) quince horas a la semana *(a week)* en la biblioteca. Yo _____ (**necesitar**) más dinero pero no _____ (**trabajar**) porque *(because)* yo _____ (**tocar**) el sa-xofón para una banda de jazz. Dos días a la semana yo _____ (**enseñar**) español a unos chicos *(kids)* de la escuela primaria. ¡Ellos _____ (**practicar**) mucho! Por la noche, Miguel y yo _____ (**estudiar**), _____ (**hablar**) por teléfono con nuestras novias o _____ (**descansar**). Los sábados yo _____ (**bailar**) en las fiestas *(parties)* con mi novia, Carmen. Los domingos mis padres y yo _____ (**visitar**) a la abuela y _____ (**pasar**) tiempo con la familia.

U. **LA VIDA ESTUDIANTIL** *(Student life)* Describe what the following people do by using appropriate phrases from the right column and conjugating the verbs correctly.

MODELO: nosotros
Nosotros descansamos por la noche.

1. mi amigo
2. yo
3. mi amiga
4. mis compañeros de clase
5. nosotros
6. el (la) profesor(a)
7. mis padres
8. ¿ ?

desear tocar la guitarra
estudiar en su cuarto
mirar Oprah en la televisión
descansar por la noche
regresar a la residencia después de la clase
pagar los libros de texto
cantar con la música del radio
escuchar la música de Marc Anthony
hablar por teléfono
comprar cuadernos en la librería *(bookstore)*

En voz alta

V. MI VIDA DIARIA (My daily routine)
In pairs, indicate whether the following statements are true or false. If a statement is false, change it to a true statement.

MODELO: Yo hablo español mucho en la clase.
E1: *Sí, yo hablo español mucho en clase.*
E2: *Sí, yo también* (also) *hablo español mucho en clase.*
o: *No, no hablo español mucho en clase.*

1. Yo descanso después de la clase.
2. Mis compañeros y yo estudiamos en la cafetería.
3. El (La) profesor(a) llega tarde a clase.
4. En clase, cantamos y bailamos.
5. Después de la clase mis compañeros regresan a casa.
6. Yo trabajo por la noche.
7. El (La) profesor(a) toca el piano en clase.
8. Nosotros practicamos el vocabulario en clase.
9. Yo tomo cinco clases este semestre.
10. Nosotros necesitamos estudiar mucho.

W. MI MADRE ME PREGUNTA (My mother asks me)
Working with a partner, practice the following questions. Take turns playing the inquisitive mom. Why would you use the **tú** form in this exercise?

MODELO: E1: ¿Cuándo estudias?
E2: *Yo estudio por la noche en mi cuarto.*

1. ¿Cuántas clases tomas este semestre?
2. ¿Cuándo regresas a casa?
3. ¿Hablas por teléfono con tu novio(a)?
4. ¿Escuchan los estudiantes a los profesores?
5. ¿Necesitamos tu padre y yo pagar la matrícula *(tuition)*?
6. ¿Trabajan tus *(your)* amigos?
7. ¿Descansas ocho horas cada noche?

X. NUEVOS COMPAÑEROS
In groups of three or four, discuss the following in Spanish.

1. where you are from
2. how many classes you are taking
3. what subjects you are studying

VOCABULARIO: *Lugares y edificios universitarios*

el campus de la universidad

la escuela

la biblioteca

la sala de clase

la cafetería

el centro estudiantil

el gimnasio

la residencia

el cuarto

la oficina

la librería

el apartamento

¿NOS ENTENDEMOS?

It is not uncommon for Spanish speakers to shorten words. For example, **la facultad** becomes **la facu**, **la universidad** becomes **la u**, and **el profesor** becomes **el profe**.

¡A practicar!

Y. ¿DÓNDE ESTÁ OSVALDO? Osvaldo is hiding in the buildings shown on the map above. After reading each clue, determine where Osvaldo is located on the campus.

MODELO: Aquí tomo un café después de las clases.
          Osvaldo está (is) *en el centro estudiantil.*

1. Aquí descanso después de las clases.
2. Aquí compro mis libros de texto.
3. Aquí estudio para los exámenes.
4. Aquí hablo con mis compañeros de clase y compro comida *(food)*.
5. Aquí escucho a la profesora y practico con mis compañeros de clase.
6. Aquí toco la trompeta para los partidos de baloncesto *(basketball games)*.

En voz alta

Z. ENTREVISTA *(Interview)* Ask a classmate about what he/she does around campus. Why is the **tú** form used in this activity?

1. ¿Estudias mucho en la biblioteca? ¿Qué estudias?
2. ¿Hablas por teléfono con personas en otras residencias? ¿Con quién hablas?
3. ¿Compras comida en el centro estudiantil? ¿Es buena la comida?
4. ¿Qué compras en la librería?
5. ¿Llegas a la universidad en auto, en autobús, en bicicleta, en motocicleta o a pie *(on foot)*?
6. Cuando regresas a tu cuarto, ¿estudias, trabajas o descansas?
7. ¿Practicas un deporte *(sport)* en el gimnasio?
8. ¿Tocas un instrumento?
9. ¿Miras muchos programas de televisión?
10. ¿Caminas mucho en el campus?

ASÍ SE DICE: *How to say what you like and what you don't like doing*

When you want to say you like doing something, use the construction **me gusta** + the infinitive form of the verb. For example, a Spanish speaker would say **me gusta escuchar música** to mean *I like to listen to music*. To make this statement negative, place **no** before **me gusta**: No me gusta escuchar música. You will learn more about using the verb **gustar** to talk about likes and dislikes in *Capítulo 3*. Here are a few more examples:

Me gusta tocar el piano.	*I like to play the piano.*
No me gusta trabajar.	*I don't like to work.*
Me gusta escuchar a mi profesor(a).	*I like to listen to my professor.*

¡A practicar!

AA. ¡ME GUSTA! ¡NO ME GUSTA! Indicate whether you like or dislike doing the following activities.

MODELO: estudiar en la biblioteca
    Me gusta estudiar en la biblioteca
  o: *No me gusta estudiar en la biblioteca.*

1. hablar con mi compañero(a) de cuarto
2. escuchar a mis profesores
3. tomar exámenes
4. bailar en las fiestas
5. practicar deportes
6. descansar mucho
7. escuchar música clásica
8. pasar tiempo con mis amigos
9. caminar a mis clases
10. regresar a casa

En voz alta

BB. MIS PREFERENCIAS *(My preferences)* Tell a classmate five things that you like to do and five things that you don't like to do.

MODELOS: *Me gusta hablar por teléfono.*
    No me gusta tomar exámenes.

In this section you will learn how to tell time and say the days of the week.

¿Qué hora es? *(What time is it?)*

This question can be answered in three ways, depending on the time.

On the hour

Es la una.	It's one o'clock.
Son las siete.	It's seven o'clock.

On the quarter or the half-hour

Son las siete **y cuarto.**	It's a **quarter past** seven.
Son las siete **y media.**	It's seven **thirty**.
Son las ocho **menos cuarto.**	It's a **quarter till** eight.

Minutes before and after the hour

Es la una **y diez.**	It's **ten past** one.
Son las ocho **menos diez.**	It's **ten till** eight.

Other time expressions

a tiempo   *on time*
ahora   *now*
tarde   *tarde*
temprano   *early*
la medianoche   *midnight*
el mediodía   *noon*

1. Use **es** to tell time between 12:31 and 1:30. Otherwise, use **son** because it refers to more than one hour (plural).

   —¿Qué hora **es?**   *What time is it?*
   —**Es** la una menos cuarto.   *It's 12:45 (a quarter till one).*
   —No. **Son** las diez y veinte.   *No. It's 10:20.*

2. After a specific time, use **de la mañana** *(in the morning/A.M.)*, **de la tarde** *(in the afternoon/P.M.)*, and **de la noche** *(in the evening/P.M.)*.

   Mi clase de computación es a   *My computer science class is at*
   las nueve **de la mañana** y mi   *nine o'clock **in the morning***
   clase de música es a las dos   *and my music class is at two*
   de la tarde.   *o'clock **in the afternoon**.*

3. To ask or tell when an event occurs, use the word **a.**

   —¿**A** qué hora trabajas?   *What time do you work?*
   —**A** las diez de la mañana.   *At ten o'clock in the morning.*

Los días de la semana
La agenda de Esther

LUNES	MARTES	MIÉRCOLES	JUEVES	VIERNES	SÁBADO	DOMINGO
de la tarde	de la mañana	de la noche	de la mañana	de la noche	de la tarde	de la tarde
tocar el violín	biblioteca	gimnasio	librería	fiesta	cuarto	centro estudiantil

el día *day*   **el fin de semana** *weekend*   **hoy** *today*
la semana *week*   **todos los días** *every day*   **mañana** *tomorrow*

¡A practicar!

CC. **¿QUÉ HORA ES?** Say the time for each of the clocks shown.

DD. **EL HORARIO DE ESTHER**
Look at Esther's busy schedule for this week and then make complete sentences out of the fragments below. Remember to conjugate each verb.

MODELO: lunes / Esther / tocar el violín / P.M.
El lunes Esther toca el violín a las cinco de la tarde.

1. martes / Esther y Helen / hablar / biblioteca / A.M.
2. miércoles / Esther / practicar volibol / gimnasio / P.M.
3. jueves / Esther / trabajar / librería / A.M.
4. viernes / Esther y Ramón / bailar / fiesta / P.M.
5. sábado / Esther / descansar / cuarto / P.M.
6. domingo / Esther y Helen / escuchar música / centro estudiantil / P.M.

En voz alta

EE. **MIS CLASES** Tell another student the days and hours of your classes. Follow the example below, but substitute your own class information for the words in **bold-faced print**.

MODELO: *Tengo mi clase de **biología** los **martes** y los **jueves**. La clase es a las **nueve de la mañana**.*

FF. **MI HORARIO PARA LA SEMANA** Now expand upon the information you gave in the previous exercise to include the following information.

1. when you arrive at school (days, times)
2. your class schedule (classes, days, times)
3. when you get home from school (days, times)
4. something about your work (place, days, times)

ENCUENTRO *cultural*

El sistema de 24 horas

Para pensar: ¿Normalmente llegas a la hora en punto a las citas? ¿a las fiestas? ¿a las cenas? ¿Piensas que es malo llegar tarde a los eventos sociales? ¿Puedes pensar en algún caso en los Estados Unidos en que se usa el sistema de 24 horas? ¿Tú lo usas para algunas cosas?

El sistema de las veinticuatro horas para dar la hora es muy común en el mundo hispánico y se usa en los sistemas de transporte (e.g., aviones, trenes y autobuses), la radio y la televisión, las invitaciones formales y los anuncios de eventos oficiales. Para usar el sistema de las 24 horas, simplemente cuenta *(count)* consecutivamente a partir del mediodía: doce *(noon)*, trece *(1:00 P.M.)*, catorce *(2:00 P.M.)*, etc.

Sistema oficial (24 horas)	**Sistema de conversación** (12 horas)
10:00 diez	las diez de la mañana
13:00 trece	la una de la tarde
23:00 veintitrés	las once de la noche

En España y en Latinoamérica, muchos eventos oficiales (servicios religiosos, eventos deportivos, citas de negocios y citas con médicos) empiezan a tiempo. Sin embargo, reuniones sociales (cenas, fiestas) comienzan 30 minutos o una hora más tarde. Para llegar a la hora correcta a una cena o fiesta, pregunta «¿en punto?».

GG. **PREGUNTAS** Answer the following questions based on the reading.

1. Give two examples of where the 24-hour system is used in the United States.
2. Use the 24-hour system to give following times.
   a. 5:30 A.M. **b.** 8:00 P.M. **c.** 1:55 A.M. **d.** 9:20 P.M.
3. Look over Rodrigo Camacho's schedule for the semester, and answer the following questions.
   a. ¿A qué hora empiezan *(begin)* las clases de Rodrigo los martes? ¿los lunes?
   b. ¿A qué hora termina Rodrigo los miércoles?
   c. ¿A qué hora es el laboratorio de física? ¿Qué días?
   d. ¿Cuándo es la clase de conversación en inglés?

La agenda de Rodrigo Camacho

lunes	martes	miércoles	jueves	viernes
10:00 cálculo, sala 505		10:00 cálculo, sala 505		10:00 cálculo, sala 505
11:00 biología molecular		11:00 biología molecular		11:00 biología molecular
	12:00 inglés, sala 303		12:00 inglés, sala 303	
	13:00 astronomía		13:00 astronomía	
16:00 física, sala 410	16:00–18:00 inglés: conversación básica	16:00 física, sala 410	16:00–18:00 inglés: conversación básica	16:00 física, sala 410
18:00–21:00 laboratorio de física, sala 411		18:00–21:00 laboratorio de física, sala 411		

http://plazas.heinle.com

Síntesis

¡A ver!

The video for this chapter contains two segments. Your narrator for this chapter, Luis, whose parents come from Ponce in Puerto Rico and who currently lives in Springfield, Massachusetts, will introduce each of the segments in Spanish. The segments deal with the main topics presented in the preliminary and first chapters of this book—greeting somebody, saying farewell, finding out basic information from somebody you have just met, and talking about your schedule.

ACTIVIDAD 1 Pre-viewing task (Segmento 1 del video)

Paso 1: In **Segmento 1 del video** you are going to see video clips from different Spanish-speaking countries. In each, people are either greeting each other or saying farewell. Make a list of the different ways that people express greetings and farewells in the video segment. Add to your list any other expressions for greetings and farewells that you already know in Spanish. You may wish to check the information given to you in the **Encuentro cultural: Meeting and Greeting Others** in **Capítulo preliminar.**

Paso 2: In small groups, exchange your list with your partners.

ACTIVIDAD 2 Pre-viewing task (Segmento 2 del video)

Paso 1: Think about the questions you would need to ask a classmate in Spanish to obtain the following information. As you do so, think also about whether you would need to ask these questions using **tú** or **usted**. Then, write down the questions on a piece of paper. Are there other ways that you can ask the same questions in Spanish, either by rephrasing the question or by making some minimal change (e.g., **¿Cómo se llama usted? ¿Cómo se llama? ¿Cuál es su apellido?**)?

primer nombre	
segundo nombre	
apellido	
edad	
número de teléfono	
lugar de origen	
dirección	

Paso 2: Now speak to two people in your class whom you do not know very well in order to obtain the information in **Paso 1**. Greet your partner before you start asking questions, and when you finish, thank him/her and say good-bye. Remember that your partner may not always respond in exactly the way you expect (e.g., you ask for the person's name expecting the whole name, and you only get the first name; in that case you would have to ask for the middle name and the family name). Therefore, you should try to react appropriately to what your partner says. Adjust your questions to fit your partner's prior responses.

Remember also to choose the correct form of address—**tú** or **usted** (e.g., if you decide to interview your instructor, you should probably use **usted,** unless he or she tells you it is OK to use **tú**).

Paso 3: In groups of three, introduce one of the people you have just met to the other member of the group.

ACTIVIDAD 3 Viewing task (Segmento 2 del video)

You are going to meet four Spanish speakers who are talking about themselves, two from Puerto Rico and two from Mexico. What information does each present us? Take notes on each of the speakers in the table below. Also, pay attention to the questions asked by the interviewer of the two Mexican speakers.

ACTIVIDAD 4 Post-viewing task (Segmento 2 del video)

In pairs, each member of the group chooses one of the speakers interviewed in **Actividad 3.** Using the information you have obtained from that speaker as you watched the video, tell your partner about this person. If your partner does not agree with you, he/she should provide his/her information. You may need to watch the video again to check your information.

¡A escribir!

Organizing your ideas

A good way to improve your writing is to organize the ideas you want to express before you actually begin composing your essay or paper.

Functions: Describing people; Introducing; Talking about the present

Vocabulary: Countries; Languages; Studies; Arts; Numbers 0–30

Grammar: Verbs: **ser;** Prepositions: **de;** Personal pronouns: **él, ella;** Articles: indefinite: **un, una**

Paso 1: Look at the chart below and familiarize yourself with the information about María Sánchez Pérez.

Nombre	María Sánchez Pérez	tu compañero(a) de clase	tú
Nación	Estados Unidos		
Lengua(s)	español e inglés		
Edad *(Age)*	19 años		
Escuela	Universidad de Miami		
Cursos	francés contabilidad periodismo economía		
Compañero(a) de clase	Francisco Javier Marina		

Paso 2: Now read the following description of María Sánchez Pérez. Note how the information in the chart above is used in this paragraph.

María Sánchez Pérez es de los Estados Unidos. Ella habla español e inglés. María tiene 19 años. Estudia en la Universidad de Miami, en Florida. Ella estudia francés, contabilidad, periodismo y economía. Estudia con un compañero de clase. Se llama Francisco Javier Marina.

Paso 3: Now interview a classmate to fill in the third column on the chart with information about him/her. Then write a similar descriptive paragraph about him/her.

Paso 4: Now fill in the chart with information about yourself. Then write a paragraph describing yourself.

Paso 5: Exchange both of your paragraphs with a classmate. Check over each other's work for mistakes and correct any mistakes that you find. Discuss the corrections and comments you made, and then return his/her paragraph.

¡A conversar!

Imagine you are at a party sponsored by the International Club at your school. An exchange student from Mexico (role-played by your partner) sits down next to you and you begin to introduce yourselves and start a conversation. Be sure to use an appropriate form of address and include the following (in Spanish) in your conversation:

1. Greet each other appropriately.
2. Introduce yourselves and shake hands.
3. Ask and tell each other where you are from.
4. Talk briefly about:
   a. your life at school (your courses, your instructors, etc.)
   b. your work or job (where you work, which days, your work schedule, etc.)
5. Now introduce your new friend to another student (a classmate) and say something interesting you learned from the first conversation.

¡A leer!

Recognizing cognates

Cognates (**Cognados**) are words that belong to different languages but are identical or very similar to each other in spelling and meaning. There are many cognates in Spanish and English. Your ability to recognize them and guess their meaning will help you read Spanish more efficiently.

Paso 1: Skim the advertisement and write down as many cognates as you can find. Then write what you think each cognate means in English. Feel free to guess if you need to. Based on the cognates you have identified, what do you think is the purpose of the ad?

Paso 2: Read over the advertisement again and answer the following questions about it.

INGLES
SU PASAPORTE PARA EL FUTURO.
Aprenda a mejorar en los EE.UU.,
Canadá o Inglaterra
Cursos intensivos para estudiantes, adultos y ejecutivos desde 2 semanas hasta un año.
• Escoja 20, 30, ó 40 lecciones por semanas.
• Grupos pequeños o individual, a todos niveles.
• Inglés especializado en su profesión.
• Hospedaje en dormitorios, hoteles o con familias.
• Altamente recomendado por referencia local

Para folletos e información favor de llamar a:
JEAN CORNELIUS LANGUAGE AND VACATION PROGRAMS
Tel. 723-9006 • 723-6796
INGLES para jóvenes 6-17 años en campamentos con deportes, actividades, cultura y excursiones en Inglaterra, Suiza, Canadá y EE.UU.

1. What is this advertisement about?
2. This ad is aimed at . . .
   a. adults.
   b. children.
   c. professional people.
   d. all of the people mentioned in a, b, and c.
3. According to the ad, in which countries could people learn English?
4. Write the Spanish equivalents for the following words.
   a. passport
   b. future
   c. courses
   d. intensive
   e. adults
   f. executives
   g. lessons
   h. groups
   i. profession
5. Write the Spanish equivalents for the following words and phrases.
   a. highly recommended
   b. specialized English
   c. from two weeks up to one year

La gente   *People*

el (la) amigo(a)   *friend*
el (la) compañero(a) de clase   *classmate*
el (la) compañero(a) de cuarto   *roommate*
el (la) estudiante   *student*
el hombre   *man*
la mujer   *woman*
el (la) novio(a)   *boyfriend/girlfriend*
el (la) profesor(a)   *professor*

Objetos de la clase   *Objects in the classroom*

el bolígrafo   *ballpoint pen*
el borrador   *eraser*
la calculadora   *calculator*
el calendario   *calendar*
la computadora   *computer*
el cuaderno   *notebook*
el diccionario   *dictionary*
el dinero   *money*
el escritorio   *desk*
el examen   *test*
el lápiz   *pencil*
la lección   *lesson*
el libro (de texto)   *(text)book*
la luz (las luces)   *light(s)*
el mapa   *map*
la mochila   *backpack*
la palabra   *word*
la pantalla   *screen*
el papel   *paper*
la pizarra   *chalkboard*
la pluma   *fountain pen*
la silla   *chair*
la tarea   *homework*
la tiza   *chalk*

Los colores   *Colors*

amarillo   *yellow*
anaranjado   *orange*
azul   *blue*
blanco   *white*
marrón   *brown*
morado   *purple*
negro   *black*
rojo   *red*
verde   *green*

Las lenguas extranjeras   *Foreign languages*

el alemán   *German*
el chino   *Chinese*
el español   *Spanish*
el francés   *French*
el italiano   *Italian*
el japonés   *Japanese*
el portugués   *Portuguese*
el ruso   *Russian*

Cursos y especializaciones   *Courses and majors*

la administración de empresas   *business administration*
el arte   *art*
la biología   *biology*
las ciencias   *science*
la computación   *computer science*
el derecho   *law*
la economía   *economics*
la educación   *education*
la filosofía   *philosophy*
la física   *physics*
la geografía   *geography*
la historia   *history*
la ingeniería   *engineering*
el inglés   *English*
la literatura   *literature*
las matemáticas   *math*
la medicina   *medicine*
la música   *music*
los negocios   *business*
el periodismo   *journalism*
la pintura   *painting*
la química   *chemistry*
la sicología   *psychology*
la sociología   *sociology*
el teatro   *theater*

Lugares y edificios universitarios   *University places and buildings*

el apartamento   *apartment*
la biblioteca   *library*
la cafetería   *cafeteria*
el campus   *campus*
el centro estudiantil   *student center*
el cuarto   *room*
la escuela   *school*
el gimnasio   *gymnasium*
la librería   *bookstore*
la oficina   *office*
la residencia   *dormitory*
la sala de clase   *classroom*
la universidad   *university*

Los días de la semana   *Days of the week*

el lunes   *Monday*
el martes   *Tuesday*
el miércoles   *Wednesday*
el jueves   *Thursday*
el viernes   *Friday*
el sábado   *Saturday*
el domingo   *Sunday*

La hora   *Time*

¿A qué hora?   *At what time?*
a tiempo   *on time*
de (por) la (mañana, tarde, noche)   *in the (morning, afternoon, evening)*
la medianoche   *midnight*
el mediodía   *noon*
¿Qué hora es?   *What time is it?*
el reloj   *clock*
tarde   *late*
temprano   *early*

Verbos

ayudar *to help*
bailar *to dance*
buscar *to look for*
caminar *to walk*
cantar *to sing*
comprar *to buy*
contestar *to answer*
descansar (por una hora) *to rest (for an hour)*
desear *to want, to wish*
dibujar *to draw*
enseñar *to teach*

entrar *to enter*
escuchar (música) *to listen (to music)*
esperar *to hope; to wait*
estudiar (en la biblioteca) *to study (in the library)*
hablar *to speak, to talk*
llamar *to call, to phone*
llegar (a clase) *to arrive (at class)*
mandar (cartas) *to send (letters)*

(no) me gusta + infinitive *I (don't) like to (do something)*
mirar *to watch*
necesitar *to need*
pagar *to pay*
pasar *to spend (time); to pass*
practicar *to practice*
preguntar *to ask (a question)*
regresar (a casa) *to return (home)*

terminar *to finish*
tocar *to touch; to play an instrument*
tomar (clases/exámenes) *to take (classes/tests); to drink*
trabajar (por la noche) *to work (at night)*
usar *to use*
viajar *to travel*
visitar *to visit*

Expresión idiomática

¡Genial! *Great!*

Expresiones temporales   *Time expressions*

ahora *now*
el día *day*

el fin de semana *weekend*
hoy *today*

mañana *tomorrow*
la semana *week*

todos los días *every day*

2

En una reunión de familia: México

Communicative goals

In this chapter you will learn how to . . .

- Define and ask about family relationships
- Indicate ownership and possession
- Describe people and things
- Indicate nationality
- Describe daily activities at home or at school

Grammar

- The use of the verb **ser**
- Agreement with descriptive adjectives
- Possessive adjectives
- Possession with **de(l)**
- Present tense of regular **-er** and **-ir** verbs
- Present tense of **tener** and certain idioms

Cultural information

- Hispanic names
- Families in the Spanish-speaking world
- Gestures

*La Plaza del Zócalo,
La Ciudad de México, México*

LA FAMILIA DE JUAN CARLOS GARCÍA MARTÍNEZ In this section you will practice talking about family relationships by learning about Juan Carlos's family. Do you know of any families like Juan Carlos's that have relatives living in two or more countries?

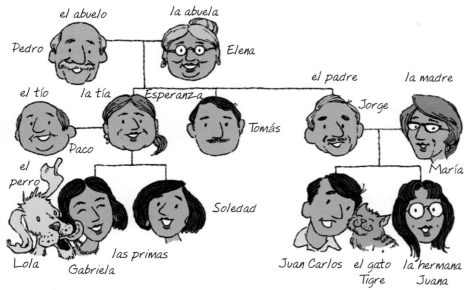

Otros parientes *Other relatives*

el apellido *last name*
el (la) esposo(a) *husband/wife*
el (la) hijo(a) *son/daughter*

el (la) nieto(a) *grandson/granddaughter*
el nombre *first name*
el (la) sobrino(a) *nephew/niece*

Las mascotas *Pets*

el pájaro *bird*
el pez *fish*

Palabras útiles

casado(a) *married*
divorciado(a) *divorced*
separado(a) *separated*
soltero(a) *single*
viudo(a) *widowed*
el (la) cuñado(a) *brother-in-law/sister-in-law*
el (la) hermanastro(a) *stepbrother/stepsister*

la madrastra *stepmother*
la madrina *godmother*
la nuera *daughter-in-law*
el padrastro *stepfather*
el padrino *godfather*
el (la) suegro(a) *father-in-law/mother-in-law*
el yerno *son-in-law*

➡ *Palabras útiles* are for recognition only; you will not be tested on these words. These words are provided to help you describe yourself and your family better.

¡A practicar!

A. **¿CIERTO O FALSO?** Study Juan Carlos's family tree above. Then decide whether the following statements are true **(cierto)** or false **(falso)**. If the statement is false, correct it to a true statement.

MODELO: Juana es la esposa de Juan Carlos.
falso: Juana es la hermana de Juan Carlos.

1. Gabriela y Soledad son hermanas.
2. Esperanza es la tía de Juan Carlos y Juana.
3. Elena es la madre de Gabriela y Soledad.
4. Paco y Tomás son los sobrinos de Juana.
5. Juan Carlos y Gabriela son sobrinas.

B. LA FAMILIA DE JUAN CARLOS Complete the following sentences with the correct relationship based on the drawing on page 47.

MODELO: Ana es *la esposa* de Jorge.

1. Juan Carlos es _____ de Juana.
2. Soledad es _____ de Esperanza y Paco.
3. Gabriela y Soledad son _____ .
4. Elena es _____ de la hija de Jorge y María.
5. La hija de Jorge y María es _____ de Esperanza.
6. Tomás es _____ de los hijos de Jorge y María.

C. EN OTRAS PALABRAS Indicate the relationships between the family members listed below.

MODELOS: yo / mi tía
Yo soy el sobrino de mi tía.

mis abuelos / mi padre
Mis abuelos son los padres de mi padre.

1. mi hermano(a) / mis abuelos
2. mi hijo(a) / mi hermano(a)
3. mi madre / mi hijo(a)
4. mis primos / mi mamá
5. yo / mis nietos

En voz alta

D. MIEMBROS DE MI FAMILIA Identify as many members of your family as you can by answering the following questions.

MODELO: ¿Quién es tu *(your)* madre?
Ella es la hija de mi (my) *abuela María.*
Ella es la esposa de mi padre.
Ella es la tía de mis primos Elena y Soldedad.

1. ¿Quién es tu abuelo(a)?
2. ¿Quién es tu primo(a)?
3. ¿Quién es tu padre?
4. ¿Quién es tu hermano(a)?
5. ¿Quiénes son tus tíos?
6. ¿Quién es tu esposo(a)?

E. ADIVINANZAS *(Riddles)* Ask a classmate the following questions. Then, add three questions of your own.

¿Quién es... ?

1. la madre de tu padre
2. el (la) hermano(a) de tu madre
3. las hijas de tus tíos
4. el (la) hijo(a) de tus padres
5. el hijo de tu hija

F. **UN ÁRBOL FAMILIAR PASO I** Create your own family tree by filling in the diagram. Add spaces as needed or list only a few members for each category.

Mis abuelos

_____	_____	_____	_____

Mis tíos   **Mis padres**   **Mis tíos**

_____   _____   _____   _____

_____   **(papá)**   **(mamá)**   _____

Mis primos   **Mis hermanos(as)**   **Yo**   **Mis primos**

_____   _____   _____   _____

_____

¿NOS ENTENDEMOS?

The forms **don** and **doña** are used before first names as titles of respect or affection (while maintaining formality); they are generally used for addressing one's elders or superiors. Juan Carlos's grandparents, for example, might be addressed as **don Pedro** and **doña Elena**.

PASO 2 Now describe your family relationships in Spanish to a partner. Your partner then will review your family tree with you before presenting it to the class.

EN CONTEXTO

Read along as you listen to the following dialog describing Juan Carlos's reunion with his grandparents, Pedro and Elena, in Mexico. Juan Carlos and his sister, Juana, live in Los Angeles and are always eager to share their experiences in the United States with their grandparents.

JUAN CARLOS:	¡Hola, abuelito! ¡Hola, abuelita! ¿Cómo están? ¡Tengo muchas cosas interesantes que quiero contarles sobre mi vida en los Estados Unidos!
ELENA:	¡Ay, qué bueno!, Carlitos. Tenemos tus cartas y tus postales, pero deseamos tener más detalles.
PEDRO:	Y ahora vives en un barrio nuevo. ¿Tienes muchos amigos allí?
JUAN CARLOS:	Sí, abuelito. Tengo muchos compañeros, ¡y dos de ellos hablan español! Los padres de mis amigos mexicanos son del D.F. y sus abuelos viven aquí. Los abuelos de mi amigo Enrique son muy simpáticos.
ELENA:	Así que no somos las únicas personas que tienen nietos en los Estados Unidos. ¿Y Juana? ¿Tiene amigas?
JUAN CARLOS:	Sí, por supuesto. Hay una familia cubana que vive cerca de nosotros en la calle 42, y ellos tienen una hija que tiene 15 años, la misma edad de Juana.
PEDRO:	¿Mi Juanita ya tiene 15 años? ¡Imposible!
ELENA:	Ves cómo tu abuelo vive en el pasado, m'ijo. Él cree que los niños nunca crecen. Y mira tú, tan alto para un chico de 16 años...
JUAN CARLOS:	¡Ay, abuelita! ¡Yo tengo 19 años!

¿NOS ENTENDEMOS?

Spanish speakers use the diminutive forms of certain nouns to express affection. Juan Carlos addresses his grandparents as **abuelito** and **abuelita** (literally, *little grandfather* and *little grandmother*). Other terms of affection commonly used in Mexico are the contractions **m'ijo** and **m'ija** (from **mi hijo, mi hija**) to mean *my son* and *my daughter*, respectively.

¿COMPRENDISTE? Based on the dialog, indicate if the following statements are **cierto** *(true)* or **falso** *(false)*. If a statement is **falso,** give the correct answer.

1. Los abuelos no tienen información sobre la vida de Juan Carlos en los Estados Unidos.
2. Juan Carlos no tiene muchos amigos en el barrio nuevo.
3. Todos los amigos de Juan Carlos hablan español.
4. Juana tiene una amiga de México.

ASÍ SE DICE: *Indicating relationships and possession*

1. One way English speakers express possession is by attaching an *'s* to a noun (the boy**'s** backpack). Spanish speakers show the same relationship by placing **de** before a noun. When using **de + el,** Spanish speakers form the contraction **del. De + la,** however, does not contract.

Juana es la hermana **de** Juan Carlos.	*Juana is Juan Carlos's sister.*
Aquí está el perro **del** abuelo.	*Here's the grandfather's dog.*
¿Dónde está el padre **de** la niña?	*Where is the girl's father?*

2. Another way to indicate relationships or ownership is to use possessive adjectives. In Spanish, possessive adjectives must match the number (singular or plural) of the nouns they describe. In the cases of **nosotros** and **vosotros,** the corresponding possessive adjectives must also match the gender (masculine or feminine) of the nouns they describe.

	Singular	Plural
my	**mi** abuelo	**mis** abuelos
your (informal)	**tu** gato	**tus** gatos
his, her, its, your (formal), *their*	**su** familia	**sus** familias
our	**nuestro** hijo **nuestra** hija	**nuestros** hijos (masculine) **nuestras** hijas (feminine)
your (informal)	**vuestro** hijo **vuestra** hija	**vuestros** hijos (masculine) **vuestras** hijas (feminine)
their, your	**su** madre	**sus** madres

¡A practicar!

H. **FOTOS DE LA FAMILIA** Complete the dialog between **la nieta** and **la abuela** as they look through the family photo album. Use **del, de la, de las,** or **de los,** as appropriate.

MODELO: **La nieta:** ¿De quién es el pájaro rojo?
La abuela: Es *del* tío Jorge.

La nieta:	¿De quiénes son los autos negros?
La abuela:	Son _____ amigos de tu padre.
La nieta:	¿Y son de los Estados Unidos?
La abuela:	Sí. Miguel es _____ ciudad de Nueva York, y Ramón es _____ estado de Florida.
La nieta:	¿Y las mujeres? ¿Son las esposas _____ muchachos?
La abuela:	No. Son amigas _____ hermana de Miguel.

I. **LAS MEMORIAS DE MAXIMILIANO** Maxmillian, Emperor of Mexico, describes his family. Complete the following paragraph with the indicated possessive adjective. Note: possessive adjectives agree in number and, in some cases, gender.

Yo tengo una familia pequeña. _____ *(My)* padres y abuelos viven en Austria, pero _____ *(our)* familia vive en México. _____ *(My)* hermano, Francis Joseph, es emperador de Austria. _____ *(His)* palacio es enorme, y hay un patio interior donde el perro pasa la mayoría de _____ *(its)* tiempo. _____ *(My)* esposa, Carlota, tiene todas _____ *(her)* amigas aquí en la ciudad. Ellas vienen a _____ *(our)* casa a comer con _____ *(their)* esposos. Muchos de _____ *(our)* amigos son de Francia.

En voz alta

J. **¿ES TU LIBRO O MI LIBRO?** Working in groups of three or four, take turns playing the role of a student suffering from temporary amnesia. When the forgetful student asks the others to whom an item in the classroom belongs, they respond in either the affirmative or negative. Use as many items as you can and consider whether you should use formal or informal possessive adjectives in this exercise.

MODELOS: libro
      E1: *¿Es mi libro?*
      E2: *No, no es tu libro. Es el libro de David.*

      bolígrafos
      E1: *¿Son mis bolígrafos?*
      E2: *No, no son tus bolígrafos. Son los bolígrafos de Karen.*

1. la mochila
2. el reloj
3. los lápices
4. el escritorio
5. el cuaderno
6. los zapatos
7. la clase de español
8. los diccionarios
9. los papeles

ENCUENTRO *cultural*

Nombres hispánicos

Éstas son unas palabras nuevas para la lectura:

el santo   *patron saint*
nacer   *to be born*
escoger   *to choose*

el nombre compuesto   *compound name*
casarse   *to get married*

En la tradición hispánica, los niños reciben más de un nombre, por ejemplo, María Rebeca, Tomás Enrique o Carlos Humberto. Algunas veces, los niños reciben el nombre del **santo** o de la **santa** dependiendo del día en que **nacen.** Por ejemplo, el 25 de julio es el día de Santiago Apóstol, así que el nombre del niño puede ser Santiago. Muchas veces, los padres **escogen** el nombre del niño o de la niña para honrar a otro miembro de la familia.

Muchos hispanos tienen dos apellidos. El primero es el apellido del padre y el segundo es el apellido de la madre: Olga González Álvarez; González es el apellido de su padre y Álvarez es el apellido de la madre. A veces solamente se usa el apellido del padre y se abrevia el apellido de la madre: Olga González A.

A veces, cuando una mujer **se casa,** ella toma el apellido de su esposo. Por ejemplo, si Olga González Álvarez se casa con Ernesto Castro Ramírez, su nombre es Olga González de Castro.

Para pensar: ¿Puedes describir el sistema de apellidos en tu país? ¿Cómo compara al sistema hispano? ¿En tu familia, hay nombres tradicionales? ¿Cuáles son?

K. **PREGUNTAS** Answer the following questions based on the reading.

1. If you apply the last-name system for Spanish speakers, how would you write your name?
2. If your sister were to marry a man named Roberto Álfaro Ramírez, what would her last name become if she were to use the Spanish system?

GRAMÁTICA I: *Present tense of the verb ser*[1]

You already learned about the forms of **ser** in the **Capítulo preliminar.**

The verb **ser** *(to be)* is used:

1. to identify essential characteristics of people and things.

   Juan **es** alto y rubio.   Juan *is tall and blond.*

   Los libros **son** interesantes.   *The books are interesting.*

---

[1] More uses of **ser** will be presented in **Capítulo 5** when **ser** is contrasted with **estar.**

2. to indicate profession or vocation.

Yo **soy** músico.	*I **am** a musician.*
Tú **eres** doctora.	*You **are** a doctor.*
Carmen **es** estudiante.	*Carmen **is** a student.*

3. to express nationality . . .

Pedro **es** mexicano.[1]	*Pedro **is** Mexican.*

. . . and origin with the preposition **de.**

Pedro **es de** México.	*Pedro **is from** Mexico.*

4. to talk about time.

Son las cinco.	*It's five o'clock.*
Es la una.[2]	*It's one o'clock.*

5. to talk about days of the week, months, and dates.

Hoy **es** lunes.	*Today **is** Monday.*
Mañana **es** el 4 de mayo.	*Tomorrow **is** May 4.*

The present tense of ser is:

yo	soy	*I am*
tú	eres	*you (informal) are*
Ud., él, ella	es	*he, she is; you (formal) are*
nosotros(as)	somos	*we are*
vosotros(as)	sois	*you (informal) are*
Uds., ellos(as)	son	*they are, you (formal) are*

¡A practicar!

L. **SER** Fill in the blanks with the appropriate form of **ser.** Remember to differentiate between formal and informal modes of address.

MODELO: Juan *es* de Puerto Rico.

1. Tú _____ mi amiga.
2. Mis padres _____ de los Estados Unidos.
3. Mi madre _____ bonita.
4. El Sr. García _____ profesor.
5. Vosotros _____ españoles.
6. Mike y Kelly _____ estudiantes.
7. Ahora _____ las 2:00 de la tarde.
8. Mis amigas _____ simpáticas.
9. Hoy _____ el ____ de _____.
10. _____ la una.

---

[1] In Spanish, adjectives of nationality are not capitalized: **Hans es alemán.**
[2] The third-person plural form of **ser** is used to express time with the exception of *one o'clock,* which uses the third-person singular.

M. **MATCHING** Choose the item on the right that best completes the statement on the left.

1. Yo soy de _____.
2. Son las _____.
3. Susana es _____.
4. Carlos es _____.
5. Hoy es _____.
6. Los exámenes de mi clase son _____.

a. difíciles
b. el veintidós de mayo
c. los Estados Unidos
d. maestro de español
e. 2:00 de la tarde
f. simpática y sincera

VOCABULARIO: *Las características físicas y la personalidad*

delgado   gordo

alta

baja

joven   nuevo   vieja

grande

pequeños

rubias   morenas

feo

bonita   guapo

corto   largo

La personalidad

amable *friendly*
antipático(a) *unpleasant*
artístico(a) *artistic*
atlético(a) *athletic*
bueno(a) *good*
extrovertido(a) *outgoing*
generoso(a) *generous*
honesto(a) *honest*

inteligente *intelligent*
irresponsable *irresponsible*
listo(a) *smart; ready*
malo(a) *bad*
paciente *patient*
perezoso(a) *lazy*
pobre *poor*
responsable *responsible*

rico(a) *rich*
simpático(a) *nice*
sincero(a) *sincere*
tacaño(a) *stingy*
tímido(a) *shy, timid*
tonto(a) *silly, foolish*
trabajador(a) *hardworking*

Palabras útiles

arrogante *arrogant*
bilingüe *bilingual*
cobarde *cowardly*
cómico(a) *humorous*
conservador(a) *conservative*
dramático(a) *dramatic*
humilde *humble*
indeciso(a) *indecisive*
intelectual *intellectual*

intuitivo(a) *intuitive*
liberal *liberal*
moderno(a) *modern*
progresivo(a) *progressive*
rebelde *rebellious*
reservado(a) *reserved*
tolerante *tolerant*
valiente *brave*

⇒ *Palabras útiles* are for recognition only; you will not be tested on these words. These words are provided to help you describe yourself and your world better.

GRAMÁTICA II: *Agreement with descriptive adjectives*

Adjectives are words that describe nouns or pronouns. In Spanish, descriptive adjectives must match the gender (masculine or feminine) and the number (singular or plural) of the noun or pronoun that they describe.

How to match adjectives with their nouns

1. Spanish adjectives agree in number and gender with the nouns they modify. Adjectives ending in **-o** change to **-a** to indicate feminine gender, and add an **-s** to indicate the plural.

	Singular	Plural
Masculine	abuelo generos**o**	abuelos generos**os**
Feminine	abuela generos**a**	abuelas generos**as**

2. Adjectives ending in **-e** or in most consonants do not change to agree in gender. For the plural of adjectives ending in **-e**, add **-s**. For the plural of adjectives ending in a consonant, add **-es**.

	Singular	Plural
Masculine	tío interesante	tíos interesant**es**
	hermano intelectual	hermanos intelectual**es**
Feminine	tía interesante	tías interesant**es**
	hermana intelectual	hermanas intelectual**es**

3. For most adjectives of nationality ending in a consonant, add **-a** to make them feminine. To form the plural, add **-es** to masculine adjectives and **-s** to feminine adjectives. Most adjectives that end in **-dor**, **-án**, **-ón**, and **-ín** also follow this pattern.

	Singular	**Plural**
Masculine	primo español	primos español**es**
	primo trabajador	primos trabajador**es**
	tío alemán	tíos aleman**es**
Feminine	prima español**a**	primas español**as**
	prima trabajador**a**	primas trabajador**as**
	tía aleman**a**	tías aleman**as**

Where to place adjectives

1. Most Spanish adjectives follow the nouns they describe.

La música **bonita** de los mariachis...   *The mariachi's **beautiful** music . . .*

Son personas **simpáticas.**   *They are **nice** people.*

2. Spanish adjectives of *quantity* precede the nouns they describe, as in English. In Spanish, when the number *one* is used to quantify a singular masculine noun, drop the **-o: un libro, un papel.**

Madonna tiene **una** hija.   *Madonna has **one** daughter.*

Yo tengo **cuatro** hermanos y **dos**   *I have **four** brothers and **two** sisters.*
hermanas.

3. The adjectives **bueno** and **malo** can be placed before or after the noun they describe. But when they precede a singular masculine noun, the **-o** is dropped: **buen** and **mal.**[1]

Billy Crystal es un **buen** cómico.
        Billy Crystal is a good comedian.
Billy Crystal es un cómico **bueno.**

Dr. Evil es un **mal** hombre.
        Dr. Evil is a bad man.
Dr. Evil es un hombre **malo.**

¡A practicar!

N. **¡NO ES ASÍ!** Complete the following sentences using the new vocabulary from this section.

MODELO: Mi mejor amigo no es antipático; es *simpático.*

---

[1] The adjective **grande** can also be used before or after the noun it describes. When it precedes a singular noun (either masculine or feminine) it drops the **-de** to become **gran.** When **gran** precedes a noun, it takes on the figurative meaning of *great* or *impressive.* When **grande** follows a noun, it assumes its more literal meaning of *large* or *big.* For example, **Es una gran casa.** *(It's a great house.)* versus **Es una casa grande.** *(It's a big house.)*

1. Mis profesores no son perezosos; son _____.
2. Los Indiana Pacers no son bajos; son _____.
3. Mi carro no es viejo; es _____.
4. Mis amigas no son feas; son _____.
5. Nosotros no somos tontos; somos _____.
6. Bill Gates no es pobre; es _____.
7. Hillary Clinton no es morena; es _____.
8. Austin Powers no es un mal hombre; es un _____ hombre.

O. **¿CÓMO ES/SON?** Describe the following people, using descriptive adjectives and the appropriate form of the verb **ser.** Use adjectives that precede a noun in at least three of your sentences.

MODELO: Bill Clinton
          Bill Clinton es alto y trabajador.

1. Ricky Martin
2. Cher
3. Michael Jordan
4. mi profesor(a) de español
5. mis compañeros de clase
6. mi mejor amigo(a)
7. yo
8. mi familia y yo
9. mis padres
10. mis hermanos(as)

En voz alta

P. **DESCRIPCIONES** Choose from the adjectives you have learned to describe what the following people are and are not like. Be sure the adjectives agree in number and, if necessary, in gender. Compare your answers with your classmates'.

MODELO: Mi madre es...   pero no es...
          Mi madre es trabajadora pero no es atlética.

1. Mi mejor amigo(a) es...   pero no es...
2. Mis abuelos son...   pero no son...
3. Mis compañeros de clase son...   pero no son...
4. Mi padre es...   pero no es...
5. Los estudiantes en esta universidad son... pero no son...
6. El (La) profesor(a) es...   pero no es...
7. Nuestro presidente es...   pero no es...
8. Yo soy...   pero no soy...

Q. **¿QUIÉN PUEDE SER?** Describe someone in the class for a classmate to identify.

MODELO: E1: *Es alta, delgada y atlética. Es morena.*
          E2: *¿Es Michelle?*
          E1: *¡Sí!*

ENCUENTRO *cultural*

Familias hispánicas

Éstos son unas palabras nuevas para la lectura:

los compadres   *co-parents*
los ahijados   *godchildren*
los padrinos   *godparents*

En la cultura hispánica la unidad social más importante es la familia. Normalmente, se mantienen íntimas relaciones entre los miembros de la familia. En el mundo hispánico la familia es los padres y los hijos, pero también es los abuelos, los tíos, los primos y los sobrinos, incluyendo hasta la segunda y tercera generaciones.

No toda la familia vive en la misma casa, pero a veces viven en el mismo barrio. Esto les permite ayudar y recibir ayuda cuando es necesario. Cuando una persona de la familia necesita ayuda, la familia da ayuda material o emocional. Por lo general, los abuelos viven con sus hijos, así contribuyen con la disciplina de los nietos y ayudan a los hijos que van a trabajar todos los días. Los abuelos son un elemento muy importante en la unión y la tradición familiar.

En el mundo hispánico la relación entre **los compadres** y **los ahijados** y **padrinos** es muy seria. Los padrinos participan en todos los eventos importantes como parte de la familia.

Para pensar: ¿Puedes describir tu familia? ¿Tienen Uds. relaciones muy íntimas o no? ¿Tienes tú padrinos, o eres tú padrino(a) de alguien? ¿Cuál es tu opinión de estas relaciones? ¿Es importante para un niño tener una familia grande o íntima?

R. **PREGUNTAS** Answer the following questions based on the reading.

1. What is the most important social unit for the Spanish-speaking culture?
2. Give two advantages and two disadvantages of being a part of a close-knit family. Explain your answers.

VOCABULARIO: *Las nacionalidades*

América del Norte
canadiense
estadounidense
mexicano(a)
norte-
americano(a)

América Central
costarricense
guatemalteco(a)
hondureño(a)
nicaragüense
panameño(a)
salvadoreño(a)

El Caribe
cubano(a)
dominicano(a)
haitano(a)
puertorriqueño(a)

América del Sur
argentino(a)
boliviano(a)
brasileño(a)
chileno(a)
colombiano(a)
ecuatoriano(a)
paraguayo(a)
peruano(a)
uruguayo(a)
venezolano(a)

Europa
alemán(a)
español(a)
francés(a)
inglés(a)
italiano(a)
ruso(a)

África
egipcio(a)
guineano(a)

Asia
chino(a)
coreano(a)
japonés(a)

¡A practicar!

S. LENGUAS Y NACIONALIDADES Identify the nationalities of the following people. In some cases, there may be various possibilities.

1. Jorge es de América del Sur y habla portugués. Él es _____.
2. Zhou es de Asia y no habla japonés. Ella es _____.
3. Paqui y Mar son de Europa y hablan español. Ellas son _____.
4. Teresita es de San Juan y habla español. Ella es _____.
5. Tito y Florentina viven en Roma. Ellos son _____.
6. Hans es de Bonn y habla alemán. Él es _____.
7. Margarita es de América del Norte y habla español. Ella es _____.
8. Pierre es de América del Norte y habla francés e inglés. Él es _____.
9. María es de América del Sur y habla español. Ella es _____.
10. Yo soy _____.
11. Mi profesor(a) es _____.

> **¿NOS ENTENDEMOS?**
> Another way to say **costarricense** is **tico(a)**. **Puertorriqueños** are also known as **boricuas**. Spaniards from **Galicia**, the northwest part of Spain, are called **gallegos**.

T. ORÍGENES Use adjectives of nationality to indicate the origins of the following items.

1. El sushi es una comida _____.
2. El croissant es _____.
3. Las pirámides más famosas son _____.
4. El kimichi es una comida _____.
5. El BMW es un automóvil _____.
6. El tango es _____.
7. Los burritos son _____.
8. Los espaguetis son _____.
9. El mejor *(The best)* café del mundo es _____.

En voz alta

U. ¿DE DÓNDE ES? Take turns saying a nationality out loud and having your partner name as many people as possible of that nationality.

Gloria Estefan

MODELO: cubano
Gloria Estefan, Fidel Castro y
José Martí son cubanos.

ENCUENTRO *cultural*

Los gestos

Los españoles y los latinoamericanos usan muchos gestos con las manos cuando hablan. Por ejemplo, hay gestos para expresar **tacaño**, **¡Cuidado!** y **¡Un momento!** Es posible tener una breve conversación con las manos.

Los turistas de otros países necesitan tener mucho cuidado con los gestos cuando visitan España o Latinoamérica. ¿Por qué? Porque los gestos no son iguales en todas las culturas. Por ejemplo, los norteamericanos usan unos gestos que no tienen equivalentes en la cultura hispánica y algunos que pueden ser ofensivos. Aquí tienes algunos gestos del mundo hispánico.

Para pensar: ¿Usas gestos? ¿Cuáles son? Con una pareja, haz todos los gestos que usas. Compáralos a los gestos del mundo hispánico.

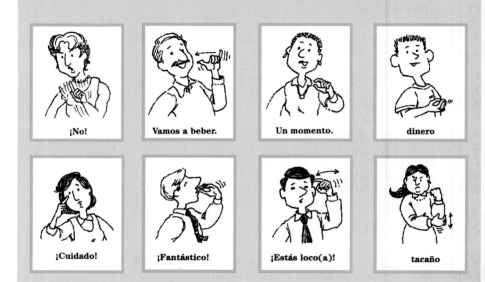

| ¡No! | Vamos a beber. | Un momento. | dinero |
| ¡Cuidado! | ¡Fantástico! | ¡Estás loco(a)! | tacaño |

V. PRÁCTICA Using some of the gestures used by Spanish speakers, work with two of your classmates to role-play the following situation: Pretend you are three students sharing an apartment and this is the first week of classes. One student wants to go out on the town; one student thinks it's a great idea; and the other student thinks it's a crazy idea and refuses to go along, but warns them to be careful.

GRAMÁTICA III: *Present tense of -er and -ir verbs*

To form the present tense of Spanish infinitives ending in **-er** and **-ir,** add the appropriate personal endings to the stem of each.

com + er *(to eat)*			viv + ir *(to live)*	
yo	com**o**	*I eat*	viv**o**	*I live*
tú	com**es**	*you (informal) eat*	viv**es**	*you (informal) live*
Ud., él, ella	com**e**	*you (formal) eat; he, she eats*	viv**e**	*you (formal) live; he, she lives*
nosotros(as)	com**emos**	*we eat*	viv**imos**	*we live*
vosotros(as)	com**éis**	*you (informal) eat*	viv**ís**	*you (informal) live*
Uds., ellos(as)	com**en**	*you (formal) eat; they eat*	viv**en**	*you (formal) live; they live*

The following are several useful **-er** and **-ir** verbs presented as phrases:

abrir (la puerta para mi abuelo)	*to open (the door for my grandfather)*
aprender (español)	*to learn (Spanish)*
asistir a (clase)	*to attend (class)*
beber (café)	*to drink (coffee)*
comprender (la tarea)	*to understand (the homework)*
creer (en la importancia de mi familia)	*to believe (in the importance of my family)*
deber (hablar con mi primo)	*(to) must (talk with my cousin)*
escribir (una carta a mi tía)	*to write (a letter to my aunt)*
leer (un libro)	*to read (a book)*
recibir (una tarjeta de mi sobrino)	*to receive (a card from my nephew)*
vender (mis libros)	*to sell (my books)*
vivir (con mis amigos)	*to live (with my friends)*

¡A practicar!

W. **MI COMPAÑERO Y YO** Complete the following paragraph with the appropriate form of the **-er** and **-ir** verbs in parentheses to learn about Tomás's roommate at UNAM.[1]

Mi compañero de cuarto se llama José Suárez. José y yo _____ **(vivir)** en un apartamento en Colonia Roma. Nosotros _____ **(asistir)** a UNAM en México. Mi compañero _____es_____ **(ser)** de Oaxaca en el sur de México. Todos los días él _____ **(recibir)** noticias *(news)* de su familia. Su hermana le _____ **(escribir)** mucho por correo electrónico *(email)*. A veces yo _____le_____ **(leer)** los mensajes *(messages)* de ella. A mi amigo no le gusta cuando yo _____abro_____ **(abrir)** sus cartas electrónicas. Mis padres a veces me _____ **(escribir)** cartas normales. Ellos no _____ **(comprender)** la tecnología nueva. Mi padre _____ **(creer)** que las computadoras son importantes, pero todavía no tienen computadora en casa. Mi amigo y yo hablamos mucho de la tecnología cuando nosotros _____ **(comer)** juntos *(together)* en la cafetería de la UNAM. José _____ **(leer)** periódicos políticos y así yo _____ **(aprender)** de él sobre los acontecimientos *(happenings)* políticos en nuestro país.

¿NOS ENTENDEMOS?

Deber is a special verb in Spanish that is used before other verbs to communicate the idea of obligation. In Spanish, as in English, when two verbs are used together the first is conjugated and the second appears in the infinitive form: Yo **debo** ir a la fiesta. *(I should [must, ought to] go to the party.)*

---

[1] UNAM stands for **la Universidad Nacional Autóctona de México.**

X. **DOS COMPAÑEROS** Complete the following paragraph with the correct form of the verb. In some cases, you will need to use the infinitive. Several words will be used more than once.

asistir a   vivir   beber   ser   comprender   comer   aprender

¡Hola! Me llamo Carlota. _bebo_____ en el D.F. _____ estudiante de la UNAM donde estudio para ser intérprete. _____ mucho de la cultura y la lengua de los norteamericanos en mis clases. Yo _____ clases con mi amigo Juan. Él _____ un compañero en la clase de inglés. Cuando nuestro profesor habla rápido en inglés, Juan no _____ bien. Mi amigo estudia mucho pero el inglés _____ difícil. Juan y yo _____ en la cafetería donde también _____ café y _____ sándwiches. Yo necesito _____ en los Estados Unidos para _____ más.

En voz alta

Y. **ACTIVIDADES DIARIAS** Construct sentences, selecting from the three categories below.

¿Quién?	¿Qué?	¿Dónde?
yo	leer el periódico	en el cuarto
mi compañero(a)	comer	en casa
tú	aprender el vocabulario	en la cafetería
el (la) profesor(a)	beber café	en clase
mis padres	escribir cartas	en la biblioteca

Z. **ENTREVISTA** Work with a partner to discuss the following questions. Report your findings to the rest of the class.

1. ¿Dónde vives ahora? ¿Con quién vives? ¿Cuál es tu dirección?
2. ¿Aprendes mucho en tus clases? ¿Debes estudiar mucho?
3. En general, ¿eres un(a) estudiante bueno(a) o malo(a)?
4. ¿Lees mucho o poco? ¿Lees novelas, el periódico o páginas en Internet?
5. ¿Dónde comes? ¿Qué tipo de comida comes?

ASÍ SE DICE: *Common uses of the verb tener*

The verb **tener** *(to have)* is frequently used to indicate possession. Another common use of **tener** is to express age.

With possession

—¿Cuántas hermanas **tienes**?   *How many sisters **do you have?***
—Yo **tengo** dos hermanas.   *I **have** two sisters.*
—¿**Tienen** familias tus hermanas?   *Do your sisters **have** families?*
—No, no **tienen** familias.   *No, **they don't have** families.*

With age

Mirta solamente **tiene 18 años** y Margarita **tiene 20 años.**
*Mirta **is only 18 years old** and Margarita **is 20 years old.***

The present tense of **tener** is formed as follows:

tener

yo	tengo	*I have*
tú	tienes	*you* (informal) *have*
usted, él, ella	tiene	*you* (formal) *have; he, she has*
nosotros(as)	tenemos	*we have*
vosotros(as)	tenéis	*you* (informal) *have*
ustedes, ellos(as)	tienen	*you* (formal) *have; they have*

The verb **tener** is used in many idiomatic expressions in Spanish. In addition to expressing age and possession, **tener** is used to express the following:

tener éxito   *to be successful*

tener hambre   *to be hungry*

tener prisa   *to be in a hurry*

tener razón   *to be right*

tener sed   *to be thirsty*

tener sueño   *to be tired/sleepy*

¡A practicar!

AA. ¿QUÉ TIENES? Provide the correct form of **tener** to complete the sentences.

MODELO: Yo *tengo* una mochila nueva.

1. Nosotros _____ una profesora nueva.
2. Tú *tienes* mucha tarea.
3. Ellos _____ el nuevo CD de Dave Mathews.
4. Vosotros _____ una fiesta cada *(each)* fin de semana.
5. Roberto estudia mucho y _____ éxito en su clase de español.
6. Después de hacer ejercicio yo *tengo* sed.
7. Mi hermanita, Paqui, *tiene* nueve años.
8. Mi profesor siempre *tiene* razón.
9. ¡Tú siempre *tienes* sueño! Debes descansar más.
10. Yo *tengo* hambre. Yo quiero un taco de Taco Bell.

BB. UNA ESCENA FAMILIAR *(A family scene)* Complete the following dialog between Juan Carlos and his mother with the appropriate idiomatic expression with **tener.**

Los padres de Juan Carlos saben cómo persuadir *(to persuade)* a su hijo. Ellos siempre _____ con él cuando el tema *(theme)* es la comida.

Mamá:	¡Juan Carlos! Tu padre nos espera en el restaurante. ¡Nosotros _____!
Juan Carlos:	Ya voy, mamá. Pero es tan tarde y yo _____.
Mamá:	¿No _____? Tú necesitas comer algo. Y yo sé que tu padre siempre _____ de una cerveza después de su trabajo.
Juan Carlos:	Sí, quiero comer algo, mamá. No comí nada *(I didn't eat anything)* en todo el día.
Mamá:	Si vamos ahora, en 15 minutos comes una hamburguesa en Sanborn's.
Juan Carlos:	Muy bien, mamá. Tú _____. Voy ahora mismo.

En voz alta

CC. CONVERSAMOS Ask the following questions of a partner and compare answers.

1. ¿Cuándo tienes sueño, en clase o por la noche?
2. ¿Tienes razón con frecuencia? ¿En qué situaciones tienes razón?
3. ¿Cuándo tienes prisa? ¿Siempre llegas a tiempo?
4. ¿Tienes mucho éxito en tu vida? ¿Tienen éxito tus compañeros(as)?
5. ¿Tenemos clase mañana?
6. ¿Tenemos mucha tarea?
7. ¿Siempre tiene razón el (la) profesor(a)?
8. ¿Tienes hambre ahora?
9. ¿Cuándo tenemos vacaciones?

DD. ¿CUÁNTOS HERMANOS TIENES? Working with a partner, ask each other questions about your families using **tener.**

MODELO: **E1:** *¿Cuántos hermanos tienes?*
          E2: *Yo tengo tres hermanos: una hermana y dos hermanos.*
          E2: *¿Tienes hermanos?*
          E1: *Sí, yo tengo una hermana. Mi hermana se llama Carolina.*
          E2: *¿Y cuántos años tiene Carolina?*
          E1: *Ella tiene 18 años.*

VOCABULARIO: *Los números 31 a 100*

	y uno
30 **treinta**	**y dos**
40 **cuarenta**	**y tres**
50 **cincuenta**	**y cuatro**
60 **sesenta**	**y cinco**
70 **setenta**	**y seis**
80 **ochenta**	**y siete**
90 **noventa**	**y ocho**
	y nueve

100 **cien/ciento**

The short form of **cien** is used before nouns and in counting. You will practice **ciento** later when you learn how to count above one hundred.

cien libros   *one hundred books*
...noventa y nueve, **cien**   *. . . ninety-nine, one hundred*

¡A practicar!

EE. **PROBLEMAS DE MATEMÁTICAS** Working with a partner, quiz each other on the following equations, taking turns reading the questions to one another.

+ **y**
− **menos**
= **son**

MODELOS: $37 + 41 =$
        E1: *¿Cuántos son treinta y siete y cuarenta y uno?*
        E2: *Treinta y siete y cuarenta y uno son setenta y ocho.*

        $50 − 25 =$
        E1: *¿Cuántos son cincuenta menos veinticinco?*
        E2: *Cincuenta menos veinticinco son veinticinco.*

1. $15 + 15 =$
2. $80 + 17 =$
3. $77 − 22 =$
4. $60 − 19 =$
5. $59 + 7 =$
6. $100 − 25 =$
7. $22 + 24 =$
8. $16 + 36 =$
9. $99 − 10 =$

En voz alta

FF. **¿QUÉ NÚMERO ES?** Working in groups of three or four, have one student think of a number between 30 and 100. The other students will try to guess the number with hints from the first student, who will guide them with **más** *(more)* or **menos** *(less)*. The first group to guess four numbers wins.

MODELO: E1: *¿Es cincuenta?*
           E2: *No, no es cincuenta. Es menos.*
           E3: *¿Es cuarenta?*
           E2: *No, no es cuarenta. Es más.*
           E1: *¿Es cuarenta y nueve?*
           E2: *¡Sí! Tienes razón.*

Síntesis

¡A ver!

ACTIVIDAD 1 Pre-viewing task (Segmento 1 del video)

Paso 1: Watch as Esmeralda, who comes from León in central Mexico, introduces the first segment of the video. Esmeralda will talk about the family in the Spanish-speaking world and show you two short video clips that will give you a sense of the importance that the family plays in the Spanish-speaking world. As you watch and listen to this introductory segment, make a list of the words and expressions that you recognize related to the family.

Paso 2: When you have finished, share your list with your partner.

ACTIVIDAD 2 Pre-viewing task (Segmento 2 del video)

You are going to meet Laura, who comes from Mexico. She is a wife and mother of two. You will see Laura at the breakfast table with her family, whom she is going to introduce to you.

Paso 1: Before you watch the video, imagine that you have to talk about your family, in Spanish, to a Spanish-speaking friend you have just made. What would you say about each member of your family? Make a list of the themes you would talk about for each person in your family (e.g., **mi hermano: su nombre, su edad, sus estudios**).

Paso 2: When you have finished, talk to your partner about your family. Make statements like the following:

> **Tengo dos hermanos. Uno se llama Pedro. Pedro tiene 15 años y es estudiante. La otra es Isabel...**

As your partner is listening to you, he/she should make reactions that signal his/her involvement in the conversation. Such reactions may be enthusiastic (e.g., **¡Genial!** [*Fantastic!*] or **¡Qué bien!** [*How nice!*]) or perhaps confirmation checks (e.g., **¿Verdad?** [*Really?*]). Your partner might also make comments such as **Mi hermana también es estudiante de la universidad.**

ACTIVIDAD 3   Viewing task (Segmento 2 del video)

Paso 1: Now watch the video segment of Laura introducing her family at the breakfast table. As you watch, find out the following information for each of the four members of the family, as well as the fifth person who appears at the end of the scene. You may not find information for all five characters on all units of information indicated in the table.

nombre	Laura			MARKos	
edad					
profesión/estudios				Arkiteo	
¿otra información?					

Paso 2: In the **¿Nos entendemos?** and **En contexto** sections of **Capítulo 2,** you are told of the use of diminutive forms of address and other phrases used to express affection, frequently with people you know very well but sometimes with people you may have just met. Can you find any examples of the use of such terms of affection in the video segment?

ACTIVIDAD 4   Post-viewing task (Segmento 2 del video)

Paso 1: Working with your partner, make statements about each member of Laura's household using the information you have obtained for **Actividad 3.**

Paso 2: How would you describe Laura's family as a whole? Would any of the adjectives listed below be used to describe the family? With your partner, give your impressions of the family, using adjectives listed below or any others you think are suitable. You may disagree with your partner (**No, no estoy de acuerdo. Para mí, es una familia muy moderna.**) or you may agree with him or her (**Sí, estoy de acuerdo.**). Make sure that you make each adjective agree in form with the noun it describes, as in the example above.

moderno	simpático	grande
humilde	arrogante	normal
conservador	interesante	pequeño
progresista	triste	
liberal	numeroso	

Paso 3: Now, with your partner, describe each of the individual members of the household, both from a physical point of view as well as from the point of view of what you imagine their personalities to be like. Again, be careful with the agreement of adjectives with the nouns they describe, and don't forget to agree or disagree with the comments made by your partner as you see fit.

¡A leer!

Skimming and scanning

Two useful reading strategies are skimming and scanning. Skimming reading material is useful for quickly getting the gist or general idea of its content. Often we reread the same material and scan it to find specific information.

Paso 1: Skim the four descriptions below to get a general understanding of what they are about. Then answer the following questions.

1. What are these descriptions about?
2. What do you suppose their purpose is?
3. In what type of publication do you think these descriptions would appear? Why do you think so?

Nombre: Marco Luis Corona
Dirección: Egido 624, Apto. 2, entre Paula y San Isidro, Chihuahua, MÉXICO
Edad: 20 años
Pasatiempos: Escuchar música, leer, coleccionar fotos de artistas, hacer amistades, correr, pasar tiempo con mis hermanos y mis primos

Nombre: Rosario Inés Arias
Dirección: Calle Variante No. 3, Código Postal 4150, Mirimire, Cuernavaca, MÉXICO
Edad: 17 años
Pasatiempos: Coleccionar postales, billetes, calco-manías, monedas y todo lo referente a mis ído-los (Chayanne, Luis Miguel y Enrique Iglesias). También me gusta leer, escuchar música y es-cribir cartas.

Nombre: Noelia Barrera Alba
Dirección: El Miramar, Apartado 3 Norte, C.P. 4300, Durango, Dgo. MÉXICO
Edad: 16 años
Pasatiempos: Tocar instrumentos musicales, salir, leer poemas e intercambiar correspondencia con chicos y chicas de todo el mundo

Nombre: Susana Prado Rivera
Dirección: Calle Guadalajara No. 5-2475, Mérida, MÉXICO
Edad: 18 años
Pasatiempos: Coleccionar postales, estampillas y todo lo relacionado con Chayanne, leer libros, escuchar música variada, aprender todo lo refe-rente a las ciencias, (especialmente la medicina), mantener correspondencia con chicos de otros países y practicar deportes

Paso 2: Scan the descriptions to answer the following questions.

1. What is the first name of the oldest person described?
2. Who enjoys . . .
   a. collecting stamps?
   b. listening to music?
   c. learning about science and medicine?
   d. collecting postcards?
   e. playing musical instruments?
   f. music by the music and film star Chayanne?

Paso 3: Imagine that Susana is your pen pal and that she has written you a letter introducing herself and her family. Scan the following excerpt from her letter in order to answer the questions below.

¡Hola! Me llamo Susana Prado Rivera. Tengo una familia grande. Hay siete personas en mi familia. Mi padre se llama Luis y mi madre se llama Josefina. Mis padres son simpáticos, honestos y trabajadores. Tengo dos hermanos menores y dos hermanas mayores. Mis hermanos se llaman Esteban y Carlos. Esteban tiene 15 años y es delgado, moreno y atlético. Carlos tiene 17 años y es alto, guapo y artístico. Mis hermanas se llaman Elena y María. Elena tiene 20 años y es soltera. María tiene 23 años y está casada. Su marido se llama Javier. Mis hermanas son intelectuales, sinceras y pacientes. Cerca de nosotros viven mi tía Teresa, la hermana de mi madre, y mi tío Felipe, su esposo.

1. How old is Susana's youngest brother?
2. What is the name of Susana's oldest sister?
3. Who does Susana describe as . . .
   a. tall, good-looking and artistic?
   b. intellectual, sincere, and pacient?
   c. nice, honest, and hard-working?

¡A escribir!

Learning Spanish word order

Word order refers to the meaningful sequence of words in a sentence. The order of words in Spanish sentences differs somewhat from English word order. Some common rules of Spanish word order are:

- Definite and indefinite articles precede nouns.
  Los gatos y **los perros** son animales.
  Tengo **un gato** y **un perro**.

- Subjects usually precede their verbs in statements.
  Mi gato es negro.

- Subjects usually follow their verbs in questions.
  ¿Tiene usted animales en casa?

- Adjectives of quantity usually precede nouns.
  ¿Cuántos animales tienes en casa?

- Adjectives of description usually follow nouns.
  El **perro marrón** se llama Bandido.

- Possession is often expressed by using **de** with a noun.
  Café es **el gato de Sara**.

Paso 1: Unscramble the words in the following sentences, then rewrite them in their correct sequence. Be sure to capitalize the first word of every sentence and to end each one with a period.

MODELO: es Anita Camacho de México
          Anita Camacho es de México.

1. es Anita una universitaria estudiante
2. Carlos Suárez su clase compañero se llama de
3. Carlos un poco y Anita hablan de inglés
4. años tienen cuántos ellos ¿?
5. Carlos 23 tiene y tiene 19 Anita
6. tiene Anita hermanos ¿?
7. José padre el es Anita de
8. gato tiene un Anita
9. Pecas llama Anita se gato de el

Paso 2: Now work with a classmate. Compare your sentences and check for errors in word order, spelling, capitalization, and punctuation.

Paso 3: Imagine that you are Susana's new pen pal and that you are writing her a letter introducing yourself and your family. You may wish to use Susana's letter in **Paso 3** of **¡A leer!** as a model. Describe your family as accurately as possible, including information such as names, ages, physical descriptions, and personality traits.

Hand in

¡A conversar!

Mi familia

Think about how you described your family in the letter you wrote to Susana in the **¡A escribir!** section above. With this in mind, now describe your family tree to your partner. Your partner should take notes and draw your family tree as you speak. Be sure to include descriptive information about specific members of your family, such as where they live, their ages, and their favorite pastimes. Later, each of you will describe your partner's family to the class.

Miembros de la familia y otros parientes   *Members of the family and other relatives*

el (la) abuelo(a)   *grandfather/grandmother*
el apellido   *last name*
el (la) esposo(a)   *husband/wife*

el (la) hermano(a)   *brother/sister*
el (la) hijo(a)   *son/daughter*
la madre (mamá)   *mother*

el (la) nieto(a)   *grandson/granddaughter*
el nombre   *first name*
el padre (papá)   *father*

el (la) primo(a)   *cousin*
el (la) sobrino(a)   *nephew/niece*
el (la) tío(a)   *uncle/aunt*

Las mascotas   *Pets*

el gato   *cat*

el pájaro   *bird*

el perro   *dog*

el pez   *fish*

Las características físicas y la personalidad   *Physical characteristics and personality*

alto(a)   *tall*
amable   *friendly*
antipático(a)   *unpleasant*
artístico(a)   *artistic*
atlético(a)   *athletic*
bajo(a)   *short (height)*
bonito(a)   *pretty*
bueno(a)   *good*
corto(a)   *short (length)*
delgado(a)   *thin*

extrovertido(a)   *outgoing*
feo(a)   *ugly*
generoso(a)   *generous*
gordo(a)   *fat*
grande   *big, large*
guapo(a)   *good-looking*
honesto(a)   *honest*
inteligente   *intelligent*
irresponsable   *irresponsible*
joven   *young*

largo(a)   *long*
listo(a)   *smart*
malo(a)   *bad*
moreno(a)   *dark-haired*
nuevo(a)   *new*
paciente   *patient*
pequeño(a)   *small*
perezoso(a)   *lazy*
pobre   *poor*
responsable   *responsible*

rico(a)   *rich*
rubio(a)   *blonde*
simpático(a)   *nice*
sincero(a)   *sincere*
tacaño(a)   *stingy*
tímido(a)   *shy, timid*
tonto(a)   *silly, foolish*
trabajador(a)   *hardworking*
viejo(a)   *old*

Las nacionalidades   *Nationalities*

alemán(a)   *German*
argentino(a)   *Argentine*
boliviano(a)   *Bolivian*
brasileño(a)   *Brazilian*
canadiense   *Canadian*
chileno(a)   *Chilean*
chino(a)   *Chinese*
colombiano(a)   *Colombian*
coreano(a)   *Korean*
costarricense   *Costa Rican*
cubano(a)   *Cuban*

dominicano(a)   *Dominican (from the Dominican Republic)*
ecuatoriano(a)   *Ecuadorean*
egipcio(a)   *Egyptian*
español(a)   *Spanish*
estadounidense   *from the United States*
francés(a)   *French*
guatemalteco(a)   *Guatemalan*

guineano(a)   *from Equatorial Guinea*
haitiano(a)   *Haitian*
hondureño(a)   *Honduran*
inglés(a)   *English*
italiano(a)   *Italian*
japonés(a)   *Japanese*
mexicano(a)   *Mexican*
nicaragüense   *Nicaraguan*
norteamericano(a)   *North American, American*

panameño(a)   *Panamanian*
paraguayo(a)   *Paraguayan*
peruano(a)   *Peruvian*
puertorriqueño(a)   *Puerto Rican*
ruso(a)   *Russian*
salvadoreño(a)   *Salvadoran*
uruguayo(a)   *Uruguayan*
venezolano(a)   *Venezuelan*

Verbos

abrir   *to open*
aprender   *to learn*
asistir a   *to attend*
beber   *to drink*
comer   *to eat*
comprender   *to understand*

creer   *to believe*
deber   *to should, must, ought*
escribir   *to write*
leer   *to read*
recibir   *to receive*

ser   *to be*
tener   *to have*
tener éxito   *to be successful*
tener hambre   *to be hungry*
tener prisa   *to be in a hurry*
tener razón   *to be right*

tener sed   *to be thirsty*
tener sueño   *to be tired, sleepy*
vender   *to sell*
vivir   *to live*

Los números 31 a 100

treinta y uno, treinta y dos, treinta y tres...   31, 32, 33 . . .

cuarenta   40
cincuenta   50
sesenta   60

setenta   70
ochenta   80
noventa   90

cien/ciento   100

Expresiones idomáticas

¡Qué bueno!   *Wonderful!*

por supuesto   *of course*

Así que...   *So . . .*

3

El tiempo libre: Colombia

Communicative goals

In this chapter you will learn how to . . .

- Describe leisure-time activities
- Express likes and dislikes
- Express plans and intentions
- Describe basic actions and places and activities in town
- Talk about seasons, the weather, and months of the year

Grammar

- The verb **gustar** + infinitive and **gustar** + noun
- The contraction **al (a + el)**
- Present tense of **ir + a(l)**
- Present tense of **hacer** and other irregular **yo** verbs
- **Saber** versus **conocer**
- The personal **a**
- Weather expressions with **hacer**
- **Tener** + **que** and **tener frío/calor**

Cultural information

- Sports in the Spanish-speaking world
- **El café**

La Plaza Bolívar, Bogotá, Colombia

LOS DEPORTES QUE PRACTICA LA GENTE ACTIVA In this section you will learn how to talk about sports and leisure-time activities.

jugar al tenis

levantar pesas

andar en bicicleta (hacer ciclismo)

caminar por las montañas

esquiar

montar a caballo

nadar (practicar natación)

patinar en línea

correr

esquiar en el agua

Otras palabras deportivas *Other sports words*

el baloncesto *basketball*
el béisbol *baseball*
el campo de fútbol (de golf) *football field (golf course)*
el fútbol (americano) *soccer (football)*

ganar *to win*
el golf *golf*
el partido *game*
el vólibol *volleyball*

Los pasatiempos *Pastimes*

bailar *to dance*
dar un paseo *to go for a walk*
hacer un picnic (planes, ejercicio) *to go on a picnic (to make plans, to exercise)*
ir... *to go . . .*
　　al cine *to the movies*
　　a tomar un café *to drink coffee*
　　a un bar *to a bar*
　　a un club *to a club*
　　a un concierto *to a concert*

　　a una discoteca *to a disco*
　　a una fiesta *to a party*
　　de compras *shopping*
mirar la tele *to watch television*
sacar fotos *to take pictures*
tocar la guitarra *to play the guitar*
tomar el sol *to sunbathe*
ver una película *to watch a movie*
visitar un museo *to visit a museum*

¿NOS ENTENDEMOS?

El baloncesto is also called **el básquetbol**, and *ball* can be called **el balón, la bola,** or **la pelota.**

➥ *Palabras útiles* are for recognition only; you will not be tested on these words. These words are provided to help you better describe the sports and pastimes you like.

Palabras útiles

la bicicleta *bicycle*	el juego *game*
la cámara *camera*	el (la) jugador(a) *player*
los esquís (acuáticos) *(water) skis*	los patines (en línea) *(in-line) skates*
el estadio *stadium*	el traje de baño *bathing suit*
las gafas de sol *sunglasses*	los zapatos de tenis (deportivos) *tennis shoes (sneakers)*

¡A practicar!

A. ASOCIACIONES ¿Qué asociaciones haces con la siguiente lista de personas?

MODELO: Garth Brooks
un concierto, tocar la guitarra, cantar

1. Michael Jordan
2. Peyton Manning
3. Mia Hamm
4. John Travolta
5. Richard Simmons
6. Pete Sampras
7. Sammy Sosa
8. Tiger Woods
9. Gabrielle Reese
10. Lance Armstrong

B. ¿EN QUÉ PUEDO SERVIRLE? *(How can I serve you?)* Ahora tú trabajas en una tienda de deportes. Adivina *(Guess)* qué deporte o pasatiempo practican tus clientes. En algunos casos *(some cases)* hay varias posibilidades.

MODELO: Un señor: Yo necesito un traje de baño.
¡Ah! Ud. nada.
o: *¡Ah! Ud. practica la natación.*

1. Dos chicos: Nosotros necesitamos una cámara.
2. Una chica: Necesito más pesas.
3. Dos señoras: ¿Dónde están los patines?
4. Una chica: Busco un casco *(helmet)* y riendas *(reins)*.
5. Dos chicos: ¿Hay zapatos de tenis en esta tienda?
6. Tu amiga: ¿Tienes gafas de sol?
7. Tu mamá: ¿Hay bicicletas a buenos precios?
8. Tus abuelos: Vamos a comprar otros esquís acuáticos.

En voz alta

C. UN FIN DE SEMANA TÍPICO Con los elementos de abajo *(items below)* hazle preguntas a un(a) compañero(a) de clase sobre lo que hace los fines de semana. Al contestar *(Upon answering)* las preguntas, cambia la oración para hacerla correcta para ti.

MODELO: tú / dar un paseo en el parque / los sábados
E1: *¿Das un paseo en el parque los sábados?*
E2: *Sí, doy un paseo en el parque los sábados con mi amiga Jill.*
o: E2: *No, mis amigas y yo hacemos un picnic los sábados.*

1. tú / bailar en las fiestas / los viernes por la noche
2. tú y tu compañero(a) de cuarto / mirar la tele / los sábados por la tarde
3. tú y tu(s) amigo(a)(s) / tomar café / los sábados por la noche
4. tú / visitar un museo / los domingos por la mañana
5. tú / andar en bicicleta / los domingos por la tarde
6. tú y tus padres / tocar el piano y cantar / los domingos por la noche

¿NOS ENTENDEMOS?

To form **sí/no** questions, make your voice rise at the end of the questions. Another way is to invert the order of the subject and verb, in addition to making your voice rise at the end of the question:

¿Miguel regresa a las seis? →

¿Regresa Miguel a las seis? →

D. DEPORTES FAVORITOS Hazle a otro(a) estudiante las siguientes preguntas sobre los deportes. ¿Hay algo que tienes en común con tu compañero(a) con respecto a sus deportes favoritos?

mi deporte

1. ¿Cuál es tu deporte favorito? ¿Qué otro deporte te gusta mucho?
2. ¿Esquías? (¿Sí? ¿Dónde esquías? ¿Con quién esquías?)
3. ¿Nadas bien o mal? ¿Dónde y con quién te gusta nadar? ¿Cuándo nadas?
4. ¿Montas a caballo? (¿Sí? ¿Es fácil o difícil montar a caballo? ¿Es más fácil montar a caballo o andar en bicicleta?)
5. ¿Haces mucho o poco ejercicio? ¿Qué tipo *(kind)* de ejercicio haces? ¿Dónde haces ejercicio normalmente?

EN CONTEXTO

Three Colombian students, Catalina, Isabel, and Gerardo, are discussing plans for an upcoming party at Catalina's apartment in Cali, Colombia. As you read the following dialog, pay attention to the form of address used among the three friends.

GERARDO: ¡Hola, Catalina! Isabel dice que usted va a tener una fiesta este fin de semana.

CATALINA: ¡Sí! Le invito a usted y a su hermano, Pepe. Ustedes tienen que venir.

GERARDO: Hmmm... ¿Cuándo es?

CATALINA: El sábado a las nueve en mi casa. Cuento con usted *(I'm counting on you)* para la música y con su hermano para sacar fotos.

GERARDO: Bueno, no sé. No toco la guitarra mucho estos días *(these days)* y...

ISABEL: ¡Venga *(Come on!),* Gerardo! Va a ser una fiesta chévere, y usted nunca practica. ¡Es un maestro de la guitarra!

GERARDO: Es un poco complicado. Yo conozco a una chica, y ya tenemos planes para ir a un club el sábado. No sé si...

CATALINA: ¡Puede venir ella *(She can come)* a pasar un buen rato *(a good time)* con nosotros!

ISABEL: Vamos a bailar mucho, y yo sé cómo le gusta bailar a su hermano.

GERARDO: Bueno, acepto. Y si toco un poquitico de música romántica, ¿no van a burlarse de mí *(you won't make fun of me?)*? Mi compañera es muy sensible,[1] y...

CATALINA: ¡Ay! ¡Qué cursi! *(How corny!)* La mujer misteriosa de Gerardo debe ser muy especial.

GERARDO: Pues sí. Creo que somos almas gemelas *(soul mates).* El otro día ella...

ISABEL: ¡Por favor, Gerardo! Basta con estas historias. Mira demasiado las telenovelas *(soap operas).*

E. ¿COMPRENDISTE? Indica si las siguientes oraciones son ciertas o falsas. Si la oración es falsa, ¡corrígela *(correct it)*!

1. A Isabel le gusta sacar fotos. F
2. Gerardo practica la guitarra todos los días. F

---

[1] **Sensible** is a false cognate that means *sensitive* rather than *sensible.*

3. La fiesta es el sábado por la noche en la casa de Isabel. T
4. La amiga de Gerardo es muy tímida. T
5. Gerardo no va a ir a la fiesta. F

ENCUENTRO *cultural*

Carlos Valderrama

Los deportes en el mundo hispánico

Éstas son unas palabras nuevas para la lectura.

el aficionado *fan*
seguir fielmente *to follow faithfully (to follow)*
la temporada de deporte (*sports season*)
En nuestra época *In our time*
comenzar *to start*
el boleto *ticket*
donar *to donate*

El fútbol es el deporte más popular en el mundo hispano. Los **aficionados** son muy apasionados y **siguen fielmente** a su equipo favorito durante la **temporada de deporte.** Este deporte es una parte esencial de la vida de muchos países hispánicos; es casi una manera de vivir.

En cada país hispánico hay ligas profesionales de fútbol. Así como en los Estados Unidos, los jugadores ganan mucho dinero. El brasileño Pelé y el argentino Diego Maradona son dos de los jugadores más famosos de fútbol del mundo hispánico. Carlos Valderrama, de Barranquilla, Colombia, es conocido por ayudar al equipo colombiano a clasificarse por tercera vez en la Copa Mundial.

El béisbol también es muy popular en el mundo hispánico, especialmente en Cuba, Puerto Rico, Panamá, la República Dominicana y Venezuela. Algunos historiadores dan crédito al cubano Nemesio Guillot por introducir el juego a Cuba en 1866 después de sus estudios en una universidad estadounidense. **En nuestra época,** el cubano José Canseco, nacido en La Habana en 1964, es uno de los grandes jugadores de béisbol de este país. El famoso dominicano Sammy Sosa **comenzó** «El domingo de Sammy Sosa» en el campo de deportes Wrigley Field. Él compra **boletos** para cada juego en Chicago y **los dona** a los niños de Chicago que normalmente no tienen dinero para ir a los juegos.

Para pensar: ¿Conoces a *(Do you know)* algún atleta hispánico? ¿Quién? ¿Qué juega? ¿Cuál es tu deporte favorito? ¿Por qué?

F. **PREGUNTAS** Contesta las siguientes preguntas a base de la lectura.

1. ¿Cuáles son los deportes más populares en el mundo hispánico?
2. ¿Cómo son los aficionados del mundo hispánico?
3. ¿Qué hace Sammy Sosa para ayudar a los niños?

GRAMÁTICA I: *Gustar + infinitive and gustar + noun*

To express likes and dislikes, Spanish speakers often use the verb **gustar** *(to be pleasing [to someone]).*

—¿Qué **te gusta** hacer?	*What do you like to do?*
—**Me gusta** correr.	*I like to go running.*
—A mi papá **le gusta** correr también.	*My Dad likes to go running, too.*
—Pero a mi madre y a mí, **nos gusta ir de compras.**	*But my mom and I like to go shopping.*
—Y a mi hermano, **le gusta** el baloncesto.	*And my brother likes basketball.*

To express to whom an action or activity—talking, running, shopping—is pleasing, use one of the following pronouns with the verb form **gusta** plus an infinitive. In the case of **gustar**, indirect object pronouns indicate *to whom* or *for whom* an action is pleasing.

me	*to me*
te	*to you* (informal)
le	*to you* (formal), *to him, to her*
nos	*to us*
os	*to you* (informal)
les	*to you* (formal and informal), *to them*

} + **gusta** + infinitive

To clarify or emphasize *to whom* something is pleasing, remember to specify the person or persons with **a** *(to)*; for example: **a Catalina** and **a tus amigos,** and remember to include the pronouns **me, te, le, nos, os,** or **les.**

—¿A Carlos **le** gusta tomar el sol?	*Does Carlos like to sunbathe?*
—Sí. También **a él le** gusta nadar.	*Yes. He also likes to swim.*
—¿A tus amigos **les** gusta tomar café?	*Do your friends like to drink coffee?*
—Sí, **les** gusta tomar café colombiano.	*Yes, they like to drink Colombian coffee.*
—¿A ustedes les gusta esquiar en el agua?	*Do you (plural) like to water ski?*
—Sí, **a nosotros nos** gusta.	*Yes, we do.*

When you use **gustar** with nouns, it changes form depending on whether you are talking about one thing or more than one thing.

A Carlos le **gusta** la piscina.
Carlos likes the swimming pool.

A Carlos le **gustan** los deportes.
Carlos likes sports.

La piscina, in the first example, is singular, so you use the singular form of **gustar: gusta. Los deportes,** in the second example, is plural, so you use the plural form of the verb **gustar: gustan.** Note that **gustar** + noun usually takes the definite article (*la* **piscina,** *los* **deportes**).

It may be helpful to think of the verb **gustar** as functioning backward.	**Instead of saying:** *I like the book.* (subject + verb + object of the verb) **Spanish speakers say:** *The book is pleasing to me.* (object of the verb + verb + indirect object pronoun)

¡A practicar!

G. LOS FINES DE SEMANA Completa los gustos de Gerardo, de Pepe y de sus amigos, usando **me, te, le, nos, os** y **les**.

1. A ti __*te*__ gusta sacar fotos.
2. A mí __*me*__ gusta tocar la guitarra.
3. A Catalina e Isabel __*les*__ gusta escuchar música.
4. A mi amiga __*le*__ gusta comer en restaurantes elegantes.
5. A la familia de Isabel __*les*__ gustan los patacones.[1]
6. A los abuelos de Catalina __*les*__ gusta recibir sus cartas.
7. Al compañero de Pepe __*le*__ gusta ir al cine con su novia.
8. A nosotros __*nos*__ gusta hacer fiestas los fines de semana.
9. A vosotros(as) __*os*__ gusta el café colombiano.

H. UN NIÑO DIFÍCIL Usa la forma correcta del verbo **gustar** y el pronombre de objeto indirecto apropiado para completar el siguiente diálogo entre una niñera *(babysitter)* y un chico problemático.

—Pepito, ¿_____ _____ mirar la tele?
—No. A mí no _____ _____ los programas de esta noche.
—Pues, yo sé que a tu hermana _____ _____ los dibujos animados *(cartoons)*.
—No es cierto. A mi hermana y a mí solamente _____ _____ ver las películas *(movies)* de horror.
—Entonces, ¿a ustedes _____ _____ las canciones de Shakira[2]? Yo tengo el nuevo CD de ella.
—No, no _____ _____ escuchar música porque a mí no _____ _____ cantar y a mi hermana no _____ _____ bailar. Por eso no _____ _____ la música.

En voz alta

I. PREFERENCIAS PERSONALES Ahora pregunta a un(a) compañero(a) si a los miembros de su familia les gustan los siguientes objetos, personas y actividades.

MODELO: el fútbol
E1: *¿A tu papá, le gusta el fútbol?*
E2: *Sí, le gusta el fútbol.*
o: E2: *No, no le gusta el fútbol. Le gusta el tenis.*

---

[1] **Patacones** are a Colombian dish made of plantains.
[2] Shakira Isabel Mebarak Ripoll is a Colombian singer of Latin-alternative folk-rock who exploded into the spotlight in 1996 with her third album, *Pies descalzos* (Bare Feet). A single off that album, **"Estoy aquí"** *("I Am Here"),* played on radio stations across Latin America.

1. la música de Shakira
2. comer
3. las películas románticas
4. el café colombiano
5. el fútbol americano
6. bailar

J. ¿Y A TU FAMILIA? Pregúntale a otro(a) estudiante qué les gusta hacer a estas personas. El (La) otro(a) estudiante escoge de la lista de las actividades a la derecha para contestar tus preguntas.

MODELO: a tu papá / jugar al tenis
   E1: *¿A tu papá le gusta jugar al tenis?*
   E2: *Sí, le gusta jugar al tenis.*
   o: E2: *No, no le gusta jugar al tenis.*

1. a tu papá   ir de compras
2. a tu mamá   mirar la televisión
3. a tus padres   jugar al tenis
4. a tu hermano(a)   patinar en línea con sus amigos
5. a tus abuelos   andar en bicicleta

K. ¿QUÉ TE GUSTA HACER? Escribe cinco oraciones sobre los pasatiempos que te gusta hacer solo(a) *(alone)*. Luego, identifica cinco lugares *(places)* que les gustan a ti y a tus amigos. Luego compara las oraciones con las de un(a) compañero(a) de clase.

MODELO: *A mí me gusta escuchar música en mi cuarto.*
   A mis amigos y a mí nos gustan las discotecas porque bailamos mucho.

GRAMÁTICA II: *The contraction a + el = al and ir a + destination or infinitive*

In **Capítulo 2** you learned how to form the contraction **del** in talking about possessive constructions. Another common contraction in Spanish is **a + el = al**. In the next section, we will be using the contraction **al** when we learn how to talk about future plans with the verb **ir** *(to go)* + the preposition **a**.

Present tense of the verb **ir** + **a** The verb **ir** has the following irregular conjugations in the present tense:		
ir *(to go)*		
yo	**voy**	*I go*
tú	**vas**	*you* (informal) *go*
Ud., él, ella	**va**	*you* (formal) *go, he/she goes*
nosotros(as)	**vamos**	*we go*
vosotros(as)	**vais**	*you* (informal) *go*
Uds., ellos(as)	**van**	*you* (formal and informal) *go, they go*

a+el = al to the
at the
a+él = To him
for him

> The construction **ir** + **a** is used in two ways:
>
> **1.** To tell where people are going, use a form of the verb **ir** plus the preposition **a**, followed by a destination
>
> —¿Adónde **van** Uds.?   *Where **are you going**?*
>
> —**Voy a** la piscina.   ***I'm going to** the pool.*
>
> —Y yo **voy al** parque.   *And **I'm going to** the park.*
>
> Remember that the preposition **a** *(to)* combines with the definite article **el** *(the)* to form the word **al** *(to the)*, as in the third example above.
>
> **2.** To express future plans, use a form of the verb **ir** plus the preposition **a**, followed by an infinitive
>
> —¿Qué **vas a hacer** ahora?   *What **are you going to do** now?*
>
> —**Voy a jugar** al tenis.   ***I'm going to play** tennis.*

¡A practicar!

L. **UNA INVITACIÓN** Completa esta conversación entre dos amigos, Ana Margarita y Fernando. Ellos van a ir a una fiesta con el grupo de estudiantes de los Estados Unidos. Usa **ir, voy, vas, va, vamos** y **van.** Luego practica la conversación con un(a) compañero(a) de clase.

Ana Margarita: ¡Hola, Fernando! ¿Adónde ___*Vas*___ ahora?
Fernando: (Yo) ___*Voy*___ al cine. ¿Quieres *(Do you want)*
         _____ conmigo?
Ana Margarita: No puedo *(I can't)*. Mi hermana y yo ___*vamos*___ al parque.
Fernando: ¿Qué ___*vas*___ a hacer este fin de semana, Ana Margarita?
Ana Margarita: ¡(Yo) ___*voy*___ a una fiesta! ¿Quieres ___*ir*___?
Fernando: Bueno, gracias. ¿Quiénes ___*van*___ con nosotros?
Ana Margarita: ___*Van*___ mi amiga Ramona y su novio, Tomás. También un grupo de estudiantes de los Estados Unidos ___*va*___ a ir.
Fernando: ¿___*vamos*___ (nosotros) en auto o en metro?
Ana Margarita: En auto. La fiesta ___*va*___ a ser en otra ciudad.

M. **¡VAMOS A CONOCER BOGOTÁ!**[1] Un grupo de estudiantes llega a Bogotá por primera vez *(for the first time)*. Tú eres el (la) profesor(a) y dices a Claire, una estudiante, lo que van a hacer los otros estudiantes en la ciudad. Usa la contracción **al** cuando es necesario.

MODELO: Megan / el Banco Nacional
           Megan va al Banco Nacional.

1. Roger y Cindy / el parque *van*   **4.** Janet y Meg / el museo *Van AL*
2. tú / el estadio *vas al*   **5.** nosotros / el centro *vamos AL*
3. Mark / la fiesta *va a*   **6.** yo / el bar *al va*

N. **¿QUÉ HACEMOS?** Es sábado y tú y tus amigos van a decidir las actividades para la noche. Escribe frases con la construcción **ir** + **a** + infinitivo.

MODELO: John / descansar en el cuarto
           John va a descansar en el cuarto.

---

[1] Santa Fé de Bogotá is the capital of Colombia. Founded in 1538, this city of over 6 million inhabitants boasts a beautiful colonial center called La Candelaria. La Avenida Pepe Sierra is the heart of the nightlife in Bogotá as it has many **clubes, bares,** and **discotecas.**

1. Helen y Claire / dar un paseo
2. nosotros / visitar los monumentos
3. Charlie / ir al cine
4. las chicas / bailar en la discoteca
5. los chicos / mirar el partido de fútbol en la tele
6. tú y Jason / sacar fotos
7. vosotros (Kevin y Mary) / tocar la guitarra en el parque
8. ¿yo?

En voz alta

O. MIS PLANES PARA EL FUTURO Habla con un(a) compañero(a) sobre lo que van a hacer.

MODELOS: E1: *Esta noche voy a descansar. ¿Y tú?*
           E2: *Voy a una fiesta esta noche.*

1. Esta noche _____.
2. Mañana _____.
3. Este fin de semana _____ y _____.
4. _____ el sábado, y el domingo _____ mucho.
5. La semana próxima _____ y el próximo viernes _____.

P. PLANES PARA UN FIN DE SEMANA Con los sujetos y los días del fin de semana de abajo, hazle preguntas a un compañero(a) de clase sobre las actividades del próximo fin de semana.

MODELO: tú / el viernes por la noche
        E1: *¿Qué vas a hacer el viernes por la noche?*
        E2: *Yo voy a ir al cine y luego yo y mis amigas vamos a una fiesta.*

1. tú / el viernes por la noche
2. tu compañero(a) de cuarto / el viernes por la noche
3. tus padres / el sábado
4. tú y tus amigo(a)s / el sábado por la tarde
5. tu profesor(a) del español / el domingo por la mañana
6. tus abuelos / el domingo por la tarde
7. tu hermano(a) / el domingo por la noche

VOCABULARIO: *Los lugares*

MACONDO, UN PUEBLO COLOMBIANO[1] In this section you will learn the names of places in a town. How does the mythical town of Macondo compare with your own?

---

[1] Macondo is the mythical town created by Colombian writer Gabriel García Márquez in his famous novel *Cien años de soledad (One Hundred Years of Solitude)*.

Palabras útiles are for recognition only; you will not be tested on these words. These words are provided to help you better describe your town.

Palabras útiles

la carnicería *butcher shop*	la peluquería *hair salon*
la ferretería *hardware store*	la joyería *jewelry store*
la frutería *fruit store*	la papelería *stationery store*
la gasolinera *gas station*	la tienda de antigüedades (de música [de discos], de ropa) *antiques (music, clothing) store*

¡A practicar!

Q. ASOCIACIONES ¿Qué lugares asocias con las siguientes actividades?

MODELO: estacionar *(to park)* el carro
            la calle

1. ir de compras
2. rezar *(to pray)*
3. ir a tomar un café
4. comer
5. mandar cartas
6. ver una película
7. nadar
8. depositar dinero
9. reunirse *(to get together)* con amigos
10. jugar deportes

R. EN MI PUEBLO HAY... NO HAY... Forma oraciones para describir los lugares en el pueblo donde vives o estudias.

MODELO: *En mi pueblo hay seis restaurantes. Mi restaurante favorito se llama Marvin's.*

1. En mi pueblo hay _____ parque(s). Se llama(n) _____, _____ y _____.
2. En mi pueblo hay _____ supermercado(s). Generalmente compro cosas en _____.

3. En mi pueblo hay _____ café(s). El café más popular es _____ .

4. En mi pueblo hay _____ cine(s). Generalmente voy al cine _____ .

5. Vivo en la calle _____ .

6. En mi pueblo hay _____ piscina(s) pública(s).

7. En mi pueblo no hay _____ , _____ ni _____ .

En voz alta

S. **¿VAS AL CINE?** Pregunta a un(a) compañero(a) de clase si él/ella va a los siguientes lugares en tu pueblo. Si tu compañero(a) va a este lugar, pregúntale lo que él/ella hace allí.

MODELO: el cáfe _____

E1: *¿Vas al café Maggie's?*

E2: *Sí, voy al café Maggie's con mis amigas.*

E1: *¿Qué hacen en Maggie's?*

E2: *Nosotros hablamos y tomamos café.*

1. la plaza _____

2. el mercado _____

3. la tienda _____

4. el centro comercial _____

5. el centro _____

6. la oficina de correos _____

7. el restaurante _____

8. el banco _____

9. la discoteca _____

10. el museo _____

ENCUENTRO *cultural*

El café en Colombia

Éstas son unas palabras nuevas para la lectura:

enorgullecerse *to take pride in something*

el mejor *the best*

la sombra *shade*

el árbol *tree*

en sí misma *in itself*

No se puede hablar de Colombia sin hablar del café. El café es uno de los productos de exportación más importantes de Colombia. Los colombianos **se enorgullecen** de que la gran parte del mundo considera el café colombiano como uno de los **mejores.**

Algunos expertos del café consideran que el mejor café se produce en áreas montañosas donde las condiciones son ideales para el café. Una de estas condiciones es la temperatura fresca, gracias a la altitud sobre el nivel del mar. Otra condición es **la sombra** de **los árboles** altos que protegen las plantas del sol. Colombia tiene muchas áreas con estas condiciones.

Además de su importancia en la economía, el café también forma una parte integral de la vida social. La presencia del café es parte de la vida diaria y es una cultura **en sí misma.** Para los colombianos, un cafecito por la mañana, por la tarde o por la noche es siempre un evento especial.

Para pensar: ¿Tomas tú café? ¿Cuándo y dónde tomas café? ¿Piensas que en los Estados Unidos tenemos también una cultura del café? ¿Adónde vas tú para tomar café? ¿Cuándo, y con quién?

T.   PREGUNTAS Contesta las siguientes preguntas a base de la lectura.

1.   ¿Cómo se considera el café colombiano en gran parte del mundo?
2.   Según los expertos, ¿cuáles son unas condiciones ideales para el café?

GRAMÁTICA III: *Verbs with irregular yo forms*

In this section you will learn how to use several verbs that describe basic actions. All the verbs given below have irregular **yo** forms but are otherwise regular in their conjugations. These verbs are also useful in describing leisure-time activities.

Present tense of the verb hacer

The verb **hacer** *(to do; to make)* is a regular -**er** verb except for the **yo** form (**yo hago**). You have already seen the verb **hacer** used in this chapter to pose questions.

¿Qué **haces** en tu tiempo libre?
What do you do in your free time?

¿Qué **hacen** tus amigos durante los fines de semana?
What do your friends do on the weekends?

Hacer is conjugated as follows:

yo	**hago**	*I do*
tú	**haces**	*you (informal) do*
Ud., él, ella	**hace**	*you (formal) do; he/she does*
nosotros(as)	**hacemos**	*we do*
vosotros(as)	**hacéis**	*you (informal) do*
Uds., ellos(as)	**hacen**	*you (formal and informal) do; they do*

Several other Spanish verbs, like **hacer,** have irregular **yo** forms only in the present indicative tense.

		yo form	
conocer	*to know; to meet*	**conozco**	**Conozco** a Carlos Suárez.
dar	*to give*	**doy**	**Doy** una fiesta el viernes.
hacer	*to do; to make*	**hago**	**Hago** mucho ejercicio.
poner	*to put (on)*	**pongo**	**Pongo** música rock en casa.
saber	*to know (how)*	**sé**	**Sé** jugar bien al béisbol.
salir	*to leave, to go out*	**salgo**	**Salgo** todos los sábados.
traer	*to bring*	**traigo**	**Traigo** mi disco compacto.
ver	*to see*	**veo**	**Veo** a mi profesora en la tienda.

The other present-tense forms of these verbs are regular with the exception of **ver,** which does not carry an accent on the -**e** of the **vosotros(as)** form as other -**er** verbs do.

¿NOS ENTENDEMOS?

Some common idioms with hacer are **hacer un viaje, hacer planes,** and **hacer una pregunta.**

	hacer	saber	conocer	dar	traer	ver	poner	salir
yo	hago	sé	conozco	doy	traigo	veo	pongo	salgo
tú	haces	sabes	conoces	das	traes	ves	pones	sales
Ud., él, ella	hace	sabe	conoce	da	trae	ve	pone	sale
nosotros(as)	hacemos	sabemos	conocemos	damos	traemos	vemos	ponemos	salimos
vosotros(as)	hacéis	sabéis	conocéis	dais	traéis	veis	ponéis	salís
Uds., ellos(as)	hacen	saben	conocen	dan	traen	ven	ponen	salen

¡A practicar!

U. **UNA CARTA DE BOGOTÁ** Claire va a escribir una carta en español a su amigo Ramón en los Estados Unidos. Ayúdala a conjugar los verbos entre paréntesis.

Querido Ramón,

¿Cómo estás? ¡Bogotá es increíble! (Yo) _____ **(salir)** mucho con mis compañeros de clase, especialmente los fines de semana cuando (nosotros) _____ **(tener)** más tiempo. Mis amigos y yo _____ **(hacer)** muchas actividades. Por ejemplo, mañana (yo) _____ **(ir)** con dos amigos a una fiesta que una amiga colombiana, Luisa Gómez, _____ **(ir)** a dar en su casa. Yo _____ **(saber)** que tú no _____ **(conocer)** a Luisa, pero ella _____ **(ser)** muy simpática y _____ **(tener)** una casa con una piscina grande. El domingo por la tarde mi amiga Anne y yo _____ **(ir)** al parque. ¿_____ **(ir)** tú y tus amigos al parque como nosotros? ¡Yo _____ **(saber)** que a ti te gusta jugar al baloncesto los domingos! Cuando Anne _____ **(ir)** al parque conmigo, ella _____ **(traer)** sándwiches y yo _____ **(traer)** fruta.

De noche, Anne y yo _____ **(ir)** a salir a tomar una cerveza. El novio de Anne _____ **(ir)** con nosotros. Su nombre es Juanjo. Ellos _____ **(salir)** casi todos los domingos.

En casa (yo) _____ **(hacer)** mucho ejercicio. Cuando Anne _____ **(hacer)** ejercicio, _____ **(poner)** música rock en la radio. Ahora [yo] _____ **(ir)** a descansar un poco.

      Abrazos,
      Claire

V. **JUANITA LA BUENA Y JUANITO EL MALO** Juanita es una chica muy buena y siempre *(always)* hace lo que debe hacer. Su hermano, Juanito, nunca *(never)* hace lo que hace su hermana. Imagínate que tú eres Juanita y escribe lo que hace tu hermano, Juanito, basado en lo que haces tú.

MODELO: Yo siempre hago mi tarea, pero Juanito nunca *hace su tarea.*

1. Yo siempre traigo dulces a mi abuela, pero Juanito nunca...
2. Yo nunca veo la tele cuando debo trabajar, pero Juanito siempre...
3. Yo nunca pongo el estéreo muy alto, pero Juanito siempre...
4. Yo siempre saludo a los estudiantes nuevos en clase, pero Juanito nunca...
5. Yo sé jugar a muchos deportes, pero Juanito...
6. Yo hago ejercicio todos los días, pero Juanito nunca...
7. Yo solamente salgo con mi novio los fines de semana, pero Juanito...
8. Yo nunca doy mi número de teléfono a personas extrañas, pero Juanito...

W. ¿CIERTO O FALSO? Decide si las siguientes oraciones con ciertas o falsas. Si la oración es falsa para ti, ¡corrígela!

MODELO: Siempre sabes la respuesta en clase.
Sí, es cierto. Yo siempre sé la respuesta en clase.
o: *No, es falso. A veces no sé la respuesta en clase.*

1. Siempre *(Always)* haces planes para el fin de semana.
2. A veces *(Sometimes)* pones la música muy alto en tu cuarto.
3. Ves la tele por lo menos *(at least)* una hora cada noche.
4. A veces traes comida a las fiestas de tus compañeros(as).
5. Conoces bien a tu profesor(a) de español.
6. Das muchas respuestas en clase.
7. Nunca *(Never)* pones tus cosas en orden.
8. Siempre traes muchos libros cuando estudias en la biblioteca.
9. Siempre sabes los planes de tu compañero(a) de cuarto.
10. Siempre sales los fines de semana.

En voz alta

X. ¿Y TÚ? Ahora forma preguntas con las oraciones de la **Actividad W** para hacérlas a un compañero(a) de clase.

MODELO: E1: *¿Siempre haces planes para el fin de semana?*
E2: *Yo siempre hago planes para el fin de semana.*

Y. ENTREVISTA Trabajando con un(a) compañero(a) de clase, hazle las siguientes preguntas con los verbos **hacer, saber, conocer, dar, traer, salir, poner** y **ver**.

1. ¿Cuándo haces planes para el fin de semana? ¿Qué vas a hacer este fin de semana? ¿Sales mucho durante la semana?
2. Cuando tienes una fiesta, ¿qué tipo de música pones? ¿Traen tus amigos comida *(food)* a la fiesta? ¿Saben tus padres que vas a tener una fiesta? ¿Sabe tu compañero(a) de cuarto? ¿Siempre conoces a todas las personas en la fiesta?
3. Cuando haces ejercicio, ¿sales de tu cuarto? ¿Ves videos cuando haces ejercicio? ¿Pones la tele o el estéreo cuando haces ejercicio?
4. ¿Haces muchos viajes? ¿Das cosas a tus padres, hermanos o amigos cuando regresas? ¿Sabes algo del sitio *(site)* que visitas antes de ir *(before you go)*?

ASÍ SE DICE: *Saber, conocer,* and *a personal*

As you have seen earlier, the verbs **saber** and **conocer** both mean *to know,* and they have irregular **yo** forms (**sé / conozco**). These verbs represent two different kinds of knowledge, however.

Use the verb **saber** to express knowing something (information) or knowing how to do something.

—¿**Sabes jugar** al tenis?   *Do you know how to play tennis?*
—No, pero **sé jugar** al golf.   *No, but I know how to play golf.*
—¿**Sabes qué?** ¡Me gusta el golf!   *Do you know what? I like golf!*

Use the verb **conocer** to express being acquainted with a person, place, or thing. Note that Spanish speakers use the preposition **a** immediately before a direct object that refers to a specific person or persons.

—¿**Conoces** Bogotá?	*Do you know Bogotá?*
—No, pero **conozco** Cali.	*No, but I know Cali.*
—¿Quieres **conocer a** mi amiga?	*Do you want to meet my friend?*
—Ya **conozco a** tu amiga Luisa.	*I already know your friend Luisa.*

Use the **a personal** with direct objects that are people. The direct object of a verb is the person or thing that receives the action of the verb. For example, in the sentence *I know Carlos,* the direct object is **Carlos.** The **a personal,** which has no English equivalent, is usually repeated before each noun or pronoun.

Conozco **a** Carlos.	*I know Carlos.*
Conozco **a** Carlos y **a** Juan.	*I know Carlos and Juan.*

¡A practicar!

Z. **CONOCER VERSUS SABER** Decide si se usa **saber** o **conocer** para hablar de las siguientes cosas.

1. jugar al tenis *S*
2. Cali *C*
3. mi amigo José Alfredo *C*
4. Fernando Botero[1] *C*
5. el arte de Botero *C*
6. Juan Valdés *C*
7. Barranquilla *C*
8. Macondo *C*
9. bailar vallenato[2] *S*
10. hablar español *S*
11. Gabriel García Márquez *C*
12. andar en bicicleta *S*

AA. **LA A PERSONAL** ¿Cuándo se usa la **a** personal? Decide si se usa la **a** personal en las siguientes frases. ¡No te olvides *(Don't forget)* de que **a + el = al**!

1. Yo no conozco _____ Bogotá.
2. Mis amigos conocen ___*a*___ mi hermano Pablo.
3. Joaquín conoce ___*a*___ la novia de Anne.
4. Julieta y Penelope conocen bien _____ la música de Carlos Vives.
5. ¿Conoces tú ___*al*___ (el) profesor de francés? ¡Es muy guapo!

En voz alta

BB. **¡YO CONOZCO... ! ¡YO SÉ... !** Ahora, habla con un(a) compañero(a) de las cosas de la lista de la **Actividad Z.**

MODELO: jugar al tenis
E1: *Yo no sé jugar al tenis. ¿Sabes tú jugar al tenis?*
E2: *Sí, sé jugar al tenis.*
o: E2: *No, no sé jugar al tenis.*

CC. **ENTREVISTA** Tú vas a entrevistar a un(a) compañero(a) de clase. Necesitas saber a quién conoce, qué lugares conoce y qué cosas sabe hacer. Escribe cuatro preguntas con **saber** y **conocer.** Después, tomen turnos *(take turns)* contestando las preguntas.

MODELO: *¿Conoces Kansas City?*
¿Sabes esquiar?
¿Conoces al presidente de los Estados Unidos?

---

[1] Fernando Botero is one of Colombia's most famous artists. He is especially known for his satirical portraits of political, military, and religious figures, whom he portrays as rotund and motionless.
[2] **Vallenato** is a type of Colombian folk music, usually played on the accordian, that celebrates everyday events, passions, and village folklore. It originated in the Magdalena Grande area of northeastern Colombia and has strongly influenced Colombian novelist Gabriel García Márquez. Carlos Vives, a Colombian musician, has become internationally famous for his **vallenato** sound.

LOS DOCE MESES Y LAS CUATRO ESTACIONES In this section you will learn how to talk about months and seasons.

Las estaciones *Seasons*

el invierno *winter* **el verano** *summer*
la primavera *spring* **el otoño** *fall*

¡A practicar!

DD. **LOS DÍAS FESTIVOS** *(Holidays)* Completa las frases con los meses y las fechas *(dates)* apropiados.

1. El Día del Trabajo es en _Septiembre._
2. El Día del Padre es en _Junio_.
3. El Día de la Madre es en _____ .
4. El Día de San Patricio es en _____.
5. El Día de Acción de Gracias *(Thanksgiving)* es en _____.
6. El primer *(first)* día del año es en _enero_.
7. La Navidad *(Christmas)* es en _____.
8. El Día de San Valentín es el 14 de _____.
9. El Día de la Independencia de los Estados Unidos es el 4 de _____.
10. Mi cumpleaños *(birthday)* es el _____ de _____.

EE. **LOS DEPORTES Y LAS ESTACIONES** ¿Con qué estaciones se asocian los siguientes deportes?

1. caminar por las montañas
2. esquiar
3. jugar al tenis
4. patinar en línea
5. esquiar en el agua

6. montar a caballo
7. tomar el sol
8. el baloncesto
9. el fútbol americano
10. el ciclismo

ASÍ SE DICE: *Weather expressions*

está nublado *it's cloudy*   **llueve** *it's raining*   **nieva** *it's snowing*

The verb **hacer** is also used to talk about the weather.

hace buen tiempo *the weather is nice*   **hace frío** *it's cold*
hace calor *it's hot*   **hace sol** *it's sunny*
hace fresco *it's chilly*   **hace viento** *it's windy*

Feminie spring

¡A practicar!

FF. **¿QUÉ TIEMPO HACE?** Mira los dibujos y completa las frases con la estación y el tiempo apropiados para cada uno.

1. En el _____ hace
   mucho _____ .

2. En el _____ hace
   _____ y _____ .

3. En la _____ hace
   _____ .

4. En el _____ hace
   _____ .

5. Mi estación favorita es _____ porque _____ .
6. No me gusta _____ porque _____ .

En voz alta

GG. **¿CUÁL ES LA FECHA? ¿EN QUÉ ESTACIÓN DEL AÑO ES? ¿QUÉ TIEMPO HACE?** Lee las siguientes fechas en español a un(a) compañero(a) de clase. Luego identifica la estación y el tiempo que hace en estas fechas en el lugar donde tú vives. También menciona qué te gusta hacer en estas fechas.

MODELO: 13/4
Es el trece de abril. Es la primavera. En abril hace sol en Barran-quilla. Me gusta dar paseos en la playa.

1.	22/12	**3.**	3/9	**5.**	29/8	**7.**	27/4
2.	25/7	**4.**	1/5	**6.**	7/10	**8.**	hoy

ASÍ SE DICE: *Idioms with tener*

In the **Capítulo preliminar** you were introduced to the verb **tener** *(to have)*, and in **Capítulo 2** you practiced some idiomatic expressions with **tener** (**tener sueño, tener sed, tener razón,** etc.). Two more idioms with **tener** are explained below.

Although Spanish speakers use **hacer** to talk about the temperature (**hace frío, hace calor**), the verb **tener** is used with **frío** and **calor** when a person expresses being hot or cold: **Yo tengo frío.** *(I am cold.)* or **Ella tiene calor.** *(She is hot.)* Consider the following examples:

Tú **tienes calor** porque hace mucho sol y no hace viento.
You are hot because it is very sunny and the wind is not blowing.

Tomás y Margarita **tienen mucho frío** porque no tienen chaquetas.
Tomás and Margarita are very cold because they don't have jackets.

The verb **tener** is also used used in the construction (**tener + que +** infinitive,) which means *to have to do something*. It is used in the same way as the verb **deber** (see **Capítulo 2**), but it carries a stronger sense of obligation. **Deber** normally carries the meaning of *should,* whereas **tener que** often means *must*. Note that both of these verb forms must be followed by an infinitive.

Yo deseo ir a la fiesta pero **tengo que estudiar.**
I want to go to the party, but I have to (must) study.

Tenemos que ir a la discoteca. ¡Hay muchos chicos guapos!
We have to (must) go to the disco. There are a lot of cute guys!

¡A practicar!

HH. **¿QUÉ TIENE JUAN?** Usa las siguientes expresiones con **tener** para explicar las condiciones físicas de Juan.

tener prisa   tener sed   tener frío
tener sueño   tener hambre   tener calor

MODELO:

Juan tiene calor.

1. _____ **2.** _____ **3.** _____

4. _____ **5.** _____

II. EN UN CAMPAMENTO Completa las siguientes oraciones con la forma apropiada de **tener que** + infinitivo para indicar lo que tienen que hacer los consejeros *(counselors)* en el campamento *(camp)*.

MODELO: los consejeros / descansar más los fines de semana
         Los consejeros tienen que descansar más los fines de semana.

1. nosotros / nadar en la mañana
2. Vince y Stephen / jugar al tenis a las 9:00
3. Wendy / patinar en línea por la tarde
4. Guadalupe / ver un video esta tarde
5. tú / hablar por teléfono con la Sra. Rogers   *tiene*
6. ¿yo?

En voz alta

JJ. LA REALIDAD Y LA FANTASÍA Trabajando con un(a) compañero(a) de clase, expresa lo que te gusta hacer en general durante los siguientes períodos y luego lo que tienes que hacer para el próximo período.

MODELO: los sábados *(Saturdays in general)* / este sábado *(this Saturday)*
         Generalmente me gusta descansar   *Este sábado tengo que*
         los sábados.   *estudiar para mi clase de*
             química.

1. los viernes por la noche / este viernes
2. los veranos / este verano
3. las tardes / esta tarde
4. los días festivos / el próximo día festivo
5. las mañanas / esta mañana
6. los fines de semana / este fin de semana

Síntesis

¡A ver!

Your narrator for the video segments in this unit is Gustavo, or as his friends and family call him, Avico. Avico comes from Manizales in Colombia, where he is a school teacher. Like many Colombians, Avico loves to spend time with his friends, especially outdoors. Avico will talk about leisure time in the Spanish-speaking world.

ACTIVIDAD 1 Pre-viewing task (Segmento 1 del video)

Paso 1: You are going to see a series of short clips showing people engaged in different types of leisure activities in the Spanish-speaking world. Make a list of as many of these activities as you can.

Paso 2: On your list, indicate which of these activities you like to do and which you do not like to do. For some of the activities, you may have no preference.

Paso 3: With your partner, talk about the activities you like to do in your spare time and those you do not like to do. In your conversation you should react in appropriate ways to your partner. You might need to make a clarification request if you do not hear or understand something, for example: **¿Cómo? ¿Qué? ¿Puedes repetirlo por favor? ¿Que te gusta? ¿Qué no te gusta?** (See **Capítulo 1** to remind yourself how to ask for clarification.) Or you can express your agreement or disagreement with what your partner says: **Ah sí, a mí me gusta ir de paseo con el perro también. A mí no; no me gusta hacer eso.**

ACTIVIDAD 2 Pre-viewing task (Segmento 2 del video)

You are going to watch a video segment in which two Mexican students, Eric and Joame, are being interviewed about what they like doing in their spare time and what they like and don't like studying. Before you listen to the interviews, carry out the following activities. These should help you to understand the video more easily.

Paso 1: Look at the photographs of Eric and Joame on the next page and guess what you think their responses might be to the following questions:

¿Qué materia te gusta estudiar? / ¿Qué materia no te gusta estudiar? / ¿Qué haces en tu tiempo libre o los fines de semana?

Paso 2: Share your suggestions with the rest of the class (e.g., **A Eric le gusta el inglés pero no le gustan las matemáticas. Le gusta salir con sus amigos en su tiempo libre.**). One student in the class makes a list on the board while the rest of the class provides their suggestions. Your instructor will listen and provide comments and reactions to your suggestions. From all the suggestions on the board, which are the most likely answers to the three questions?

ACTIVIDAD 3   Viewing task (Segmento 2 del video)

Paso 1: Watch the interviews of Eric and Joame in **Segmento 2 del video.** As you watch, fill out the table below with the necessary information. You may need to watch the segment more than once.

	¿Qué materia le gusta estudiar?	¿Qué materia no le gusta estudiar?	¿Qué hace en su tiempo libre o los fines de semana?

Paso 2: Working with a partner, check the information you have in your table. Then share your answers with the rest of the class. Who made the most accurate guess in **Actividad 2**?

Paso 3: Watch the interviews with Eric and Joame again and this time pay attention to the questions that the interviewer asks. Notice how she poses questions that depend on how Eric and Joame respond to previous questions. Make a note of some of these questions and then share them with the rest of the class.

ACTIVIDAD 4   Post-viewing task (Segmento 2 del video)

Paso 1: Using the information you have obtained in **Actividad 3,** role-play the interviews with Eric and Joame with your classmate. Use the questions that you identified in **Paso 3** together with any other questions that you think necessary.

Paso 2: Now interview your partner to find out what subjects he/she likes studying and what he/she likes to do in his/her spare time and at the weekends. Remember to make your questions appropriate for the ways in which your partner responds to earlier questions. Also, if you wish to ask further questions about a particular topic with your partner, try to think of one or two relevant questions (as the interviewer did in **Segmento 2 del video**).

¡A escribir!

Combining sentences

Learning to combine simple sentences into more complex ones can help you improve your writing style immensely. In Spanish, there are several words you can use to combine sentences and phrases:

y	*and*	**que**	*that; which; who*
pero	*but*	**o**	*or*

Functions: Writing a letter (informal); Describing people; Talking about the present

Vocabulary: Sports; Leisure; Board games; Family members; Animals: Domestic; University

Grammar: Verbs: **ser, tener;** Articles: contractions **al, del**

Paso 1: Read the following letter that Esther wrote to her pen pal in the United States about what she is doing during her summer vacation. Circle all of the connectors used in the following sentences.

Querida Kelly:

¿Qué tal? ¿Cómo estás?

De momento, estoy de vacaciones y tengo mucho tiempo libre. Me gusta practicar muchos deportes, como el tenis, la natación, el ciclismo y el baloncesto. Pero cuando llueve, veo videos o miro la tele en casa.

También paso mucho tiempo con mi amigo Carlos. Carlos tiene 23 años y es un chico muy simpático. Nos gusta salir por la noche los fines de semana e ir a las discotecas que están en el centro. Nos gusta bailar y caminar por la ciudad. ¡Bogotá es preciosa!

Bueno, en pocos minutos van a llegar mis padres. Vamos al cine hoy para ver una película.

Espero recibir tu carta pronto. Tu amiga,

Esther

Paso 2: Now that you have seen how connectors were used in the above letter, combine the following sets of sentences, using **y, pero,** and **que** appropriately.

M O D E L O S : Estudio en la Universidad de Bogotá. Me gustan mis clases.
Estudio en la Universidad de Bogotá y me gustan mis clases.

Tengo muchos amigos. Son muy simpáticos.
Tengo muchos amigos que son muy simpáticos.

1. Me gusta practicar deportes. No tengo mucho tiempo libre.
2. Mi amiga corre todos los días. Es muy atlética.
3. Carlos es mi compañero. Toma mucho café.
4. Deseo mirar un partido de fútbol en la tele. Tengo que estudiar.
5. Tengo muchos amigos. Esquían en el invierno.

Paso 3: Now, using Esther's letter as a model, write in Spanish to one of your classmates about your favorite pastimes and leisure activities. Be sure to include a description of what you like to do in your free time, and mention who (if anyone) you like to do these activities with. Then exchange letters with your classmate. This will give you an excellent opportunity to learn more about what your classmates like to do in their free time.

¡A leer!

Using context to predict content

Efficient readers use effective strategies for guessing the meaning of unfamiliar words and phrases in a reading selection. For example, they rely on what they already know about the reading topic (background information); they guess what the reading will be about (prediction); and they use ideas they understand in the passage (context). In this section you will practice using these three reading strategies.

Paso 1: Background information

1. What do Julia Roberts and Richard Gere have in common?
2. Where do people usually read about them?

Paso 2: Prediction

1. First, look at the reading and read the large, boldfaced title at the top center. Then, read the subtitles in smaller boldfaced type.
2. What do you suppose the descriptions are about?

Paso 3: Context

1. Skim the reading without stopping and try to understand the gist of its content.
   a. In general, what opinion does the author express toward these three movies?
   b. Which movie would you prefer to see, and why?

2. Scan the descriptions and complete the following tasks.
   a. Underline the words and phrases that indicate the author's favorable opinion of these three films.
   b. Name the film that features much young talent.
   c. Name the film that deals with romance.

La guía del cine

Runaway Bride Nueve años después de haber confeccionado la dudosa pero popular *Pretty Woman,* Julia Roberts y Richard Gere vuelven a trabajar junto al director Garry Marshall para preparar otro romántico soufflé. *Runaway Bride* nos presenta una historia más dulce que la anterior, aunque usted no lo crea. Logra penetrar un territorio genuinamente emocional que *Pretty Woman* no se atrevió a tocar.

American Pie Una comedia juvenil que focaliza en la obsesión de los adolescentes norteamericanos con la virginidad y el modo en que la obsesión se agudiza a la fecha de graduación de escuela superior, concentrando todas las expectativas en el «senior prom».

Esta comedia tiene mucho talento joven, bajo la dirección de los hermanos Paul y Chris Weitz, que debutan en la realización tras créditos como guionistas de *Antz.*

Universal Soldier: The Return Van Damme salta por primera vez en su carrera al territorio de las segundas partes. Más de 20 películas a su nombre, incluyendo éxitos como la original *Universal Soldier, Timecop, Double Impact, Hard Target* y *Nowhere to Run,* Jean-Claude Van Damme define la acción en su forma más pura. Constantemente emprende nuevos e imaginativos proyectos que ponen de relieve su carisma y su energía. Así se presenta en su película más reciente.

¡A conversar!

Many times, the weather affects what we feel like doing. One day may be better for going to the theater or for doing indoor activities, while another may be better for getting some exercise. With a classmate, discuss in Spanish what you personally like to do on weekends or during your free time in the following situations:

- when it's hot
- when it's raining
- when it's snowing
- anytime (regardless of the weather!)

Be prepared to share what your partner likes do in his/her free time depending on the weather conditions.

Los deportes   *Sports*

andar en bicicleta   *to ride a bike*
el baloncesto   *basketball*
el béisbol   *baseball*
caminar por las montañas   *to hike/walk in the mountains*
el campo de fútbol (de golf)   *football field (golf course)*

el ciclismo   *cycling*
correr   *to run*
esquiar (en el agua)   *to (water) ski*
el fútbol (americano)   *soccer (football)*
ganar   *to win*
el golf   *golf*

jugar (ue) al tenis   *to play tennis*
levantar pesas   *to lift weights*
montar a caballo   *to go horseback riding*
nadar   *to swim*
la natación   *swimming*

el partido   *game*
patinar (en línea)   *to (in-line) skate*
el vólibol   *volleyball*

Los pasatiempos   *Pastimes*

bailar   *to dance*
dar un paseo   *to go for a walk*
hacer un picnic (planes, ejercicio)   *to go on a picnic (to make plans, to exercise)*

ir...   *to go . . .*
   a un bar   *to a bar*
   a un club   *to a club*
   a un concierto   *to a concert*
   a una discoteca   *to a disco*
   a una fiesta   *to a party*

   al cine   *to the movies*
   de compras   *shopping*
mirar la tele   *to watch television*
sacar fotos   *to take pictures*
tocar la guitarra   *to play the guitar*

tomar el sol   *to sunbathe*
ver una película   *to watch a movie*
visitar un museo   *to visit a museum*

Los lugares   *Places*

el banco   *bank*
el café   *café*
la calle   *street*
el centro   *downtown*
el centro comercial   *mall*

el cine   *movie theater*
la iglesia   *church*
el mercado (al aire libre)   *(outdoor) market*
el museo   *museum*

la oficina de correos   *post office*
el parque   *park*
la piscina   *pool*
la plaza   *plaza*

el restaurante   *restaurant*
el supermercado   *supermarket*
la tienda   *store*

Verbos

conocer   *to know; to meet*
dar   *to give*
gustar   *to be pleasing (to someone)*

hacer   *to do; to make*
poner   *to put (on)*
saber   *to know (how)*
salir   *to leave, to go out*

tener calor   *to be hot*
tener frío   *to be cold*
tener que   *to have to (do something)*

traer   *to bring*
ver   *to see*

Los meses del año   *Months of the year*

enero   *January*
febrero   *February*
marzo   *March*

abril   *April*
mayo   *May*
junio   *June*

julio   *July*
agosto   *August*
septiembre   *September*

octubre   *October*
noviembre   *November*
diciembre   *December*

Las estaciones   *Seasons*

el invierno   *winter*

el otoño   *fall*

la primavera   *spring*

el verano   *summer*

El tiempo   *Weather*

está nublado   *it's cloudy*
hace buen tiempo   *the weather is nice*

hace calor   *it's hot*
hace fresco   *it's cool*
hace frío   *it's cold*

hace sol   *it's sunny*
hace viento   *it's windy*
llueve   *it's raining*

nieva   *it's snowing*

Expresión idiomática

¡Chévere!   *Cool!*

PLAZAS

BIENVENIDOS A *PLAZAS*, UNA PUBLICACIÓN QUE DESCRIBE EL PANORAMA DE LOS PAÍSES DE HABLA ESPAÑOLA.

¿El ambiente festivo o académico?

¿Necesitas 100.000 pesos? Tenemos un trabajo para ti

¿Sociable o tímido? Las dos características en una sola nacionalidad

La batalla de los sexos

Nueva visión artística: Modelos delgadas desempleadas

En esta edición vas a conocer a personas, lugares y aspectos culturales de Colombia, México y los Estados Unidos y vas a comparar tus ideas y opiniones con las de nuestros autores. Participa con nosotros y vas a ver que a pesar de *(in spite of)* nuestras diferencias, tenemos mucho en común.

¿El ambiente festivo o académico?

Nuestros 30 millones de vecinos *(neighbors)* latinos viven en muchas partes de los Estados Unidos. Hay grupos latinos en numerosas regiones del país y, aunque *(even though)* tienen en común el idioma, cada grupo conserva su nacionalismo particular. Los estados con una población grande de latinos son California, Florida, Illinois, Nueva York y Texas. Vamos a examinar tres aspectos diferentes de la influencia latina en los Estados Unidos.

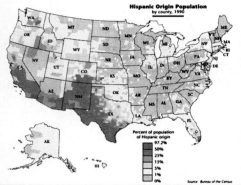

Hispanic Origin Population
by county, 1990

Percent of population of Hispanic origin
97.2%
50%
25%
15%
5%
1%
0%

Source: Bureau of the Census

Loco, loco, loco Vamos a calle Ocho

¿Te gustan los conciertos? ¿Te gusta la música caribeña? ¿Te gusta comer platos típicos de Cuba? Si te gustan las fiestas enormes, el Festival de calle Ocho es para ti. Aproximadamente 1,2 millones de personas van al Festival de calle Ocho en Miami en marzo. Es posible escuchar música de más de 30 grupos musicales toda la tarde y toda la noche en este festival que ocupa un espacio de 27 cuadras *(street blocks)*.

¿Qué fiestas anuales celebran en tu ciudad?
¿Participas en estas fiestas?
¿Cuáles son algunos aspectos interesantes de estas fiestas?

...Y ahora, un mensaje serio

La Universidad de San Francisco tiene una oficina que se llama «Center for Latino Studies in the Americas». Este centro ofrece un programa de estudios latinoamericanos. Los estudiantes tienen la oportunidad de tomar clases de identidades políticas, estudios culturales, crítica literaria, justicia económica, olas *(waves)* de migración y religión.

Este programa revela el interés que existe por la cultura latina en los Estados Unidos. El centro auspicia *(sponsors)* conciertos, lecturas *(readings)* de poesía, exposiciones de arte, charlas sobre temas históricos y contemporáneos, programas de radio —todo sobre la presencia de los latinos en los Estados Unidos y su relación con las Américas.

Muchas universidades ofrecen un certificado o una especialización en estudios latinoamericanos.
¿Qué programas similares tiene tu universidad?
¿Organiza tu universidad actividades relacionadas con las culturas latinas?
¿Qué porcentaje de la población en tu universidad es latino?

Center for Latino Studies in the Americas

CELASA e-mail:
celasa@usfca.edu
voice mail: 415-422-2940
fax: 415-422-2346
www.usfca.edu/celasa

Marzo en Miami, abril en San Antonio

Otra fiesta popular es la Fiesta San Antonio, celebrada en abril en la magnífica ciudad tejana.

La fiesta dura *(lasts)* diez días, con más de 150 eventos. Hay desfiles *(parades)* iluminados de noche, conciertos, actividades deportivas, fuegos artificiales *(fireworks)* y, por supuesto, mucho para comer.

Esta fiesta tiene sus orígenes en el año 1891, en honor de los héroes que lucharon por *(fought for)* la libertad de Texas. También reconoce la diversidad cultural de la ciudad.

Más de 3,5 millones de personas participan en esta celebración, además de *(in addition to)* los 75.000 voluntarios que hacen posible estas actividades tan ricas en historia y cultura.

¿Cómo comparas el Festival de calle Ocho con la Fiesta San Antonio?
En la ciudad donde vives, ¿hay una cultura / varias culturas que tiene(n) celebraciones anuales?
¿Cuáles son unas fiestas anuales que se celebran *(are celebrated)* en este país?

¿Necesitas 100.000 pesos? Tenemos un trabajo para ti.

Nuestra corresponsal, Silvia Jiménez, tiene una copia de la agenda del presidente de México. La fecha es el 23 de agosto y creemos que vas a aprender mucho sobre las actividades del presidente. ¿Podrías *(Would you be able)* hacer este trabajo? Si respondes que sí, el salario que corresponde con el trabajo es **100.000 pesos, ¡por UN mes!**

Y ahora tú...

Los editores aquí en *Plazas* tenemos una oportunidad para ti. ¡Necesitamos tu colaboración! El presidente tiene la tarde libre del día de su cumpleaños debido a *(due to)* la cancelación de un evento especial. Ahora, tú eres uno(a) de los asistentes que prepara el horario del presidente. ¿Qué planes preparas para el período de las 1300 horas a las 1800 horas? Si los consejeros políticos seleccionan tus planes, vas a recibir **100.000 pesos** y un viaje de diez días con todos los gastos pagados *(all-expenses-paid trip)* a las ciudades mexicanas más populares. ¡Buena suerte!

MIÉRCOLES, 23 DE AGOSTO

800	Hacer ejercicios en el gimnasio presidencial
900	Tomar café con esposa, leer el periódico y documentos del Tratado de Libre Comercio de Norteamérica (NAFTA)
1000	Llegar a la oficina para una reunión (meeting) con los delegados de las Naciones Unidas
1300	Almorzar con los delegados
1400	Asistir a la conferencia del Departamento de Educación sobre (about) la violencia en las escuelas públicas
1600	Regresar a la oficina para firmar (sign) documentos y para practicar un discurso (speech) titulado «Las economías latinoamericanas: ¿Dónde está México?» El discurso es para la cumbre (summit) económica en Santa Fe de Bogotá a fin de mes. Van a participar en esta cumbre todos los presidentes de Latinoamérica.
1800	Hablar con los consejeros (advisors) políticos sobre el día de hoy y sobre los planes para mañana
1900	Cenar (Have dinner) con su familia

Oficina del Presidente
Plaza central
México D.F.

Recomendaciones de los consejeros políticos:
- Busca información biográfica del presidente de México en el Internet.
- Considera las actividades típicas de nuestro presidente.
- Incluye una actividad divertida (fun) para su cumpleaños.
- Consulta un periódico mexicano para buscar noticias de actualidad o interesantes para ti.

MÉXICO

Ciudad de México

¿Sociable o tímido?

Las dos características en una sola nacionalidad

Octavio Paz (1914–1998), gran poeta y ensayista mexicano, recibió el Premio Nóbel de Literatura en 1990. Esta selección es de su ensayo sobre el perfil *(profile)* del mexicano, *El laberinto de la soledad* (1959).

¿Cierto o *falso?*

- En la cultura mexicana hay muchas fiestas, celebraciones y ceremonias.

- Los mexicanos dependen de su imaginación y de su sensibilidad cuando celebran.

- Las fiestas religiosas no son muy importantes.

- Una característica de las fiestas es la danza.

- Los mexicanos compran frutos y otros objetos en las plazas.

El solitario mexicano ama *(loves)* las fiestas y las reuniones públicas. Todo es ocasión para reunirse *(get together)*. Cualquier pretexto es bueno para interrumpir la marcha *(passing)* del tiempo y celebrar con festejos y ceremonias hombres y acontecimientos *(events)*. Somos un pueblo ritual. Y esta tendencia beneficia a nuestra imaginación tanto como a nuestra sensibilidad, siempre afinadas y despiertas *(lively)*. El arte de la Fiesta, envilecido *(underappreciated)* en casi todas partes, se conserva intacto entre nosotros. En pocos lugares del mundo se puede vivir con un espectáculo parecido *(similar)* al de las grandes fiestas religiosas de México, con sus colores violentos, agrios y puros, sus danzas, ceremonias, fuegos de artificio *(fireworks)*, trajes insólitos *(unusual clothing)* y la inagotable *(endless)* cascada de sorpresas de los frutos dulces *(sweet)* y objetos que se venden esos días en plazas y mercados.

- ¿Cómo celebras tu cumpleaños? ¿Con quiénes?

- ¿Participas en la conmemoración del 5 de mayo?

- ¿Qué hay en una piñata?

- ¿Qué tipo de música escuchas en tu día festivo favorito?

COLOMBIA

La batalla de los sexos

¿Quiénes dominan, los hombres o las mujeres?

Hablamos con 475 estudiantes de la Universidad Nacional de Colombia de sus opiniones sobre las características y las cualidades del novio o de la novia ideal. Ahora, vamos a ver las descripciones de los estudiantes:

Los muchachos buscan una muchacha		Las muchachas buscan un muchacho	
bonita	38%	inteligente	46%
simpática	23%	romántico	22%
inteligente	21%	guapo	19%
de buena familia	18%	generoso	13%

El momento de la verdad

13–16 puntos: Vas a tener mucho éxito en tu vida, pero eres muy serio(a) y necesitas divertirte *(to have fun)* un poco más. La vida es muy corta.

9–12 puntos: Eres aventurero(a) y no te gusta la vida aburrida. Debes tener cuidado. Recuerda *(Remember)* que hay consecuencias para todo.

5–8 puntos: Tienes muchos amigos. Dependes mucho de las emociones, y debes ser más realista.

4 puntos: Eres muy popular. Eres un poco superficial y las apariencias son más importantes que las personalidades. No es posible comprar la felicidad.

¿Coincides con los estudiantes? ¿Cómo es el novio o la novia ideal?

Identifica cuatro características del (de la) novio(a) ideal, en orden de importancia. Luego, mira a ver cuántos puntos corresponden a cada *(each)* característica. Al final, suma *(add)* los puntos para ver qué personalidad mejor te corresponde.

1 punto	2 puntos
fuerte	caballero/dama
guapo/bonita	generoso(a)
participa en deportes	romántico(a)
rico(a)	sensible

3 puntos	4 puntos
machista	cordial
perezoso(a)	disciplinado(a)
rebelde	inteligente
rudo(a)	responsable

NUEVA VISIÓN ARTÍSTICA:

1932 Nace en 1932 en Medellín e inicia su carrera artística como ilustrador de un periódico a los 17 años.

Viaja por *(throughout)* Colombia, a Madrid, Nueva York, Los Ángeles y París.

1979 Tiene su primera *(first)* exposición en un museo, y no en una galería, en 1979 en Washington, D.C.

Después tiene numerosas exposiciones en museos de diferentes países como Colombia, Japón, Estados Unidos e Italia.

En 1999 recibe una invitación de Florencia, Italia, para celebrar sus 50 años de artista con una exposición de pinturas y esculturas.

1999 Reside ahora parte del año en París y parte en Monte Carlo.

Uno de los artistas colombianos contemporáneos más famosos es Fernando Botero.

Modelos delgadas desempleadas

¿Cómo es Fernando Botero?

Informe especial: Fernando Botero y otros artistas visitan tu universidad para una exposición de arte moderno. Antes de la exposición, todos los artistas van a hablar con los estudiantes. ¡Los compañeros de clase ya empezaron *(began)* a preguntar! Continúa la conversación con preguntas originales.

RAMÓN:	Sr. Botero, quiero ser artista. ¿Qué me recomienda usted?
FERNANDO BOTERO:	Les recomiendo a los artistas jóvenes trabajar con gran pasión todos los días.
GRACIELA:	Sr. Botero, ¿por qué no pinta usted las figuras delgadas?
FERNANDO BOTERO:	Pinto las figuras gordas porque me gusta el volumen en la pintura, a diferencia de la pintura plana *(flat)* del pasado. Considero mi arte **pintura volumétrica.**
RAMÓN:	¿Cuál es la fuente *(source)* de su inspiración?
FERNANDO BOTERO:	Yo simplemente creo *(create)* arte. No creo en la pintura como forma de crítica política ni social. El arte debe ser original.
GRACIELA:	¿Le gusta ser famoso?
FERNANDO BOTERO:	Creo que ser famoso es un gran honor.
MARGARITA:	Cuéntenos, por favor, de algo que le gusta y de algo que no le gusta.
FERNANDO BOTERO:	Mi compositor favorito es Mozart y definitivamente el Internet es un gran misterio.

En la casa: España

Communicative goals

In this chapter you will learn how to . . .

- Describe the features of your home or personal residence
- Talk about furniture and appliances
- Describe household chores
- State locations and describe feelings
- Describe actions in progress
- Count from 100 and higher

Grammar

- Present tense of stem-changing verbs: e to **ie**; o to **ue**; e to **i**
- Present tense of **estar**
- The verb **estar** with adjectives
- The present progressive
- Idioms **tener ganas de, tener celos/miedo/paciencia**

Cultural information

- Antonio Gaudí
- Housing in Latin America and Spain

La Plaza Mayor, Madrid, España

EN LA CASA DE LA TROYA, SANTIAGO DE COMPOSTELA, ESPAÑA[1] In this section you will practice talking about household rooms and furniture by learning about a famous student residence in Santiago de Compostela, Spain, that houses students from the medical school. Are there any student houses on your campus? How do they compare with doña Rosa's? Do the houses have special themes?

➡ *Palabras útiles* are for recognition only; you will not be tested on these words.

Palabras útiles

el apartamento, el departamento *apartment*
el balcón *balcony*
la chimenea *fireplace, chimney*
el condominio *condominium*
el cuadro *painting*

el hogar *home*
el techo *roof*
la terraza *terrace*
el tocador *dresser*
la vivienda *housing*

¿NOS ENTENDEMOS?

La alcoba, el cuarto, la recámara, and **la pieza** are all synonyms for **el dormitorio** (which does not mean *dormitory*). In some parts of the Spanish-speaking world, **el condominio,** means *apartment complex,* making the term somewhat of a false congnate.

¡A practicar!

A. ¿Y DÓNDE PONGO LOS MUEBLES NUEVOS? Ayuda a doña Rosa a instalar los muebles *(furniture)* que está comprando para la Casa de la Troya. Indica el cuarto apropiado para cada mueble.

MODELO: Usted debe poner el estante en *el dormitorio.*

1. Es lógico poner el sillón en ___*la SALA*___.
2. Usted debe poner la cama y la cómoda en ___*dormitorio*___, ¿no?
3. El sofá debe estar en ___*SALA*___.
4. ¿La ducha, la bañera, el inodoro y el lavabo? En ___*EL CUARTO Baño*___, ¡por supuesto!

---

[1] La Casa de la Troya is Santiago de Compostela's most famous student residence. It provided lodging for students studying at the medical school and is the birthplace of Santiago's most prestigious student musical group. Musical groups from different university schools are called **tunas** and feature talented musicians who dress up in medieval costumes to serenade young women.

5. Es necesario poner la mesa y las sillas en _el comedor_

6. El coche va en _El Garaje._

B. **EN OTRAS PALABRAS** Identifica los cuartos o los muebles que corresponden a las siguientes descripciones.

1. Es el cuarto donde la gente come. _Comedor_
2. Es un lugar subterráneo. _Sotano_
3. Es un mueble que usamos para escribir cartas. _
4. Conecta el primer piso al segundo piso.
5. Sirve para ver nuestra imagen.
6. Es donde preparamos la comida.

En voz alta

C. **LUGARES PREFERIDOS** Habla con un(a) compañero(a) de clase sobre las siguientes actividades. Dile en qué lugar de la casa te gusta hacer cada actividad.

MODELO: leer libros
           Me gusta leer libros en el dormitorio.

1. estudiar   **4.** comer solo(a)   **7.** descansar
2. comer con la familia   **5.** hablar por teléfono   **8.** jugar a las cartas
3. mirar la tele   **6.** escuchar música

D. **LA FAMILIA REAL ESPAÑOLA** España es uno de los pocos países que tiene una familia real *(royal family)*.[1] Juan Carlos I es el rey *(king)* y Sofía, su esposa, es la reina *(queen)*. Los reyes tienen tres hijos: Elena, Cristina y Felipe. Elena y Cristina están casadas; el esposo de Elena es Don Jaime de Marichalar y el esposo de Cristina es Don Iñaki Urdangarín. Felipe sigue soltero. Usando tu imaginación, describe cómo es el Palacio Real.

MODELO: *El Palacio Real es muy elegante. Hay quince dormitorios y tres*
           cocinas. Los muebles también son elegantes. Las camas son
           grandes y altas, etc.

---

[1] Spain is a parliamentary monarchy; the King is the official head of state and head of the armed forces, while the members of the two-chamber parliament, or **Cortes** in Spanish, are elected by the general public. The Prime Minister has to be unanimously elected by the members of the **Cortes**. The current Prime Minister of Spain is José María Aznar.

LA VIDA MODERNA In this section you will practice talking about household appliances.

el refrigerador — la lavadora — la secadora — la estufa — el despertador — el horno de microondas — el lavaplatos — la plancha — la aspiradora — la tostadora

¡A practicar!

E. LOS ELECTRODOMÉSTICOS Indica el objeto que no va con el resto del grupo y explica por qué es diferente.

MODELO: la tostadora, el horno de microondas, *la aspiradora*
La aspiradora es diferente porque no se usa para cocinar.

1. el despertador, la estufa, el refrigerador
2. la aspiradora, la lavadora, el lavaplatos, el horno de microondas
3. la lavadora, la secadora, el refrigerador, la plancha
4. el horno de microondas, la estufa, la tostadora, el lavaplatos

F. ¿QUÉ HAY EN TU CASA? Completa las siguientes oraciones con los muebles y aparatos domésticos de tu casa o residencia.

MODELO: En el cuarto de baño hay *un lavabo, un inodoro, una bañera y unas toallas.*

1. En mi casa hay _____ (#) dormitorios y _____ (#) cuartos de baño.
2. Hay _____ (#) puertas y _____ (#) ventanas.
3. En la cocina hay _____.
4. En el dormitorio hay _____.

5. En la sala hay _____.
6. En el comedor hay _____.
7. En el garaje hay _____.
8. ¿Tienes un jardín? ¿una piscina? ¿una chimenea? ¿una terraza?

En voz alta

G. ¡ES LA CASA DE MIS SUEÑOS! Describe la casa de tus sueños *(dreams)* a un(a) compañero(a) de clase. ¡Usa tu imaginación!

MODELO: *La casa de mis sueños tiene tres pisos.*
Hay una cocina muy grande.
Hay un gimnasio en el sótano.
La casa tiene un jardín con plantas exóticas.

EN CONTEXTO

In the ¡**A ver!** section of the **Síntesis,** you will meet Francisco and Miguel, who eventually become roommates. Before that encounter, however, Francisco shares some of his thoughts on the disastrous apartment he sees before arriving at Miguel's place.

En la calle...

FRANCISCO: Hmmm... el césped *(lawn)* no está cortado. Y las plantas del patio están muertas *(dead)*. Espero que el apartamento esté en mejores condiciones.

En la sala...

FRANCISCO: ¡Ay! ¡Dios mío! ¡Es un desastre el apartamento! Hay ropa por todos lados, y en el sillón hay un mogollón de libros. Deben ser estudiantes las personas que viven aquí. A ver si está bien la cocina.

En la cocina...

FRANCISCO: ¡Qué barbaridad! Todos los platos están sucios. Y todavía no han quitado la mesa *(they have not cleared the table)*. Parece que nadie limpia aquí. Y para colmo *(And on top of that)*, ¡un saco de basura en el lavabo!... No sé cómo viven aquí.

En el dormitorio...

FRANCISCO: No veo la cama... Ah, allí está. Apenas la veo debajo de la ropa. Y ni siquiera *(not even)* un libro en el estante. Creo que todos están en el sillón en la sala. El radio debe estar para entretener *(to entertain)* a las cucarachas.

En el cuarto de baño...

FRANCISCO: La gente de este piso son unos sinvergüenzas *(shameless people)*. Mira cómo está la bañera... huele mal aquí. No puedo vivir entre esta gente... Estoy más cómodo en un jardín zoológico. Y el alquiler está super alto. En fin, ya me voy ... ¡No soporto más! *(I can't take it anymore!)*

¿NOS ENTENDEMOS?

Spanish speakers say ¡**Dios mío!** *(Oh my gosh!)* to express amazement in either a positive or negative context. ¡**Qué barbaridad!** *(How atrocious!)* is reserved to express disgust and/or outrage. Among teens and young adults in Spain, it's common in informal speech to use **un mogollón** to mean *a lot.* Young Spaniards are also likely to use the adverb **super** to add emphasis to a quality or condition. In Spain, the word **piso** is used to mean *apartment* instead of **el apartamento.**

H. **¿COMPRENDISTE?** ¿Cuáles son algunos de los problemas que Francisco encuentra con el apartamento? Escribe una lista de cuatro o cinco cosas que están mal.

MODELO: *El césped no está cortado.*

1.   4.

2.   5.

3.

ENCUENTRO *cultural*

Gaudí y su obra

Éstas son unas palabras nuevas para la lectura:

la obra maestra *masterpiece*
la superficie plana *flat surface*
la redondez *roundness*
el espacio abierto *open spaces*
ondulado *wavy*

la esquina *corner*   **el candado** *lock*   **el ascensor** *elevator*

Antoni Gaudí i Cornet (1852–1926) es conocido como uno de los más prestigiosos arquitectos internacionales en la arquitectura catalana. Entre sus **obras maestras** está la Iglesia San Feliu de les Corts de Sarriá y el Palacio Güell. La dedicación de Gaudí es notable en sus creaciones como Casa Clavet, Casa Batlló y Casa Milá. Estas grandes estructuras reducen al mínimo la tradición lineal y **las superficies planas** por el uso de **la redondez** y la irregularidad de **espacios abiertos** y un techo y balcones **ondulados.** La más famosa de sus obras es La Sagrada Familia, una iglesia considerada como la obra más importante de Gaudí. Esta iglesia incompleta está en Barcelona.

La última obra civil de Gaudí es la Casa Milá, también conocida como La Pedrera. Es una de sus mejores y más ambiciosas creaciones. Este edificio es un apartamento y está en Barcelona también. Tiene acceso al techo, donde la gente puede ir de noche para ver la magnífica vista de la ciudad mientras toma un refresco y escucha música. La Pedrera tiene seis escaleras, dos torres para la ventilación y siete chimeneas. La Pedrera está diseñada alrededor de dos patios, uno circular y otro elíptico. El patio circular está en **la esquina** del Paseo de Grácia, y el otro en la calle Provença. Las puertas, **los candados,** los muebles, y **los ascensores** muestran la dedicación y la participación de Gaudí en los detalles más pequeños de los edificios. El edificio está abierto para el turismo y hay una variedad de exhibiciones y eventos culturales.

Para pensar: ¿Qué piensas del estilo de Gaudí? ¿Es similar o diferente de la arquitectura en tu ciudad?

I. **PREGUNTAS** Contesta las siguientes preguntas a base de la lectura.

1. ¿Por qué es muy conocido Gaudí?
2. ¿Qué ciudad tiene muchos edificios de Gaudí?
3. Esta lectura habla de la Casa Milá. ¿Dónde está? ¿Tiene otro nombre? ¿Puedes mencionar algo especial de esta casa?

GRAMÁTICA I: *Present tense of stem-changing verbs: e to ie; o to ue; e to i*

In this section you will learn how to conjugate verbs that have a spelling change—either **e** to **ie**, **o** to **ue**, or **e** to **i**—in the stem of the verb. A stem is the part of an infinitive to which one adds personal endings. For example, the stem of **hablar** is **habl-**. Several types of vowel changes occur in the stem of certain verbs in the present tense.

The following verbs change their stem vowel from **e** to **ie**, except in the **nosotros(as)** and **vosotros(as)** forms.

comenzar (ie)	pensar (ie)	querer (ie)	preferir (ie)
(to begin)	*(to think)*	*(to want; to love)*	*(to prefer)*
comienzo	pienso	quiero	prefiero
comienzas	piensas	quieres	prefieres
comienza	piensa	quiere	prefiere
comenzamos	pensamos	queremos	preferimos
comenzáis	pensáis	queréis	preferís
comienzan	piensan	quieren	prefieren

Two verbs that have stem changes from e to ie have an irregular yo form. You have already learned the endings for tener in Capítulo preliminar and in Capítulo 2.

tener (ie)	venir (ie)
(to have)	*(to come)*
tengo	**vengo**
tienes	vienes
tiene	viene
tenemos	venimos
tenéis	venís
tienen	vienen

Other frequently used e-to-ie stem-changing verbs are:

cerrar (ie)   *to close*
empezar (ie)   *to begin*
entender (ie)   *to understand*
perder (ie)   *to lose; to miss (a function)*

The following verbs change their stem vowel from **o** to **ue**, except in the **nosotros(as)** and **vosotros(as)** forms. **Jugar** is the only **u-to-ue** stem-changing verb in Spanish.

jugar (ue)	almorzar (ue)	poder (ue)	volver (ue)	dormir (ue)
(to play)	*(to have lunch)*	*(to be able)*	*(to return)*	*(to sleep)*
juego	almuerzo	puedo	vuelvo	duermo
juegas	almuerzas	puedes	vuelves	duermes
juega	almuerza	puede	vuelve	duerme
jugamos	almorzamos	podemos	volvemos	dormimos
jugáis	almorzáis	podéis	volvéis	dormís
juegan	almuerzan	pueden	vuelven	duermen

Other frequently used **o-to-ue** stem-changing verbs are:

contar (ue)   *to count; to tell*
costar (ue)   *to cost* (used in third-person singular and plural forms)
llover (ue)   *to rain* (used in third-person singular form)
morir (ue)   *to die*

The following **-ir** verbs change their stem vowel from **e** to **i**, except in the **nosotros(as)** and **vosotros(as)** forms.

servir (i)	pedir (i)	decir (i)
(to serve)	*(to ask for)*	*(to say; to tell)*
sirvo	pido	digo[1]
sirves	pides	dices
sirve	pide	dice
servimos	pedimos	decimos
servís	pedís	decís
sirven	piden	dicen

Other frequently used **e-to-i** stem-changing verbs are:

seguir (i)   *to continue; to follow*
conseguir (i)   *to get, to obtain*

¡A practicar!

J.   **ENTREVISTA CON DOÑA ROSA**   Raquel Navarro es reportera. Quiere escribir un artículo sobre la gente anciana. En este momento ella está hablando con doña Rosa. Completa su conversación, usando la forma apropiada de los siguientes verbos: **comenzar, pensar, preferir, querer, tener, venir.**

---

[1] The **yo** form of **decir** is irregular.

Raquel:	Yo _____ hablar con usted sobre su vida, doña Rosa. ¿Está bien?
Doña Rosa:	Por supuesto. ¿_____ (nosotras) con mi vida personal?
Raquel:	Muy bien. ¿_____ usted muchos hijos?
Doña Rosa:	Sí, _____ cuatro. Dos de ellos viven aquí conmigo.
Raquel:	Y los otros... ¿_____ a visitarla frecuentemente?
Doña Rosa:	Bueno, no _____ frecuentemente porque viven en Madrid.
Raquel:	Sé que los estudiantes la tienen muy ocupada. Pero ¿qué hace durante el día para divertirse?
Doña Rosa:	Me gusta mirar la tele. (Yo) _____ ver telenovelas.
Raquel:	¿_____ usted una telenovela favorita, doña Rosa?
Doña Rosa:	Claro que sí, señorita. Se llama «Decepción y amor». El programa _____ en una hora. ¿_____ tú verlo conmigo este tarde?
Raquel:	Sí, gracias. Me gusta mucho este programa. ¡Qué guay! *(Cool!)* ¿Y qué _____ usted de las telenovelas españolas, doña Rosa?
Doña Rosa:	Bueno, pues... me gustan mucho, pero mi hija _____ las telenovelas norteamericanas porque son menos melodramáticas.

K. ¿CIERTO O FALSO?
Ahora tienes que corregir *(correct)* algunos de los errores en el artículo de Raquel antes de publicarlo en el periódico *(newspaper)*. Si la oración es falsa, ¡corrígela!

MODELO: Doña Rosa: «Yo tengo tres hijos.»
           Es falso. Doña Rosa tiene cuatro hijos.

1. Doña Rosa: «Mis hijos vienen a visitarme frecuentemente.»
2. Raquel: «Su hija la tiene muy ocupada.»
3. Doña Rosa: «Prefiero el noticiero *(news program)*.»
4. Doña Rosa: «No tengo un programa favorito.»
5. Doña Rosa: «Pienso que las telenovelas españolas son malas.»
6. Doña Rosa: «Nosotros preferimos ver las telenovelas británicas.»

L. PLANES PARA EL SÁBADO.
Beti y su compañero Tomás, dos estudiantes de medicina, están hablando de sus planes. Completa su conversación con la forma correcta de los siguientes verbos: **almorzar, dormir, jugar, poder** y **volver**.

Beti:	¿Por qué no _____ (nosotros) al tenis esta tarde?
Tomás:	Yo no _____ bien al tenis, Beti. Y después de mi accidente, no _____ hacer mucho ejercicio por una semana.
Beti:	Pues, vamos a ir al cine. ¿Qué te parece? Nosotros _____ ver la nueva película de Almodóvar.[1]
Tomás:	Bien. Antes del cine, ¿_____ (nosotros) en la calle Franco?[2] Conozco un restaurante nuevo.
Beti:	¡Perfecto! Y después de almorzar, nosotros _____ a casa. Yo siempre _____ la siesta.
Tomás:	¿Cómo? Tú _____ dormir la siesta, si quieres, pero a mí no me gusta.

---

[1] Pedro Almodóvar is one of Spain's most famous filmmakers. He has directed over 12 films, including *All About My Mother*, which won an Academy Award for Best Foreign Language Film in 2000.
[2] *La calle Franco* is one of the more popular streets for dining in Santiago de Compostela. The street is in the old part of the city where car traffic is prohibited. It features numerous street musicians and other attractions.

M. UNA FIESTA EN LA CASA DE LA TROYA Ramón quiere tener una fiesta para sus amigos en la casa de doña Rosa la noche del sábado. Con los fragmentos de abajo, forma oraciones completas para narrar *(to narrate)* la historia *(story)*. Luego pon los eventos en un orden lógico.

¡LA FIESTA VA A SER GENIAL! ¡PARECE QUE TODOS MIS COMPAÑEROS DE CLASE VIENEN!

1. _____ su hermano / venir / Madrid / ayudar
2. _____ doña Rosa / pensar que / los chicos / salir temprano / la fiesta
3. _____ Ramón y doña Rosa / comenzar a / hacer planes
4. _____ Ramón: «¡pensar / tener/ fiesta estupenda!»
5. _____ Ramón: «mi novia y yo / poder / preparar / unas tapas riquísimas[1]»
6. _____ Ramón / querer / invitar / muchas personas
7. _____ doña Rosa: «Ramón / entonces / tener que / limpiar / la casa»
8. _____ Ramón / preferir / tener / fiesta / en casa
9. _____ Ramón / saber que / nadie / dormir / su fiesta

En voz alta

N. ¿ES VERDAD? Responde a las siguientes observaciones, indicando si son aplicables a ti.

MODELO: Tú siempre pides mucha comida en la cafetería.
No es verdad. Yo no pido mucha comida en la cafetería.

1. Tú y tus amigos(as) siempre decís cosas buenas sobre los profesores.
2. Tus amigos sirven comida exótica en las fiestas.
3. Tu profesor(a) de español pide demasiada tarea.
4. Tú siempre dices la verdad a tus compañeros de clase.
5. Tú siempre pides ayuda cuando no entiendes una cosa.
6. Vosotros pedís trabajos extras de los profesores.
7. Los restaurantes de la universidad sirven buena comida.

O. ENCUENTRA A ALGUIEN QUE... Encuentra a alguien en tu clase que haga las siguientes cosas. Con las siguientes frases, forma preguntas para tus compañeros(as) para saber si ellos(as) hacen o no hacen esas cosas.

MODELO: querer una casa con chimenea
E1: *¿Quieres una casa con chimenea?*
E2: *Sí, yo quiero una casa con chimenea.*

1. almorzar en la terraza
2. preferir una casa a un apartamento
3. pensar tener una fiesta en la casa de sus padres
4. poder preparar comida riquísima

---

[1] **Tapas** are small portions of food, like appetizers, that are frequently served at parties or at bars along with beverages. A favorite **tapa** in Spain is **tortilla española,** a potato omelette.

- tener que lavar los platos
- pedir postres *(desserts)* en los restaurantes
- decir comentarios atrevidos *(bold)* a miembros del sexo opuesto
- servir comida deliciosa en las fiestas

ENTREVISTA: PREGUNTAS SOBRE LA VIVIENDA Hazle las siguientes preguntas sobre su vivienda a un(a) compañero(a) de clase.

- ¿Prefieres vivir en un apartamento, una casa o una residencia? ¿Almuerzas
en casa *(at home)* o en una cafetería? ¿Vienen tus padres a visitarte con
frecuencia?
- ¿Cierras las ventanas de tu dormitorio por la noche? ¿Duermes bien cuando
estás solo(a) en casa? ¿Pueden visitarte tus amigos a cualquier hora *(at
any time)*?
- ¿Tienes muchas fiestas en tu casa? ¿En qué cuarto prefieres estar con tus
amigos en una fiesta? ¿Pierdes muchas fiestas porque tienes que estudiar?
¿Puedes tener fiestas en un patio o en un jardín? ¿A qué hora vuelves de una
fiesta generalmente?
- ¿Pierdes muchas cosas en tu dormitorio? ¿Puedes estudiar bien en tu dormitorio? ¿Duermes fácilmente en tu dormitorio? ¿Qué muebles tienes en tu
dormitorio? ¿Qué aparatos domésticos tienes?

VOCABULARIO: *Los quehaceres domésticos*

LOS QUEHACERES DE DOÑA ROSA Y LOS ESTUDIANTES In this section you will
learn how to talk about household chores.

LIMPIAR LA CASA

barrer el piso

hacer la cama

sacar la basura

lavar las ventanas

poner la mesa

quitar la mesa

lavar los platos

pasar la aspiradora

lavar la ropa

cortar el césped

planchar la ropa

regar las plantas

¡A practicar!

¿NOS ENTENDEMOS?

Many of the household chores you have just learned have synonyms that are used often. **Fregar (ie) los platos** means *to wash the dishes;* **tirar la basura** means *to take out the garbage (trash);* and **tender (ie) la cama** means *to make the bed.*

Q. LOS QUEHACERES DE DOÑA ROSA Y LOS ESTUDIANTES Completa las siguientes oraciones para identificar los quehaceres domésticos de doña Rosa y los estudiantes.

1. Manuel y David: «Nosotros _____ la mesa antes de comer.»
2. Carlos _____ la mesa después de comer.
3. Doña Rosa y Marcos _____ los platos en la cocina.
4. Doña Rosa: «Pepe, tú _____ la basura.»
5. Manuel y David _____ la casa los fines de semana.
6. Ramón: «Yo _____ el césped y _____ las plantas en junio, julio y agosto.»
7. Los estudiantes _____ la cama todas las mañanas.
8. La hija de doña Rosa _____ la ropa y _____ el piso.
9. Si está de buen humor *(in a good mood)*, doña Rosa _____ la aspiradora.

R. LA SECCIÓN FEMENINA[1] Carmen Franco, la esposa de Francisco Franco,[2] tiene muchos quehaceres en su casa. ¿Qué tiene que hacer Carmen?

MODELO: La cama está desordenada *(messy).*
          Carmen tiene que hacer la cama.

1. Los platos están sucios *(dirty).*
2. La basura está llena *(full).*
3. La ropa está arrugada *(wrinkled).*
4. La casa está sucia.
5. El piso está sucio.
6. Las plantas están secas *(dry).*

En voz alta

S. ¿QUÉ HACES PARA LIMPIAR LA CASA? Pregúntale a un(a) compañero(a) de clase si hace los siguientes quehaceres. Si tu compañero(a) no hace el quehacer, debe indicar quién lo hace.

MODELO: sacar la basura
          E1: *¿Sacas la basura?*
          E2: *No, no saco la basura. Mi padre saca la basura.*

1. poner la mesa
2. lavar los platos
3. planchar la ropa
4. lavar la ropa
5. pasar la aspiradora
6. hacer la cama
7. cortar el césped
8. barrer el piso
9. regar las plantas

T. ENTREVISTA Trabajando con un(a) compañero(a) de clase, hazle las siguientes preguntas sobre los quehaceres domésticos que él (ella) hace en casa.

1. ¿Tienes muchos quehaceres domésticos? ¿Cuáles son?
2. ¿Te gusta cocinar? ¿poner la mesa? ¿quitar la mesa? ¿lavar los platos?

---

[1] In 1934 the **Sección Femenina** was created with the idea that the venue for woman's political participation was the home. This controversial movement claimed that if women took power in the home they could reform Spain by being good mothers and wives.
[2] Francisco Franco was the dictator of Spain from 1939 to 1975 after having risen to power during the Spanish Civil War (1936–1939). A very controversial figure, Franco is praised by some for saving Spain from a bitter civil war, while he is criticized by others for being a fascist dictator with ties to Hitler and Mussolini during World War II.

3. ¿Qué hace(n) tu(s) hermanos(as)?
4. ¿Quién en la familia plancha la ropa? ¿Usas la lavadora y la secadora?
5. ¿Cuántas veces al mes limpias la casa? ¿el refrigerador?
6. ¿Tienes que cortar el césped?
7. ¿Quién en la familia riega las plantas?
8. ¿Tienes que barrer el piso? ¿el patio? ¿el garaje?

ENCUENTRO *cultural*

Viviendas en Latinoamérica y España

Éstas son unas palabras nuevas para la lectura:

el cartón *cardboard*
el piso *floor*

Para pensar: ¿Vives en una ciudad grande o en un pueblo pequeño? ¿Es más común vivir en un apartamento o en una casa en tu ciudad? ¿Cuál prefieres tú?

En Latinoamérica y España, las viviendas varían según el país, la región, el clima, la posición económica y el gusto de las personas. La arquitectura varía desde pequeñas casas coloniales hasta edificios de apartamentos muy altos, o desde condominios hasta casas de adobe o de **cartón.** Los edificios altos tienen una forma de numerar los **pisos** que es diferente de la que usamos en los Estados Unidos. Lo que nosotros llamamos el primer piso, ellos llaman la planta baja. Lo que nosotros llamamos el segundo piso, ellos llaman el primer piso.

Es difícil encontrar una casa típica del mundo hispánico. El estilo de las casas depende de la región. Madrid, la capital de España, tiene casi 3 millones de habitantes. No hay mucho espacio, y por eso los apartamentos son las viviendas más comunes para mucha gente, así como en las ciudades grandes de los Estados Unidos.

U. **COMPRENSIÓN** Contesta las siguientes preguntas a base de la lectura.

1. ¿Cómo es la arquitectura de las viviendas en Latinoamérica y España?
2. ¿Cuáles son las viviendas más comunes en las ciudades grandes de Latinoamérica y España?

GRAMÁTICA II: *The verb estar*

The verb *to be* in English is translated in Spanish by either the verb **ser** or **estar.** As you learned in **Capítulo 2, ser** is used to identify essential or inherent characteristics, profession, nationality, origin, time, and dates. The verb **estar** has two primary functions.[1]

---

[1] You will receive more practice in distinguishing between the uses of **ser** and **estar** in **Capítulo 5.**

To state where people are, use **estar en** + a location.

¿Dónde **está** papá?   *Where **is** Dad?*

Está en el comedor.   *He's **in** the dining room.*

To describe how people are feeling, use **estar** + an adjective.

¿Cómo **estás**, Elena?   *How **are you**, Elena?*

Estoy muy cansada.   *I'm very tired.*

The present tense of **estar** has an irregular **yo** form; the other forms have regular **-ar** endings, but with accents on every form except the **nosotros(as)** form.

estar *(to be)*

yo	estoy	*I am*
tú	estás	*you (informal) are*
Ud., él, ella	está	*you (formal) are; he/she is*
nosotros(as)	estamos	*we are*
vosotros(as)	estáis	*you (informal) are*
Uds., ellos(as)	están	*you (formal) are; they are*

Here are some adjectives commonly used with estar to describe emotional and physical states:

aburrido(a)	*bored*	**limpio(a)**	*clean*
contento(a)	*happy*	**nervioso(a)**	*nervous*
desordenado(a)	*messy*	**ocupado(a)**	*busy*
emocionado(a)	*excited*	**ordenado(a)**	*neat*
enfermo(a)	*sick*	**preocupado(a)**	*worried*
enojado(a)	*angry*	**sucio(a)**	*dirty*
furioso(a)	*furious*	**triste**	*sad*

Estar can also be used with the adverbs **bien** and **mal**.

¿Cómo estás?   *How are you?*

Yo **estoy bien (mal).**   *I'm **well (bad).***

¡A practicar!

V.   **¿DÓNDE ESTÁ OSVALDO?** Basado en la información, indica dónde están Osvaldo y su esposa Silvia. Varias respuestas son posibles.

MODELO: Silvia y Osvaldo almuerzan juntos.
             Están en el comedor.

1. Osvaldo duerme profundamente *(deeply)*.
2. Silvia comienza a leer una novela.
3. Osvaldo piensa cortar el césped.
4. Silvia y Osvaldo juegan a las cartas.
5. Osvaldo empieza a cantar una canción.
6. Silvia y Osvaldo vuelven de sus trabajos y cierran la puerta.
7. Silvia piensa en los ingredientes de una comida especial.
8. Osvaldo cierra con llave *(locks)* el coche.

W. ¿CÓMO ESTÁ(N)? Mira los siguientes dibujos y decide cómo están las personas. Usa la forma apropiada de los adjetivos de la lista en la página 116 y el verbo **estar**.

1.

2.

3.

4.

5.

6.

7.

8.

X. ¡NO HAY LUZ! No hay electricidad en la casa y tienes que decidir dónde están las siguientes personas basándote en los objetos que se encuentran en cada cuarto. Usa una de las formas de **estar + en.** En algunos casos hay varias posibilidades.

MODELO: Michelle / el horno
            Michelle está en la cocina.

1. John y Clyde / el despertador
2. nosotros / el inodoro
3. tú / el coche *(car)*
4. vosotros / el sillón
5. Keith / plantas
6. Mary y Susan / la cómoda
7. yo / la secadora
8. nosotros / la estufa

En voz alta

Y. **SITUACIONES Y EMOCIONES** Trabajando con un(a) compañero(a) de clase, tomen turnos *(take turns)* identificando sus emociones en las siguientes situaciones, y expliquen *(explain)* por qué.

MODELO: Cuando hace sol, estoy...
Cuando hace sol, estoy muy contento; me gusta mucho el sol.

1. Cuando recibo una mala nota *(bad grade)*, estoy...
2. Cuando tengo que hablar en español, estoy...
3. Cuando mi familia y yo limpiamos la casa todo el día, estamos...
4. Cuando mi hermano tiene que limpiar el cuarto de baño, está...
5. Cuando estoy con mis amigos, nosotros estamos...
6. Cuando mi compañero(a) pierde un documento en la computadora, está...
7. Cuando los estudiantes no tienen clase, están...
8. Cuando el (la) profesor(a) corrige nuestros exámenes, está...

Z. **ESCULTURAS DE BARCELONA** Inventa una historia *(story)* sobre estas fotos de esculturas famosas en Barcelona con **estar** y otros verbos para describir la situación y las emociones representadas. La foto a la izquierda es una escultura de Antonio Gaudí y forma parte de su obra maestra, La Sagrada Familia (a la derecha).

ASÍ SE DICE: *Describing actions in progress*

The present progressive tense is used to describe actions in progress. To form the present progressive, use a present-tense form of **estar** plus a present participle, which is formed by adding **-ando** to the stem of **-ar** verbs and **-iendo** to the stem of **-er** and **-ir** verbs.

estoy			
estás		estud**iando**	*(studying)*
está	+	com**iendo**	*(eating)*
estamos		escrib**iendo**	*(writing)*
estáis			
están			

Two irregular present participles are **leyendo** *(reading)* and **trayendo** *(bringing)*. Verbs that end in **-ir** and have a stem change, such as the verbs **dormir, pedir,** and **servir,** change in the stem from **o** to **u** or from **e** to **i** (forming **durmiendo, pidiendo,** and **sirviendo,** respectively).

While Spanish speakers often use the simple present tense to describe routine or habitual actions, they use the present progressive tense to describe what is happening right now. Compare the two examples:

1. Happens habitually

Generalmente, Lorena **come** con su familia en casa.

Generally, Lorena eats with her family at home.

2. Happening right now

Pero en este momento Lorena **está comiendo** en una cafetería.

But right now Lorena is eating in a cafeteria.

¡A practicar!

AA. ¿QUÉ ESTÁN HACIENDO? Eres fotógrafo(a) y estás explicando tus fotos de la Casa de la Troya. Usa el presente progresivo (**estar + participio presente**) para describir las acciones de las personas en cada foto.

MODELO: Ramón / bailar
Ramón está bailando.

1. doña Rosa / cantar
2. nosotros / poner la mesa
3. los estudiantes / limpiar la casa
4. tú / dormir
5. vosotros(as) / servir la comida
6. Beti y Tomás / pensar en los planes para el fin de semana

7. Carlos / quitar la mesa
8. la hija de doña Rosa / planchar la ropa
9. yo / pasar la aspiradora
10. Miguel / leer el periódico

En voz alta

BB. ¡ACTUEMOS! En grupos de tres personas, tomen turnos actuando y adivinando varios quehaceres domésticos. Una persona hace pantomima y los otros del grupo indican qué está haciendo usando el presente progresivo.

ASÍ SE DICE: *More idioms with tener*

As you learned in **Capítulos 2** and **3,** in certain cases you can also use the verb **tener** + a noun to describe how people are feeling.

—¿**Tienes sueño,** mamá?	*Are you sleepy, Mom?*
—Sí, **tengo mucho sueño.**[1]	*Yes, I'm very sleepy.*
—¿**Tienes hambre?**	*Are you hungry?*
—Sí, **tengo mucha hambre.**	*Yes, I'm very hungry.*

Here are four more expressions you can use with **tener:**

tener celos	*to be jealous*
tener ganas de	*to feel like (doing something)* (used with an infinitive)
tener miedo (de)	*to be afraid (of)*
tener paciencia	*to be patient*

To express *very* with the **tener** expressions, use a form of the adjective **mucho,** which must match the gender (masculine or feminine) and number (singular or plural) of its noun, as in the examples above.

¡A practicar!

CC. EN OTRAS PALABRAS Usando una expresión con el verbo **tener,** indica que
tienen las siguientes personas.

MODELO: Mercedes: «Yo quiero ir al cine.»
Mercedes tiene ganas ver una película.

1. Manolo dice: «Allí está Ramón hablando con mi novia.»
2. Milagros y Maite dicen: «Nosotras podemos esperar; no tenemos prisa.»
3. Yo digo: «¡Ayyyy! ¡Un perro grande!»
4. Tú dices: «Yo quiero ir a la discoteca.»

En voz alta

DD. ¿QUÉ HACES CUANDO TIENES... ? Trabajando con un(a) compañero(a) de
clase, forma preguntas usando expresiones con **tener.** Luego contesta las preguntas de la otra persona.

MODELO: E1: *¿Qué haces cuando tienes miedo por la noche?*
E2: *Cuando tengo miedo por la noche, yo cierro las ventanas.*

VOCABULARIO: *Los números 100 y más*

100	**cien (ciento + número)**	800	**ochocientos(as)**
200	**doscientos(as)**	900	**novecientos(as)**
300	**trescientos(as)**	1.000	**mil**
400	**cuatrocientos(as)**	2.000[1]	**dos mil**
500	**quinientos(as)**	200.000	**doscientos(as) mil**
600	**seiscientos(as)**	1.000.000	**un millón**
700	**setecientos(as)**	2.000.000	**dos millones**

Use numbers 1–2000 to state a specific year in Spanish.

1835 **mil ochocientos treinta y cinco**

1998 **mil novecientos noventa y ocho**

Use the preposition **de** to connect the day, the month, and the year.

Nací *(I was born)* el 24 **de** junio **de** 1979.

Note that when writing numbers, Spanish uses a period where English uses a
comma, and vice versa.

Spanish: **$1.500,75**   English: **$1,500.75**

This is not the case when writing years. Years are written as follows, without
commas:

1999   1969   1492

¡A practicar!

EE. ACONTECIMIENTOS HISTÓRICOS Empareja cada oración con el año correcto. Años históricos: ~~mil doscientos siete~~, ~~mil cuatrocientos noventa y dos~~, mil
~~quinientos diecinueve~~, ~~mil seiscientos cinco~~, mil seiscientos siete, ~~mil setecientos~~

---

[1] Use **mil** to express numbers over 1,000.

setenta y seis, mil ochocientos sesenta, mil novecientos cincuenta y siete, mil novecientos setenta y seis, mil novecientos noventa y dos, dos mil uno

1. Hernán Cortés llegó a México en _1_ 5 _1_ 9 .
2. Los rusos lanzaron el *Sputnik* en 1 _9 5_ 7 .
3. Abraham Lincoln fue elegido presidente en _1_ 8 6 _0_.
4. Los peregrinos fundaron Jamestown en _1_ 6 _0_ 7 .
5. Cristóbal Colón llegó al Nuevo Mundo el 12 de octubre de _1_ 4 _9_ 2 . En el año 1 _9_ 9 _2_ se celebró el quinto centenario de este descubrimiento.
6. Los Estados Unidos declararon su independencia de Inglaterra el 4 de julio de _1_ 7 7 _6_ . Luego, doscientos años más tarde, en el año _1_ 9 _7_ 6 , los norteamericanos celebraron el bicentenario de este acontecimiento.
7. En el año 2 _0_ 0 _0_ comenzamos otros 1.000 años de historia de nuestro mundo.
8. *El Poema del mio Cid*[1] fue escrito en 12 _0 7_ .
9. Miguel de Cervantes Saavedra publicó *Don Quijote de la Mancha*[2] en _1_ 6 _0_ 5.
10. El año de nacimiento de mi papá es _1924_, y el de mi mamá es _1926_. El año de mi nacimiento es _1953_.

FF. **OBRAS MAESTRAS**[3] Doña Rosa busca algunas obras de arte para decorar su casa. Como eres vendedor(a) de arte, tienes que escribir los números del precio en pesetas para cada obra.

MODELO: *The Triangular Hour* de Salvador Dalí
87.329.200,00 ptas.

ochenta y siete millones trescientos veintinueve mil, doscientas pesetas

1. *Las Meninas* de Diego de Velásquez 655.450.150,00 ptas.

---

[1] *El poema del mío Cid* is Spain's oldest epic poem written in medieval Spanish. The poem is anonymous and relates the heroic deeds of *El Cid* during the Crusades. *El Cid* was Rodrigo Diáz de Vivar, a commander under King Alfonso VI of Castile in the eleventh century.
[2] *El ingenioso hidalgo Don Quijote de la Mancha* (The Ingenious Gentleman Don Quixote of the Mancha) is Spain's most famous work of literature and is widely considered to be the first "novel" as we know the

2. *Duelo a garrotazos* de Francisco Goya 25.745.285,00 ptas.

3. *Guernica* de Pablo Picasso 975.475.110,00 ptas.

genre today. The novel is based on the escapades of a squire, who believes himself to be a knight after reading too many novels of chivalry, and his faithful servant, Sancho Panza. Don Quijote and Sancho Panza are universal icons of the ideal and the mundane.
[3] **Salvador Dalí** (1904–1989) is most famous for his particular surrealist style which features interior landscapes of the unconscious. Diego Velásquez (1599–1660) was the official court painter for Philip IV. *Las Meninas,* featuring one of Philip's daughters posing for her portrait, is his most famous work as it depicts the artistic process itself. Francisco Goya (1746–1828) was the court painter for King Fernando VII. *Duelo a garrotazos* (Duel with Cudgels) reflects a particularly violent moment in Spain's history. **Pablo Picasso** (1881–1973) was one of the early innovators of cubism in Spain. *Guernica* is a national treasure of Spain depicting the horrors of modern warfare suffered by the inhabitants of Guernica, bombed by the Germans on the eve of WWII.

En voz alta

GG. **¿CÓMO SE DICE... EN ESPAÑOL?** Escribe los siguientes números y luego exprésalos a un(a) compañero(a) de clase.

MODELO: la fundación de esta universidad
1825 mil ochocientos veinticinco

1. la población de esta ciudad
2. el año de tu nacimiento
3. el número de estudiantes en esta universidad
4. la cantidad de dinero que tienes en el banco
5. la población de la Ciudad de México
6. el número de días en el año
7. el número de cartas electrónicas que recibes en un año
8. 100 x (tu edad)
9. 1000 x (el número de chicas en esta clase)
10. 1000 x (el número de chicos en esta clase) − 50

HH. **¿CUÁNTO CUESTA?** *(How much is it?)* Estás en Tecnolandia, una tienda de electrodomésticos en Santiago. Doña Rosa quiere unas cosas nuevas para la Casa de la Troya, y tú tienes que comprarlas. Tienes 40.000 pesetas para comprarlo todo. ¿Qué vas a comprar? ¿Puedes comprar todo lo que ella quiere? Habla con dos compañeros(as) de clase sobre qué van a comprar, qué no van a comprar y por qué.

MODELO: *Yo compro la aspiradora por 19.450 pesetas, el microondas por 15.633, la tostadora por 2.545 y los dos despertadores por 1.294. Así gasto 38.922 pesetas. No puedo comprarlo todo.*

Doña Rosa quiere:

una aspiradora nueva
dos despertadores
una tostadora
un sillón
un refrigerador
un horno de microondas

Tecnolandia ofrece:

Aspiradora Kirby, 19.450 ptas.
Despertador Timex, 647 ptas.
Tostadora Krupps, 2.545 ptas.
Sillón Chico Flojo, 10.999 ptas.
Refrigerador Whirlpool, 33.985 ptas.
Microondas Sony, 15.663 ptas.

Síntesis

¡A ver!

La narradora de los segmentos de video del **Capítulo 4** es Conchita, quien vive en Torrelavega en el norte de España. Conchita nos va a presentar el tema principal de este capítulo, el hogar en el mundo hispánico. Nos va a hablar sobre su propia casa en la provincia de Santander y luego presentarnos los dos segmentos de video.

ACTIVIDAD 1 Pre-viewing task (Segmento 1 del video)

As you create your description of Laura's house, agree or disagree appropriately with your partner's opinions.

Paso 1: Escucha a Conchita hablar de la casa. Mira el primer segmento que consiste en una serie de fotos y un clip muy corto, todo de la casa de la familia de Laura, a quienes conocimos en el **Capítulo 2**. Recuerda que Laura vive en la Ciudad de México. Mientras escuchas y miras, haz una lista de todas las partes de la casa que reconoces.

Paso 2: Comparte tu lista con el resto de la clase.

Paso 3: ¿Cómo es la casa de Laura? Descríbela con tu compañero(a) de clase. Utiliza adjetivos descriptivos como **grande, pequeño, bonito, amplio, cómodo, oscuro,** etc. ¡Cuidado con la forma de los adjetivos!

ACTIVIDAD 2 Pre-viewing task (Segmento 2 del video)

Paso 1: Eres estudiante en Madrid, la capital de España. Buscas un piso o una casa para vivir. No te importa vivir con otras personas, con otros estudiantes. Ves en el periódico anuncios de unos sitios interesantes. Vas a llamar por teléfono para pedir información. ¿Qué preguntas vas a hacer antes de ir a ver el sitio? Haz una lista de estas preguntas. Utiliza las sugerencias indicadas en la siguiente tabla, añadiendo otras preguntas necesarias en la columna 3.

MODELO: *¿Cuántos dormitorios tiene la casa? ¿Cuánto es el alquiler?*

Las habitaciones	Otras cosas	¿Algo más?
dormitorios cocina baños sala de estar comedor jardín garaje patio ¿ ?	el alquiler los gastos (electricidad, gas, etc.) el número de inquilinos *(renters)*	

Alquileres...

Alquilo piso céntrico. 4 dormitorios. 2 baños, 1 en suite. Cocina completa. Lavadero, garaje. Muy buen estado. Cerca de estación de metro. Alquiler: 80.000 pesetas mensuales, gastos incluidos.

Piso amplio con vistas al parque. Sin muebles. Terraza, 3 dorm., 2 baños, cocina-comedor. Garaje para dos coches. Llamar tardes después de las 8. Precio: 75.000 pesetas mensuales. Sin gastos.

Apartamento en edificio torre de lujo. 1 dormitorio y medio. Equipado para 3 personas. Cocina-comedor, completa, microondas. Living amplio. Terraza con vistas excelentes. Céntrico. Sin garaje.

Paso 2: En parejas, haz la conversación telefónica entre tú, el (la) estudiante y el (la) dueño(a) de la casa o del piso. Utiliza tu lista de preguntas preparadas. Tu compañero(a) (el [la] dueño[a]) debe utilizar uno de los anuncios para responder a tus preguntas. Cuando terminas, cambia de papel (role) con tu compañero(a).

Ask for clarifications if you do not understand or do not catch what the other person says to you. Remember the best way of asking for a clarification in Spanish is ¿Cómo? Or you can be more specific by repeating the question with a rising intonation.

ACTIVIDAD 3 Viewing task (Segmento 2 del video)

En el **Segmento 2 del video** vas a conocer a Miguel, que tiene un piso en el centro de Madrid. Miguel es estudiante de periodismo en la Universidad Complutense de Madrid. También trabaja como traductor de comics. Busca un nuevo compañero de piso.

Paso 1: Mira el **Segmento 2 del video.** Miguel enseña su piso a Francisco Gutiérrez, que busca compartir piso. Mira el plano del piso de Miguel y determina el nombre de cada una de las habitaciones.

Paso 2: Compara tu plano del piso de Miguel con el de tu compañero(a) de clase. Haz preguntas como las siguientes:

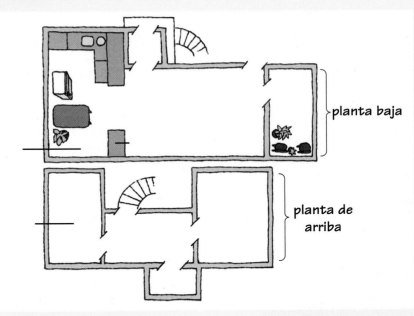

planta baja

planta de arriba

MODELO: —¿Cuál es esta habitación?
—Creo que es el dormitorio de Miguel.
—¿Qué es esto?
—No sé. A lo mejor es la cocina.
—¿Dónde está el dormitorio de Miguel?
—Creo que está aquí.

If you are uncertain of your answer to your partner's question, indicate that you are uncertain:
No estoy seguro(a). *(I'm not sure.)* Use an expression indicating tentative opinion, for example:
A lo mejor / Quizás / Tal vez es... *(Perhaps it is . . .)* Or say:
Creo que es... *(I think it is . . .)*

ACTIVIDAD 4 Post-viewing task (Segmento 2 del video)

Paso 1: Dibuja un plano de tu propia casa, indicando en español los nombres de cada una de las habitaciones.

Paso 2: Describe tu casa a tu compañero(a). Empieza tu descripción indicando dónde se encuentra *(where it is located)*, continúa con una descripción de la misma casa y termina con el jardín, patio, garaje, etc.

MODELO: *La casa de mis padres está en el campo. Aquí está el plano de la casa. Esta es la planta de arriba. Tiene tres dormitorios...*

¡A leer!
Clustering words

Reading one word at a time is inefficient because it slows down your reading speed. Reading one word at a time can also lead to a great deal of frustration, as in many instances you will not know the meaning of every word in a given passage. It is more efficient to read meaningful groups or clusters of words.

Paso 1: Read the following advertisement to get the gist of its content.

70 m²

Un espacio integrado da vida a este apartamento, que tiene tres zonas útiles: la sala de estar, el comedor y una cocina. También hay un dormitorio independiente. El equipo de decoradores de Estudio 48 ha realizado la distribución del espacio y los muebles. La mayor parte del mobiliario incorpora estructuras modulares y piezas extensibles, que pueden adaptarse a distintas situaciones. Predominan los materiales duraderos, de fácil mantenimiento y limpieza. Los diseñadores han utilizado colores vivos sin despojar a la vivienda de su atmósfera funcional, límpia y desahogada.

Paso 2: Based on what you read in the above advertisement, answer the following questions.

1. ¿Qué parte del apartamento no se menciona en el artículo?
   a. la sala de estar   c. el comedor
   b. el garaje   d. la cocina
2. ¿Han decorado el apartamento con muebles de muchos colores vivos?
   a. Sí   b. No

Paso 3: Now reread the passage at your usual reading speed and try to pull out information you may have missed during the first reading. Concentrate on reading clusters of three or four words, as indicated by the red circles that appear in the body of the text. Then complete the following checklist.

Según el artículo, en el apartamento hay...

_____ un dormitorio independiente   _____ muchos espejos
_____ un balcón   _____ una chimenea
_____ una atmósfera funcional y limpia   _____ piezas de colores vivos

Paso 4: As you read the advertisement, circle clusters of words that appear in meaningful groups. Also, use the pictures provided for additional clues about the content of the passage.

Concepto urbano

El salón se convierte en el núcleo central del piso. El interiorista ha desarrollado un único espacio abierto distribuido en diferentes zonas, aprovechando al máximo su amplitud y la luz natural. El sofá tiene forma de ele, con *chaise longue*,

tapizado en algodón crudo. Frente al estar se ha creado un ambiente polivalente que funciona como comedor y zona de trabajo. La mesa y la librería las ha diseñado Santiago Nin en DM pintado en el mismo tono que las paredes. La estantería, además de la luz

que lleva incorporada, se ilumina con apliques instalados en su parte superior. Jarrones de cerámica mongol, de La Compañía Francesa de Oriente y de China. Las sillas, de Philippe Starck, se utilizan en el comedor y en el estar, cerrando la zona de reunión.

Paso 5: Read the paragraph again, being sure to pay attention to the word clusters you identified in **Paso 4.** Then answer the following questions.

1. ¿Cuáles son los muebles más importantes del piso?
2. ¿Cómo es el sofá? Descríbelo.
3. ¿Te gusta el «concepto urbano» de esta sala? ¿Por qué?

¡A escribir!

Writing topic sentences

The first step in writing a well-structured paragraph is to formulate a clear, concise topic sentence. A good topic sentence has the following characteristics:

- It comes at the beginning of a paragraph.
- It states the main idea of the paragraph.
- It focuses on only one topic of interest.
- It makes a factual or personal statement.
- It is neither too general nor too specific.
- It attracts the attention of the reader.

Functions: Writing an introduction; Describing objects

Vocabulary: House: bathroom, bedroom, furniture, kitchen, living room

Grammar: Verbs: **estar, tener;** Progressive tenses; Position of adjectives

Paso 1: Below you will find five possible topic sentences for a paragraph about housing in the Hispanic world. Discuss the sentences with a classmate. In your opinion, which is the best sentence to begin the paragraph? Why? There is no one correct answer, so you and your classmate may have different opinions.

1. Los apartamentos son las viviendas más comunes.
2. Se encuentran viviendas en calles muy angostas.
3. En el mundo hispánico, hay muchos tipos de viviendas.
4. La planta baja es lo que nosotros llamamos el primer piso.
5. Hay muchas ciudades coloniales en ciertos países hispánicos.

Paso 2: Write a topic sentence for a paragraph describing your own house or apartment. Next, write five or six sentences to develop the idea stated in your topic sentence. Then, find a classmate and read each other's paragraph. Discuss how you might improve the topic sentence. You may use the following checklist questions as a guide:

Does the topic sentence . . .

1. come at the beginning of the paragraph? _____ yes _____ no
2. state the main idea of the paragraph? _____ yes _____ no
3. focus on only one topic of interest? _____ yes _____ no
4. make a factual or personal statement? _____ yes _____ no
5. seem neither too general nor too specific? _____ yes _____ no
6. attract the attention of the reader? _____ yes _____ no

¡A conversar!

Paso 1: Imagine that you have the opportunity to build the home of your dreams—**el hogar de tus sueños.** In the chart below, jot down a list of characteristics describing your ideal residence. What type of residence is it (e.g., an apartment, a house, or a condominium)? How many floors and rooms are there? Is there a garden, a terrace, a patio . . .

El hogar de mis sueños	
¿Qué tipo de residencia es?	
¿Cuántos pisos hay?	
¿Cuántos cuartos hay?	
¿Qué otras características tiene el hogar?	

Paso 2: Now pair up with a partner and compare your dream houses. Instead of just showing your descriptions from the chart above, you should ask each other questions to find out specific information about your ideal residences (e.g., **¿Cuántos dormitorios hay en el hogar de tus sueños? ¿Hay una chimenea en la sala?,** etc.). Try to incorporate the following ideas into your conversation:

- the most important aspects of each of your dream houses
- some things that your dream houses have in common
- significant differences between your dream houses

La casa   *The house*

la bañera   *bathtub*
la cocina   *kitchen*
el comedor   *dining room*
el cuarto de baño   *bathroom*
el dormitorio   *bedroom*

la ducha   *shower*
la escalera   *stairs*
el garaje   *garage*
el inodoro   *toilet*
el jardín   *garden*

el lavabo   *bathroom sink*
la pared   *wall*
el piso   *floor*
la puerta   *door*
la sala   *living room*

el sótano   *basement*
la ventana   *window*

Los muebles   *Furniture*

la alfombra   *carpet*
el armario   *wardrobe, armoire, closet*
la cama   *bed*

la cómoda   *dresser*
el escritorio   *desk*
el espejo   *mirror*
el estante   *bookshelf*

la lámpara   *lamp*
la mesa   *table*
la mesita   *coffee (side) table*

la silla   *chair*
el sillón   *easy chair, arm chair*
el sofá   *sofa, couch*

Los electrodomésticos   *Appliances*

la aspiradora   *vacuum cleaner*
el despertador   *alarm clock*
la estufa   *stove*

el horno (de microondas)   *(microwave) oven*
la lavadora   *washing machine*

el lavaplatos   *dishwasher*
la plancha   *iron*
el refrigerador   *refrigerator*

la secadora   *clothes dryer*
la tostadora   *toaster*

Los quehaceres domésticos   *Chores*

barrer el piso   *to sweep the floor*
cortar el césped   *to mow the lawn*
hacer la cama   *to make one's bed*

lavar (los platos, la ropa, las ventanas)   *to wash (dishes, clothes, windows)*
limpiar la casa   *to clean the house*
pasar la aspiradora   *to vacuum*

planchar (la ropa)   *to iron (clothes)*
poner la mesa   *to set the table*
quitar la mesa   *to clear the table*

regar (ie) las plantas   *to water the plants*
sacar la basura   *to take out the garbage*

Los números 100 y más   *Numbers 100 and higher*

100	cien (ciento + número)	500	quinientos(as)	900	novecientos(as)	200.000	doscientos(as) mil
200	doscientos(as)	600	seiscientos(as)	1.000	mil	1.000.000	un millón
300	trescientos(as)	700	setecientos(as)	2.000	dos mil	2.000.000	dos millones
400	cuatrocientos(as)	800	ochocientos(as)	20.000	veinte mil		

Adjetivos

aburrido(a)   *bored*
contento(a)   *happy*
desordenado(a)   *messy*
emocionado(a)   *excited*

enfermo(a)   *sick*
enojado(a)   *angry*
furioso(a)   *furious*

limpio(a)   *clean*
ocupado(a)   *busy*
ordenado(a)   *neat*

preocupado(a)   *worried*
sucio(a)   *dirty*
triste   *sad*

Expresiones idiomáticas

tener celos   *to be jealous*

tener ganas de   *to feel like (doing something)*

tener miedo (de)   *to be afraid (of)*

tener paciencia   *to be patient*

Verbos

almorzar (ue)   *to have lunch*
cerrar (ie)   *to close*
comenzar (ie)   *to begin*
conseguir (i)   *to get, to obtain*
contar (ue)   *to count; to tell*
costar (ue)   *to cost*

empezar (ie)   *to begin*
entender (ie)   *to understand*
decir (i)   *to say; to tell*
dormir (ue)   *to sleep*
jugar (ue)   *to play*
llover (ue)   *to rain*

morir (ue)   *to die*
pedir (i)   *to ask for*
pensar (ie)   *to think*
perder (ie)   *to lose; to miss (a function)*
poder (ue)   *to be able*

preferir (ie)   *to prefer*
querer (ie)   *to want; to love*
seguir (i)   *to continue; to follow*
servir (i)   *to serve*
venir (ie)   *to come*
volver (ue)   *to return*

Communicative goals

In this chapter you will learn how to . . .

- Identify parts of the body
- Describe daily routines and hygienic practices
- Talk about what you have just done
- Talk about illnesses and conditions relating to health
- Give advice on health and suggest treatments for illness
- Make comparisons

Grammar

- Reflexive verbs and pronouns
- **Acabar de** + infinitive
- **Tener** idioms related to health
- The verb **doler**
- **Ser** versus **estar**
- Affirmative informal commands
- Comparatives

Cultural information

- Health and the environment in Bolivia
- Coca, an Andean tradition
- Paraguayan herbal remedies

La Plaza San Francisco, La Paz, Bolivia

EN EL CENTRO DE SALUD RURAL ANDINO In this section you will learn how to talk about parts of the body by learning about Juan Carlos Guarabia and his work at the Andean Rural Health Center in Montero, Bolivia.[1] Does your university sponsor trips to developing countries to assist with public health care?

ReFlexivos

El cuerpo humano

el pelo — la cabeza
las orejas — los ojos
la boca — la nariz
la garganta — los dientes
— la cara
el cuello

el brazo
el codo

los pulmones
el corazón
la espalda

el estómago
la mano

los dedos

las piernas
las rodillas

el oído

los tobillos
los pies
los dedos de pie

la piel

¿NOS ENTENDEMOS?

Some useful expressions that name parts of the body are: **hablar por los codos** *(to talk a lot)*, **tener mucha cara** *(to have a lot of nerve)*, and **tomárselo a pecho** *(to take it to heart)*.

¿NOS ENTENDEMOS?

El cabello is another word for *hair*.

Palabras útiles

las cejas *eyebrows*
el cerebro *brain*
el hígado *liver*
el hueso *bone*
la lengua *tongue*

el páncreas *pancreas*
las pestañas *eyelashes*
los riñones *kidneys*
las uñas *fingernails*

➥ *Palabras útiles* are for recognition only; you will not be tested on these words. They are provided to help you better describe yourself.

¡A practicar!

A. **¡NO ES LÓGICO!** Identifica la palabra que no va con el grupo y explica por qué.

MODELO: los dedos, las manos, *los dientes*
Los dientes son parte de la cabeza; los dedos y las manos son parte del brazo.

---

[1] Montero is a medium-sized city in the tropical, lowland region of Bolivia, an hour north of Santa Cruz (Bolivia's second-largest city). Montero is currently experiencing a large influx of people from surrounding rural areas who hope to improve their lives by migrating to the city.

1. la boca, la cabeza, (el brazo)
2. el corazón, (el pelo), el estómago
3. los pulmones, la nariz, el oído
4. los dedos, las rodillas, los tobillos
5. la garganta, la cara, el estómago
6. las piernas, los pies, (los codos), los dedos de pie
7. el brazo, el codo, los dientes, las manos
8. los ojos, la boca, (la espalda), las orejas, los dientes

B. **ASOCIACIONES** ¿Qué parte del cuerpo humano asocias con las siguientes actividades?

MODELO: respirar
la nariz, la boca, los pulmones

1. hablar
2. comer
3. pensar

4. escribir
5. beber
6. caminar

7. escuchar
8. leer

C. **ANATOMÍA 101** Tienes que enseñar una clase de anatomía para Juan Carlos pero tu dibujo no tiene los nombres de las partes del cuerpo. Escribe los nombres en los espacios.

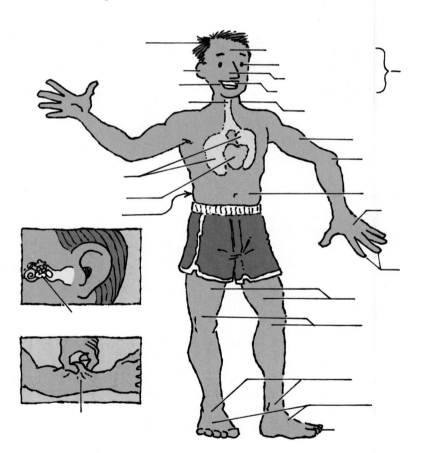

En voz alta

D. RETRATOS (Portraits) DE LA CLASE Descríbele a un(a) compañero(a) de clase los atributos físicos de otra persona de la clase mientras tu compañero(a) dibuja a esa persona. Después de dibujar, tu compañero(a) tiene que adivinar (guess) la identidad de la persona.

MODELO: E1: *Tiene piernas cortas. Su pelo es negro y largo. Tiene ojos azules. Tiene una cara bonita y un poco redonda* (round). *Es delgada y baja.*
E2: *¿Es Cathy?*
E1: *¡Sí!*

EN CONTEXTO

La señora Mendoza y su hija, Carolina, están en una clínica rellenando *(filling out)* una historial clínica *(medical history)* y hablando con el doctor Chávez. Carolina piensa que está muy enferma.

DR. CHÁVEZ:	¿Cómo se siente su hija hoy, señora Mendoza?
SRA. MENDOZA:	Dice que está muy mal y que no puede asistir a la escuela. Lleva tres días en cama mirando la tele.
DR. CHÁVEZ:	Hmmm... Carolina, ¿te duele el estómago?
CAROLINA:	¡Ayyy! Sí, me duele mucho el estómago.
DR. CHÁVEZ:	¿Tienes fiebre?
SRA. MENDOZA:	Dice que sí, pero cuando le tomo la temperatura tiene 37 grados, o sea, normal.
DR. CHÁVEZ:	Vamos a ver... ¿Tienes dolor de cabeza?
CAROLINA:	¡Sí! Y tengo tos *(cough)*, y estoy mareada *(dizzy)* y... y...
DR. CHÁVEZ:	Parece que estás muy grave, Carolina. Tenemos que operarte inmediatamente. Creo que tienes la *escuelacitis*. Es una condición del cerebro.
CAROLINA:	¿Una operación? ¿El cerebro? Pues... la verdad es que ahora me encuentro *(I'm feeling)* un poco mejor.

School ideas

E. ¿COMPRENDISTE? Contesta las siguientes preguntas a base del diálogo.

1. ¿Está realmente enferma Carolina?
2. ¿Tiene síntomas verdaderos *(real symptoms)*?
3. ¿Por qué recomienda una operación el doctor Chávez?
4. ¿Por qué se siente mejor Carolina al final?

> **¿NOS ENTENDEMOS?**
>
> Spanish speakers use the verb **llevar** *(to carry)* to indicate how long someone has been experiencing a condition, for example: **Carolina lleva tres días en cama. Llevar** is also used to indicate how long someone has been living in a certain place: **Nosotros llevamos dos años en Bolivia.** *(We've been living in Bolivia for two years.)* The expression **o sea** is frequently used in daily speech to provide further clarification, such as saying *I mean* or *in other words.*

ENCUENTRO *cultural*

La Paz, Bolivia

Bolivia: El ambiente y la salud

Éstas son unas palabras nuevas para la lectura:

el mareo *dizziness*
el (la) viajero(a) *traveler*
la subida *climb*
el esfuerzo físico *physical exertion*
la debilidad *weakness*   **el jadeo** *panting*   **subir** *to climb, to go up*

Para pensar: ¿A ti te gustan las montañas? ¿Conoces alguna ciudad o algún lugar en las montañas? ¿Cómo te sientes cuando vas allí?

La Paz, la capital de Bolivia, es la capital más alta del mundo a cuatro kilómetros *(two miles)* sobre el nivel del mar. Debido a la altitud de unos 3.000 metros *(10,000 feet)* en la región del altiplano, muchas personas sufren de **mareos,** no sólo **los viajeros** sino también los habitantes de Bolivia que no viven en el altiplano. La severidad del mareo está relacionada con la altitud, la rapidez de **la subida, el esfuerzo físico** y la aclimatación. Una persona puede tener varios síntomas de mareos al mismo tiempo: dolor de cabeza, insomnio, náuseas, **debilidad** y **el jadeo.** Estos síntomas pueden empezar a las 48 horas después de subir, pero a veces empiezan más tarde. Los síntomas desaparecen dentro de uno a siete días después de acostumbrarse a la altura, pero el descenso es el único tratamiento.

La mejor manera de aclimatarse es empezar a **subir** a un nivel intermedio en intervalos de dos a cuatro días. Es importante descansar antes de seguir subiendo. El jadeo, la falta de aire y el pulso acelerado son indicaciones serias de que hay que parar y descansar. Es importante beber mucho líquido y comer carbohidratos. Para el dolor de cabeza y la fiebre se puede tomar aspirina. Una persona debe consultar con un médico antes de tomar medicamentos especiales.

F. **PREGUNTAS** Contesta las siguientes preguntas a base de la lectura.

1. ¿Cuál es la característica geográfica que hace especial la capital de Bolivia? ¿Cómo afecta la salud?
2. ¿Cuáles son algunos síntomas al subir a mucha altitud?

GRAMÁTICA I: *Reflexive pronouns and present tense of reflexive verbs*

A reflexive construction consists of a verb and a reflexive pronoun. In English, reflexive pronouns end in *-self* or *-selves;* for example: *myself, yourself, ourselves.* In Spanish, reflexive pronouns are used with certain verbs (called reflexive verbs) that reflect the action back to the subject of a sentence, meaning that the subject of the verb also receives the action of the verb. In the following example, notice how Juan Carlos is both the subject and recipient (object) of the action of getting himself up.

Subject   Pronoun   Verb
  ↓   ↓   ↓

Juan Carlos   **se**   levanta   a las 8:00.
Juan Carlos gets (himself) up at 8:00.

To form reflexive constructions

Use a reflexive pronoun (e.g., **me**) with its corresponding verb form (e.g., **levanto**), according to the subject of the sentence (e.g., **yo**).	Yo **me levanto** a las 10:00. *I get up at 10:00.*

levantarse (*to get up*)

yo	**me** levanto	*I get up*
tú	**te** levantas	*you* (informal) *get up*
Ud., él, ella	**se** levanta	*you* (formal) *get up; he/she gets up*
nosotros(as)	**nos** levantamos	*we get up*
vosotros(as)	**os** levantáis	*you* (informal) *get up*
Uds., ellos(as)	**se** levantan	*you* (formal and informal) *get up; they get up*

Place reflexive pronouns as follows:

• **Place the pronoun in front of the conjugated verb.**	Juan Carlos **se levanta** a las 8:00. *Juan Carlos **gets up** at 8:00.*
• **When an infinitive or a present participle is used reflexively, either place the pronoun before the conjugated verb or attach it to the infinitive or to the present participle.**	Sara **se va a levantar** pronto. *or* Sara **va a levantarse** pronto. *Sara **is going to get up** soon.* Sara **se está levantando** ahora. *or* Sara **está levantándose** ahora.[1] *Sara **is getting up** now.*

When the action is performed on a person other than the subject of the verb, a reflexive pronoun is not used. Compare these two examples.	**Me despierto** a las 8:00. *I wake up at 8:00.* **Despierto a mi mamá** a las 8:00. *I wake up my mom at 8:00.*

When reflexive verbs are used with parts of the body or with articles of clothing, use the definite article (el, la, los, las), as shown in the following examples.	Juan Carlos se cepilla **los** dientes. *Juan Carlos brushes **his** teeth.* Sara está poniéndose **el** pijama. *Sara is putting on **her** pajamas.* Tomás va a quitarse **los** jeans. *Tomás is going to take off **his** jeans.*

---

[1] When a reflexive pronoun is attached to a present participle (e.g., **levantándose**), an accent mark is added to maintain the correct stress.

Verbos reflexivos de las actividades diarias y la higiene personal

acostarse (ue) *to go to bed*	**maquillarse** *to put on makeup*
afeitarse *to shave*	**peinarse** *to comb one's hair*
bañarse *to take a bath*	**pintarse** *to put on makeup*
cepillarse los dientes *to brush*	**ponerse (la ropa)** *to put on (one's*
one's teeth	*clothes)*
cuidar(se) *to take care (of oneself)*	**quitarse (la ropa)** *to take off (one's*
despertarse (ie) *to wake up*	*clothes)*
dormirse (ue) *to fall asleep*	**secarse (el cuerpo)** *to dry off (one's*
ducharse *to take a shower*	*body)*
lavarse *to wash up*	**vestirse (i)** *to get dressed*
levantarse *to get up*	

¡A practicar!

G. **LOS DOMINGOS POR LA MAÑANA** Completa las siguientes oraciones usando las formas apropiadas de los verbos entre paréntesis y tu información personal.

MODELO: **(afeitarse)** Todos los días Juan Carlos *se afeita* y yo nunca *me afeito.*

1. **(levantarse)** Los domingos Juan Carlos y Sara _____ a las 8:00, y Tomás, su hijo, _____ a las 9:00. Yo _____ .
2. **(cepillarse)** Después, el esposo y la esposa siempre _____ los dientes, pero a veces Tomás no _____ los dientes. Y yo _____ .
3. **(ducharse)** Juan Carlos y Tomás se bañan, pero Sara prefiere _____ . Yo prefiero _____ .
4. **(vestirse)** Juan Carlos y Sara _____ elegantemente y Tomás _____ de jeans. Yo _____ . A veces, mis amigos y yo _____ .
5. **(peinarse)** Después, Juan Carlos y Sara _____ bien, pero Tomás no _____ porque es un poco perezoso. Y yo _____ .

H. **¡QUÉ MUJER MÁS OCUPADA!** Para comprender las actividades diarias que tiene Sara durante la semana, completa la siguiente descripción conjugando los verbos de la lista. Puedes usar los verbos más de una vez.

pintarse	entrar	secarse	despertarse
levantarse	ir	tener	vestirse
ponerse	peinarse	ducharse	bañarse

¡Hola! Yo soy Sara, y ¡soy una mujer muy ocupada! Los días de trabajo, _____ a las 7:00. Mi esposo y yo _____ a las 7:15. Primero, yo _____ al baño donde _____ por diez minutos. Cuando _____ más tiempo, _____ . Después, _____ bien todo el cuerpo y _____ el pelo. Normalmente, mi esposo, Juan Carlos, _____ en el baño. Mientras él _____ , yo _____ elegantemente, _____ la cara y _____ un poco de perfume. Mi hijo Tomás es bastante grande —él _____ solo.

lavar	almorzar	salir	trabajar
tomar	desayunar	hablar	volver
caminar	cepillarse	peinar	
levantar	bañar	lavarse	

Antes de desayunar, yo siempre _____ a mi hija de tres años, Sarita.
A Sarita, yo la _____ , le _____ la cara y la _____ .
Ella acaba de aprender a _____ los dientes sola. Después, Sarita, Juan
Carlos, Tomás y yo _____ y _____ un poco. Luego yo
_____ los dientes y _____ de mi casa. Yo _____ al
hospital donde _____ como enfermera hasta *(until)* la 1:00 de la tarde.
Luego _____ a casa. Yo _____ las manos y _____
con mi familia. Después de comer, Tomás y Juan Carlos _____ los
platos. Normalmente, mis hijos _____ una siesta.

I. **LAS ACTIVIDADES DIARIAS DE TOMÁS** Basado en los dibujos, explícale a
un(a) compañero(a) de clase lo que está haciendo Tomás en este momento. Luego
explica lo que va a hacer mañana.

MODELOS: *Tomás está despertándose a las 6:00.*
   o: *Tomás se está despertando a las 6:00.*

   Tomás se va a despertar mañana a las 6:00.
   o: *Tomás va a despertarse mañana a las 6:00.*

1.

2.

3.

4.

5.

En voz alta

J. **PREFERENCIAS PERSONALES** Hablando con un(a) compañero(a) de clase, compara lo que hacen estas personas los días de la semana con lo que hacen los fines de semana.

MODELO: levantarse: yo
Los días de la semana me levanto a las 6:00, pero los fines de semana, me levanto a las 9:00.

1. peinarse: mi mejor amigo(a) y yo
2. vestirse: tú
3. maquillarse: mis hermanas
4. acostarse: mi hermanito de tres años
5. dormirse: yo

K. **TUS ACTIVIDADES DIARIAS** Con un(a) compañero(a) de clase, háganse y contesten las siguientes preguntas.

1. ¿A qué hora te levantas normalmente? ¿Te levantas inmediatamente después de despertarte? ¿Te bañas o te duchas? ¿Prefieres bañarte por la mañana o por la noche? ¿Desayunas con tu compañero(a) de cuarto/casa? O si vives con tu familia, ¿desayunas con tu familia? ¿Siempre te cepillas los dientes después del desayuno?
2. ¿Cómo te vistes los días de semana? ¿Qué tipo de ropa te pones los fines de semana? Si eres mujer, ¿te maquillas todos los días? Si eres hombre, ¿te afeitas los fines de semana?
3. En general, ¿te gusta cuidarte? ¿Te peinas durante el día, o solamente antes de salir? ¿Siempre te lavas las manos antes de comer? ¿A qué hora almuerzas normalmente? ¿Duermes la siesta a veces después del almuerzo?
4. De noche, ¿comes algo para la cena? ¿Ayudas a lavar los platos después? ¿A qué hora te gusta acostarte? ¿Siempre te quitas la ropa antes de acostarte? Normalmente, ¿te duermes fácilmente? En general, ¿miras la tele o lees algún libro antes de dormir?

L. **MIS ACTIVIDADES DIARIAS** Descríbele tu rutina diaria a un(a) compañero(a) de clase. Tu compañero(a) debe dibujar tus actividades y usar el dibujo para explicarlas a la clase.

ASÍ SE DICE: *How to talk about things you have just finished doing*

Acabar de + infinitive is a very convenient way of talking about things that have just taken place without having to use the past tense. Literally, **acabar de** + infinitive means *to have just finished doing something.* It is used with an infinitive to show that something has recently been done.

Juan Carlos **acaba de ver** a tres pacientes.

*Juan Carlos **has just seen** three patients.*

When used with a reflexive verb in the infinitive, you have the option of putting the pronoun before **acabar de** or tagging it on the end of the infinitive.

Sara **acaba de bañarse**.
Sara **se acaba de bañar.**   }   *Sara **has just bathed.***

¡A practicar!

M. MAMÁ, ¡ACABO DE HACERLO! Tu mamá sugiere varias actividades para algunas personas. Dile que ya están hechas *(are done)*, usando **acabar de.**

MODELO: ¿Por qué no te bañas?
          Yo ~~acabo~~ acabo de bañarme.

[handwritten: acabamos se / se acaban la fiesta]

1. ¿Por qué tú y tu hermana menor no se cepillan los dientes?
2. ¿Por qué no se visten para la fiesta tus amigos?
3. ¿Por qué no se afeita tu padre?
4. ¿Por qué no tomas una siesta?
5. ¿Por qué no se peina tu mejor amiga?

N. ¡ADIVINA LO QUE ACABA DE HACER ESA GENTE! Las siguientes personas acaban de hacer algo. Tú y un(a) compañero(a) de clase tienen que adivinar lo que acaban de hacer basándose en la información que tienen.

MODELO: Sara sale del baño. Tiene el pelo mojado.
          Sara acaba de bañarse.

1. Tomás se levanta de la cama.
2. Sarita y Tomás se levantan de la mesa. Son las 8:00 de la mañana.
3. Juan Carlos sale de su cuarto. Tiene puesta ropa elegante para una fiesta.
4. El doctor Chávez entra por la puerta de la clínica. Son las 9:00 de la mañana.
5. La señora Martínez sale del consultorio del doctor Chávez.
6. Juan Carlos y Sara están en la cama y apagan la luz.

En voz alta

O. ¿QUIÉN ACABA DE... ? Tienes dos minutos para buscar a alguien de tu clase que acabe de hacer las siguientes cosas. Después de encontrar a alguien para cada categoría, pídele que firme *(sign)* tu lista. Al final del juego, cuéntales a tus compañeros(as) lo que acabas de aprender.

MODELO: acabar de pasar dos horas estudiando
          Tú: *Susie, ¿acabas de pasar dos horas estudiando?*
          Susie: *Sí, acabo de pasar dos horas estudiando.* (Susie signs
                  your paper.)
    o: Susie: *No, no acabo de pasar dos horas estudiando.* (Susie
                  doesn't sign your paper and you look for someone else.)
          Al final: *Susie acaba de estudiar dos horas. John y Heather aca-
                  ban de levantarse tarde antes de venir a clase...*

CATEGORÍAS

1. comer algo
2. cepillarse los dientes
3. llegar a clase de prisa

4. ver al doctor
5. tomar aspirina
6. tomar una ducha rápida

VOCABULARIO: *La salud*

EN LA CLÍNICA DEL CENTRO DE SALUD RURAL ANDINO In this section you will learn how to talk about common illnesses and discuss treatments and remedies. In the drawing on the following page, Dr. Carlos Dardo Chávez, the director of the clinic, is busy treating patients.

la pastilla
la paciente
el antibiótico
la sala de espera
la farmacia
la receta
el jarabe
la aspirina
la medicina
la sala de emergencia
el médico
la ambulancia
la enfermera

Los problemas médicos

la alergia *allergy*
el catarro *cold*
congestionado(a) *congested*
el dolor (de oídos, de cabeza) *pain, ache (earache, headache)*

la enfermedad *illness*
mareado(a) *dizzy*
el resfriado *cold*
el síntoma *symptom*

Verbos relacionados con la salud

doler(le) (ue) (a alguien) *to be painful (to someone)*
enfermarse *to get sick*
estar enfermo(a) *to be sick*
estar sano(a) *to be healthy*
estornudar *to sneeze*
examinar *to examine*
guardar cama *to stay in bed*
resfriarse *to catch a cold*
sentirse (bien/mal) *to feel (good/bad)*

tener dolor de cabeza *to have a headache*
tener escalofríos *to have chills*
tener fiebre *to have a fever*
tener gripe *to have a cold*
tener náuseas *to be nauseous*
tener tos *to have a cough*
tomarle la temperatura (a alguien) *to take (someone's) temperature*
toser *to cough*

¡A practicar!

P. ¿QUÉ RECOMIENDAS? El doctor Chávez te explica algunos casos para ver lo que recomiendas para tratar *(to treat)* cada enfermedad de la lista. Empareja cada enfermedad con el tratamiento *(treatment)* apropiado.

MODELO: *Una persona que tiene catarro debe tomar jarabe.*

Una persona que tiene...	debe...
1. fiebre	tomar un jarabe
2. gripe	descansar un poco
3. dolor de cabeza	tomar Pepto Bismol
4. tos	tomar antibióticos
5. un problema grave	tomar aspirina
6. dolor de estómago	hablar con un(a) médico
7. náuseas	ir a una clínica
8. escalofríos	guardar cama

handwritten notes: duele [thing] · me te le nos les · duelen · more then on thng hurts

En voz alta

Q. **¿QUÉ HACES PARA CUIDARTE?** Con un(a) compañero(a) de clase, forma preguntas sobre las siguientes enfermedades para averiguar *(to find out)* lo que hacen las personas en cada caso.

MODELO: tú / tener tos
E1: *¿Qué haces cuando tienes tos?*
E2: *Yo tomo un jarabe y descanso más.*

1. tu mejor amigo(a) / estar congestionado(a)

2. tú / estar mareado(a)

3. tú y tu compañero(a) de cuarto / enfermarse

4. tus hermanos(as) / resfriarse

5. tu profesor(a) / enfermarse gravemente

6. tú / estornudar

R. **CONVERSACIÓN SOBRE LA SALUD** Con un(a) compañero(a) de clase, contesten las siguientes preguntas sobre la salud.

1. ¿Qué haces cuando tienes catarro? ¿Tomas algún medicamento? ¿Tienes escalofríos cuando tienes un catarro?

2. ¿Tienes dolor de cabeza con mucha o poca frecuencia? ¿Qué haces cuando tienes dolor de cabeza? ¿Tomas aspirina?

3. ¿Qué haces cuando tienes náuseas? ¿Tomas Pepto Bismol? ¿Te sientes mareado(a)? Si tienes náuseas, ¿guardas cama?

4. ¿Estás resfriado(a) con más frecuencia en el verano o en el invierno? ¿Te da fiebre a veces? ¿Qué otros síntomas tienes cuando estás resfriado(a)? ¿Estornudas a veces? ¿Tienes tos?

5. ¿Cómo te sientes hoy? ¿Te sientes bien, mal o más o menos? ¿Estás sano(a), o tienes una enfermedad? ¿Estás congestionado(a)? ¿Estás tomando algún medicamento?

ASÍ SE DICE: *How to talk about painful conditions*

The verb **doler** *(to be painful, to hurt)* is used like the verb **gustar,** with indirect object pronouns (**me, te, le, nos, os,** and **les**) and only the third-person singular and plural forms of the verb (**duele** and **duelen**). Rather than saying *My leg hurts*, Spanish speakers say *My leg is painful to me* (**Me duele la pierna**). As with reflexive verbs, when one is using **doler** to talk about a body part, the definite articles (**el, la, los, las**) are used.

Me duele el estómago.
A Lorena **le duelen** los pies.
A nosotros **nos duelen** las manos.

*My stomach **hurts**.*
*Lorena's feet **hurt**.*
*Our hands **hurt**.*

¡A practicar!

S. **¿QUÉ LE DUELE?** Completa las siguientes oraciones con la forma correcta del verbo **doler** y el pronombre de objeto indirecto apropiado.

MODELO: A Esteban *le duele la mano.*

1. A mí _____.

2. A Carolina y Susi _____.

3. A ellos _____.

4. A ti _____.

5. A nosotros _____.

En voz alta

T. **EN LA SALA DE EMERGENCIAS** Habla con otro(a) estudiante: una persona es el (la) médico y la otra persona es su paciente. El (La) paciente tuvo *(had)* un accidente y le duelen muchas partes de su cuerpo. El (La) médico tiene que preguntar qué le duele y recomendar un tratamiento. Recuerda que entre doctor y paciente, normalmente se usa la forma de **usted.** Después, comparte el diálogo con la clase.

MODELO: Médico: *¿Qué le duele?*
Paciente: *Me duele el brazo, me duelen las piernas y me duele el cuello.*
Médico: *Usted tiene que guardar cama por una semana y tomar pastillas para el dolor.*

ENCUENTRO *cultural*

Coca: Una tradición de la cultura andina

Éstas son unas palabras nuevas para la lectura:

cultivar *to plant*
la hoja *leaf*
masticar *to chew*
el sabor *flavor*
el cansancio *tiredness*

La coca es una planta que crece en los países andinos. Los nativos del imperio Tahuantinsuyo,[1] ubicado en lo que hoy llamamos Bolivia, Perú, Ecuador y el norte de la Argentina, **cultivaban** la planta. En los Andes, ninguna otra planta es más apreciada por los indios que la coca. **Las hojas** se usan para medicina folklórica y en ritos religiosos indígenas. No las **mastican** por **el sabor,** sino por su efecto fisiológico y psicológico. Los andinos usan las hojas de la coca para aliviar el dolor de cabeza, el mareo y el soroche.[2] Masticar las hojas también sirve para mitigar condiciones como **el cansancio,** el hambre y la sed. Por virtud de su profundo significado místico y mitológico en la religión, la cultura, la salud y el trabajo, la hoja de la coca es un símbolo poderoso en la identidad del indígena andino.

Para pensar: Muchas personas en los Estados Unidos toman bebidas y pastillas con cafeína para mantenerse alertas. ¿Cómo es similar y/o diferente el uso de la hoja de coca en la cultura andina?

U. **PREGUNTAS** Completa las siguientes oraciones a base de la lectura.

1. En las culturas andinas, el uso más común de las hojas de la coca es...
a. tomar. **b.** masticar. **c.** beber.
2. Los andinos usan las hojas de la coca para...
a. aliviar el dolor de cabeza.
b. ritos religiosos.
c. el cansancio.

GRAMÁTICA II: *Ser versus estar*

As you have learned, the verbs **ser** and **estar** both mean *to be,* but they are used to express different kinds of information. In this section you will learn how to differentiate between uses of **ser** and **estar.**

---

[1] From the Inca empire that was divided into four regions (Antisuyo, Collasuyo, Contisuyo, and Chinchasuyo)
[2] Quechua word that means *altitude sickness*

The verb **ser** often implies a fundamental quality that describes the essence of a person, thing, place, or idea. Use **ser** to express the following information:

• **Identification**	Soy Dr. Carlos Dardo Chávez.
• **Origin**	Soy de Bolivia.
• **Nationality**	Soy boliviano.
• **Profession**	Soy médico.
• **Marital status**	Soy soltero.
• **Physical features**	Soy alto.
• **Personality traits**	Soy inteligente.
• **Ownership**	El perro **es** de Tomás.
• **Time of day**	**Son** las 2:00 de la tarde.
• **Dates**	**Es** sábado. **Es** el 24 de junio.
• **Intentions**	**Es** para ti, Sara. **Es** para tu cumpleaños.
• **Impersonal statements**	**Es** importante comer frutas y vegetales.
• **Location of events**	La fiesta de los voluntarios **es** en mi casa.

The verb **estar** often indicates a state or condition of a person, thing, place, or action, which may be the result of a change or a deviation from the norm. Use **estar** to express the following information:

• **Location of people**	**Estoy** en casa.
• **Location of things**	Mi casa **está** en Monteros.
• **Location of places**	Monteros **está** en Bolivia.
• **Marital status**	No **estoy** casada.[1]
• **Physical condition**	**Estoy** cansada.
• **Emotional condition**	**Estoy** preocupada.
• **Action in progress**	**Estoy** trabajando.

¡A practicar!

V.   ¿SER O ESTAR? Indica si debes usar **ser** o **estar** para expresar en español la idea de *to be* en las siguientes frases.

MODELO: I'm tall.
          ser

1. He is frustrated.
2. She is resting.
3. The Quechua and the Aymara are the two largest indigenous groups of Bolivia.
4. Hugo Banzer Suárez is the president of Bolivia.
5. The city of La Paz is the capital of Bolivia.
6. La Paz is in the Andes.
7. It is necessary to rest at high altitudes.
8. Lake Titicaca is the highest navigable lake in the world.
9. Bolivians are very friendly.
10. The classical guitar concert is in Santa Cruz.
11. The book about Simón Bolívar is for you!
12. Where are my glasses?

W.   LA FIESTA DE LOS VOLUNTARIOS Completa la siguiente descripción y conversación con las formas apropiadas de **ser** y **estar.**

---

[1] The verb **estar** is not usually followed by a noun. Because the words **soltero(a)** and **viudo(a)** are nouns the verb **ser** is used with them to describe marital status; for example: **Soy soltera.** Here, **estar** is used because **casado(a)** is an adjective.

Hoy ___es___ sábado, el 24 de junio. ___son___ las 2:00 de la tarde.
Hace calor y ___esta___ lloviendo un poco. La temperatura ___esta___
a 26 grados centígrados. Juan Carlos, su familia y unos amigos del Centro de
Salud Rural Andino ___estan___ comiendo un pastel con Roberto, un volun-
tario de los Estados Unidos. La fiesta ___es___ en su apartamento.
Roberto ___esta___ hablando con su amiga Rachel.

—Mmm. ¡Qué pastel más rico, Rachel!
—¿Te gusta? ___es___ tu pastel favorito.
—Pero ___esta___ tan grande, Rachel.
—Sí, cómo no. Muchas personas ___esta___ aquí hoy.
—Perdón, ¿dónde ___esta___ el Dr. Chávez?
—Él ___esta___ durmiendo ahora, Roberto.
—¿___esta___ enfermo?
—No, él ___esta___ un poco cansado.
—Él ___esta___ trabajando mucho en estos días.
—Sí. Él ___es___ muy dedicado.

X. **¿QUIERES SER VOLUNTARIO?** Escribe una carta de cuatro párrafos a Juan
Carlos del Centro de Salud Rural Andino, explicando que quieres trabajar como
voluntario el verano que viene. Las siguientes frases contienen ideas útiles.

Querido Juan Carlos,

Párrafo 1: Tus datos personales (de dónde eres, tu nacionalidad, tu estado
civil, tu edad, tu fecha de nacimiento, tu personalidad)

Párrafo 2: Tus estudios (nombre de tu escuela, tus cursos, tus profesores), tu
trabajo (dónde trabajas, qué haces) y tu estado emocional

Párrafo 3: Tu familia (sus nombres, sus edades, el estado civil de cada persona, las características físicas y emocionales de cada persona)

Párrafo 4: Tus amigos, tus pasatiempos (deportes y otras actividades) y tus
otros gustos (tus posesiones materiales, tu comida favorita)

En voz alta

Y. **DATOS PERSONALES** Con un(a) compañero(a) de clase, háganse preguntas
con los verbos **ser** y **estar** sobre los siguientes temas.

1. **La personalidad:** Ask about his/her personality in general and his/her emotional and physical state today.
2. **El pueblo:** Ask about his/her hometown, where it is, what it looks like, and
whether it's big or small.
3. **La familia:** Ask about his/her family (size, ages, physical features, personalities).
4. **La fiesta ideal:** Ask about the date, the location, and the time. For whom is
the party?

Z. **ENCUENTRA A ALGUIEN QUE...** Tienes dos minutos para buscar a una persona en tu clase para las siguientes categorías. Después de encontrar a alguien
para cada categoría, pídele que firme *(sign)* tu lista. Al final del juego, cuenta a
tus compañeros(as) lo que acabas de aprender. Ten cuidado con el uso de **ser** y
estar en esta actividad.

MODELO: estar con dolor de estómago hoy
Tú: *Brian, ¿estás con dolor de estómago hoy?*
Brian: *Sí, estoy con dolor de estómago.* (Brian signs your paper.)

o: Brian: *No, no estoy con dolor de estómago.* (Look for someone else for this category.)

Al final: *Brian está con dolor de estómago hoy. Cecilia está con dolor de cabeza. Bob es estudiante de medicina.*

1. estar enfermo(a)
2. ser una persona muy sana
3. estar con dolor de cabeza

4. ser estudiante de medicina
5. estar congestionado(a)
6. ser fumador(a) *(smoker)*

GRAMÁTICA III: *Affirmative informal or tú commands*

In this section you will learn how to form affirmative informal or **tú** commands. Spanish speakers use affirmative informal commands mainly to tell children, close friends, relatives, and pets to do something. You have already seen these commands in the direction lines of each exercise telling you **(tú)** what to do.[1]

For most Spanish verbs, use the **él/ella** verb forms of the present indicative.			
Infinitive	él/ella	**tú command**	
hablar	habla	**habla**	*speak*
comer	come	**come**	*eat*
escribir	escribe	**escribe**	*write*
cerrar	cierra	**cierra**	*close*
dormir	duerme	**duerme**	*sleep*

Eight verbs have irregular affirmative **tú** commands.			
decir:	**di**	salir:	**sal**
hacer:	**haz**	ser:	**sé**
ir:	**ve**	tener:	**ten**
poner:	**pon**	venir:	**ven**

—**Ven** conmigo al mercado.
Come with me to the market.

—Sí, pero **ten** paciencia, Elena.
Yes, but be patient, Elena.

Attach pronouns to affirmative **tú** commands. If the command form has two or more syllables, it carries an accent mark over the stressed vowel to retain the stress of the verb.

—¡**Levántate**, Keri.
Get up, Keri!

—¡Ay! Tengo prisa. **Dúcharte** más tarde¿vale?
Oh! I'm in a hurry. Shower later, okay?.

¡A practicar!

AA. **CONFLICTOS ENTRE AMIGAS** En Asunción, Paraguay, hay otra clínica hermana *(sister clinic)* del Centro de Salud Rural Andino en Bolivia. Dos chicas,

---

[1] To form the **vosotros** command, replace the final **-r** in the infinitive with **-d: hablar → hablad, comer → comed, escribir → escribid.** You will learn how to form negative informal commands in **Capítulo 11** when you learn the subjunctive mood.

Elena y Keri, son voluntarias en esta clínica paraguaya. Completa la siguiente conversación entre ellas, usando los mandatos informales de la lista. Puedes usar los verbos más de una vez.

ten	ponte	ven	come
espera	dime	deja	

Elena: Ay, Keri, _come_ estos chocolates luego. Vamos a la clínica. Tengo mucho trabajo allá.

Keri: _espera_ diez minutos más, Elena. Quiero comer uno más antes de irnos.

Elena: Pues, ya comiste mucho. _deja_ de comer tanto, o vas a estar muy gorda. Vamos ya.

Keri: ¿No me oyes, Elena? _ten_ paciencia. ¿No puedes esperar dos minutos?

Elena: _ven_ en dos minutos entonces. Te espero, te espero. Voy a fumar un cigarrillo en la sala.

Keri: Elena, _espera_ afuera. Sabes que el humo (smoke) me molesta bastante.

Elena: Bueno, ¿qué puedo hacer? _dime_, ¿qué puedo hacer?

Keri: _deja_ de fumar, Elena. Tú me criticas por comer mucho chocolate, pero tú también te estás dañando la salud con los cigarrillos. Bueno, si no quieres enfermarte, _____ tu chaqueta —¡hace mucho frío!— y vamos a la clínica.

BB. **CONSEJOS PARA ELENA** Antes de salir para Paraguay, una amiga paraguaya de Elena le da algunos consejos sobre su viaje. ¿Qué le dice su amiga? Contesta usando mandatos informales afirmativos.

MODELO: hablar / solamente en español
Habla solamente en español.

1. tener / cuidado con comidas extrañas _ten_
2. llevar / una botella de Pepto Bismol _lleva_
3. dormir / mucho _dorma_
4. tomar / solamente agua mineral _toma comer_
5. comer / en restaurantes vegetarianos _comer_
6. tomar / café solamente por la mañana _toma_
7. salir / para hacer ejercicio con mucha frecuencia _sal_
8. ir / al gimnasio para levantar pesas dos veces a la semana _va_
9. dormir / la siesta en el parque cuando hace sol _dorme_
10. tratar / de no fumar mucho _trata_

En voz alta

CC. **¿QUÉ RECOMIENDAS?** Ahora un estudiante universitario de Paraguay te escribe una carta. Pide consejos para tener una experiencia positiva en tu universidad en los Estados Unidos. Dale consejos para cuidar la salud durante su viaje y para tener una experiencia buena en tu universidad. Trabajando con un(a) compañero(a) de clase, haz una lista de mandatos afirmativos y luego practícalos con el (la) otro(a) estudiante.

MODELO: *Come en la cafetería Watkins. ¡La comida en la otra cafetería es horrible y te puedes enfermar!*

ENCUENTRO *cultural*

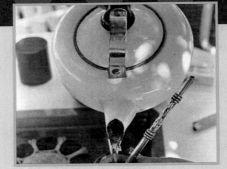

Hierbas de Paraguay

Éstas son unas palabras nuevas para la lectura:

la hierba   *herb*
encontrar   *to find*
el hierro   *iron*
el remedio casero   *home remedy*

Para pensar: ¿Cuáles son algunas hierbas y otros remedios no farmacéuticos que se venden en los Estados Unidos? ¿Dónde se venden esas cosas? ¿Por qué piensas que muchas personas tienen interés en estos productos? ¿Qué piensas tú del uso de las hierbas y otros productos similares?

En el Paraguay, como en otros países de América del Sur, hay una gran variedad de **hierbas** y otras plantas que tienen usos medicinales y nutritivos. Por ejemplo, muchas hierbas se usan para el té y otras se usan como ingredientes para cocinar. Así como los exploradores **encontraron** la papa, hoy en día estamos descubriendo y usando muchas hierbas que los nativos han usado por siglos *(have used for centuries)*.

Dos hierbas de uso común son la stevia y el mate (o yerba mate). La planta stevia es originaria de Paraguay y las hojas tienen un sabor refrescante; son mucho más dulces que el azúcar. Varios estudios dicen que la hoja de stevia contiene proteína, fibra, carbohidratos y **hierro.** En la cultura guaraní, el té de stevia es un remedio natural para el resfriado y la gripe, y se usa para aliviar la fiebre, la tos, el dolor de garganta y las alergias. También usan stevia para lavarse la boca, para cepillarse los dientes y para cuidar la piel.

El mate es una hierba para **remedios caseros** de la cultara guaraní. El mate se cultiva en Paraguay, y se usa para preparar té en Paraguay, Uruguay, Argentina y en otros países. Se mezcla el mate con agua caliente y se bebe para las alergias, la bronquitis, el asma, el dolor de cabeza, la indigestión y la pérdida de peso.

DD. **PREGUNTAS** Contesta las siguientes preguntas a base de la lectura.

1. ¿Puedes nombrar unas plantas que tienen usos medicinales en Paraguay?
2. ¿Cómo son las hojas de la hierba stevia?
3. ¿Qué enfermedades se curan con las hierbas medicinales?

GRAMÁTICA IV: *Comparisons*

In this section you will learn how to make comparisons in Spanish. English speakers make comparisons either by adding the ending **-er** to an adjective (e.g., *warmer*) or by using the words *more* or *less* before an adjective (e.g., *more interesting, less expensive*). Spanish speakers make comparisons in the following manner:

Comparisons of inequality

Use **más** *(more)* or **menos** *(less)* before an adjective, an adverb, or a noun, and use **que** *(than)* after it.

$$\left.\begin{array}{c} \text{más} \\ \\ \text{menos} \end{array}\right\} + \left\{\begin{array}{l} \textit{adjective} \text{ (tímido)} \\ \textit{adverb} \text{ (pronto)} \\ \textit{noun} \text{ (hambre)} \end{array}\right\} + \quad \textbf{que}[1]$$

Keri quiere comer **más pronto que** Elena.
*Keri wants to eat **sooner than** Elena.*

Creo que Keri es **menos tímida que** Elena y es **más impaciente.**
*I think Keri is **less shy than** Elena and is **more impatient.***

Hoy Elena tiene **menos hambre que** Keri.
*Today Elena is **less hungry than** Keri.*

Use **más que** or **menos que** after a verb form.

Elena trabaja mucho.
Elena works a lot.

Elena trabaja **más que** Keri.
*Elena works **more than** Keri.*

Irregular comparatives

mejor(es) *better*
peor(es) *worse*
menor(es) *younger*
mayor(es) *older*

—El tiempo en Asunción es **mejor que** en La Paz.
*The weather in Asunción is **better than** in La Paz.*

—Sí, pero la humedad en Asunción es **peor que** en La Paz.
*Yes, but the humidity in Asunción is **worse than** in La Paz.*

—Keri es **mayor que** Elena, ¿verdad?
*Keri is **older than** Elena, right?*

—Sí. Elena es **menor que** Keri, y Keri es **mayor que** Elena.
*Yes. Elena is **younger than** Keri, and Keri is **older than** Elena.*

Comparisons of equality

Use **tan**[2] *(as)* before an adjective or an adverb and **como** *(as)* after it.[3]

$$\text{tan} \quad + \left\{\begin{array}{l} \textit{adjective} \text{ (nublado)} \\ \textit{adverb} \text{ (frecuentemente)} \end{array}\right\} + \quad \textbf{como}[4]$$

—A veces está **tan** nublado en La Paz **como** en Asunción.
*Sometimes it is **as** cloudy in La Paz **as** in Asunción.*

—También llueve **tan** frecuentemente en La Paz **como** en Sucre.
*Also, it rains **as** frequently in La Paz **as** in Sucre.*

---

[1] Use the preposition **de** *(than)* before a number; for example: Beti tiene **más de diez** amigos. *(Beti has more than ten friends.)*

[2] **Tan** can also be used by itself to show a great degree of a given quality; for example: ¡**Qué día tan perfecto!** *(What a perfect day!)*

[3] Note that one can make comparisons with verbs; for example: **Estudias tanto como yo.** *(You study as much as I do.)*

[4] One can change a comparison of equality to one of inequality by using the word **no** before a verb; for example: **No llueve tanto en La Paz como en Asunción.** *(It doesn't rain as much in La Paz as in Asunción.)*

Use **tanto(a)** *(as much)* or **tantos(as)**[1] *(as many)* before a noun and **como** *(as)* after it.

$$\left.\begin{array}{l}\textbf{tanto} \text{ (dinero)}\\ \textbf{tanta} \text{ (nieve)}\\ \\ \textbf{tantos} \text{ (días)}\\ \textbf{tantas} \text{ (fiestas)}\end{array}\right\} + \quad \textbf{como}$$

—¿Hace **tanto** calor en Potosí **como** en Concepción?
*Is it **as hot** in Potosí **as** in Concepción?*

—Sí. Y hay **tantas** nubes en Potosí **como** en Concepción.
*Yes. And there are **as many** clouds in Potosí **as** in Concepción.*

—¿Tiene Paraguay **tantos** días de sol **como** Bolivia?
*Does Paraguay have **as many** sunny days **as** Bolivia?*

—¡No! Y Paraguay no tiene **tanta** nieve **como** Bolivia.
*No! And Paraguay does not have **as much** snow **as** Bolivia.*

¡A practicar!

EE. **COMPARACIONES** Usando la información que sigue, haz comparaciones entre la clínica de Paraguay, la clínica de Bolivia y la gente que trabaja en las dos. Usa **más, menos, mayor** o **menor.**

MODELO: Hay seis enfermeras en la clínica de Paraguay. Hay diez enfermeras en la clínica de Bolivia.
Hay más enfermeras en la clínica de Bolivia que en la clínica de Paraguay.
o: *Hay menos enfermeras en la clínica de Paraguay que en la clínica de Bolivia.*

1. La clínica de Paraguay es pequeña. La clínica de Bolivia es grande.
2. La clínica de Paraguay tiene 490 pacientes. La clínica de Bolivia tiene 540 pacientes.
3. La clínica de Paraguay tiene 20 voluntarios. La clínica de Bolivia tiene 64.
4. Juan Carlos tiene 39 años. Su esposa Sara tiene 29.
5. Sarita tiene 5 años. Su hermano Tomás tiene 14 años.
6. Elena trabaja 38 horas por semana. Su amiga Keri trabaja 42 horas por semana.
7. El doctor Chávez tiene 20 años de experiencia. El doctor Fernández sólo tiene 12 años de experiencia.
8. En tu opinión, ¿qué clínica es mejor? ¿Qué clínica es peor?

FF. **LOS INTERESES DE KERI Y ELENA** Keri y Elena tienen muchos intereses en común. Completa las siguientes oraciones apropiadamente, usando **tan, tanto, tanta, tantos** o **tantas.**

MODELO: Keri es *tan* inteligente como Elena.

1. Keri tiene ___*tanta*___ energía como Elena.
2. Keri trabaja ___*tanto*___ como su amiga.
3. Elena hace ___*tantos*___ actividades como Keri.
4. Y Elena hace ___*tanto*___ ejercicio como Keri.
5. Keri juega al tenis ___*tan*___ bien como Elena.

---

[1] **Tanto(a)(s)** can also be used without **como**... to show a great amount of something; for example: ¡Hace **tanto calor!** *(It's so hot!)*

6. También Keri está ___tan___ contenta como Elena.
7. Elena tiene ___tantos___ amigos como Keri.
8. A Elena le gusta ir al cine ___tanto___ como a Keri.

En voz alta

GG. **¿CÓMO ERES TÚ?** Completa las siguientes oraciones con un(a) compañero(a) de clase.

MODELO: Soy tan inteligente como *Einstein*.

1. Soy tan inteligente como _____.
2. Estoy tan sano(a) como _____.
3. Estoy tan ocupado(a) como _____.
4. Hablo inglés tan bien como _____.
5. Hago tanto ejercicio como _____.
6. Tengo tantos problemas de salud como _____.

HH. **LO QUE HAGO YO** Usa las siguientes frases para describir tu situación personal a un(a) compañero(a) de clase. Usa **más/menos... que** o **tan... como** en cada oración.

MODELO: Nado más (el invierno / el verano)
        Nado más en el invierno que en el verano.
    o: *Nado menos en el invierno que en el verano.*
    o: *Nado más en el verano que en el invierno.*

1. Camino más/menos (el invierno / el verano)
2. Duermo más/menos (cuando hace frío / cuando hace calor)
3. Me ducho más/menos frecuentemente (el verano / el invierno)
4. Me enfermo más/menos (la primavera / el otoño)
5. Tengo más/menos dolores de cabeza (durante el semestre / durante las vacaciones)
6. Tomo más/menos bebidas (cuando hace calor / cuando hace fresco)
7. Me pongo un suéter tan frecuentemente (diciembre / mayo)
8. Trabajo tan bien (cuando hace mal tiempo / cuando hace buen tiempo)

II. **DOS AMIGAS Y TÚ** Compara a Elena con su amiga Keri, y luego comparáte tú con las dos. Hazle preguntas a un(a) compañero(a) de clase según el modelo.

MODELOS: ¿Quién es más joven?
        Elena es más joven que Keri.

        ¿Eres tú menor o mayor que Keri?
        Soy menor que Keri; tengo 20 años.

Persona	Edad	Trabajo en la clínica	Libros de medicina	Intereses
Elena	23	8 horas al día	12	libros, arte, conciertos
Keri	26	9 horas al día	12	vólibol, tenis, rap, fiestas
tú				

1. ¿Quién es mayor? ¿Eres tú menor o mayor que Elena? ¿Cuántos años tienes tú?
2. ¿Quién tiene más libros de medicina? ¿Tienes tú más o menos libros que Keri?
3. ¿Quién es más trabajador(a)? ¿Eres tú más o menos trabajador(a) que Keri? ¿Cuántas horas estudias o trabajas tú al día?
4. ¿Quién practica menos deportes? ¿A qué deportes juegas tú? ¿Qué otros intereses tienes tú?

Síntesis

¡A ver!

El **Capítulo 5** se centra en el tema de la salud. El narrador de este capítulo se llama Juan, y trabaja de médico en el centro de salud rural en Montero, Bolivia. El trabajo de Juan lo lleva a otros países hispánicos, especialmente a zonas rurales donde no hay servicios médicos apropiados. Juan nos habla de la medicina y de la salud.

ACTIVIDAD 1 **Pre-viewing task (Segmento 1 del video)**

Paso 1: En el primer segmento del video vas a ver una serie de fotos y clips cortos, todos relacionados con la salud y la medicina. Juan, un médico boliviano y nuestro narrador videográfico para este capítulo, nos explica todo. En la siguiente tabla apunta cualquier palabra *(any word)* que oyes o que ves en las imágenes relacionada con la medicina tradicional o con la medicina moderna. Algunas de las palabras pueden ser de las dos categorías.

Medicina tradicional	Medicina moderna
MODELO: *tienda naturista* *enfermo(a)*	*cirujano* *enfermo(a)*

Paso 2: Con un(a) compañero(a) de clase, explica la relación que tiene cada palabra en la tabla del **Paso 1** con su categoría de medicina tradicional o medicina moderna.

MODELOS: tienda naturista: *Es donde la gente compra plantas medicinales y otros alimentos medicinales.*

enfermo(a): *Es una persona que no se siente bien de salud.*

ACTIVIDAD 2 **Pre-viewing task (Segmento 2 del video)**

En el **Segmento 2 del video,** una médico chilena la hace un examen médico a una joven paciente que se llama Natalia. Aquí hay una serie de fotos de la médico en su consultorio con Natalia.

As you carry out this task in Spanish remember to agree or disagree with your partner or ask for clarifications if necessary.

Antes de ver el segmento, haz la siguiente actividad.

Paso 1: Estás sufriendo de una gripe fuerte. Decides ir a consultar con un(a) médico. Escribe una lista de los síntomas que tienes.

MODELOS: *Tengo un dolor de cabeza. (Me duele mucho la cabeza.)*
No como nada. No tengo nada de hambre. Normalmente como bien.

Paso 2: En tu opinión, ¿qué recomendaciones te va a hacer el (la) médico? Al lado de cada uno de los síntomas que apuntaste *(that you wrote down)* en el **Paso 1**, escribe una posible recomendación o consejo *(piece of advice)* del (de la) médico.

MODELO: 1. *Usted tiene que tomar (Usted debe tomar... / Usted va a tomar...) estas pastillas antiinflamatorias cinco veces al día durante dos semanas.*
2. *Debe (Tiene que / Va a) guardar cama durante una semana.*

> Remember that some of the ways of giving advice in Spanish are **Debe...**, **Tiene que...**, **Va a...** —each followed by the infinitive of the verb.

Paso 3: En parejas, utilicen la información que tienen de los **Pasos 1** y **2** para crear un diálogo entre el (la) paciente y el (la) médico. Tu compañero(a) de clase hace el papel del (de la) médico. Al terminar, cambien de papel.

ACTIVIDAD 3   Viewing task (Segmento 2 del video)

Paso 1: Después de hacerle a Natalia un examen, la doctora le prepara una receta médica. Le recomienda unos medicamentos y además le da una serie de sugerencias. ¿Cuáles son? Rellena la tabla de abajo con la información que falta *(missing information)*.

Medicamentos	Motivo	Dosis
1.	para la garganta	
2.		una pastilla cada ocho horas por siete días
3. paracetamol		

Otras sugerencias
•
•
• reposar
•

Paso 2: Comparte tu información con un(a) compañero(a) de clase.

ACTIVIDAD 4   Post-viewing task (Segmento 2 del video)

Natalia, la joven paciente de nuestra escena videográfica, informa a la médico que su madre también está sufriendo de la misma enfermedad que ella. La madre de Natalia no puede ir a ver a la médico porque no puede faltar a *(can't miss)* su trabajo. La médico decide llamar por teléfono a la madre de Natalia para darle algunos consejos.

Utilizando la información que tienes de la **Actividad 3** y trabajando con un(a) compañero(a), crea el diálogo telefónico que tiene la médico con la madre de Natalia.

> Before you start, think about the following: form of address (**tú** or **usted**) to be used in the dialog and ways of expressing advice in Spanish. As you create your dialog, react to your partner in appropriate ways. You might use the device used by the doctor in the video scene to check that her patient is following her advice and explanations: ¿**Ya?** *(OK? Understand? Follow?)*

¡A leer!

Recognizing Spanish affixes

An affix is added to the beginning (prefix) or to the end (suffix) of a word stem to create a new word. Knowing the meaning of Spanish affixes can significantly increase your ability to read Spanish effectively.

Paso 1: Escribe el significado en inglés de los prefijos y los sufijos españoles que siguen. Mira la lista de ejemplos para ayudarte a comprender el significado de cada afijo.

Español	Inglés	Ejemplos
Prefijos		
auto-	*self-*	**auto**control, **auto**defensa, **auto**estima
mono-	*mono- (one)*	**mono**lingüe, **mono**polio
mal-	_____	**mal**tratar, **mal**estar
bi-	_____	**bi**lingüe, **bi**cicleta, **bi**mestre
tri-	_____	**tri**lingüe, **tri**ángulo, **tri**mestre
im-	_____	**im**posible, **im**paciente, **im**parcial
in-	_____	**in**necesario, **in**mortal, **in**creíble
Sufijos		
-mente	_____	especial**mente**, rápida**mente**
-ado, -ada	_____	ocup**ado**, motoriz**ado**, divorci**ada**
-oso, -osa	_____	maravill**oso**, gener**oso**, fabul**osa**
-dad, -tad	_____	oportuni**dad**, ciu**dad**, liber**tad**
-ción, -sión	_____	conversa**ción**, ac**ción**, televi**sión**

Paso 2: Vas a leer un texto sobre la automedicación. Basándote en lo que sabes de los afijos españoles, ¿qué significa **la automedicación**? Escribe una definición en inglés en tus propias palabras.

Paso 3: Antes de leer el texto, piensa en tu propia experiencia y contesta la pregunta que sigue.

¿Qué haces cuando te enfermas?

- Voy a hablar con un(a) médico, quien me da una receta.
- Voy a la farmacia para comprar medicina.
- Le pido unas pastillas a un(a) amigo(a).
- Tomo una combinación de varias pastillas o medicinas.
- Tomo la dosis *(dose)* necesaria de la medicina, según las instrucciones.

Paso 4: Ahora lee el texto. Usa lo que sabes sobre los afijos españoles para ayudarte a comprenderlo.

1. Escribe los equivalentes en inglés de las palabras que siguen.
   - **a.** malestar
   - **b.** anticoagulantes
   - **c.** indicadas
   - **d.** previamente
   - **e.** antialérgico
   - **f.** malformaciones

2. Escribe los equivalentes en español de las expresiones que siguen.
   - **a.** secondary effects
   - **b.** dangerous combinations
   - **c.** miniature adult

Nunca debes automedicarte más de cinco días seguidos: si persisten las molestias, ve al médico.

Los cinco mandamientos de la automedicación

1. **Lee el prospecto cuidadosamente.**
Sigue las instrucciones al pie de la letra, incluida la posología (dosificación): tomar más dosis de las indicadas no hará que el fármaco sea más eficaz, pero aumentará los efectos secundarios. Y es necesario tomarlo cuando se indica —antes o después de las comidas—, porque de ello dependerá también su eficacia.

2. **Sigue tratamientos a corto plazo.**
No debes superar los cinco o siete días. Si pasado este tiempo persiste el malestar, debes acudir al médico.

3. **Ten cuidado con las combinaciones peligrosas.**

Muchas veces asociar dos medicamentos es jugar con fuego. Una sustancia puede limitar el efecto de otra o acentuarla. Por ejemplo, los anticoagulantes unidos a la aspirina elevan el riesgo de hemorragia, y un tranquilizante más un antialérgico aumenta la somnolencia.

4. **Evita la automedicación en niños y mujeres embarazadas.**
Un niño no es un adulto en miniatura y darle un fármaco sin consultar previamente al médico puede ser arriesgado, sobre todo si tiene menos de 6 años. En todo caso, sólo deben utilizarse medicamentos infantiles y calculando bien la dosis, en función de la edad y el peso. En

cuanto a las mujeres embarazadas también es necesario ser prudentes, ya que la mayoría de los fármacos pueden pasar al feto, que no tiene medios para defenderse y destruirlos —se calcula que un 3% de las malformaciones que sufren los neonatos se deben a esta causa.

5. **Pide consejo a tu farmacéutico.**
No todos los fármacos funcionan de la misma forma en todas las personas, de manera que lo que le ha ido muy bien a un amigo o a un familiar tuyo puede no servirte a ti o incluso llegar a resultarte perjudicial. El farmacéutico puede jugar aquí un gran papel como asesor.

¡A conversar!

Consejos

Paso 1: Estudiante A: Imagínate que te sientes enfermo(a). Decides llamar a tu amigo(a) por teléfono para quejarte *(to complain)* de los síntomas que tienes.

Paso 2: Estudiante B: Tu amigo(a) se siente enfermo(a) y te llama por teléfono para quejarse. Dale consejos sobre los síntomas que te describe.

Paso 3: Después, cambien de papel y hagan la actividad de nuevo, empleando síntomas y remedios nuevos.

MODELO: E2: *Diga.*
E1: *Hola, habla...*
E2: *Hola. ¿Cómo estás?*
E1: *Muy mal. Me duele mucho la cabeza y el estómago. Creo que estoy enfermo(a).*
E2: *¡Qué lástima! Debes descansar. Toma dos aspirinas y duerme una siesta.*
Luego,...

¡A escribir!

Using a bilingual dictionary

A bilingual dictionary is a useful tool that, when used properly, can enhance the quality, complexity, and accuracy of your writing in Spanish. Here are some suggestions to help you use your bilingual dictionary properly.

1. When you look up the Spanish equivalent of an English word, you will often find several meanings for the same word, often appearing like this:

   cold: *n.* frío, catarro, resfriado
           adj. frío

2. In larger dictionaries, the Spanish equivalents may appear in a phrase or sentence to clarify their meaning and use.

   cold: *n.* frío *(low temperature)*; catarro *(illness)*; resfriado *(illness)*
           adj. frío

3. Pay attention to certain abbreviations in your dictionary that will tell you what type of word you have found. Notice the abbreviations *n.* and *adj.* in the examples above, indicating that the word is a noun or an adjective. Some of the more common abbreviations you will find are the following:

n. noun	*adj.* adjective
adv. adverb	*conj.* conjunction
prep. preposition	*v.* verb

4. Looking up a lot of different words in a bilingual dictionary when you are writing is inefficient. If you insist on looking up too many words as you write, you may become frustrated or feel like you want to give up altogether. It is wiser and faster to use the phrases you already know in Spanish as much as possible, rather than trying to translate too many new words you don't know from English to Spanish. You will learn more and more new words as you continue reading and listening to the language.

Paso 1: Busca las siguientes palabras inglesas en tu diccionario bilingüe y escribe sus equivalentes españoles en una hoja de papel.

1. wall (e.g., in a house)
2. to grade (e.g., to correct)
3. bank (e.g., of a river)

Paso 2: Indica si las palabras son sustantivos *(nouns)*, verbos, adjetivos, adverbios, etcétera.

Paso 3: Compara tus respuestas con las de un(a) compañero(a) de clase.

Paso 4: Ahora, imagínate que tienes un(a) amigo(a) que siempre tiene problemas de salud, pero a él (ella) no le gustan nada los médicos ni las clínicas ni los hospitales. Por eso, tú tienes que explicarle algunos remedios caseros que él (ella) puede usar en casa en vez de ir al médico. Usando mandatos informales, escribe una carta a tu amigo(a) para darle unos consejos sobre remedios caseros para los síntomas a continuación. Usa tu diccionario cuando es necesario para buscar nuevas palabras.

dolor de garganta
la gripe
dolor de estómago
dolor de cabeza
la tos

Querido(a) _____:

Pues entiendo que a ti no te gusta nada ir a ver a los médicos. Por eso, te voy a recomendar unos remedios caseros de mi madre. Para el dolor de garganta, toma té con limón o miel y...

Para el dolor de cabeza, toma dos aspirinas y...
Para la tos,...
Para el dolor de estómago,...

El cuerpo humano   *The human body*

la boca   *mouth*
los brazos   *arms*
la cabeza   *head*
la cara   *face*
los codos   *elbows*
el corazón   *heart*
el cuello   *neck*

los dedos   *fingers*
los dedos de pie   *toes*
los dientes   *teeth*
la espalda   *back*
el estómago   *stomach*
la garganta   *throat*
las manos   *hands*

la nariz   *nose*
el oído   *inner ear*
los ojos   *eyes*
las orejas   *(outer) ears*
el pelo   *hair*
la piel   *skin*
las piernas   *legs*

los pies   *feet*
los pulmones   *lungs*
las rodillas   *knees*
los tobillos   *ankles*

Las actividades diarias y la higiene personal   *Daily activities and personal hygiene*

acabar de + infinitive   *to have just (done something)*
acostarse (ue)   *to go to bed*
afeitarse   *to shave*
bañarse   *to take a bath*
cepillarse los dientes   *to brush one's teeth*

cuidar(se)   *to take care (of oneself)*
despertarse (ie)   *to wake up*
dormirse (ue)   *to fall asleep*
ducharse   *to take a shower*
lavarse   *to wash up*
levantarse   *to get up*
maquillarse   *to put on makeup*

peinarse   *to comb one's hair*
pintarse (la cara)   *to put on makeup*
ponerse   *to put on*
quitarse   *to take off*
secarse   *to dry off*
vestirse (i)   *to get dressed*

La salud   *Health*

la ambulancia   *ambulance*
el antibiótico   *antibiotic*
la aspirina   *aspirin*
el (la) enfermero(a)   *nurse*
la farmacia   *pharmacy*

el jarabe   *cough syrup*
la medicina   *medicine*
el (la) médico   *physician, doctor*
el (la) paciente   *patient*
la pastilla   *pill*

la receta   *prescription*
la sala de emergencia   *emergency room*
la sala de espera   *waiting room*

Los problemas médicos   *Medical problems*

la alergia   *allergy*
el catarro   *cold*
congestionado(a)   *congested*

el dolor (de oídos, de cabeza)   *ache, pain (earache, headache)*
la enfermedad   *illness*

mareado(a)   *dizzy*
el resfriado   *cold*
el síntoma   *symptom*

Verbos relacionados con la salud   *Health-related verbs*

doler(le) (ue) (a alguien)   *to be painful (to someone)*
enfermarse   *to get sick*
estar enfermo(a)   *to be sick*
estar sano(a)   *to be healthy*
estornudar   *to sneeze*
examinar   *to examine*

guardar cama   *to stay in bed*
resfriarse   *to catch a cold*
sentirse (bien/mal)   *to feel (good/bad)*
tener dolor de cabeza   *to have a headache*
tener escalofríos   *to have chills*
tener fiebre   *to have a fever*

tener gripe   *to have a cold*
tener náuseas   *to be nauseous*
tener tos   *to have a cough*
tomarle la temperatura (a alguien)   *to take (someone's) temperature*
toser   *to cough*

Comparativos   *Comparatives*

más... que   *more . . . than*
menos... que   *less . . . than*
tan... como   *as . . . as*

tanto(a)... como   *as much . . . as*
tantos(as)... como   *as many . . . as*
mayor   *older*

mejor   *better*
menor   *younger*
peor   *worse*

6

Vamos a comer: Venezuela

Communicative goals

In this chapter you will learn how to . . .

- Talk about foods and beverages for breakfast, lunch, and dinner
- Extend invitations
- Order food in a restaurant
- Talk about events occurring in the past
- Make superlative statements

Grammar

- Demonstrative adjectives
- Demonstrative pronouns
- Preterite of regular verbs
- Superlatives

Cultural information

- Typical Venezuelan foods
- Venezuelan restaurants

La Plaza Bolívar, Caracas, Venezuela

EL MENÚ DEL RESTAURANTE DE DOÑA MARGARITA In this section you will practice talking about foods by learning about doña Margarita's restaurant, El Criollito, on the east side of Caracas.

El Criollito

Para empezar	**To begin with**
las arepas (la especialidad de la casa)[1]	arepas (the house specialty)
la ensalada de la casa (lechuga, tomate, huevo duro)	house salad (lettuce, tomato, hard-boiled egg)
la sopa de verduras	vegetable soup
el pan (tostado)	bread (toast)
Platos principales	**Main dishes**
La carne	**Meats**
la carne de res (bistec) con arroz y champiñones	beef (steak) with rice and mushrooms
las chuletas de cerdo en salsa de tomate	pork chops in tomato sauce
el sándwich de jamón y queso	ham and cheese sandwich
el pavo con verduras	turkey with vegetables
el pollo asado	roast chicken
la hamburguesa (con queso) y papas fritas	hamburger (cheeseburger) with french fries
Mariscos y pescado del día	**Shellfish and fish of the day**
la langosta	lobster
los camarones fritos	fried shrimp
los calamares fritos	fried calamari (squid)
Bebidas	**Beverages**
el agua mineral con/sin gas	carbonated/noncarbonated mineral water
el café	coffee
la cerveza	beer
el jugo de fruta	fruit juice
la leche	milk
los refrescos	soft drinks
el té (helado)	(iced) tea
el vino (blanco, tinto)	(white, red) wine
Postres	**Desserts**
las frutas: manzana, naranja, banana	fruit: apples, oranges, bananas
el flan casero	homemade caramel custard
el helado	ice cream

¿NOS ENTENDEMOS?

In Spain, **las papas** are referred to as **las patatas**.

¿NOS ENTENDEMOS?

There are four ways to order coffee in Venezuela: **un negrito** (black espresso coffee served in a demitasse), **un marroncito** (**un negrito,** with a little milk added), **un blanquito** (more milk than coffee), and **café con leche** (espresso with hot milk added and served in a teacup). **La gaseosa** is another term for **el refresco**.

¿NOS ENTENDEMOS?

Various countries use different words for *bananas:* **el plátano** in Spain and Latin America, **la banana** in some Latin American countries, **el guineo** in Puerto Rico, and **el cambur** in Venezuela.

Las comidas *Meals*

almorzar (ue) *to have (eat) lunch*
el almuerzo *lunch*
la cena *dinner, supper*
cenar *to have (eat) dinner (supper)*
desayunar *to have (eat) breakfast*
el desayuno *breakfast*

Los condimentos *Condiments*

el aceite *oil*
la mantequilla *butter*
la pimienta *pepper*
la sal *salt*
el vinagre *vinegar*

[1] **Arepas** are flat pancakes made from white corn flour, water, and salt. They are deep-fried or baked and are filled with butter, meat, or cheese. **Arepas** are very popular in Venezuela and Colombia.

¡A practicar!

A. UN MENÚ DESORGANIZADO Doña Margarita está planeando el menú para su restaurante. Ayúdala a encontrar la comida que no pertenece al grupo.

1. las chuletas, los camarones, el helado, el pescado
2. el vino tinto, el té, la cerveza, el vino blanco
3. el bistec, los calamares, la langosta, el pescado
4. el pavo, la carne de res, el pollo, los huevos
5. los champiñones, las papas, las manzanas
6. la mantequilla, el helado, el flan
7. la sal, el vinagre, el aceite, los sándwiches
8. la ensalada, el pan tostado, la sopa, el pollo asado

B. ¿QUÉ BEBIDAS TE APETECEN? Escogiendo de la lista de bebidas a la derecha, completa las siguientes oraciones para expresar tus preferencias.

1. Para el desayuno, prefiero tomar...   leche
2. Cuando estudio en casa, tomo...   café
3. Cuando tengo mucha sed, bebo...   té
4. Para el almuerzo, me gusta beber...   vino tinto/blanco
5. En las fiestas siempre tomo...   agua mineral
6. Los fines de semana me gusta tomar...   jugo de tomate
7. Para la cena prefiero beber...   un refresco
8. Cuando estoy en el cine, tomo...   una cerveza

En voz alta

C. ¿QUÉ PREFIERES? Pregúntale a otro(a) estudiante cuáles son sus preferencias.

MODELO: té helado o té caliente
         E1:   *¿Prefieres té helado o té caliente?*
         E2:   *Prefiero té caliente.*
   o: E2:   *Prefiero té caliente por la mañana.*
   o: E2:   *No me gusta ni el té caliente ni el té helado.*

¿Prefieres...

1. vino tinto o vino blanco?
2. jugo de naranja o jugo de tomate?
3. sopa de verduras o sopa de tomate?
4. pan con mantequilla o pan con mermelada?
5. helado de chocolate o helado de vainilla?
6. pollo con ensalada o pollo con papas fritas?

D. ENTREVISTA Hazle las siguientes preguntas a otro(a) estudiante sobre sus hábitos a la hora de comer.

1. el desayuno: ¿A qué hora desayunas? ¿Desayunas solo(a) o con otras personas? ¿Qué prefieres tomar por la mañana: café, té, leche o jugo? ¿Qué te gusta comer para el desayuno?
2. el almuerzo: Normalmente, ¿dónde almuerzas? ¿Con quién te gusta comer al mediodía? ¿A qué hora? ¿Qué comes para el almuerzo?
3. la cena: Normalmente, ¿a qué hora cenas? ¿Cenas con tu familia, con otras personas o solo(a)? ¿Comes mucho o poco en la cena? Por ejemplo, ¿qué comes?

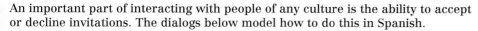

ASÍ SE DICE: *Accepting and declining invitations*

An important part of interacting with people of any culture is the ability to accept or decline invitations. The dialogs below model how to do this in Spanish.

—Voy a **hacer una fiesta.**　　　*I'm going **to have a party.***
—**¿En qué fecha?**　　　*On what date?*
—El 30 de noviembre.　　　*On November 30th.*
—**Ay, no puedo ir.**　　　*Darn, I can't go.*

—**¿Quieres ir** al restaurante　　　*Do you want to go to the restaurant*
　El Criollito?　　　　　*El Criollito?*
—**¿Cuándo?**　　　*When?*
—**Esta noche.**　　　*Tonight.*
—**No puedo** ir hoy. **Ya tengo planes.**　　　*I can't go today. I already have plans.*
—**Vamos** este fin de semana **entonces.**　　　*Let's go this weekend then.*
—**Bien.** Gracias, *me encantaría.*　　　*Okay. Thanks, I'd love to.*
—De nada.　　　*You're welcome.*

En voz alta

E.　**UNA INVITACIÓN** Conversa con un(a) compañero(a) de clase para hacer planes para una comida durante el fin de semana.

Estudiante A	Estudiante B
1. Saluda a tu amigo(a).	**2.** Contéstale a tu amigo(a). Pregúntale cómo está él o ella. Invita a tu amigo(a) a un almuerzo en casa el sábado.
3. Dile que no puedes aceptar su invitación. Explica los planes que ya tienes.	**4.** Reacciona a lo que dice tu amigo(a). Invítalo(la) al almuerzo otro día.
5. Acepta la invitación. Dale las gracias a tu compañero(a). Pregúntale sobre la invitación.	**6.** Responde a sus preguntas.
7. Pregúntale si su familia va a estar en el almuerzo.	**8.** Contesta si tu familia va a estar en el almuerzo, o no.
9. Dile gracias y adiós.	**10.** Contesta y dile adiós.

EN CONTEXTO

El siguiente diálogo tiene lugar *(takes place)* en el restaurante El Criollito de doña Margarita. Doña Margarita está sirviendo a sus primeros clientes *(customers)*, Rosa y Simón, y quiere servirles una cena perfecta.

DOÑA MARGARITA: ¡Bienvenidos al Criollito! ¿Quieren sentarse adentro o en la terraza?

ROSA: En la terraza. ¡Las flores que tienen allí son muy bonitas!

DOÑA MARGARITA: Gracias. Por aquí, entonces. Pasen.

*****

DOÑA MARGARITA: ¿Está bien? El camarero les trae el menú en seguida.

SIMÓN: ¡Perfecto!

*****

EL CAMARERO: ¡Buenas tardes! Aquí tienen el menú. ¿Les apetece *(Would you like)* tomar algo?

ROSA: Para mí, un jugo de naranja con hielo.

SIMÓN: Y para mí, una cerveza.

EL CAMARERO: Muy bien. ¿Les traigo un plato de arepas para empezar? ¡Es la especialidad de la casa!

SIMÓN: ¡Cómo no! *(Of course!)*

*****

EL CAMARERO: Aquí están las arepas.

SIMÓN: ¡Huelen *(They smell)* riquísimo!

ROSA: ¡Son para chuparse *(to lick)* los dedos!

EL CAMARERO: Están muy frescas. La cocinera acaba de prepararlas. ¿Quieren pedir algo del menú?

ROSA: Sí. Vamos a ver. Yo quisiera los calamares fritos. ¿Están frescos?

EL CAMARERO: Sí, señora. Los recibimos esta mañana. Los preparamos con una salsa especial. Seguro que le van a gustar. ¿Y para el señor?

SIMÓN: Quisiera el bistec bien asado *(well done)* con champiñones.

¿NOS ENTENDEMOS?

Spanish speakers use several expressions to indicate their enjoyment of a meal; for example: **¡Son para chuparse los dedos!** *(They're finger-licking good!)* and **¡Huele riquísimo!** *(It smells delicious!)*. It is also quite common to use the diminutive form when requesting common beverages such as **un cafecito** *(coffee)* or **una cervecita** *(beer)*. In Latin America, it is more appropriate to use **(yo) quisiera...** *(I would like*—the past subjunctive form of the verb **querer)** when ordering food. In Spain, it is more common to use the more direct **(yo) quiero...**

*****

EL CAMARERO:	¿Algo más? ¿Postre? ¿Café?
SIMÓN:	Un cafecito y la cuenta *(the check)*, por favor.
ROSA:	Tú siempre dices eso, mi amor. No nos mataría *(wouldn't kill us)* un postre de vez en cuando.

F. **¿COMPRENDISTE?** Identifica la frase del diálogo que establece los siguientes hechos.

MODELO: Es por la tarde.
El camarero dice «¡Buenas tardes!».

1. A Rosa le gusta sentarse en la terraza.
2. Rosa y Simón van a comer arepas.
3. Las arepas están muy sabrosas *(tasty)* y frescas.
4. Simón pide un plato del menú.
5. Rosa no va a comer un postre.

ENCUENTRO *cultural*

La comida típica venezolana

Éstas son unas palabras nuevas para la lectura:

la tajada   *slice*
mechado(a)   *shredded*
el manjar   *delicacy*
el chipichipi   *a thumbnail-size clam*
la concha   *shell*
el ajo   *garlic*
la cebolla   *onion*

la harina de maíz   *corn flour*
rellenar   *to stuff*
molido(a)   *ground*
el aguacate   *avocado*

Para pensar: ¿A ti te gusta probar *(to try)* comidas de otros países? ¿Quieres probar una arepa? ¿Quieres probar el pabellón? ¿Por qué sí o no? ¿Probaste alguna vez un plátano frito? ¿Te parece extraño preparar un plato principal con fruta? ¿Qué relleno para arepas te parece *(seems)* ser el más sabroso? ¿Por qué?

¿NOS ENTENDEMOS?

The Spanish-speaking world has many words for *beans*. **Las caraotas** in Venezuela, **los frijoles** in Mexico, and **las judías** in Spain are just a few examples.

El plato más típico de Venezuela es el pabellón. El pabellón, que se considera como el plato nacional de Venezuela, lleva cuatro ingredientes: caraotas negras, arroz blanco, **tajadas** de plátano frito y carne **mechada.**

Como Venezuela está situada en el Mar Caribe y tiene muchos ríos y lagos, los mariscos son muy comunes. Un **manjar** muy apreciado en Venezuela es la sopa de **chipichipi.** Esta sopa está preparada con los chipichipis en **la concha.** Para comer los chipichipis es necesario usar las manos para sacar la carne de la concha. La sopa también tiene **ajo,** cilantro, **cebollas,** tomates, sal y puré de tomate.

Una comida muy popular en Venezuela es la arepa. La arepa es una torta de **harina de maíz** del mismo tamaño y forma que un *English muffin.* Se puede preparar las arepas en el horno o se puede freírlas. Para servir la arepa, se **rellena** al gusto individual. Algunos rellenos son carne mechada, carne **molida,** huevos fritos, jamón, queso, atún u otros mariscos. Un relleno muy popular se llama Reina Pepiada —es una ensalada de **aguacate.** Las arepas son tan populares que hay areperas —un tipo de restaurante que se especializa en arepas— en todos los pueblos pequeños y las ciudades grandes.

G. **PREGUNTAS** Contesta las siguientes preguntas a base de la lectura.

1. Nombra unas comidas muy típicas de Venezuela.
2. ¿Qué lleva la sopa chipichipi? ¿El pabellón? ¿Las arepas?

GRAMÁTICA I: *Demonstrative adjectives and pronouns*

In this section you will learn how to specify people, places, things, and ideas.

Demonstrative adjectives

You can use demonstrative adjectives to point out a specific noun. These adjectives must agree in gender (masculine or feminine) and number (singular or plural) with the noun to which they refer.

Singular		Plural	
este(a) *this*		**estos(as)** *these*	
ese(a) *that*		**esos(as)** *those*	
aquel (aquella) *that (over there)*		**aquellos(as)** *those (over there)*[1]	
este queso *this cheese*		**estos** huevos *these eggs*	
esta fruta *this fruit*		**estas** papas *these potatoes*	
ese bistec *that steak*		**esos** tomates *those tomatoes*	
esa leche *that milk*		**esas** verduras *those vegetables*	
aquel restaurante *that restaurant*		**aquellos** camareros *those waiters*	
aquella mesa *that table*		**aquellas** arepas *those arepas*	

Demonstrative pronouns are used in place of nouns and must agree with them in gender (masculine or feminine) and number (singular or plural). These forms all carry accents to distinguish them from the demonstrative adjectives:

---

[1] To point out people, things, and places that are far from the speaker and from the person addressed and to indicate something from a long time ago, Spanish speakers use forms of the demonstrative adjective **aquel**. For example: **Esta cena hoy es deliciosa, esa cena en el restaurante el mes pasado fue increíble y *aquella* cena en la casa de Margarita fue inolvidable.**

	Singular	Plural
	éste(a)	**éstos(as)**
	ése(a)	**ésos(as)**
	aquél (aquélla)	**aquéllos(as)**

—¿Quieres ese pescado?   *Do you want that fish?*
—Sí, **ése**.   *Yes, **that** one.*

—¿Son tuyos aquellos platos sucios?   *Are those dirty plates (over there) yours?*
—Sí, **aquéllos** son míos.   *Yes, **those** are mine.*

Neuter demonstrative pronouns
The words **esto** *(this)*, **eso** *(that)*, and **aquello** *(that over there)* can refer either to nonspecific things that are not yet identified or to ideas that were already mentioned.

—¿Qué es **esto**, mamá?   *What's **this**, Mom?*
—Es una lechosa.   *It's a papaya.*

—¿Sabes cocinar **eso**, papá?   *Do you know how to cook **that**, Dad?*
—Sí, pero es difícil.   *Yes, but it's difficult.*

—¿Qué es **aquello** que se ve a lo lejos?   *What is **that** (very far away)?*
—Es un calamar.   *It's a squid.*

¡A practicar!

H. **¡QUÉ RICA ESTÁ LA COMIDA DE MI MAMÁ!** Doña Margarita está cocinando para su familia. Aquí tienes los comentarios de su esposo Jorge y sus dos hijas, Matilde y Elena, sobre la comida. Completa sus comentarios, usando apropiadamente **este, esta, estos** o **estas**.

MODELO: Jorge: ¡*Esta* comida está rica!

Elena: ¡Mmmm! _____ queso es mi favorito.
Matilde: Bueno, ¡y qué rica está _____ sopa!
Jorge: Querida, ¡_____ arepas están fabulosas!
Elena: ¡Y _____ pescado está rico también!
Matilde: ¡Ay! _____ café está muy delicioso.
Margarita: Están muy ricos _____ mariscos, ¿eh?
Elena: _____ arroz está bueno, ¿verdad?

I. **DE COMPRAS** Ahora doña Margarita, Jorge y Matilde están hablando de la comida de un supermercado.

Paso 1: Completa sus comentarios, usando apropiadamente **ese, esa, esos** o **esas**.

Doña Margarita: _____ vino tinto es excelente, querido.
Jorge: Bueno, y _____ cerveza alemana también.
Doña Margarita: _____ mantequilla tiene muchas calorías, Matilde.
Matilde: _____ postres también, mamá. ¡Pero qué ricos!
   ¡Mira, mamá! _____ papas son muy grandes.
Doña Margarita: Sí, pero mira _____ tomates. Son pequeños.
Matilde: ¡Mira, mira, papá! _____ pollos son muy feos.
Jorge: ¡Uf! Y _____ pescado también. ¡Vamos a casa!

¿NOS ENTENDEMOS?

When you say **La comida está rica** as opposed to **La comida es rica,** you are saying that the food is particularly good-tasting as opposed to rich in consistency.

Paso 2: Matilde ve unas cosas exóticas en el supermercado que ella no reconoce. Le pregunta a su papá qué son usando **eso** y **esto.**

Matilde: ¡Papá! ¿Qué tienes en la mano? ¿Qué es _____?
Jorge: _____ es queso azul. Es muy rico.
Matilde: Y _____ que tengo en la mano, ¿qué es?
Jorge: _____ es un plátano. Parece ser una banana enorme, ¿verdad?

En voz alta

J. EN LA TIENDA Matilde y su mamá, Margarita, están en una tienda de comidas especiales. Cuando Matilde sugiere *(suggests)* una cosa, su mamá indica que quiere otra. Mira el dibujo de abajo para esta actividad, y con un(a) compañero(a) de clase, hagan los papeles de Margarita y Matilde.

M O D E L O : queso canadiense / queso holandés
Matilde: *¿Quieres este queso canadiense?*
Doña Margarita: *No. Prefiero aquel queso holandés.*
Matilde: *¿Aquél?*
Doña Margarita: *Sí, aquél.*

1. café colombiano / café brasileño
2. cerveza alemana / cerveza mexicana
3. bistec argentino / bistec chileno
4. naranjas españolas / naranjas chilenas
5. vino tinto / vino blanco

K. **PREFERENCIAS** Ahora responde a las preguntas de Matilde usando pronombres demostrativos (**éste, ésta, ése, ésa, aquél, aquélla**).

MODELO: ¿Quieres este café brasileño?
Sí, quiero éste.

1. ¿Quieres este queso canadiense?
2. ¿Quieres aquel vino blanco?
3. ¿Necesitas esas verduras para la sopa?
4. ¿Vas a usar esas naranjas chilenas?
5. ¿Quieres un poco de ese vino tinto para la salsa?
6. ¿Usas estas verduras?
7. ¿Vas a llevar aquella cerveza mexicana?

VOCABULARIO: *El restaurante*

EN EL RESTAURANTE EL CRIOLLITO In this section you will learn vocabulary and expressions associated with eating in a restaurant.

Adjetivos

caliente   *hot (temperature)*
fresco(a)   *fresh*
ligero(a)   *light (meal, food)*
pesado(a)   *heavy (meal, food)*
rico(a)   *delicious*

Verbos

cocinar   *to cook*
dejar una (buena) propina   *to leave a (good) tip*
desear   *to wish, to want*
pedir (i)   *to order (food)*
picar   *to eat appetizers, to nibble*
preparar   *to prepare*
recomendar (ie)   *to recommend*

Expresiones idiomáticas

¡Buen provecho!   *Enjoy your meal!*
¡Cómo no!   *Of course!*
Estoy a dieta.   *I'm on a diet.*
Estoy satisfecho(a).   *I'm satisfied.*
La cuenta, por favor.   *The check, please.*
No puedo más.   *I can't (eat) any more.*

¿Qué te apetece?   *What would you like (to eat)?*
¡Salud!   *Cheers!*
Te invito.   *It's on me (my treat).*
Yo quisiera...   *I would like . . .*

¡A practicar!

L.   **IMPRESIONES DE PEPE** Pepe el camarero siempre les sirve a don Fernando y a doña Olga cuando ellos vienen a comer al restaurante El Criollito. Completa el párrafo siguiente sobre sus impresiones de la pareja. Usa las siguientes frases, palabras y expresiones:

yo te invito	ensalada	agua mineral
¿qué les apetece?	propina	algo ligero
picar	menú	piden
está a dieta		

Hola. Sí, yo llevo muchos años trabajando aquí en El Criollito. Conozco bien a Fernando y a Olga —son clientes muy buenos. Siempre empiezo preguntándoles «_____». Don Fernando siempre pide ver el _____. Después, él siempre pide _____ para _____. Les gustan mucho los mariscos —casi siempre _____ la langosta o el pescado. Claro, ¡doña Margarita tiene el mejor pescado de Caracas! Como doña Olga es un poco gorda, siempre _____. Por eso, normalmente ella pide _____ para beber y una _____ para comer con su plato principal. Realmente son unas personas especiales y muy románticas. Al final de su comida, don Fernando siempre le dice a su esposa: «_____, cariño», y me deja una buena _____.

M. **UN CAMARERO CONFUNDIDO** Pepe, el camarero del restaurante de doña Margarita, está un poco confundido. Ayúdalo a poner en orden las frases que él les dice a los clientes.

_____ Les traigo la cuenta ahora mismo.
_____ ¿Qué les apetece?
_____ De postre hay fruta, helados y flan casero.
_____ ¿Y para beber?
_____ ¿Dos para cenar?

_____ Recomiendo los mariscos.
_____ ¡Buenas noches!
_____ ¡Buen provecho!
_____ ¿Desean algo más?
_____ Gracias, señores, y muy buenas noches.
_____ Aquí tienen el menú.

En voz alta

N. ¿CÓMO SE DICE... EN ESPAÑOL? Hazle las siguientes preguntas a un(a) compañero(a) de clase. Tu compañero(a) tiene que contestar apropiadamente. Recuerda que los camareros y clientes normalmente usan **Ud.** para conversar.

MODELO: Can I see the menu?
E1: *¿Puedo ver el menú?*
E2: *Aquí está el menú.*

1. What's the house specialty?
2. What do you recommend?
3. Do you have soft drinks?
4. Do you like the food?

5. What's for dessert?
6. Can you bring us the check?
7. It's my treat.

O. ESCENAS EN UN RESTAURANTE Trabajando con un(a) compañero(a) de clase, hagan el papel de un(a) cliente y un(a) camarero(a) en un resturante. Usen las expresiones que acaban de aprender y las comidas de los menús en las páginas 159 y 179.

ENCUENTRO *cultural*

Los restaurantes en Venezuela

Como los Estados Unidos, Venezuela tiene restaurantes de todo tipo. Por ejemplo, hay areperas y pizzerías que sirven comida las 24 horas. Aparte de la comida típicamente venezolana, hay muchos restaurantes que sirven platos de otras partes del mundo —es muy común comer comida china, italiana y hasta mexicana en Venezuela.

Muchos restaurantes venezolanos sirven a la carta, y algunos sirven un plato del día. Una comida entera en un restaurante elegante consiste normalmente en una entrada (algo ligero para comenzar), el plato principal (carne o pescado con papas o vegetales) y al final, un postre. El postre puede ser tan simple como un poco de fruta como lechosa —el nombre venezolano para papaya— o tan elegante como un *crème brûlée*.

Después de la comida viene la sobremesa. Como en los países hispánicos la comida es algo que se toma en serio, la sobremesa es el tiempo que la gente pasa a la mesa después de comer —normalmente se conversa, y a veces se toma un café o un coñac también. El café no se sirve con la comida como en los Estados Unidos. En los restaurantes venezolanos el café es lo último que se sirve, normalmente después del postre.

Para pensar: Esta lectura habla de una comida en un restaurante típicamente venezolano (con la entrada, el plato principal y el postre). Con un(a) compañero(a), hablen de cómo es normalmente una comida en un restaurante «típicamente» estadounidense. En tu familia, ¿cómo es una comida elegante? ¿Tomas café después de comer? ¿Siempre hay postre?

P. PREGUNTAS Contesta las siguientes preguntas a base de la lectura.

1. Compara la información sobre los restaurantes venezolanos con lo que tú sabes de los restaurantes estadounidenses.
2. ¿Qué plato principal pedirías *(would you order)* en un restaurante venezolano?

GRAMÁTICA II: *Preterite of regular verbs*

Spanish speakers use the preterite tense to describe what occurred in the past.

> To form the preterite for most Spanish verbs, add the following endings to the verb stem. Note the identical endings for **-er** and **-ir** verbs.

	hablar	comer	vivir
yo	hablé	comí	viví
tú	hablaste	comiste	viviste
Ud., él, ella	habló	comió	vivió
nosotros(as)	hablamos	comimos	vivimos
vosotros(as)	hablasteis	comisteis	vivisteis
Uds., ellos(as)	hablaron	comieron	vivieron

> **-Ar** and **-er** stem-changing verbs have no stem change in the preterite; use the same verb stem as you would for the **nosotros** form.[1]

pensar: pensé, pensaste, pensó, pensamos, pensasteis, pensaron

volver: volví, volviste, volvió, volvimos, volvisteis, volvieron

—**Pensé** mucho en doña Margarita.

I thought a lot about doña Margarita.

—¿Cómo está?

How is she?

—Está bien. **Trabajó hasta** tarde en el restaurante. **Volvió** a casa a las 10:00.

*She's fine. **She worked** late in the restaurant. **She returned** home at 10:00.*

> Verbs ending in **-car, -gar,** and **-zar** have a spelling change in the **yo** form of the preterite tense.
>
> **c** changes to **qu**   **g** changes to **gu**   **z** changes to **c**
>
> tocar → to**qué**   llegar → lle**gué**   comenzar → comen**cé**
>
> Observe in the following paragraph the verbs in **bold** that exhibit a spelling change.

---

[1] You will learn the preterite conjugations for stem-changing **-ir** verbs in **Capítulo 7**.

Ayer visité a don Fernando y a doña Olga. Salí de casa con mucha hambre, y tomé el autobús a su casa. **Llegué** a las 2:00 y **almorcé** con su familia. Después, **toqué** la guitarra y **saqué** unas fotos de los hijos de Fernando y Olga. Más tarde, **jugué** a las cartas con toda la familia.

*Yesterday I **visited** don Fernando and doña Olga. I left the house hungry and took the bus to their house. I **arrived** at 2:00 and **had lunch** with the family. Afterward, I **played** the guitar and **took** some photos of Fernando and Olga's kids. Later, I **played** cards with the family.*

Verbs ending in **-ir** and **-er** that have a vowel before the infinitive ending require the following change in the **usted/él/ella** and **ustedes/ellos/ellas** forms of the preterite tense: the **i** between the two vowels changes to **y.**

	creer	leer	oír
Ud., él/ella	creyó	leyó	oyó
Uds., ellos(as)	creyeron	leyeron	oyeron

Observe in the following paragraph the verbs in **bold** that exhibit a spelling change.

Antes de acostarse, Margarita y su esposo Jorge **leyeron** un poco, luego se durmieron. A las 6:00 de la mañana, sonó el despertador y Margarita se despertó para abrir el restaurante. Jorge no **oyó** nada y se levantó una hora después. Cuándo llegó tarde al trabajo, nadie **creyó** su historia.

*Before going to bed, Margarita and her husband Jorge **read** a bit, then they went to sleep. At 6:00 in the morning, the alarm sounded and Margarita woke up to open the restaurant. Jorge didn't **hear** anything and got up an hour later. When he arrived at work late, nobody **believed** his story.*

Uses of the preterite

Spanish speakers use the preterite tense to express the beginning and completion of past actions, conditions, and events. Basically, the preterite is used to tell what did or did not happen or to tell what someone did or did not do.

Observe the use of the preterite in the following paragraph.

Ayer Jorge **se despertó** un poco tarde porque no **oyó** su despertador. Margarita **llamó** a su esposo dos veces y finalmente él **se levantó.** Luego Jorge **se duchó** y **desayunó** con sus dos hijas, Matilde y Elena.

*Yesterday, Jorge **woke up** a little late because he didn't **hear** his alarm clock. Margarita **called** her husband two times and finally **he got up.** Then, Jorge **showered** and **ate breakfast** with his two daughters, Matilde and Elena.*

Some expressions referring to the past:

anoche   *last night*
anteayer   *the day before yesterday*
ayer   *yesterday*
(la semana, el mes, el año) pasado(a)   *last (week, month, year)*

¡A practicar!

Q. CÓMO PREPARAMOS AREPAS Doña Olga explica cómo ella, su esposo Fernando y sus tres hijos, Alberto, Pedro y Óscar, prepararon las arepas ayer. Escribe su historia con la siguiente información.

MODELO: nosotros / entrar / en la cocina / para preparar arepas
Nosotros entramos en la cocina para preparar arepas.

1. mi esposo Fernando / leer / la receta
2. yo / comenzar / a buscar / los ingredientes
3. mi hijo Óscar / mezclar *(to mix)* / la harina de maíz con agua
4. mis hijos Pedro y Alberto / formar / las arepas
5. nosotros / meter *(to put)* / las arepas / en el horno
6. Fernando / limpiar / la cocina
7. yo / sacar / todas las arepas
8. Óscar, Pedro y Alberto / comer / las arepas / rápidamente

R. CÓMO NOS CONOCIMOS Doña Margarita recuerda cuándo conoció a su esposo. Completa las siguientes oraciones con el pretérito.

1. yo / conocer / a Jorge en 1998
2. nosotros / comenzar a / salir inmediatamente
3. él / invitarme / a cenar en un restaurante elegante
4. después, nosotros / ver / la película *Hombres en negro*
5. él / decidir estudiar / en la universidad
6. yo también / tomar / varias clases sobre negocios y culinaria
7. nosotros / casarse / en 2000
8. los padres de Jorge / comprar / un restaurante para nosotros
9. el restaurante / costar / mucho dinero
10. Jorge, Pepe el camarero y yo / abrir / el restaurante en el verano de 2000

S. UN SECRETO Alberto, el hijo mayor de Olga y Fernando, está secretamente enamorado de Matilde, la hija de doña Margarita. Una noche, él va con sus hermanos a la casa de Matilde y le dan una serenata *(serenade)*. Usando los verbos de la lista, completa el siguiente párrafo en que Matilde describe lo que pasó.

creer	oír *(to hear)*	invitar	despertarse
apagar	volver	recibir	acostarse
cerrar	leer	hablar	
llamar	llegar	cantar	

Anoche, yo _____ un poco antes de dormir. A las 11:00, yo _____ la luz y _____. ¡Siempre estoy cansada después de trabajar en el restaurante con mamá! Una hora después, a las 12:00, _____. Mi hermana Elena y yo _____ algo fuera de la casa. Cuando yo _____ a la ventana para mirar, ¡no lo _____! ¡Óscar, Alberto y Pedro! Bueno. La semana pasada, yo _____ una carta de Alberto en que él me _____ de su amor por mí. Y ayer, él me _____ por teléfono y me _____ a cenar con él. ¡Ay, ay ay! ¡Yo no quiero ser la novia de Alberto! Pero anoche, él y sus dos hermanos me _____ una canción de amor. Elena y yo _____ la ventana y _____ a acostarnos. ¡Esos muchachos!

En voz alta

I. LO QUE YO HICE Dile a otro(a) estudiante lo que tú hiciste[1] *(you did)* la semana pasada. A continuación hay varias posibilidades que puedes usar si las necesitas.

MODELO: En casa...
   a. levantarse tarde   *Yo me levanté tarde.*
   b. lavarse el pelo   *Me lavé el pelo.*
   c. limpiar mi dormitorio   *Limpié mi dormitorio.*
   d. cenar con mi familia   *Cené con mi familia.*

1. En el trabajo...
   a. no trabajar mucho   **c.** hablar con mi jefe(a)
   b. recibir un cheque   **d.** conocer a otro(a) empleado(a)
2. En la universidad...
   a. jugar a un deporte   **c.** aprender mucho español
   b. comer en la cafetería   **d.** tomar un examen difícil
3. En el restaurante...
   a. pedir algo para picar   **c.** comer pescado frito
   b. beber agua mineral   **d.** pagar la cuenta

J. AYER YO... ¿Qué comió tu compañero(a) ayer? Pregúntale lo que comió y después, cuéntale lo que tú comiste. Pide muchos detalles —no sólo lo que comió, sino también con quién comió, cuánto, a qué hora, dónde, si lo preparó él/ella, etcétera.

MODELO: el desayuno
   E1: *¿Qué comiste para el desayuno?*
   E2: *Comí cereales con leche.*
   E1: *¿Dónde desayunaste?*
   E2: *Desayuné en casa.*
   E1: *¿Bebiste algo?*
   E2: *Sí, bebí café con leche y jugo de naranja.*

1. el desayuno   **2.** el almuerzo   **3.** la cena

K. ¿QUIÉN COMIÓ CAMARONES? Tienes dos minutos para buscar a alguien de tu clase que haya hecho *(has done)* las siguientes cosas. Después de encontrar a alguien para cada categoría, pídele que firme *(sign)* tu lista. Al final del juego, cuéntales a tus compañeros(as) de clase lo que acabas de aprender.

MODELO: comer camarones ayer
       Tú: *Bonnie, ¿comiste camarones ayer?*
   Bonnie: *Sí, comí camarones ayer.* (Bonnie signs your paper.)
            No, no comí camarones ayer. (Bonnie doesn't sign and you look for someone else.)
    Al final: *Bonnie comió camarones ayer.*

1. comer hamburguesa anteayer
2. oír música venezolana alguna vez
3. leer un libro de recetas la semana pasada
4. tocar la guitarra anoche
5. llegar tarde a clase el mes pasado
6. pagar la cuenta en un restaurante ayer
7. comenzar un libro nuevo la semana pasada
8. preferir comer en casa

Hacer is an irregular verb in the preterite. Its full conjugation will be presented in **Capítulo 7.**

W. LA ÚLTIMA VEZ QUE COMÍ EN UN RESTAURANTE Habla con un(a) compañero(a) de clase sobre la última vez que comiste en un restaurante con tus amigos o con tu familia. Después, pregúntale sobre su última experiencia en un restaurante. Acuérdate de usar la forma **tú.** Piensa en las siguientes preguntas: ¿En qué restaurante comiste? ¿Con quién? ¿Qué pidieron ustedes? ¿Comieron postre? ¿Qué bebieron? ¿Les gustó la comida? ¿Comieron demasiado? ¿Quién pagó la cuenta?

MODELO: *La semana pasada, mis amigos y yo comimos en el restaurante Molina. Yo pedí arepas para picar y después, para el plato principal, pedí calamares fritos. Mi compañera de cuarto comió el pescado del día. Bebimos vino blanco y agua mineral. No comí nada de postre, pero mis amigos tomaron café después de la comida. Nos gustó mucho la comida. Mi mejor amiga pagó la cuenta.*

GRAMÁTICA III: *Superlatives*

English speakers single out someone or something from a group by adding the ending *-est* to an adjective (e.g., *warmest*), or by using the phrases *the most* or *the least* with an adjective (e.g., *the most elegant, the least expensive*). Spanish speakers form superlatives by using a definite article before the person or thing being compared + **más** *(most)* or **menos** *(least)* + an adjective. To introduce the group to which the person or thing is being compared (*the most/least . . . in the class/world/city*, etc.), the preposition **de** + noun is used.

el (sobrino)
la (familia)   **más**
                    +   + *adjective* (+ **de** + *noun*)
los (amigos)   **menos**
las (compañeras)

—Estoy muy feliz.   *I'm very happy.*
—¿Por qué, Margarita?   *Why, Margarita?*
—Porque tengo **la familia más**   *Because I have **the most intelligent***
   inteligente, el esposo más   ***family, the handsomest husband,***
   guapo, los amigos más   ***the most generous friends,** and*
   generosos y **el restaurante**   *the most popular restaurant*
   más popular de Caracas.   *in Caracas.*

Irregular superlatives

el (la, los, las)	mejor(es)	*best*
el (la, los, las)	peor(es)	*worst*
el (la, los, las)	menor(es)	*youngest*
el (la, los, las)	mayor(es)	*oldest*

—¡El Criollito es **el mejor** restaurante   *El Criollito is **the best** restaurant*
   de Caracas!   *in Caracas!*
—Sí. El otro, El Mesón, es **el peor**   *Yes, and the other, El Mesón, is **the***
   restaurante **de** Caracas.   ***worst** restaurant **in** Caracas.*
—Elena es **la menor** de las niñas   *Elena is **the youngest** of Margarita*
   de Margarita y Jorge.   *and Jorge´s girls.*
—Matilde es **la mayor.**   *Matilde is **the oldest.***

¡A practicar!

X. DOS RESTAURANTES Compara El Criollito con otro restaurante de Caracas, El Mesón.

MODELO: En El Criollito, Margarita pone música popular. En El Mesón, el dueño pone música clásica. (moderno)
En El Criollito, Margarita pone la música más moderna. En El Mesón, el dueño pone la música menos moderna.

1. Pepe el camarero, en El Criollito, es muy simpático. El camarero en El Mesón es antipático *(mean).* (simpático)
2. Doña Margarita tiene un menú muy grande con 20 platos principales. El dueño de El Mesón tiene un menú de solamente 14 platos. (grande)
3. El Criollito tiene muchos clientes porque es un restaurante muy popular. El otro restaurante, El Mesón, tiene pocos clientes. (popular)
4. Doña Margarita es una señora de 45 años. El dueño de El Mesón tiene 60 años. (mayor)
5. Las arepas en El Criollito están siempre ricas. Las arepas en El Mesón están horribles. (rico)
6. En tu opinión, ¿qué restaurante es el mejor de los dos? ¿Qué restaurante es el peor?

En voz alta

Y. ¡VAMOS A VOTAR! Usando el superlativo, escribe cuatro oraciones que describan a cuatro estudiantes diferentes de tu clase de español, según las cuatro categorías de la lista. Luego, lee tus frases en voz alta sin decir el nombre de la persona que describes. El resto de la clase tiene que adivinar de quién hablas.

MODELO: *(Janice) es la estudiante más generosa de la clase.*
(Greg) es el estudiante menos tímido de la clase.

> **Categorías de personalidad:**
>
> | más contento(a) | menos perezoso(a) |
> |---|---|
> | menos tímido(a) | el (la) mayor |
> | más generoso(a) | el (la) menor |

Síntesis

¡A ver!

El tema central del **Capítulo 6** es la comida. Pedro, el narrador videográfico de este capítulo, es cocinero de un restaurante famoso en Caracas, la capital de Venezuela. En los segmentos de video que vamos a ver, Pedro nos habla de la importancia que tiene la comida en el mundo hispánico.

ACTIVIDAD 1 Pre-viewing task (Segmento 1 del video)

Paso 1: Mira el primer segmento del video. Es una serie de clips muy cortos sobre algunas de las comidas que tienen su origen en el Nuevo Mundo. En un papel haz una lista de las comidas mencionadas, por ejemplo: **papa** *(potato)*.

Paso 2: Vuelve a mirar el primer segmento. Esta vez apunta cualquier información *(jot down any information)* que oyes o que ves en los clips videográficos sobre las comidas de tu lista.

Paso 3: Comparte tu lista con tu compañero(a) de clase. Explica la información que tienes sobre los alimentos, por ejemplo: **papa—En este país la papa es típica con la hamburguesa.**

ACTIVIDAD 2 Pre-viewing task (Segmento 2 del video)

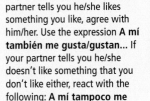

Remember to react appropriately as you create your dialog. If your partner tells you he/she likes something you like, agree with him/her. Use the expression **A mí también me gusta/gustan...** If your partner tells you he/she doesn't like something that you don't like either, react with the following: **A mí tampoco me gusta/gustan...**

Paso 1: ¿Qué es lo que a ti te gusta comer y lo que no te gusta comer? Haz dos listas, una de tus cosas favoritas y la otra de las cosas que no te gusta comer.

Paso 2: Explica a tu compañero(a) de clase las cosas que te gusta comer y las que no te gusta comer. Selecciona el grado de gusto (de muy positivo a muy negativo) de la lista a continuación.

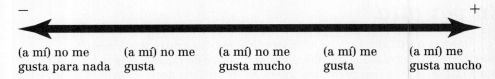

| (a mí) no me gusta para nada | (a mí) no me gusta | (a mí) no me gusta mucho | (a mí) me gusta | (a mí) me gusta mucho |

ACTIVIDAD 3 Viewing task (Segmento 2 del video)

Paso 1: Mira el **Segmento 2 del video** y apunta en la hoja del camarero lo que piden Laura y su amiga para comer en el restaurante Los Arcos. Consulta el siguiente menú para ayudarte. No tienes que saber el significado de todos los platos en el menú.

Paso 2: Apunta en la misma hoja del camarero los precios de cada plato que piden las dos mujeres y luego haz la suma en pesos para cada cliente, y el total de la cuenta.

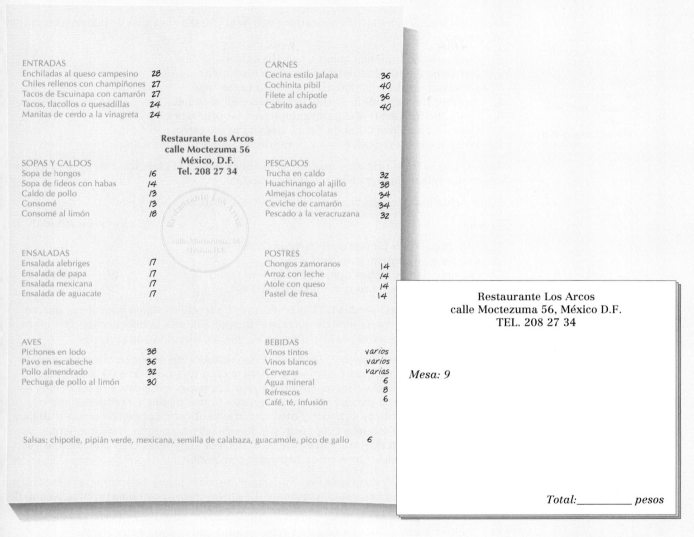

ENTRADAS
Enchiladas al queso campesino 28
Chiles rellenos con champiñones 27
Tacos de Escuínapa con camarón 27
Tacos, tlacollos o quesadillas 24
Manitas de cerdo a la vinagreta 24

CARNES
Cecina estilo Jalapa 36
Cochinita pibil 40
Filete al chipotle 36
Cabrito asado 40

Restaurante Los Arcos
calle Moctezuma 56
México, D.F.
Tel. 208 27 34

SOPAS Y CALDOS
Sopa de hongos 16
Sopa de fideos con habas 14
Caldo de pollo 13
Consomé 13
Consomé al limón 18

PESCADOS
Trucha en caldo 32
Huachinango al ajillo 38
Almejas chocolatas 34
Ceviche de camarón 34
Pescado a la veracruzana 32

ENSALADAS
Ensalada alebriges 17
Ensalada de papa 17
Ensalada mexicana 17
Ensalada de aguacate 17

POSTRES
Chongos zamoranos 14
Arroz con leche 14
Atole con queso 14
Pastel de fresa 14

Restaurante Los Arcos
calle Moctezuma 56, México D.F.
TEL. 208 27 34

Mesa: 9

AVES
Pichones en lodo 38
Pavo en escabeche 36
Pollo almendrado 32
Pechuga de pollo al limón 30

BEBIDAS
Vinos tintos *varios*
Vinos blancos *varios*
Cervezas *varias*
Agua mineral 6
Refrescos 8
Café, té, infusión 6

Salsas: chipotle, pipián verde, mexicana, semilla de calabaza, guacamole, pico de gallo 6

*Total:*_____ *pesos*

ACTIVIDAD 4   Post-viewing task (Segmento 2 del video)

Paso 1: Imagínate que vas a cenar en el mismo restaurante que Laura. ¿Qué pides para comer y para beber? Apunta en un papel lo que quieres pedir (1) de primer plato, (2) de segundo plato, (3) de postre y (4) para beber.

Paso 2: Trabajando con tu compañero(a) de clase, crea un diálogo entre tú y el camarero en el cual él te pregunta lo que quieres comer y beber para la cena.

To attract the waiter's attention you might need the following expressions: **Oiga, por favor,...** ; **Mesero, por favor; Camarero, por favor.**

¡A escribir!

Adding details to a paragraph

In **Capítulo 4**, you learned how to write a topic sentence for a paragraph. The other sentences in the paragraph should contain details that develop the main idea stated in the

Functions: Appreciating food; Stating a preference
Vocabulary: Food; Food: restaurant
Grammar: Verbs: **gustar**

topic sentence. The following procedure will help you develop a well-written paragraph in Spanish:

1. Write a topic sentence about a specific subject.
2. List some details that develop your topic sentence.
3. Cross out any details that are unrelated to the topic.
4. Number the remaining details in a clear, logical order.
5. Write the first draft of a paragraph based on your work.
6. Cross out any ideas that do not contribute to the topic.
7. Write the second draft of your paragraph as clearly as possible.

Paso 1: Lee la frase principal que sigue. Después, indica si cada frase de la lista de detalles está relacionada o no con la frase principal.

Frase principal: Mi restaurante favorito es Chez Claude.

Detalles	¿Frase relacionada?	
El restaurante Chez Claude sirve comida francesa.	Sí	No
Mis amigos y yo comemos en casa a veces.	Sí	No
Chez Claude tiene muchos tipos de refrescos.	Sí	No
Los precios son altos pero la comida es deliciosa.	Sí	No

Paso 2: Lee el párrafo siguiente. Vas a ver que el párrafo contiene unas ideas que no están relacionadas con la idea de la frase principal. Elimina la información que no es importante. Para hacer el párrafo más corto, puedes combinar unas frases.

Mi restaurante favorito es Freddie's. Es un restaurante pequeño que sirve comida norteamericana. Mi madre siempre prepara la cena en casa a las 6:00. En Freddie's me gusta pedir sándwiches de jamón y queso. Las papas fritas siempre están muy ricas. A veces yo pido papas fritas en otros restaurantes también. Freddie's tiene muchos tipos de refrescos, licuados y otras bebidas deliciosas. Las personas que trabajan en el restaurante son muy simpáticas y el servicio es muy bueno. Hay una tienda de ropa muy cerca donde me gusta ir de compras. Por lo general, creo que Freddie's es un restaurante muy interesante. ¡Me gusta comer allí!

Paso 3: ¿Cuál es tu restaurante favorito? Sigue los siete pasos de arriba para escribir un párrafo en español sobre este restaurante. Después, trabaja con un(a) compañero(a) de clase. Uds. deben...

- Eliminar los detalles que no están relacionados con la frase principal.
- Añadir *(Add)* unos detalles, si es necesario.
- Corregir los errores de vocabulario, de gramática o de ortografía *(spelling)*.

¡A conversar!

Con un(a) compañero(a) de clase, imagínense que están en un restaurante en Venezuela. Uno(a) es el (la) cliente y el (la) otro(a) es el (la) camarero(a).

1. Greet the server.
2. The server asks you if you would like something to drink.
3. Say that you're very thirsty. Order something to drink from the menu.
4. The server takes your order and goes to get your drink.
5. Say you're hungry.

CAFÉ SOL

SOPAS		POSTRES	
Consomé	1.300	Quesos variados	1.600
Sopa del día	1.350	Fruta	1.300
Sopa de pescado	1.400	Pastel de chocolate	1.750

PLATOS PRINCIPALES		BEBIDAS	
Pollo de la casa	1.900	Agua mineral	1.250
Pollo al limón	2.200	Vino	1.300
Bistec con papas fritas	2.500	Café	1.200
Hamburguesa Sol	2.100	Té	1.200

6. The server tells you about the house specialty and explains some of the items on the menu to you.

7. Order something to eat from the menu.

8. The server asks how your meal is and asks if you would like coffee or dessert.

9. Order dessert and coffee, if you wish.

¡A leer!

Improving your reading efficiency

Reading efficiently involves a great deal of guessing. By considering several organizational features of a passage, you can often make intelligent guesses about the content of the passage even before you begin reading it. You should use all of the information available to you, including titles, subtitles (if any are present), and pictures, to help you get an idea of the topic of the reading. You should also skim over the passage before reading it in order to get the gist of the reading.

Prereading strategies

Paso 1: Read the *title* of the following poem.
What do you think the main topic of the poem is?

Paso 2: Look at the accompanying *image*.
How does this image complement the title of the poem?
Now guess what the poem is about.

Skimming

Paso 3: Skim the poem to get the gist of it. Then complete the following sentences.

1. El tema principal del poema es...
   a. la cebolla.
   b. el tomate.
   c. la fruta.
   d. la carne.

2. El tomate es...
  a. un alimento sin importancia.
  c. una fruta poco conocida.
  b. una carne muy conocida.
  d. un alimento importante.
3. El tomate y las cebollas se unen con...
  a. la sal y las papas.
  c. la pimienta y el asado.
  b. las papas y el asado.
  d. la pimienta, la sal y el perejil.

Oda al tomate

La calle se llenó de tomates,
mediodía,
verano,
la luz
se parte
en dos mitades (halves)
de tomate,
corre
por las calles
el jugo.
En diciembre
se desata (is untied)
el tomate,
invade
las cocinas,
entra por los almuerzos,
se sienta
reposado (quiet)
en los aparadores (shop windows),
entre los vasos,
las mantequilleras,
los saleros azules.
Tiene
luz propia,
majestad benigna.
Debemos, por desgracia,
asesinarlo:
se hunde (sinks into)
el cuchillo
en su pulpa viviente,
es una roja
víscera,
un sol
fresco,

profundo
inagotable,
llena las ensaladas
de Chile,
se casa alegremente
con la clara cebolla...
y para celebrarlo
se deja
caer
aceite,
hijo
esencial del olivo,
sobre sus hemisferios entreabiertos,
agrega (adds)
la pimienta
su fragrancia,
la sal de su magnetismo:
son las bodas
del día
el perejil (parsley)
levanta
banderines (small flags)
las papas
hierven vigorosamente,
el asado
golpea con su aroma
en la puerta,
¡es hora!
¡vamos!
y sobre la mesa, en la cintura
del verano,
el tomate,
astro de tierra,
estrella

repetida
y fecunda (fruitful),
nos muestra
sus circunvoluciones,
sus canales,
la insigne plentitud
y la abundancia
sin hueso (bone),
sin coraza,
sin escamas ni espinas,
nos entrega
el regalo
de su color fogoso
y la totalidad de su frescura.

Pablo Neruda
(Odas elementales, 1954)

Paso 4: Scan the poem for the information you need to answer the following questions.

1. Tres comidas mencionadas por el autor son _____, _____ y _____.
2. En las ensaladas, el tomate se casa alegremente con _____.
3. El _____ se usa para poder ver la pulpa roja del tomate.
4. El _____ es el hijo esencial del olivo.
5. El tomate nos entrega su color _____ y su _____.

Impresiones personales

Paso 5: ¿Qué impresión tienes de este poema? Explica tu respuesta.

(Creo que el poema es [interesante/aburrido/descriptivo] porque...)

Paso 6: Piensa en tu comida favorita y luego escribe un poema breve (de 15 a 30 palabras) sobre ella.

Oda a _____

Las comidas   *Meals*

el almuerzo   *lunch*

la cena   *dinner, supper*

el desayuno   *breakfast*

Las bebidas   *Beverages*

el agua (f.) mineral con/sin gas   *carbonated/non-carbonated mineral water*

el café   *coffee*
la cerveza   *beer*
el jugo de fruta   *fruit juice*

la leche   *milk*
el refresco   *soft drink*
el té (helado)   *(iced) tea*

el vino (blanco, tinto)   *(white, red) wine*

Los platos principales   *Main dishes*

el bistec   *steak*
los calamares (fritos)   *(fried) squid*
los camarones (fritos)   *(fried) shrimp*
la carne (de res)   *meat (beef)*

la chuleta (de cerdo)   *(pork) chop*
el jamón   *ham*
la langosta   *lobster*
los mariscos   *shellfish, seafood*

el pavo   *turkey*
el pescado   *fish*
el pollo (asado)   *(roast) chicken*

Las frutas y los vegetales   *Fruits and vegetables*

el arroz   *rice*
el champiñón   *mushroom*
la lechuga   *lettuce*

la manzana   *apple*
la naranja   *orange*
las papas (fritas)   *(french fried) potatoes*

las verduras   *vegetables*

Otras comidas   *Other foods*

el huevo duro   *hard-boiled egg*
el pan (tostado)   *bread (toast)*

el queso   *cheese*
la salsa   *sauce*

Los cognados

la banana, la ensalada, la fruta, la hamburguesa, el tomate, el sándwich, la sopa

Los condimentos   *Condiments*

el aceite   *oil*
la mantequilla   *butter*

la pimienta   *pepper*
la sal   *salt*

el vinagre   *vinegar*

Los postres   *Desserts*

el flan (casero)   *(homemade) caramel custard*

el helado   *ice cream*

El restaurante

el (la) camarero(a)   *waiter (waitress)*
la cuenta   *check, bill*

la especialidad de la casa   *house specialty*

el menú   *menu*

Adjetivos

caliente   *hot (temperature)*
fresco(a)   *fresh*

ligero(a)   *light (meal, food)*
pesado(a)   *heavy (meal, food)*

rico(a)   *delicious*

Verbos

almorzar (ue)   *to have (eat) lunch*
cenar   *to have (eat) supper (dinner)*

cocinar   *to cook*
dejar una (buena) propina   *to leave a (good) tip*

desayunar   *to have (eat) breakfast*
desear   *to wish, to want*
pedir (i)   *to order (food)*

picar   *to eat appetizers*
preparar   *to prepare*
recomendar (ie)   *to recommend*

VOCABULARIO ESENCIAL 🎧

Expresiones idiomáticas

¡Buen provecho! *Enjoy your meal!*
¡Cómo no! *Of course!*
Estoy a dieta. *I'm on a diet.*

Estoy satisfecho(a). *I'm satisfied. I'm full.*
La cuenta, por favor. *The check, please.*

No puedo más. *I can't (eat) any more.*
¿Qué te apetece? *What would you like (to eat)?*

¡Salud! *Cheers!*
Te invito. *It's on me (my treat).*
Yo quisiera... *I would like . . .*

Expresiones adverbiales de tiempo

anoche *last night*
anteayer *the day before yesterday*
ayer *yesterday*

(la semana, el mes, el año) pasado(a) *last (week, month, year)*

Superlativos irregulares

el (la, los, las) mejor(es) *best*
el (la, los, las) peor(es) *worst*

el (la, los, las) menor(es) *youngest*

el (la, los, las) mayor(es) *oldest*

PLAZAS

BIENVENIDOS A *PLAZAS*, UNA PUBLICACIÓN QUE DESCRIBE EL PANORAMA DE LOS PAÍSES DE HABLA ESPAÑOLA.

Mi casa es tu casa, y mi palacio es tu palacio

Si buscas un lugar en donde cenar, visita Tasca del Mar

¿Estás enfermo? Consulta con nuestra curandera, doña Esmeralda

Con las cámaras esperando

Cinco hijas y su madre siempre están en su casa

ESPAÑA

Madrid

Andalucía

Granada

Mi casa es tu casa, y mi palacio es tu palacio

Los turistas que visitan España ven una arquitectura bastante diversa. ¿Por qué hay tanta diversidad? En parte es porque la historia de España tiene una rica combinación de varias culturas. Una influencia principal en el sur de España, en la región que se llama Andalucía, es la influencia árabe, por la invasión de los árabes, y la subsiguiente *(subsequent)* ocupación del sur de España, desde el siglo VIII hasta el XV. Los reyes de los diferentes grupos árabes se establecieron en las ciudades andaluzas más grandes. En los reinos *(kingdoms)* regionales, piensa en dónde viven los reyes: ¿en un apartamento? ¿en una casa? ¿en un palacio? ¿en un condominio?

Uno de los palacios más famosos, y el mejor conservado, es la Alhambra, que se encuentra en la ciudad de Granada, el antiguo centro político y aristocrático musulmán en el este de Andalucía. Con la construcción principal del palacio (1333–1391), los visitantes de hoy pueden apreciar esta residencia de la familia real *(royal)*. Las salas enormes con techos altos, los dormitorios y los cuartos de los sirvientes son sólo algunas partes del palacio que hoy se conservan. Además, el clima árido es una consideración en la construcción de estos palacios en el sur de España. Por eso, las fuentes *(fountains)*, los baños, los patios interiores sombreados *(shaded)* y los extensos jardines sirven de ejemplo de cómo los reyes se adaptaron al calor tan intenso de Andalucía. La Alhambra es una verdadera joya *(gem)* de la construcción árabe que muestra la influencia extranjera *(foreign)* en la arquitectura del pasado que podemos apreciar hoy.

¿Similar o *diferente?*

Con la ausencia de reyes en los Estados Unidos, ¿qué tipos de residencias existen para las personas de importancia histórica? ¿Puedes nombrar unos ejemplos?

Busca información sobre la Alhambra en el Internet para comparar su estructura con los ejemplos que acabas de nombrar.

Además de los palacios, encuentra información sobre las otras secciones de importancia histórica alrededor de *(around)* la Alhambra. ¿Existen ejemplos de estas secciones en los Estados Unidos?

Si buscas un lugar en donde cenar, visita Tasca del Mar

Si quieres comer en un restaurante popular y buscas porciones grandes a precios razonables, acabo de encontrar un lugar perfecto en la zona cultural de Caracas. En Tasca del Mar tus amigos y tú pueden seleccionar de una variedad de platos de un menú muy interesante. Sus especialidades son el pescado y los mariscos, pero también sirven unas carnes riquísimas. Para empezar, yo pedí las arepas de queso y mi compañera comió la sopa de langosta, los dos platos con un sabor muy fresco. Después, nosotros pedimos dos selecciones del menú de las especialidades del día: el atún a la parrilla que comí estuvo *(was)* delicioso, y a mi compañera le gustaron mucho los camarones al ajillo. De postre mi compañera y yo comimos un pastel de frutas tropicales.

El restaurante es un lugar alegre, con música en vivo de un guitarrista y un flautista que forman una combinación ecléctica. Las paredes están pintadas a mano con colores brillantes y dan la sensación de un chalet tropical. La comida es tan magnífica como bien presentada y el servicio es tan bueno como en los restaurantes de primera categoría. Tasca del Mar es nuestra primera recomendación para una noche divertida con amigos en un ambiente ameno *(pleasant atmosphere)* que aún *(still)* te deja con suficiente dinero para ir al cine después de comer.

¿Cuál es tu restaurante favorito?

- Llama por teléfono a un(a) amigo(a) e invítalo(la) a cenar contigo en tu restaurante favorito.

- Describe el restaurante y la comida que sirven.

- Dile dónde está y haz los planes para llegar.

- Después de tu visita, prepara una reseña *(review)* como la que acabas de leer sobre Tasca del Mar. Incluye información sobre los platos, el ambiente, los precios y la calidad de la comida.

Caracas

VENEZUELA

¿Estás enfermo?

Consulta con nuestra curandera, doña Esmeralda

Si buscas alternativas en la medicina, mira la lista de doña Esmeralda, una curandera boliviana famosa que lleva tres años en los Estados Unidos y que desea compartir *(to share)* con nosotros sus sugerencias para tres condiciones de salud comunes. Mira la lista para ver cómo doña Esmeralda puede ayudarte. Las recomendaciones de doña Esmeralda sólo curan las enfermedades si los enfermos tienen una fe *(faith)* implícita en las capacidades de los curanderos.[1]

Enfermedad	Recomendaciones de doña Esmeralda
Alergias a los perros o gatos	Baña el animal en un té de rosas caliente y luego sécalo con plumas *(feathers)* de pollo por 30 minutos.
Dolor de cabeza	Pon tu fruta favorita en el horno microondas por 15 segundos. (Lávala primero.) Luego, córtala en dos pedazos *(pieces)*. Pon los pedazos al lado de las orejas y di «Adiós dolor». Si tienes dolor de estómago, puedes usar un vegetal en vez de *(instead of)* una fruta.
Resfriado	Para esta condición no hay cura, sólo alivio de tus síntomas. Acuéstate en el sofá. Cierra los ojos y piensa en unas vacaciones ideales. Luego, levanta los pies al aire y vas a sentir un poco de alivio porque acabas de soltar *(release)* un poco de la energía negativa que acompaña el resfriado.

La Paz

BOLIVIA

Sucre

- ¿Recomiendan unos tratamientos especiales los miembros de tu familia para ciertas enfermedades? ¿Qué recomiendan y quién los recomienda?

- ¿Qué le recomiendas a una persona con náuseas?

- ¿Te gustaría *(Would you like)* visitar a un(a) curandero(a)? ¿Por qué?

- ¿Por qué cree la gente en las capacidades de los curanderos?

[1] En casos de enfermedades graves, o de enfemedades que duran *(last)* más de cuatro días, los editores de *Plazas* recomiendan una consulta con tu médico.

Con las cámaras esperando

Ayer celebramos el primer día de actividades del concurso de Miss Universo. ¿Saben Uds., queridos lectores de **Plazas,** que en los últimos 30 años Miss Venezuela ha ganado *(has won)* el concurso cuatro veces? Representa el número más alto de cualquier otro país. Las candidatas de Venezuela ganaron en 1979, 1981, 1986 y 1996. Por eso, nuestras cámaras captaron ayer la imagen de una de las mujeres más bonitas del mundo. Vamos a ver las actividades de Miss Venezuela de este año durante su primer día con las demás *(other)* candidatas.

Claudia Moreno, la candidata que representa Venezuela este año, se levantó a las 6:00 de la mañana para comenzar su día ocupado. Se arregló para la primera actividad del día, un desayuno con todas las chicas del concurso. Primero se cepilló los dientes. Entonces, se duchó, se secó y se arregló el pelo. Luego se maquilló porque todas las chicas del concurso saben que hay cámaras por todas partes. Decidió ponerse ropa casual, porque iba *(she was going)* a esperar hasta por la noche para ponerse su ropa más elegante. Cuando estaba preparada, se miró al espejo y bajó *(went down)* al comedor principal del hotel. ¡Cuánta gente estaba *(was)* allí, esperando a ver a su chica favorita y tomar unas fotos o pedir su autógrafo! El concurso será *(will be)* televisado el domingo por la noche. ¿Va a ganar otra Miss Venezuela?

- Según las fotos, ¿tiene Claudia buenas probabilidades de ganar el título de Miss Universo?

- ¿Por qué crees que las señoritas de Venezuela ganan frecuentemente este concurso?

- ¿Cuál es tu opinión de estos concursos?

- ¿Vas a ver el programa el domingo?

- Mira la rutina de Claudia. ¿Cómo es similar a tu rutina? ¿Cómo es diferente?

Cinco hijas y su madre que siempre están en su casa

Uno de los más conocidos poetas y dramaturgos españoles del siglo XX es Federico García Lorca (1898–1936). Estudió en Granada y en Madrid. Viajó por toda España, por los Estados Unidos y la América del Sur. Es autor de numerosos poemas y obras teatrales, famosos por su lirismo y su preocupación *(concern)* por la muerte y por el conflicto humano.

Uno de los dramas más populares, su última creación dramática, se llama *La casa de Bernarda Alba*. Se trata de *(It's about)* de una viuda y sus hijas, y capta la esencia de la vida aislada y solitaria de esta familia, bajo el estricto control de la madre, Bernarda Alba. Lorca describe con sencillez *(simplicity)* el escenario *(stage)* de los tres actos.

La casa de Bernarda Alba

Acto primero Habitación blanquísima del interior de la casa de Bernarda. Muros (Paredes) gruesos. Puertas en arco con cortinas de yute. Sillas de anea. Cuadros con paisajes *(landscapes)* inverosímiles de ninfas o reyes de leyenda. Es verano. Un gran silencio umbroso *(shadowed)* se extiende por la escena. Al levantarse el telón *(curtain)*, está la escena sola.

Acto segundo Habitación blanca del interior de la casa de Bernarda. Las puertas de la izquierda dan a los dormitorios. Las hijas de Bernarda están sentadas en sillas bajas cosiendo *(sewing)*.

Acto tercero Cuatro paredes blancas ligeramente *(slightly)* azuladas del patio interior de la casa de Bernarda. Es de noche. El decorado ha de ser *(should be)* una perfecta simplicidad. Las puertas iluminadas por la luz de los interiores dan un tenue fulgor (esplendor delicado) a la escena. En el centro, una mesa con un quinqué *(oil lamp)*, donde están comiendo Bernarda y sus hijas. La Poncia las sirve. … Al levantarse el telón hay un gran silencio, interrumpido por el ruido de los platos y los cubiertos.

● ¿Qué tipo de ambiente *(atmosphere)* crea Lorca con las introducciones a los actos? ● ¿Parece auténtico este ambiente? ● ¿Cuál es la importancia de la luz y de los colores para este drama? ¿Por qué crees que Lorca los menciona? ● ¿A qué se refiere la diferencia entre las referencias a «blanquísimo», «blanco» y «blanco ligeramente azulado»? ● La acción se enfoca *(focuses)* en el diálogo en la casa. ¿De qué piensas que hablan las hijas?

De compras: Argentina

Communicative goals

In this chapter you will learn how to . . .

- Talk about shopping for clothing
- Make selections and talk about sizes and other preferences while shopping
- Make emphatic statements about possession
- Talk about past events with common irregular and stem-changing verbs
- Talk about elapsed time since an event took place in the past
- Simplify expressions using direct object pronouns
- Describe ongoing or habitual actions in the past

Grammar

- Stressed possessive adjectives and pronouns
- Preterite of irregular and stem-changing verbs
- The verb form **hace** + time (ago)
- Direct object pronouns
- Imperfect of regular and irregular verbs

Cultural information

- Shopping in Buenos Aires
- Tango

La Avenida 9 de Julio y el Obelisco, Buenos Aires, Argentina.

LA ROPA DE ÚLTIMA MODA EN BUENOS AIRES In this section you will learn how to talk about clothing and related accessories by looking at pages from a fashion magazine. What kinds of clothing are fashionable for people today? Do you think fashions in Spanish-speaking countries are ahead of or behind styles currently popular in the United States?

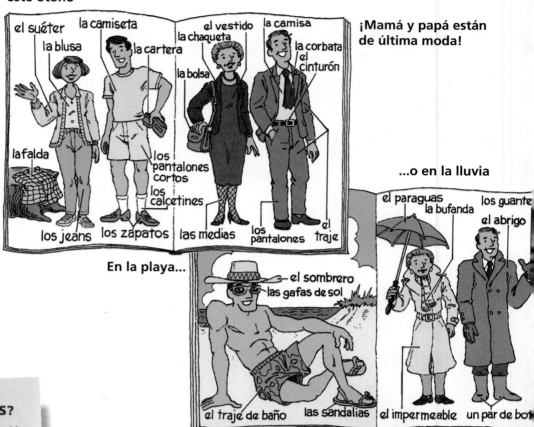

Para chicas y chicos este otoño

el suéter · la camiseta · la blusa · la cartera · la falda · los pantalones cortos · los calcetines · los jeans · los zapatos · el vestido · la chaqueta · la bolsa · las medias · la camisa · la corbata · el cinturón · los pantalones · el traje

¡Mamá y papá están de última moda!

...o en la lluvia

el paraguas · la bufanda · los guantes · el abrigo · el impermeable · un par de botas

En la playa...

el sombrero · las gafas de sol · el traje de baño · las sandalias

Estilos y telas   *Styles and fabrics*

de cuadros   *plaid*
de lunares   *polka-dotted*
de rayas   *striped*
es de...
   algodón   *cotton*
   cuero   *leather*
   lana   *wool*
   seda   *silk*

¡A practicar!

A. **¿PARA HOMBRES O MUJERES?** Decide si los siguientes artículos se asocian más con los hombres, las mujeres o con ambos *(both)*. Luego, trata de encontrar una persona en la clase que lleve los mismos artículos de ropa.

MODELO: la bufanda
Es para los hombres y las mujeres. Soledad lleva una bufanda.

1. la blusa
2. la camisa
3. las botas
4. los pantalones de lana

5. la mini-falda
6. los guantes
7. los calcetines
8. las medias

B. **ASOCIACIONES** ¿Cuál es la palabra que no pertenece al grupo?

1. la cartera, la bolsa, el paraguas, el abrigo
2. la chaqueta, los pantalones cortos, la camiseta, el suéter
3. el sombrero, las medias, los zapatos, las sandalias
4. el traje, el vestido, el cinturón, la corbata
5. los guantes, el traje de baño, el impermeable, el abrigo

En voz alta

C. **TUS PREFERENCIAS** Con un(a) compañero(a) de clase, habla de tus preferencias. Después de contestar sus preguntas, pregúntale a él/ella las suyas.

MODELO: botas moradas de cuero / zapatos de tenis
E1: *¿Cuál prefieres tú, unas botas moradas de cuero o unos zapatos de tenis?*
E2: *Hmmm, yo prefiero unas botas moradas. No me gustan mucho los zapatos de tenis. ¿Y tú?*

1. bufanda de cuadros / bufanda de lana
2. sombrero de vaquero / gorra de béisbol
3. mini-falda / falda larga
4. guantes de seda / guantes de algodón
5. abrigo de lana / chaqueta de esquiar
6. pantalones de cuero / jeans
7. traje o vestido formal / ropa cómoda
8. pantalones cortos / pantalones largos

D. **LA ROPA Y EL CLIMA** Hazle estas preguntas a otro(a) estudiante sobre qué ropa se necesita para las siguientes situaciones.

1. Es octubre, hace sol y no hace viento. Tú y dos amigos quieren montar en bicicleta en el parque. ¿Qué ropa van a ponerse?
2. Tú y tu mejor amigo(a) piensan ir de vacaciones a Mar del Plata[1] por dos semanas en enero cuando hace buen tiempo allí. ¿Qué ropa van a llevar?
3. Una amiga te invita a esquiar en Bariloche[2] por cinco días. Tú aceptas la invitación y ahora tienes que decidir qué ropa vas a llevar.

---

[1] Mar del Plata is a beachside resort about 250 miles south of Buenos Aires. It is one of Argentina's largest tourist attractions and receives over 6 million visitors each year.
[2] San Carlos de Bariloche is known as the **Suiza de las Américas** *(Switzerland of the Americas)* as it is a mountain town rich with European influences and winter attractions, especially skiing.

E. **ESTOY PENSANDO EN UNA PERSONA** Un(a) estudiante va a pensar en otro(a) estudiante sin revelar quién es. Los otros estudiantes tienen que averiguar *(to find out)* la identidad de la persona haciendo preguntas de tipo **sí** o **no.**

MODELO: E1: *¿Lleva esta persona botas de cuero?*
　　　　　 E2: *No, no lleva botas de cuero.*
　　　　　 E3: *¿Lleva esta persona zapatos de tenis?*
　　　　　 E2: *Sí, esta persona lleva zapatos de tenis.*
　　　　　 E3: *¿Es Raymond?*
　　　　　 E2: *Sí, es él.*

EN CONTEXTO

Hoy es sábado, el 18 de diciembre. Julio y Silvia Sepúlveda y su hijo están en un almacén (tienda) en la calle Florida[1] en Buenos Aires. Silvia está probándose *(trying on)* un vestido blanco que quiere llevar a una fiesta que van a dar la semana que viene. Julio está esperándola con su hijo, Juan Carlos.

SILVIA: ¿Qué te parece este vestido, Julio? ¿Cómo me queda? *(How does it fit me?)*

JULIO: ¡Me gusta mucho! Te queda muy bien. Estás muy elegante.

SILVIA: Gracias. Me gusta este color porque va bien con las joyas *(jewelry)* que me diste *(you gave me)* para mi cumpleaños. Creo que el vestido va a ser perfecto para nuestra fiesta, ¿verdad?

JULIO: ¡Claro que sí! ¿Recuerdas la fiesta estupenda que dieron *(gave)* Jorge y Hortensia el año pasado?

SILVIA: Nunca voy a olvidarla. ¡Cómo nos divertimos!, ¿no? Comimos tantas cosas ricas y conocimos a mucha gente.

JULIO: Sí, sí. La fiesta fue *(was)* fabulosa. Bueno, ahora voy a pagar el vestido con mi tarjeta de crédito. ¿Cuánto cuesta, Silvia?

SILVIA: Menos de 100 pesos. Es un buen precio, ¿no crees, Julio?

JULIO: Pues... creo que sí. Oye, Silvia, tenemos que volver a la zapatería *(shoe store)* para cambiar estos zapatos que le compramos a Juan Carlos la semana pasada. Le quedan un poco grandes.

SILVIA: Bueno. Y después vamos a casa porque Juan Carlos tiene hambre y estoy cansada de tanta actividad.

> **¿NOS ENTENDEMOS?**
>
> In Spanish the preposition *for* is often included in the verb itself. Silvia, for example, **paga el vestido** *(pays **for** the dress)*. Other verbs that function like this are **buscar** *(to look **for**)*, **pedir** *(to ask **for**)*, and **esperar** *(to wait **for**)*.

F. **¿COMPRENDISTE?** Contesta las siguientes preguntas a base del diálogo.

1. ¿Dónde están los Sepúlveda en este momento?
2. ¿Qué están haciendo allí?
3. Y después, ¿qué van a hacer?
4. Silvia (compró/recibió/pagó) unas joyas.
5. Su vestido es (blanco/verde/rojo/negro).
6. La zapatería es un tipo de (tienda/comida/ropa).
7. La fiesta va a ser en la casa de los (Reynosa/Sepúlveda).
8. Los zapatos de Juan Carlos son relativamente (viejos/nuevos).

---

[1] **La calle Florida** is a pedestrian-only street that features many boutiques and shops.

ENCUENTRO *cultural*

De compras en Buenos Aires

Éstas son unas palabras nuevas para la lectura:

bullicioso(a) *busy*
las antigüedades *antiques*
la artesanía *handicrafts*
lujoso(a) *luxurious*

Para pensar: En tu ciudad, ¿hay barrios conocidos por productos especiales? ¿Cuáles son? ¿Qué hay en estos barrios? ¿Hay ferias de artesanía o de arte de vez en cuando? ¿Vas tú a veces a estas ferias?

Con casi 13 millones de habitantes, Buenos Aires es una gran metrópolis y una de las mayores ciudades en el mundo. También es la ciudad más elegante y **bulliciosa** en Sudamérica y es, hasta cierto punto, la esencia de la variedad de lo argentino. Entre la construcción moderna y una actividad dinámica, hay viejas tradiciones. Uno se fascina por la atmósfera, la personalidad individual de cada barrio, la cordialidad de la gente y la gran selección de su cultura y las oportunidades de comercio.

En los barrios de San Telmo y Recoleta, hay **antigüedades** a mejores precios que en los Estados Unidos o Europa. Hay objetos de **artesanía** de todo el país y especialmente de la Pampa hay cuero, abrigos de piel y ropa. Hay mercados como la Feria de San Pedro Telmo, que es la más popular; también hay ferias los sábados, domingos y días festivos en el parque Lezama y en la Plaza Intendente Alvear.

En la calle Florida y la avenida Santa Fe siempre hay mucha gente de compras. La mayoría de las boutiques **lujosas** están en el barrio de la Recoleta. Hay también otras zonas comerciales sobre las avenidas Cabildo, Mitre y Avellaneda. Numerosas tiendas de barrio tienen telas y ropa a buen precio.

G. **PREGUNTAS** Contesta las siguientes preguntas a base de la lectura.

1. ¿Cómo es la ciudad de Buenos Aires?
2. ¿Qué se puede comprar a mejores precios en Buenos Aires que en los Estados Unidos o Europa?
3. ¿Dónde se encuentra la mayoría de las boutiques lujosas?

ASÍ SE DICE: *Making emphatic statements about possession*

Possessives are used to express ownership. In **Capítulo 2** you learned how to indicate possession by using **de** (El **vestido es** *de* **Silvia.**) and by using unstressed possessive adjectives: **mi(s), tu(s), su(s), nuestro(a)(s), vuestro(a)(s), su(s).** In English, we place emphasis on the possessive by using intonation *(This is **my***

dress.) or by using the form *of mine, of his, of hers,* etc. In Spanish, emphasis is placed on the possessive by using the stressed forms, identified below:

mío(a)(s)	*my, (of) mine*
tuyo(a)(s)	*your, (of) yours*
suyo(a)(s)	*your, of yours; his, (of) his; her, (of) hers, its*
nuestro(a)(s)	*our, (of) ours*
vuestro(a)(s)	*your, (of) yours*
suyo(a)(s)	*your, (of) yours; their, (of) theirs; his (of) his; her (of) hers*

The stressed possessive adjective must follow the noun.

Unstressed:	Éstos son mis guantes.	*These are my gloves.*
Stressed:	Estos guantes son **míos.**	*These are **my** gloves.*
		*These gloves are **mine.***

Unstressed:	Es su blusa.	*It's her blouse.*
Stressed:	Es una blusa **suya.**	*It's **her** blouse.*
		*It's a blouse **of hers.***

The stressed possessives often function as pronouns, substituting for the omitted noun. When used as a pronoun, stressed possessive adjectives are preceded by a definite or indefinite article.

Silvia no tiene chaqueta.	*Silvia doesn't have a jacket.*
Le doy **la mía.**	*I'll give her **mine.***

Mi camiseta está sucia.	*My shirt is dirty.*
Préstame **una tuya.**	*Lend me one **of yours.***

¡A practicar!

H. ¿A QUIÉN LE CORRESPONDE? Llena los espacios con la forma correcta del adjetivo posesivo.

MODELO: Es mi falda. Es *mía.*

1. Son los zapatos de Tamara. Son _____.
2. Es la corbata de Sebastián. Es _____.
3. Son tus pantalones. Son _____.
4. Es mi chaqueta. Es _____.
5. Son las sandalias de Mauricio. Son _____.
6. Son nuestros trajes. Son _____.

I.   CONFUSIÓN EN LA LAVANDERÍA Dos chicas acaban de lavar la ropa y tienen que separar las prendas *(articles)* de ropa. Utiliza la forma apropiada del adjetivo posesivo o pronombre posesivo enfático entre paréntesis.

—Esos pantalones no son _____ *(mine);* son _____ *(yours).*
—¡Imposible! Son muy grandes. Son de Mary. Son _____ *(hers).*
—Y esa camiseta, ¿también es _____ *(hers)?* No, esa camiseta es _____ *(mine).*
—¡Ay! Me olvidé de separar estos jeans de mi blusa blanca. ¡Mira la blusa _____ *(mine)!*
—No importa. Te presto la _____ *(mine)* para la fiesta esta noche.

En voz alta

J. **¿DE QUIÉN SON... ?** Con un(a) compañero(a) de clase, contesten las siguientes preguntas para decir de quién son estas cosas.

MODELO: E1: ¿Éstos son mis guantes?
E2: *Sí, son los tuyos.*

1. ¿Éstas son mis botas?
2. ¿Éstas son nuestras camisas?
3. ¿Éstos son nuestros suéteres?
4. ¿Éstos son sus trajes de baño (de ellos)?
5. ¿Éstas son sus gafas de sol (de Uds.)?
6. ¿Ésta es mi blusa?
7. ¿Éste es tu cinturón?
8. ¿Éste es su sombrero (de él)?

K. **¿ES TUYA?** Usando el vocabulario que ya sabes de este capítulo, haz ocho preguntas a dos compañeros(as) de clase sobre las prendas de ropa que encuentras en la clase.

MODELO: E1: *Jason, ese abrigo, ¿es tuyo?*
E2: *No es mío. Es de mi compañero de cuarto. Es un abrigo suyo.*

GRAMÁTICA I: *Irregular preterite verbs*

In this section you will learn how to express past conditions or talk about past events with common irregular verbs and with stem-changing verbs.

> As you know, Spanish speakers use the preterite tense to express the beginning and ending/completion of past actions, conditions, and events. Some Spanish verbs have irregular verb stems in the preterite. Their endings have no accent marks, unlike regular preterite verbs.

dar:	di	diste	dio	dimos	disteis	dieron
hacer:	hice	hiciste	hizo[1]	hicimos	hicisteis	hicieron
poder:	pude	pudiste	pudo	pudimos	pudisteis	pudieron
poner:	puse	pusiste	puso	pusimos	pusisteis	pusieron
saber:	supe	supiste	supo	supimos	supisteis	supieron
querer:	quise	quisiste	quiso	quisimos	quisisteis	quisieron
venir:	vine	viniste	vino	vinimos	vinisteis	vinieron
estar:	estuve	estuviste	estuvo	estuvimos	estuvisteis	estuvieron[2]
tener:	tuve	tuviste	tuvo	tuvimos	tuvisteis	tuvieron
decir:	dije	dijiste	dijo	dijimos	dijisteis	dijeron[3]
traer:	traje	trajiste	trajo	trajimos	trajisteis	trajeron
ser/ir:[4]	fui	fuiste	fue	fuimos	fuisteis	fueron

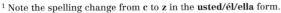

[1] Note the spelling change from **c** to **z** in the **usted/él/ella** form.
[2] **Andar** also follows this pattern: **anduve, anduviste, anduvo, anduvimos, anduvisteis, anduvieron.**
[3] Note that both the preterite stems of **decir** and **traer** end in **-j.** With these two verbs, the **-i** is dropped in the **ustedes/ellos/ellas** form to become **dijeron** and **trajeron,** respectively.
[4] Note that the preterite forms for **ir** and **ser** are identical; context clarifies their meaning in a sentence.

Note that **poder, poner, saber, querer, venir, estar,** and **tener** share the same endings:

pud-
pus-
sup-
quis-
vin-
estuv-
tuv-

-e
-iste
-o
-imos
-isteis
-ieron

—Trabajé en Macy's por un día. **Fui** dependiente.	I worked at Macy's for one day. **I was** a salesclerk.
—¿Cómo? ¿Qué pasó?	Huh? What happened?
—No me gustó, pero **pude** comprar unas medias a un precio reducido.	I didn't like it, but **I was able** to buy some stockings at a reduced price.

Since the preterite tense is used to express the beginning or the completion of past actions, conditions, and events, it takes on a special meaning with some of the verbs that convey states or conditions. The preterite forms of **poder, saber, querer,** and **tener que** are translated into English as the following:[1]

pude	I could (and did)	**no pude**	I (tried and) could not
supe	I found out	**no supe**	I never knew
tuve que	I had to (and did)	**no tuve que**	I didn't have to (and didn't)
quise	I wanted to (and did)	**no quise**	I refused to

—Fui a cambiar estos zapatos, pero **no pude.**	I went to exchange these shoes, but **I couldn't** (didn't succeed).
—¿Qué pasó, Silvia?	What happened, Silvia?
—El dependiente **no pudo** cambiarlos.	The salesclerk **couldn't** exchange them.
—Pero ¿por qué?	But why?
—Porque **supo** que los compré en liquidación.	Because he **found out** I bought them on clearance.

The preterite of **hay** is **hubo.**

—**Hubo** un robo hoy en esta tienda.	**There was** a robbery today in this store.
—¿Qué pasó?	What happened?
—No sé, pero **hubo** policías investigando toda la mañana.	I don't know, but **there were** police officers investigating all morning.

---

[1] The underlying principle of the preterite tense is to express the completion or the beginning of past actions, conditions, and events. This principle governs the verbs **poder, saber, querer,** and **conocer** just as it governs all other Spanish verbs.

¡A practicar!

L. **CONFESIONES DE UNA ESPOSA** Silvia fue de compras un sábado con su amiga sin avisar *(without telling)* a su esposo Julio. Conjuga los verbos entre paréntesis para completar su historia.

1. Silvia _____ (**levantarse**) temprano.
2. Ella le _____ (**decir**) a su esposo que iba a visitar *(was going to visit)* a una amiga.
3. Silvia y su amiga Andrea _____ (**ir**) a la calle Florida.
4. Silvia _____ (**traer**) las tarjetas de crédito de su esposo a las tiendas.
5. Las dos amigas _____ (**entrar**) en la tienda más lujosa de Buenos Aires.
6. Ellas _____ (**saber**) en seguida que todas las prendas estaban rebajadas.
7. Las dos _____ (**ponerse**) muy felices.
8. Las dependientes _____ (**estar**) muy simpáticas con ellas.
9. Con las tarjetas de crédito de su marido, Silvia _____ (**poder**) comprar mucha ropa.
10. Silvia _____ (**tener que**) confesar la verdad a su esposo.
11. Cuando su marido _____ (**saber**) lo que _____ (**hacer**), él _____ (**ponerse**) furioso.

M. **¡POBRE DE JULIO!** Julio, el esposo de Silvia, supo de las compras de su esposa aquella misma noche. Él nos cuenta cómo lo supo y cómo se sintió después de saberlo. Completa los siguientes párrafos con formas apropiadas del pretérito de los infinitivos.

Ayer por la noche yo _____ (**saber**) que mi esposa Silvia _____ (**ir**) de compras con su amiga Andrea. Por la mañana, ella no me _____ (**decir**) nada de las compras.

Ella _____ (**salir**) a las 9:00 de la mañana. Primero, ella y Andrea _____ (**ir**) a la calle Florida donde las dos _____ (**comprar**) zapatos nuevos. Después, ellas _____ (**tomar**) un café en la Recoleta. En la Recoleta, ellas _____ (**entrar**) en muchas tiendas muy caras y _____ (**encontrar**) vestidos nuevos y regalos para sus familias. Lo peor es que Silvia _____ (**usar**) nuestra tarjeta de crédito para esas compras. Cuando ella _____ (**venir**) a casa anoche, me _____ (**confesar**) la verdad. «Lo siento, Julio, pero ¡Andrea y yo _____ (**encontrar**) unas rebajas fantásticas en la Recoleta, y no _____ (**poder**) resistir!»

Primero, yo _____ (**estar**) muy enojado con ella. Pero después, ella me _____ (**hacer**) un regalo muy bonito— ¡una cartera de cuero! Yo le _____ (**dar**) un beso muy fuerte. Nosotros _____ (**tener**) una cena deliciosa de pizza a la piedra[1] con nuestro hijo, Juan Carlos. La noche _____ (**ser**) muy buena. Todos _____ (**acostarse**) contentos a las 10:00 de la noche.

En voz alta

N. **RECUERDOS DE LAS COMPRAS** Forma cinco oraciones escogiendo de los siguientes elementos para describir un viaje a un centro comercial. Debes conjugar todos los verbos en el pretérito.

---

[1] **Pizza a la piedra** is a very popular dish in Buenos Aires. The pizza is cooked with the crust directly on a stone surface over a wood fire, which makes the crust have a more crispy consistency than when baked on a pan. A famous **pizzería** in the microcenter of Buenos Aires is called **Los Inmortales**.

MODELO: *Mi papá estuvo enojado porque yo usé su tarjeta de crédito.*

mis amigos y yo	ir	un gran centro comercial
mi papá	comprar	una ganga
yo	haber	unos regalos
tú	traer	unas rebajas *(sales)*
nosotros	saber	un traje o un vestido nuevo
ellos	ponerse	tarjeta de crédito
	usar	algo interesante
	estar enojado(a)	un robo
	poder	

O. **ENTREVISTA: UNA FIESTA ESTUPENDA** Trabajando con un(a) compañero(a) de clase, forma preguntas con los verbos entre paréntesis para hacerle preguntas a la otra persona sobre varias detalles de una fiesta especial.

MODELO: cuándo (ir)
E1: *¿Cuándo fuiste a una fiesta estupenda?*
E2: *Fui el fin de semana pasado.*

1. tipo de celebración (ser) (fiesta de cumpleaños, etc.)
2. dónde (ser)
3. ropa (vestirse)
4. hora de la fiesta (comenzar)
5. tu llegada (llegar)
6. cuántos invitados (estar)
7. regalos (llevar)
8. nuevos amigos (conocer)
9. actividades (hacer)
10. una sorpresa (haber)

P. **DE COMPRAS** Descríbele a un(a) compañero(a) de clase una experiencia que ocurrió cuando fuiste a un centro comercial. Considera las siguientes preguntas en tu historia.

- ¿Adónde y con quién fuiste?
- ¿Llevaste las tarjetas de crédito?
- ¿Qué compraste?
- ¿Por qué compraste eso?
- ¿Cuánto costó (costaron)?
- ¿Pudiste encontrar alguna ganga *(bargain)*?

- ¿Hiciste algún regalo con lo que compraste?
- ¿Qué más hiciste allí?
- ¿Estuviste contento(a) con tus compras?
- ¿Dijiste algo a tus padres de tus compras? ¿a tu novio(a) o esposo(a)?

VOCABULARIO: *De compras*

EN LAS TIENDAS DE LA RECOLETA[1] In this section you will practice shopping vocabulary and expressions by learning more about one of the most famous shopping areas in Buenos Aires.

---

[1] In Buenos Aires the most luxurious boutiques can be found in the Recoleta neighborhood. Other popular shopping areas in Buenos Aires are the **calle Florida, Alto Palermo,** and **Galerías Pacífico.** The **avenida Santa Fe** also offers boutiques with very elegant clothing and accessories.

el cheque   *check*
el (la) dependiente   *salesclerk*
el descuento   *discount*
el efectivo   *cash*
la liquidación   *sale (Lat. Am.),*
   reduction (in price)

el número   *shoe size*
el por ciento   *percent*
la rebaja   *sale (Spain), reduction (in price)*
la talla   *size (clothing)*
la tarjeta de crédito   *credit card*

Verbos

cambiar   *to change*
costar (ue)   *to cost*
gastar   *to spend (money)*
hacer juego con   *to match*
llevar   *to wear; to carry*
mostrar (ue)   *to show*

pagar   *to pay for*
ponerse   *to put on*
probarse (ue)   *to try on*
quedarle (a uno)   *to fit (someone)*
rebajar   *to reduce (in price)*
usar   *to wear; to use*

Adjetivos

barato(a)   *inexpensive, cheap*
caro(a)   *expensive*

grande   *big*
pequeño(a)   *small*

Expresiones idiomáticas

¿Cómo me queda?   *How does it look?*
¿Cuánto le debo?   *How much do I owe you?*
¡Es una ganga!   *It's a bargain!*

¡Está de última moda!   *It's the latest style!*
¡Me quedan muy pequeños!   *They're too small!*

---

[1] Sizes in European and in some Latin American countries run on an entirely different scale. In this case a 36 would be equivalent to a woman's size 8.

¡A practicar!

Q. **¡ES UNA GANGA!** A Silvia le fue muy bien en las tiendas de la Recoleta. Termina el siguiente párrafo con las palabras de la lista siguiente.

hace juego	rebajas	probarse
por ciento	queda	de última moda
descuentos	talla	cara

Cuando Silvia vio unas _____ en su tienda favorita, no pudo resistir y entró. ¡Había *(There were)* _____ de hasta el 20 _____! Silvia decidió _____ una blusa que estaba _____.

La dependiente le dijo «Es su _____, señora. La blusa le _____ divinamente. Además, la blusa _____ con los patalones que lleva.» «Me gusta mucho», dijo Silvia. «¿Es muy _____?»

cuánto le debo	rebajamos	gastar
efectivo	cuesta	estilos
tarjeta de crédito		

La dependiente le respondió, «No. Hoy nosotros _____ todas las prendas que ve en esta sección. La blusa le _____ treinta pesos. Tenemos otros _____, pero son más caros.» Entonces Silvia le dijo, «No puedo _____ más de 30 pesos. Voy a llevar la blusa.» «¿Algo más?», le preguntó la dependiente. «No», dijo Silvia. «¿_____ por la blusa?» La dependiente pensó un segundo y luego añadió, «Si usted paga en _____, le puedo bajar el precio un poquito más.» «Lo siento», dijo Silvia. «Creo que tengo que pagar con _____. No tengo suficiente efectivo.»

En voz alta

R. **¡ME ENCANTA ESTA CHAQUETA ANARANJADA!** Estás de compras con Rolanda, una persona de muy mal gusto. Ella te sugiere muchas cosas, y tú le tienes que decir (¡sin insultarla!) que no te gustan. Usa excusas como **es demasiado caro(a), me queda grande/chico/mal, no es mi color, no está de moda, no hace juego con mi...** ¡Trata de usar una excusa diferente cada vez! Tu compañero(a) toma el papel de Rolanda.

MODELO: una chaqueta anaranjada
            Rolanda: *¿Por qué no compras esta chaqueta anaranjada?*
            Tú: *Bueno, realmente no es mi color.*

1. un bikini de lunares talla 1
2. unas gafas de sol rojas
3. unos zapatos verdes
4. una corbata amarilla brillante
5. un traje morado de poliéster talla 60
6. una camisa roja y amarilla
7. unas medias de rayas
8. un sombrero de cowboy
9. una minifalda muy corta
10. unas botas de piel de cocodrilo

LAS TALLAS DE ROPA

DAMAS[1]

Vestidos / Trajes

Norteamericano	6	8	10	12	14	16	18	20
Argentino	34	36	38	40	42	44	46	48

Calcetines / Pantimedias

Norteamericano	8	8½	9	9½	10	10½
Argentino	0	1	2	3	4	5

Zapatos

Norteamericano	6	6½	7	8	8½	9
Argentino	36	37	38	38½	39	40

CABALLEROS

Trajes / Abrigos

Norteamericano	36	38	40	42	44	46
Argentino	46	48	50	52	54	56

Camisas

Norteamericano	14	14½	15	15½	16	16½	17	17½	18
Argentino	36	37	38	39	41	42	43	44	45

Zapatos

Norteamericano	5	6	7	8	8½	9	9½	10	11
Argentino	37½	38	39½	40	41	42	43	44	46

S. **EN UNA TIENDA DE ROPA** Habla con otro(a) estudiante: una persona es el (la) dependiente y la otra persona es su cliente.

Dependiente	**Cliente**
1. Greet your customer.	**2.** Answer appropriately.
3. Ask how you can help.	**4.** Say what you want to try on.
5. Inquire about size(s) using the chart.	**6.** Respond to the question(s).
7. Find the correct size(s).	**8.** Decide whether or not to buy.
9. Ask about form of payment.	**10.** State method of payment.
11. End the conversation.	**12.** Respond appropriately.

T. **SITUACIONES** Con un(a) compañero(a) de clase, escojan una de las siguientes situaciones. Intenten usar expresiones que están estudiando en esta sección. Después, cambien de compañero(a) y hagan otro diálogo.

ESTUDIANTE 1: You are a new employee in a shoe store. You want to impress your boss and make many commissions. Try to convince your customer to buy two pairs (**pares**) of shoes and several pairs of socks.

ESTUDIANTE 2: You are a frugal customer. You want to buy an inexpensive pair of shoes. Once you find a pair you like, buy only the shoes.

Verbos útiles: vender, gastar, rebajar, mostrar, probarse

[1] You might notice that the sizes used throughout Argentina are the same as sizes in Europe. Buenos Aires is known as the Paris of South America due to its strong economic, cultural, and historical ties to Europe.

ESTUDIANTE 1: You are going to a semiformal party with one of your best friends. You want to really dress up for the occasion because you enjoy wearing beautiful well-made clothes and clothing accessories, and you want to create a good impression at the party. Telephone your friend to convince him/her to dress as well as you do.

ESTUDIANTE 2: You are an easy-going person who takes life as it comes. You like to dress casually no matter what the occasion, and you don't like to spend a great deal of money, especially on the latest fashions in clothing and clothing accessories. Express these feelings when your friend speaks with you over the phone.

Verbos útiles: vestirse formalmente, hacer una buena impresión, vestirse cómodamente, no gastar mucho dinero

ESTUDIANTE 1: Your friend is trying on an awful-looking suit or dress for his/her college graduation. You want to be polite but convince him/her not buy it. Use as many excuses as you can.

ESTUDIANTE 2: You're buying a suit or dress for graduation. You have eccentric tastes and have finally found the perfect polka-dotted pattern. Be determined to buy it. Use as many arguments as you can.

Verbos útiles: quedarle bien (mal), hacer juego con

ENCUENTRO *cultural*

Para pensar: ¿Sabes tú bailar algún baile típico de tu región, o conoces bailes especiales? ¿Cómo se llama(n)? ¿Te gusta bailarlos? ¿Conoces ya el tango? ¿Sabes bailarlo?

El tango argentino

Éstas son unas palabras nuevas para la lectura:

el patrón   *pattern*
la Caminata   *the Walk*
el paso   *(dance) step*
el Paseo   *the Stroll*
la Caza   *the Chase*
la Cunita   *the Cradle, or Rock step*   **sin esfuerzo alguno**   *effortless*

Es difícil hablar de Argentina sin mencionar el tango. Para bailar bien el tango hay que tener instinto. Pero, para encontrar tu instinto del tango tienes que aprender todas las reglas básicas. El **patrón** más básico del tango es **la Caminata.** Algunos otros **pasos** de este baile argentino son **el Paseo,** la Cadencia, **la Caza** y **la Cunita.**

Lo más complicado del tango es el ritmo. En el tango los movimientos de la mujer deben ocurrir una fracción de segundo después de los del hombre. Los pasos de la mujer son precisos y parecen ser **sin esfuerzo alguno.** Todos los impulsos de la mujer son dirigidos por indicaciones que el hombre hace con gestos sutiles con la mano derecha que descansa sobre la espalda de la mujer. El tango es hermoso cuando dos personas pueden integrar la pasión y el drama en el baile. El tango toma tiempo y sentimiento; no es necesario tener talento acrobático ni un vestido increíblemente elegante para bailar el tango.

Este baile argentino apareció en 1911, y la canción más famosa del tango es «La Cumparsita». Para el año 1924, el tango fue sin duda el baile más popular de Buenos Aires, y sigue hoy como el baile nacional de Argentina.

U. PREGUNTAS Contesta las siguientes preguntas a base de la lectura.

1. ¿Cuántos patrones básicos del tango puedes nombrar?
2. ¿Qué es necesario para bailar el tango?
3. ¿Cuál es la canción más famosa del tango?

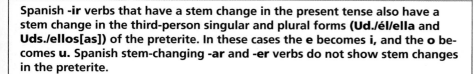

GRAMÁTICA II: *Preterite of stem-changing verbs*

Spanish **-ir** verbs that have a stem change in the present tense also have a stem change in the third-person singular and plural forms (**Ud./él/ella** and **Uds./ellos[as]**) of the preterite. In these cases the **e** becomes **i**, and the **o** becomes **u**. Spanish stem-changing **-ar** and **-er** verbs do not show stem changes in the preterite.

servir *(to serve)*   **divertirse** *(to have fun)*

Present	Preterite	Present	Preterite
(i)	(i)	(ie)	(i)
s**i**rvo	serví	me div**ie**rto	me divertí
s**i**rves	serviste	te div**ie**rtes	te divertiste
s**i**rve	s**i**rvió	se div**ie**rte	se div**i**rtió
servimos	servimos	nos divertimos	nos divertimos
servís	servisteis	os divertís	os divertisteis
s**i**rven	s**i**rvieron	se div**ie**rten	se div**i**rtieron

dormir *(to sleep)*

Present	Preterite	Present	Preterite
(ue)		(u)	
d**ue**rmo	dormimos	dormí	dormimos
d**ue**rmes	dormís	dormiste	dormisteis
d**ue**rme	d**ue**rmen	d**u**rmió	d**u**rmieron

Here are other **-ir** stem-changing verbs that exhibit the same changes as the three verbs shown above. Many of these you have already learned. (The first vowel in the parentheses represents the stem change in the present tense, and the second vowel represents the stem change in the preterite.)

conseguir (i, i)   *to get, to obtain*
despedir(se) (i, i) (de)   *to say good-bye (to)*
dormirse (ue, u)   *to fall asleep*
morir(se) (ue, u)   *to die*
pedir (i, i)   *to request, to order; to ask for*
preferir (ie, i)   *to prefer*
reírse (i, i)[1]   *to laugh*
sentirse (ie, i)   *to feel*
sonreír (i, i)[2]   *to smile*
sugerir (ie, i)   *to suggest*
vestirse (i, i)   *to get dressed*

---

[1] The spelling of the third-person forms of **reírse** undergoes the following simplification: **ri-ió->rió**; **ri-ieron->rieron**.
[2] The third-person forms of **sonreír** are simplified in the same manner as **reírse**.

¡A practicar!

V. **UN DÍA DE TRABAJO PARA JULIO** Julio es el gerente *(manager)* de un almacén grande en Buenos Aires. Él nos explica la rutina de un día típico. Cambia las oraciones del presente al pasado.

MODELO: Yo consigo permiso del jefe Luis para las rebajas de otoño.
Yo conseguí permiso del jefe Luis para las rebajas de otoño.

1. Yo me visto con traje y me pongo el sombrero.
2. Yo me despido de mi esposa a las 7:00 de la mañana.
3. Cuando llego a la tienda, los dependientes me piden el horario para la próxima semana.
4. Yo prefiero abrir la tienda un poco temprano.
5. Los clientes me sonríen cuando entran en la tienda.
6. Dos chicos se divierten con sus madres.
7. Ellos se ríen mucho de los chistes de Julio.
8. Yo y el dependiente sugerimos unas botas negras a un señor mayor.
9. Yo me siento bien cuando el dependiente nuevo sirve bien a sus clientes.
10. Cuando yo vuelvo a casa, mi esposa y yo nos dormimos temprano.

W. **UNA PEQUEÑA FIESTA DE SILVIA Y JULIO** El sábado pasado Silvia y Julio dieron una fiesta en su apartamento en Buenos Aires para celebrar su aniversario con unos amigos. Silvia describe los preparativos y lo que pasó en la fiesta.

El sábado durante el día, nosotros _____ **(tener)** que prepararnos para la fiesta. Primero, Julio y Juan Carlos _____ **(tener)** que limpiar la casa. Mientras tanto *(Meanwhile)*, yo _____ **(ir)** de compras para la comida. En el mercado, yo _____ **(conseguir)** unas comidas riquísimas. Dos dependientes me _____ **(sugerir)** empanadas de carne para picar en la fiesta.

A las 7:00, Julio y yo _____ **(ducharse)**, luego _____ **(vestirse)**. Yo _____ **(ponerse)** un vestido largo de cuadros, y Julio _____ **(vestirse)** elegantemente también. A las 8:30 _____ **(llegar)** los primeros invitados. Yo _____ **(servir)** unos sándwiches, pero una amiga mía _____ **(preferir)** no comer nada. Un señor _____ **(pedir)** una cerveza y su esposa _____ **(preferir)** tomar vino; Julio les _____ **(servir)** estas dos bebidas. Todos _____ **(divertirse)** mucho en la fiesta: los invitados _____ **(bailar)** y _____ **(cantar)** hasta la 1:00 de la madrugada. Cuando los invitados _____ **(salir)**, Julio y yo _____ **(acostarse)** y _____ **(dormir)** bien porque _____ **(trabajar)** mucho para dar una fiesta divertida.

En voz alta

X. **ENTREVISTA: UNAS COMPRAS MEMORABLES** Haz las siguientes preguntas a un(a) compañero(a) de clase. Luego describe a la clase las experiencias de la persona.

1. ¿Adónde fuiste? ¿Con quién fuiste? ¿Cómo te vestiste para ir de compras?
2. ¿Preferiste ir a un centro comercial grande o a tiendas pequeñas? ¿A qué hora llegaste (llegaron ustedes) a tu (su) destino? ¿Se divirtieron tú y tus amigos? ¿Se rieron mucho durante las compras? ¿Pediste algo especial en alguna tienda? ¿Comieron y bebieron Uds. algo durante las compras? ¿Qué quisiste hacer tú, pero tus amigos no quisieron hacerlo?

3. ¿Después de cuánto tiempo saliste para volver a casa? ¿Te cansaste mucho haciendo compras? ¿A qué hora te acostaste cuando llegaste a casa? ¿Te sentiste contento(a) con lo que compraste? ¿Por qué sí o no? ¿Te dormiste inmediatamente o no? ¿Por qué?

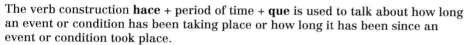

ASÍ SE DICE: *How to tell how long something has been happening*

The verb construction **hace** + period of time + **que** is used to talk about how long an event or condition has been taking place or how long it has been since an event or condition took place.

To indicate how long something has been happening, Spanish speakers use the construction **hace** + period of time + **que** + present tense.

—**¿Cuánto tiempo hace que vives** en Buenos Aires?   *How long have you been living in Buenos Aires?*

—**Hace seis años que vivo** aquí.   *I've been living here for six years.*

To express how long ago an action or state occurred, Spanish speakers use the verb form **hace** + period of time + **que** + preterite tense.

—**¿Cuánto tiempo hace que se mudaron** ustedes de la Argentina?   *How long ago did you move from Argentina?*

—**Hace un año que nos mudamos.** **(Nos mudamos hace un año**.)   *We moved a year ago.*

The question **¿Cuánto tiempo hace que... ?** can be used to ask about either (1) a period of time that continues into the present or (2) the amount of time since an event took place. The only feature that distinguishes the first scenario from the second is the choice of the present tense versus the past tense. Note the different implications for the following questions:

—**¿Cuánto tiempo hace que estudias** medicina?   *How long have you been studying medicine?* (You continue to study or be a student.)

—**¿Cuánto tiempo hace que estudiaste** medicina?   *How long has it been since you studied medicine?* (You are no longer studying or no longer a student.)

¡A practicar!

Y. **¿CUÁNTO TIEMPO HACE QUE... ?** Completa las siguientes oraciones con el período de tiempo apropiado y la conjugación correcta del verbo en el presente.

MODELO: Hace *un año* que yo *estudio* (estudiar) español.

1. Hace _____ que mi compañero(a) de cuarto y yo _____ (vivir) juntos.
2. Hace _____ que yo no _____ (vivir) con mis padres.
3. Hace _____ que el (la) profesor(a) _____ (enseñar) en esta universidad.

4. Hace _____ que nosotros _____ **(practicar)** español en esta sala.

5. Hace _____ que esta universidad _____ **(ofrecer)** clases.

6. Hace _____ que yo _____ **(leer)** novelas.

Z. **HECHOS IMPORTANTES** ¿Cuánto tiempo hace que los siguientes aconte-cimientos *(events)* ocurrieron en el pasado?

MODELO: yo / ir a la universidad por primera vez
Hace tres años que yo fui a la universidad por primera vez.

1. yo / conocer a mi mejor amigo(a)

2. la princesa Diana / morir

3. el nuevo milenio / empezar

4. los Denver Broncos / ganar el campeonato de fútbol americano

5. tu novio(a) / decirte que te quiere

6. yo / venir a la universidad para estudiar

7. mis amigos y yo / ponernos ropa elegante para una fiesta

8. tu mamá / darte un regalo especial

9. los compañeros de clase / divertirse en la clase de español

10. yo / sentirme realmente frustrado(a)

En voz alta

AA. ¿HACE CUÁNTO TIEMPO QUE... ? Pregúntale a un(a) compañero(a) de clase cuánto tiempo hace que hace o que hizo las siguientes cosas.

MODELO: estar con tu novio(a)
E1: *¿Hace cuánto tiempo que estás con tu novio(a)?*
E2: *Hace seis meses que estoy con mi novio(a).*
o: E1: *¿Hace cuánto tiempo que estuviste con tu novio(a)?*
E2: *Hace dos semanas que estuve con mi novio(a). Nosotros nos dejamos.* (We broke up.)

1. vivir en esta ciudad

2. conocer a tu mejor amigo(a)

3. dar un regalo a alguien

4. ir de compras

5. estudiar español

6. ir a la biblioteca

BB. **ENTREVISTA** Forma preguntas para hacer a otro(a) estudiante usando **¿Cuánto tiempo hace que... ?** para pedir información sobre los siguientes artícu-los. Debes hacer dos preguntas adicionales sobre cada artículo.

MODELO: ropa nueva
E1: *¿Cuánto tiempo hace que compraste ropa nueva? ¿Qué com-praste? ¿De qué color es (son)?*

1. unas gafas de sol

2. un paraguas

3. un regalo para alguien

4. un traje o vestido elegante

5. una bolsa o una cartera

6. algo de lunares

In this section you will learn how to simplify expressions by substituting direct objects with direct object pronouns.

Direct object pronouns

All sentences have a subject and a verb. Many sentences also have an object that receives the action of the verb. For example, in the sentence below, the direct object (**la blusa**) receives the action of the verb (**compró**) performed by the subject (**Silvia**).

Subject	**Verb**	**Direct Object**
Silvia	compró	la blusa.
Silvia	*bought*	*the blouse.*

The direct object of a sentence is usually a person or a thing and it answers the questions *whom?* or *what?* in relation to the sentence's subject and verb.

Julio llamó a su **mamá**.	*Whom did he call?* *(his mom)*
Silvia compró **la blusa**.	*What did she buy?* *(a blouse)*

In Spanish, as in English, a direct object pronoun may be used in place of a direct object noun.

Singular		**Plural**	
me	*me*	**nos**	*us*
te	*you* (informal)	**os**	*you* (informal)
lo	*you* (formal); *him; it* (masculine)	**los**	*you* (formal); *them* (masculine)
la	*you* (formal); *her; it* (feminine)	**las**	*you* (formal); *them* (feminine)

Julio llamó a su **mamá**.	Él **la** llamó.
*Julio called his **mother**.*	*He called **her**.*

Silvia compró **las blusas**.	Ella **las** compró.
*Silvia bought the **blouses**.*	*She bought **them**.*

In the preceding sentences, the direct object pronouns **la** and **las** replace the direct object nouns **mamá** and **las blusas**, respectively. In the following example, see how **los** replaces **los Renoysa**, **lo** replaces **el suéter**, and **las** replaces **las sandalias**.

—Julio, ¿conoces a **los Reynosa**?	—Sí, **los** conozco.
*Julio, do you know **the Reynosas**?*	*Yes, I know **them**.*

—Silvia, ¿lavaste mi **suéter**?	—No, no **lo** lavé.
*Silvia, did you wash my **sweater**?*	*No, I didn't wash **it**.*

—Papá, ¿dónde están mis **sandalias**?	—**Las** tengo aquí.
*Dad, where are my **sandals**?*	*I have **them** here.*

Place the pronoun in front of the conjugated verb.

—¿Cambiaste los pantalones, Julio?	—Sí, **los cambié** anoche.
Did you exchange the pants, Julio?	*Yes, **I exchanged them** last night.*

In negative sentences, place the **no** in front of the pronoun.

—¿Me llamaste, Silvia?	—No, Julio. **No te** llamé.
Did you call me, Silvia?	*No, Julio. I did **not** call **you**.*

When the direct object pronoun is used with an infinitive or a present participle, place it either before the conjugated verb or attach it to the infinitive or the present participle. (A written accent is needed to retain the stressed vowel of a present participle when a direct object pronoun is attached to it.)[1]

Lo voy a llamar mañana.
     or   *I'm going to call him tomorrow.*
Voy a **llamarlo** mañana.

Lo estoy llamando ahora.
     or   *I'm calling him now.*
Estoy llamándolo ahora.

The direct object pronoun **lo** can be used to stand for actions or ideas in general.

—Julio, compré tres blusas nuevas.   —¡No puedo creer**lo**!
Julio, I bought three new blouses.   *I can't believe it! (it = the fact that Silvia bought three new blouses)*

¡A practicar!

CC. **EL ASISTENTE DE JULIO** Julio está trabajando en la tienda con su nuevo asistente, Rogelio. Están hablando de dónde poner la ropa nueva que acaba de llegar. Completa las conversaciones con los pronombres **lo, la, los** o **las**.

MODELO: —Julio, ¿va a poner los pantalones de lana aquí?
                  —No, voy a poner*los* allí.

1. —Julio, ¿usted vendió la última blusa de seda?
 —Sí, _____ vendí ayer.
2. —Rogelio, ¿terminó con las cuentas de ayer?
 —Pues... no, Julio. Yo estoy haciéndo_____ ahora.
3. —Julio, ¿encontró los nuevos suéteres de algodón?
 —No, todavía estoy buscándo_____.
 —Yo creo que _____ puso allí, al lado de los trajes de baño.
4. —Julio, mañana tengo que llevar a mi hermano al hospital. No puedo venir a trabajar hasta mediodía.
 —¡Yo no _____ creo! ¡Ud. no tiene hermanos!

DD. **CONVERSACIONES DOMÉSTICAS** Completa los siguientes diálogos con los pronombres apropiados.

En casa

Silvia: ¿Conoces a Ramón Sarmiento, Julio?

Julio: Pues... sí, _____ conozco un poco. ¿Por qué?

Silvia: Porque Ramón y su esposa _____ (a nosotros) invitaron a una fiesta.

Julio: ¿_____ (a nosotros) invitaron? Hmm... _____ conocimos el año pasado, ¿no?

Silvia: Sí, en una fiesta, pero nunca _____ visitamos. ¿Vamos a la fiesta?

Julio: Sí, cómo no. Vamos.

Silvia: Pues, si vamos, ¡me voy a comprar aquel vestido rojo que encontré ayer en la Recoleta! ¿Puedo comprárme_____, Julio?

Julio: Ay, ay, ay. Sí, mi amor, cómprate_____.

---

[1] With reflexive verbs in the infinitive form, the direct object pronoun is placed after the reflexive pronoun at the end of the verb. For example: **Voy a probarme el suéter. Voy a probármelo.** Affirmative commands also require that the direct object pronoun be attached to the verb. You will learn more about commands and placement of pronouns in **Capítulos 8** and **11**.

En la fiesta

Silvia: Gracias por tu invitación, Ramón. _____ recibimos la semana pasada.

Ramón: De nada, Silvia. ¿Conocen ustedes a mis hijas?

Julio: Pues no... Creo que no _____ conozco.

Ramón: Bueno, ésta es Angelina y ésta es Berta.

Berta: Mucho gusto.

Silvia: Berta, ¿no _____ recuerdas? Soy la señora Sepúlveda. _____ conocí hace dos años.

Berta: Ah, sí, señora Sepúlveda. Ahora _____ recuerdo.

En voz alta

EE. **¿QUÉ QUIERES?** Tu compañero(a) va a ofrecerte las siguientes cosas. Responde indicando si quieres comprar el objeto o no, sustituyendo el sustantivo *(noun)* por el pronombre *(pronoun)* apropiado.

MODELO: las camisetas

E1: *¿Quieres comprar las camisetas?*
E2: *Sí, las quiero comprar.*
o: E2: *Sí, quiero comprarlas.*
o: E2: *No, no las quiero comprar.*
o: E2: *No, no quiero comprarlas.*

1. el abrigo
2. las corbatas de seda
3. la chaqueta de los Kansas City Royals
4. el súeter de algodón
5. las medias de seda
6. las gafas de sol negras
7. los zapatos de tenis de Adidas
8. la blusa de Versace

FF. **¿CÓMO ME QUEDAN?** Ahora tu compañero(a) va a escoger cuatro artículos de la **Actividad EE.** Va a preguntarte si quieres probártelos o no. Al contestar cada pregunta, debes usar un pronombre de complemento directo.

MODELO: el abrigo

E1: *¿Quieres probarte el abrigo?*
E2: *No, no quiero probármelo.*
o: E2: *No, no me lo quiero probar.*
o: E2: *Sí, quiero probármelo.*
o: E2: *Sí, me lo quiero probar.*

GRAMÁTICA IV: *The imperfect tense*

Spanish speakers use the imperfect tense to describe past actions, conditions, and events that were in progress or that occurred habitually or repetitiously.

> **To form the imperfect, add the following endings to the verb stem. Note the identical endings for -er and -ir verbs.**

	jugar	hacer	divertirse	
yo	jugaba	hacía	me	divertía
tú	jugabas	hacías	te	divertías
Ud., él, ella	jugaba	hacía	se	divertía
nosotros(as)	jugábamos	hacíamos	nos	divertíamos
vosotros(as)	jugabais	hacíais	os	divertíais
Uds., ellos(as)	jugaban	hacían	se	divertían

Only three Spanish verbs are irregular in the imperfect:

	ir	ser	ver
yo	iba	era	veía
tú	ibas	eras	veías
Ud., él, ella	iba	era	veía
nosotros(as)	íbamos	éramos	veíamos
vosotros(as)	ibais	erais	veíais
Uds., ellos(as)	iban	eran	veían

—¿**Ibas** mucho de compras cuando **eras** niña?

Did you used to go shopping a lot when you were a little girl?

—¿**Veías** mucha ropa en las tiendas?

Did you used to see a lot of clothes in the stores?

—Sí. Mi familia y yo **veíamos** mucha ropa.

Yes. My family and I saw lots of clothes.

The imperfect tense of **hay** is **había**.

—¿**Había** muchas personas en el centro comercial?

Were there a lot of people at the mall?

—Sí, Silvia. **Había** mucha gente.

Yes, Silvia. There were many people.

Talking about the past: The preterite and the imperfect[1]

You have learned that Spanish speakers use the preterite tense to describe the beginning or completion of past actions, conditions, and events. For example, notice how Silvia uses the preterite to tell what happened at her home this morning.

Esta mañana mi despertador **sonó** a las 7:00 como siempre. **Me levanté, fui** al baño, **me duché** y **me vestí.** Luego, **desperté** a Juan Carlos y **preparé** el desayuno. **Comimos** fruta y pan tostado y **tomamos** café. Después, **nos lavamos** los dientes y **salimos** de casa. **Fuimos** en colectivo[2] al centro.

This morning my alarm went off at 7:00 as always. I got up, went to the bathroom, showered, and got dressed. Then, I woke up Juan Carlos and prepared breakfast. We ate fruit and toast, and we drank coffee. Next, we brushed our teeth and left the house. We went downtown by bus.

Spanish speakers use the imperfect tense to express actions, conditions, and events that were in progress at some focused point in the past. For example, notice how Silvia uses the imperfect tense to tell what was going on when she got off the bus with her son.

---

[1] You will learn more about distinguishing between the preterite and the imperfect in **Capítulo 8.**
[2] The easiest and most common way of getting around Buenos Aires is by buses called **colectivos.**

Cuando nos bajamos del autobús, **hacía** un poco de frío y **llovía.** Juan Carlos no **quería** ir de compras conmigo porque todavía **estaba** cansado.

When we got off the bus, it was cold and it was raining. Juan Carlos didn't want to go shopping with me because he was still tired.

Spanish speakers also use the imperfect to describe actions, conditions, and events that occurred habitually or repetitiously in the past. Notice how Silvia uses the imperfect to describe how her life was when she was a girl.

Cuando **era** niña, todo **era** diferente de lo que es ahora. Yo **tenía** menos responsabilidades y creo que **estaba** más contenta. Todos los sábados **me levantaba** tarde porque no **había** mucho que hacer en casa. Luego **iba** a la cocina, **me servía** un vaso de leche y **miraba** la tele. Por la tarde mis amigas y yo **jugábamos** juntas.

When I was a child, everything was different than it is now. I had fewer responsibilities and I think I was happier. Every Saturday I would get up late because there wasn't much to do at home. Then, I would go to the kitchen, I would serve myself a glass of milk, and I would watch TV. In the afternoon my friends and I would play together.

Yo **quería** ir de compras ayer. Pero no **podía** salir de casa porque **tenía** que lavar la ropa y limpiar el apartamento.

I wanted to go shopping yesterday. But I couldn't get out of the house because I had to wash the clothes and clean the apartment.

The imperfect tense can be translated in different ways, depending on the context. For example, read the following paragraph and notice the English meaning of the forms in parentheses.

De niña yo **vivía** *(I lived)* en un pueblo cerca de Buenos Aires. Los sábados mi mamá y yo **íbamos** *(used to go)* de compras al centro donde **mirábamos** *(we would look at)* muchas cosas en las tiendas. Un sábado, cuando **caminábamos** *(we were walking)* en la plaza, vimos un festival de música cerca de la plaza.

¡A practicar!

GG. **QUERIDO ABUELO** Cambia los verbos de la siguiente lista al imperfecto para completar el primer párrafo de una carta que Silvia le escribió a su abuelo.

| r | estar | poder | llamar |
| ener | escribir | querer | trabajar |

¿Cómo estás, abuelito? Yo _____ escribirte antes pero no lo _____ hacer porque _____ tantos quehaceres aquí en casa para prepararnos para la fiesta. Julio, Juan Carlos y mi trabajo ocupan casi todo mi tiempo. Ayer Julio _____ preguntándome sobre ti y le dije que _____ a escribirte muy pronto. Recuerdo que te _____ cartas y que te _____ por teléfono más frecuentemente cuando no _____ tanto como ahora.

HH. **SILVIA DE NIÑA** Silvia está contándole a Juan Carlos algunas cosas que ella hacía de niña. ¿Qué le dice a su hijo?

MODELO: yo / jugar al vólibol
          Yo jugaba al vólibol.

1. mi familia y yo / vivir en un rancho 20 kilómetros al norte de Buenos Aires
2. (nosotros) no / tener auto pero / tener muchos caballos
3. tu abuelo / ser agricultor también / comprar y / vender caballos
4. mi mamá / trabajar en casa
5. mis dos hermanos y yo / divertirse mucho / andar en bicicleta / montar a caballo e / ir a jugar a diferentes lugares
6. (nosotros) nunca / aburrirse porque / haber muchas cosas que hacer
7. antes de acostarnos por la noche mi mamá nos / leer o nos / contar historias sobre cuando ella / ser niña
8. a veces, mi papá / tocar el acordeón y nos / cantar viejas canciones italianas[1]
9. yo / querer mucho a mis padres y muchas veces les / decir que (yo) no / poder vivir sin ellos

II. ¿PRETÉRITO O IMPERFECTO? Julio está conversando con Juan Carlos en la sala sobre cómo llegaron a vivir en Buenos Aires. Completa su conversación, indicando los verbos correctos entre paréntesis.

Juan Carlos: Papá, ¿dónde (vivieron/vivían) tú y mamá después de casarse?

Julio: (Vivimos/Vivíamos) por un año y medio con mis padres cerca de Buenos Aires porque no (tuvimos/teníamos) mucho dinero.

Juan Carlos: ¿Qué tipo de trabajo (hiciste/hacías), papi?

Julio: (Trabajé/Trabajaba) como dependiente en un almacén. (Vendí/Vendía) zapatos allí. Nosotros (ganamos/ganábamos) poco dinero, pero (fue/era) suficiente para vivir.

Juan Carlos: ¿Cuándo (vinieron/venían) ustedes a vivir aquí en Buenos Aires?

Julio: Dos meses después de que (naciste/nacías), hijo.

Juan Carlos: ¿(Fue/Era) en diciembre?

Julio: Sí. Luego, tú, mamá y yo (pasamos/pasábamos) la Navidad *(Christmas)* juntos en esta casa. ¿Recuerdas eso?

Juan Carlos: ¿Cómo voy a recordar si solamente (tuve/tenía) cuatro meses?

En voz alta

JJ.   CUANDO YO TENÍA DIEZ AÑOS... Trabajando con un(a) compañero(a) de clase, tomen turnos terminando las siguientes oraciones con la información apropiada sobre su niñez *(childhood)*.

1. Cuando yo tenía diez años, mi familia y yo vivíamos en...
2. Nuestra casa (apartamento) era...
3. Mi papá trabajaba en... y mi mamá...
4. En general, mis padres...
5. Yo me divertía mucho. Por ejemplo...
6. Yo tenía un(a) amigo(a), que se llamaba...
7. A veces, él (ella)... y yo...
8. También nosotros...

---

[1] Around the turn of the twentieth century, many Italians immigrated to Argentina. People of Italian descent still make up a large portion of the Argentine population.

KK. **¿QUÉ HACÍAS?** Dile a otro(a) estudiante lo que hacías durante los tiempos indicados.

MODELO: Anoche a las 11:00...
Anoche a las 11:00 yo dormía.

1. Ayer a las 10:00 de la mañana...
2. Ayer a las 4:00 de la tarde...
3. Anoche a las 11:00...
4. Esta mañana a las 7:30...
5. Hoy, antes de venir a clase,...

LL. **ENTREVISTA** Hazle estas preguntas a un(a) compañero(a) de clase.

1. La familia: ¿Dónde y con quién vivías cuando tenías seis años? ¿Cuántos hermanos tenías? ¿Quién era el menor? ¿y el mayor? ¿Qué tipo de trabajo hacía tu papá? ¿Trabajaba tu mamá también? (¿Sí? ¿Dónde? ¿Qué hacía ella?) ¿Cuándo visitabas a tus tíos y a tus abuelos? ¿Qué otras cosas hacías con tu familia?
2. Las posesiones: De niño(a), ¿tenías una bicicleta? (¿Sí? ¿De qué color era?) ¿Tenías un perro o un gato? (¿Sí? ¿Cómo se llamaba?) ¿Qué otras cosas tenías? ¿Cuál era la cosa más importante que tenías?
3. Los amigos: ¿Tenías muchos o pocos amigos en la escuela primaria? ¿Cómo te divertías con ellos? ¿Cómo se llamaba tu mejor amigo o amiga en la escuela secundaria? ¿Dónde vivía? ¿Qué hacían ustedes juntos(as)? ¿Tenías novio(a)? (¿Sí? ¿Cómo se llamaba? ¿Cómo era él/ella?)
4. Los pasatiempos: De adolescente, ¿cómo pasabas el tiempo cuando no estudiabas o trabajabas? ¿Practicabas algún deporte? ¿Cuál? ¿Con qué frecuencia ibas al cine? ¿Qué tipo de películas veías? ¿Qué programas de televisión mirabas? ¿Qué otras cosas hacías para divertirte?

Síntesis ◆◆◆

¡A ver!

El tema central del **Capítulo 7** es la compra. Isabel, una estudiante argentina que nació en Córdoba en el centro del país, es la presentadora videográfica de este capítulo. En los segmentos que vamos a ver, Isabel nos habla de una variedad de establecimientos comerciales. En el segundo segmento compramos ropa con Laura y su amiga en una tienda de moda en México, D.F.

ACTIVIDAD 1   Pre-viewing task (Segmento 1 del video)

You can also look on page 82 of **Capítulo 3** for store names.

Paso 1: Vas a ver una serie de fotografías de tiendas en el mundo hispánico. Haz una lista de las tiendas que ves. Si no sabes el nombre de una tienda, pregunta a tu compañero(a) de clase de la siguiente forma: **¿Cómo se llama en español la tienda donde venden medicamentos y cosas para la salud?**

Paso 2: Con tu compañero(a) de clase, uno dice el nombre de una de las tiendas de su lista, y el otro explica lo que venden en esa tienda.

> M O D E L O :   E1: *farmacia*
> E2: *Una farmacia es donde venden medicamentos, cosas para la salud y cosas para la higiene.*

ACTIVIDAD 2   Pre-viewing task (Segmento 2 del video)

Paso 1: Tus padres te dan dinero para comprar ropa nueva. Decides comprarte cosas para el trabajo. Tienes dinero suficiente para tres prendas *(articles)*. Apunta en una hoja la siguiente información:

- los nombres de las tres cosas que te gustaría comprar
- el color de cada prenda
- la talla que llevas de cada prenda
- información sobre la tela de cada prenda

Paso 2: Explica a tu compañero(a) de clase lo que vas a comprarte. Tu compañero(a) te hace preguntas para obtener la mayor información posible sobre cada prenda y reacciona positiva o negativamente a las prendas que vas a comprar. Aquí hay algunas expresiones útiles:

Reacciones positivas	Reacciones negativas
¡Qué bonito(a)!	Pues, no me gusta mucho...
¡Qué lindo(a)!	Pues, ¿qué te voy a decir? *(Well, what can I say?)*
¡Qué precioso(a)!	
¡Chévere!	¡Que no me gusta... !
¡Qué bien!	¡Qué aburrido! *(How boring!)*
¡Me encanta!	Pues, no hace juego con...

ACTIVIDAD 3   Viewing task (Segmento 2 del video)

Mira el **Segmento 2 del video** en el cual Laura y su amiga van de compras en el centro de México D.F. ¿Qué compró Laura de ropa? Apunta en una lista las cosas que compró. Incluye toda la información posible sobre cada prenda: nombres de prendas, colores, estilos, telas, tallas, precios, etcétera. ¿Coincide alguna de las prendas que Laura compró con una que a ti te gustaría comprar?

ACTIVIDAD 4   Post-viewing task (Segmento 2 del video)

Compara la información que tienes sobre las compras que hizo Laura con la que tiene tu compañero(a) de clase. Traten de hablar de todos los aspectos de las compras.

¡A conversar!

De compras

Paso 1: ESTUDIANTE 1: El cumpleaños de tu mamá es en una semana y tienes que comprarle un regalo. Decides ir de compras a una tienda de ropa; en la tienda, hablas del precio y de la talla de varias prendas de ropa (i.e., vestidos, blusas, camisas, etc.) con el (la) dependiente. Después de hablar de varias prendas de ropa, cómprale una a tu madre. Paga con tarjeta de crédito.

ESTUDIANTE 2: Trabajas en una tienda de ropa. Tienes que hablar con un(a) cliente que busca un regalo de cumpleaños para su madre. Habla con él (ella) de los precios de varias prendas de ropa.

Paso 2: Después, cambien de papel y hagan la actividad de nuevo, empleando nuevas prendas de ropa.
   E2: Buenos días, señor (señorita). ¿En qué puedo servirle?
   E1: Buenos días. Busco un regalo para mi madre. ¿Cuánto cuesta esta blusa?
   E2: Cuesta 20 dólares...
   E1: ...

¡A escribir!

Editing your writing

Editing your written work is an important skill to master when learning a foreign language. You should plan on editing what you write several times. When checking your compositions, consider the following areas:

1. Content
   a. Is the title of your composition captivating? Would it cause readers to want to read further?
   b. Is the information you wrote pertinent to the assigned topic?
   c. Is your composition interesting? Does it capture reader interest?

Functions: Talking about past events; Talking about recent events; Sequencing events
Vocabulary: Clothing; Fabrics; Colors; Stores and products
Grammar: Verbs: irregular preterite; Personal pronouns; Indirect objects **le, les**

2. Organization

    a. Does each paragraph in the essay have a clearly identifiable main idea?

    b. Do the details in each paragraph relate to a single idea?

    c. Are the sentences in the paragraph ordered in a logical sequence?

    d. Is the order of the paragraphs correct in your composition?

3. Cohesion and style

    a. Does your composition as a whole communicate exactly what you are trying to convey?

    b. Does your composition "flow" easily and smoothly from beginning to end?

    c. Are there transitions between the different paragraphs you included in your composition?

4. Style and accuracy

    a. Have you chosen the precise vocabulary words you need to express your ideas?

    b. Are there grammatical errors in your composition (i.e., subject-verb agreement; adjective-noun agreement; errors with verb forms or irregular verbs, etc.)

    c. Are there spelling errors in your composition (including capitalization and punctuation)?

If you consider these factors as you edit your written work, the overall quality of your compositions can increase drastically!

Paso 1: Antes de escribir, piensa en la última vez que fuiste de compras. Contesta las siguientes preguntas.

- ¿Qué compraste?
- ¿Adónde fuiste de compras? (¿Cómo se llaman las tiendas?)
- ¿Cuánto dinero gastaste en las compras que hiciste?

Paso 2: Ahora, escribe una composición breve (de dos o tres párrafos) sobre la última vez que fuiste de compras. En tu composición, incluye la información que usaste para contestar las preguntas en **Paso 1.**

Paso 3: Ahora, tienes que corregir tu composición. Usa las preguntas de la sección de arriba (partes 1, 2, 3 y 4 de *Editing your writing*) como guía de correción. Luego, entrégale la composición al (a la) profesor(a).

¡A leer!

Using background knowledge to anticipate content

The better you can anticipate what you will read, the easier you will be able to understand the main ideas in a reading passage. In addition to looking at the pictures, titles, and subtitles that accompany a text, you should also think about what you already know about the topic.

Paso 1: Antes de leer el texto que sigue, mira los siguientes elementos.

1. la foto

    a. ¿Quiénes son estas personas?

    b. ¿Qué prendas de ropa llevan?

    c. ¿Cuál es la estación del año según la foto?

2. el título

    a. ¿Qué ideas asocias con la estación del año mencionada en el título?

    b. El verbo **alterar** es sinónimo de **cambiar** *(to change)*. Según el título, ¿qué está cambiando?

Paso 2: El texto que vas a leer trata de la moda. Antes de leer, piensa en lo que ya sabes sobre la moda.

1. ¿Cuáles son los estilos y las telas más populares hoy en día?
2. ¿Cuáles son los colores más populares?
3. ¿Cuáles son las tiendas de ropa más populares?

Paso 3: Antes de leer el texto, lee las preguntas que siguen. Después, lee el texto y contesta las preguntas.

1. ¿Cómo se describen los tres estilos principales mencionados en el texto? Rellena el cuadro que sigue con algunas palabras y expresiones.

el *sport* urbano	el *cyberchic*	el *neohippy*

2. Según el texto, ¿cuáles son los tejidos (telas) más populares? ¿Cuáles son los colores más populares?
3. Entre los tres estilos que se describen en el texto, ¿cuál prefieres tú? ¿Por qué?

La primavera la moda altera
Todo lo que se llevará esta próxima temporada

Durante décadas, la moda masculina y femenina no parecían guardar conexión. Sin embargo, en los últimos años, los diseños se han aproximado lo justo en cuanto a tendencias —si no en formas, sí en estilos, colores y tejidos.

En la próxima temporada primavera-verano, esa relación va a ser evidente por el paralelismo entre los guardarropas de estío de ambos sexos.

En términos generales, se puede hablar de una tendencia clara hacia un corte sencillo, muy estructurado, con preferencia de tejido sobre la forma, que se ha plasmado en las pasarelas a través de tres estilos: el sport urbano, el cyberchic y el neohippy.

El primero, inspirado principalmente en las prendas técnicas deportivas y en las náuticas, se llevará la palma.

Triunfan los combinados de blanco y negro, los ácidos naranja y amarillo.

El segundo —resultado de la ciencia ficción y la eclosión tecnológica que define el siglo— es una apuesta clara por las formas atrevidas, los tejidos de aspecto técnico y las fibras artificiales. Se aleja, no obstante, de la visión apocalíptica de los diseños futuristas de otros tiempos y adquiere un aspecto más sofisticado.

Por último, el neohippy representa la vuelta a lo natural, lo rústico y lo étnico y una recuperación de materiales y fibras nobles. Esta tendencia se presenta como vía formal de escape frente a una sociedad que se imagina dominada por las máquinas, y responde a las nuevas filosofías de humanización de la persona.

En la misma línea, los diseñadores han trabajado con fibras naturales y artificiales. Ambas se mezclan y es el resultado final —después de tratadas— lo que hace que adopten un aspecto u otro, también con aspectos brillantes y tornasolados. Al mismo tiempo, la piel, el algodón, el lino y la seda vuelven a primera línea.

En colores, el blanco desplaza al gris. Su mezcla más exitosa es con el negro.

Y frente a los tonos neutros, llegan los ácidos, jugosos como el naranja o el amarillo, que se combinan con otros tan poco sutiles —aunque sí muy atractivos— como el fucsia, los jades e, incluso, los ultravioletas.

La ropa   *Clothing*

el abrigo   *overcoat*
la blusa   *blouse*
las botas   *boots*
la bufanda   *scarf*
los calcetines   *socks*
la camisa   *shirt*
la camiseta   *T-shirt*
la chaqueta   *jacket*

el cinturón   *belt*
la corbata   *necktie*
la falda   *skirt*
los guantes   *gloves*
el impermeable   *raincoat*
los jeans   *blue jeans*
las medias   *stockings*
los pantalones (cortos)   *pants (shorts)*

las sandalias   *sandals*
el sombrero   *hat*
el suéter   *sweater*
el traje   *suit*
el traje de baño   *swimsuit*
el vestido   *dress*
los zapatos   *shoes*

Los accesorios   *Accessories*

la bolsa   *purse, bag*
la cartera   *wallet*

las gafas de sol   *sunglasses*
el paraguas   *umbrella*

Estilos y telas   *Styles and fabrics*

de cuadros   *plaid*
de lunares   *polka-dotted*
de rayas   *striped*

es de..
   algodón   *cotton*
   cuero   *leather*

lana   *wool*
seda   *silk*

De compras   *Shopping*

el cheque   *check*
el (la) dependiente   *salesclerk*
el descuento   *discount*
el efectivo   *cash*

la liquidación   *sale (Lat. Am.), reduction (in price)*
el número   *shoe size*
el por ciento   *percent*

la rebaja   *sale (Spain), reduction (in price)*
la talla   *size (clothing)*
la tarjeta de crédito   *credit card*

Verbos

cambiar   *to change*
costar (ue)   *to cost*
gastar   *to spend (money)*
hacer juego con   *to match*

llevar   *to wear, to carry*
mostrar (ue)   *to show*
pagar   *to pay for*
ponerse   *to put on*

probarse (ue)   *to try on*
quedarle (a uno)   *to fit (someone)*
rebajar   *to reduce (in price)*
usar   *to wear; to use*

Adjetivos

barato(a)   *inexpensive, cheap*

caro(a)   *expensive*

grande   *big, large*

pequeño(a)   *small*

Expresiones idiomáticas

¿Cómo me queda?   *How does it look?*
¿Cuánto le debo?   *How much do I owe you?*
¡Es una ganga!   *It's a bargain!*

¡Está de última moda!   *It's the latest style!*
¡Me quedan muy pequeños!   *They're too small!*

un par de...   *a pair of . . .*

Fiestas y vacaciones: Guatemala y El Salvador

Communicative goals

In this chapter you will learn how to . . .

- Talk about holidays and vacations
- Describe changes in emotion
- Recognize and employ different strategies to talk about the past
- Talk about the beach and the countryside
- Use affirmative and negative expressions
- Ask questions to obtain information about people and events

Grammar

- **Ponerse** + adjective
- Preterite and imperfect tenses contrasted
- Affirmative and negative expressions
- Summary of interrogative words

Cultural information

- Santo Tomás de Chichicastenango
- El santo patrón de El Salvador

*La Plaza San Salvador,
San Salvador, El Salvador*

CELEBRANDO EL DÍA DE SANTO TOMÁS EN CHICHICASTENANGO, GUATEMALA[1]
In this section you will learn how to talk about parties and celebrations while learning about the festivities surrounding a Mayan holiday in a small, Guatemalan mountain town.

¿NOS ENTENDEMOS?

Generally, when people toast in Spanish they say **¡Salud!** In Spain, however, it is common to say **¡Salud, amor y pesetas, y tiempo para gozarlos!** *(Health, love, and money, and time to enjoy them!)*. Another word for **la fiesta** and **la celebración** is **el festejo,** which comes from the verb **festejar** *(to celebrate)*.

¿NOS ENTENDEMOS?

Un(a) **fiestero(a)** is a *party-going person* while un(a) **aguafiestas** is a *party pooper.* **El desfile** is another word for **la procesión.**

cumplir años *to have a birthday*	**portarse bien (mal)** *to behave well (poorly)*
dar (hacer) una fiesta *to give a party*	**reaccionar** *to react*
pasarlo bien (mal) *to have a good (bad) time*	**recordar (ue)** *to remember*
	reunirse con *to get together with*

Sustantivos

el cumpleaños *birthday*   **el día feriado** *holiday*

Expresión idiomática

¡Felicitaciones! *Congratulations!*

---

[1] The people of Santo Tomás de Chichicastenango combine ancient Mayan beliefs with a Christian ideology in their celebration of the Winter Solstice, the shortest day of the year. In the Northern Hemisphere, this event takes place on December 21st. In this small Guatemalan village, the inhabitants celebrate the day of their patron saint with processions and dances. The festivities of the day are also directed to the pagan Sun god who is honored in order that he continue to bless the town with light and warmth.

Palabras útiles: Días festivos del mundo hispánico

el Cinco de Mayo   *Cinco de Mayo*
el Día de la Raza   *Columbus Day*
el Día de los Muertos   *Day of the Dead*[1]
el Día de los Reyes Magos   *Day of the Magi*
   (Three Kings)
el Día de Todos los Santos   *All Saints' Day*
   (November 2nd)

el día del santo   *saint's day (the saint for*
   whom one is named)
la Pascua   *Easter, Passover, Christmas*[2]
la Navidad   *Christmas*
la Noche Vieja   *New Year's Eve*
la Nochebuena   *Christmas Eve*
la Semana Santa   *Holy Week*[3]

➥ These holiday names in Spanish are provided for your information. You will not be tested on these words, but you should be able to recognize them.

¡A practicar!

A.   UN CUMPLEAÑOS Escoge la palabra apropiada para completar las siguientes frases.

1. Ayer fue el disfraz/cumpleaños de Tomás.
2. Hubo una fiesta de sorpresa/anfitriona con todos sus amigos y parientes.
3. Vinieron muchos brindis/invitados a la fiesta.
4. Sus parientes le dieron regalos/velas.
5. Su esposa le preparó un día feriado/pastel de cumpleaños muy grande con muchas velas/celebraciones.
6. Su esposa Marta y su amiga Tulia fueron las anfitrionas/procesiones de la fiesta.
7. La hermana de Tomás, Claudia, ofreció cohetes/entremeses a los invitados que tenían hambre.
8. Los niños pequeños se portaron/recordaron bien.
9. Todos los invitados lo pasaron bien/lo pasaron mal en esa máscara/celebración.

B.   ¡UNA FIESTA DE SORPRESA PARA TOMÁS! Este año Tomás cumplió 30 años. Describe los preparativos *(preparations)* que hizo su esposa para la fiesta de sorpresa conjugando los verbos apropiados en el pretérito.

llorar	hacer un brindis	reunirse
disfrazarse	cumplir años	reaccionar
asustarse	dar una fiesta	recordar
celebrar	divertirse	gritar

Este año mi esposa Marta _____ de sorpresa para mi cumpleaños. _____ todos mis amigos en mi casa y cuando entré a la fiesta, mis amigos me _____ «¡Feliz cumpleaños!» Una niña _____ por el ruido y _____. Mi mejor amigo Rodrigo _____ con champán. Mi esposa Marta _____ de una manera muy sentimental —ella _____ todos nuestros cumpleaños de los últimos cinco años juntos. A las 12:00 de la noche, mi amigo Rodrigo y su esposa Claudia _____ de un matrimonio muy viejo para hacernos imaginar nuestra vida del futuro. Normalmente, no me gusta mucho _____, pero este año nosotros _____ bien y todos _____ muchísimo.

---

[1] Although this day is a rough equivalent of Halloween, it is celebrated in Hispanic countries on November 1st and is a more solemn occasion to honor and remember one's ancestors.
[2] Notice that **Pascua** means *Easter, Passover,* and *Christmas. Easter* is sometimes referred to as **la Pascua Florida** while *Christmas* is referred to as **la Pascua Navideña.**
[3] **Semana Santa** is Guatemala's largest celebration, featuring processions and celebrations throughout the country.

En voz alta

C. MI DÍA FERIADO FAVORITO Con un(a) compañero(a) de clase, hablen sobre su día feriado favorito.

1. ¿Cuál es tu día feriado favorito? ¿Por qué?
2. ¿Cómo celebras esta ocasión especial?
3. ¿Das una fiesta en tu casa?
4. ¿Vas a algún lugar por la noche?
5. ¿Preparas una comida o bebida especial?
6. ¿Cómo te pones emocionalmente para esta fiesta?
7. ¿Qué hiciste el año pasado para celebrar este día?
8. ¿Recibiste algunos regalos durante ese día? ¿Diste algunos regalos?

D. UNA MUJER CÍNICA Esperanza, una amiga de Marta, es muy cínica con respecto a *(with regard to)* las fiestas de familia. Discute con dos compañeros(as) de clase para ver si son ciertas o falsas las opiniones de ella para Uds.

MODELO: Es mejor acostarse temprano durante la Noche Vieja.
E1: *No es cierto para mí. Nosotros siempre nos acostamos tarde durante la Noche Vieja.*
E2: *Es cierto para mí. Mi familia se acuesta antes de la medianoche.*
E3: *En mi familia, depende del año. Este año nos acostamos tarde pero el año pasado nos acostamos temprano.*

1. Siempre recibo regalos raros *(strange)* o inútiles.
2. La época de la Navidad puede ser un poco deprimente *(depressing)*.
3. No me gusta hacer cola *(to stand in line)* en las tiendas antes de las fiestas de diciembre.
4. Recibo cartas de personas que solamente quieren presumir de *(to brag about)* sus familias.
5. Las fiestas son una invención de Hallmark para ganar dinero.
6. Hay demasiados días festivos.
7. No recuerdo un cumpleaños divertido.
8. Mis amigos nunca reaccionan como quiero cuando abren mis regalos.

ASÍ SE DICE: *How to describe changes in emotion*

To show a change of emotion in Spanish, use the expression **ponerse** + adjective (*to become, to get* + adjective).

Yo **me pongo contenta** cuando es mi cumpleaños.

*I **become happy** when it's my birthday.*

Tomás **se puso enojado** cuando él y su esposa discutieron.

*Tomás **got angry** when he and his wife fought.*

¡A practicar!

E. **¿QUÉ PASA CON ESTA GENTE?** Completa las siguientes frases para describir las emociones de las personas en los dibujos. Usa la expresión **ponerse** + adjetivo.

MODELO: Tomás / furioso
Tomás se pone furioso.

1. Marta / contenta

2. tú / triste

3. nosotros / asustados

4. Uds. / cansados

En voz alta

F. **¿CÓMO TE PONES?** Dile a un(a) compañero(a) de clase cómo reaccionas en las siguientes situaciones.

MODELO: Estás en una fiesta y tu novio(a) está bailando con otra persona.
Me pongo furioso(a) y grito.

1. Das una fiesta y se acaba *(runs out)* toda la comida en media hora.
2. Es tu cumpleaños y tus amigos te hacen una fiesta de sorpresa.
3. Estás en una fiesta y los invitados no se ríen, no se sonríen, ni apenas *(barely)* hablan.
4. Estás en una fiesta y alguien te vuelca *(spills)* una bebida sobre tu camisa/vestido.
5. No recuerdas que hoy es el cumpleaños de tu mejor amigo(a).
6. Estás en una fiesta brava *(wild)* y alguien apaga las luces.

Bienvenida, la madre de Tomás, decidió visitar a su hijo y a su esposa en Chichicastenango sin avisarles. Presta atención al uso del pretérito y del imperfecto.

   Ayer fue domingo, el 20 de diciembre. Eran las 11:40 de la mañana y la temperatura en Chichicastenango estaba a 14 grados centígrados y llovía. Marta estaba duchándose y Tomás se estaba vistiendo porque muy pronto iban a ir a la iglesia. De repente *(Suddenly)*, sonó el teléfono y Tomás fue a contestarlo.

—¿Bueno?

—¡Hola, hijo! Habla tu mamá.

—Mamá, ¿cómo estás?

—Bien, bien. Acabo de llegar de Quezaltenango.[1] Estoy aquí en la estación de autobuses.

—¡Mamá! ¿Estás aquí en Chichicastenango?

—Sí, hijo. Decidí venir a última hora *(at the last minute)*. Hace seis meses que no los veo.

—¡Qué bueno, mamá! Voy a la estación a...

—No, mi hijo. Puedo ir a tu casa en taxi porque vives muy lejos de la estación y tengo mucho equipaje.

—Bueno. Entonces te esperamos aquí en casa, ¿eh?

—Sí, sí. Nos vemos pronto. Hasta luego, hijo.

—Hasta luego, mamá.

Bienvenida salió de la estación con su maleta, encontró un taxi y se subió. Luego ella le dio al taxista la dirección de la casa de Marta y Tomás. Mientras Bienvenida y el taxista iban a la casa, conversaban sobre el mal tiempo, pero el taxista estaba tan cansado que casi se durmió dos veces.

   De repente, ¡pum! El taxi chocó con *(crashed into)* un autobús que venía de otra calle y los dos vehículos pararon *(stopped)* inmediatamente. El taxista estaba tan cansado que no vio el autobús. Afortunadamente, nadie se lastimó, pero Bienvenida estaba nerviosa.

   Dos horas más tarde, el taxi llegó finalmente a la casa de Marta y Tomás, quienes esperaban a Bienvenida en la puerta. Ella salió del taxi y todos se saludaron con abrazos y besos.

G. **¿COMPRENDISTE?** Indica si las siguientes oraciones son ciertas o falsas. Si la oración es falsa, ¡corrígela!

1. Hacía mal tiempo el día en que llegó Bienvenida.
2. Bienvenida causó el accidente entre el taxi y el autobús.
3. Bienvenida llegó rápidamente a la casa de su hijo.
4. Ella llegó en otoño.
5. La madre de Tomás no tenía miedo de nada.
6. Tomás estaba triste cuando su mamá lo llamó.

---

[1] Quezaltenango is a small city located west of Guatemala City in the mountainous region of the country.

ENCUENTRO *cultural*

Chichicastenango

Éstas son unas palabras nuevas para la lectura:

el altiplano occidental *western highlands*
llevar a cabo *to take place*
la herencia *heritage*
orar *to pray*
quemar *to burn*
el alma *(f.)* *soul*
sagrado(a) *sacred*

Santo Tomás de Chichicastenango es un centro comercial muy importante para los indígenas del **altiplano occidental.** Está a solamente 87 millas de la Ciudad de Guatemala y se conoce por el mercado que se **lleva a cabo** cada jueves y domingo.

En Chichicastenango se puede ver **la herencia** maya en todo su esplendor. En la Iglesia de Santo Tomás se celebran una mezcla de ritos católicos y paganos. En las escaleras de la iglesia la gente **ora** y **quema** incienso de copal. Una vez dentro de la iglesia, ofrecen velas y flores a **las almas** de los muertos mientras invocan a los santos de toda clase de fuerzas naturales.

En Chichicastenango también está el Monasterio de Santo Domingo, el lugar donde encontraron el *Popol Vuh,* el libro **sagrado** de los mayas.

Para pensar: ¿Conoces algún lugar similar a Chichicastenango? ¿Tienes interés en ir a visitar «Chichi»? ¿Por qué sí o por qué no?

H. **PREGUNTAS** Contesta las siguientes preguntas a base de la lectura.

1. ¿Cómo se llama el centro comercial muy importante para los indígenas del altiplano occidental?
2. ¿Qué se celebra en la iglesia de Santo Tomás?
3. ¿Qué hace la gente en los escalones de la iglesia?

GRAMÁTICA I: *The preterite and imperfect tenses contrasted*

The choice of using the preterite tense or the imperfect tense is not arbitrary. The choice depends on how a speaker or writer views the past actions, conditions, and events that he/she describes.

> Spanish speakers use the preterite tense to describe the beginning or completion of past actions (e.g., what happened or did not happen; what someone did or did not do), conditions, and events.

- **Actions that were completed in the past**

Tulia **conoció** a Marta el año pasado en la casa de una amiga. Tulia **sugirió** la idea de la fiesta de sorpresa para Tomás. El día de la fiesta, Tulia **se puso** un vestido largo y bonito y **se pintó** la cara. Después, ella **salió** de su casa y **anduvo** a la casa de Marta y Tomás.

*Tulia **met** Marta last year at a friend's house. Tulia **suggested** the idea of a surprise party for Tomás. The day of the party, Tulia **put on** a long, pretty dress and **put on makeup**. Later, she **left** her house and **walked** to Marta and Tomás's house.*

- **Events that began and/or were completed in the past**

Allí los invitados **celebraron** el cumpleaños de Tomás. Muchas personas **estuvieron** en la fiesta: todos los parientes y amigos de la familia. A las 9:00 de la noche un conjunto musical **empezó** a tocar. La fiesta **fue** maravillosa; a Tomás le **gustó** mucho. A la 1:00 de la mañana, los invitados **volvieron** a sus casas.

*There, the guests **celebrated** Tomás's birthday. Many people **were** at the party: all of the family's relatives and friends. At 9:00 at night a band **began** to play. The party **was** marvelous; Tomás **enjoyed** it a lot. At 1:00 in the morning, the guests **left** for their houses.*

- **Conditions that began and/or were completed in the past**

Después de llegar a su casa, Tulia **se sintió** cansada y un poco enferma, pero al día siguiente ella **estuvo** mucho mejor.

*After arriving at her house, Tulia **felt** tired and a little ill, but the next day she **was** much better.*

The imperfect is used for describing past actions, conditions, and events that occurred *habitually* or *repetitiously* in the past.

Cada verano mi esposa y yo **íbamos** de vacaciones a un país extranjero. **Comíamos** en restaurantes diferentes, **montábamos** en bicicleta y **jugábamos** al tenis cerca de nuestro hotel. Ay, ¡cómo **nos divertíamos**!

*Every summer my wife and I **would go** on vacation to a foreign country. We **would eat** at different restaurants, we **would ride** bikes, and we **would play** tennis near our hotel. Oh, what fun we **would have**!*

The imperfect is also used for describing actions, conditions, and events that were in progress at some focused point in the past. The person describing them tells what was happening, often when something else was going on at the same time.[1]

El verano pasado Marta y yo fuimos a El Salvador.[2] El día que salimos **hacía** buen tiempo. Mientras **esperábamos** en la estación de tren, mi esposa **leía** el periódico y yo **miraba** a la gente despidiéndose de sus parientes.

*Last summer Marta and I went to El Salvador. The day we left the weather **was** great. While we **were waiting** in the train station, my wife **read** the newspaper and I **watched** people saying good-bye to their families. We **were** a bit tired.*

Spanish speakers also use the imperfect to describe past actions, conditions, and events that were anticipated or planned.

Queríamos quedarnos un día más en El Salvador pero no **teníamos** dinero.

*We **wanted** to stay another day in El Salvador but we didn't **have** the money.*

---

[1] To describe two simultaneous actions that were occurring in the past, Spanish speakers often use **mientras** *(while)* to join the two clauses in the imperfect tense.
[2] El Salvador is the small country to the south of Guatemala and is one of its major trading partners. It boasts a varied landscape including beaches on the Pacific coast, mountains and volcanos in the center and north, and the famous **el bosque El Imposible** *(Impossible Forest)*. Salvadorans refer to themselves as **guanacos**.

Spanish speakers often use the preterite and imperfect together to describe past experiences within the framework of the time they occurred. The imperfect is used to indicate what was taking place when another action in the preterite interrupts the event. (This phenomenon is exemplified by the last sentence of the following paragraph.)[1]

El segundo día de las vacaciones en El Salvador, **eran** las 2:15 de la tarde y Tomás y Marta **tenían** mucha hambre. Por eso, **fueron** al restaurante Torremolinos. Marta le **preguntó** a su marido si ellos **podían** sentarse en la terraza como **hicieron** el año pasado cuando **almorzaron** allí. Tomás le **dijo** al camarero que su esposa **quería** sentarse en la terraza porque a ella le **gustaba** el papagayo que tenían allí. Tomás y Marta **hablaban** sobre los acontecimientos de aquel día cuando **vino** el camarero con los entremeses.

*On the second day of the trip in El Salvador, it **was** 2:15 in the afternoon and Tomás and Marta **were** very hungry. So, they **went** to the restaurant Torremolinos. Marta **asked** her husband if they **could** sit on the terrace as they **did** last year when they **ate** lunch there. Tomás **told** the waiter that his wife **wanted** to sit on the terrace because she **liked** the papagayo they **had** out there. Tomás and Marta **were talking** about the events of that day when the waiter **came** with the appetizers.*

The following parameters may be used to distinguish between the use of the preterite and imperfect tenses:

Preterite	**Imperfect**
single, completed action (what someone did or didn't do)	habitual action or event (expresses the idea in English of something you *used to do* or *would always do* in the past)
Marta **dio** una fiesta de sorpresa para su marido con amigos especiales.	Tomás y Marta siempre **celebraban** los cumpleaños.
*Marta **gave** a surprise party for her husband with special friends.*	*Tomás and Marta always **celebrated** (**used to celebrate**) birthdays.*
highlighted, main action	background action or description that sets the stage for preterite action (including time, location, mood, age, weather, and physical and emotional states)
Cuando Tomás **llegó** a casa, **hacía** buen tiempo y **era** de noche. (Pret.) (Imp.) (Imp.) *When Tomás **arrived** at home, it **was** nice out and it **was** nighttime.*	
beginning or end of an event	middle of an event or emphasis on indefinite continuation of event
A las 11:00 de la noche **empezó** a llover.	En la fiesta todos los invitados **hablaban** y **comían**.
*At 11:00 at night, it **began** to rain.*	*At the party, all the guests **talked** and **ate**.*

---

[1] To describe an ongoing action in the imperfect that is interrupted by an event in the preterite, Spanish speakers often use the word **cuando** to introduce the preterite action.

When the verb **ir** is used in the imperfect with the preposition **a** + infinitive, it translates in English as *was/were going to do something*. The implication is usually that something happened later that prevented the intended action from taking place. For example, **Yo iba a mirar la tele, pero un amigo me llamó pidiéndome ayuda.** (*I was going to watch TV, but a friend called asking for help.*)

action that interrupts another action or event	ongoing event or action in the past that is interrupted

Los invitados **cantaban** cuando Tomás **entró** en la sala.
              (Imp.)   (Pret.)

*The guests **were singing** when Tomás **entered** the room.*

Verbs that normally refer to states or conditions (**saber, querer, tener, poder**) take on a special meaning in the preterite:

Preterite	**Imperfect**
supe *I found out*	**sabía** *I knew*
quise *I wanted to* (and did)	**quería** *I wanted to* (outcome undetermined)
pude *I was able to* (and did)	**podía** *I was able to* (outcome undetermined)
tuve que *I had to* (and did)	**tenía que** *I had to* (outcome undetermined)
tuve *I got, received*	**tenía** *I had (in my possession)*

The preterite is often used with verbs associated with time expressions such as **ayer, anteayer, anoche, una vez, dos veces, el mes pasado,** and **de repente** *(suddenly)*.	The imperfect is often used with time expressions such as **todos los días, cada semana, siempre, frecuentemente, de niño(a),** and **de joven.**

¡A practicar!

I.   ¿PRETÉRITO O IMPERFECTO? Decide si las siguientes oraciones en inglés requieren *(require)* el pretérito, el imperfecto o ambos *(both)*. Explica por qué es necesario usar cada forma que escoges.

1. We used to go to downtown to watch the parades.
2. My brother would always wear a costume.
3. When I was ten, my Aunt Jeanie had a big party for my mother.
4. It was a nice day, and we were all very excited.
5. We were all having a good time, when my aunt brought in a large birthday cake.
6. My mom began to cry.
7. It was a wonderful party.

J.   LA PRIMERA CITA DE TOMÁS Y MARTA Lee el siguiente párrafo una vez y luego conjuga los verbos entre paréntesis en el pretérito o el imperfecto según el contexto.

Marta _____ (**estar**) leyendo un libro en su apartamento cuando Tomás la _____ (**llamar**) por teléfono. Tomás le _____ (**preguntar**) si _____ (**querer**) ir al parque con él. Marta le _____ (**decir**) que sí, aunque _____ (**tener**) mucho que leer para la semana próxima. Tomás _____ (**venir**) a las 3:00 y los dos _____ (**salir**) juntos al parque. Mientras ellos _____ (**caminar**), los dos _____ (**hablarse**) cariñosamente. Los dos _____ (**sentirse**) muy contentos porque _____ (**hacer**) buen tiempo y _____ (**ser**) sábado. ¡No

_____ (tener) que levantarse temprano el día siguiente! En el parque ellos _____ (sentarse) en un banco y _____ (mirar) a la gente. Cuando ellos _____ (observer) a una pareja vieja en otro banco, un señor se les _____ (acercar) con unos globos grandísimos. El señor les _____ (explicar) que él los _____ (vender) en el parque todos los sábados. Tomás le _____ (comprar) uno a Marta y los dos _____ (reírse).

Ahora contesta las siguientes preguntas sobre la primera cita de Tomás y Marta.

1. ¿Qué hacía Marta cuando Tomás la llamó?
2. ¿Qué le preguntó Tomás?
3. ¿Qué tenía que hacer Marta para la semana próxima?
4. ¿A qué hora vino Tomás al apartamento?
5. ¿Por qué se sentían contentos Tomás y Marta en el parque?
6. ¿Qué hicieron ellos en el parque?
7. ¿Por qué se les acercó un señor en el parque?

K. MÁS PRETÉRITO O IMPERFECTO Recuerda que las palabras **tener que, saber, querer** y **poder** tienen significados diferentes en el pretérito y el imperfecto. Decide qué forma —pretérito o imperfecto— es necesaria para completar las siguientes frases. Después, pon el verbo en el tiempo necesario.

MODELO: Ayer cuando Tomás llegó a casa, él *supo* (saber) que había una fiesta para su cumpleaños.

1. Ayer antes de la fiesta yo _____ (tener) que limpiar la casa. Lo hice. Yo _____ (saber) que _____ (ir) a tener muchos invitados.
2. Ayer por la tarde nosotros _____ (saber) que los padres de Tomás _____ (querer) venir a la fiesta pero no _____ (poder).
3. El año pasado, nosotros _____ (tener) que hacer planes con más tiempo porque _____ (querer) tener mucha gente para la celebración.

L. UNA ESCENA EXTRAORDINARIA Completa el siguiente párrafo, usando correctamente el pretérito o el imperfecto de los verbos dados.

ver	correr	ir	caminar	estar
leer	dar	escuchar	lavar	cantar

Un miércoles a las 4:30 de la tarde, Marta _____ los platos del almuerzo en la cocina y _____ mientras su esposo la _____ y _____ el periódico en la sala. De repente, Tomás _____ un anuncio en el periódico. Después de verlo, Tomás _____ tan contento que _____ rápidamente a la cocina con el periódico en la mano.

El próximo sábado a las 11:00 de la mañana, la pareja _____ al centro de la ciudad donde Tomás _____ un discurso *(speech)* a los ciudadanos de Chichicastenango. ¡Tomás _____ a ser el próximo alcalde *(mayor)* del pueblo!

En voz alta

M. OCASIONES MEMORABLES Hazle las siguientes preguntas a un(a) compañero(a) de clase y luego comparen sus respuestas.

1. ¿Cuándo fue la primera vez que enviaste una tarjeta *(card)* a una persona para el día de San Valentín? ¿Cómo reaccionó la persona? ¿Cómo te sentías en aquel momento? ¿Recibiste alguna vez flores de otra persona?

2. Cuando eras joven, ¿qué hacías para celebrar el Día de Acción de Gracias *(Thanksgiving)*? ¿Comías mucho pavo?
3. ¿Cuál fue el cumpleaños más memorable para ti? ¿Con quién celebraste? ¿Recibiste algunos regalos especiales? ¿Lo pasaste muy bien?
4. ¿Ibas a la iglesia para la Pascua cuando eras joven?
5. ¿Gritaste «¡Feliz año nuevo!» el año pasado a la medianoche de la Noche Vieja? ¿Qué hacías cuando tocó el reloj las 12:00?

N. HABÍA UNA VEZ... Forma un grupo con dos o tres compañeros(as) de clase. Luego una persona comienza con la siguiente oración: «Había una vez una bruja *(witch)* que vivía sola en una casa vieja y oscura... » Las otras personas del grupo toman turnos para continuar el cuento lógicamente hasta su desenlace. Usa tu imaginación y el vocabulario de este capítulo para crear un cuento interesante.

VOCABULARIO: *La playa y el campo*

DE VACACIONES EN LA COSTA DEL SOL, EL SALVADOR[1] In this section you will learn vocabulary and expressions to talk about outdoor activities at the beach and in the countryside.

pescar · hacer camping · caminar por las montañas · el lago · el río · pasear en canoa · hacer una parrillada · broncearse/tomar el sol · la crema bronceadora · el balneario · la playa · la costa · correr las olas · el océano/el mar · pasear en velero · bucear · hacer esnórquel

¡A practicar!

O. ASOCIACIONES Selecciona la palabra que no va con el resto del grupo y explica por qué.

1. el océano, el mar, las montañas, el río, el lago
2. hacer camping, hacer una parrillada, bucear
3. el balneario, la playa, caminar por las montañas, la costa
4. pasear en canoa, broncearse, tomar el sol, la crema bronceadora

---

[1] El Salvador's Costa del Sol, situated about 40 miles to the east of San Salvador, is considered the country's most exclusive beach, offering a full range of tourist amenities.

P. **¿QUÉ HACE ESTA GENTE?** Mira los dibujos a continuación y describe lo que estas personas están haciendo. Usa el vocabulario que acabas de aprender.

MODELO:

Tomás corre las olas.

Tomás

1. nosotros

2. José Carlos y Eva

3. tú

4. yo

5. Marta

6. Lucho

En voz alta

Q. **PROBLEMAS Y SOLUCIONES** Conversa con otra persona. Estudiante 1 es un(a) cliente en el balneario Hotel Playa de Tesoro y Estudiante 2 es el (la) director(a) de actividades para el balneario. El (La) director(a) debe ofrecer una solución lógica a los problemas del (de la) cliente. Luego, cambien de papel y hagan otra conversación.

MODELO: E1: No me gusta nadar en el mar.
E2: *Usted puede nadar en nuestra piscina.*

1. Quiero ir a la playa, pero no tengo traje de baño.
2. Tengo hambre y quiero comer unas pupusas.[1]
3. No sé bucear, pero quiero ver cómo es debajo del mar.
4. Quiero aprender a bucear, pero no sé adónde ir.
5. Siempre tengo miedo de broncearme mucho cuando voy a la playa.
6. Me gusta pasear en canoa, pero no quiero ir solo(a).
7. Quiero jugar al vólibol en la playa, pero no tengo pelota *(ball)* ni conozco a nadie aquí.

---

[1] **Pupusas,** the Salvadoran counterpart to the Venezuelan **arepa,** are thick corn tortillas stuffed with cheese, beans, or pork.

8. ¿Es seguro *(safe)* nadar en el río o es mejor nadar en el océano?
9. Mi hijo quiere pescar, pero no sabemos dónde y no tenemos el equipo.
10. Quiero hacer algo romántico (aventurero) con mi novio(a).

R. **¡A PASARLO BIEN!** Trabaja con otro(a) estudiante. Imagínense que ustedes van a pasar un fin de semana en un balneario o en el campo. Primero, hagan una lista de las actividades que ustedes van a hacer en ese lugar el sábado y el domingo. Luego hagan una lista de todo lo que ustedes van a llevar. Traten de *(Try to)* usar el vocabulario de este capítulo y del **Capítulo 3.** Al terminar, expliquen el itinerario a la clase.

MODELO:

Actividades	Cosas para llevar
sacar fotos	*una cámara*
tomar el sol	*un traje de baño*
comer mariscos	*200 dólares*

ENCUENTRO *cultural*

El santo patrón de El Salvador

Éstas son unas palabras nuevas para la lectura:

honrar *to honor*
la coronación de una reina *crowning of a queen*
el circo *circus*

El Salvador es predominantemente católico. Por eso, casi todas las fiestas tienen un significado religioso. La Navidad y la Pascua son populares, pero la fiesta que les gusta más a los niños es la Fiesta del Salvador del Mundo. Ésta es la fiesta que **honra** al santo patrón de la ciudad de San Salvador, la capital del país. En la religión católica, el santo patrón sirve como protector espiritual de una región. El festival de la ciudad de San Salvador se llama las Fiestas Agostinas, y empezaron a celebrarlo en el siglo XVI, casi inmediatamente después de la conquista española.

Cada año se celebran las Fiestas Agostinas desde el 1 de agosto hasta el 6 de agosto en San Salvador. Esta fiesta es tan popular que se celebra también en toda la nación. Las Fiestas Agostinas no están completas sin la feria, las procesiones, **la coronación de una reina, el circo,** los cohetes y muchos caramelos. Toda la gente va a las celebraciones en las iglesias —ésa es la parte más emocionante de las celebraciones y es la parte más querida del festival de la capital.

Para pensar: En el pueblo o ciudad donde tú creciste, ¿hay un festival especial? Si no, ¿conoces alguna ciudad que tiene una celebración especial todos los años? Explica lo que sabes de los festivales anuales de tu propia experiencia o de la experiencia de otras personas.

S. PREGUNTAS Contesta las siguientes preguntas a base de la lectura.

1. ¿Qué son las Fiestas Agostinas?
2. ¿Qué eventos incluye esa celebración?

ASÍ SE DICE: *Affirmative and negative expressions*

Here are some useful affirmative and negative expressions.

algo	*something, anything*	**nada**	*nothing, not anything*
alguien	*somebody, anybody*	**nadie**	*nobody, no one*
algún, alguno(a)	*some, any*	**ningún, ninguno(a)**	*none, not any*
o... o	*either . . . or*	**ni... ni**	*neither . . . nor*
siempre	*always*	**nunca**	*never*
también	*also, too*	**tampoco**	*neither, not either*

In a negative Spanish sentence, at least one negative word comes before the verb. Sometimes there are several negative words in one sentence.

—¿Quieres beber **algo** antes del masaje, Marta?   *Do you want to drink **something** before your massage, Marta?*

—**No, no** quiero **nada**, gracias.   *No, I don't want **anything**, thank you.*

—¿Hay **alguien** con el masajista ahora?   *Is there **someone** with the massage therapist now?*

—**No, no** hay **nadie**, Marta.   *No, there's **no one**, Marta.*

Omit the word **no** if a negative word precedes the verb.

no + verb + negative word	negative word + verb
No viene nadie conmigo a nadar.	**Nadie viene** conmigo a nadar.

Nobody is coming with me to swim.

no + verb + negative word	negative word + verb
No voy nunca al gimnasio.	**Nunca voy** al gimnasio.

I never go to the gym.

The words **algún, alguno, alguna, algunos,** and **algunas** are used as adjectives and pronouns; use **algún** before a masculine singular noun.

—¿Hay **algún** traje de baño para mí, Marta?   *Is there **any** swimsuit for me, Marta?*

—No, pero tengo **algunos** zapatos de tenis para ti.   *No, but I have **some** tennis shoes for you.*

—No hay restaurante **alguno** en este pueblo.   *There is not a single restaurant in this town.*

The plural forms **ningunos** and **ningunas** are not used often;[1] instead, use the singular form, and use **ningún** before a masculine singular noun.

—¿Cuántos campos de fútbol hay aquí?   *How many soccer fields are there here?*

—No hay **ningún** campo de fútbol aquí.   *There aren't **any** soccer fields here.*

⟫

---

[1] **Ningunos** and **ningunas** are only used with nouns that always come in pairs or are always plural. For example: **¿Hay algunos zapatos de tenis para mí? No, no hay ningunos.** *(Are there any tennis shoes for me? No, there aren't any.)* Other nouns that always come in pairs or are always plural are **guantes, calcetines, medias, pantalones,** and **vacaciones.**

—¿A qué hora viene mi entrenador?   *What time is my trainer coming?*
—No tengo **ninguna** idea, Tomás.   *I have **no** idea, Tomás.*
—¿Cuántas piscinas tiene el bal-   *How many swimming pools does the*
neario?   *resort have?*
—No tiene **ninguna**.   *It doesn't have **any**.*

Express *neither* with a subject pronoun (**yo, tú, usted, él, ella**, etc.) + **tampoco**.

—Nunca voy al gimnasio.   *I never go to the gym.*
—Yo **tampoco**.   *Me **neither**.*

Place **ni** before a noun or a verb to express the idea of *neither . . . nor*.

—¿Quieres ir a correr o a levantar   *Do you want to go running or lift*
pesas?   *weights?*
—No quiero **ni** ir a correr **ni** levantar   *I want **neither** to go running **nor** to*
pesas.   *lift weights.*

¡A practicar!

T.   **IDEAS OPUESTAS** Forma una oración con el significado opuesto sustituyendo las palabras afirmativas con palabras negativas.

MODELO: Yo siempre estoy con mi familia para la Noche Vieja.
                Yo nunca estoy con mi familia para la Noche Vieja.

1. Hay algunos libros sobre el Día de los Muertos en la biblioteca.
2. Alguien en el balneario sabe correr las olas.
3. Tomás quiere bucear también.
4. Marta tiene algo para su esposo.
5. Rita quiere bucear o hacer esnórquel.
6. Siempre es divertido pasear en velero.

U.   **ENTRE ESPOSOS** Completa las dos siguientes conversaciones, usando **algo, nada, alguien, nadie, o... o, ni... ni, también, tampoco, siempre** y **nunca**.

—Tomás, voy al supermercado porque no hay casi _____ en el refrige-
rador. ¿Quieres comer _____ especial esta noche?
—No, gracias, Marta. No quiero comer _____ porque comí mucho en el
almuerzo.
—Pero, ¿qué te pasa, Tomás?
—_____. Es que no tengo hambre, Marta.
—Bueno. Hasta luego.
(Más tarde...)
—¡Hola, Tomás! Conocí a _____ en el supermercado. Y _____
es una persona que te conoce a ti.
—Ah, ¿sí? Debe ser _____ un amigo _____ un compañero de
trabajo. ¿Cuál es?
—Bueno, no es _____ un amigo _____ un compañero tuyo. Se
llama Lucía.
—¿Cómo? ¿Lucía? No conozco a _____ con ese nombre. Y no tengo
muchas amigas _____.
—¿No? Pues, ella me dijo que fue tu novia.
—¿Mi novia? Marta, _____ estás inventando cosas.
—Yo _____ invento historias sobre tus «mujeres». ¿No recuerdas a
Lucía? Era tu novia cuando tenía 14 años.
—Ah sí, ahora recuerdo, era muy amable conmigo y con mi mamá.

V. **ENFRENTE DEL HOTEL PLAYA DE TESORO** Completa la siguiente conversación, usando **algún, alguna, algunos, algunas, ningún, ninguna** y **ninguno**.

—Perdón, estoy buscando la piscina pública.
—¿Cómo? No hay _____ por aquí, señor.
—_____ amigos me dijeron que hay una piscina pública cerca de un mercado.
—No. No hay _____ mercado por aquí. Hay una piscina, pero es privada. La piscina pública está lejos.
—¿Está abierta o cerrada?
—No tengo _____ idea, señor.
—¿Hay un teléfono aquí?
—Aquí no hay _____. _____ día van a instalar un teléfono público aquí. Pero por el momento no hay _____teléfono público en esta zona.
—Muchas gracias.
—De nada.

W. **DE MAL HUMOR** Tú estás de mal humor hoy y, por eso, siempre les contestas negativamente a tus amigos que te hacen las siguientes preguntas.

MODELO: E1: ¿Quieres salir conmigo? (nadie)
         E2: *No quiero salir con nadie.*

1. ¿Quieres estudiar conmigo? (nunca)
2. ¿No quieres estudiar conmigo? (nadie)
3. ¿Te gusta correr las olas o esquiar en el agua? (ni... ni)
4. ¿Haces ejercicio? (ningún)
5. ¿Qué vas a hacer hoy? (nada)
6. ¿Quieres nadar en la piscina? (ninguna)
7. ¿Prefieres ir a mi casa? (Tampoco)

En voz alta

X. **¿ES VERDAD O NO?** Conversa con un(a) compañero(a) de clase. Una persona lee las siguientes oraciones y la otra persona responde apropiadamente a cada situación. Luego, cambien de rol.

MODELO: (Nada / Nunca) hace frío en la Ciudad de Nueva York.
         E1: *Nunca hace frío en la Ciudad de Nueva York.*
         E2: *No tienes razón. En la Cuidad de Nueva York hace frío en*
             el invierno.

1. El profesor (nadie / nunca) habla con nosotros fuera de clase.
2. Creo que los estudiantes en esta universidad no tienen (ningún / ninguno) interés en la política *(politics)*.
3. El profesor tiene un trabajo, pero tú no tienes (ninguno / tampoco).
4. En Guatemala, (algún / nunca) hace frío en el invierno.
5. (Nadie / Algunos) residentes de esta ciudad son de El Salvador.
6. Yo no estudio mucho para esta clase y tú (tampoco / también).
7. Las clases de esta universidad no son (o / ni) interesantes (o / ni) muy aburridas.

Y. **MÁS PREGUNTAS** Hazle las siguientes preguntas en español a un(a) compañero(a) de clase. Luego, hagan la actividad de nuevo diciendo lo opuesto de lo que dijeron antes.

MODELO: Are there some students from other countries in this class?
E1: *¿Hay algunos estudiantes de otros países en esta clase?*
E2: *Sí, hay algunos. Hay dos estudiantes de Inglaterra y una de Japón.*
o: E2: *No, no hay ningún estudiante de otro país en esta clase.*

1. Do you want to go to the moon **(la luna)** someday?
2. Do you like to study in the afternoon or in the evening?
3. Do some of your friends study on the weekends?
4. Do you always watch television in the evenings?
5. Do some of your friends speak German?
6. _____ likes to speak in Spanish. Do you also like to speak in Spanish?

ASÍ SE DICE: *Interrogative words*

Throughout *Plazas* you have been using interrogative words to ask for information about people and events. Below is a summary of interrogative words and examples of their uses.

¿Adónde? *Where (to)?*	**¿Adónde vas?** *Where are you going?*
¿Dónde? *Where?*	**¿Dónde está el balneario?** *Where is the beach resort?*
¿De dónde? *From where?*	**¿De dónde eres tú?** *Where are you from?*
¿Cómo? *How?*	**¿Cómo lo hiciste?** *How did you do it?*
¿Cuándo? *When?*	**¿Cuándo es la fiesta?** *When is the party?*
¿Cuánto(a)? *How much?*	**¿Cuánto cuestan los entremeses?** *How much are the hors d'oeuvres?*
¿Cuántos(as)? *How many?*	**¿Cuántas personas vienen a la fiesta?** *How many people are coming to the party?*
¿Quién(es)? *Who?*	**¿Quién es ella?** *Who is she?*
¿De quién(es)? *Whose?*	**¿De quién es la fiesta?** *Whose party is it?*
¿Por qué? *Why?*	**¿Por qué quieres ir a la playa?** *Why do you want to go to the beach?*
¿Para qué? *For what purpose?*	**¿Para qué ahorras tu dinero?** *Why are you saving your money?*
¿A qué hora? *At what time?*	**¿A qué hora es la fiesta?** *What time is the party?*
¿Qué? *What? Which?*	**¿Qué quieres comer?** *What do you want to eat?*
¿Cuál(es)? *What? Which one(s)?*	**¿Cuál es tu plato favorito?** *What is your favorite dish?*

¿Cuál(es)? is used much more frequently than the English word *Which?* and can mean both *What?* and *Which?* **¿Cuál(es)?** cannot be used when the next word in the question is a noun. In such cases, **¿Qué?** must be used.

¿Qué libro quieres?	**Which** book do you want?
¿Cuál de los dos libros quieres?	**Which** of the two books would you like?
¿Cuál es la fecha?	**What** is the date?
¿Qué hora es?	**What** time is it?

As you can see, the choice of whether to use **¿Qué?** or **¿Cuál?** depends on the syntax of the question. Use **¿Qué?** before a verb to ask for a definition or explanation.

¿**Qué** quieres?	*What do you want?*
¿**Qué** es un balneario?	*What is a balneario?*
¿**Qué** es esto?	*What is this?*

¡A practicar!

Z. **PREGUNTAS DE UN TURISTA** Dos turistas están hablando en la Costa del Sol, El Salvador. Un turista le hace muchas preguntas al otro. Indica la palabra interrogativa correcta para completar cada pregunta.

1. ¿De dónde / Dónde está el Hotel Tesoro de la Playa?
2. ¿Cómo / Cuándo son los cuartos en ese hotel?
3. ¿Cuánto / Cuántas cuesta el alojamiento *(lodging)* en el hotel?
4. ¿Con quiénes / cuántas personas compartes tu cuarto?
5. ¿Qué / Quiénes van contigo a la discoteca esta noche?
6. ¿Dónde / Quién es tu novia? ¿Es Luisa o Mónica?
7. ¿A qué / Adónde hora empiezan los fuegos artificiales *(fireworks)*?
8. ¿Para qué / Por qué no quieres ir con nosotros a ver los fuegos artificiales?
9. ¿Cuál / Qué es tu playa favorita en El Salvador?
10. ¿Dónde / Adónde vas en las próximas vacaciones con tu familia?

AA. *¿QUÉ O CUÁL(ES)?* Escoge la palabra correcta y luego haz la pregunta a un(a) compañero(a) de clase.

1. ¿_____ es el amor?
2. ¿_____ es tu grupo de música favorito?
3. ¿_____ clase tienes después de esta clase?
4. ¿_____ son los videos más recientes que viste en las últimas tres semanas?
5. ¿_____ es el Internet?
6. ¿_____ es tu número de teléfono?
7. ¿En _____ residencia estudiantil vives?
8. ¿_____ es la capital de El Salvador?
9. ¿_____ ciudad es la capital de Guatemala?

En voz alta

BB. ¿**CUÁNDO ES LA FIESTA?** Conversa con un(a) compañero(a) de clase. Una persona va a inventar detalles sobre una fiesta y la otra persona va a hacerle todas las preguntas posibles sobre esa fiesta.

Síntesis

¡A ver!

El **Capítulo 8** se centra en el tema de las fiestas y las vacaciones. Los segmentos de video de este capítulo los presenta Jaime, que es de la ciudad de Quetzaltenango en Guatemala. En el primer segmento, vas a ver una serie de clips cortos de diversas fiestas en el mundo hispánico. El segundo segmento se trata del famoso festival del Día de los Muertos en México.

ACTIVIDAD 1   Pre-viewing task (Segmento 1 del video)

Paso 1: Algunos clips que vas a ver en el primer segmento se tratan de festejos muy típicos de las culturas hispánicas. Otros son típicos no sólo de las culturas hispánicas sino también de otras culturas. Organiza las celebraciones que ves en los clips según si son típicas en tu cultura o no.

Celebraciones típicas en mi cultura	Celebraciones que *no* son típicas en mi cultura
1 *la fiesta de cumpleaños*	
2	
3	
4	
5	
6	
7	
8	

Paso 2: Compara tu lista con la de un(a) compañero(a) de clase y expliquen las diferencias que hay entre sus listas.

ACTIVIDAD 2   Pre-viewing task (Segmento 2 del video)

Paso 1: Tal vez ya sabes algo del famoso Día de los Muertos, una celebración importante en México. Antes de ver el segundo segmento de video que trata de este festejo en México, apunta en una hoja una lista de lo que ya sabes del Día de los Muertos.

Paso 2: En grupos de tres o cuatro, compartan la información que tienen sobre el Día de los Muertos. Primero seleccionen a un(a) secretario(a) del grupo para escribir una lista definitiva de información. Después cada estudiante del grupo lee su lista de información —el primero lee toda su lista, el segundo lee sólo lo que es nuevo, etcétera. Finalmente, dicten al (a la) secretario(a) la lista definitiva del grupo.

Use Spanish as much as possible to carry out the tasks indicated in **Paso 2.** You should be able to ask who wants to be the group secretary: **¿Quién quiere ser... ?** You should also be able to indicate how much new information you can add to the list: **No tengo nada más...** Then indicate to the rest of the group what you think should be included in the final list of information.

ACTIVIDAD 3   Viewing task (Segmento 2 del video)

Paso 1: Mira el segmento del video sobre el Día de los Muertos en México. Averigua si el video confirma o desmiente *(disproves)* la información que apuntó tu grupo en la **Actividad 2.**

Paso 2: La celebración del Día de los Muertos en México se realiza entre el 31 de octubre y el 2 de noviembre. Vuelve a mirar el segmento de video y apunta en la tabla de abajo cualquier información sobre lo que se festeja cada uno de los días de esta fiesta mexicana.

el 31 de octubre	el 1 de noviembre	el 2 de noviembre

ACTIVIDAD 4   Post-viewing task (Segmento 2 del video)

En los mismos grupos que formaron para la **Actividad 2,** comparen la información que todos apuntaron en la tabla de la **Actividad 3.**

¡A escribir!

Writing a descriptive paragraph

A descriptive paragraph contains sentences that describe people, places, and/or things. In this section, you will learn to write a descriptive paragraph in Spanish about one of your family's activities and how often they do it.

To express how often you or others do something, you can use adverbs of frequency; several of these adverbs are the same as the positive and negative expressions you learned earlier in this chapter. Some common adverbs of frequency are:

Functions: Expressing time relationships; Linking ideas; Talking about habitual actions

Vocabulary: Time expressions

a veces *sometimes*
cada año *each (every) year*
dos veces a la semana *twice a week*
muchas veces *often*
nunca *never*

raras veces *rarely, infrequently*
siempre *always*
todos los días *every day*
una vez al mes *once a month*

You can also modify these expressions to express a wide variety of time frames: **dos veces al mes, tres veces a la semana, cada mes,** and so on.

For example, read the following paragraph. As you read, circle the adverbs of frequency as they appear.

Todos los días a las 7:00 de la mañana mi hermano menor David y yo desayunamos con nuestros padres. David y yo siempre tomamos leche y yo como pan tostado con mermelada y, a veces, un huevo frito. Mi papá siempre toma café, y a mi mamá le gusta tomar chocolate caliente. Una vez al mes mi familia y yo desayunamos en un restaurante. Muchas veces vamos al restaurante La Cocina Guatemalteca porque nos gusta la comida allí.

Ahora, escribe un párrafo que describe una actividad (o unas actividades) que tú y tu familia hacen juntos. Usa los adverbios que has aprendido para indicar con qué frecuencia Uds. hacen estas actividades.

¡A conversar!

Entrevista a un(a) compañero(a) de clase sobre las vacaciones que él (ella) hacía con su familia de niño(a). Luego de cambien de papel. Usen el tiempo imperfecto para hablar de acciones habituales (repetidas).

Como guía, Uds. pueden usar las siguientes preguntas:

- ¿Adónde iban ellos? ¿Por qué?
- ¿Cuánto tiempo pasaban ellos allí?
- ¿Qué actividades hacían?
- ¿Qué aspecto de esas vacaciones le gustaba más (a su compañero[a])? ¿Por qué?

¡A leer!

Guessing meaning from word roots

Up to this point, you have learned a large number of new Spanish words. You are also able to recognize a large number of cognates, even if these words are new to you. Using this knowledge, you can guess the meaning of even more new Spanish words if you know the meaning of their roots. For example, in this chapter you learned the word **sorpresa;** based on your knowledge of this word, what would you guess that the verb **sorprender** means?

Words like **sorpresa** and **sorprender** that have the same root (e.g., **sorpr-**) are called "word families" because such words are closely related to one another.

Now look at the following list of words; these new words have the same word root as some of the new vocabulary items you learned in this chapter (refer to the vocabulary list at the end of the chapter if necessary). Can you guess the meanings of these new words based on the word root they contain?

_____ 1. asustado

_____ 2. campamento

_____ 3. el recuerdo

_____ 4. la despedida

a. memento; souvenir

b. good-bye; farewell

c. scared; frightened

d. camp; campsite

Paso 1: Antes de leer el artículo, contesta las siguientes preguntas.

1. Mira el mapa, la foto, el título y los subtítulos de la siguiente lectura. ¿Qué tipo de información contiene este artículo?
2. Consulta el mapa de nuevo. ¿Cuáles de los subtítulos se refieren a los nombres de regiones geográficas (e.g., ciudades, lagos, montañas, regiones, etc.) en Guatemala? Escribe una lista de estos nombres.

Paso 2: Identifica las palabras que contienen la misma **raíz** *(word root)*. ¿Puedes adivinar qué significan estas palabras?

_____	**1.** la altitud	**a.**	traído
_____	**2.** viajar	**b.**	cercano
_____	**3.** pervivir	**c.**	pueblo
_____	**4.** traer	**d.**	altura
_____	**5.** cerca	**e.**	vivir
_____	**6.** población	**f.**	baños
_____	**7.** bañarse	**g.**	viajero

Paso 3: Ahora, lee el artículo con cuidado. Luego, contesta las siguientes preguntas.

1. Según el artículo, ¿aproximadamente cuántos dialectos indígenas se hablan en Guatemala?
2. ¿Qué documentación es necesaria para viajar a Guatemala?
3. ¿Qué tipo de museo es el Museo Popol Vuh en la capital de Guatemala?
4. ¿Cómo se llama la ciudad más importante en la zona central del altiplano?
5. ¿Dónde está el castillo de San Felipe?
6. ¿Qué tipos de cosas puede comprar un viajero en Guatemala?

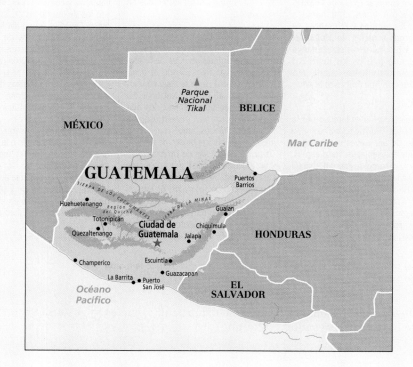

Guía del Viajero

Guatemala

SITUACIÓN

Se trata del país más septentrional de América Central. Limita al Norte y al Oeste con México, al Noroeste con Belice y al Este con Honduras y El Salvador. Tiene una costa atlántica de 117 kms. y un litoral pacífico de 332. Ocupa un área de 131.800 kms², dos veces la superficie de Suiza.

POBLACIÓN

La mitad de los ocho millones de habitantes del país pertenecen a los más de 20 grupos indígenas descendientes de los antiguos mayas. En la capital, la más grande de América Central, viven 1.300.000 habitantes.

IDIOMA

Aunque el español es el oficial, se hablan alrededor de 28 dialectos indígenas entre los que destacan el quiché, cakchiquel, kekchí y el mam.

DOCUMENTACIÓN

Sólo el pasaporte **en regla.**

QUÉ SE DEBE VER

GUATEMALA, CAPITAL Y ALREDEDORES

En la ciudad merece la pena visitar tres museos: el de *Arqueología y Etnología,* en Finca La Aurora, zona 13. El *Museo Ixchel,* del traje indígena, en la 4ª avenida 16–27, zona 10. Y el *Museo Popol Vuh,* de arte maya colonial, en la avenida de la Reforma 8–60, sexto piso, zona 9. En la llamada zona 1: destaca la plaza Mayor, donde está la Catedral, el Palacio Nacional, el pintoresco Mercado Central. En la zona 2, el Parque Minerva, zona residencial, y el «mapa en relieve» del país a gran escala.

A unos 25 kms. de la capital: *el lago Amatitlán.* Hay una vista panorámica excepcional desde el Parque de las Naciones Unidas. El volcán Pacaya, junto al pueblo de San Vicente Pacaya,

con sus continuas erupciones constituye todo un espectáculo.

La ciudad de Antigua, declarada por la UNESCO Monumento de las Américas, conserva magníficos edificios del siglo XVI y XVIII. Es famosa su Semana Santa.

EL LAGO AMATITLÁN

A unos 25 kms. de la ciudad de Guatemala es, según muchos, uno de los lagos más hermosos del mundo. Doce pueblos indígenas habitan en sus **orillas,** destacando Panajachel, centro turístico de la región, y las **aldeas** de Santiago Amatitlán, Santa Catarina Palopó y San Pedro La Laguna. Es muy interesante asistir al día de mercado en Sololá, en la parte alta del lago.

QUETZALTENANGO

En la zona central del altiplano destaca Quetzaltenango, la segunda ciudad en importancia del país, a más de 2.300 metros de altura. Cerca está la aldea de *Zunil,* y *Fuentes Georginas,* ambas con baños termales y antiguas iglesias coloniales. *Salcajá,* es la cuna del jaspe y en *Totonicapán* se pueden comprar coloridos **huipiles** bordados con flores. Son también famosas las **mantas** y **alfombras** de lana, hechas a mano, de *Momostenango.* A 10 kms. de Quetzaltenango se encuentra uno de los mercados más auténticos y típicos donde pervive el trueque: *San Francisco el Alto.*

EL QUICHÉ

Este Departamento es famoso por la población de *Chichicastenango* y su mercado de los jueves y domingos, que reúne artesanías de todo el país. En el cerro cercano de Pascual Abaj (O Turkaj) se realizan ritos prehistóricos mayas. Hacia el Norte se halla *Santa Cruz del Quiché,* la capital de este Departamento. En las afueras se encuentran las ruinas de *Utatlán,* última capital de los mayas quichés.

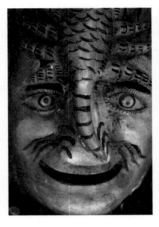

HUEHUETENANGO

La sierra de los Cuchumatanes alcanza aquí los 4.000 metros de altitud. En medio de valles y abruptas quebradas están las aldeas de *Todos Santos Cuchumatán* y *San Mateo Ixtatán,* famosas por sus **tejidos,** tradicionales y rituales mayas. En el área denominada triángulo ixil, merece la pena conocer los pueblos indígenas de *Nebaj, Chajul y Cotzal,* detenidos en el tiempo.

LA RUTA MAYA

En la selva del Petén se ocultan las ruinas más impresionantes de la civilización maya, *Tikal.* Desde el aeropuerto de Santa Elena se llega en unos 45 minutos al Parque Nacional del Petén. Se necesitan mínimo dos días para visitar este centro religioso, sus pirámides, palacios, amplias avenidas, juegos de pelota y el Museo de Tikal.

Otras ruinas son las de *Uaxactún,* 25 kms. al Norte de Tikal, por un camino casi intransitable en época de lluvias. El pueblecito de *Sayaxché,* 61 kms. al Sudoeste de *Flores,* es la base para visitar las ruinas mayas del Sudoeste del Petén. Los yacimientos más interesantes son *El Ceibal* a 17 kms. de

Sayaxché. A lo largo del río de la Pasión hay otros sitios arqueológicos para los más aventureros como *Aguateca, Dos Pilas* y *Tamarindito,* cerca del lago Petexbatún.

LAGO IZABAL

Situado al Noroeste de la carretera del Atlántico, destaca en él el Castillo de San Felipe, que data de 1652, construido para defenderse de los piratas.

EL CARIBE

La ciudad de Livingstone está habitada por los descendientes de los esclavos traídos desde África. Pintoresco lugar de cocoteros y casas pintadas de chillones colores. Excursiones por el río Dulce, a la reserva *Natural de Chocón-Machacas.* Y a los *Siete Altares,* cataratas y pozas a lo largo de la Bahía de Amatique.

QUÉ COMPRAR

Lo más famoso de Guatemala son sus textiles, hechos de forma artesanal en los telares primitivos de cintura o palitos. Los huipiles o camisas bordadas de las indígenas son la prenda más llamativa y colorista. Los más bonitos son los de las aldeas de San Antonio Aguas Calientes, Santa María de Jesús, Santiago Atitlán y los de Nebaj de Chajul. Son conocidos los chalés jaspeados de Salcajá o Totonicapán, y las cintas bordadas del pelo de Aguacatán. Los sacos o bolsos de hombre de Sololá y los pantalones bordados con aves de Santiago Atitlán o San Pedro la Laguna.

Hay también máscaras muy originales de la Danza del Venado o la Conquista que se venden en el mercado de Chichicastenango. En la capital se puede comprar artesanía de todo tipo: huipiles, joyas de jade y plata, tallas de madera, máscaras en el Mercado Central (detrás de la Catedral).

---

en regla *in order* **las orillas** *banks (of the lake)* **la aldea** *village, town* **el huipil** *traditional woman's tunic* **la manta** *blanket*
la alfombra *rug carpet, floor covering* **el tejido** *weaving, fabric*

Paso 4: De los sitios y ciudades descritos en el artículo, ¿cuáles te gustaría visitar? ¿Cuáles te parecen interesantes? ¿Por qué?

Fiestas y celebraciones   *Holidays and celebrations*

asustarse *to be frightened*
celebrar *to celebrate*
cumplir años *to have a birthday*
dar (hacer) una fiesta *to give a party*

disfrazarse *to wear a costume*
gritar *to shout*
hacer un brindis *to make a toast*
llorar *to cry*

pasarlo bien (mal) *to have a good (bad) time*
ponerse + adjective *to become, to get + adjective*
portarse bien (mal) *to behave well (poorly)*

reaccionar *to react*
recordar (ue) *to remember*
reunirse con *to get together with*

Sustantivos

el anfitrión *host*
la anfitriona *hostess*
el brindis *toast*
la celebración *celebration*
los cohetes *rockets*
el cumpleaños *birthday*

el día feriado *holiday*
el disfraz *costume*
los entremeses *hors d'oeuvres*
la fiesta (de sorpresa) *(surprise) party*
el (la) invitado *guest*
la máscara *mask*

el pastel *cake*
la procesión *parade*
los regalos *gifts*
las velas *candles*

La playa y el campo   *The beach and the country*

el balneario *beach resort*
la costa *coast*
la crema bronceadora *suntan lotion*

el lago *lake*
el mar *sea*
el océano *ocean*

el río *river*

Pasatiempos

broncearse (tomar el sol) *to get a suntan*
bucear *to scuba dive*
caminar por las montañas *to hike in the mountains*

correr las olas *to surf*
hacer camping *to go camping*
hacer esnórquel *to snorkel*
hacer una parrillada *to have a cookout*

pasear en canoa/velero *to go canoeing/sailing*
pescar *to fish*

Expresiones afirmativas

algo *something, anything*
alguien *somebody, someone, anybody, anyone*

algún, alguno(a) *some, any*
o... o *either . . . or*
siempre *always*

también *also, too*

Expresiones negativas

nada *nothing, not anything, at all*
nadie *nobody, no one*

ningún, ninguno(a) *none, not any*
ni... ni *neither . . . nor*

nunca *never*
tampoco *neither, not either*

Palabras interrogativas

¿A qué hora? *At what time?*
¿Adónde? *Where (to)?*
¿Cómo? *How?*
¿Cuál(es)? *What? Which one(s)?*
¿Cuándo? *When?*

¿Cuánto(a)? *How much?*
¿Cuántos(as)? *How many?*
¿Dónde? *Where?*
¿De dónde? *From where?*
¿De quién(es)? *Whose?*

¿Para qué? *For what purpose?*
¿Por qué? *Why?*
¿Qué? *What? Which?*
¿Quién(es)? *Who?*

Expresión idiomática

¡Felicitaciones! *Congratulations!*

De viaje por el Caribe: La República Dominicana, Cuba y Puerto Rico

Communicative goals

In this chapter you will learn how to . . .

- Talk about air travel, other types of transportation, and lodging
- Simplify expressions using in-direct object pronouns and direct and indirect object pronouns together
- Talk about getting around in the city
- Give directions and express desires using formal commands
- Recognize statements of volition and influence

Grammar

- Indirect object pronouns
- Double object pronouns
- Formal commands
- The subjunctive mood

Cultural information

- La República Dominicana
- Cuba
- Puerto Rico

La Plaza de Armas, Viejo San Juan, Puerto Rico

EN EL AEROPUERTO LAS AMÉRICAS[1] In this section you will learn vocabulary and expressions used for traveling by airplane. The drawing below represents a typical scene in the Dominican Republic's main airport.

EL AEROPUERTO

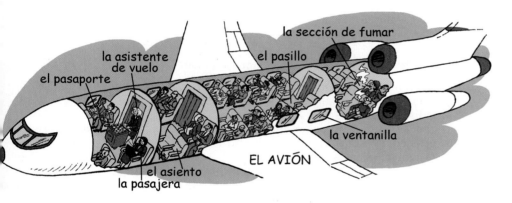

EL AVIÓN

el boleto (billete) de ida *one-way ticket*
el boleto (billete) de ida y vuelta *round-trip ticket*
el viaje *trip*
el vuelo (sin escala) *(nonstop) flight*

Verbos

abordar *to board*
bajar(se) (de) *to get off*
facturar el equipaje *to check the luggage*
hacer escala (en) *to make a stop (on a flight) (in)*
hacer la(s) maleta(s) *to pack one's suitcase(s)*

ir en avión *to go by plane*
pasar (por) *to go through*
recoger *to pick up, to claim*
viajar *to travel*
volar *to fly*

Expresiones idiomáticas

¡Bienvenido(a)! *Welcome!*

¡Buen viaje! *Have a nice trip!*

> **¿NOS ENTENDEMOS?**
>
> While a *passenger* is **un(a) pasajero(a)**, a *traveler* is **un(a) viajero(a).**

---

[1] Santo Domingo is the capital city of the Dominican Republic. The international airport is called **Las Américas**, and it is about 20 minutes east of Santo Domingo.

¿NOS ENTENDEMOS?

In Latin America, the words **boleto** and **billete** are used to talk about an airplane ticket. In Spain it is more common to use **el pasaje**, which is also used in Latin America.

Palabras útiles

abrochar el cinturón de seguridad   *to buckle the seat belt*
la aerolínea   *airline*
aterrizar   *to land*
la cabina   *cabin*
con destino a   *departing for*

la demora   *delay*
despegar   *to take off*
el (la) piloto   *pilot*
procedente de   *arriving from*
la salida de emergencia   *emergency exit*

¡A practicar!

A. UN VIAJE EN AVIÓN A SANTO DOMINGO Teresita, una mujer puertorriqueña, hizo un viaje a Santo Domingo para visitar a unos familiares el verano pasado. Pon sus acciones en un orden lógico.

_____ Pasó por la aduana.
_____ Se bajó del avión.
_____ Facturó el equipaje.
_____ Abordó el avión con destino a Santo Domingo.
_____ Fue a la agencia de viajes.
_____ Compró un boleto de ida y vuelta.
_____ Hizo las maletas.
_____ Recibió una invitación de sus parientes en Santo Domingo.
_____ Buscó su asiento de ventanilla en la sección de no fumar.
_____ Recogió su equipaje.

B. DEFINICIONES Identifica la palabra definida.

1. la gente que paga para viajar en avión _____
2. el lugar en que se aborda el avión _____
3. la lista de los días y las horas de vuelos _____
4. el documento para poder entrar en otro país_____
5. el asiento desde el cual se puede ver hacia afuera _____
6. el equipaje que se factura _____
7. el lugar donde se ve lo que hay en las maletas _____
8. la tienda donde se compran los boletos de avión _____
9. el boleto que se compra cuando uno no quiere volver _____
10. lo que uno les dice a los amigos antes de viajar _____

a. de ida
b. la aduana
c. la puerta
d. el horario
e. las maletas
f. ¡Buen viaje!
g. el pasaporte
h. los pasajeros
i. la ventanilla
j. la agencia de viajes

C. NUESTRA LUNA DE MIEL Teresita y su esposo Manny fueron a La Habana[1] para pasar su luna de miel *(honeymoon)*. Escoge de las siguientes palabras para completar el párrafo.

agente de viajes   salida   viaje
equipaje de mano   asiento de pasillo   hacer escala
inmigración   asistente de vuelo   ir en avión
llegada   vuelo sin escalas   Bienvenidos

El mes pasado, Manny y yo fuimos a La Habana, Cuba, para nuestra luna de miel. No queríamos ir en barco, preferíamos _____. Nuestro

---

[1] In December of 1999, the first charter flight in more than 30 years left New York for Havana, Cuba. During most of the Castro regime, travel to Cuba for American citizens has been extremely limited. As o December 1999, it became legal for some people to go to Cuba from the U.S.—citizens with familial rela tions in Cuba, researchers, and medical personnel.
[2] Cubana: Empresa Consolidada de Aviación is the national airline of Cuba.

_____ nos reservó un _____ en la aerolínea Cubana.[2] Yo estaba contenta porque a mí no me gusta _____. Tampoco me gusta ver afuera del avión cuando vuelo, así que yo pedí el _____. A la _____ del vuelo, dimos nuestros pasaportes y boletos al _____. No teníamos muchas maletas, pero Manny llevó _____ con las cosas más necesarias. Durante el vuelo, esperamos con mucha expectativa la _____. Al llegar a La Habana, el piloto anunció «¡_____ a Cuba!» Tuvimos que pasar por la _____, pero fue fácil. Total, nuestra luna de miel en La Habana fue el mejor _____ de mi vida.

En voz alta

D. **MIS PREFERENCIAS** Indica tus preferencias personales a un(a) compañero(a) de clase.

1. Normalmente, cuando compro un boleto de avión, pago...
2. En general, prefiero viajar por la noche/mañana/tarde porque...
3. Para pasar el tiempo durante el vuelo, normalmente yo...
4. Generalmente, cuando viajo en avión prefiero un asiento...
5. Cuando el vuelo tiene una demora de más de una hora ...
6. Por lo general, cuando hago un viaje de dos semanas o más, llevo...

E. **¿QUÉ OPINAS?** Léele las siguientes oraciones a otro(a) estudiante, quien debe decirte si está de acuerdo o no, y por qué.

MODELO: E1: Es mejor pedir un vuelo sin escalas que con escalas.
            E2: *Estoy de acuerdo.*
            E1: *¿Por qué?*
            E2: *Porque los pasajeros llegan más rápidamente.*

1. Es mejor sentarse en la ventanilla que en el pasillo de un avión.
2. Es difícil viajar en avión con un bebé o con un niño pequeño.
3. Es buena idea llevar poco equipaje cuando se viaja en avión.
4. Es preferible pagar un boleto de avión antes de viajar que después de viajar.
5. Es importante sentarse cerca de una puerta de emergencia en el avión.
6. Es más interesante sentarse en la sección de clase turística que en primera clase.

F. **ENTREVISTA** Hazle a otro(a) estudiante las siguientes preguntas sobre sus experiencias de viaje. Luego, formen sus propias preguntas usando el vocabulario nuevo.

1. ¿Tienes pasaporte? ¿Sí? ¿Cuándo conseguiste *(did you acquire)* tu pasaporte? o: ¿No? ¿Piensas conseguir un pasaporte algún día? ¿Por qué?
2. ¿A qué países viajaste en los últimos cuatro años? ¿Cuál es tu país favorito? ¿Qué países quieres visitar algún día? ¿Por qué?
3. Normalmente, ¿llevas mucho o poco equipaje cuando viajas?
4. ¿Cuándo fue la última vez que viajaste en avión? ¿Adónde fuiste? ¿Por qué fuiste a ese lugar?
5. ¿Prefieres sentarte en el pasillo o al lado de la ventanilla cuando viajas en avión? ¿Por qué?
6. En un vuelo internacional, ¿prefieres sentarte en la sección de fumar o en la sección de no fumar?

G. **EN EL AEROPUERTO** Haz esta actividad con otros(as) dos estudiantes. Dos personas son pasajeros en el aeropuerto, y la otra persona es el (la) agente de la aerolínea.

AGENTE	**PASAJEROS**
1. Greet your passengers.	2. Respond appropriately.
3. Find out where they are going.	4. Answer the question.
5. Ask for their tickets and passport.	6. Do what the agent asks and say something appropriate.
7. Ask their seating preference (smoking/nonsmoking; window/aisle).	8. Answer, then ask if your plane will leave on time.
9. Answer the question, then check in their luggage.	10. Ask how the weather is at your destination.
11. Respond, then say where they should board the airplane.	12. Ask for directions to your departure gate.
13. Explain, then return their travel documents.	14. Ask what time it is. Express appreciation.
15. Respond, then wish them a good trip.	16. Express your appreciation.
17. Say good-bye.	18. Answer appropriately.

EN CONTEXTO

Sharon y su amiga Kate son estudiantes de la Universidad Internacional de la Florida en Miami donde han estudiado español por tres años. Ahora ellas están de vacaciones en Santo Domingo visitando la Ciudad Colonial.[1] Lo que sigue es una parte del diario que grabó Sharon en su grabadora.

27 de junio

Ahora Kate y yo estamos en el Hotel Montesinos. Cuando llegamos aquí anoche, estábamos tan cansadas que nos acostamos inmediatamente. Esta mañana caminamos por la ciudad colonial y vimos algunas plazas e iglesias coloniales. En una librería compramos tarjetas postales y se las mandamos a nuestros padres y amigos. Luego tomamos un autobús al Fuerte del Ángulo desde donde vimos el puerto. Yo saqué una foto de Kate enfrente de la fortaleza. Cuando volvamos a Florida, se la voy a dar a ella. Espero que salga bien. En la Plaza de la Hispanidad conocí a Eduardo Pérez, a su esposa Gabriela y a sus dos hijas. Se los presenté a Kate cuando ella volvió de la Plaza España donde hacía algunas compras. Ellos nos invitaron a su casa. Ojalá que podamos visitarlos antes de volver.

28 de junio

Hoy visitamos muchas iglesias como la Capilla de Nuestra Señora de los Remedios. Por la tarde, fuimos al mercado de artesanías en el Parque Colón para comprar algunos recuerdos. Yo compré un anillo *(ring)* y unos aretes *(earrings)*, y se los di a Kate. Luego, ella compró un sombrero y una camiseta muy bonita, ¡y me los dio a mí! Allí en el parque conocimos a Juan Ochoa Valderrama y José Hernández Lillo, que son empleados del Museo Casas Reales. Juan tiene 23 años y José tiene 20. Ellos nos invitaron a tomar café en un pequeño restaurante donde charlamos por dos horas. Antes de salir, Juan nos invitó a una fiesta en su casa. Hemos estado en Santo Domingo solamente dos días y ya tenemos seis amigos. ¡Qué simpáticos son los dominicanos!

---

[1] The Dominican Republic was the first European colony of the New World. Its capital, Santo Domingo, is home to the first Spanish fortresses, hospitals, and churches. It is also the site of the first colonial cathedral and university.

H. ¿COMPRENDISTE? Contesta las siguientes preguntas a base de la lectura.

1. Según **En contexto,** ¿cuáles son algunos sitios de interés turístico que ofrece Santo Domingo?
2. Haz una lista de los lugares que Sharon y Kate visitaron durante su estancia *(stay)* en Santo Domingo y las actividades que ellas hicieron allí.

> MODELO: Lugares Actividades
> *Hotel Montesinos* *Durmieron en ese hotel.*
> *una librería* *Compraron tarjetas postales allí.*

3. Escribe uno o dos párrafos con un resumen de lo que hicieron Sharon y Kate, usando la información de la lista que acabas de escribir.
4. Imagínate que tú estás en Santo Domingo ahora. De las cosas que Sharon y Kate vieron e hicieron en esta isla, ¿cuáles te gustaría ver y hacer?
5. ¿Qué impresiones tienes de Kate y Sharon?

ENCUENTRO *cultural*

La República Dominicana

Éstas son unas palabras nuevas para la lectura:

el merengue   *type of dance and music*
la tambora   *type of drum*
la güira   *percussion instrument scraped by a metal rod*
la bachata   *type of dance*   **disfrutar**   *to enjoy*   **ruidoso**   *noisy*

La República Dominicana está en la misma isla que la República de Haití. Los habitantes tienen una herencia taína, europea y africana.[1] Según los historiadores, los taínos llamaban a la isla «Quisqueya» antes de la llegada de los españoles.

La música (y baile) más popular en la isla es **el merengue.** Este ritmo domina la vida musical de la República Dominicana. El merengue tradicional se toca por un grupo de tres personas. Los instrumentos necesarios son una **tambora,** un acordeón y una **güira.** También, la salsa es muy popular. Hay discotecas en cada pueblito donde bailan muchos otros bailes populares, como la **bachata,** que es la música ranchera dominicana.

El turismo es muy importante para la economía de esta isla, y millones de personas la visitan cada año. Muchos van en avión o en barco. Los turistas **disfrutan** de las extensas playas de las aguas cristalinas y el clima soleado pero agradable. Para el transporte, los turistas se divierten alquilando los motoconchos, un tipo de motocicleta. Aunque el viaje puede ser muy **ruidoso,** por 25 centavos americanos *(US$0.25)* por persona, pueden subir hasta tres personas. Por tres o cuatro dólares se puede viajar en carros públicos, o conchos.

Para pensar: ¿Quieres ir algún día a esta isla? ¿Por qué sí o no? Compara la herencia de las razas diferentes de la República Dominicana con la herencia en los Estados Unidos. ¿Es muy diferente? ¿similar? Explica tu respuesta.

---

[1] The Taino were the indigenous peoples who inhabited the island when the Spaniards arrived. The African presence on the island, as in the case of Puerto Rico and Cuba, stems from the years when the colonizers brought slaves from Africa to work the island plantations.

PREGUNTAS Contesta las siguientes preguntas a base de la lectura.

1. ¿Cuáles son los orígenes étnicos de la gente de la República Dominicana?
2. ¿Qué es el merengue? ¿En qué consiste un grupo que toca merengue?
3. ¿Cuáles son algunas opciones de transporte para los turistas en la República Dominicana?

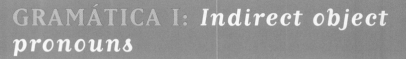

GRAMÁTICA I: *Indirect object pronouns*

All sentences have a subject and a verb. As you learned in **Capítulo 7**, many sentences also have a direct object or a pronoun that replaces the direct object (the direct object pronoun).

Subject	Verb	Direct Object	Subject	D.O.P.	Verb
↓	↓	↓	↓	↓	↓
Manny	compró	**un boleto.**	Manny	**lo**	compró.

*Manny bought a **ticket**.*　　　　　*Manny bought **it**.*

Some sentences also have an indirect object.

Subject	I. O. P.	Verb	Direct Object	Indirect Object
↓	↓	↓	↓	↓
Manny	le	compró	un boleto	**a su esposa.**

*Manny bought a ticket **for his wife**.*

Indirect object pronouns refer to people already mentioned as indirect objects; that is, the pronoun tells *to whom* or *for whom* the action of the verb is performed.

To whom did he give the tickets?

Manny **le** dio los boletos **a su esposa.**　　*Manny gave the tickets **to his wife**.*
Él **le** dio los boletos.　　　　　　　　　　*He gave the tickets **to her**.*

For whom did she buy the souvenirs?

Teri **les** compró recuerdos **a sus**　　　　*Teri bought souvenirs **for her**
　hermanos.　　　　　　　　　　　　　　　　brothers.*
Ella **les** compró los recuerdos.　　　　　　*She bought the souvenirs **for them**.*

In the sentences above, the indirect object pronouns **le** and **les** replace the indirect object nouns **esposa** and **hermanos**, respectively.

Formation and placement of indirect object pronouns

Singular		Plural	
me	*to/for me*	**nos**	*to/for us*
te	*to/for you* (informal)	**os**	*to/for you* (informal)
le	*to/for you* (formal), *him, her*	**les**	*to/for you* (formal), *them*

Indirect object pronouns are placed in the same positions as direct object pronouns.

1. Place the pronoun in front of the conjugated verb.

—¿Marta **te dio** esa maleta?   *Did Marta **give you** that suitcase?*

—Sí. También **me compró** estos sombreros.   *Yes. **She** also **bought me** these hats.*

2. In negative sentences, place the **no** in front of the pronoun.

—Le di el sombrero a mi esposo.   *I gave my husband the hat.*

—¿Por qué **no nos** diste uno?   *Why **didn't** you give **us** one?*

3. When the pronoun is used with an infinitive, a present participle, or an affirmative command, either place it before the conjugated verb or attach it to the infinitive, the present participle, or the command.[1]

Le voy a escribir.
Voy a escribir**le**.   *I'm going to write to **him**.*

Le estoy escribiendo ahora.
Estoy escribiéndo**le** ahora.   *I'm writing to **him** now.*

¡Escríbe**le** ahora!   *Write to **him** now!*

Because **le** and **les** have different meanings, you may add the expressions **a él, a ella, a usted, a ellos, a ellas,** or **a ustedes** to the sentence for clarification or emphasis.

For clarification

—¿**Le** prometiste el viaje **a él** o **a ella**?   *Did you promise the trip **to him** or **her**?*

—**Le** prometí el viaje **a ella**.   *I promised the trip **to her**.*

For emphasis

—¿**A quién le** está regalando este recuerdo?   ***To whom** are you giving this souvenir?*

—Estoy regalándo**le** este recuerdo **a usted**.   *I'm giving this souvenir **to you**.*

Indirect object pronouns are normally used with the verbs **dar** *(to give)* and **decir** *(to say; to tell)*. Other verbs that frequently employ indirect object pronouns are:

escribir *to write*	**preguntar** *to ask a question*
explicar *to explain*	**prestar** *to lend*
hablar *to speak*	**prometer** *to promise*
mandar *to send*	**recomendar (ie)** *to recommend*
ofrecer (zc)[2] *to offer*	**regalar** *to give (as a gift)*
pedir (i) *to request; to ask for*	**servir (i)** *to serve*

---

[1] A written accent is needed to mark the stressed vowel of a present participle or an affirmative command when an indirect object pronoun is attached to it.
[2] The **yo** form of **ofrecer** is **ofrezco**.

¡A practicar!

J. **OBJETOS INDIRECTOS** Rellena los espacios en blanco con el pronombre de objeto indirecto apropiado.

MODELO: Yo *les* escribo cartas. (a mis padres)

1. Mis amigos _____ piden ayuda. (a mí)
2. Yo _____ ofrezco ayuda. (a mis amigos)
3. Mi mejor amigo(a) _____ regala cosas. (a mí)
4. Yo _____ hago preguntas. (a mis compañeros de clase)
5. Tu compañero(a) de cuarto _____ explica tareas difíciles. (a ti)
6. El profesor _____ recomienda películas interesantes. (a nosotros)
7. Yo _____ prometo hacer muchas cosas con él (ella). (a mi novio[a])
8. Los padres _____ prestan dinero. (a los hijos)
9. Manny _____ habla. (al asistente de vuelo)
10. El consejero del hotel _____ recomendó aquel restaurante cubano. (a nosotros)
11. El camarero allí _____ sirvió dos mojitos cubanos.[1] (a mí)
12. Teri _____ escribió dos tarjetas postales durante el viaje. (a sus padres)

K. **EN UNA TIENDA EN EL AEROPUERTO** Teri y Manny deciden al último momento comprarle un recuerdo de Cuba al hermano de Teri. Rellena los espacios en blanco conjugando los verbos entre paréntesis (si es necesario) y colocando *(placing)* el pronombre de objeto indirecto en el lugar apropiado.

MODELO: Dependiente: ¿Puedo *ayudarles* (ayudar/les)?

Dependiente:	Hola, ¿en qué puedo _____ (servir/les)?
Teri:	Queremos _____ (comprar/le) un regalo a mi hermano.
Dependiente:	Bien. ¿Qué tipo de regalo _____ (buscar/le)?
Teri:	Pues, a mi hermano y a mí _____ (gustar/nos) mucho la ropa.
Dependiente:	¿Ropa? ¿Qué tipo de ropa _____ (gustar/les) a Uds., por ejemplo?
Teri:	Bueno, el año pasado él _____ (regalar/me) un sombrero típico de Perú y ahora quiero _____ (dar/le) a él un sombrero típico cubano.
Manny:	Y a mí _____ (gustar/me) mucho las guayaberas.[2] Teri, ¿no quieres _____ (dar/le) a tu hermano una guayabera como ésta?
Teri:	Hmm, es verdad que necesito _____ (hacer/te) un regalo de boda a ti todavía. ¿Por qué no _____ (comprar/te) esa guayabera a ti? Pero creo que _____ (ir a gustar/le) más a mi hermano el sombrero.
Dependiente:	Comprendo. Bueno, ¿a Ud. _____ (gustar/le) éste?
Teri:	¡Sí! Él _____ (ir a decir/nos) «¡Muchas gracias!» ¿Puedo _____ (probar/me) el sombrero? Mi esposo puede _____ (regalar/me) uno también.
Manny:	Y tú _____ (poder/me) regalar la guayabera, ¿no?

---

[1] A **mojito cubano** is a Cuban drink made with rum, sugar, and mint leaves. Supposedly, it was the writer Ernest Hemingway's preferred drink during his stay in Cuba.
[2] A **guayabera** is a typical dress shirt worn by men in the Caribbean. They are usually made of lightweight material and have four pockets embroidered on the front.

L. ¡AYÚDANOS! Teri y Manny están muy cansados después de su luna de miel y te piden ayuda. Explica lo que tú haces por ellos, y ellos por ti, usando el pronombre de objeto indirecto apropiado.

MODELO: (a ellos) hacer las reservas para el vuelo
            Les hago las reservas para el vuelo.

1. (a Teri) bajar las maletas
2. (a ellos) llamar un taxi
3. (a Manny) prestar dinero para el taxi
4. (a Teri) ofrecer ayuda con las maletas en el aeropuerto
5. (a ellos) ayudar a facturar el equipaje
6. (al agente) preguntar el horario
7. (a Teri y Manny) prometer escribir una carta
8. (a mí) Manny y Teri regalar un recuerdo de La Habana
9. (a nosotros) Teri dar un beso
10. (a Manny) decir «Buen viaje»
11. (a mí) Manny y Teri dar una guayabera cubana por mi ayuda
12. (a nosotros) Manny pedir una Coca-Cola para todos

En voz alta

M. UN ESPOSO ANSIOSO En el aeropuerto Manny está preocupado con todos los detalles *(details)* del viaje. Teri lo tranquiliza *(reassures him)*, explicándole que ella ya *(already)* hizo varias cosas. ¿Cómo responde Teri a las preocupaciones de Manny?

MODELO: ¿Les compramos los regalos a nuestros amigos?
            Ya les compramos regalos ayer.

1. ¡Ay! Me olvidé de confirmarnos el vuelo.
2. ¡Caramba! Yo quería comprarme una camiseta de Cuba.
3. También quise comprarte una caja de puros *(box of cigars)* de aquí.
4. ¿Le preguntaste al agente si está a tiempo el vuelo?
5. Tenemos que mandarle una tarjeta postal a mi abuelo.
6. Tenemos que explicarle al agente de vuelo que llevamos mucho equipaje.

N. ESCENAS INSÓLITAS

Paso 1: Describe a un(a) compañero(a) de clase la escena insólita *(unusual)* de cada dibujo usando la frase verbal.

MODELO: ofrecer consejos sobre su técnica
            *Steffi Graf le ofrece consejos
            sobre su técnica a Venus Williams.*

Venus y Steffi

Verónica y el profesor

1. explicar la tarea

Romeo y los padres de Julieta

2. ofrecer flores

Einstein y nuestra clase

3. pedir ayuda con un problema

Bill Gates y yo

Fidel Castro y tú

Bill Clinton y nosotros

4. prestar 5 millones

5. dar una caja de puros cubanos

6. decir la verdad

Paso 2: Después de terminar esta actividad, hazla otra vez usando el tiempo progresivo (**estar** + gerundio).

MODELO: *Steffi Graf le está ofreciendo (está ofreciéndole) consejos sobre su técnica a Venus Williams.*

O. **PREGUNTAS PERSONALES** Con un(a) compañero(a), tomen turnos formando preguntas con las siguientes frases. Ustedes tienen que contestarse el uno al otro.

MODELO: escribirles muchas cartas a tus amigos
E1: *¿Les escribes muchas cartas a tus amigos?*
E2: *Sí. Les escribo muchas cartas a mis amigos.*

1. darles un poco de dinero a algunos de tus amigos
2. comprarle cosas bonitas a tu mejor amigo(a)
3. hacerle muchos favores a tu papá o a tu mamá
4. pedirle perdón a la gente cuando no tienes razón
5. escribirles cartas a amigos en otros estados
6. mandarle flores a tu novio(a)
7. ofrecerles bebidas a tus amigos cuando te visitan en casa
8. hacerme preguntas en esta clase

ENCUENTRO *cultural*

Cómo viajar a Cuba

Éstas son unas palabras nuevas para la lectura:

el Tratado de Libre Comercio (TLC) *North American Free Trade Agreement (NAFTA)*
los (las) demás *others*
el yate *yacht*
la orilla *shoreline*
el crucero *cruise liner*

Sólo hay dos maneras de viajar a Cuba porque es una isla: por avión y por mar. Todos los vuelos internacionales llegan a la nueva terminal internacional del aeropuerto José Martí. Hasta el año 1999 no había vuelos directos entre los Estados Unidos y Cuba y el turismo está efectivamente prohibido por **el Tratado de Libre Comercio (TLC),** que no deja a los ciudadanos estadounidenses gastar dinero en Cuba.

Los que sí pueden gastar dinero en Cuba (sólo para gastos relacionados con el viaje, como hoteles y comida) son los funcionarios del gobierno, los periodistas, las personas con familia en Cuba, los académicos y los que viajan para actividades humanitarias. Las **demás** personas tienen que obtener un permiso especial del departamento de la Tesorería de los Estados Unidos. La gente que tiene permiso de viajar a Cuba sólo puede gastar 100 dólares por día.

Hasta hace pocos años muchos **yates** mantenían su distancia de **la orilla** de las costas cubanas por miedo de ataques guerrilleros contra Castro, pero ahora Cuba les ofrece una cariñosa recepción a los visitantes por mar. Los yates de muchos países se paran en las marinas de la isla. Muchos **cruceros** vienen de otras islas caribeñas, Europa o el Canadá.

Para pensar: ¿Conoces a gente de Cuba, o a gente que ha visitado Cuba? ¿Puedes nombrar a alguien famoso de Cuba? ¿Para la gente de los EE.UU., ¿por qué es difícil visitar Cuba?

P. **PREGUNTAS** Contesta las siguientes preguntas a base de la lectura.

1. ¿Pueden los estadounidenses viajar a Cuba?
2. Vamos a suponer que tú quieres hacer un viaje de los Estados Unidos a Cuba. Haz una lista de las cosas que tienes que hacer, según la ley de los Estados Unidos.

GRAMÁTICA II: *Double object pronouns*

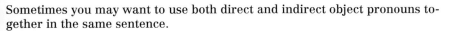

Sometimes you may want to use both direct and indirect object pronouns together in the same sentence.

Indirect object pronouns always precede direct object pronouns.

Indirect before Direct

me	
te	lo
le (se)	la
nos	los
os	las
les (se)	

The indirect object pronouns **le** and **les** always change to **se** when they are used together with the direct object pronouns **lo, la, los,** and **las.**

Teri le compró **un regalo a su hermano.**	Teri bought *a gift for her brother.*
Se lo compró ayer en el aeropuerto.	She bought *it for **him*** yesterday in the airport.
También le compró **una camiseta a su madre.**	She also bought *a shirt for her mother.*
Teri **se la** compró en una tienda en el centro.	Teri bought *it for her* in a store downtown.

In verb phrases, pronouns may be placed before conjugated verbs or attached to infinitives or present participles, but they always come before negative commands. Pronouns must be attached to affirmative commands; when two pronouns are attached, an accent mark is written over the stressed vowel.

Teri quiere comprarle un sombrero a Humberto.	Teri wants to buy Humberto a hat.
Se lo va a comprar hoy. Va a comprár**selo** hoy.	She's going to buy *it for him* today.
Se lo está comprando ahora. Está comprándo**selo** ahora.	She is buying it *for him* now.
Teri, **no se lo** compres allí. Teri, cómpra**selo** en esa tienda.	Teri, don't buy *it for him* there. Teri, buy *it for him* in that store.

¡A practicar!

Q. **OBJETOS DIRECTOS E INDIRECTOS** Lee las siguientes preguntas. Subraya el objeto directo y haz un círculo alrededor del objeto indirecto. Después, sustitúyelos con los pronombres de objeto directo e indirecto necesarios.

MODELO: ¿Venden los agentes de viaje <u>los boletos</u> (a los turistas?)
Sí, *se los* venden.

1. ¿Le explicó Manny a Teri los detalles del viaje?
Sí, _____ _____ explicó.

2. ¿Le trajo Teri regalos a sus hermanos?
No, no _____ _____ trajo.

3. ¿Le prometió Manny un viaje a Cuba a Teri?
Sí, _____ _____ prometió.

4. ¿Le compró Teri una guayabera a Manny?
Sí, _____ _____ compró.

5. ¿Compró Teri una guayabera a su mamá?
No, no _____ _____ compró.

6. ¿Teri y Manny nos trajeron un recuerdo a nosotros?
Sí, _____ _____ trajeron.

7. ¿El abuelo de Teri le escribió una carta a ella?
No, no _____ _____ escribió.

8. ¿Manny va a prestarte a ti su nueva guayabera?
No, no _____ _____ va a prestar.
No, no va a prestár_____.

9. ¿Teri me va a dar a mí un libro sobre Cuba?
Sí, ella _____ _____ va a dar.
Sí, ella va a dár_____.

R. **SUSTITUCIÓN** Teri está muy nerviosa con los preparativos de su viaje, y por eso se pone muy mandona *(bossy)* con Manny. Para cada situación, cambia el verbo a un mandato de **tú.** Sustituye los objetos directos e indirectos con los pronombres necesarios.

MODELO: mandar la carta a mi mamá / *¡Mándasela!*

1. plancharme la blusa
2. servirnos el desayuno
3. mandar el dinero a Visa
4. prepararte las maletas (las maletas de Manny)
5. dar comida a los perros
6. comprar una maleta nueva para mí (para Teri)

En voz alta

S. **PREGUNTAS DE LA MADRE** La madre de Manny le hace preguntas sobre el viaje. Una persona va a leer las preguntas de la madre y la otra persona indica cómo responde Manny a las preguntas usando pronombres de objeto directo y de objeto indirecto.

MODELO: ¿Compraste un regalo para tu padre?
Sí, mamá, se lo compré.
o: *No, mamá, no se lo compré.*

1. ¿Trajiste las fotos de La Habana para mí?
2. ¿Le dijiste «gracias» al recepcionista del hotel?
3. ¿Hiciste una reserva en el hotel para nosotros para el año que viene?
4. ¿Le regalaste las guayaberas a la familia de Teri?
5. ¿Tienes un recuerdo del viaje para ti?
6. ¿Trajo Teri tu pasaporte para ti?
7. ¿Compró Teri un sombrero para ti?
8. ¿Recogiste las maletas para ti y para Teri?

T. **ENTREVISTA** Hazle las siguientes preguntas a otro(a) estudiante. Intenta usar pronombres de objeto directo e indirecto cuando sea posible.

1. Cuando necesitas dinero para un viaje, ¿a quiénes se lo pides? (¿Y te lo dan?) Y tus padres, ¿te dan mucho o poco dinero? ¿Se lo pides con mucha o con poca frecuencia?
2. Cuando vas de viaje, ¿a quiénes les compras regalos? ¿Qué cosas les compras? ¿A quiénes les compraste regalos la última vez que viajaste?
3. ¿Te gusta escribir cartas si estás de viaje? ¿Mandas cartas o tarjetas postales? ¿Alguien te escribe a ti? ¿Cuándo fue la última vez que escribiste una tarjeta postal? ¿A quién la escribiste, y por qué?
4. Cuando vas de viaje, ¿compras recuerdos para ti? ¿Qué tipo de cosas te compras?

VOCABULARIO: *El hotel*

EN EL HOTEL NACIONAL DE CUBA, LA HABANA In this section you will learn vocabulary and expressions associated with lodging by observing scenes from Teri and Manny's honeymoon in La Habana.

---

[1] The monetary unit in Cuba is the Cuban peso, but as a tourist you cannot spend this currency. The tourist facilities on the island only accept U.S. dollars. One dollar is currently worth 210,000 Cuban pesos.

la cama sencilla (doble) *single (double) bed*
la recepción *front desk*
la reserva *reservation*

Adjetivos

arreglado(a) *neat, tidy*
cómodo(a) *comfortable*
limpio(a) *clean*

privado(a) *private*
sucio(a) *dirty*

Verbos

quedarse *to stay*
quejarse *to complain*
registrarse *to register*

¡A practicar!

U. DEFINICIONES Busca una palabra de la lista de vocabulario que va con cada definición de abajo.

MODELO: Nosotros dormimos en esta cosa.
la cama

1. Es una cama para una persona.
2. Entramos en esto para subir o bajar.
3. En este lugar uno se registra.
4. Es una cama para dos personas.
5. Es un baño que no hay que compartir con otros.
6. Es una máquina que enfría el cuarto.
7. Es la persona que trabaja en la recepción.
8. Es un hotel muy lujoso *(luxurious)*.
9. Es un objeto de metal que abre la puerta.
10. Cuando la criada *(maid)* acaba de limpiar el cuarto, el cuarto está...
11. Cuando nadie limpia el cuarto, el cuarto está...
12. Mucha gente hace esto con el agente de viajes para tener un cuarto o un vuelo durante las vacaciones.

En voz alta

V. ¡BIENVENIDO A LA HABANA! Conversa con un(a) compañero(a) de clase.

CLIENTE	RECEPCIONISTA
1. Greet the receptionist.	2. Return the greeting.
3. Ask for a single room with a private bath.	4. Ask how many days he/she is going to stay.
5. Find out how much the room costs.	6. Inform your guest about your various room rates.
7. Ask about the hotel facilities.	8. Answer your guest's questions.
9. Describe the kind of room you want.	10. Respond, then say the number and floor of the room.
11. Express your appreciation.	12. Respond, then say something to make your guest feel welcome.

W. SITUACIONES Lee cada problema. Luego habla con un(a) compañero(a) de clase de la mejor solución para resolverlo.

1. Tú y tu amigo(a) acaban de llegar al aeropuerto de una ciudad latinoamericana. Ustedes hablan con un agente de viajes para ayudarles a encontrar un cuarto barato en la ciudad. El agente les informa que el cuarto más barato cuesta 40 dólares, pero ustedes no quieren pagar más de 25 dólares. Son las 10:00 de la noche y ustedes están muy cansados.
2. Después de entrar en su cuarto de hotel, ustedes se duchan, miran las noticias de la televisión y luego se acuestan. A las 3:00 de la mañana un ruido tremendo los despierta. Una pareja en otro cuarto comienza a hablar muy alto y ustedes no pueden dormir.

MANNY ESTÁ SOLO EN EL VIEJO SAN JUAN, PUERTO RICO[1] In this section, you will learn how to ask for and give street directions.

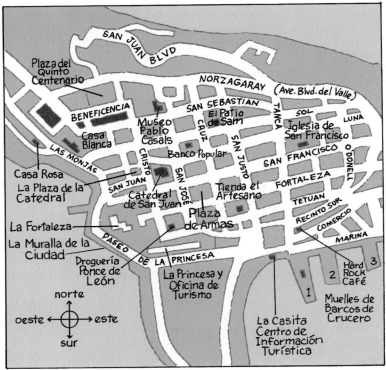

¿NOS ENTENDEMOS?

There are two ways to say *map* in Spanish: **el plano** and **el mapa**.

¿NOS ENTENDEMOS?

In Spain, it is more common to say **recto** (*straight ahead*), whereas in Latin America, **derecho** is more commonly used. Likewise in Spain, it is more common to say **la manzana**, instead of **la cuadra**, for *block*.

La Plaza de Armas está en el centro de la ciudad. **Hacia** *(Toward)* el **sur** de la ciudad el Paseo de la Princesa está **detrás de** *(behind)* la Muralla de la Ciudad *(City Wall)*. En el **norte** de la ciudad el Patio de Sam está **entre** *(between)* las calles San Justo y Cruz. Los Muelles de Barcos de Crucero están **enfrente de** *(across from)* la calle Marina. La Plaza de la Catedral está **a la izquierda de** *(on the left of)* la Catedral de San Juan. La Catedral de San Juan está **a la derecha de** *(on the right of)* la Plaza de la Catedral. El mar está **al lado de** *(next to)* los Muelles de Barcos de Crucero. El Museo Pablo Casals está **cerca del** *(near)* Patio de Sam. San Juan Bulevard está **delante de** *(in front of)* la calle Norzagaray. El aeropuerto está **lejos de** *(far from)* la ciudad.

CÓMO PEDIR INDICACIONES Manny está en la Plaza de Armas y busca la Casa Blanca.

Manny:	**Perdón,** ¿dónde está la Casa Blanca?	*Excuse me, where is the Casa Blanca?*
Señor:	Está en la calle Monjas. **Suba tres cuadras** en la calle San José. **Doble** en la calle Sol, **cruce** la calle y **siga**[2] **derecho**.	*It's on Monjas Street. **Go up three blocks** on San José Street. **Turn on Sol Street, cross the street,** and **continue straight ahead.***
Manny:	¿Eso es **hacia** el **este**, verdad?	*That is **going toward the east**, right?*
Señor:	No, es **hacia** el **oeste**.	*No, it's **toward** the west.*
Manny:	Muchísimas gracias.	*Thank you very much.*

---

[1] Puerto Rico is a commonwealth of the United States. Puerto Ricans are U.S. citizens but do not have the right to vote in national elections, as they do not pay federal taxes.
[2] **Suba, doble, cruce,** and **siga** are formal commands that you will be learning later in this chapter.

El transporte y otros lugares en la ciudad   *Transportation and other places in the city*

la estación de trenes   *train station*   la terminal de autobuses   *bus station*
el puerto   *port*

Verbos

cruzar   *to cross*   en barco   *by boat*   en tren   *by train*
doblar   *to turn*   en bicicleta   *by bike*   parar(se)   *to stop*
ir...   *to go . . .*   en coche   *by car*   seguir (i)   *to continue*
  a pie   *on foot*   en metro   *by subway*   subir(se) (a)   *to go up*
  en autobús   *by bus*   en taxi   *by taxi*

Adverbios

cerca   *near*   hasta   *up to, until*
demasiado   *too much*   lejos   *far (away)*

¡A practicar!

X. OPUESTOS Indica el opuesto de cada palabra indicada.

MODELO: a la izquierda   *a la derecha*

1. norte   **2.** lejos de   **3.** delante de   **4.** detrás de   **5.** oeste   **6.** entre

Y. LUGARES Y TRANSPORTE Usa una palabra del vocabulario para completar las siguientes frases.

1. Tengo mucha prisa; no quiero tomar el autobús y no tengo tiempo para ir a pie. Voy a pedir un _____ .

2. Compré un boleto ayer para el tren que sale a las 5:00. ¿Dónde está la _____?

3. No sé dónde está la estación, pero tengo aquí un _____ de la ciudad. Podemos mirarlo, si quieres.

4. Voy desde el Viejo San Juan a Ponce[1] en autobús. Pero no sé dónde está la _____ .

5. Uy, hay mucho tráfico. Yo quiero cruzar la ciudad por debajo de la tierra —voy _____ .

En voz alta

Z. ¿DÓNDE ESTÁ? Trabajas en una oficina de turismo en el Viejo San Juan, y tienes que indicar a los turistas dónde están los siguientes lugares en el mapa de la página 259. Usa **al lado de, cerca de, delante de, detrás de, enfrente de, entre** y **lejos de**.

MODELO: el aeropuerto
          El aeropuerto está lejos del centro de la ciudad.

1. la Plaza del Quinto Centenario
2. el Patio de Sam
3. el Banco Popular
4. la droguería Ponce de León
5. la Catedral de San Juan
6. la calle San Francisco
7. el Museo Pablo Casals
8. la Fortaleza

AA. EN ESTA CIUDAD Pregúntale a un(a) compañero(a) dónde están varios lugares en la ciudad o pueblo donde estudias.

MODELO: ¿Dónde está la Iglesia Gobin?
          Está al lado de East College, en la calle Locust.

---

[1] Ponce is the second-largest city in Puerto Rico and is a popular tourist destination.

ENCUENTRO *cultural*

Encuentro cultural: Puerto Rico

Éstas son unas palabras nuevas para la lectura:

la isla *island*
rodeado(a) *surrounded*
las murallas de piedra *stone walls*

Para pensar: ¿Conoces Puerto Rico? ¿Qué piensas de un país con dos lenguas oficiales? ¿Qué sabes de la situación política de Puerto Rico?

Puerto Rico es **una isla** muy pequeña. Tiene solamente 158 kilómetros de largo y 58 kilómetros de ancho, y es una de las áreas más densamente pobladas del mundo. Puerto Rico tiene casi 4 millones de habitantes. El primer idioma de la isla es español, pero como es oficialmente una parte de los Estados Unidos, también se habla inglés. En 1993, el español y el inglés se declararon como los idiomas oficiales de la isla. Es el único país de habla hispana que tiene el inglés como lengua oficial.

Puerto Rico es una mezcla de lo muy nuevo y lo muy viejo. Tiene cosas de la vida de los Estados Unidos y al mismo tiempo conserva las influencias formales de lo español. El Viejo San Juan, un barrio de la ciudad San Juan, es uno de los barrios coloniales mejor conservados de las Américas. El barrio está casi totalmente **rodeado** de **murallas de piedra** hechas por los españoles.

Para viajar dentro del país, también hay aeropuertos pequeños en Aguadilla y Ponce. Para otras formas de transporte dentro de la isla, hay carros públicos y taxis, y hay muchas agencias de viajes que alquilan carros a muy buen precio.

¿NOS ENTENDEMOS?

Puertorriqueños sometime refer to themselves as **boricuas**. This term comes from the Taino name for the island, **Borinquen**.

BB. **PREGUNTAS** Contesta las siguientes preguntas a base de la lectura.

1. ¿Cuáles son las lenguas oficiales de Puerto Rico? ¿Cómo es Puerto Rico especial en ese sentido?
2. ¿Qué es y cómo es el Viejo San Juan?

GRAMÁTICA III: *Formal commands*

In **Capítulo 5** you learned how to form familiar affirmative commands. In this section you will learn how to form formal affirmative and formal negative commands.

Formal commands
When we give advice to others or ask them to do something, we often use commands such as *Take bus No. 25* and *Give me your address*. Spanish speakers use formal commands when they address people as **usted** or **ustedes**.

To form formal commands for most Spanish verbs, drop the **-o** ending from the present tense **yo** form and add the following endings to the verb stem: **-e/-en** for **-ar** verbs; **-a/-an** for **-er** and **-ir** verbs. To form the negative, simply place **no** before the verb.

	Infinitive	Present-tense **yo** form	**usted**	**ustedes**
-ar verbs	hablar	hablo	habl**e**	habl**en**
-er verbs	volver	vuelvo	vuelv**a**	vuelv**an**
-ir verbs	venir	vengo	veng**a**	veng**an**

Vengan a visitarme pronto en San Juan. **Come** to visit me soon in San Juan.

No olvide mi dirección. **Don't forget** my address.

Verbs ending in **-car, -gar,** and **-zar** have a spelling change: the **c** changes to **qu, g** changes to **gu,** and **z** changes to **c,** respectively.

Infinitive	Present-tense **yo** form	**usted**	**ustedes**
sacar	saco	sa**que**	sa**quen**
llegar	llego	lle**gue**	lle**guen**
comenzar	comienzo	comien**ce**	comien**cen**

Saque una foto de nosotros. **Take** a picture of us.

Lleguen a tiempo, por favor. **Arrive** on time, please.

No comience a caminar todavía. **Don't start** walking yet.

Several irregular verbs vary from the pattern above.

Infinitive	**usted**	**ustedes**
dar	**dé**	**den**
estar	**esté**	**estén**
ir	**vaya**	**vayan**
saber	**sepa**	**sepan**
ser	**sea**	**sean**

Sean buenos estudiantes. **Be** good students.

Vaya al banco. **Go** to the bank.

In affirmative commands, attach reflexive and object pronouns to the end of the command, thus forming one word. If the command has three or more syllables, write an accent mark over the stressed vowel. In negative commands, place the pronouns separately in front of the verb.

Póngase el abrigo. **Put on** your overcoat.

No se lo ponga. **Don't put it on.**

Cómprelo ahora. **Buy it** now.

No lo compre mañana. **Don't buy it** tomorrow.

¡A practicar!

CC. ENTRE AMIGOS Manny está hablando por teléfono con Jorge, un amigo que quiere visitarlo con su esposa. Manny está dándoles instrucciones para llegar en autobús a su apartamento. Completa la siguiente conversación con las formas correctas de los verbos entre paréntesis.

—Primero, _____ (salir) ustedes de su hotel. Luego _____ (caminar) dos cuadras a la derecha hasta la calle Fonseca. Allí _____ (doblar) a la izquierda y _____ (ir) una cuadra más hasta la calle de Plata.

—Hasta la calle de Plata, ¿dices, Manny?

—Sí, Jorge. Luego _____ (ir) ustedes al otro lado de esa calle y _____ (esperar) el autobús número 32.

—¿El autobús 32, Manny?

—Correcto, amigo. _____ (Tomar/lo) hasta la avenida Buena Vista. _____ (Bajarse) allí en esa avenida.

—¿Cómo sabemos dónde está la avenida Buena Vista?

—Bueno, _____ (preguntar/le) ustedes al chófer del autobús. _____ (Decir/le) que quieren bajarse en la avenida Buena Vista. Pues, _____ (bajarse) allí y _____ (cambiar) a otro autobús... el número 19. _____ (Subirse) a ese autobús y _____ (tomar/lo) hasta la calle San Juan.

—¿Está lejos esa calle?

—No, Jorge. Está a como siete cuadras más o menos. _____ (Saber) Uds. que no es muy difícil. Entonces _____ (seguir) ustedes todo derecho hasta la calle San Juan. Luego _____ (salir) del autobús y en esa esquina les espero. ¿Qué te parece?

—Pues, es un poco complicado. Pero nos vemos pronto.

—Claro que sí. Hasta luego, Jorge.

¿NOS ENTENDEMOS?

You can soften commands to make them sound more like requests than demands, by using **usted** or **ustedes** after the command form. **Pasen ustedes por aquí.** (*Come this way.*) **No hable usted tan rápido.** (*Don't speak so fast.*) When you want people to do something, but you wish to say so tactfully, ask a question or make a simple statement with reference to your wish rather than using a direct command. For example, suppose you are a dinner guest at a friend's house. The dining room is uncomfortably hot, and you want a window opened or the air conditioner turned on. You might say: **Hace un poco de calor, ¿no?**

DD. **CONSEJOS PARA TURISTAS EN SANTO DOMINGO** Completa los mandatos de un guía turístico para la ciudad de Santo Domingo usando mandatos formales.

MODELO: (ustedes) caminar para ver todo lo que ofrece la ciudad
Caminen para ver todo lo que ofrece la ciudad.

1. (usted) salir temprano del hotel
2. (usted) ir a un mercado cercano
3. (usted) no sacar fotos sin pedir permiso
4. (ustedes) descansar un poco por la tarde
5. (ustedes) no subirse a un autobús sin saber la ruta
6. (usted) no andar en bicicleta; es muy peligroso
7. (ustedes) pararse para las procesiones
8. (usted) no cruzar las calles sin mirar en las dos direcciones
9. (ustedes) ser buenos con la gente de la ciudad, y ellos les van a tratar bien a Uds.

En voz alta

EE. **SUGERENCIAS** Manny y Teri te explican cómo se sienten. Dales sugerencias en forma de mandatos. Haz mandatos de **Ud.** o **Uds.** para cada situación.

MODELO: Nosotros estamos cansados de caminar y tomar el autobús.
¡Tomen Uds. un taxi entonces!

1. Yo tengo muchas ganas de comer comida china.
2. Queremos quedarnos en un hotel lujoso.
3. Necesito cambiar dinero. ¿Dónde está el banco?
4. Tengo ganas de beber algo.
5. Necesito comprar regalos para mi familia.
6. Necesitamos confirmar nuestro vuelo.
7. No sabemos cómo agradecerle a Ud.

FF. **¡BIENVENIDOS A MI UNIVERSIDAD!** Imagínate que tú trabajas como guía estudiantil en tu universidad. Tú eres responsable de acompañar a un grupo de profesores españoles (dos o tres de tus compañeros[as] de clase), quienes te hacen preguntas sobre varios lugares que quieren visitar. Contesta según el plano.

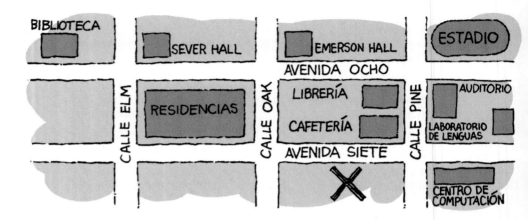

MODELO: Profesor Martínez: Busco una librería. ¿Hay una por aquí?
Tú: *Cómo no, profesor. Está cerca de Emerson Hall.*
Camine usted... Luego vaya...

1. Señor Lozano: Perdón, ¿dónde está la cafetería de la universidad?
2. Señorita Guzmán y señora Ortiz: Estamos buscando la biblioteca.
3. Profesor Corral: Perdón, ¿dónde dijo usted que puedo encontrar el laboratorio de lenguas?
4. Profesores García y Gutiérrez: Perdón, ¿hay un centro de computación por aquí?
5. Doctora Letrán: ¿Me puede decir dónde está el estadio, por favor?

GG. **UN CONSEJERO DE LA UNIVERSIDAD** Trabajen en grupos de tres personas. Una persona es un(a) consejero(a) para la universidad. Los otros estudiantes van a presentarle un problema que tienen. El (La) consejero(a) entonces va a ofrecer consejos en forma de mandatos formales.

MODELO: E1: *No puedo estudiar en mi cuarto.*
E2: *Vaya a la biblioteca para estudiar.*
E3: *Mi compañero de cuarto y yo siempre llegamos tarde a nuestra primera clase.*
E2: *Levántense más temprano.*

ASÍ SE DICE: *The subjunctive mood*

Thus far in *Plazas* you have been learning the indicative mood of the present and past tenses. The indicative mood is used to state facts and ask questions objectively. A second mood exists in Spanish called the subjunctive mood. The subjunctive is used to express more subjective concepts as well as to make statements about wishes, wants, and emotions. The subjunctive is also used to express doubt, uncertainty, or negation. You will learn more about the subjunctive mood beginning with **Capítulo 11.** The formation of the subjunctive follows the same procedure as that of formal commands. For now, you should at least be able to recognize the subjunctive mood and have a basic understanding of why the subjunctive is used. Here are a few examples of the subjunctive mood and the contexts that cause it:

volition/influence	Yo quiero que tú **vayas** al banco.
	*I want you **to go** to the bank.*
emotion	Siento que no **vengas** al mercado conmigo.
	*I'm sorry you won't be **coming** to the market with me.*
doubt	Ella duda que Ramón **coma** con nosotros.
	*She doubts that Ramon **will eat** with us.*
negation/denial	No es cierto que Pedro **sepa** hablar italiano.
	*It's not true that Pedro **knows how** to speak Italian.*

HH. **RECONOCER EL SUBJUNTIVO** Mira las siguientes frases y explica por qué usan el subjuntivo *(volition, emotion, doubt, or negation)*. Subraya el verbo en subjuntivo en cada caso.

1. Estoy triste de que tengamos que irnos de Santo Domingo.
2. Pero me alegro de que hagamos muchos viajes.
3. El año que viene, quiero que tú y yo vayamos a la playa en Puerto Rico.
4. Yo dudo que mi papá tenga bastante dinero para pagarnos el viaje.
5. Yo no creo que sea necesario hacer las reservas con un año de antelación *(one year in advance)*.
6. No es que San Juan no me guste, sino que prefiero la playa.
7. Yo deseo que mis hijos conozcan las islas del Caribe este invierno.

Síntesis

¡A ver!

El **Capítulo 9** tiene como tema principal el viaje y el alojamiento. La presentadora videográfica de este capítulo es Graciela, una joven cubana nacida en la capital de La Habana. Graciela estudia turismo en la Universidad de la Habana. En los segmentos de video que vamos a ver, Graciela enseña primero una serie de fotos sobre el transporte. Después vamos a ver cómo se piden indicaciones en Puerto Rico y en España.

ACTIVIDAD 1   Pre-viewing task (Segmento 1 del video)

Paso 1: En el **Segmento 1 del video** vas a ver una serie de imágenes de medios de transporte, todas tomadas en el mundo hispanohablante. Haz una lista de estos medios de transporte y organízalos según las categorías indicadas en la tabla.

Medios de transporte en los cuales me gusta viajar	Medios de transporte en los cuales NO me gusta viajar	No tengo opinión

Both partners should speak about a form of transport before moving on to the next one in the list. Remember to react to what your partner says. You may agree with his/her opinion: **Pues sí, a mí me gusta también ir en barco. Hace tres años fui en un crucero desde Miami hasta Puerto Rico con mis padres.** You may disagree with your partner: **Pues yo no..., A mí no...** Remember also to react to any anecdotal information your partner may give you: **¡Qué interesante! ¡Qué suerte!**

Paso 2: Con un(a) compañero(a) de clase, hablen de cada medio de transporte dando una explicación de los motivos por los cuales les gusta o no les gusta viajar en ellos. Si no tienes opinión sobre el medio de transporte explícaselo a tu compañero(a). Si tienes alguna anécdota que contar, habla de ello también.

MODELO: *El verano pasado viajé en avión por primera vez.*

ACTIVIDAD 2   Pre-viewing task (Segmento 2 del video)

Aquí hay un plano del centro de San Juan, la capital de la isla de Puerto Rico. Te encuentras andando por la calle Topasio hacia la avenida Apolo (ver la señal de **Estás aquí** en la parte superior derecha del plano). Paras a una persona en la calle para pedir indicaciones de cómo llegar a los lugares marcados en la lista. Con un(a) compañero(a) de clase, practiquen los diálogos correspondientes.

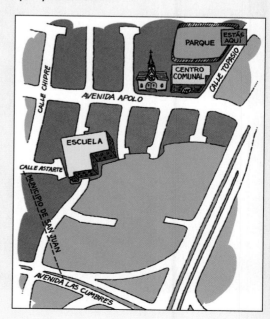

Don't forget to use a suitable expression to gain somebody's attention when you stop them in the street to ask for directions: **Disculpe... Perdone... Oiga, por favor...** would be useful, followed by your inquiry.

1.   la casa de un amigo en la calle Astarte
2.   el parque que queda al lado de la avenida Las Cumbres
3.   la iglesia más cercana
4.   la entrada principal de la escuela primaria

ACTIVIDAD 3 Viewing task (Segmento 2 del video)

Vas a ver dos clips cortos en este segmento del video, uno filmado en San Juan, Puerto Rico, el otro filmado en Madrid, España. Los dos clips muestran a gente que está pidiendo indicaciones de cómo llegar a un lugar. Presta atención en los dos clips a la forma del verbo que utilizan los locutores, especialmente en su elección de utilizar **tú** o **usted.**

Paso 1: Mira el primer clip y averigua dónde está la calle Santa Rita en el plano. Márcala en el plano.

Paso 2: Mira el segundo clip. Miguel busca alguna forma económica para llegar a Alcalá de Henares desde el centro de Madrid. ¿Cuál es la recomendación de la persona a quien le pide información Miguel? Apunta la lista de instrucciones que le da el señor de la parada de autobuses. Aquí están los sitios mencionados en la conversación: Alcalá de Henares, Cuatro Caminos, avenida América.

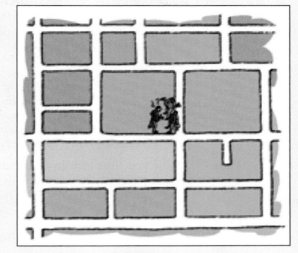

ACTIVIDAD 4 Post-viewing task (Segmento 2 del video)

Paso 1: Averigua con tu compañero(a) de clase primero la localización de la calle Santa Rita en San Juan y después las recomendaciones del señor de la parada de autobuses en Madrid.

Paso 2: Hagan un *role play* de los dos clips que vieron para la **Actividad 3.**

¡A escribir!
Giving directions

If you're traveling in a Spanish-speaking country or city, chances are you might need to get directions at some point. And if someone happens to ask you how to get somewhere, you yourself might even have to give directions! The most important element of explaining to someone how to get from one place to another is accuracy. If you explain your directions clearly and concisely, people will be able to follow them easily.

Here are six basic requirements for giving directions to a place:

1. Choose the easiest route.
2. Be very clear in your directions.
3. Give the directions in chronological order.
4. Use linking expressions such as **Primero..., Luego..., Después de eso..., Entonces..., Usted debe..., Después...,** and **Finalmente...**
5. Identify clearly visible landmarks such as:

la avenida	*avenue*	**el cruce de caminos**	*intersection*
el bulevar	*boulevard*	**el edificio**	*building*
la calle	*street*	**el letrero**	*sign*
el camino	*road*	**el puente**	*bridge*
la colina	*hill*	**el semáforo**	*traffic light*

ATAJO

Functions: Asking for and giving directions; Linking ideas; Expressing distance; Expressing location

Vocabulary: City; Directions and distance; Means of transportation; Metric systems and measurements

Grammar: Verbs: imperative: **usted(es), ser** and **estar, tener** and **haber;** Negation: **no, nadie, nada;** Interrogative adverbs: **¿dónde?, ¿adónde?**

6. Include a sketch of the route.

MODELO: *Para llegar a mi casa desde el aeropuerto, siga estas indicaciones. Primero, siga la calle del aeropuerto hasta la salida. Allí está un letrero que dice «STOP». Luego doble a la derecha y siga por el bulevar Man O' War dos kilómetros hasta el primer semáforo, donde hay un cruce de caminos. Entonces, doble a la izquierda y siga por el camino Parkers Mill dos kilómetros (pasando debajo de un puente) hasta la calle Lane Allen. En esa calle, doble a la derecha y siga otros dos kilómetros (pasando un semáforo) hasta el segundo semáforo. Después, doble a la izquierda en el camino Beacon Hill y siga derecho medio kilómetro hasta el Camino Normandy. Doble a la izquierda y vaya a la cuarta casa a la derecha. Allí vivo yo, y ¡allí tiene su casa!*

Paso 1: Escribe una composición en la cual le explicas a un viajero hispanohablante cómo ir del aeropuerto o de la estación de autobuses de tu ciudad hasta tu residencia. Antes de empezar, vuelve a leer los seis puntos y el párrafo de arriba.

Paso 2: Corrige tu composición. Puedes consultar la siguiente lista:

___ easiest route   ___ visible landmarks

___ clear directions   ___ correct punctuation

___ chronological order   ___ correct grammar

___ linking expressions   ___ correct spelling

Paso 3: Intercambia tu composición y tu dibujo con los de un(a) compañero(a) de clase. Corrijan sus párrafos, y después discutan los cambios que son necesarios.

¡A conversar!

Conversa con un(a) compañero(a) de clase.

Paso 1:

Estudiante A: Tú estás en una ciudad hispánica donde vas a visitar a una familia que te invitó a comer para una ocasión especial. Tú no sabes dónde está el apartamento de la familia y, por eso, le haces algunas preguntas al padre (a la madre). Necesitas saber cómo llegar allí en autobús (dónde debes subirte y bajarte).

Estudiante B: Tú eres el padre (la madre) del (de la) estudiante que invitó a un(a) amigo(a) a comer con tu familia. Ahora tú le das la información que te pide. Escucha bien lo que quiere y sé cortés.

Paso 2:

Estudiante A: Tú decidiste tomar un taxi para llegar al apartamento de tus amigos hispánicos. Ahora antes de subir al taxi, habla con el (la) taxista para confirmar la distancia y negociar el costo.

Estudiante B: Tú tienes diez años de experiencia como taxista. Está lloviendo y es de noche; por eso, la tarifa (el costo) es diferente a la del día cuando hace buen tiempo. Habla ahora con tu cliente.

¡A leer!

Using format clues

Printed material often contains different kinds of cues that can help you skim, scan, and guess meaning. For example, some words and phrases appear in large, boldface, or italic print to attract the reader's attention; some words are repeated several times to persuade the reader; and other words appear together with a graphic design to help the reader remember a particular concept.

Paso 1: Lee la lectura rápidamente y contesta las preguntas generales que siguen.

1. ¿Cuál es el país que se menciona en la lectura?
2. ¿Cuál es la capital de este país?
3. La lectura presenta cierta información organizada en cuatro secciones, sobre la capital. ¿Cómo se llaman estas cuatro secciones?

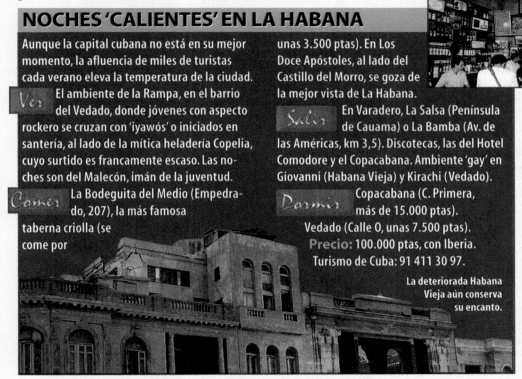

NOCHES 'CALIENTES' EN LA HABANA

Aunque la capital cubana no está en su mejor momento, la afluencia de miles de turistas cada verano eleva la temperatura de la ciudad.

Ver El ambiente de la Rampa, en el barrio del Vedado, donde jóvenes con aspecto rockero se cruzan con 'iyawós' o iniciados en santería, al lado de la mítica heladería Copelia, cuyo surtido es francamente escaso. Las noches son del Malecón, imán de la juventud.

Comer La Bodeguita del Medio (Empedrado, 207), la más famosa taberna criolla (se come por unas 3.500 ptas). En Los Doce Apóstoles, al lado del Castillo del Morro, se goza de la mejor vista de La Habana.

Salir En Varadero, La Salsa (Península de Cauama) o La Bamba (Av. de las Américas, km 3,5). Discotecas, las del Hotel Comodore y el Copacabana. Ambiente 'gay' en Giovanni (Habana Vieja) y Kirachi (Vedado).

Dormir Copacabana (C. Primera, más de 15.000 ptas). Vedado (Calle 0, unas 7.500 ptas). **Precio:** 100.000 ptas, con Iberia. Turismo de Cuba: 91 411 30 97.

La deteriorada Habana Vieja aún conserva su encanto.

Paso 2: Lee la lectura otra vez y contesta las preguntas específicas que siguen.

1. Según el título de la lectura, La Habana se conoce por sus noches «calientes». ¿Por qué razón está elevada la temperatura de la ciudad?
   a. la falta de aire acondicionado **c.** la afluencia de miles de turistas
   b. el clima del Caribe
2. Según la lectura, ¿cuál de los siguientes lugares **no** se puede ver en el barrio del Vedado?
   a. el Malecón **c.** la heladería Copelia
   b. el museo de Bob Marley
3. De los dos hoteles que se mencionan, ¿cuál es el más barato? ¿Cuánto cuesta en pesetas españolas?

VOCABULARIO ESENCIAL 🎧

Viajar en avión   *Airplane travel*

la aduana   *customs*
el aeropuerto   *airport*
la agencia de viajes   *travel agency*
el (la) agente de viajes   *travel agent*
el asiento   *seat*
el (la) asistente de vuelo   *flight attendant*

el avión   *plane*
el boleto (billete) de ida   *one-way ticket*
el boleto (billete) de ida y vuelta   *round-trip ticket*
el equipaje (de mano)   *(carry-on) baggage, luggage*
el horario   *schedule*

la inmigración   *passport control*
la llegada   *arrival*
la maleta   *suitcase*
el (la) pasajero(a)   *passenger*
el pasaporte   *passport*
el pasillo   *aisle*
la puerta   *gate*

la salida   *departure*
la sección de (no) fumar   *(non)smoking section*
la ventanilla   *window*
el viaje   *trip*
el vuelo (sin escala)   *(non-stop) flight*

Verbos

abordar   *to board*
bajar(se) (de)   *to get off*
facturar el equipaje   *to check the luggage*

hacer escala (en)   *to make a stop (on a flight) (in)*
hacer la(s) maleta(s)   *to pack one's suitcase(s)*

ir en avión   *to go by plane*
pasar (por)   *to go through*
recoger   *to pick up, to claim*
viajar   *to travel*
volar   *to fly*

En el hotel   *In the hotel*

el aire acondicionado   *air-conditioning*
el ascensor   *elevator*
la cama sencilla (doble)   *single (double) bed*

el cuarto   *room*
el hotel de cuatro estrellas   *four-star hotel*
la llave   *key*
la recepción   *front desk*

el (la) recepcionista   *receptionist*
la reserva   *reservation*

Adjetivos

arreglado(a)   *neat, tidy*
cómodo(a)   *comfortable*

limpio(a)   *clean*
privado(a)   *private*

sucio(a)   *dirty*

Verbos

registrarse   *to register*

quedarse   *to stay*

quejarse de   *to complain about*

Indicaciones   *Directions*

a la derecha de   *to the right of*
a la izquierda de   *to the left of*
al lado de   *next to*
cerca de   *near*

delante de   *in front of*
derecho   *straight*
detrás de   *behind*
enfrente de   *across from*

entre   *between*
el este   *east*
hacia   *toward*
lejos de   *far from*

el norte   *north*
el oeste   *west*
el sur   *south*

Otros lugares en la ciudad y el transporte   *Other places in the city and transportation*

la cuadra   *city block*
la estación de trenes   *train station*

el puerto   *port*
la terminal de autobuses   *bus station*

Verbos

cruzar   *to cross*
doblar   *to turn*
ir...   *to go . . .*
  a pie   *on foot*

en autobús   *by bus*
en barco   *by boat*
en bicicleta   *by bike*
en coche   *by car*

en metro   *by subway*
en taxi   *by taxi*
en tren   *by train*
parar(se)   *to stop*

seguir (i)   *to continue*
subir   *to go up*

Adverbios

cerca   *near*

demasiado   *too much*

hasta   *up to, until*

lejos   *far (away)*

Expresiones idiomáticas

¡Bienvenido(a)!   *Welcome!*

¡Buen viaje!   *Have a nice trip!*

Perdón.   *Excuse me.*

PLAZAS

...y el encuentro para la hispanidad

BIENVENIDOS A *PLAZAS*, UNA PUBLICACIÓN QUE DESCRIBE EL PANORAMA DE LOS PAÍSES DE HABLA ESPAÑOLA.

En esta edición de *Plazas,* presentamos las experiencias de un grupo de estudiantes que pasó el semestre en el mar para conocer mejor varias regiones de Latinoamérica. Los estudiantes salieron de Tampa, Florida hacia su primer puerto de escala en Puerto Rico.

La magia de los magos

¿En qué ocasiones compras regalos para los miembros de tu familia o para tus amigos?

Para ti, ¿es mejor regalar o recibir regalos? ¿Es mejor ser invitado(a) o anfitrión (anfitriona)? ¿Por qué?

¿Cuál es tu día feriado favorito?

¿En qué aspectos ves la importancia de la religión en estos días feriados en los países hispanos?

¿En qué aspectos entra o no entra la religión en los días feriados que celebras tú?

Escoge *(choose)* uno de los días festivos del mundo hispano que aparecen en la página 221 y prepara un informe breve sobre cuándo y cómo se celebra.

Drew Hoffman nos describe una tradición típica de los países latinos.

6 de enero

Hoy acabo de regresar de la casa de Sonimar Pardo, una estudiante de la Universidad de Puerto Rico. Su familia me invitó a pasar el Día de los Reyes Magos en su casa. En los países hispanos, esta fiesta es uno de los días favoritos de los niños y de los adultos también. Como esta fiesta es desconocida *(unknown)* para mí, me explicaron que el origen de la tradición se encuentra en la Biblia. Los tres Reyes Magos vinieron del Oriente para la adoración del Niño Jesús y de regalo le trajeron incienso, oro y mirra. Los tres Reyes se llamaban Melchor, Gaspar y Baltasar. Melchor fue un hombre mayor de barba blanca, Gaspar un joven rubio y Baltasar un hombre de raza negra y de barba espesa *(thick).* Se cree que la diversidad en las razas se adoptó durante el transcurso de *(throughout)* los siglos para simbolizar la universalidad del cristianismo.

Había muchos regalos esta mañana, como es la tradición, para imitar la generosidad que estos magos tuvieron al adorar al Niño Jesús. En preparación de la llegada de los Reyes Magos, los hermanitos de Sonimar dejaron hierba *(grass)* para los caballos anoche para que los caballos comieran antes de seguir a la próxima casa. Sus hermanitos se levantaron muy temprano esta mañana para ver qué regalos recibieron de los Reyes. ¡Qué sorpresa! ¡Los caballos comieron toda la hierba! Por supuesto, este día no fue sólo para los niños. Los adultos también se hicieron regalos y todos lo pasamos muy bien. Aunque es la primera vez que celebré este día feriado, la celebración me mostró la importancia que las tradiciones tienen para la familia.

¿Quién puede dormir con tanto que ver?

Después de pasar tres días en Puerto Rico, la próxima parada los llevó a Santo Domingo en la República Dominicana y luego a La Habana en Cuba. Lizzie Reubens y Alec Davis comparan los hoteles donde se quedaron en estas dos ciudades.

12 de enero (Lizzie)

Primero, recogimos nuestro equipaje antes de salir del barco y tomamos un taxi para llegar a "Paraíso del Caribe", un hotel de tres estrellas en Santo Domingo. El taxista nos dijo que era un hotel popular. En realidad, así era. El recepcionista nos dio la llave de nuestro cuarto y cuando llegamos, vimos que teníamos una vista impresionante del mar. No nos importó para nada subir los cuatro pisos en escalera porque el ascensor no funcionaba ni tener un cuarto sin baño privado porque el hotel no estaba muy lleno. ¡Por lo menos había aire acondicionado! En realidad, fue para nosotros una parada *(stop)* en el paraíso porque estábamos rodeados *(surrounded)* por tanta belleza *(beauty)* natural.

16 de enero (Alec)

La semana siguiente pasamos por uno de los puertos principales de Cuba y fuimos en autobús hacia el hotel "Santa Cruz", otro hotel de tres estrellas. Sin embargo, este hotel estaba un poco más lejos de la costa y no había cuartos con vista del mar. Nos gustó más el hotel en Santo Domingo, pero la ventaja de este hotel en La Habana fue su ubicación *(location)* ideal. Cerca del hotel, encontramos un restaurante cubano típico. Al cruzar la calle, había un parque con muchas fuentes *(fountains)* y plantas tropicales que hasta ese momento sólo habíamos visto *(had seen)* en las fotos de una de nuestras profesoras. Después de explorar un poco más, descubrimos que detrás del hotel había una plaza magnífica. Lo curioso era que no vimos a mucha gente paseando ni niños jugando en esta plaza. Aún así, Lizzie y yo nos sentamos en un banco *(bench)* en la plaza para escribir en nuestros diarios.

En las dos ciudades nos dimos cuenta *(realized)* que los hoteles ocupan un lugar de segunda importancia cuando hay tantos lugares nuevos que conocer.

¿Cuál de los dos hoteles prefieres?

Cuando viajas, ¿es más importante que el hotel tenga muchos servicios o cuartos más económicos?

En el Caribe, ¿te gustaría quedarte en un hotel con vista del mar o en un hotel en la ciudad?

★ La Habana

CUBA

HAITÍ **REPÚBLICA DOMINICANA**

★ Santo Domingo

PUERTO RICO

La peor pesadilla:
¡empacar!

Como un proyecto especial, Debbie Williams preparó una lista de la ropa que los viajeros deben incluir cuando hacen la maleta. Una vez en Guatemala, ella se dio cuenta *(realized)* que trajo demasiado para el viaje y quiere ayudar a los estudiantes de los próximos semestres a empacar sólo lo más esencial.

8 de febrero

Ropa: Acuérdense que pueden lavar la ropa a medida que *(as)* sea necesario. Con esto en mente, no necesitan llevar tanta ropa. Con tres o cuatro camisetas y la misma cantidad de pantalones cortos, ya tienen suficiente ropa de día. De noche, prepárense para unas temperaturas más bajas, para lo cual deben incluir dos suéteres y dos pares de pantalones. Recomiendo que sean de algodón. Otra cosa, no olviden su cinturón favorito. Por supuesto van a necesitar unos trajes de baño, pero como no ocupan tanto espacio pueden llevar dos o tres.

Accesorios: Además de sandalias y zapatos para el bote, incluyan un sombrero y mucha crema bronceadora para protegerse del sol. Las gafas de sol deben ser de una calidad excelente para protegerles los ojos de los peligrosos *(dangerous)* rayos del sol. Como es una vida sencilla *(simple)*, no es necesario llevar todas las comodidades *(comforts)* de casa.

Lo mejor de todo es que si les hace falta *(you need)* algo en particular siempre lo pueden comprar en el próximo puerto.

MÉXICO

BELICE

GUATEMALA

Ciudad de Guatemala
★

HONDURAS

EL SALVADOR

(¿Te gustaría pasar un semestre (12 a 15 semanas) con esta cantidad de ropa?

(¿Cuánto equipaje llevas normalmente cuando vas de viaje?

(¿Qué recomendaciones tienes para el viajero que siempre lleva demasiado?

(¿Es suficiente lo que incluye Debbie en su lista? ¿Qué falta *(is missing)*? ¿Qué se puede eliminar?

Gigante salvadoreño durmiente

Claribel Alegría

Después de visitar Guatemala, los cinco estudiantes fueron de excursión por El Salvador, donde podían apreciar la belleza natural y majestuosa de los lugares que visitaron. El lugar que más impresionó a Mackenzie Reynolds fue la ciudad de Santa Ana y la excursión al volcán Izalco[1]. Ella tomó muchas fotos y en una de las tiendas donde ella compró un refresco, el dueño (owner) le dijo que una poeta escribió varios poemas sobre el volcán. La poesía de Claribel Alegría refleja el testimonio de su pueblo salvadoreño. Aunque nació en Nicargua (1924), vivió mucho tiempo en El Salvador y se identifica culturalmente con este país. Es conocida por su retrato (portrayal) del apasionado espíritu humano a la luz del (in light of) conflicto humano y los críticos la clasifican como una escritora representativa de la literatura salvadoreña de nuestros tiempos. El poema favorito de Mackenzie es de la colección *Flores del volcán*, escrita en 1982.

- ¿Cómo expresa Alegría el tono nostálgico del poema?
- ¿Parece realista o artísica esta descripción? Explica.
- ¿Qué logra (accomplish) la poeta con la repetición de los versos que comienzan con la palabra «y»?
- ¿En qué aspectos es similar esta descripción a una descripción de la naturaleza de tu ciudad o pueblo? ¿En qué aspectos es diferente?

Flores del volcán

Catorce volcanes se levantan
en mi país memoria
en mi país mito
que día a día invento.
Catorce volcanes de follaje y piedra
   (stone)
donde nubes extrañas se detienen
y a veces el chillido (screech)
de un pájaro extraviado (lost bird).
¿Quién dijo que era verde mi país?
es más rojo
es más gris
es más violento:
el Izalco que ruge (roars)
exigiendo más vidas.
Los eternos chacmol
que recogen la sangre
y los que beben sangre
del chacmol
y los huérfanos (orphans) grises
y el volcán babeando (spewing)
toda esa lava incandescente
y el guerrillero muerto
y los mil rostros (faces) traicionados
y los niños que miran para contar la
   historia.

[1]The volcano Izalco, which forms part of the Central American volcanic chain, is a few miles west from Santa Ana, the second-largest city in El Salvador and the city where Claribel Alegría spent the first two decades of her life. Because Izalco was such an active volcano, with regular eruptions between 1770 and 1958, it is dubbed the "lighthouse of the Pacific."

Mar del Plata, tiempo de oro

Un mes y varias paradas después, los estudiantes siguieron hacia el sureste, hasta llegar a la costa de Argentina. Pararon en una ciudad que se llama Mar del Plata[1], que comparte *(shares)* su nombre con la playa inmensa de esta ciudad. Aquí tenemos las impresiones de Rick Morgan.

25 de marzo

En la costa del Océano Atlántico, uno de los balnearios sudamericanas más famosos es el de Mar del Plata. De tantas actividades que podíamos hacer, Debbie y yo decidimos hacer el esnórquel y Lindsey y Mackenzie decidieron pasear en velero. Nos pusimos mucha crema bronceadora porque sabíamos que íbamos a pasar casi todo el día en el sol. Debbie también puso la crema en su bolsa para más tarde. Además de poder participar en todas estas actividades acuáticas, la ciudad de Mar del Plata ofrece para los visitantes calles peatonales *(pedestrian)* con muchas tiendas y restaurantes, galerías y un casino. Y la vida nocturna *(night life)* ... ¡es bárbara *(awesome)!* Aunque estábamos muy cansados después de un día con tantas actividades, no queríamos perder para nada esta parte tan integral de la vida en Mar del Plata. Empezamos con una parrillada[2] en el restaurante que estaba enfrente del casino y de ahí seguimos a un lugar que se llama "Los Alfajores" para bailar y hablar toda la noche. Mañana, vamos a continuar con nuestra excursión en Villa Gesell, un lugar popular entre la gente joven para hacer el camping. Debo terminar aquí porque nos reunimos mañana a las siete.

- ¿En qué deportes acuáticas participas?
- ¿Qué piensas del horario de los estudiantes?
- ¿Qué te gusta del camping? ¿Qué no te gusta?
- ¿Qué más te gustaría hacer en Mar del Plata?

---

[1] Mar del Plata, a city in the province of Buenos Aires, is also the name of one of the most popular beach and resort areas in Argentina. Mar del Plata is located on the Northern Atlantic coast, about 230 miles from the capital city of Buenos Aires. The beaches of Mar del Plata extend for about five miles. People from all around Argentina vacation in this region during the summers, leaving their homes in the interior of the country to spend time at the beach's coastal waters. Groups of students often meet here for holidays and families vacation here as well.

[2] To go out for **una parrillada** is much more than going out to eat dinner at a restaurant. This tradition in Argentine cuisine reflects the fact that beef dominates many Argentine menus, as servers walk around the restaurant with large skewers of meat (anything from fine cuts to intestines) and place the meat chunks on the diner's plate.

Las relaciones sentimentales: Honduras y Nicaragua

Communicative goals

In this chapter you will learn how to . . .

- Talk about relationships and courtship
- Describe recent actions, events, and conditions
- Describe reciprocal actions with reflexive pronouns
- Talk about receptions and banquets
- Use adverbs to qualify actions
- Use the Spanish equivalents of *who, whom, that,* and *which*

Grammar

- The present perfect tense
- The reciprocal **se**
- Adverbs
- Relative pronouns

Cultural information

- Los novios hispánicos
- Las bodas hispánicas

Una plaza sin nombre, Tegucigalpa, Honduras

EL NOVIAZGO DE FRANCISCO MORAZÁN Y CELIA HERRERA In this section you will learn vocabulary associated with courtship and marriage and how to talk about intimate relationships by following the courtship of Francisco Morazán and his wife, Celia Herrera de Morazán.[1]

Cuando se conocieron, fue **el amor a primera vista.**

Se llevaron bien durante la **primera cita.**

TE QUIERO. Y YO A TI.

Se declararon **su amor** el uno a otro.

Un año después de **enamorarse,** decidieron **casarse.**

En **la boda los novios se besaban** mientras las madres **se abrazaban** y los padres **se daban la mano.**

Los invitados **tiraron** arroz cuando **los recién casados** salieron de la iglesia para su **luna de miel.**

Sustantivos

la **amistad** friendship	la **flor** flower	la **separación** separation
el **cariño** affection	el **matrimonio** marriage	la **vida** life
el **compromiso** engagement	el **noviazgo** courtship	
el **divorcio** divorce	el **ramo** bouquet	

Verbos

amar to love	**romper (con)** to break up (with)
divorciarse (de) to get divorced (from)	**salir (con)** to go out (with)
querer to love	**separarse (de)** to separate (from)

¿NOS ENTENDEMOS?

Some other ways of talking about romantic breakups are **dejar a alguien** and **cortar con alguien.** You can also say that a relationship ended by stating the following: **Se acabó (terminó) la relación.** *(The relationship has ended.)*

¡A practicar!

A. **ETAPAS DE UN AMOR FRACASADO** No todas las parejas tienen el mismo éxito que Francisco y Celia. Pon los siguientes eventos de un amor fracasado en un orden lógico.

---

[1] Francisco Morazán (1792–1842), a Honduran soldier and statesman, is considered a national hero of Honduras. Morazán was the guiding force behind the Central American Federation (1823–1839), which united Costa Rica, El Salvador, Guatemala, Honduras, and Nicaragua. Disputes between liberals and conservatives and among the five national groups finally broke up the federation in 1839. Morazán was also president of Costa Rica for a few months before he was assassinated in 1842.

_____ el compromiso   _____ la amistad
_____ el divorcio   _____ el matrimonio
_____ la separación   _____ el noviazgo

B. **DEFINICIONES** Encuentra la palabra de la lista a la derecha que va con la definición a la izquierda.

1. _____ cuando dos personas empiezan a quererse
2. _____ tener una boda
3. _____ hacer planes con otra persona para salir o hacer algo a una hora determinada
4. _____ cuando dos personas se enamoran la primera vez que se ven
5. _____ tener mucho amor por alguien es como tenerle mucho _____
6. _____ cuando dos personas nunca pelean y se divierten mucho juntos
7. _____ una muestra *(sign)* de amor con los labios
8. _____ una muestra de amor con los brazos
9. _____ cuando dos personas se casan, prometen pasar toda _____ juntos
10. _____ cuando dos personas siempre pelean y no les gusta estar juntos
11. _____ lo que los invitados hacen con el arroz después de la boda
12. _____ cuando una pareja decide no seguir juntos
13. _____ tener una persona en la vida con quien ir al cine, a fiestas, etcétera, sin estar casados
14. _____ cuando una pareja casada se separa legalmente para terminar su matrimonio para siempre
15. _____ dos verbos que señalan el amor
16. _____ una manera de saludar a una persona con la mano

a. separarse
b. casarse
c. llevarse bien
d. darse la mano
e. amar
f. divorciarse
g. romper con alguien
h. querer
i. tirar
j. abrazarse
k. besarse
l. llevarse mal
m. enamorarse
n. el amor a primera vista
o. la cita
p. la vida
q. el cariño
r. salir con alguien

C. **PREPARACIONES PARA UNA BODA** Completa el párrafo con palabras y frases apropiadas de la lista.

flores   luna de miel   novia   recién casados   boda   ramo   novio

Normalmente, las preparaciones para una _____ consumen mucho tiempo y mucha energía. Primero, la _____ tiene que comprar su vestido. También ella pide las _____ de una florería, así como el _____ que ella va a llevar al altar de la iglesia. El _____ compra un traje nuevo o puede alquilar *(rent)* un smoking *(tuxedo)*. Finalmente, los novios planean la _____, según el dinero que tienen. A veces, los _____ van a otro país, pero frecuentemente lo pasan bien cerca de su casa.

En voz alta

D. **ENTREVISTA** Pregúntale a otro(a) estudiante las siguientes preguntas sobre el matrimonio y comparen sus respuestas.

1. ¿Eres soltero(a) o estás casado(a)?
2. Si eres soltero(a), ¿tienes novio(a) ahora? Si estás casado(a), ¿cuándo y dónde te casaste?
3. Para ti, ¿es importante casarse en nuestra sociedad? ¿Por qué?
4. Para ti, ¿qué es una familia? En tu opinión, ¿qué futuro tiene la familia en nuestra sociedad?
5. ¿Por qué hay tanto divorcio en nuestro país?
6. ¿Qué se puede hacer para tener éxito en el matrimonio?
7. Para ti, ¿cuál es el lugar ideal para casarse?
8. ¿Cuál es el lugar ideal para pasar una luna de miel?

¿NOS ENTENDEMOS?

El (La) amigo(a) and **el (la) novio(a)** are two Spanish words that do not have an exact English equivalent. **Amigo(a)** is used for *friend, girlfriend,* or *boyfriend.* **Novio(a)** is used for *fiancé/fiancée, groom/ bride.* **El (La) amigovio(a)** is a slang term comprised of the words **amigo(a)** and **novio(a)** to mean a little more than just friends. In Chile the word **el (la) pololo(a)** can be used to say *boyfriend/girlfriend,* as can the word **el (la) enamorado(a)** in Ecuador.

E. **ENCUENTRA A ALGUIEN...** Busca a una persona en tu clase para cada una de las siguientes descripciones. Pon las firmas *(signatures)* de las personas en un papel. Al final, compara tus respuestas con las de los otros estudiantes de la clase.

MODELO: Estoy casado(a).
          E1: *¿Estás casada?*
          E2: *Sí, estoy casada. Y tú, ¿estás casado?*
          E1: *No, no estoy casado.* (E2 signs E1's paper.)

1. Estoy casado(a)
2. Tengo novio(a).
3. No quiero casarme nunca.
4. Me gusta salir, pero no tengo ganas de tener una relación seria.
5. No creo en el matrimonio.
6. No creo en el divorcio.
7. Pienso que la idea de la familia está cambiando en los Estados Unidos.
8. Quiero (Tuve) una boda grande.

F. **UNA BODA MEMORABLE** Descríbele a un(a) compañero(a) de clase una boda memorable a la que tú asististe. En tu descripción, debes contestar las siguientes preguntas.

1. ¿Cómo se llamaban los novios?
2. ¿Cuándo y dónde fue la boda?
3. ¿Qué tiempo hacía ese día?
4. ¿Quiénes estuvieron allí?
5. ¿Con quién fuiste tú a la boda?
6. ¿A qué hora comenzó la ceremonia?
7. ¿Qué pasó después de esa ceremonia?
8. ¿Qué comieron los novios y sus invitados?
9. ¿Qué cosa interesante pasó en la recepción?
10. ¿Dónde pasaron los novios su luna de miel?

EN CONTEXTO

El 14 de marzo Munci Pujol, la novia de Jorge Goytisolo, recibió una invitación de su amigo Felipe. Luego Munci llamó por teléfono a Jorge.

—Aló.
—Hola, Jorge, ¿cómo estás?
—Bien, mi amor. ¿Qué tal?
—Muy bien. Oye, Jorge, ¿sabes qué? He recibido *(I have received)* muy buenas noticias de mi amigo Felipe Vega. Se va a casar el próximo mes con Marisol Flores.
—¡No me digas! ¿Es la mujer con quien *(with whom)* estuvo Felipe en el cine la semana pasada?
—Sí, la misma. Él me ha hablado *(He has spoken to me)* mucho de ella. Parece muy simpática. Según él, ellos se quieren *(they love each another)* locamente.
—¿Cuándo es la boda?
—Han decidido casarse el 16 de abril en la iglesia de San Jacinto. Es la iglesia que está en frente del restaurante El Alba. ¿Quieres ir al casamiento conmigo?
—Pues, claro que sí, Munci. ¡Muchas gracias! Pero, ¿sabes qué? Nunca he asistido *(I have attended)* a una boda.
—No importa. Yo te explico todo. Vamos a pasarlo bien. Bueno, ahora voy a llamar a Felipe para felicitarlo. Chau, Jorge.
—Chau, Munci.

G. **¿COMPRENDISTE?** Contesta las siguientes preguntas con oraciones completas.

1. ¿Cuál es el tema principal de este diálogo?
2. ¿Cuál sería un título apropiado para el diálogo?
3. ¿Por qué llamó Munci a su novio?
4. ¿Conoce Jorge a Marisol? ¿Por qué sí, o por qué no?
5. ¿Están muy enamorados Felipe y Marisol?
6. ¿Va a ser la primera vez que Jorge va a una boda?

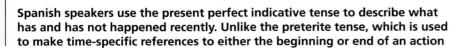

ENCUENTRO *cultural*

Los novios hispánicos

Las costumbres tradicionales de salir en pareja están cambiando rápidamente en Latinoamérica y en España pero, por lo general, todavía son distintas de las costumbres norteamericanas. Por ejemplo, los jóvenes hispánicos comienzan a participar en actividades coeducacionales en grupos alrededor de los 14 años. Ellos salen juntos al cine, a fiestas, a la playa y a eventos deportivos. Generalmente, los jóvenes hispánicos comienzan a salir en parejas a una edad mayor que la de la mayoría de los jóvenes norteamericanos, y aún así están más restringidos que éstos. A veces, ya a los 18 o 19 años, salen en pareja. Al contrario de lo que creen muchas personas, la costumbre de salir en pareja acompañados con un chaperón o una chaperona ya no existe en los países de habla española, y en Latinoamérica y en España, como en muchas otras culturas, muchos jóvenes prefieren una unión libre. En varios casos, el costo de un matrimonio es mucho, y la anulación es difícil de obtener, especialmente por la iglesia católica.

Para pensar: Por lo general, ¿a qué edad salen en parejas los jóvenes de tu país? ¿Qué beneficios hay en salir en grupo? ¿Cuáles son algunas limitaciones de salir en grupo? ¿Y de salir en parejas? Cuando tú estabas en la escuela secundaria, ¿salías en grupo con tus amigos? ¿Qué hacían tú y tus amigos juntos? ¿Salías en pareja?

H. **PREGUNTAS** Contesta las siguientes preguntas a base de la lectura.

1. ¿Qué tipo de actividades hacen los hispanos jóvenes cuando salen en grupos?
2. ¿Cuándo empiezan a salir en parejas?
3. Nombra dos razones por qué algunas parejas prefieren vivir juntos antes de casarse.

GRAMÁTICA I: *The present perfect tense*

Spanish speakers use the present perfect indicative tense to describe what has and has not happened recently. Unlike the preterite tense, which is used to make time-specific references to either the beginning or end of an action or event in the past, the present perfect merely establishes the fact that an action has taken place sometime in the past before the present. The emphasis is placed on the fact that the action took place, not *when* it took place. Consider the following examples:

Present perfect	Yo **he comido.**	*I have eaten.* (past action with no specific reference to time)
Preterite	Yo **comí** a las 7:00.	*I ate at 7:00.* (past action with specific reference to time)

How to form the present perfect
Use the present-tense forms of the auxiliary verb **haber** *(to have)* with the past participle of a verb.

Present of **haber** + past participle:

yo	**he** *I have*	
tú	**has** *you* (inf.) *have*	
Ud., él, ella	**ha** *you* (form.) *have; he/she has*	**hablado** *spoken*
nosotros(as)	**hemos** *we have*	**comido** *eaten*
vosotros(as)	**habéis** *you have*	**vivido** *lived*
Uds., ellos(as)	**han** *you have; they have*	

How to form past participles
1. Add **-ado** to the stem of **-ar** verbs, and **-ido** to the stem of **-er** and **-ir** verbs.

-ar verb	stem + **-ado**		**-er/-ir** verb	stem + **-ido**	
hablar	habl**ado** *spoken*		comer	com**ido** *eaten*	
pensar	pens**ado** *thought*		vivir	viv**ido** *lived*	
llegar	lleg**ado** *arrived*		dormir	dorm**ido** *slept*	

—¿**Has hablado** con el nuevo novio de Ana? — *Have you spoken to Ana's new boyfriend?*
—No, pero ellos **han venido** a la casa de mi hermano antes. — *No, but they have come to my brother's house before.*
—¿Y todavía **no se han conocido**? — *And you still haven't met each other?*
—No, pero creo que él **ha vivido** en Tegucigalpa por muchos años. — *No, but I believe he has lived in Tegucigalpa for many years.*

2. Several **-er** and **-ir** verbs have an accent mark on the **i** of their past participles.

leer	le**ído** *read*		traer	tra**ído** *brought*
creer	cre**ído** *believed*		reír	re**ído** *laughed*

—Te **he traído** un regalo, Celia. — *I've brought a gift for you, Celia.*
—¿Qué me **has traído**, mi amor? — *What have you brought me, my love?*
—Un ramo de flores. — *A bouquet of flowers.*

3. Other verbs have irregular past participles.

abrir	**abierto**	*opened*		morir	**muerto**	*died*
decir	**dicho**	*said; told*		poner	**puesto**	*put*
escribir	**escrito**	*written*		ver	**visto**	*seen*
hacer	**hecho**	*done; made*		volver	**vuelto**	*returned*

—¿Qué **han hecho** ustedes hoy?   *What **have you done** today?*
—**Hemos visto** una película.   *We **have seen** a movie.*
—**He escrito** algunas cartas.   *I **have written** some letters.*

¡A practicar!

I. EN UNA TERRAZA EN LAS ISLAS BAHÍAS, HONDURAS[1] Completa la siguiente conversación durante la luna de miel de Francisco y Celia con la forma correcta de **haber: he, has, ha, hemos** o **han.**

Camarero: ¿_____ estado Uds. en estas islas antes?
Celia: Sí, señor. Nosotros _____ venido aquí antes.
Camarero: Oiga, señora, ¿_____ visto nuestras flores en la terraza?
Celia: Sí, sí. Yo las _____ visto.
Camarero: Y luego, ¿por qué _____ venido Uds. aquí esta tarde?
Celia: Pues, _____ decidido pasar la tarde entre las flores.
Francisco: Mejor dicho, tú _____ decidido venir aquí, Celia.
Celia: Sí, Francisco. Pero también nosotros _____ comido bien aquí.

J. UNA SITUACIÓN COMPLICADA, O EL AMOR DE UN PERRO Clementina, una niña de diez años, ha encontrado un perro en la calle. Ella se ha enamorado del perro e intenta explicárselo a sus padres. Completa las siguientes conversaciones entre dos padres y su hija, usando los participios de los verbos indicados.

1. ver / escribir / hacer / encontrar
Padre: ¿Qué has _____ hoy, hija?
Clementina: He _____ algunas cartas y he _____ este perrito en la calle.
Padre: ¡Ay! ¿Qué has _____? ¿Lo ha _____ tu madre?

2. morir / jugar / dar / enamorar
Clementina: Papá, creo que el perro ha _____.
Padre: No, está durmiendo. Tú le has _____ muchas galletas. *(cookies)*
Madre: Ella ha _____ mucho con el perrito hoy, ¿verdad?
Padre: Sí, porque se ha _____ de él.

3. abrir / decir / poner / comer / volver
Padre: ¿Qué tienes en la mano, hija?
Clementina: Más galletas. El perro ya ha _____ las otras. He _____ una caja *(box)* nueva.
Madre: ¿Qué te hemos _____, hija? El perrito no quiere más.
Padre: Sí, niña. Nos has _____ en una situación difícil. ¿Qué van a decir los dueños *(owners)* si su perro no ha _____ a su casa esta tarde?

---

[1] **Las Islas Bahías** are located off the Caribbean coast in Honduras and are a very popular tourist destination. There are three main islands in the group, and the government of Honduras has established somewhat strict laws to protect the environment there. They suffered devastating damage from Hurricane Mitch in 1998.

K. **MIS QUERIDOS AMIGOS...** Celia está escribiéndoles a sus amigos sobre algunas actividades que ella y Francisco han hecho en las Islas Bahías. ¿Qué les dice en su carta?

MODELO: Yo *he hecho* (**hacer**) mucho ejercicio aquí.

Yo _____ (**nadar**) en la piscina de nuestro hotel y _____ (**jugar**) al tenis con Francisco. Él _____ (**montar**) en bicicleta dos veces esta semana. Desafortunadamente yo no _____ (**comprar**) muchas cosas aquí porque no _____ (**ir**) a ninguna tienda. (**Yo**) _____ (**estar**) muy ocupada.

Francisco y yo _____ (**divertirse**) mucho. Esta tarde _____ (**almorzar**) en un buen restaurante. Francisco y yo _____ (**pasar**) toda la tarde en una terraza magnífica. En la terraza _____ (**ver**) unas flores estupendas. Durante nuestro tiempo en la terraza, yo _____ (**leer**) el periódico. El camarero nos _____ (**traer**) mucha comida. Pienso que él _____ (**creer**) que teníamos mucha hambre. Nosotros _____ (**reírse**) mucho de él. En total, lo _____ (**pasar**) muy bien aquí en esta ciudad maravillosa.

L. **MI LUNA DE MIEL** Imagínate que estás en tu luna de miel. Escribe una carta a un(a) amigo(a) que lee español y descríbele lo que tú y tu esposo(a) han hecho durante sus vacaciones. También hazle algunas preguntas para saber de sus actividades recientes. Trata de usar el vocabulario que has aprendido en esta sección.

Párrafo 1: Información introductoria (tu salud, el tiempo, el viaje, el hotel)
Párrafo 2: Actividades durante tu luna de miel
Párrafo 3: Preguntas para tu amigo(a) (sobre su familia, sus actividades)

En voz alta

M. **RECIENTEMENTE...** Habla con otro(a) estudiante, completando las siguientes oraciones.

MODELO: En mi clase de español, mi profesor (no) ha...
En mi clase de español, mi profesor no ha *dado muchos exámenes.*

1. En mis clases yo (no) he...
2. En la residencia, mis amigos y yo (no) hemos...
3. Mi mejor amigo y su novia (no) han...
4. En casa (no) he...
5. En mi familia, nosotros hemos...
6. En mi trabajo, mis compañeros de trabajo (no) han...
7. El último fin de semana, he...

N. **CHARLA** Hazle las siguientes preguntas a un(a) compañero(a) de clase. También puedes hacerle otras preguntas, según sus respuestas.

1. ¿Has visitado a tu(s) amigo(a)/novio(a)/abuelo(a)/padres/... recientemente? ¿Sí? ¿Qué han hecho Uds.?
2. ¿Has ido a un centro comercial esta semana? ¿Sí? ¿Qué día fuiste allí? ¿A qué hora? ¿Con quién fuiste allí? ¿Qué hiciste (hicieron Uds.) en el centro comercial?
3. ¿Has visto la película «_____»? ¿Sí? ¿Dónde la viste? ¿Te gustó o no? ¿Por qué?
4. ¿Has jugado al _____ esta semana? ¿Sí? ¿Dónde y con quién jugaste? ¿A qué otro deporte has jugado recientemente? ¿Te gusta mucho ese deporte? ¿Por qué?
5. ¿Has leído el periódico hoy? ¿Sí? ¿Qué aprendiste leyendo el periódico?

O. **¡ADIVINEN UDS.!** Cada estudiante de tu clase de español va a escribir en un papel pequeño una acción que él o ella ha hecho recientemente. Luego van a formar grupos de cinco o seis personas. Mientras cada persona muestra *(shows)* con gestos (pantomima) lo que escribió una persona del grupo, sus compañeros del grupo tratan de *(try to)* adivinarlo; luego esa persona dice si los otros lo adivinaron o no.

MODELO: E1: [Lee un periódico.]
           E2: *¿Has leído un periódico?*
           E1: *¡Sí! ¡Bravo!*

ASÍ SE DICE: *Describing reciprocal actions*

Spanish speakers express the idea of *each other* or *one another* with the plural reflexive pronouns **se, nos,** and **os.** Verbs that are not normally reflexive are frequently used to express reciprocal actions. Consider the following examples:

Osvaldo y Lola **se miran** el uno al otro.[1]   *Osvaldo and Lola **look at one another.***
Mi novia y yo **nos besamos.**   *My girlfriend and I **kiss each other.***
¿**Se conocen?**   *¿Do you (they) **know one another?***

¡A practicar!

P. **LA HISTORIA DE AMOR ENTRE UNA NIÑA Y SU PERRO** Completa las siguientes frases para terminar la historia de amor entre Clementina y el perro que encontró en la calle. Usa el pretérito.

MODELO: Clementina y el perro / encontrarse / en la calle
           Clementina y el perro se encontraron en la calle.

1. Clementina y el perro / verse / una tarde de julio en la calle
2. no hablarse / pero / ellos mirarse profundamente
3. inmediatamente / la chica y el perro / enamorarse
4. ellos / abrazarse / besarse / mucho aquella tarde
5. Clementina explicó a sus padres: «El perro y yo / enamorarse»

---

[1] The phrase **el uno al otro** *(one another, each other)* is sometimes added to reciprocal actions for emphasis.

Q. MIS RELACIONES SENTIMENTALES Forma preguntas con las siguientes frases para hacerle a un(a) compañero(a) de clase sobre sus relaciones sentimentales.

MODELO: tú y tus amigos / verse frecuentemente
           E1: *¿Se ven tú y tus amigos frecuentemente?*
           E2: *Sí, nos vemos frecuentemente los fines de semana.*

1. tú y tus padres / hablarse por teléfono una vez a la semana
2. tú y tu mejor amigo(a) / escribirse durante las vacaciones
3. tú y tus abuelos / conocerse muy bien; respetarse
4. tú y tus hermanos / ayudarse con problemas económicos
5. tú y tu compañero(a) de cuarto / hablarse sinceramente
6. tú y tu novio(a) / mirarse cariñosamente; quererse
7. tú y tus compañeros de clase / darse la mano en clase

En voz alta

R. ¿LA PAREJA IDEAL? Indica si estás de acuerdo con las siguientes cualidades de la pareja ideal. Si no estás de acuerdo, explica por qué.

MODELO: Ellos nunca se miran a los ojos cuando se hablan.
           No es una cualidad de la pareja ideal, porque dos personas de una
           pareja ideal siempre se miran cuando se hablan.

1. Ellos se comunican todas sus ideas y opiniones.
2. Ellos se ayudan con problemas difíciles.
3. Ellos siempre se dicen la verdad.
4. Ellos no discuten con frecuencia.
5. A veces se besan en público.
6. Se enamoraron el uno del otro a primera vista.
7. Nunca se separan cuando van juntos a una fiesta.
8. Se casan después de un noviazgo largo.
9. Siempre se tiran objetos cuando están enojados.

VOCABULARIO: *La recepción*

LA RECEPCIÓN DE RUBÉN Y RAFAELA EN MANAGUA, NICARAGUA[1] In this section you will practice vocabulary used to describe receptions and banquets. Below are scenes from the wedding reception of Rubén Darío,[2] Nicaragua's most famous literary talent, and his bride Rafaela Contreras in the National Palace in Managua in 1890.

---

[1] Managua is the capital and largest city of Nicaragua. It is located in the west central part of the country along the south shore of Lake Managua. It was chosen to be the capital of Nicaragua in 1857 in order to resolve a dispute over the location of the capital between the then larger cities of Granada and León.
[2] Rubén Darío is Nicaragua's most famous poet. He is credited with introducing **el modernismo,** an innovative poetic aesthetic, to European intellectual circles at the end of the nineteenth century. He was born in Metapa, Nicaragua, in 1867 and his original name was Félix Rubén García.

Todas las personas importantes de Managua **asistieron a la recepción** para Rubén y Rafaela.

La recepción de **la pareja tuvo lugar** en una sala en el Palacio Nacional.

Los invitados felicitaban a **la pareja** mientras entraba en la sala. Más tarde el presidente del país le hizo un brindis especial.

El banquete era elegante con todos los invitados **vestidos de gala. La orquesta** de la ciudad tocó para la celebración.

Rafaela tiró el ramo de flores y una chica de 20 años lo **agarró**. Todos **aplaudieron**.

Rubén tenía celos de un viejo amigo de Rafaela que la **acompañaba** a ella toda la noche. Cuando Rafaela bailaba con su amigo, Rubén les interrumpió y así **terminó** la celebración.

¡A practicar!

S. **¿EN QUÉ PALABRA ESTOY PENSANDO?** Busca la palabra apropiada del nuevo vocabulario que vaya con cada definición a continuación.

1. dos palabras que refieren a la fiesta que se da después de una boda
2. un grupo de dos personas
3. el grupo musical que toca en fiestas o en conciertos
4. con elegancia
5. Los _____ se refiere a la gente que va a una boda o a otro evento.

T. **LA PERSPECTIVA DE UN MÚSICO** Félix, un miembro de la orquesta que tocó para los recién casados, narra la historia de la recepción. Usa los siguientes verbos para terminar su relato, escogiendo entre el pretérito o el imperfecto.

terminar   asistir a   felicitar   tener lugar   aplaudir   acompañar   agarrar

Más de 300 personas _____ la recepción para Rubén y Rafaela. La celebración _____ en el elegante Palacio Nacional. Nosotros, los músicos, _____ a un cantante en una canción de amor cuando los novios entraron. Todos los invitados _____ con felicidad. El presidente les _____ con un brindis. Una chica joven _____ el ramo de flores que Rafaela tiró. La fiesta _____ bruscamente cuando Rubén y Rafaela se fueron.

En voz alta

U. **DIÁLOGO** Danira está organizando la recepción para la boda de su mejor amiga, Gabriela. Con un(a) compañero(a), hagan los papeles de Danira y Gabriela y hablen de los planes para la fiesta. Formen preguntas con la información dada.

MODELO: Danira: *¿Dónde quieres tener la recepción, Gabriela?*
              Gabriela: *Yo quiero tener la fiesta en la sala de baile del Club Náutico.*

Preguntas de Danira	Respuestas de Gabriela
¿Dónde?	Sala de baile, Palacio Nacional
¿Cuántos invitados?	350 personas
¿Cena o no? ¿De qué?	Cena de cinco platos: mariscos, carne, ensalada, queso y postre; vino blanco
¿Tipo de ropa?	Ropa muy formal y elegante
¿Tipo de música?	Merengue
¿Baile?	¡Baile!
¿Tirar arroz?	No tirar arroz

V. **ENTREVISTA** Con un(a) compañero(a) de clase, contesten las siguientes preguntas sobre las bodas.

1. ¿Estás casado(a)? Si no, ¿piensas casarte algún día? ¿Cómo vas a celebrar? Si estás casado(a), ¿cómo celebraste la boda? ¿Hubo una fiesta grande? ¿Quién vino? ¿Qué llevaste tú? ¿Qué llevaron los invitados?
2. ¿Fuiste a una boda alguna vez? ¿De quién? ¿Lo pasaste bien? ¿Hubo mucha gente? ¿Qué tipo de ropa se vistió? ¿Dónde tuvo lugar la boda?
3. ¿Fuiste alguna vez a una recepción o banquete para celebrar una boda? ¿Hubo una orquesta? ¿un baile? ¿Cómo trataron los invitados a los novios? ¿Les tiraron mucho arroz? ¿Bailaron juntos los novios?

ENCUENTRO *cultural*

Las bodas hispánicas

Éstas son unas palabras nuevas para la lectura:

comprometidos   *engaged*
estar de acuerdo   *to agree*
el (la) juez   *judge*
prometer   *to promise*
cumplir con   *to honor*
los testigos   *witnesses*
firmar   *to sign*

Para pensar: ¿Qué impresiones tienes de las bodas hispánicas? ¿Cómo son las bodas norteamericanas en comparación con las hispánicas?

Cuando dos novios piensan casarse, es posible que estén **comprometidos** por varios años mientras trabajan y ahorran dinero para alquilar un apartamento y comprar muebles. Muchas veces, posponen la boda hasta terminar sus estudios.

Es común que el novio le pida la mano de su novia al padre de ella. Si éste **está de acuerdo,** las dos familias comienzan a planear juntas la boda. Muchos matrimonios en Latinoamérica y en España consisten en dos ceremonias oficiales, una civil y otra religiosa. Tradicionalmente, la ceremonia más importante para los novios y sus familias es la religiosa. A veces, la ceremonia civil tiene lugar en la casa de la novia o del novio, y participan en ella algunos familiares y amigos íntimos de las dos familias. **Un(a) juez** casa a los novios, leyendo palabras de un texto oficial. Después de que se **prometen cumplir con** todas las responsabilidades del matrimonio, los novios están casados oficialmente. Luego ellos y sus **testigos firman** los documentos correspondientes.

W. **PREGUNTAS**   Contesta las siguientes preguntas a base de la lectura.

1.   ¿Por qué dura mucho el noviazgo en los países hispánicos?
2.   Describe las dos ceremonias que hay en una boda hispánica.

ASÍ SE DICE: *Using adverbs to qualify actions*

An adverb is a word that modifies a verb, an adjective, or another adverb. It may describe *how, when, where, why,* or *how much.* You already know many adverbs such as **muy, ayer, siempre, después, mucho, bien, mal, tarde, temprano, mejor,** and **peor.**

For most Spanish adverbs, add **-mente** *(-ly)* to an adjective.

natural	**naturalmente**	*naturally*
frecuente	**frecuentemente**	*frequently*

If an adjective ends in **-o**, change the **-o** to **-a,** then add **-mente.**

perfecto	**perfectamente**	*perfectly*

If an adjective has an accent mark, the adverb retains it.

fácil **fácilmente** *easily*   rápido **rápidamente** *rapidly*

Adverbs modifying a verb are generally placed immediately after the verb, whereas adverbs modifying adjectives or other adverbs are placed directly before them.

Ellos salieron **rápidamente** de la sala.   *They left the room **quickly**.*
Rubén estaba **muy** enojado.   *Rubén was **very** mad.*

¡A practicar!

X. **MÁS IMPRESIONES DE LA RECEPCIÓN** Da más énfasis a las siguientes oraciones. Primero convierte la palabra en adverbio, y luego incorpórala en la oración.

MODELO: fabuloso / Rafaela se vestía.
fabulosamente / Rafaela se vestía fabulosamente.

1. puntual / El carruaje *(carriage)* nupcial llegó a la recepción.
2. fácil / La chica agarró el ramo de flores.
3. constante / La orquesta tocaba.
4. estupendo / Rafaela y su amigo bailaban.
5. inmediato / Rubén se puso enojado.
6. tranquilo / El amigo de Rafaela le habló a Rubén.
7. paciente / Rafaela intentó calmar a su esposo.
8. total / Los invitados estaban sorprendidos.
9. feliz / La recepción no terminó.
10. rápido / Rafaela y Rubén salieron.

En voz alta

Y. **¿CÓMO HACES ESAS COSAS?** Con un(a) compañero(a), busquen el adverbio que corresponda con las palabras de abajo para describir cómo Uds. hacen las siguientes cosas. **¡OJO!** Algunas de las palabras no requieren cambios —ya son adverbios.

MODELO: jugar con niños pequeños
E1: *¿Cómo juegas con niños pequeños?*
E2: *Juego pacientemente con niños pequeños. ¿Y tú?*
E1: *Yo juego mal con niños pequeños; no me gustan los niños.*

natural	frecuente	bien	perfecto	paciente	mal
tarde	rápido	mejor	fácil	peor	

1. hablar con gente del sexo opuesto
2. conducir
3. hablar español
4. estudiar para mis clases
5. tocar el piano
6. bailar

ASÍ SE DICE: *Adverbial expressions of time and sequence*

In previous chapters, you learned many of the following adverbs and adverbial expressions with their English equivalents.

Use the following adverbs to express how often something is done.

a veces *sometimes*   **otra vez** *again*
dos (tres, etc.) veces *twice (three times, etc.)*   **una vez** *once*
muchas veces *very often*

cada día (semana, mes, etc.) *each (every)*
  day (week, month, etc.)
(casi) siempre *(almost) always*
nunca *never*

solamente *only, just*
todos los años (días, meses,
  etc.) *every year (day,*
  month, etc.)

—Hablo con mi novio **todos los días.**
—**Siempre** voy con él al cine los fines
de semana.

*I talk to my boyfriend **every day.***
*I **always** go to the movies with him on*
the weekends.

Use the following adverbs to express the order of events.

primero *first*
luego *then*

entonces *then; so*
después *afterward*

finalmente *finally*
por fin *at last, finally*

—¿Adónde vamos **primero,** mi amor?
—Al cine. **Luego** a la discoteca.
—¿Y **después**?
—Volvemos a casa.

*Where are we going **first,** my love?*
*To the movies. **Then** to the disco.*
*And **afterward**?*
We're going back home.

¡A practicar!

Z. **ADVERBIOS** Completa las siguientes frases con la siguiente lista de adverbios.

| nunca | cada | una vez | dos veces | a veces |
| siempre | muchas veces | otra vez | solamente | todos los días (años) |

1. Me gusta mucho ser soltero. Yo no quiero casarme _____.
2. Elizabeth Taylor se ha casado _____.
3. El matrimonio puede ser muy aburrido. Las parejas hablan de lo mismo _____, y van de vacaciones al mismo lugar _____.
4. Rafaela quiere todavía a su viejo amigo. Le habla _____ día por teléfono.
5. Rubén es un señor muy celoso. Cuando él ve a su esposa hablando con otros hombres, él _____ se pone furioso.
6. —¿Cómo? ¡No puedo creerlo! ¿Estás bailando _____ con tu viejo amigo, Rafaela?
7. —Sí, bailé con él la noche de nuestra boda, y también hoy bailo con él. Nosotros hemos bailado _____.
8. —Pero Rafaela, yo pensaba que Uds. _____ bailaron una vez.
9. —Rubén, yo te amo mucho. Pero me gusta ver a mi viejo amigo también _____.
10. El amor es una cosa que ocurre solamente _____ en la vida.

AA. **UN FRACASO AMOROSO** Luis Eduardo cuenta de una relación amorosa que terminó mal para él. Pon el relato en orden. Después, vuelve a contar la historia y añade palabras como **primero, un día, entonces, después, finalmente, por fin** y **luego** para hacerla más completa.

_____ Me fui corriendo de su casa. Me puse muy triste —¡yo quería casarme con esta chica!
_____ ¡La encontré en los brazos de mi hermano, Raúl!
_____ La invité a cenar conmigo.
_____ Yo me enamoré seriamente de ella.
_____ Salí temprano del trabajo, y me paré en su casa para sorprenderla.
_____ Conocí a Raquel, la mujer más guapa del mundo, el año pasado.
_____ Fuimos a tomar un café y hablamos toda la noche.
_____ Decidí romper con ella para siempre.
_____ Empezamos a salir todas las noches.

¿NOS ENTENDEMOS?

Married couples are referred to as **el matrimonio.** Some Hispanic countries use the word **el matrimonio,** rather than the more common words **la boda** or **el casamiento,** for *wedding.*

En voz alta

BB. **ACTIVIDADES FAMILIARES** Cuéntale a otro(a) estudiante algunas actividades que hacen tus parientes. Escoge un elemento de cada una de las tres columnas para hacer tus oraciones.

MODELO: *Mi papá me llama por teléfono frecuentemente.*

¿Quién(es)?	¿Qué hace(n)?	¿Con qué frecuencia?
mi papá (mamá)	venir a visitarme	a veces
mi tío(a)	escribirme una carta	casi cada mes
mi esposo(a)	llamarme por teléfono	una vez al día
mi novio(a)	darme un regalo bonito	frecuentemente
mi hermano(a)	jugar al béisbol (golf)	todos los años
mi(s) _____	ir de compras (al cine)	cada fin de semana

CC. **LOS FINES DE SEMANA** Completa las siguientes oraciones conversando con un(a) compañero(a) de clase.

1. Cuando era niño(a), me gustaban los fines de semana porque...
   A veces los sábados por la mañana mis amigos y yo íbamos a...
   Luego, por la tarde íbamos a... donde...
   Por la noche nos gustaba..., pero nunca...
   Casi todos los domingos por la mañana me levantaba a las...
   Primero,... Luego,... Después,...
   Por la tarde me gustaba..., pero muchas veces prefería..., y siempre...
   Los domingos por la noche..., entonces yo..., y finalmente...

2. Todavía me gustan los fines de semana porque...
   A veces los sábados por la mañana mis amigos y yo vamos a...
   Luego, por la tarde vamos a... donde...
   Por la noche nos gusta...
   Casi todos los domingos por la mañana me levanto a las...
   Primero,... Luego,... Después,...
   Por la tarde me gusta..., pero muchas veces prefiero...
   Los domingos por la noche..., y por fin...

GRAMÁTICA II: *Relative pronouns*

Relative pronouns are used in joining two clauses together. There are four primary relative pronouns in English: *who, whom, that,* and *which.* Their Spanish equivalents are words you already know.

que refers to people and things
quien refers only to people
lo que refers to an entire idea, concept or situation

¿Quién es el hombre **que** hablaba contigo?
　↑　　　　　　↑
(first clause)　(second clause)

*Who is the man **who** was talking with you?*

Ella es la mujer con **quien** yo bailaba.
　↑　　　　　　↑
(first clause)　(second clause)

She is the woman I was dancing with.
*(lit., She is the woman **with whom** I was dancing.)*

No sabemos **lo que** él hizo en la fiesta
　↑　　　　　　↑
(first clause)　(second clause)

*We don't know **what** he did at the party.*

In distinguishing between the use of the relative pronouns **que** or **quien**, both of which can be used to refer to people, Spanish speakers use **quien** *(who/whom)* only when it is preceded by a preposition or when it functions as an indirect object of the sentence. Compare the following examples:

Es una mujer **que** tiene muchos amigos.	*She is a woman **who** has many friends.*
Es la mujer **con quien** yo bailaba.	*She is the woman I was dancing with. (She is the woman **with whom** I was dancing.)*
(quien preceded by the preposition **con)**	
Es la mujer **a quien** yo le di el regalo.	*She is the woman **to whom** I gave the gift.*
(quien as an indirect object pronoun)	

The relative pronouns **que** and **quien** carry accents when they are used in interrogative or exclamatory sentences.

¿Con **quién** sales ahora?	***Whom** are you going out with now?*
¡**Qué** mujer tan interesante!	***What** an interesting woman!*

¡A practicar!

DD. **UNA MUJER MISTERIOSA** Usa el pronombre relativo apropiado para completar las siguientes oraciones.

1. ¿Quién es la mujer _____ lleva el vestido azul?
2. Creo que es la mujer con _____ Ramón hablaba el otro día.
3. Me gustan las mujeres _____ tienen ese aire misterioso.
4. Dicen que es la mujer _____ se divorció de Juan Medellín porque él era pobre.
5. ¡_____ dicen es mentira! Juan salía con una chica _____ era la amiga de esa mujer.
6. ¿_____ dices? Él me dijo que siempre le fue fiel *(faithful)* a la mujer con _____ se casó.
7. No debes confiar en *(trust)* _____ dice él ni en _____ dicen las otras personas. Yo lo vi a él con la otra mujer, _____ lo besaba detrás del teatro este verano.

En voz alta

EE. **LO QUE NECESITAMOS ES EL AMOR** Completa las siguientes preguntas con **que, lo que** o **quien.** Después, contéstalas con un(a) compañero(a) de clase para expresar sus opiniones personales.

MODELO: E1: ¿Tu mejor amiga es la persona *que* sabe más de ti?
         E2: *Sí, mi mejor amiga sabe todos mis secretos.*
      o: E2: *No, yo le cuento más a mi mamá que a mi mejor amiga.*

1. ¿Es el matrimonio _____ da felicidad en la vida?
2. ¿El divorcio es _____ está destruyendo nuestra sociedad?
3. ¿Te quieres casar con una persona _____ tiene los mismos gustos que tú?
4. ¿Con _____ quieres compartir tus secretos más íntimos?
5. ¿_____ es la persona que menos quieres en el mundo? ¿Por qué?

Síntesis

¡A ver!

El **Capítulo 10** explora el tema de las relaciones íntimas. La presentadora de los segmentos de video se llama Cecilia, que trabaja para la televisión nicaragüense en la que es presentadora de un programa para jóvenes. Cecilia nació en Chinandega, pueblo en el que viven todavía sus padres, aunque Cecilia ahora vive en la capital de Managua. En los segmentos de video que vamos a ver, Cecilia nos habla de las relaciones entre familiares y entre amigos en el mundo hispánico.

ACTIVIDAD 1   Pre-viewing task (Segmento 1 del video)

Paso 1: En este segmento del video vas a ver una serie de clips cortos y fotografías que se enfocan en *(that focus on)* la interacción y la relación entre amigos y familiares. ¿Qué verbos se pueden utilizar en español para describir el tipo de interacción y/o el tipo de relación que observas en cada clip o fotografía? Haz una lista de estos verbos tratando de incluir en tu lista por lo menos un verbo del tipo «acción o relación recíproca» para cada clip o fotografía. Mira la siguiente lista de verbos de este tipo como ejemplos.

abrazarse   *to hug*
acompañarse   *to accompany each other*
ayudarse   *to help each other*
besarse   *to kiss each other*
conocerse   *to know each other; to meet*
darse la mano   *to shake hands*
hablarse   *to talk with each other*

llevarse bien (mal)   *to get along well (poorly) with each other*
mirarse   *to look at each other*
quererse   *to love each other*
saludarse   *to greet each other*
tocarse   *to touch each other*

Paso 2: Vuelve a ver el mismo segmento, y con un(a) compañero(a) de clase, haz una descripción de cada clip o foto; enfoca en la interacción y/o la relación entre los amigos o familiares que se observa en ello. Utiliza en tu descripción los verbos que tienes en tu lista e incluye por lo menos un verbo del tipo «acción o relación recíproca».

ACTIVIDAD 2   Pre-viewing task (Segmento 2 del video)

Paso 1: ¿Qué recuerdos tienes de los (las) novios(as) o amigos(as) íntimos *(close friends)* que tenías cuando estabas en la escuela? Apunta en un papel una lista de los nombres de dos o tres de ellos. Para cada persona, apunta también un lugar y una cosa que identificas con esa persona (por ejemplo: Anabel, el hospital de Springfield, un collar de tres piedras preciosas).

Paso 2: Para esta actividad, trabaja en grupos de tres personas. Haz preguntas para averiguar *(to find out)* la identificación de las personas, los lugares y las cosas que cada miembro del grupo ha apuntado en su lista. Si tienes alguna foto contigo para ayudar con tu descripción, utilízala.

As you listen to your companions' descriptions, you should react with exclamations. Remember, an exclamation can take the following forms: ¡**Qué** + *adjective*! (¡**Qué interesante!**, ¡**Qué bonito!**) or ¡**Qué** + *noun* + **más** + *adjective*! (¡**Qué regalo más bonito! ¡Qué nombre más interesante! ¡Qué lugar más romántico!**).

MODELO: E1: *¿Quién es esta chica?*
E2: *Anabel es la chica con quien salía cuando tenía 16 años y la que llevé al Prom en el año 1999.*
E3: *¿Y qué significa para ti el hospital de Springfield?*
E2: *Es el lugar donde los dos trabajábamos los fines de semana.*
E1: *¿Y el collar de piedras preciosas? ¿Qué significado tiene para ti?*
E2: *Es lo que le compré para el Prom.*

ACTIVIDAD 3   Viewing task (Segmento 2 del video)

En el **Segmento 2 del video** vas a ver a Laura con sus dos niños mirando unas fotos de cuando su madre era niña. En la siguiente tabla termina las frases indicadas en la segunda columna como respuesta a cada una de las preguntas:

1. ¿Quién es Marián de la primera foto?	Es la amiga con quien...
2. ¿Cuál es el parque de la segunda foto?	Es el sitio en el que...
3. ¿A qué fiesta hace referencia Laura en la tercera foto?	Es la fiesta en la que...
4. ¿Quién es el señor Treviño de la cuarta foto?	Es el señor de quien...
5. ¿Quiénes son las personas en la quinta foto?	Son... con quienes..

ACTIVIDAD 4   Post-viewing task (Segmento 2 del video)

Con tu compañero(a) de clase, hablen de las fotos de Laura cuando era niña. ¡Ojo con las formas de los verbos que utilizas!

¡A escribir!

Writing a summary

A good summary tells the reader the problem and the events that lead to the solution in a narrative. The following is a list of important features that one should include in a summary:

- An interesting title
- When and where the action takes place
- The main characters (if applicable)
- The problem, conflict, or action at the center of the narrative
- The solution or resolution to the problem or conflict (if applicable)

Lee la siguiente lectura, «La boda de Javier y María Jesús». Después, contesta las preguntas.

La boda de Javier y María Jesús

Llegó el 18 de abril, el día de la boda. A las 7:00 de la tarde más de 100 parientes y amigos de María Jesús y Javier asistieron a la ceremonia religiosa en la Catedral de Poneloya (un pueblo en la costa de Nicaragua). Poco después, llegó Javier, quien llevaba un elegante traje negro. Estaba muy contento, pero un poco nervioso. A las 7:50 llegó el señor Cabral con su bonita hija vestida de blanco. A Javier le parecía un ángel.

Pronto empezó la marcha nupcial. Los novios caminaron lentamente hacia el altar donde el padre Contreras celebró la misa y casó a Javier y María Jesús. Cuando el padre les dijo que ya eran esposos, los dos jóvenes se besaron. Luego ellos salieron de la catedral y los invitados les tiraron arroz, los abrazaron y los besaron. Entonces todos fueron al restaurante Antonio donde tuvo lugar la recepción.

Cuando Javier y su nueva esposa entraron en el restaurante, los invitados los aplaudieron y sacaron fotos de ellos. Después de un brindis a los recién casados, María Jesús, Javier y sus invitados entraron en un salón comedor donde tuvieron un banquete maravilloso: consomé de verduras, ensalada mixta, filete de pollo asado, vino tinto y vino blanco y café con leche.

Después de cenar, la banda comenzó a tocar música moderna y todos los invitados empezaron a bailar, hasta el abuelo de Javier, un señor amistoso de 84 años. Más tarde, María Jesús les tiró su ramo de flores a las solteras; su hermana Leticia lo agarró. Entonces Javier le quitó la liga *(garter)* a María Jesús y se la tiró a los solteros. Un primo de María Jesús la agarró. Luego Leticia y el primo bailaron juntos y todos los aplaudieron.

Más tarde, Javier y María Jesús cortaron el pastel nupcial, que a los invitados les gustó muchísimo. Después de otro brindis por el papá de Javier, todos aplaudieron de nuevo y les dijeron «Felicidades» a la nueva pareja. Entonces, todo el mundo tomó una copa de champán en honor de Javier y María Jesús. Después, la fiesta duró hasta las 5:30 de la mañana. Todo el mundo lo pasó muy bien.

Functions: Writing about characters; Writing about theme, plot, or scene; Expressing a need

Vocabulary: Prose; Punctuation marks

Verbs: Irregular preterite; Imperfect

Paso 1: Escribe la siguiente información en una hoja de papel:
  a. Escribe un nuevo título para el cuento.
  b. ¿Dónde tuvo lugar el acontecimiento?
  c. ¿Cuándo ocurrió el acontecimiento?
  d. ¿Quiénes son los personajes principales del cuento?
  e. ¿Cuál es el suceso central del cuento?

Paso 2: Empleando la información que apuntaste en **Paso 1,** escribe un breve resumen de la lectura.

Paso 3: Ahora, vuelve a leer el resumen y corrígelo, teniendo en cuenta el contenido, la organización, la gramática y la ortografía.

¡A leer!

Summarizing a reading passage

Summarizing in English a reading passage that you have read in Spanish can help you synthesize its most important ideas. Some guidelines for writing this type of summary are as follows:

- Underline the main ideas in the reading passage.
- Circle the key words and phrases in the passage.
- Write the summary of the passage in your own words.
- Do not include your personal reactions to the summary.

- Avoid the following common errors in writing a summary:
  - too long/short
  - too many details
  - main ideas not expressed
  - key ideas not emphasized
  - wrong key ideas

Correo de amor

Querido Calixto:

No estoy segura de que me pueda ayudar. Hace seis meses cumplí 20 años y tengo una vida social saludable. Disfruto de ser soltera y nunca pensé que me gustaría cambiar. Eso fue hasta hace poco. Hay un joven llamado Pedro que es guapo, muy bueno y con un gran sentido del humor. Cada vez que nos vemos el cielo se me abre. Sé que él me desea y yo a él, tanto que deseo gritar. Pero hay un problema: él se ve con mi amiga Lisa. Están saliendo desde hace un tiempo y no les ha ido mal. Lo que quiero decir es que a ella le gusta Pedro, pero no lo quiere; se ve con él por no estar sola. Pero mientras tanto, yo estoy loca por Pedro.

Calixto, Lisa es una vieja amiga y me muero si ella se enfada conmigo por robarle su novio, pero temo que él se aleje y que yo pierda la oportunidad de vivir la vida con un hombre que me atrae tanto. ¿Debo decirle a Lisa cómo me siento, debo decírselo a Pedro y dejar que él sea el que decide? Por favor, Calixto, apúrese. Me estoy volviendo loca, especialmente cuando los veo juntos y me digo que Pedro sería más feliz conmigo.

«Enamorada del novio de una Amiga»

Estimada «Enamorada... »

Estás corriendo el riesgo de perder una buena amiga. Desde aquí, no estoy seguro si esa amistad con Lisa puede pasar esta prueba. Si crees que puedes hacerlo, pregúntaselo. Esto te da dos alternativas: dejar que Pedro hable con Lisa acerca de la situación de sus relaciones y su deseo de entablar una relación contigo, o esperar pacientemente que ellos rompan su amistad amorosa, de la forma que sea. Quizás Lisa te sorprenda y deje a Pedro, pero esto es una línea muy fina. Por favor, déjame saber qué ha pasado. Me gustaría también saber de otros lectores que se encuentren en la misma situación.

Paso 1: Lee las dos cartas y subraya las ideas principales.

Paso 2: Lee cada carta una vez más. Luego, marca con un círculo las palabras y las expresiones claves.

Paso 3: Escribe un resumen en inglés de la primera carta. Indica cuál es el problema principal de la autora.

Paso 4: Escribe un resumen en inglés de los consejos de Calixto.

Paso 5: Vuelve a leer rápidamente las dos cartas y busca la información necesaria para completar las frases que siguen:

Primera carta

1. (Un chico / Una chica) escribió esta carta.
2. Esta persona (es soltera / está casada).
3. (Él / Ella) tiene (miedo / hambre / razón).
4. Esta persona le pide (dinero / amor / consejos) a Calixto.
5. Pedro y Lisa son (amigos / novios / esposos).

Segunda carta

6. Calixto es (optimista / pesimista / neutral) en su respuesta.
7. Es probable que Calixto sea (menor / mayor) que sus lectores.
8. De las dos alternativas que ofrece Calixto, la (primera / segunda) es mejor.

Reacciones personales

9. ¿Qué piensas del problema de la persona que escribió la primera carta? ¿Has tenido este problema también? ¿Cómo lo resolviste?
10. ¿Qué piensas de los consejos de Calixto? ¿Qué consejos tienes tú?

¡A conversar!

Paso 1: ¿Cómo fue la última boda a la que asististe? Descríbele la última boda a la que asististe a un(a) compañero(a) de clase. Incluye la siguiente información:

- ¿Cuándo fue?
- ¿Quiénes se casaron?
- ¿Dónde tuvo lugar?
- ¿Quiénes asistieron a la boda? ¿Qué relación tienes con la pareja?
- ¿Cómo fue? ¿Lo pasaron bien los invitados? ¿Hubo una banda? ¿Bailaron los invitados?
- ¿Hubo otro aspecto importante o divertido de la boda?

Paso 2: Después, cambien de papel y hagan la actividad de nuevo.

Las relaciones sentimentales *Relationships*

la amistad *friendship*
el amor *love*
la boda *wedding*
el cariño *affection*
la cita *date (social)*
el compromiso *engagement*

el divorcio *divorce*
la flor *flower*
la luna de miel *honeymoon*
el matrimonio *marriage*
el noviazgo *courtship*
la novia *bride*

el novio *groom*
el ramo *bouquet*
los recién casados *newlyweds*
la separación *separation*
la vida *life*

Verbos

abrazar(se) *to hug (each other)*
amar *to love*
besar(se) *to kiss (each other)*
casarse (con) *to get married, to marry*
darse la mano *to shake hands*

divorciarse (de) *to get divorced (from)*
enamorarse (de) *to fall in love (with)*
llevarse bien (mal) (con) *to get along well (poorly) (with)*
querer *to love*

romper (con) *to break up (with)*
salir (con) *to go out (with)*
separarse (de) *to separate (from)*
tirar *to throw*

La recepción

el banquete *banquet*   **los invitados** *guests*   **la orquesta** *band*   **la pareja** *couple*

Verbos

acompañar *to accompany*
agarrar *to catch*
aplaudir *to applaud*

asistir (a) *to attend (a function)*
felicitar *to congratulate*
tener lugar *to take place*

terminar *to end*

Adverbios

a veces *sometimes*
cada día (semana, etc.) *every day (week, etc.)*
casi (siempre) *(almost) always*
después *afterward*
dos (tres, etc.) veces *twice (three times, etc.)*

entonces *then; so*
finalmente *at last, finally*
luego *then*
muchas veces *very often*
nunca *never*
otra vez *again*
por fin *finally*

primero *first*
solamente *only, just*
todos los años (días, meses, etc.) *every year (day, month, etc.)*
una vez *once*

Participios pasados

abierto *opened*
dicho *said; to be*
escrito *written*

hecho *done; made*
muerto *died*
puesto *put*

visto *seen*
vuelto *returned*

Expresiones idiomáticas

a primera vista *at first sight*   **vestido(a) de gala** *dressed elegantly*

El mundo del trabajo: Panamá

Communicative goals

In this chapter you will learn how to . . .

- Talk about professions, the office, and work-related activities
- Make statements about motives, intentions, and periods of time
- Describe the job hunt, benefits, and personal finances
- Make informal requests
- Express desires and intentions

Grammar

- The prepositions **por** and **para**
- Negative **tú** commands
- Formation of the present subjunctive
- The subjunctive mood and volition

Cultural information

- El canal de Panamá
- Protocolo en los negocios en el mundo hispánico

La Plaza del Monumento Francés, la Ciudad de Panamá, Panamá

EN UNA OFICINA EN PANAMÁ[1] In this section you will learn to talk about professions in the working world.

la cocinera

el ingeniero

el banquero

el dentista

la fotógrafa

la mujer de negocios

la peluquera

el policía

el plomero

el siquiatra

el (la) abogado(a) *lawyer*	**el (la) maestro(a)** *teacher*
el (la) arquitecto(a) *architect*	**el (la) obrero(a)** *worker, laborer*
el (la) carpintero(a) *carpenter*	**el (la) periodista** *journalist*
el (la) contador(a) *accountant*	**el (la) programador(a)** *programmer*
el (la) empleado(a) *employee*	**el (la) traductor(a)** *translator*
el (la) gerente *manager*	**el (la) veterinario(a)** *veterinarian*
el (la) jefe *boss*	

Palabras útiles

el (la) accionista *stockbroker*	**el (la) mecánico(a)** *mechanic*
el (la) analista de sistemas *systems analyst*	**el (la) ranchero(a)** *rancher*
el (la) bombero(a) *firefighter*	**el (la) reportero(a)** *reporter*
el (la) cajero(a) *cashier*	**el (la mujer) soldado** *soldier*
el (la) comerciante *merchant*	**el (la) técnico** *technician*
el (la) criado(a) *servant; maid*	**el (la) vendedor(a)** *salesperson*
el (la) electricista *electrician*	

➡ You will not be tested on these **Palabras útiles;** they are for recognition only. However, they are provided in case your career is not listed in **Vocabulario.**

---

[1] Panama is one of the most strategically located countries in Central America. As early as the sixteenth century, the idea of building a canal in Panama to connect the Atlantic and Pacific Oceans was debated. After declaring its independence from Spain in 1821, Panama became part of **la Gran Colombia,** a territory comprising what is today known as Ecuador, Colombia, and Venezuela. Motivated by interest in ratifying a treaty that would allow the Panama Canal to be built, the United States helped Panama gain its independence from Colombia in 1903.

¡A practicar!

A. ¿A QUIÉN VAS A LLAMAR? Tú trabajas para una agencia de empleo en la Ciudad de Panamá y estás tratando de identificar las profesiones que tus clientes buscan. Lee las siguientes descripciones y decide cúal de las profesiones mejor corresponde a cada situación.

MODELO: hombre / preparar comida en el Restaurante Gorditos
un cocinero

1. mujer / enseñar a chicas activas en la escuela Nuestra Señora de las Lágrimas
2. mujer / sacar fotos de la boda de nuestra querida hija, Alejandra
3. hombre o mujer / escribir documentos legales
4. mujer / recibir y contar dinero de nuestros clientes en el Banco Central
5. hombre / ayudar en el diseño *(design)* de un nuevo centro comercial
6. mujer / ayudar a nuestros clientes con problemas emocionales
7. mujer / escribir artículos cortos sobre la moda para *La Prensa*[1]
8. mujer / supervisar un departamento de una compañía
9. hombre / ayudar con las finanzas de una gran corporación
10. mujer / construir un nuevo cuarto en una residencia personal

B. ¡UNA NIÑERA DESESPERADA! Tu amiga Dora está cuidando a los dos hijos de su hermana Susana. Te llama pidiendo consejos para las siguientes situaciones. ¿A quién debe llamar Dora?

1. ¡El lavabo de la cocina está atascado *(clogged)* y hay agua por todos lados!
2. ¡Miguelito acaba de romperse dos dientes!
3. ¡Tomás me cortó el pelo cuando me dormí en el sofá!
4. ¡Miguelito le dio una patada *(kicked)* a la computadora y ahora no funciona!
5. ¡Tomás robó unos juguetes *(toys)* de una tienda y el gerente está aquí y está muy enojado!
6. ¡Los niños le dieron chocolate al perrito!
7. ¡Tomás y Miguelito tienen hambre y yo quemé *(burned)* la cena!
8. ¡Las instrucciones para el televisor solamente están en francés!

En voz alta

C. IMPRESIONES DEL MUNDO DE TRABAJO Da tus impresiones de las siguientes profesiones a un(a) compañero(a) de clase, escogiendo de la siguiente lista de adjetivos. Explica tu respuesta. Puedes modificar los adjetivos con adverbios como **muy, un poco** y **demasiado.**

MODELO: el hombre (la mujer) de negocios
E1: *Yo creo que ser hombre de negocios es aburrido.*
E2: *Pues, yo pienso que ser hombre de negocios es interesante. Los hombres de negocios siempre viajan y ganan mucho dinero. Yo quiero ser hombre de negocios algún día.*

interesante / aburrido   creativo / rutinario   exigente *(demanding)*/ fácil
peligroso / seguro   variado / monótono   prestigioso / ordinario   flexible / rígido
divertido / arduo

1. el (la) veterinario(a)	3. el (la) peluquero(a)	5. el (la) maestro(a)
2. el (la) obrero(a)	4. el (la) periodista	6. el (la) abogado(a)

---

[1] *La Prensa* is a daily newspaper in Panama with one of the highest circulation numbers in the country.

D.   ENCUESTA En grupos de cuatro o cinco personas, háganse las siguientes preguntas. Comparen sus respuestas para después compartirlas con toda la clase.

MODELO: *En nuestro grupo, hay dos personas que quieren ser abogados, una*
que quiere ser ingeniera y una que quiere ser mujer de negocios.
Tres de nosotros queremos trabajar en una compañía pequeña, y
una persona quiere trabajar por su cuenta. Pensamos que la profe-
sión más peligrosa es ser policía. La profesión más aburrida para
nosotros es la de contador(a). A todos nosotros nos importa ganar
mucho dinero. El trabajo más lucrativo es ser abogado(a).

1.   ¿Qué profesión te interesa para después de la universidad?
2.   ¿Quieres trabajar en una compañía pequeña, una compañía grande, por tu
cuenta *(for yourself)*, para el gobierno, o... ?
3.   ¿Qué trabajo te parece el más peligroso de todos?
4.   ¿Qué trabajo te parece el más aburrido de todos?
5.   ¿Te importa ganar mucho dinero en el trabajo? En tu opinión, ¿cuál es el
trabajo más lucrativo?

E.   ENTREVISTA Trabajando con dos compañeros(as) de clase, háganse las siguientes preguntas sobre las profesiones.

1.   ¿Tienes un trabajo ahora? ¿Qué haces? ¿Cuántas horas a la semana trabajas?
2.   Cuando te gradúes de la universidad, ¿qué quieres hacer? ¿Por qué? ¿Qué
clases te dan preparación para tus planes en el futuro?
3.   ¿Cuáles son las profesiones más populares entre tus amigos?
4.   ¿Cuáles son las carreras de mayor prestigio en nuestra sociedad? ¿de menor
prestigio? ¿Hay alguna profesión que te guste pero que no vas a hacer
porque no es prestigiosa?
5.   Pensando en los miembros de tu clase, ¿cuáles son las profesiones más
apropiadas para algunos de ellos?

EN CONTEXTO

Julián Darío está solicitando un puesto *(applying for a job)* en una oficina de abogados. Lo que sigue es parte de la entrevista con Carlos Infante Garrido, el jefe de la empresa.

—Buenos días, Julián. Siéntate.

—Gracias, Sr. Garrido. Ud. es muy amable.

—Gracias a ti, Julián, por venir *(for coming)* a charlar con nosotros. Tienes un currículum *(résumé)* fabuloso para un hombre tan joven.

—Pues, he tenido algunas oportunidades buenas.

—No seas tan modesto. Tienes todas las cualidades que esperamos de un abogado que trabaja para nosotros. ¿Y quieres trabajar para nosotros?

—¡Sí, señor! Espero que Uds. no ofrezcan el puesto a otro candidato sin considerar lo que puedo contribuir.

—¡No te preocupes *(Don't worry)*, Julián! La verdad es que no hemos encontrado a la persona adecuada todavía. Quiero que nuestros abogados tengan ciertas sensibilidades, que sean dedicados, responsables y, sobre todo, profesionales con los clientes.

—Pues, le juro *(I swear)* que puedo satisfacerlo con respecto a *(with regard to)* estas cualidades. Por ejemplo, soy muy trabajador y...

—Ya lo sé, Julián. Tu currículum lo dice todo. ¡No me digas más! *(Say no more!)* El puesto es tuyo, si lo quieres.

Note how Carlos uses **tú** to address a subordinate while Julián uses **Ud.**, a sign of respect in addressing a superior. It is important to remember to use **Ud.** in business situations.

F. **¿COMPRENDISTE?** Contesta las siguientes preguntas con oraciones completas.

1. ¿Por qué está tan impresionado el jefe con Julián?
2. ¿Por qué piensa Carlos que Julián es modesto?
3. ¿Hay otros candidatos que Carlos está considerando?
4. Para Carlos, ¿qué atributos son importantes para los abogados que trabajan en su empresa *(firm)*?
5. ¿Cree Julián que él puede hacer el trabajo?
6. ¿Cómo termina la entrevista? ¿Recibe Julián el puesto?
7. ¿Piensas tú que Carlos debe hacerle más preguntas a Julián?

ENCUENTRO *cultural*

El canal de Panamá

Éstas son unas palabras nuevas para la lectura:

angosto(a) *narrow*
rodear *to surround*
marítimo *having to do with the sea*
el embarque *shipping*
proveer *to provide*

La construcción del canal de Panamá por los Estados Unidos duró siete años (1907–1914) y la administración del canal estuvo a cargo de los Estados Unidos hasta 1999, cuando se pasó al gobierno panameño. El canal de Panamá se sitúa en el punto más **angosto** entre el Océano Pacífico y el Océano Atlántico. El canal es actualmente la única vía de comunicación que conecta los dos grandes océanos, el mar Caribe al norte y el océano Pacífico al sur. Desde que existe este canal, los barcos tienen una ruta mucho más corta y entonces más económica para transportar productos de un lado a otro de las Américas.

El canal ha producido más trabajos, contratos e ingresos para el gobierno que ninguna otra actividad económica de la nación. La economía más activa está concentrada en la área urbana central de Panamá que **rodea** el canal.

Ahora, como la economía de la región es más diversa, el canal no es tan importante como antes. Otras actividades, como los servicios **marítimos,** la industria y **el embarque** ahora juntos **proveen** más trabajos e ingresos por impuestos que el canal. Sin embargo, el canal sigue funcionando, ahora bajo el control de los panameños.

Para pensar: Los barcos que usan el canal pueden tardar más de 15 horas en cruzar. ¿Te gustaría pasar por el canal en barco? ¿Por qué sí o por qué no? Los Estados Unidos pagó la construcción del canal pero está en el país de Panamá. En tu opinión, ¿es lógico que Panamá haya recibido el control del canal? Explica tu respuesta.

G. **PREGUNTAS** Contesta las siguientes preguntas a base de la lectura.

1. ¿Cuál es la vía que conecta el mar Caribe con el océano Pacífico?
2. ¿Qué ha producido el canal?
3. ¿Qué otros trabajos proveen ahora más recursos financieros que el canal?

Uses of **por**

You may have noticed that the prepositions **por** and **para** have different uses and meanings. The preposition **por** has a wider range of uses than **para**. In general, **por** conveys the underlying idea of a cause, reason, or source behind an action.

1. Duration of time *(for, in, during)*

—¿**Por** cuánto tiempo viviste en Panamá?

—Viví allí **por** más de tres años.

(For) How long did you live in Panama?

*I lived there **for** more than three years.*

—¿Trabajas en la clínica todo el día?

—Sí, **por** la mañana y **por** la tarde.

Do you work in the clinic all day?

*Yes, **during** the morning and **during** the afternoon.*

2. Motion *(through, along)*

—¿Quieres caminar conmigo **por** la oficina para conocer a la gente?

*Would you like to walk **through** the office with me to meet the people?*

3. General area *(around)*

—Perdón, ¿hay una fotocopiadora **por** aquí?

—Sí, señora. Hay una **por** allí.

*Excuse me, is there a copy machine **around** here?*

*Yes, ma´am. There is one **over there**.*

4. In exchange *(for)*

—¿Desea cambiar esta máquina de escribir?

—Sí, **por** una computadora, por favor.

Would you like to exchange this typewriter?

*Yes, **for** a computer, please.*

5. Value or cost *(for)*

—¿Cuánto pagaste **por** los servicios del abogado?

—Le pagué $500 **por** su tiempo.

*How much did you pay **for** the lawyer´s services?*

*I paid him $500 **for** his time.*

6. In place of *(for)*

—Yo no sabía que trabajas aquí, Tomás.

—Trabajo **por** Juan, que está muy enfermo.

I didn´t know you worked here, Tomás.

*I´m working **for (substituting for)** Juan, who is very ill.*

7. Gratitude *(for)*

—Gracias **por** toda su ayuda, Sr. Navarro.

—De nada. ¡Buena suerte con el proyecto!

*Thanks **for** all your help, Mr. Navarro.*

You´re welcome. Good luck with the project!

8. On behalf of *(for)*

—Hola, Miguel. Vengo a verte **por** parte de mis hijos.

*Hello, Miguel. I´ve come to see you **on behalf of** my kids.*

9. Mistaken identity *(for)*

—En Panamá me tomaron **por** canadiense.

—¿Sabes qué? ¡Me tomaron **por** mexicana!

*In Panama, they took me **for** a Canadian.*

*You know what? They took me **for** a Mexican!*

10. Unit of measurement *(by, per)*

—La secretaria escribe más de 60 palabras **por** minuto.

*The secretary writes more than 60 words **per** minute.*

11. Reason *(because of)*

—¡Hombre, viniste muy tarde a la oficina!

Wow, you arrived late at the office!

—Llegué tarde **por** el tráfico tan tremendo.

*I arrived late **because of** all the traffic.*

12. Purpose *(for, after)* followed by noun

—¿Vas a la oficina **por** tu cheque?

*Are you going to the office **for** your check?*

—Sí, y después voy a la tienda **por** comida.

*Yes, and afterward I'm going to the store **for** some food.*

13. Idiomatic expressions

Por favor. *Please.*	**Por casualidad...** *By the way . . .*
¡Por Dios! *¡Oh my gosh!*	**¡Por supuesto!** *Of course!*
Por eso... *That's why . . .*	**por ejemplo** *for example*

Uses of **para**

In general, **para** conveys the underlying idea of purpose (goal), use, and destination.

1. Recipient *(for)*

—Estos papeles son **para** la jefe.

*These papers are **for** the boss.*

2. Employment *(for)*

—¿**Para** quién trabajas ahora?

For whom do you work now?

—Trabajo **para** mi papá en su oficina.

*I work **for** my father in his office.*

3. Specific time *(by, for)*

—¿**Para** cuándo necesita el dinero, señora?

(For) When do you need the money, ma'am?

—Lo necesito **para** el próximo sábado.

*I need it **by (for)** next Saturday.*

4. Destination *(to, for)*

—¿**Para** dónde sales mañana por la tarde?

(To) Where are you going tomorrow afternoon?

—Salgo **para** la costa.

*I'm leaving **for** the coast.*

5. Purpose *(in order to)* + infinitive

—¿Por qué estudias español?

Why do you study Spanish?

—Lo estudio **para** hablar con mis clientes.

*I study it **in order to** speak with my clients.*

6. Member of a group *(for)*

—**Para** un chico de diez años, él es muy responsable.

For a ten-year-old, he is very responsible.

7. To show one's opinion *(for)*

—**Para** Elena, es mejor trabajar por la mañana.

For Elena, it is better to work in the morning.

—**Para** mí, el peluquero tiene un trabajo fascinante.

For me (In my opinion), the hairstylist has a fascinating job.

¡A practicar!

H. *¿POR O PARA?* Escoge entre **por** o **para** para completar las siguientes oraciones y explica por qué. Luego, hazle las preguntas a un(a) compañero(a) de clase.

1. ¿Vives por/para trabajar o trabajas por/para vivir?
2. ¿Prefieres trabajar por/para la mañana o por/para la tarde?
3. ¿Pasas por/para el campus universitario todos los días?
4. ¿Vas a trabajar por/para una compañía multinacional o por/para una compañía pequeña?
5. Por/Para ti, ¿cuál es la profesión menos agradable?
6. ¿Trabajaste alguna vez por/para una persona que estaba enferma?
7. ¿Por/Para cuánto tiempo estudias en esta universidad?
8. ¿Cuánto pagaste por/para tus libros este semestre?
9. ¿Por/Para dónde vas al final del semestre?
10. ¿Por/Para cuándo necesitas entregar tu próximo trabajo escrito?
11. Por/Para los estudiantes de esta universidad, ¿es fácil encontrar trabajo durante el año académico?

I. **UNA ENCUESTA** Elena va al Banco Central. Una empleada le hace algunas preguntas. Con un(a) compañero(a) completen la conversación, usando las preposiciones **para** o **por** en el diálogo. Luego, dramaticen la escena para la clase.

EMPLEADA

1. ¿—————— qué viene Ud. aquí, señora?
3. ¿—————— qué decidió Ud. venir aquí esta mañana?
5. Generalmente ¿cuándo viene aquí —————— usar nuestros servicios?
7. Cuánto paga —————— los servicios de este banco?
9. ¿Le parece razonable?
11. ¡Muy bien! ¿—————— casualidad, conoce Ud. a nuestra cajera, Susana?
13. ¡Ah! —————— eso se parecen tanto. Permítame una última pregunta, —————— favor: ¿Qué impresión tiene Ud. del Banco Central?
15. Gracias —————— su cooperación.

ELENA

2. —————— el servicio rápido y porque es muy conveniente.
4. —————— depositar dinero.
6. Los sábados —————— la mañana.
8. Quince balboas[1] —————— mes.
10. Sí, —————— mí está muy bien. Y voy a abrir otra cuenta *(account)* —————— mi hija en un año.
12. Sí, alguien me tomó —————— ella el otro día. ¡Ja, ja! Ella es mi hermana.
14. —————— mí, es un banco fabuloso.
16. De nada, señora.

En voz alta

J. **¿QUÉ SABES TÚ DE PANAMÁ?** Con otro(a) estudiante, hagan una conversación usando la siguiente información. Estudiante 1 tiene unas preguntas sobre

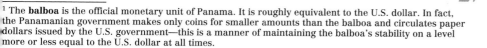

---

[1] The **balboa** is the official monetary unit of Panama. It is roughly equivalent to the U.S. dollar. In fact, the Panamanian government makes only coins for smaller amounts than the balboa and circulates paper dollars issued by the U.S. government—this is a manner of maintaining the balboa's stability on a level more or less equal to the U.S. dollar at all times.

Panamá. Estudiante 2 tiene una lista de información sobre Panamá y tiene que buscar la respuesta para cada pregunta. Noten el uso de **por** y **para** en las preguntas y en las respuestas.

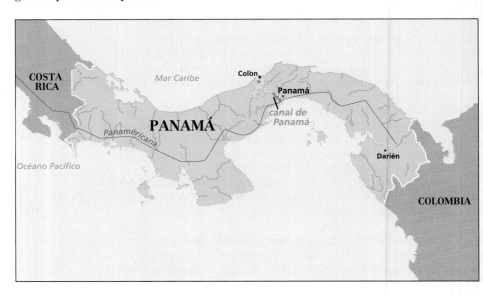

Estudiante 1

1. ¿Hay que pasar **por** otros países **para** llegar a Panamá desde los Estados Unidos?
2. ¿Hay un sitio **por** donde los barcos pueden pasar del océano Atlántico al Pacífico en Panamá?
3. **Para** los turistas, ¿hay playas bonitas en Panamá?
4. ¿Hay algún lugar especial **para** hacer compras?
5. ¿Se puede viajar **por** Panamá en autobús?
6. ¿Pasa la Panamericana **por** Panamá?

Estudiante 2

a. El Canal de Panamá es el único sitio **por** donde los barcos pueden pasar del océano Atlántico al Pacífico.[1]
b. **Para** llegar a Panamá desde los Estados Unidos, hay que pasar **por** México y toda Centroamérica.
c. La Panamericana cruza casi todo el país de Panamá, excepto **por** 150 kilómetros de la región de Darién, donde es imposible construir carreteras.[2]
d. La Zona Libre de Colón es un lugar especial **para** mayoristas *(wholesalers)* donde no hay impuestos de importación.[3]

---

[1] **El canal de Panamá,** or the Panama Canal, was first put into use in 1914. The United States controlled and ran the canal during the entire twentieth century. On December 31, 1999, the canal was officially handed over to Panama. During the last years of U.S. control, as much as 93% of the workforce running the canal was Panamanian. Thus, the transfer was quite smooth. The Panama Canal affords travel by sea from the Atlantic to the Pacific Oceans (or vice versa) without having to go around the entire continent of South America—thus saving thousands of miles and unnecessary time at sea for ocean transport.

[2] **La Panamericana,** or the Panamerican Highway, is a highway that begins at Fairbanks, Alaska, and continues almost without interruption down to Tierra del Fuego in Argentina. There is only one area where this highway could not be built: the highway is missing a stretch of about 150 kilometers between Panama and Colombia. This break in the road is called the Darien Gap.

[3] **La Zona Libre de Colón,** or the Colón Free Trade Zone, is located in Colón. It is an enclosed commercial park where companies can import and export goods—normally on a wholesale level—without great governmental interference and without having to pay international duties. Colón is a port city located at the entrance of the Panama Canal on the Caribbean coast. It is also famous for its bazaars, beautiful beaches, and colonial Spanish fortress.

e. Panamá tiene un sistema bastante bueno de autobuses **para** viajar alrededor del país.

f. La Isla Taboga es un lugar en Panamá donde hay mucha historia y que tiene una playa muy bonita. Hay varias playas en el país, y también es un país con mucha historia.

VOCABULARIO: *La oficina, el trabajo y la búsqueda de un puesto*

SOLICITANDO UN PUESTO EN LA OFICINA DE INFANTE GARRIDO Y GARRIDO: ABOGADOS In this section you will learn how to talk about a typical office environment and work-related activities. You will also learn words and expressions related to the job search.

| los beneficios *benefits* | la entrevista *interview* | el salario/sueldo *salary* |
| la empresa *corporation; business* | el puesto *job, position* | la solicitud *application (form)* |

Verbos

contratar *to hire*	llamar por teléfono *to make a phone call*	renunciar *to resign*
dejar *to quit*		reunirse *to meet*
despedir (i) *to fire*	llenar *to fill out (a form)*	solicitar un puesto *to apply for a job*
imprimir *to print*	pedir un aumento *to ask for a raise*	
jubilarse *to retire*		

Expresiones idiomáticas

de tiempo completo *full-time*   de tiempo parcial *part-time*

¿NOS ENTENDEMOS?

The following words can be useful when filling out a Spanish job application: **la letra de molde** *(print)*, **el estado civil** *(marital status)*, **actual** *(current, present)*, **el sueldo mensual** *(monthly salary)*, **el puesto desempeñado** *(position held)*.

¡A practicar!

K. EMPAREJAR Empareja la definición a la derecha que mejor corresponda a cada una de las palabras o frases a la izquierda.

1. _____ jubilarse
2. _____ de tiempo completo
3. _____ la solicitud
4. _____ solicitar un puesto
5. _____ la impresora
6. _____ imprimir
7. _____ despedir

a. trabajar desde las 8:00 hasta las 5:00 todos los días
b. producir un documento escrito de una computadora
c. algo que se conecta con la computadora
d. dejar de trabajar después de muchos años
e. el formulario que entregas con el currículum
f. eliminar una persona de la empresa
g. buscar una posición nueva

L. UN DÍA EN LA VIDA DE SOFÍA Sofía es la secretaria en la oficina de Infante Garrido y Garrido. Completa la historia de abajo con las palabras de la lista para describir un día en su trabajo. En algunos casos vas a tener que conjugar los verbos.

imprimir	pedir un aumento	beneficios
reunirse	puesto	candidato
llenar	sala de conferencias	fax
correo electrónico	renunciar	
llamar por teléfono	tiempo parcial	

1. Yo tengo un _____ en la oficina de Infante Garrido y Garrido.
2. Aunque el sueldo no es muy alto, los _____ que me dan son buenos.
3. ¡El problema es que me dan demasiado que hacer! Tengo que contestar cuando alguien _____.
4. Paso mucho tiempo trabajando con el _____ cuando la gente manda documentos urgentes.
5. También, yo tengo que contestar los mensajes que vienen en la computadora por _____. A veces necesito _____ los mensajes para mi jefe porque él no sabe usar la computadora.
6. A veces, me hacen _____ formularios muy importantes, y me pongo nerviosa.
7. Estoy cansada de trabajar tanto, estoy pensando _____ si no encontramos a alguien más para ayudarme.
8. Buscamos un _____ para un puesto de _____ para ayudarme por la mañana.
9. Además, los jefes de la oficina van a _____ en la _____ para hablar de mí esta tarde —yo les acabo de _____ de sueldo. ¡A ver qué pasa!

M. EL CASO DE UN EMPLEADO DESPEDIDO Escogiendo de la lista de palabras, completa la siguiente narrativa sobre el nuevo empleado de Infante Garrido y Garrido. En algunos casos, vas a tener que conjugar los verbos. ¿Puedes explicar por qué se usa el imperfecto en los casos indicados?

sueldo	despedir	proyectos	jubilarse	computadora
contratar	reunión	entrevista	informe	
fotocopiadora	dejar	currículum	empresa	

La oficina de Infante Garrido y Garrido _____ a Julián Darío el año pasado. Julián **tenía** un _____ impresionante y le cayó muy bien a Carlos durante la _____. Por eso, Carlos le ofreció un _____ muy bueno y una _____ nueva. Julián lo aceptó y él y su esposa se mudaron a la Ciudad de Panamá para poder estar más cerca de la _____. Durante el primer mes el jefe **estaba** muy contento con el trabajo de Julián. Carlos pensó que por fin **podía** _____ sin preocupaciones.

Los problemas empezaron el segundo mes cuando Julián faltó a una _____ importante y empezó a entregar *(to turn in)* documentos tarde. Además, dejaba documentos importantes en la _____ y en dos ocasiones no firmó testamentos *(wills)*. Por encima, Carlos encontró el _____ anual, qué él mismo escribió sobre los _____ del año pasado, en la basura de Julián. Carlos lo _____ al día siguiente. Julián le dijo que él **iba** a _____ el puesto de cualquier modo.

En voz alta

N. ADIVINANZAS Con un(a) compañero(a), tomen turnos describiendo las palabras en la lista sin usar la misma palabra. Tu compañero(a) tiene que adivinar *(guess)* la palabra que estás describiendo.

MODELO: el currículum
E1: *Es un papel en que un candidato escribe todos los trabajos que él o ella ha tenido. Un candidato les da este papel a las compañías donde quiere trabajar.*
E2: *¿Es el currículum?*
E1: *¡Sí!*

E1
los beneficios
la fotocopiadora
el fax
la sala de conferencias

E2
despedir
un trabajo de tiempo completo
pedir un aumento
la entrevista

O. PARA SOLICITAR UN PUESTO Con un(a) compañero(a) de clase, hablen de lo que se necesita para conseguir un trabajo. Después, hagan una lista de los pasos *(steps)*. Usen las sugerencias de abajo para inspiración. **¡OJO!** Las sugerencias no están en orden —es necesario cambiarlas un poco para tu lista.

MODELO: *1. Es necesario preparar un currículum para describir tu experiencia de trabajo.*
2. Hay que buscar una compañía interesante para ti.
3. Tienes que escribirle una carta al jefe de la compañía.
4. ...

- preparar el currículum
- hacer preguntas sobre la empresa, el puesto y el sueldo
- contestar un anuncio en el periódico
- ir a la oficina
- celebrar
- llenar una solicitud

- pedir cartas de recomendación y referencias personales
- comprar un traje/vestido nuevo
- conocer a los otros empleados
- presentarse al jefe y contestar preguntas
- levantarse temprano y vestirse cuidadosamente

P. LA ENTREVISTA Con un(a) compañero(a), hagan una entrevista de trabajo entre un(a) candidato(a) y el (la) jefe de Infante Garrido y Garrido. A la izquierda, hay una lista de información para el (la) candidato(a). A la derecha hay información para el (la) jefe. Formen preguntas y respuestas con la información.

El (La) candidato(a)
Información sobre ti:
Tienes mucha experiencia.
Has trabajado tres años en una oficina.
Nunca vienes tarde al trabajo.

El (La) jefe
Quieres saber si el (la) candidato(a)...
tiene experiencia.
tiene más de dos años de experiencia.
es responsable, confiable.

Nunca pides días de vacaciones.

¿   ?

Tú quieres saber si la compañía...

ofrece un buen sueldo.

es una compañía con buena reputación.

ofrece beneficios.

tiene un puesto disponible *(available)* de tiempo completo.

El final de la entrevista:

Decide si el trabajo te interesa o no.

Explica al (a la) jefe tus razones.

necesita mucho tiempo libre.

¿   ?

Información sobre la compañía/el puesto:

El puesto paga $500 al mes.

La compañía tiene más de 40 años de experiencia.

La compañía tiene un buen plan de seguro médico.

Buscamos a alguien para un puesto de tiempo parcial.

El final de la entrevista:

Decide si el (la) candidato(a) te interesa o no.

Ofrécele el trabajo si quieres, o explícale por qué no le quieres ofrecer el trabajo.

ENCUENTRO *cultural*

Protocolo en los negocios en el mundo hispánico

Éstas son unas palabras nuevas para la lectura:

la falta   *lack*
el apretón de manos   *handshake*
la jerarquía   *hierarchy*

Para pensar: ¿Tienes trabajo o has tenido trabajo en el pasado? ¿Cómo tratabas a la gente en tu trabajo? ¿Notas una diferencia entre cómo los empleados se tratan en el mundo hispánico y en los Estados Unidos?

Muchas veces las interacciones personales entre los hispanos en el mundo de los negocios son más formales que en los Estados Unidos. Las expresiones informales que a veces pasan en este país —llamar a un cliente por su primer nombre, por ejemplo— pueden ser interpretadas como **una falta** de respeto en el mundo hispánico. Es más común en el mundo hispánico llamar a un colega por su título y apellido que por su nombre de pila. Por ejemplo, a la Srta. Susana González, es más común llamarla «Srta. González» que «Susana».

Los colegas generalmente se dan el saludo y la despedida al principio del día y al final. Es más común usar el más formal «Buenos días» que «Hola», que se considera menos formal. Ésta también es la manera de saludar a los clientes.

Muchas reuniones de negocios empiezan y terminan con **un apretón de manos**. La distancia que la gente mantiene es generalmente menor que en los Estados Unidos, especialmente en una conversación muy animada.

La jerarquía en los negocios hispánicos es normalmente bien definida. Los subordinados generalmente saludan al director mayor usando su título y su apellido, y le tratan de Ud. aunque el superior puede usar el **tú** con los subordinados. Los colegas del mismo nivel pueden usar **tú** o **Ud.**, dependiendo de la diferencia de la edad y el grado de la familiaridad entre ellos. Algunos jefes tratan a sus empleados de **Ud.** como un medio para mantener una distancia de respeto.

Q. **PREGUNTAS** Contesta las siguientes preguntas a base de la lectura.

1. ¿Cuál es un comportamiento apropiado entre los hispanos en el mundo de negocios?
2. ¿Cómo empieza y termina una reunión de negocios en el mundo hispánico?
3. ¿Cómo saludan los subordinados a sus jefes en el mundo hispánico?

GRAMÁTICA II: *Negative tú commands*

Formation of negative informal commands

In **Capítulo 5** you learned how to form affirmative informal commands. To form negative informal commands, you'll be using the same strategy as you would to form either affirmative or negative formal commands.

Recall from **Capítulo 9** that to form both affirmative and negative formal commands for most Spanish verbs, you drop the **-o** ending from the present-tense **yo** form and add the following endings to the verb stem: **-e/-en** for **-ar** verbs; **-a/-an** for **-er** and **-ir** verbs. Remember that there are also spelling changes for verbs ending in **-car, -gar,** and **-zar** and that there are irregular verbs such as **dar, estar, ir, saber,** and **ser.**

The chart below, demonstrating all the command forms for the verbs **hablar, comer, vivir, dormir,** and **ir,** graphically illustrates the similarities among the negative informal command forms and all the formal command forms.

Infinitive	Informal command (tú/vosotros)		Formal command (Ud./Uds.)	
	(+)	(−)	(+)	(−)
hablar	habla	**no hables**	**hable**	**no hable**
	hablad	**no habléis**	**hablen**	**no hablen**
comer	come	**no comas**	**coma**	**no coma**
	comed	**no comáis**	**coman**	**no coman**
vivir	vive	**no vivas**	**viva**	**no viva**
	vivid	**no viváis**	**vivan**	**no vivan**
dormir	duerme	**no duermas**	**duerma**	**no duerma**
	dormid	**no durmáis**	**duerman**	**no duerman**
ir	ve	**no vayas**	**vaya**	**no vaya**
	id	**no vayáis**	**vayan**	**no vayan**

As you can see from the chart above, only the affirmative informal commands (**habla/hablad, come/comed, vive/vivid, duerme/dormid,** and **ve/id**) deviate from the endings used in the remaining command forms.

Another way to interpret the similarities shared among the negative familiar command forms and all of the formal command forms is to understand that these structures are conjugated in the same way as present subjunctive forms, which you saw in *Capítulo 9.*

As with negative formal commands, place reflexive or object pronouns before the negated verb.

—No **te** olvides de escribirme.	*Don't forget to write me.*
—No **le** hables.	*Don't talk **to him**.*
—¿Debo llamarte?	*Should I call you?*
—No, no **me** llames.	*No, don't call **me**.*

¡A practicar!

R. ¡TANTOS CONSEJOS! Antes de su entrevista con la empresa de Infante Garrido y Garrido, José recibió muchos consejos de su familia y sus amigos. Pon los verbos de abajo en forma de mandato *(command)* negativo para completar lo que dijeron los amigos y la familia de José.

1. No _____ **(decir)** tonterías *(silly things)* durante la entrevista.
2. No _____ **(fumar)** en la oficina.
3. No _____ **(hablar)** demasiado de tu familia.
4. No _____ **(comer)** por una hora antes de la entrevista.
5. No _____ **(dormirte)** durante la entrevista.
6. No _____ **(contestar)** las preguntas personales.
7. No _____ **(olvidarte)** de llamar a tus padres después.
8. No _____ **(hacer)** muchas preguntas sobre los beneficios y la duración de las vacaciones.

S. ¿HACER O NO HACER? Forma mandatos informales con los elementos de abajo decidiendo si son cosas que tu amigo(a) debe o no debe hacer durante su primer mes en un puesto nuevo. ¡OJO! Los mandatos tienen que ser lógicos.

MODELO: invitar / un(a) empleado(a) del sexo opuesto / salir contigo
No invites a un(a) empleado(a) del sexo opuesto a salir contigo durante tu primer mes.

1. entregar / los documentos / a tiempo
2. conocer / solamente / las personas importantes
3. salir / temprano / la oficina
4. responder / el correo electrónico
5. pedir / favores especiales / la recepcionista
6. trabajar / horas extras
7. vestirse / con ropa cómoda
8. pedir / un aumento de sueldo
9. contratar / un asistente
10. prepararse / las reuniones

En voz alta

T. EL COMPORTAMIENTO *(BEHAVIOR)* PROFESIONAL Con un(a) compañero(a) de clase, decidan el comportamiento apropiado con respecto a los siguientes temas en un ambiente profesional. Usen mandatos informales —uno afirmativo y otro negativo— para expresar su posición.

MODELO: la fotocopiadora
No la uses para proyectos personales.
o: *Úsala solamente para proyectos relacionados con tu trabajo.*

1. los otros empleados	5. la hora del almuerzo	9. las vacaciones
2. el (la) jefe	6. las reuniones	10. la computadora
3. tu oficina	7. los clientes	
4. el teléfono	8. el salario	

U. **PROBLEMAS Y CONSEJOS** Imagínate que eres un(a) consejero(a) para un programa de servicio cívico para tu universidad. Varios estudiantes vienen a tu oficina para contarte problemas con sus trabajos en organizaciones y empresas de la comunidad. ¿Qué consejos puedes darles? Da por lo menos un mandato positivo y uno negativo. Trata de ser diplomático(a) con ellos.

MODELO: Anne dice que su jefe no está contenta con la calidad de su trabajo.
Anne, escúchame bien. Habla con tu jefe sobre lo que puedes hacer para mejorar. No hagas tu trabajo demasiado rápido.

1. Linda es muy tímida con los clientes. No le gusta hablar con otras personas.
2. Jim no se lleva bien con los otros empleados de Animals-R-Us. Ellos dicen que él es diferente.
3. Rich no tiene el tiempo suficiente para su trabajo y sus estudios.
4. Mónica tiene problemas con la puntualidad. No puede llegar a tiempo a su trabajo.
5. Howard trabaja en una escuela primaria y dice que los maestros no lo respetan.
6. María trabaja por la tarde en el hospital. Su jefe quiere que ella trabaje por la mañana.
7. Francine dice que no puede aprender el nuevo sistema en la computadora donde trabaja.
8. Teri siempre está estudiando cuando debe estar ayudando a los clientes en la tienda.

VOCABULARIO: *Las finanzas personales*

EN EL BANCO NACIONAL DE PANAMÁ In this section you will learn how to talk about your personal finances.

Sustantivos

la cuenta corriente *checking account*	**la cuenta de ahorros** *savings account*	**el préstamo** *loan*

Verbos

ahorrar *to save*	**pagar en efectivo** *to pay in cash*	**rebotar** *to bounce (a check)*
pagar a plazos *to pay in installments*	**prestar** *to loan*	

¿NOS ENTENDEMOS?

Another way to say **la factura** *(bill)* is **la cuenta**.

¡A practicar!

V. DEFINICIONES Empareja cada una de las palabras de abajo con su definición.

a. pagar en efectivo
b. pagar a plazos
c. depositar
d. pedir dinero prestado
e. el cajero automático
f. pagar las facturas
g. el cheque
h. ahorrar
i. préstamo
j. la tarjeta de crédito

1. _____ Es un papel pequeño que usas para pagar algo. No es dinero, pero representa dinero de tu cuenta.

2. _____ Es cuando tú no gastas tu dinero, sino que *(but rather)* lo pones en el banco para usar otro día.

3. _____ Es algo plástico que usas para pagar en tiendas y restaurantes. Si no pagas la cuenta cada mes, tienes que pagar mucho interés.

4. _____ Es el acto de poner dinero en el banco.

5. _____ Cada mes mandas cheques por correo para pagar la electricidad, tus tarjetas de crédito, el gas, etc.

6. _____ Eso es lo que haces si pagas poco a poco por algo, por ejemplo, si compras una bicicleta y pagas $50 por mes durante seis meses en vez de pagar $300 inmediatamente.

7. _____ Es una máquina del banco que puedes usar para sacar dinero de tu cuenta las 24 horas del día.

8. Muchos estudiantes tienen que pedir un _____ para estudiar; en otras palabras, ellos tienen que _____.

9. _____ Eso es cuando no usas crédito o un cheque para pagar, sino dólares, balboas, pesetas, etc.

W. ¿QUÉ HAGO CON TANTO DINERO? La mamá de Dora acaba de ganar la lotería. Dora le da consejos sobre qué hacer con el dinero que ganó. Completa su conversación con las siguientes palabras.

sacar   presupuesto   cuenta corriente   cuenta de ahorros   prestar

Mamá: Dora, ¡no sé qué hacer con tanto dinero! Quiero abrir una _____, así voy a poder escribir muchos cheques sin preocupaciones.

Dora: Bueno, mamá, está bien, pero también quieres ahorrar parte de tu dinero, ¿no? ¿Por qué no abres una _____ también?

Mamá: Pero hija, si es necesario, ¿puedo _____ dinero de esa cuenta?

Dora: Claro, mamá. ¿Sabes cuánto dinero usas cada semana? Debes tener un plan. Tú necesitas escribirte un _____ que incluya todos tus gastos.

Mamá: Gracias por tu ayuda, hija.

Dora: De nada, mamá. Quiero lo mejor para ti. A propósito, ¿me podrías _____ unas balboas para el alquiler *(rent)*?

En voz alta

X. **ENTREVISTA** Habla con un(a) compañero(a) de clase sobre las siguientes preguntas. ¿Quién tiene más éxito con las finanzas personales?

1. ¿Les prestas dinero a tus amigos con frecuencia? ¿Cuánto prestaste la última vez? ¿La persona te devolvió *(returned)* el dinero? Cuando sales con tus amigos(as), ¿quién paga la cuenta generalmente?
2. ¿Tienes un presupuesto mensual *(monthly)*? ¿Tienes el dinero suficiente al final del mes? ¿Cuánto dinero necesitas para actividades divertidas cada semana?
3. ¿Tienes un trabajo? ¿Quieren tus padres que pagues parte de la matrícula para la universidad? ¿Pediste algunos préstamos?
4. ¿Tienes algunas tarjetas de crédito? ¿Usas las tarjetas solamente para urgencias o con más frecuencia? ¿Puedes pagar todo el monto *(balance)* de tu tarjeta al final del mes? ¿Cuándo fue la última vez que pagaste con tarjeta de crédito?

Y. **SITUACIONES EN EL BANCO** Trabajando con un(a) compañero(a) de clase, inventen un diálogo para una de las siguientes situaciones. Usen el vocabulario nuevo de este capítulo.

1. Quieres abrir una cuenta corriente en el banco pero solamente tienes $20 para abrirla.
2. Según el banco, tienes $100 menos en tu cuenta de ahorros de lo que tú pensabas. Crees que es un error por parte del banco.
3. Perdiste tu tarjeta de cajero automático. Quieres saber si alguien la usó para sacar dinero de tu cuenta.

GRAMÁTICA III: *Formation of the present subjunctive and statements of volition*

At the end of **Capítulo 9** you learned that the present tense has both an indicative mood and a subjunctive mood. You have used the present indicative to state facts, describe conditions, express actions, and ask questions. In this section you will learn more about the subjunctive mood and how Spanish speakers use it to express what they want others to do.

As you recall from **Capítulo 9,** the most common use of the subjunctive mood is for influence—in the form of wanting, hoping, demanding, preferring, recommending and prohibiting: the first subject/verb combination (clause) of a sentence influences the second subject/verb combination. Note that, with few exceptions, the subjunctive only appears in dependent clauses.

Carlos **quiere que José trabaje** más.   *Carlos **wants José to work** more.*

In the example above, the first clause **(Carlos quiere...)** causes the subjunctive in the second (dependent) clause **(...que José trabaje)** because the first clause is a statement of *causing* or *volition*. This is the type of subjunctive situation you'll be practicing later in this section.

Forming the present subjunctive

Although you already know how to form the present subjunctive—using the same procedure as you would to form formal and negative informal commands—the process is reviewed as follows.

To form the present subjunctive of most verbs, drop the **-o** from the present indicative **yo** form, then add the endings shown.

	-ar verbs	**-er** verbs	**-ir** verbs
	lavarse	hacer	escribir
yo	me lave	haga	escriba
tú	te laves	hagas	escribas
Ud., él, ella	se lave	haga	escriba
nosotros(as)	nos lavemos	hagamos	escribamos
vosotros(as)	os lavéis	hagáis	escribáis
Uds., ellos(as)	se laven	hagan	escriban

The stem of verbs that end in **-car, -gar,** and **-zar** have a spelling change to maintain pronunciation.

	sacar (c → qu)	llegar (g → gu)	comenzar (z → c)
	saque	llegue	comience
	saques	llegues	comiences
	saque	llegue	comience
	saquemos	lleguemos	comencemos
	saquéis	lleguéis	comencéis
	saquen	lleguen	comiencen

—¿Quieres que yo **saque** los documentos?

Do you want me to take out the papers?

—Sí, recomiendo que **comencemos** ahora.

Yes, I recommend that we begin now.

Stem-changing verbs that end in **-ar** and **-er** have the same stem changes **(ie, ue)** in the present indicative and in the present subjunctive. Pay special attention to the **nosotros** and **vosotros** forms.

pensar (e → ie)		poder (o → ue)	
Present Indicative	**Present Subjunctive**	**Present Indicative**	**Present Subjunctive**
pienso	piense	puedo	pueda
piensas	pienses	puedes	puedas
piensa	piense	puede	pueda
pensamos	pensemos	podemos	podamos
pensáis	penséis	podéis	podáis
piensan	piensen	pueden	puedan

—¿Qué te dijo la jefe?

What did the boss tell you?

—Ella insiste en que yo **vuelva** a Colón.

She insists that I return to Colón.

Stem-changing verbs that end in **-ir** have the same stem changes **(ie, ue)** in the present indicative and in the present subjunctive. However, the **nosotros** and **vosotros** forms have a stem change **(e** to **i, o** to **u)** in the present subjunctive.

divertirse (ie)		dormir (ue)	
Present Indicative	Present Subjunctive	Present Indicative	Present Subjunctive
me divierto	me divierta	duermo	duerma
te diviertes	te diviertas	duermes	duermas
se divierte	se divierta	duerme	duerma
nos divertimos	nos divirtamos	dormimos	durmamos
os divertís	os divirtáis	dormís	durmáis
se divierten	se diviertan	duermen	duerman

—Espero que **te diviertas** en la Isla Taboga.

*I hope **you have fun** on Taboga Island.*

The verbs **pedir** and **servir** have the same stem change **(e** to **i)** in the present indicative and in the present subjunctive. The **nosotros** and **vosotros** forms have an additional stem change **(e** to **i)** in the present subjunctive.

pedir (i)		servir (i)	
Present Indicative	Present Subjunctive	Present Indicative	Present Subjunctive
pido	pida	sirvo	sirva
pides	pidas	sirves	sirvas
pide	pida	sirve	sirva
pedimos	pidamos	servimos	sirvamos
pedís	pidáis	servís	sirváis
piden	pidan	sirven	sirvan

—Deseo que **sirvamos** a los clientes con respeto.
—¿Quieres que yo **pida** una reunión con los empleados?

*I want us **to serve** the clients with respect.*
*Do you want me **to request** a meeting with the employees?*

Some verbs have irregular forms in the present subjunctive because their stems are not based on the **yo** form of the present indicative.

dar	estar	ir	saber	ser
dé	esté	vaya	sepa	sea
des	estés	vayas	sepas	seas
dé	esté	vaya	sepa	sea
demos	estemos	vayamos	sepamos	seamos
deis	estéis	vayáis	sepáis	seáis
den	estén	vayan	sepan	sean

—¿Permites que le **dé** yo el número de la oficina en Panamá?	*Do you permit me **to give** him the number of the office in Panama?*
—Sí. Y quiero que él **sepa** el número en Colón también.	*Yes. And I want him to **know** the number in Colón also.*

The subjunctive form of **hay** is **haya,** which is invariable.

Espero que **haya** muchos candidatos para el puesto.	*I hope that **there are** many candidates for the position.*

Using the present subjunctive with verbs of volition

The examples given in the section above demonstrate several common verbs of volition that cause the subjunctive to be used in the dependent clause. These verbs include the following:

desear *to wish; to want*	**permitir** *to permit*	**querer (ie)** *to want*
insistir en *to insist*	**preferir (ie, i)** *to prefer*	**recomendar (ie)** *to recommend*
mandar *to command*	**prohibir** *to prohibit; to forbid*	
pedir (i, i) *to request*		

A verb of volition is followed by a verb in the subjunctive when the subject of the dependent clause is different from that of the independent clause. The two clauses are linked together by the word **que** *(that).*

Change of subject

(Carlos) **quiere que**	(José) **trabaje** más.
Independent clause	Dependent clause

In sentences that have no change of subject, an infinitive—not the subjunctive—follows the verb of volition. Compare the following sentences.

No change of subject	Change of subject
José **prefiere trabajar** ahora.	Carlos **prefiere que José trabaje** ahora.
*José **prefers to work** now.*	*Carlos **prefers that José work** now.*

Place pronouns before conjugated verbs in the present subjunctive.

—Deseamos que **te diviertas.**	*We want **you to have fun.***
—Y yo insisto en que **me escribas.**	*And I insist that **you write to me.***
—¿Quieres mi dirección?	*Do you want my address?*
—Sí, recomiendo que **me la des** ahora.	*Yes, I recommend that **you give it to me** now.*

¡A practicar!

Z. **¿QUÉ QUIERE MI JEFE?** ¿Qué dice José sobre lo que quiere el jefe de él y de los otros empleados? Termina cada oración con un verbo apropiado de la lista.

llegue   termine   conteste   dé   llame

Mi jefe quiere que yo...

1. _____ informes mensuales *(monthly).*
2. _____ a tiempo a la oficina.

3. _____ a mis clientes por teléfono cada semana.
4. _____ mi trabajo antes de salir de la oficina.
5. _____ el correo electrónico.

nos comuniquemos   tengamos   no hablemos   nos vistamos

Mi jefe prefiere que nosotros...

6. _____ reuniones cortas.
7. _____ de una manera profesional.
8. _____ de nuestros proyectos fuera de la oficina.
9. _____ mucho entre nosotros.

imprima   haga   salga   no trabaje

Mi jefe recomienda que Sofía...

10. _____ las fotocopias.
11. _____ todos los documentos antes de las reuniones.
12. _____ durante los fines de semana.
13. _____ de la oficina durante su almuerzo.

AA. **CONSEJOS PARA DORA** Dora tiene una hermana, Susana, que trabaja en un banco. Susana le da consejos a su hermana sobre las finanzas personales. Completa la historia con la forma correcta del verbo entre paréntesis.

Dora, yo quiero que tú _____ (**abrir**) una cuenta de ahorros. No quiero que tú y tu esposo _____ (**seguir**) con tantos problemas económicos. Insisto en que tú _____ (**dejar**) de pagar a plazos cuando compras cosas. Prefiero que tú me _____ (**pedir**) prestado el dinero, o sugiero que no _____ (**comprar**) cosas tan caras. Te recomiendo que tú _____ (**enseñar**) a tu hijo a ahorrar más dinero. No queremos que él _____ (**tener**) problemas luego con el dinero. Espero que todos Uds. _____ (**saber**) que estas ideas son buenas para Uds.

BB. **MI TRABAJO EN LA UNIVERSIDAD** Forma oraciones completas con las siguientes palabras. A veces vas a usar el infinitivo en la segunda cláusula.

MODELO: mis padres / prohibir / yo / trabajar / la semana
          Mis padres prohíben que yo trabaje durante la semana.

1. el consejero / recomendar / los estudiantes / no hablar por teléfono / sus amigos
2. mi jefe / pedir / yo / no usar / la fotocopiadora / asuntos personales
3. los profesores / esperar / los gerentes / dar / a nosotros / un sueldo bueno
4. yo / querer / aprender / mi experiencia
5. nosotros / preferir / no trabajar / los sábados
6. la profesora / insistir / nosotros / estudiar / antes / salir para el trabajo
7. yo / desear / encontrar / trabajo / tiempo completo
8. mi madre / recomendar / yo / buscar / trabajo / tiempo parcial

En voz alta

CC. **PREFERENCIAS** Trabajando con un(a) compañero(a) de clase, terminen las siguientes oraciones con información relevante a sus experiencias como estudiantes. Luego, hazle preguntas a tu compañero(a) sobre algunas de las oraciones para recibir más información.

MODELO: El profesor quiere que nosotros...
E1: *El profesor quiere que nosotros estudiemos mucho.*
E2: *¿Por qué quiere el profesor que estudiemos mucho?*
E1: *Porque quiere que hablemos mejor el español.*

1. Mi mejor amigo(a) prefiere que yo...
2. Mis padres no recomiendan que mi mejor amigo(a)...
3. Mi compañero(a) de cuarto insiste en que nosotros...
4. El presidente de la universidad prefiere que los estudiantes...
5. Yo quiero que mis amigos....
7. Mi novio(a) no permite que nosotros...
8. Mi consejero(a) espera que yo...
9. Los estudiantes prefieren que los profesores...

DD. MAMÁ SIEMPRE SABE MÁS Tu mamá te quiere dar muchos consejos sobre tus finanzas personales. Explícale a un(a) compañero(a) lo que tu mamá quiere que hagas según la información de abajo. Usa los verbos de voluntad para comenzar las frases: **desear, insistir en, mandar, pedir, permitir, preferir, prohibir, querer, recomendar.**

1. ahorrar más dinero
2. pagar las cuentas a tiempo
3. dejar de comprar a plazos
4. pedir préstamos para la universidad
5. servir comida barata para mis fiestas
6. llegar temprano para mi trabajo
7. dar un poco de dinero a la caridad *(charity)* cada semana
8. ir a los cajeros automáticos para sacar dinero
9. saber ahorrar bien mi dinero
10. ser inteligente con los asuntos de las finanzas personales

EE. ASPIRACIONES ¿Qué aspiraciones tienes en cuanto al dinero? Contesta las siguientes preguntas. Puedes usar las sugerencias de abajo o usar otros verbos de voluntad presentados en este capítulo.

1. ¿Quieres mejorar tu posición económica? ¿Cómo quieres hacerlo?
Yo quiero... Espero...
2. ¿Qué consejos les da tu madre a ti y a tus hermanos sobre el dinero?
Mi mamá quiere que nosotros... Ella desea que nosotros... Ella no quiere que nosotros...
3. ¿Qué le dices tú a tu novio(a) o esposo(a) sobre el dinero?
Yo le mando que él/ella... Yo le recomiendo que él/ella... Yo le prohíbo que él/ella...
4. ¿Qué le dices tú a tu compañero(a) de clase en cuanto a sus finanzas personales?
Yo deseo que él/ella... Yo recomiendo que él/ella...
5. ¿Qué les dice un contador a sus clientes sobre las finanzas personales?
Yo recomiendo que Uds.... Yo insisto en que Uds....

FF. ¿QUÉ DICES TÚ? Con un(a) compañero(a), hablen de lo que les gusta y lo que es importante para Uds. en un trabajo. Tomen turnos recomendando trabajos y explicando por qué.

MODELO: E1: *Me gustan las matemáticas y quiero trabajar con el dinero.*
E2: *Recomiendo que seas contador(a) porque los contadores tienen que comprender muy bien las matemáticas.*

Síntesis

¡A ver!

El tema principal del **Capítulo 11** es el mundo laboral y se enfoca en Panamá. El presentador videográfico se llama Humberto, quien trabaja en la sección de divisas en un banco de la capital de Panamá.

ACTIVIDAD 1   Pre-viewing task (Segmento 1 del video)

Paso 1: En el primer segmento del video vas a ver una serie de clips cortos en los cuales todas las personas hablan de su trabajo o su profesión. Identifica el trabajo o profesión de cada persona.

Paso 2: Organiza la lista de trabajos/profesiones que has identificado en **Paso 1** según las tres categorías en la siguiente tabla y según tu opinión personal.

Trabajos menos deseados	Trabajos aceptables	Trabajos ideales

Paso 3: Con un(a) compañero(a) de clase, habla de los trabajos de la tabla que menos te gustaría tener y los que más te gustaría tener. En cada caso explica por qué. ¿Cuáles son los trabajos que sólo te parecen aceptables? ¿Por qué no te interesan mucho? En el diálogo hazle preguntas a tu compañero(a) para averiguar *(to find out)* sus opiniones sobre los trabajos.

M O D E L O :   *¿Por qué no te gustaría ser conductor de autobuses? Me parece un trabajo interesante en el cual estás al aire libre todo el día.*

ACTIVIDAD 2   Pre-viewing task (Segmento 2 del video)

Paso 1: Estás interesado(a) en ser camarero(a) en un restaurante en el pueblo donde vives durante las vacaciones. En una entrevista para este puesto, ¿qué preguntas puedes hacer para informarte del trabajo? Y, ¿qué preguntas te puede hacer a ti el (la) entrevistador(a)? Haz dos listas de estas posibles preguntas.

Paso 2: ¿Qué preguntas tiene tu compañero(a) de clase en su lista? Intercambia ideas con él/ella.

ACTIVIDAD 3   Viewing task (Segmento 2 del video)

Vas a ver a Marisol, a quien conociste en el **Capítulo 6** cuando preparaba arroz con gandules con su tía en Puerto Rico. Marisol tiene planes de trabajar durante las vacaciones y se entrevista para un puesto de camarera en el restaurante El Batey en el centro de San Juan, Puerto Rico. Averigua la siguiente información sobre el puesto de trabajo que solicita Marisol.

Experiencia de Marisol como camarera	
Motivo por el cual necesitan una nueva camarera en el restaurante El Batey	
Horario de trabajo	
Total de horas a la semana	
Sueldo base por hora	
Sueldo mensual aproximado (incluyendo propinas [tips])	
Fecha de comienzo del trabajo	
Número de candidatos para el puesto (excluyendo a Marisol)	

ACTIVIDAD 4   Post-viewing task (Segmento 2 del video)

Paso 1: Comprueba tus respuestas de la **Actividad 3** con las de un(a) compañero(a) de clase.

Paso 2: Haz el diálogo de la entrevista con tu compañero(a). Uno hace el papel de Marisol y el otro hace el papel de la dueña del restaurante. Utiliza la información de la **Actividad 3** como en el modelo.

MODELO: Dueña del restaurante: *Marisol, ¿tienes experiencia como camarera? Veo en tu currículum que la tienes.*
Marisol: *Sí, trabajé durante dos veranos en el restaurante del Hotel Galería en San Juan.*

¡A leer!

Guessing unfamiliar words and phrases

When you read a passage in English and come to an unfamiliar word or phrase, you probably try to guess its meaning from context or skip over it and continue reading. When learners of Spanish as a foreign language read literature in Spanish, they will likely encounter a number of unfamiliar vocabulary items. However, if you can transfer your ability to guess word meaning from context over to Spanish, your reading comprehension will increase significantly, as will your reading speed.

Take a few mintues to skim the following passage, which contains a brief introduction to the author (a Panamanian writer) and an excerpt from a short story that he wrote. After skimming the introduction and the excerpt, complete the following exercises. While reading the passage, try to incorporate as many of the reading strategies you have learned up to this point as you can!

Paso 1: Lee el siguiente fragmento del cuento corto «El Jefe» por Dimas Lidio Pitty y luego usa el contexto para determinar el significado de las siguientes palabras y expresiones.

_____ **1.** unánime   **a.** incendiar, pegar fuego
_____ **2.** ocupar   **b.** parte del cigarrillo que se pone en la boca
_____ **3.** adelanto   **c.** por todas las personas
_____ **4.** encender   **d.** pasar
_____ **5.** boquilla   **e.** avance; progreso

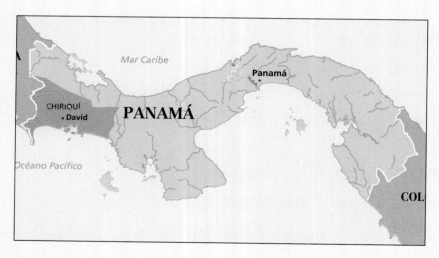

Dimas Lidio Pitty es cuentista panameño, nacido en la provincia de Chiriquí. Hizo estudios en Santiago de Chile y luego en la Universidad de Panamá. Entre sus obras más importantes se destacan *Camino de las cosas* (1965) y *El país azul, Cuentos y poemas para niños* (1968). Es considerado como una de las más auténticas voces de la última generación de escritores panameños.

El Jefe

(fragmento)

por Dimas Lidio Pitty

Cuando llega a la oficina, todos lo observan atentamente. Después de recibir la ad- *finding out about, informing*
miración unánime el jefe ocupa algunos minutos en enterarse de° lo ocurrido antes de *himself about*
las 10:30, su hora habitual de llegada. Seguidamente dicta una nota y habla por teléfono *is in the habit of*
con varias personas (otro jefe, amigos —acostumbra° llamar a su esposa para pregun-
tarle si durmió bien— quizás el ministro, en casos especiales al presidente). A conti-
nuación va a la cafetería y pide un vaso de jugo.

Al regreso, conversa con la secretaria del ministro y con la secretaria del vice-ministro.
De paso saluda al director de relaciones públicas. Porque es conveniente, claro, que sean
conocidos los adelantos introducidos por él en provecho de la administración pública y
en beneficio del país.

De vuelta a su despacho,° firma la nota y ordena su envío. Luego enciende uno de sus *personal office*
cigarrillos importados (extralargos, con boquilla de lujo°) y... *deluxe, fancy*

Paso 2: Ahora, vuelve a leer el fragmento y luego contesta las siguientes preguntas.

1. ¿Qué pasa cuando entra el jefe en la oficina?
2. ¿A qué hora llega el jefe a la oficina cada día?
3. Según el cuento, ¿con quién habla el jefe?

Paso 3: Ahora contesta las preguntas a continuación.

1. ¿Te parece típica la rutina del jefe (por ejemplo, su hora de llegada, las cosas que hace por la mañana, etc.)?
2. Al final del fragmento, el jefe acaba de encender un cigarrillo en su despacho. En tu opinión, ¿cómo pasa el resto del día el jefe? ¿Qué cosas hace?

¡A escribir!

Writing from an idea map

An idea map is a tool for organizing your ideas before you begin developing them in a composition. In this section you are going to write about the job of your dreams with the aid of an idea map.

Paso 1: Escribe las palabras **Mi empleo ideal** en una hoja de papel. Esto es el título de tu composición.

Paso 2: Escribe una palabra clave bajo el título. Vas a incluir esta idea en la frase princi- pal de tu párrafo.

Paso 3: Escribe unas ideas relacionadas a este tema. Estas ideas son los detalles que apoyan *(support)* a la frase principal.

Paso 4: Dibuja unas líneas para asociar las ideas que se corresponden. Puedes seguir el siguiente modelo:

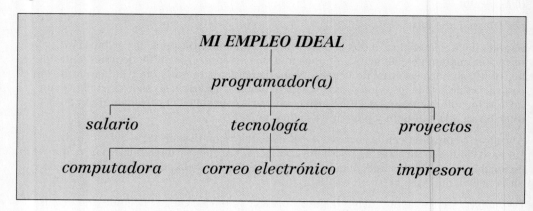

Paso 5: Basándote en el mapa que has dibujado, haz una lista de frases que puedes incluir en un párrafo sobre el tema principal. Al escribir las frases, debes considerar las siguientes preguntas:

    a. ¿Al lector le va a interesar la información?
    b. ¿Tienes bastante información para un párrafo?
    c. ¿Puedes limitar la información a sólo un párrafo?

Paso 6: Sigue los **Pasos 2** a **5** para desarrollar las ideas necesarias para unos párrafos más.

Paso 7: Ahora escribe una composición sobre tu empleo ideal, usando el mapa como guía. Usa el tiempo presente para describir el empleo.

MODELO: Mi empleo ideal

    Quiero ser programador(a). Generalmente las empresas les ofrecen un salario muy bueno a los (las) programadores(as). Tienen muchas oportunidades para trabajar en proyectos interesantes. Trabajan con la tecnología todos los días. Siempre usan las computadoras y las impresoras y reciben correo electrónico con mucha frecuencia.

Functions: Expressing hopes and aspirations; Expressing intention

Vocabulary: Professions, trades, working conditions

Grammar: Verbs: present

¡A conversar!

Paso 1: Con un(a) compañero(a) de clase, habla de un puesto que has tenido. Si no has tenido un puesto, puedes describir el de otra persona que conoces. Incluye la siguiente información:

- ¿Qué trabajo hiciste?
- ¿Cuándo fue?
- ¿Qué responsabilidades tuviste?
- ¿Cuánto fue el salario?
- ¿Trabajaste con muchas personas o solo(a)?
- ¿Te gustó el trabajo? ¿Por qué sí o por qué no?

Paso 2: Después, cambien de papel y hagan la actividad de nuevo.

Las profesiones y los oficios   *Professions*

el (la) abogado(a)   *lawyer*
el (la) arquitecto(a)   *architect*
el (la) banquero(a)   *banker*
el (la) carpintero(a)   *carpenter*
el (la) cocinero(a)   *cook, chef*
el (la) contador(a)   *accountant*
el (la) dentista   *dentist*
el (la) empleado(a)   *employee*
el (la) fotógrafo(a)   *photographer*

el (la) gerente   *manager*
el hombre (la mujer) de negocios   *businessperson*
el (la) ingeniero(a)   *engineer*
el (la) jefe   *boss*
el (la) maestro(a)   *teacher*
el (la) obrero(a)   *worker; laborer*
el (la) peluquero(a)   *hairstylist*
el (la) periodista   *journalist*

el (la) plomero(a)   *plumber*
el (la) (mujer) policía   *police officer*
el (la) programador(a)   *programmer*
el (la) siquiatra   *psychiatrist*
el (la) traductor(a)   *translator*
el (la) veterinario(a)   *veterinarian*

La oficina, el trabajo y la búsqueda de trabajo   *The office, work, and the job hunt*

los beneficios   *benefits*
el (la) candidato(a)   *candidate, applicant*
la computadora   *computer*
el correo electrónico   *email*
el currículum   *résumé*
la empresa   *corporation; business*

la entrevista   *interview*
el fax   *fax machine*
la fotocopiadora   *photocopier*
la impresora   *printer*
el informe   *report*
el proyecto   *project*

el puesto   *job, position*
la reunión   *meeting*
la sala de conferencias   *conference room*
el salario/el sueldo   *salary*
la solicitud   *application (form)*

Verbos

contratar   *to hire*
dejar   *to quit*
despedir (i)   *to fire*
imprimir   *to print*

jubilarse   *to retire*
llamar por teléfono   *to make a phone call*
llenar   *to fill out (a form)*

pedir un aumento   *to ask for a raise*
renunciar   *to resign*
reunirse   *to meet*
solicitar un puesto   *to apply for a job*

Expresiones idiomáticas

de tiempo completo   *full-time*

de tiempo parcial   *part-time*

Las finanzas personales   *Personal finances*

el cajero automático   *ATM*
el cheque   *check*
la cuenta corriente   *checking account*

la cuenta de ahorros   *savings account*
la factura   *bill*
el préstamo   *loan*

el presupuesto   *budget*
la tarjeta de crédito   *credit card*

Verbos

ahorrar   *to save*
depositar   *to deposit (money)*
pagar a plazos   *to pay in installments*

pagar en efectivo   *to pay in cash*
pedir prestado   *to borrow*
prestar   *to loan*

rebotar   *to bounce (a check)*
sacar   *to withdraw (money)*

El medio ambiente: Costa Rica

Communicative goals

In this chapter you will learn how to . . .

- Talk about rural and urban locales and associated activities and problems
- Use the subjunctive to express emotion and make impersonal statements
- Talk about the conservation and exploitation of natural resources
- Use the subjunctive to state uncertain, doubtful, or ideal situations
- Talk about a nature preserve, animals, and endangered species

Grammar

- The present subjunctive with emotion, impersonal expressions, and **ojalá**
- The present subjunctive following verbs and expressions of doubt and uncertainty
- The present subjunctive in adjective clauses

Cultural information

- Costa Rica ecológica
- Monteverde y Tortuguero

La Plaza de la Basílica de Nuestra Señora de los Ángeles, Cartago, Costa Rica

GOLFITO[1] Y SAN JOSÉ,[2] COSTA RICA[3] In this section you will learn how to talk about rural and urban areas and the associated activities and problems.

la sobrepoblación *overpopulation*

el transporte público *public transportation*

Verbos

cultivar *to cultivate, to grow (plants)*
llevar una vida tranquila *to lead a peaceful life*

regar (ie) *to irrigate; to water*
sembrar (ie) *to plant*

Adjetivos

acelerado(a) *accelerated*
bello(a) *beautiful*

denso(a) *dense*
tranquilo(a) *tranquil, peaceful*

Palabras útiles

el árbol *tree*
la frontera *border*
el llano *plain*

el paisaje *landscape*
el valle *valley*
el volcán *volcano*

---

[1] Golfito is a small port town of 14,000 inhabitants located on the southern tip of Costa Rica. The town is almost entirely surrounded by lush, forested hills. Golfito is world famous for sport fishing and its natural beauty. Golfito developed into a major port in the 1930s when the United Fruit Company set up operations there along the Pacific Coast.
[2] San José is the capital city of Costa Rica. San José lies in the mountainous center of the country. Population estimates range from 300,000 inhabitants to a million, depending on which suburbs are included. The city is subject to frequent earthquakes because of its location in a zone of tectonic activity.
[3] Since gaining its independence from Spain in 1821, Costa Rica has been one of Latin America's long-standing democracies. After an armed conflict in 1948, Costa Rica abolished the army to ensure democratic rule.

➥ *Palabras útiles* are for recognition only; you will not be tested on these words. However, they are provided as useful words for talking about the environment.

¡A practicar!

A. LA LLEGADA A SAN JOSÉ Termina la historia de Mario escogiendo la palabra adecuada.

1. Cuando Mario llegó a (la metrópolis / el arroyo) de San José, se dio cuenta de que la vida era mucho más (tranquila / acelerada) de lo que él había experimentado *(had experienced)* en el campo.
2. Había mucho (arroyo / tráfico) en las (carreteras / colinas), y no estaba acostumbrado al ruido causado por los coches.
3. Miró los grandes (campesinos / rascacielos) y pensó en los hermosos árboles del bosque que él había abandonado *(had abandoned)*.
4. Miró la (basura / finca) en las calles y el humo *(smoke)* de las fábricas y pensó en la tierra prístina de su finca.
5. ¡Y cuánta gente! Seguro que la (selva / sobrepoblación) era la fuente *(source)* de los problemas (urbanos / densos), pensó Mario.

B. ASOCIACIONES ¿Con qué se asocian las siguientes palabras? Empareja cada palabra o frase de la primera columna con la palabra o frase más lógica de la segunda columna.

¿NOS ENTENDEMOS?

While la finca is understood
throughout most of the Spanish-speaking world to mean
farm, some regions use other
terms. In Mexico, **el rancho** is
used to mean *ranch* or *farm.* **La
hacienda** is also used in Mexico
and in other Latin American
countries to mean *farm* usually
with an estate manor on it. **La
granja** is commonly used in
Spain to refer to small family
farms, while **la chacra** is used in
countries such as Costa Rica.

1. _____ el bosque
2. _____ bello
3. _____ las cataratas
4. _____ el campesino
5. _____ denso
6. _____ sembrar, cultivar
7. _____ el transporte público
8. _____ la selva
9. _____ tranquilo
10. _____ el rascacielos
11. _____ la metrópolis

a. la Ciudad de México, Tokio, Nueva York
b. con muchas plantas y vegetación
c. Johnny Appleseed
d. bonito
e. pacífico, sin ruido
f. Caperucita Roja *(Little Red Riding Hood)*
g. el edificio Empire State
h. una persona del campo
i. el autobús, el tren, el metro
j. Niágara, Iguazú, el Salto del Ángel
k. Tarzán

C. ÉRASE UNA VEZ... Completa la siguiente historia sobre la vida rural de Mario, un campesino tico, usando las palabras de la lista.

regar	llevaba una vida tranquila	selva	cultivaba
agricultor	finca	colinas	tierra	arroyo

Érase una vez un _____ joven y trabajador que cultivaba un pedazo de _____ en la _____ tropical de Costa Rica. El hombre industrioso se llamaba Mario, y _____ muchos plátanos cada año. No tenía que _____ las plantas porque llovía muchísmo en aquella región. Mario _____ y exitosa. Había un lago en su _____ donde él pescaba durante los fines de semana. También corría un _____ bonito entre unas _____ verdes donde él descansaba después de trabajar. A pesar de la belleza de su finca, Mario sufría de la soledad del lugar. Por eso un día decidió vender sus propiedades y se fue para la ciudad para encontrar un trabajo en el centro urbano de San José.[1]

---

[1] Throughout the late nineteenth and the entire twentieth centuries, there has been mass movement in Latin America from the countryside to urban centers. This population shift is due in part to industrialization in the cities, where many jobs have become available, as well as to a decline in the world market for small-scale production of farm produce.

En voz alta

D. **LOS PROBLEMAS DE MI PUEBLO** Trabajando con un(a) compañero(a) de clase, pongan los siguientes temas en orden de mayor a menor importancia con referencia al pueblo donde Uds. viven. Después de establecer los problemas más importantes, indiquen lo que recomiendan para resolver tres de ellos. ¿Cuáles son los temas que no son problemáticos para su pueblo?

MODELO: el tráfico
El tráfico en nuestra ciudad es un problema muy grande. Recomendamos que más gente camine o ande en bicicleta en vez de ir en coche. También sugerimos que las personas vayan juntas al trabajo en vez de una sola persona en cada coche.

1. el transporte público
2. el ruido
3. la basura
4. la sobrepoblación
5. las fábricas
6. las metrópolis
7. los rascacielos

E. **OPINIONES** Completa las siguientes oraciones con el vocabulario de esta sección para expresar tus opiniones sobre las siguientes ideas a un(a) compañero(a) de clase.

MODELO: Trabajar en una finca (no) es fácil porque... *es necesario levantarse muy temprano todos los días. Es desagradable trabajar con los animales y la tierra. Hay mucho trabajo físico, y uno se cansa fácilmente.*

1. (No) Me gusta vivir en la ciudad porque...
2. La vida rural (no) es atractiva para mí porque...
3. Lo que más me impresiona de la metrópolis es/son...
4. Cuando voy al campo, prefiero estar en... porque...
5. La última vez que estuve en una ciudad grande vi...
6. La última vez que estuve en un parque natural había...

F. **ENTREVISTA** Con un(a) compañero(a) de clase, háganse preguntas sobre los siguientes temas.

1. ¿Has pasado tiempo en una ciudad grande? ¿Cuándo? ¿Qué ciudad(es)? ¿Te gustó? ¿Qué hiciste allá? ¿Cómo se compara esa ciudad con el lugar donde vives?
2. ¿Has pasado tiempo en el campo? ¿Cuándo? ¿Con quién? ¿Te gustó? ¿Es muy diferente del lugar donde vives? ¿Qué hiciste allá?
3. ¿Cómo es el lugar donde vives tú? ¿Es más rural o más urbano? ¿Quieres vivir en una ciudad grande algún día? ¿O prefieres el campo o un pueblo más pequeño? ¿Cuáles son las ventajas de vivir en una ciudad grande? ¿Cuáles son las ventajas de vivir en el campo?

¿NOS ENTENDEMOS?

In English, the world *people* is plural while its Spanish equivalent, **la gente**, is singular. When you want to express *people* in the sense of *nation* or *national group*, use the term **el pueblo**.

Rona y Luis Grandinetti son hermanos pero tienen ideas muy diferentes sobre el lugar ideal donde quieren vivir en el futuro.

RONA: Luis, ¿no te molesta el tráfico de San José? No entiendo por qué te gusta tanto esta ciudad.

LUIS: No me molesta para nada. Me gusta que las calles estén llenas de gente y de actividad.

RONA: Pues, te digo que prefiero que vivamos en otro lugar. Quiero vivir en un pueblo pequeño cerca del mar, un lugar que tenga aire puro y un medio ambiente sano *(healthy)*.

LUIS: La vida del campo es bella, pero no tiene ni las oportunidades ni los servicios de una ciudad grande. Con tu afán *(desire)* de ir al cine todos los fines de semana, yo dudo que la vida rural sea tan atractiva como piensas tú.

RONA: ¿Y cómo sabes tú? No has pasado mucho tiempo en el campo. Hiciste camping una vez, ¿y ya eres experto? Y no tengo que ir al cine todos los fines de semana.

LUIS: Así que, ¿quieres ser campesina? ¿Quieres vivir con los monos *(monkeys)* y los insectos? ¿Y si ves una culebra *(snake)*?

RONA: ¡Ay! Ojalá que *(I wish that)* fueras *(you were)* más sensible. No quiero vivir en la selva. Solamente quiero llevar una vida tranquila. Necesito vivir en un sitio donde no haya tanto ruido, ni contaminación, ni rascacielos, ni carreteras.

LUIS: Pues, es importante que decidas de una vez. El mes pasado estabas convencida de que querías vivir en Tokio, y ahora empiezas con estas fantasías de la vida rural.

RONA: Es mejor que uno tenga ilusiones. Tú no puedes imaginarte la vida fuera de tu cuarto.

G. **¿COMPRENDISTE?** Contesta las siguientes preguntas en oraciones completas.

1. ¿Por qué no está contenta Rona?
2. Según Luis, ¿cuáles son algunas ventajas *(advantages)* de vivir en la ciudad?
3. ¿Sabe Luis mucho de la vida rural?
4. Según Rona, ¿cuál es el lugar ideal para ella?
5. ¿Por qué sospechamos *(we suspect)* que Rona es un poco indecisa?

H. **¡AHORA TE TOCA A TI!** ¿Te identificas más con la posición de Rona o la de Luis? Prepara cinco argumentos para vivir en el campo o en la ciudad, y luego debate tu posición con una persona que tenga la opuesta *(opposite)* posición.

ENCUENTRO *cultural*

Costa Rica ecológica

Éstas son unas palabras nuevas para la lectura:

la orquídea   *orchid*
los mamíferos   *mammals*
el perezoso con   *three-toed sloth*
   tres dedos
el quetzal   *bird with long beautiful feathers found in Central America*
talar   *to cut down (trees)*

Costa Rica, un país de sólo 19.653 millas cuadradas, está situado en Centroamérica. Tiene un poco más de 3,5 millones de habitantes y tiene un paisaje variado, lo cual quiere decir que tiene una biodiversidad increíble. Hay montañas, costas, ríos, volcanes y varios tipos de bosques y selvas tropicales donde viven más de 700.000 especies de flora y fauna. Más de 2.000 variedades de **orquídeas** y cientos de miles de especies de insectos, incluyendo una innumerable cantidad de tipos de mariposas, viven en los varios ecosistemas del país. También hay **mamíferos** interesantes que viven allí, como **el perezoso con tres dedos**, y diversos tipos de aves, como **el quetzal**. La vida silvestre costarricense es un verdadero tesoro natural.

Como en muchos países menos desarrollados, la industria más común en Costa Rica era la agricultura. Desafortunadamente, eso significaba **talar** árboles para cultivar la tierra. En una época la deforestación llegó a ser el problema medioambiental más grave para este país pequeño pero de gran valor ecológico. Los seres humanos destruyeron tantas áreas naturales que pusieron en peligro de extinción muchas especies de flora y fauna. Afortunadamente, el gobierno del país reconoció el problema y empezó a resolverlo.

Ahora, Costa Rica se encuentra en una situación ecológica privilegiada. En 1970 el gobierno costarricense estableció un sistema de parques nacionales con el fin de proteger las áreas de vida silvestre del país. Hoy en día, ¡el 28 por ciento de todo el territorio del país se encuentra protegido de una manera u otra! Costa Rica es el país con el mayor porcentaje de tierra protegida en el mundo. Hay reservas biológicas, refugios naturales (públicos y privados) y también parques nacionales. Los esfuerzos del gobierno han llegado a tal punto que el ecoturismo ahora reemplaza la agricultura como primera industria en el país. Así asegura el bienestar no sólo de sus habitantes humanos, sino también de los animales y las plantas.

Para pensar: ¿Crees que es necesario establecer áreas protegidas para conservar la naturaleza? ¿Tenemos algo parecido en EE.UU.? ¿Te interesa conservar la naturaleza? ¿Crees que el ecoturismo ha beneficiado nuestro país?

I.   PREGUNTAS Basándote en la lectura, contesta las siguientes preguntas con oraciones completas.

1. ¿Qué hace el gobierno costarricense para proteger el medio ambiente?
2. Describe cómo los seres humanos casi destruyeron el medio ambiente en Costa Rica.
3. ¿Cuánto territorio en Costa Rica está protegido y cómo?

In the previous chapter, you learned how to use the present subjunctive to express wishes, intentions, preferences, advice, suggestions, and recommendations. Spanish speakers also use verbs of emotion with the subjunctive to express their emotions and opinions.

Verbs of emotion and impersonal expressions

The list below contains verbs of emotion for expressing feelings and impersonal expressions for expressing opinions.

Verbs of emotion	Impersonal expressions[1]
alegrarse (de) *to be glad*	**es bueno (malo)** *it's good (bad)*
esperar *to hope*	**es importante** *it's important*
gustar *to like*	**es (im)posible** *it's (im)possible*
molestar *to bother*	**es lógico** *it's logical*
preocuparse (de) (por)	**es mejor** *it's better*
to worry (about)	**es necesario** *it's necessary*
quejarse (de) *to complain*	**es ridículo** *it's ridiculous*
sentir (ie) *to be sorry*	**es una lástima** *it's a shame*
sorprender *to surprise*	
tener miedo de *to be afraid*	

Use these verbs and impersonal expressions exactly as you did with the verb **querer** and other verbs of volition.

One subject	Change of subject
Mario espera encontrar una vida mejor.	**Mario espera que la ciudad ofrezca** una vida mejor.
*Mario **hopes to find** a better life.*	*Mario **hopes that the city offers** a better life.*
Es importante tener un trabajo bueno.	**Es importante que Mario tenga** un trabajo bueno.
*It's **important to have** a good job.*	*It's **important that Mario have** a good job.*

Ojalá

You have learned that one way to express your desires and hopes is to use verbs like **querer, desear,** and **esperar.** Another way to express those feelings is to use the expression **ojalá (que)** with the subjunctive. This expression has several English equivalents including *let's hope that, I hope that,* and *if only,* all of which refer to some pending, unrealized action in the future. **Ojalá (que)** is always followed by the subjunctive, whether there is a change of subject or only one subject. The word **que** is often used after **ojalá** in writing, but it is usually omitted in conversation.

---

[1] The impersonal expressions **es obvio que, es cierto que, es seguro que,** and **es verdad que** do not cause the subjunctive in the subordinate clause because of their strong affirmative meanings: *Es obvio* que Mario *tiene* mejores oportunidades en la ciudad.

ojalá (que) + subjunctive	
Ojalá lo pases bien en Costa Rica.	*I hope you have a good time* in Costa Rica.
Ojalá haga buen tiempo allá.	*Let's hope* the weather is good there.
Ojalá que recibas esta carta.	*I hope you receive* this letter.

¡A practicar!

J. **ENTRE HERMANOS** Completa la siguiente conversación entre Rona y Luis Grandinetti, dos jóvenes de la ciudad, usando los verbos apropiados entre paréntesis.

Rona: Es una lástima que no te (gustar / guste) pasar más tiempo al aire libre. Es bueno (disfrutar / disfrutes) de la naturaleza para relajarte.

Luis: No me gusta que (criticarme / me critiques) por lo que hago en mi tiempo libre. ¿Necesito (decirte / te diga) lo que tú debes hacer? Siento que no me (comprender / comprendas), Rona.

Rona: Te comprendo perfectamente. Es lógico que no te (gustar / guste) la naturaleza. Siempre estás mirando la tele.

K. **DOS HERMANOS** Completa las siguientes oraciones para conocer un poco mejor a Luis y a Rona.

MODELO: Rona tiene 15 años. Es mejor que ella _____ (ir a fiestas / expresar sus opiniones).
Es mejor que ella vaya a fiestas.
o: *Es mejor que ella exprese sus opiniones.*

1. A Rona no le gusta ver los programas deportivos. Es posible que ella _____ (no ser deportista / no practicar ningún deporte / preferir escuchar discos compactos / pasar mucho tiempo hablando por teléfono).
2. Rona es una estudiante excelente en el colegio donde tiene muchos amigos. Es bueno que ella _____ (estudiar todos los días / tocar el piano / tener muchos amigos / ser una chica popular).
3. A veces, Luis y su hermana Rona tienen conflictos. Es lógico que ellos _____ (no siempre estar de acuerdo / discutir mucho en casa / expresar sus opiniones / darse consejos el uno al otro con cariño).

L. **OJALÁ QUE...** Haz oraciones completas con las frases de abajo usando la forma correcta del subjuntivo del verbo.

1. ojalá que / los granjeros *(farmers)* / seguir produciendo comida para el mundo
2. ojalá / no haber / tanto tráfico esta mañana como ayer
3. ojalá que / nosotros / tener / más opciones de transporte público el año que viene
4. ojalá / Uds. / ir a la ciudad el año que viene
5. ojalá / yo / poder ir al campo / para ver a mis primos

En voz alta

M. **¡OJALÁ!** Usando la expresión **ojalá,** descríbele diez deseos que quieres realizar dentro de tres años a un(a) compañero(a) de clase. Luego, cambien de papel.

MODELO: *Ojalá que yo encuentre trabajo.*
Ojalá que yo viva en Hawai.

N. **¿QUÉ TE PARECE?** Primero, escribe tus opiniones positivas y negativas sobre la posibilidad de vivir en una ciudad grande. Luego léele tus opiniones a otro(a) estudiante, quien debe reaccionar positiva o negativamente.

MODELO: E1: *Es mejor que vivas en la ciudad porque hay más oportunidades culturales.*
E2: *No estoy de acuerdo. Solamente los ricos tienen acceso a los eventos culturales.*

Opiniones positivas	Opiniones negativas
1. Me alegro de (que)...	**8.** Me quejo de (que)...
2. Es bueno (que)...	**9.** Me soprende (que)..
3. Es mejor (que)...	**10.** Me molesta (que)...
4. No es malo (que)...	**11.** Es malo (que)...
5. Me gusta (que)...	**12.** Es ridículo (que)...
6. Es importante (que)...	**13.** Es terrible (que)...
7. Espero (que)...	**14.** Es una lástima (que)...

O. **TUS OPINIONES** Escribe tus reacciones a los siguientes temas. Luego forma un grupo con otros dos o tres estudiantes y discutan sus opiniones sobre estos temas.

MODELO: En la ciudad: la sobrepoblación
E1: *Es necesario que tengamos familias más pequeñas.*
E2: *No estoy de acuerdo. Ojalá que los padres tengan la libertad de tener familias grandes.*

1. En la ciudad: el tráfico
2. En el campo: las tierras rurales
3. En la ciudad: las oportunidades
4. En el campo: la tranquilidad
5. En la ciudad: muchos servicios
6. En el campo: poca gente, nada que hacer como diversión
7. En la ciudad: eventos culturales
8. En el campo: la naturaleza, los animales y las plantas

P. **UN DEBATE** Formen grupos de cuatro personas. Dos del grupo tienen que hacer una lista de las ventajas de vivir en una ciudad. Los otros dos tienen que escribir una lista de las ventajas de vivir en el campo. Después, hagan un debate entre las dos parejas del grupo.

VOCABULARIO: *La conservación y la explotación*

LA DESTRUCCIÓN Y LA CONSERVACIÓN DEL MEDIO AMBIENTE In this section you will learn how to talk about the destruction and the conservation of the environment.

la capa de ozono *ozone layer*
la ecología *ecology*

la escasez *lack, shortage*
el medio ambiente *environment*

la naturaleza *nature*
el petróleo *petroleum*

Verbos

acabar *to run out*
desarrollar *to develop*
destruir *to destroy*

explotar *to exploit*
recoger *to pick up*
reforestar *to reforest*

resolver (ue) *to solve, to resolve*

Adjetivos

contaminado(a) *polluted*

destruido(a) *destroyed*

puro(a) *pure*

Expresión idiomática

¡No arroje basura! *Don't litter!*

¿NOS ENTENDEMOS?

While the verb **reciclar** means *to recycle,* **el reciclaje** is *recycling.* Although recycling is not as widespread a practice in the Hispanic world as in other countries, awareness and participation are growing. Costa Rica leads Latin America in its recycling efforts.

¡A practicar!

Q. DEFINICIONES Empareja cada palabra o frase con su definición.

1. _____ acabar
2. _____ resolver
3. _____ explotar
4. _____ el aire
5. _____ la capa de ozono
6. _____ el desarrollo

7. _____ puro

a. encontrar la solución de un problema
b. no contaminado
c. construir nuevos edificios
d. usar todo de algo
e. aprovechar de algo, usarlo sin pagar el precio
f. una parte de la atmósfera que se está destruyendo
g. lo que respiramos

R. UN CHICO MUY MALO Jorge, un niño muy malcriado *(badly behaved)*, no entiende toda la preocupación con el medio ambiente. Él habla de sus opiniones sobre la ecología. Escoge de las palabras de abajo para completar sus pensamientos.

| destruir | naturaleza | conservar | petróleo | energía solar |
| contaminación | reciclar | recursos naturales | arrojar | ecología |

Yo no comprendo todas las preocupaciones sobre la _____ . Yo sé que yo no debo _____ basura en el suelo, pero a veces no hay dónde ponerla. No veo por qué necesitamos _____ el papel y otras cosas. Tampoco me gusta la idea de usar el poder *(power)* del sol, o la _____ , para las casas. Yo no creo que vayamos a _____ el medio ambiente. La _____ siempre existe. Tenemos muchos _____ como el aire, el agua y el _____ . No tengo ganas de _____ nada. Yo sé que el mundo puede sobrevivir. ¿Para qué preocuparme por la _____ ?

S. ¿POR EL BIEN O MAL DEL MEDIO AMBIENTE? Abajo hay una lista de palabras asociadas con el medio ambiente. En grupos de tres o cuatro estudiantes, divídan la lista en dos columnas. La primera columna debe tener las palabras que se asocian con los problemas del medio ambiente. La segunda columna debe incorporar palabras que sugieren ayuda al medio ambiente. Luego, miren los dos grupos de palabras que escogieron. Hablen de por qué algunos términos son buenos o malos para el medio ambiente.

MODELO: E1: *La deforestación es malo para el medio ambiente porque significa la destrucción de las selvas y los bosques.*
E2: *Mi grupo seleccionó reforestar como algo bueno para el medio ambiente porque puede salvar los bosques y las selvas.*

1. recoger basura
2. reforestar
3. el desperdicio
4. la destrucción
5. proteger
6. la escasez de los recursos naturales
7. reciclar aluminio
8. conservar
9. proteger
10. el desarrollo
11. la energía solar
12. contaminar

En voz alta

T. CONSEJOS PARA NUESTROS HIJOS Termina los siguientes consejos que los padres les dan a sus hijos con respecto a problemas del medio ambiente.

MODELO: la naturaleza: Es recomendable que
Es recomendable que conservemos la naturaleza.

1. el agua: Es necesario que...
2. las latas *(cans)* de aluminio: Es mejor que...

3. la basura: Es importante que...
4. los periódicos *(newspapers)*: Es lógico que...
5. la capa de ozono: Es importante que...

U. PROBLEMAS Y SOLUCIONES Usando el vocabulario de esta sección, indica a un(a) compañero(a) de clase cómo podemos resolver los siguientes problemas globales. Intenta usar el subjuntivo en tus respuestas.

MODELO: la escasez de los recursos naturales
Es importante que conservemos y reciclemos.

1. la contaminación del aire
2. la sobrepoblación
3. la escasez de energía
4. la destrucción de las selvas tropicales
5. la dependencia mundial del petróleo
6. el arrojamiento *(dumping)* de basura en el océano
7. el desperdicio nuclear

V. PRIORIDADES Imagínate que eres el (la) presidente de los Estados Unidos y tus consejeros te dan una lista de medidas *(measures)* posibles que tienes que evaluar. Indica la urgencia de cada situación con las siguientes letras: necesidad **(N)**, prioridad **(P)**, importante pero no urgente **(I)**, no es importante **(NI)**. Solamente puedes marcar tres cosas como **necesidades.** Luego, explica tus decisiones a dos de tus consejeros (miembros de tu clase). Ellos deben persuadirte de que cambies de opinión si no están de acuerdo.

MODELO: prohibir el uso de coches privados
(P) Yo creo que es necesario que prohibamos el uso de coches priva-dos. Pienso que todo el mundo debe usar el transporte público para evitar la contaminación.

1. poner multas *(fines)* a los individuos que arrojan basura en las carreteras
2. acabar con la destrucción de la capa de ozono
3. reducir los desperdicios de los centros urbanos
4. desarrollar la energía solar
5. controlar mejor la contaminación de los ríos
6. evitar *(to avoid)* el consumo de los recursos naturales
7. sembrar más árboles en los centros urbanos
8. hacer leyes *(laws)* más estrictas para proteger la ecología de las selvas tropicales

W. ENTREVISTA Haz las siguientes preguntas a un(a) compañero(a) de clase y comparen sus respuestas.

1. En tu opinión, ¿cúal es el problema ecológico más grave que tenemos ahora? ¿Es posible que encontremos una solución para este problema? ¿Haces algo para aliviar este problema?
2. ¿Qué haces para conservar nuestros recursos naturales? ¿Reciclas? ¿Andas en bicicleta o vas a pie para gastar menos gasolina? ¿Bajas el termostato en invierno o usas menos el aire acondicionado en verano?
3. ¿Depende nuestra sociedad demasiado del petróleo? ¿Es posible tener desarrollo económico y conservar energía a la vez? ¿En qué sentido es la crisis ecológica un problema de dimensiones internacionales? ¿Qué debemos enseñar a nuestros hijos para que no tengan los mismos problemas que nosotros?

ENCUENTRO *cultural*

Monteverde y Tortuguero

Éstas son unas palabras nuevas para la lectura:

el acercamiento *encroachment*
el bosque nuboso *cloud forest*

Entre las muchas áreas bajo protección en Costa Rica, hay la Reserva Biológica Bosque Nuboso Monteverde y el Parque Nacional Tortuguero.

Para combatir el inminente **acercamiento** y población de seres humanos al área, unos científicos establecieron Monteverde en 1972 con unas solas 328 hectáreas. Mantenida únicamente con fondos privados, la reserva ahora abarca unas 10.500 hectáreas de naturaleza protegida.

Como **el bosque nuboso** es un hábitat muy raro, era importantísimo conservar las más de 100 especies de mamíferos, 400 especies de aves, 120 especies de anfibios y reptiles y las más de 2.500 especies de plantas que dependen de este medio ambiente único para vivir. Entre la flora y fauna protegidas hay orquídeas, jaguares, ocelotes y quetzales.

El Parque Nacional Tortuguero se encuentra en la costa caribeña al norte del país muy cerca de la frontera con Nicaragua. La protección de la tortuga verde motivó la creación del parque en donde viven seis de las ocho especies marinas de tortugas del mundo. El parque también protege muchas otras especies de plantas y animales como el manatí y el cocodrilo.

Ambos Monteverde y Tortuguero han sido reconocidos internacionalmente por sus esfuerzos en proteger el medio ambiente y educar a la gente de la importancia de la naturaleza.

Para pensar: En tu región, ¿hay hábitats y ecosistemas únicos como en Monteverde y Tortuguero? ¿Te gustaría visitar Tortuguero o Monteverde? Explica por qué.

X. PREGUNTAS Basándote en la lectura, contesta las siguientes preguntas con oraciones completas.

1. ¿Por qué fueron establecidas como áreas de conservación Monteverde y Tortuguero?

2. ¿Cuáles son algunas de las especies protegidas en la reserva y el parque?

GRAMÁTICA II: *Using the subjunctive to state uncertain, doubtful, or hypothetical situations*

Present subjunctive following verbs and expressions of uncertainty

Spanish speakers also use the subjunctive mood to express doubt, uncertainty, disbelief, unreality, nonexistence, and indefiniteness.

You can use the following verbs and expressions to communicate uncertainty; they are used like those shown in **Gramática I**.

dudar *to doubt*
Dudo que Rona **conserve** energía.

I doubt that Rona conserves energy.

es dudoso *it's doubtful*
Es dudoso que **haya** mucha agua pura.

It's doubtful that there is much pure water.

no creer *not to believe*
No creo que **salvemos** el planeta.

I don't believe that we will save the planet.

no es cierto[1] *it's uncertain*
No es cierto que **tengamos** suficientes recursos naturales.

It's not true that we have enough natural resources.

no estar seguro (de) *to be uncertain*
No estoy seguro de que **ayude** el reciclaje.

I'm not sure that recycling helps.

no pensar *to not think*
No pienso que **debamos** seguir así.

I don't think that we should continue like this.

Present subjunctive following adjective clauses that express hypothetical situations

Spanish speakers use the indicative mood after **que** to refer to people and things they are *certain about* and *believe to be true*. Consider the following example:

Me llamo Rona Grandinetti. Vivo en San José, una ciudad grande. **Sé** que el aire **está** contaminado aquí. **Creo** que **hay** demasiados autos que contaminan el aire. **No dudo** que **necesitamos** más transporte público.

Rona tells us that she lives in San José, a large city. She also knows that the air is polluted there, caused by too many cars in the city. She has no doubt that San José needs more public transportation. Since Rona knows these facts or feels certain about them, she uses verbs in the indicative after **que***.*

Spanish speakers use the subjunctive mood after **que** when they describe hypothetical people, places, things, or conditions, or when they do not believe that they exist at all. These types of structures are called *adjective clauses* because they qualify the preceding noun. In the following example, **una ciudad** is qualified by the clause **que sea tan bonita como Golfito**. Note that this particular use of the indicative or the subjunctive does not depend on the concept conveyed by the verb in the independent clause.[2]

➤➤

---

[1] Although the subjunctive is not used after the impersonal expression **es cierto que**, it is required after the negative form because it expresses doubt. The verb **pensar** also requires the subjunctive when it is negated.
[2] ¡OJO! Use the **a personal** before a direct object that refers to a specific person (in the indicative). If the person referred to is not specified, however, omit the **a personal**, except before **alguien, nadie, alguno,** and **ninguno.**

¿Conoces **a alguien** que vaya a la conferencia?   (a + **alguien**)
Conozco **a María Cristina** que es estudiante.   (a + *specific person*)
But: Necesito **un amigo** que vaya conmigo.   (omit a + *nonspecific person*)

Quiero vivir en **una ciudad que sea** tan bonita como Golfito. Busco **una ciudad que no tenga** mucha gente y **que esté** cerca del mar.

Now Rona tells us about an idealized city that she is searching for. The city must have certain qualifications such as being in a beautiful location, not having a lot of people, and being near the sea. Since it is indefinite or uncertain that Rona will find such a city, she uses the subjunctive after **que**.

¡A practicar!

Y. **UNA CONVERSACIÓN SINCERA ENTRE LUIS Y RONA** Completa la siguiente conversación entre Luis y Rona, usando los verbos apropiados entre paréntesis.

Rona: ¿Crees que tú y Leticia (van / vayan) a participar en el proyecto de conservación?

Luis: Pues, sé que Leticia (quiere / quiera) hacerlo, pero no estoy seguro que ella (está / esté) preparada para pasar sus vacaciones en la conservación del medio ambiente.

Rona: ¿Dudas que tú (quieres / quieras) ayudar?

Luis: No, quiero ayudar, pero necesitamos más tiempo para pensarlo. Ella me dijo que yo (debo / deba) pensarlo bien. Ella piensa que la conservación (es / sea) una cosa seria. Y tú, ¿crees que (debes participar / debas participar) en el proyecto?

Rona: Pues, claro que sí. Pero es dudoso que (paso / pase) todo mi tiempo en eso.

Z. **UNAS VACACIONES ECOLÓGICAS** Rona y Luis fueron a Golfito para participar en un proyecto de conservación ecológica en el Parque Nacional Piedras Blancas.[1] Se quedaron en un hotel donde se quejaron un poco de algunas cosas que encontraron. ¿Qué le dijeron al recepcionista?

MODELO: ¿hay un cuarto / tener dos camas?
 E1: *¿Hay un cuarto que tenga dos camas?*
 E2: *Sí, hay un cuarto que tiene dos camas.*
 o: *No, no hay un cuarto que tenga dos camas.*

Antes de ver el cuarto:
1. ¿no tiene Ud. otros cuartos / costar un poco menos?
2. ¿puede Ud. darnos un cuarto / estar en el tercer piso?
3. ¿es posible darnos un cuarto / tener una vista al mar?
4. ¿hay alguien / poder ayudarnos con las maletas?

Después de ver el cuarto:
5. deseamos un cuarto / no ser tan feo como ése
6. buscamos un empleado / poder darnos más toallas
7. queremos otro cuarto con una ducha / funcionar mejor

---

[1] The Piedras Blancas National Park was established in 1991 in an effort to preserve one of the last unprotected lowland tropical rainforests on the Pacific coast of Central America. Before the declaration of the park, deforestation was taking place, causing irreversible damage to the Esquinas Forest. While logging has ceased almost completely, some of the land in the park still belongs to private owners who can legally request logging permits until that land is all owned by the national parks system.

AA. **DOS AMIGOS** Con otro(a) estudiante, completa las siguientes conversaciones entre Luis y su amigo Jorge, como en el modelo.

MODELO: Luis: mis padres creen / (yo) reciclar mucho
               Jorge: ¿Cómo? no creo / (tú) reciclar mucho porque...
               Luis: *Mis padres creen que reciclo mucho.*
               Jorge: *¿Cómo? No creo que recicles mucho porque eres perezoso.*

1. Jorge: creo / ir (yo) a participar en el proyecto de conservación
   Luis: dudo / (tú) participar porque...
   Jorge: no creo / (tú) tienes razón porque...
2. Jorge: quiero / tú y yo volver a Golfito en mayo
   Luis: es dudoso / (nosotros) volver porque...
3. Jorge: mis padres creen / (yo) ser perezoso
   Luis: no dudo / (tú) ser perezoso porque...
4. Luis: Rona no está segura / sus amigos querer participar en el proyecto
   Jorge: no hay duda / ellos querer participar porque...

En voz alta

BB. **LA CIUDAD IDEAL** Describe a un(a) compañero(a) de clase cinco atributos de tu ciudad ideal utilizando el vocabulario de este capítulo.

MODELO: *Quiero vivir en una ciudad donde no haya contaminación, que tenga un buen sistema de transporte público y que sea bonita.*

CC. **¿QUÉ CREES TÚ?** Describe tus ideas sobre los siguientes temas a un(a) compañero(a) y discutan sus respuestas. Expresen sus creencias con las siguientes frases: **Creo que... Dudo que... No creo que... Es dudoso que... Estoy seguro(a) de que... Es obvio que...**, etcétera.

MODELO: la ecología
            Creo que la ecología es muy importante.
     o: *No creo que debamos seguir destruyendo la ecología.*

1. el aire y el agua
2. el reciclaje
3. los recursos naturales
4. la deforestación
5. la capa de ozono
6. el universo
7. el medio ambiente
8. la construcción de carreteras grandes
9. ¿ ?

DD. **EL FUTURO INCIERTO** No hay nada más incierto que el futuro, pero es importante hacer planes. Conversa con un(a) compañero(a) de clase sobre tus ambiciones.

MODELO: *Algún día quiero vivir en un lugar que esté cerca del mar...*

1. Algún día quiero vivir en un lugar que...
2. Para vivir allí sé que..., pero dudo que...
3. No estoy seguro(a) que... en ese lugar, pero creo que...
4. En ese lugar, hay...
5. Por eso, estoy seguro(a) de que...

EN LA RESERVA BIOLÓGICA DE GOLFITO[1] In this section you will learn about animals on a wildlife reserve. Which of the following animals would you expect to find in the tropical rain forests of Golfito?[2]

¿NOS ENTENDEMOS?

La víbora and **la serpiente** are synonyms for **la culebra.**

➥ These *Palabras útiles* are provided for recognition only; you will not be tested on these words.

Palabras útiles

el búho *owl*	el hipopótamo *hippopotamus*
el caimán *alligator*	la mariposa *butterfly*
el camello *camel*	la pantera *panther*
la cebra *zebra*	el rinoceronte *rhinoceros*
el ciervo *deer*	el zorro *fox*

¡A practicar!

EE. ¿DÓNDE VIVEN LOS ANIMALES? En grupos de tres o cuatro, hablen de dónde viven los siguientes animales —en el agua, los árboles, la tierra o el aire. Más de una respuesta puede ser correcta.

---

[1] The Golfito Reserve is in a wilderness area with a lot of rain. The forest is very thick, with species that are similar to those within the Osa Peninsula. Many animals such as butterflies, toucans, monkeys, scarlet macaws, tapirs, parrots, boas, sloths, and jaguars call the reserve home. The reserve is important for the conservation of the water supply for the city of Golfito.

[2] A large variety of birds and snakes are to be found in the lush woods of Golfito, Costa Rica. Though rare, coral snakes and vipers live in the forest and their bites can be life threatening. The vipers grow to more than six feet long and are characterized by a triangular head.

1. la culebra
2. el mono
3. el ave
4. el elefante
5. el león

6. el oso
7. el lobo
8. el gorila
9. el tigre

FF. **RICKY EL GUARDAPARQUES** Ricky trabaja en la reserva como guarda-parques. Completa la historia de abajo con las siguientes palabras para terminar su historia.

culebra   en peligro de extinción   especies   naturalistas   tigre
león   guardaparques   elefantes   aves   gorila   monos

¡Hola! Me llamo Ricky, y trabajo como _____ aquí en la Reserva Biológica de Golfito. Aquí tenemos muchas _____ de plantas y animales diferentes. Mi trabajo es interesante, porque me gusta mucho la naturaleza.

Todos los días, veo _____ que vuelan en el cielo *(sky)*. En los árboles viven muchos _____ que juegan colgándose de las ramas *(hanging on the branches)*. En el agua, muchas veces hay _____ gigantescos y grises. ¡Éstos se bañan con el agua de sus troncos! También, tengo la oportunidad de ver a muchos animales que están _____. Si mantengo el silencio, a veces puedo ver al rey de la selva, el _____. También hay un _____ que parece un gato muy grande con rayas. Cuando camino, tengo que cuidarme de no pisar *(step on)* una _____ venenosa —viven aquí en la selva y son muy peligrosas. Otro animal que vive aquí es el _____. Se parece mucho al mono, y al ser humano, pero es más grande.

Muchas veces, tenemos _____ que vienen a visitar la reserva para estudiar los animales y las plantas. ¡Me fascina mi trabajo!

En voz alta

GG. **YO ESTOY PENSANDO EN UN ANIMAL...** Un miembro de la clase va a escoger un animal de la lista de vocabulario. Los otros estudiantes solamente pueden hacer preguntas de **sí** o **no** para adivinar el animal. La persona que adivine correctamente toma el siguiente turno.

MODELO: E1: *¿Vive en el agua?*
           E2: *No. Pero a veces anda por el agua.*
           E3: *¿Es un animal peligroso?*
           E1: *Sí. Puede ser muy peligroso.*
           E2: *¿Es una culebra?*
           E1: *¡Sí!*

HH. **¡PELIGRO DE EXTINCIÓN!** Los siguientes animales están en peligro de extinción. En grupos de tres personas, hablen de lo que podemos hacer para salvar estos animales. (Por ejemplo, ¿podemos controlar la población de otros animales que son sus depredadores? ¿Podemos tratar de criarlos *(raise them)* en una reserva o en un parque zoológico?). Traten también de adivinar por qué están en peli-gro. Después, busquen información en el Internet o en una enciclo-pedia para averiguar sus adivinanzas.

1. el gorila
2. el oso panda
3. el tigre de Bengala

4. el lobo
5. el elefante
6. el león

Síntesis

¡A ver!

Elena nos va a presentar el video del **Capítulo 12** que se centra en el tema del medio ambiente, de su destrucción por el hombre y en los esfuerzos que se están empezando a ver en el mundo para salvarlo. Elena es de Costa Rica, concretamente de Cartago que está cerca de la capital de San José. El gobierno de Costa Rica ha hecho avances importantes en reconocer la necesidad de tomar medidas ecológicamente beneficiosas.

ACTIVIDAD 1   Pre-viewing task (Segmento 1 del video)

Paso 1: En el primer segmento del video vas a ver una serie de diez fotografías y clips cortos sobre paisajes *(landscapes)* de diversos lugares en el mundo hispánico. Identifica el tipo de paisaje representado en cada fotografía o clip. Escucha bien las descripciones de Elena, la presentadora del segmento.

M O D E L O :   *zona de montañas en Chile, selva amazónica, zona urbana, etcétera.*

Paso 2: Compara tu lista con la de un(a) compañero(a) de clase.

Paso 3: Entre los diez paisajes representados en las fotografías y los clips, selecciona los dos más atractivos y los dos menos atractivos como lugar de residencia desde tu punto de vista. En cada caso explica a tu compañero(a) de clase tu selección y justifica por qué sí o por qué no te gustaría vivir allí.

ACTIVIDAD 2   Pre-viewing task (Segmento 2 del video)

Paso 1: Cada ciudad grande (Los Ángeles o Atlanta, por ejemplo) hoy en día sufre de problemas de contaminación de muchos tipos. Haz una lista de estos problemas.

Paso 2: Entre todos, hagan una lista definitiva de estos problemas. Uno(a) de la clase apunta la lista en la pizarra mientras los otros hacen sugerencias. ¡Ojo que no se repitan sugerencias!

Paso 3: ¿Qué posibilidades hay de encontrar alguna solución a cada uno de los problemas que aparecen en la lista? ¿Qué sugerencias tienes tú para resolver el problema? Trabaja con un compañero(a) de clase para hacer una lista de estas sugerencias y después compartan sus ideas con el resto de la clase.

M O D E L O :   *Sugiero que haya más parques y más árboles en zonas urbanas.*

ACTIVIDAD 3   Viewing task (Segmento 2 del video)

El segundo segmento del video trata del problema de la contaminación ambiental en la Ciudad de México. El locutor del segmento ofrece dos razones por las cuales existe el grave problema. También nos explica cuatro medidas que se han tomado para buscar una solución al problema. Mira el segmento y rellena la siguiente tabla con la información que falta.

Orígenes del problema de la contaminación ambiental en la Ciudad de México	1. 2.
Medidas que se han tomado en busca de una solución al problema de la contaminación ambiental en la Ciudad de México	1. 2. 3. 4.

ACTIVIDAD 4   Post-viewing task (Segmento 2 del video)

Paso 1: Compara tus respuestas de la **Actividad 3** con las de tu compañero(a) de clase.

Paso 2: Entre todas las soluciones que has oído tanto en la **Actividad 2** como en la **Actividad 3**, ¿cuáles son las más interesantes? Haz una selección personal de tres soluciones o sugerencias que te convencen.

Paso 3: Entre todos, hagan una selección definitiva de tres soluciones, defendiendo los méritos de cada una de ellas.

¡A escribir!

Writing a persuasive essay

In this section you will learn to write an essay in which you try to convince your reader of your point of view regarding a particular environmental issue. Writers often use the following words and phrases to connect ideas in this type of composition.

To express opinions
creo que   *I believe*
pienso que   *I think*
en mi opinión   *in my opinion*

To show contrast
pero   *but*
aunque   *although*
por otro lado   *on the other hand*

To support opinions
primero   *first*
una razón   *one reason*
por ejemplo   *for example*

To summarize
por eso   *therefore*
finalmente   *finally*
en conclusión   *in conclusion*

Paso 1: Formula tu opinión sobre uno de los temas que siguen.

- El mejor lugar para vivir (en el campo, en la ciudad, etc.)
- El mejor medio de transporte (el coche, la bicicleta, el autobús, el tren, etc.)
- El problema global más grave (la contaminación del aire, la sobrepoblación, la destrucción de las selvas tropicales, etc.)
- La mejor manera de resolver los problemas del medio ambiente (controlar la contaminación de los ríos, reciclar, desarrollar la energía solar, etc.)
- El mejor lugar para los animales (en estado salvaje o en un refugio natural)

Paso 2: Escribe un ensayo en el cual das tu opinión sobre el tema que has escogido. Debes mencionar dos razones con detalles que apoyan tu posición. Por fin, escribe una conclusión. Tu ensayo debe tener cuatro párrafos. Puedes seguir el esbozo *(outline)* y el modelo que siguen, los cuales tratan de este tema: **El mejor medio de transporte.**

 I. Introducción (dar tu opinión sobre el tema)
   El mejor medio de transporte es el autobús.

 II. Primera razón a favor de tu opinión
   Hay menos coches en la carretera cuando las personas viajan en autobús.
   El autobús reduce la contaminación del aire.

 III. Segunda razón a favor de tu opinión
   Una persona puede leer y descansar mientras viaja en autobús.
   El autobús reduce el estrés de los pasajeros.

 IV. Conclusión
   Todos deben viajar en autobús.

MODELO: *Creo que el mejor medio de transporte es el autobús. El autobús tiene varios aspectos positivos.*

  Una razón es que el autobús nos ayuda a conservar el medio ambiente. Cuando las personas viajan en autobús, no tienen que usar el coche. Si hay menos coches en la carretera, hay menos contaminación del aire. Por eso, el autobús no contamina el medio ambiente tanto como los coches.

  Otra razón es que el autobús es mejor para el bienestar de las personas. Por ejemplo, una persona puede leer y descansar mientras viaja en autobús. Esto reduce el estrés de los pasajeros.

  En conclusión, pienso que el autobús es el mejor medio de transporte. Es bueno para el medio ambiente y para los pasajeros.

Functions: Persuading; Expressing an opinion; Agreeing and disagreeing; Comparing and contrasting

Vocabulary: Animals; Automobile; Health: diseases and illnesses; Means of transportation; Violence

Grammar: Verbs: subjunctive; **pero, sin (que), nada más que**

¡A conversar!

Paso 1: Habla con un(a) compañero(a) de clase acerca de los problemas ambientales que existen en el mundo contemporáneo. Debes hacerle las preguntas que siguen.

- ¿Te preocupas poco o mucho por los problemas del medio ambiente?
- ¿Qué problemas te molestan más? ¿Por qué?
- ¿Quiénes son algunas personas que hacen mucho para proteger la naturaleza? ¿Las conoces personalmente?
- ¿Qué hicieron esas personas para conservar el medio ambiente?
- En tu opinión, ¿qué responsabilidades tenemos para conservar los recursos naturales?

Paso 2: Entonces, cambien de papel. Luego, preséntale a la clase un informe sobre las respuestas de tu compañero(a).

¡A leer!

Understanding the writer's perspective

In many cases, you can use information you know about the author, his/her background, or his/her previous works to give you some perspective on the reading. Often this information can be useful in interpreting themes or messages that the author is attempting to convey via literature. Fortunately, many literary works (novels, collections of short stories, collections of poems, etc.) contain an introduction that gives at least some biographical information about the author, and in many cases provides some insight into the nature of the author's literary production.

For example, consider the following short story, written by the well-known Latin American short story writer Horacio Quiroga. A typical introduction to the author is provided. Does the introduction to the author provide you with information you can use to interpret the short story that follows?

Paso 1: Lee el siguiente párrafo sobre el autor Horacio Quiroga. Entonces, contesta las siguientes preguntas.

1. ¿Dónde nació el autor? ¿Dónde murió?
2. ¿Qué autores famosos han tenido una influencia importante en la obra de Quiroga? ¿Conoces algo de estos autores (su vida, su obra, etc.)?
3. ¿Tuvo Quiroga mucho contacto con la naturaleza durante su vida? ¿Cómo?
4. ¿Qué temas literarios de Quiroga se mencionan?

> Horacio Quiroga fue un escritor uruguayo considerado como un maestro del cuento corto. Aunque nació en Uruguay (1878), se trasladó a Argentina en 1901, donde vivió hasta su muerte (1937). Durante su vida, publicó varias colecciones de cuentos cortos, incluidos *Cuentos de la Selva* (1918), *Anaconda* (1921) y *El desierto* (1924). Influyeron en su obra autores de renombre mundial, como Kipling, Poe y Chekov. Quiroga vivió muchos años en la selva, donde tuvo que enfrentar muchas dificultades relacionadas con la naturaleza salvaje en la que vivió. Por esa experiencia, uno de sus temas preferidos era la relación tenue y difícil entre el hombre y la naturaleza. En muchos de sus cuentos Quiroga ilustra una situación en la que hay una confrontación inherente entre los seres humanos y la naturaleza que los rodea. Muchas veces, esta confrontación resulta en la muerte, la cual es otro tema muy común en varias obras del escritor.

Paso 2: Ahora, lee el cuento «Los cazadores de ratas», escrito por Quiroga. Entonces, organiza los acontecimientos de acuerdo a la historia.

_____ El hijo de la pareja se muere.
_____ Las víboras se dan cuenta de *(notice)* la presencia de la familia por primera vez.
_____ Las víboras descubren que hay ratas viviendo en el rancho de la pareja.
_____ Una de las víboras pica *(bites)* al hijo del matrimonio.
_____ El hombre mata a una de las víboras de cascabel.
_____ La familia construye un rancho en la zona donde viven las víboras.

Los cazadores de ratas

Una siesta de invierno, las víboras de cascabel,° que dormían extendidas sobre la greda,° se arrollaron bruscamente al oír insólito° ruido. Como la vista no es su agudeza particular,° las víboras se mantuvieron inmóviles, mientras prestaban oído.

—Es el ruido que hacían aquéllos... —murmuró la hembra.°
—Sí, son voces de hombres; son hombres —afirmó el macho.°

Y pasando una por encima de la otra se retiraron veinte metros. Desde allí miraron. Un hombre alto y rubio y una mujer rubia y gruesa se habían acercado° y hablaban observando los alrededores. Luego, el hombre midió el suelo a grandes pasos, en tanto que la mujer clavaba estacas° en los extremos de cada recta. Conversaron después, señalándose mutuamente distintos lugares, y por fin se fueron.

—Van a vivir aquí —dijeron las víboras.
—Tendremos que irnos.

En efecto, al día siguiente llegaron los colonos con un hijo de tres años y una carreta° en que había catres,° cajones,° herramientas° sueltas y gallinas° atadas a la baranda. Durante semanas trabajaron todo el día. La mujer se interrumpía para cocinar, y el hijo, un osezno° blanco, gordo y rubio, ensayaba de un lado a otro su infantil marcha de pato.°

Tal fue el esfuerzo de la gente aquella, que al cabo de un mes tenían pozo,° gallinero,° y rancho. Después, el hombre se ausentó por todo un día, volviendo al siguiente con ocho bueyes,° y la chacra comenzó.

Las víboras, entretanto, no se decidían a irse de su tierra natal. Solían llegar hasta la linde° del pasto,° y desde allí miraban el trabajo del matrimonio. Un atardecer en la que la familia entera había ido a la chacra, las víboras, animadas por el silencio, se aventuraron a cruzar el pasto y entraron en el rancho.

Pero allí había ratas; y desde entonces tomaron cariño a la casa.° Llegaban todas las tardes hasta el límite del patio y esperaban atentas a que aquélla quedara sola. Y a más, debían precaverse de° las gallinas con pollos, cuyos gritos, si las veían, delatarían su presencia.°

De este modo, una tarde en que la larga espera las había distraído, fueron descubiertas por una gallineta, que después de mantener un rato el pico° extendido, huyó a toda ala abierta, gritando. Sus compañeras comprendieron el peligro sin ver, y la imitaron.

El hombre, que volvía del pozo, se detuvo al oír los gritos. Miró un momento, y se encaminó al sitio sospechoso. Al sentir su aproximación, las víboras quisieron huir, pero únicamente la hembra tuvo el tiempo necesario, y el colono encontró sólo al macho. El hombre echó una rápida ojeada alrededor° buscando un arma° y llamó, los ojos fijos en el gran rollo obscuro.

—¡Hilda! ¡Alcánzame la azada!° ¡Es una serpiente de cascabel!

La mujer corrió y entregó ansiosa la herramienta a su marido.

Tiraron luego lejos, más allá del gallinero, el cuerpo muerto, y la hembra lo halló por casualidad al otro día. Cruzó y recruzó cien veces por encima de él, y se alejó al fin, yendo a instalarse como siempre en la linde del pasto, esperando pacientemente a que la casa quedara sola.

El próximo día, la víbora había cerrado los ojos para echar una siesta, cuando de pronto fue descubierta de nuevo por las gallinetas, que quedaron esta vez girando en torno suyo, gritando todas a contratiempo. La víbora se mantuvo quieta, prestando oído. Sintió al rato ruido de pasos... la Muerte. Creyó no tener tiempo de huir, y se aprestó con toda su energía vital a defenderse.

rattlesnakes/ground, clay (soil)
unusual, unaccustomed
strong suit, sharpest sense

female
male

moved closer, approached

put stakes in the ground (as markers)

wagon, cart
cots, light beds/boxes/tools/ hens
bear cub (figuratively, small child)
duck
well/henhouse

oxen

edge/pasture, grazing land

they took a liking to the house

to be on their guard against
would give them away

beak

took a quick look around/ weapon

hoe

En la casa dormían todos menos el chico. Al oír los gritos de las gallinetas, apareció en la puerta, y el sol quemante le hizo cerrar los ojos. Titubeó° un instante, perezoso, y al fin se dirigió con su marcha de pato a ver a sus amigas las gallinetas. En la mitad del camino se detuvo, indeciso de nuevo, evitando el sol con el brazo. Pero las gallinetas continuaban sus gritos, y el osezno rubio avanzó.

He hesitated

De pronto, el chico lanzó un grito y cayó sentado. La víbora, presta de nuevo a defender su vida, se deslizó° dos metros y se replegó. Vio a la madre y los brazos desnudos asomarse inquieta; la vio correr hacia su hijo, levantarlo y gritar aterrada.

slipped away

—¡Otto, Otto! ¡Lo ha picado° una víbora!

bitten

Vio llegar al hombre, pálido, y lo vio llevar en sus brazos a la criatura atontada.° Oyó la carrera de la mujer al pozo, sus voces. Y al rato, después de una pausa, su alarido° desgarrador:

dazed, stupefied
shriek, scream, cry

—¡Hijo mío!...

Paso 3: Teniendo en cuenta la historia, contesta las siguientes preguntas.

1. En tu opinión, ¿cuál es el tema más importante de la historia? Explica tu respuesta.
2. ¿Qué comentario hace Quiroga acerca de la relación entre el hombre y la naturaleza?
3. ¿Te gusta el cuento? ¿Tendrías interés en leer otros cuentos cortos de Quiroga?

La geografía rural y urbana   *Rural and urban geography*

el (la) agricultor(a) *farmer*	**la carretera** *highway*	**el rascacielos** *skyscraper*	**el tráfico** *traffic*
el arroyo *stream*	**la catarata** *waterfall*	**el ruido** *noise*	**el transporte público** *public*
la basura *trash*	**la colina** *hill*	**la selva** *jungle*	*transportation*
el bosque *forest*	**la fábrica** *factory*	**la sobrepoblación** *over-*	
el (la) campesino(a) *farm*	**la finca** *farm*	*population*	
worker, peasant	**la metrópolis** *metropolis*	**la tierra** *land, earth*	

Verbos

cultivar   *to cultivate; to grow (plants)*
llevar una vida tranquila   *to lead a peaceful life*

regar (ie)   *to irrigate; to water*
sembrar (ie)   *to plant*

Adjetivos

acelerado(a)   *accelerated*
bello(a)   *beautiful*

denso(a)   *dense*
tranquilo(a)   *tranquil, peaceful*

La conservación y la explotación   *Conservation and exploitation*

el aire *air*	**la destrucción** *destruction*	**la naturaleza** *nature*
la capa de ozono *ozone layer*	**la ecología** *ecology*	**el petróleo** *petroleum*
la contaminación *pollution*	**la energía solar** *solar energy*	**los recursos naturales** *natural resources*
el desarrollo *development*	**la escasez** *lack, shortage*	
el desperdicio *waste*	**el medio ambiente** *environment*	

Verbos

acabar *to run out*	**desarrollar** *to develop*	**reciclar** *to recycle*
conservar *to conserve*	**destruir** *to destroy*	**recoger** *to pick up*
construir *to construct*	**explotar** *to exploit*	**reforestar** *to reforest*
contaminar *to pollute*	**proteger** *to protect*	**resolver (ue)** *to solve, to resolve*

Adjetivos

contaminado(a)   *polluted*
destruido(a)   *destroyed*
puro(a)   *pure*

Los animales y el refugio natural   *Animals and the wildlife preserve*

el ave *bird*	**el gorila** *gorilla*	**el mono** *monkey*
la culebra *snake*	**el (la) guardaparques** *park ranger*	**el (la) naturalista** *naturalist*
el elefante *elephant*	**el león** *lion*	**el oso** *bear*
las especies *species*	**el lobo** *wolf*	**el tigre** *tiger*

Expresiones idiomáticas

¡No arroje basura!   *Don't litter!*
en peligro de extinción   *in danger of extinction*

Lugar de encuentro para la hispanidad

PLAZAS

BIENVENIDOS A *PLAZAS*, UNA PUBLICACIÓN QUE DESCRIBE EL PANORAMA DE LOS PAÍSES DE HABLA ESPAÑOLA.

La feria de trabajo
te quiere reclutar

**La luna de miel
inolvidable**

Cuidemos nuestro
planeta

Perspectivas del trabajo

Cuando una carrera
no es suficiente...

La feria de trabajo te quiere reclutar

Para la feria de trabajos en la universidad este fin de semana, queremos anunciar algunos de los puestos vacantes para las cuales se buscan empleados profesionales, responsables y entusiastas. Los sueldos son negociables, de acuerdo con la experiencia del (de la) candidato(a). Aquí puedes ver una selección de oportunidades.

Plaza vacante	Cualificaciones	Descripción del trabajo
 Guardaparques	Deseo para trabajar al aire libre y para trabajar con un sinnúmero de animales y plantas tropicales.	Trabajar los fines de semana, de viernes por la tarde a domingo por la noche, en uno de los parques nacionales de Costa Rica. Colaborar con la creación de un programa de conservación de la belleza natural del parque.
Planificador de bodas	Atención al detalle y experiencia con la planificación bajo presión.	Organizar todos los detalles de la boda para los recién comprometidos económicamente afortunados: invitaciones, música, banquetes, flores, etc.
 Fotógrafo	Ojo creativo para capturar imágenes en blanco y negro. Experiencia con todos los aspectos de la fotografía.	Trabajar para una revista de viajes y acompañar a los reporteros y otros fotógrafos que viajan por todo el mundo. Ser responsable por el diseño (design) de las secciones en blanco y negro que suplementan las fotos a colores.

¿Cuál puesto te gustaría solicitar? ¿Por qué?

¿Qué sueldo recomiendas para los candidatos?

¿Cuáles son otras cualificaciones y/o descripciones de estos trabajos que sugieres incluir?

La luna de miel inolvidable

Maricarmen Mendoza y José Domínguez se casaron la semana pasada y ahora están de luna de miel. Han preparado todo el viaje con mucho cuidado porque quieren que sea un viaje inolvidable. Como Maricarmen es periodista para un periódico pequeño y José es maestro, sus sueldos no son tan altos y han pedido un préstamo para ayudarles con los gastos de la luna de miel. Maricarmen ha soñado toda la vida con visitar la América Central porque su familia es de León[1], una ciudad cerca de la costa del Pacífico en Nicaragua. Van a comenzar en Honduras y seguir hacia el sur para ver lugares de interés en Nicaragua, Costa Rica y Panamá.

Pensaron depender mayormente de los cajeros automáticos para sus gastos diarios pero decidieron que querían cambiar un poco de su dinero por la moneda *(currency)* local antes de llegar a cada país. Para su transacción pidieron la cotización *(exchange rate)* para la moneda de los países que iban a visitar, entre ellos: **la lempira** en Honduras, **el nuevo córdorba** en Nicaragua, **el colón** en Costa Rica y **el balboa** en Panamá. El cajero en el banco les ayudó con la transacción y les explicó que fácilmente podían usar los cajeros automáticos. ¡Qué problema! Dejaron su tarjeta bancaria en casa y ahora necesitan buscar alternativas. Definitivamente, esta luna de miel será inolvidable.

- ¿Qué les recomiendas a Maricarmen y a José para resolver su problema?
- ¿Has tenido un viaje inolvidable? ¿En cuáles aspectos fue inolvidable?
- ¿Has pedido préstamos? ¿Para qué son los préstamos generalmente?
- ¿Con qué frecuencia usas el cajero automático?

Consulta un mapa para ver cuáles son algunas ciudades principales de estos países y sugiere un itinerario para Maricarmen y José.

Busca las cotizaciones de las monedas locales para indicar cuánto de la moneda local el matrimonio va a recibir al cambiar su dinero.

[1] Visitors who travel to León are most likely to see the bullet-riddled murals dedicated to the cause of the Sandanistas during the revolutionary war begun in 1978. The city is also known for its colonial arquiteture, including the largest cathedral in Central America, that has been spared from damage that other cities have not so fortunately avoided due to earthquakes. The city is located to the northwest of Managua.

Cuidemos nuestro planeta

Violeta Barrios de Chamorro, la primera mujer elegida presidente en un país centroamericano (Nicaragua, 1990–1997), se dedica a muchas causas sociales, humanas y políticas. Chamorro, quien nació en Rivas, Nicaragua, en 1929, habló con uno de nuestros corresponsales de **Plazas,** Enrique Maldonado, sobre sus actividades relacionadas con la conservación del medio ambiente con el fin de estimular interés en la creación de programas de reciclaje y de protección de recursos naturales.

PLAZAS: ¿Por qué se interesa Ud. en las cuestiones ambientales?

VIOLETA CHAMORRO: Creo que nuestro medio ambiente debe ser protegido y para esto necesitamos que la comunidad nos apoye *(support)*. Tenemos mucha destrucción del medio ambiente y los niveles de contaminación están cada día más altos.

PLAZAS: ¿Qué ha hecho Ud. para combatir estos problemas?

VIOLETA CHAMORRO: He establecido un programa que se llama «Fundación Violeta Barrios de Chamorro» que, además de ser una organización que se propone respetar y reconocer los derechos civiles, se dedica a mejorar la calidad de vida de los ciudadanos de nuestro país.

PLAZAS: En su opinión ¿cuál es el problema ambiental más serio?

VIOLETA CHAMORRO: No pienso que la gente sepa cuáles son las consecuencias de sus acciones. Si no comenzamos hoy a proteger hoy lo que necesitamos para mañana, toda la destrucción, toda la contaminación, toda la basura y todos los desperdicios van a causar la destrucción del medio ambiente.

PLAZAS: ¿Qué podemos hacer nosotros?

VIOLETA CHAMORRO: Es importante que tengamos una visión hacia el futuro para implementar programas de protección del medio ambiente y de conservación de los recursos naturales. Podemos reciclar, utilizar energía solar, participar en programas de recoger basura o simplemente no participar en actividades que puedan causar la destrucción de nuestro planeta. Ojalá que podamos resolver este problema con la cooperación de todos.

- ¿Qué futuro ves para nuestro planeta en términos del medio ambiente?
- ¿Qué sugieres que hagamos para conservar energía?
- ¿Eres parte del problema o parte de la solución para la protección del medio ambiente? ¿Cómo?

Perspectivas del trabajo

Carmen Naranjo, escritora costarricense nacida en 1931, se ha destacado por sus contribuciones literarias en forma de poema, novela y cuento. Uno de los temas principales es el amor al ser humano que la escritora explora en términos de la frustración humana, el aislamiento, el abandono y la soledad. En la novela *Responso por el niño Juan Manuel* (1971), Naranjo depende del diálogo y del monólogo interior para mostrar la soledad que rodea a Juan Manuel, ya mayor, y sus amigos.

—Estaba pensando en algún tema de interés para conversar. Debe estar aburrido de tanto silencio...

—Nunca me aburro, los viejos tenemos esa cualidad. Lo malo es que aburrimos a los demás...

—¿En qué trabaja?

—Hago todo lo que es posible hacer a mi edad. Arreglo jardines, cuido casas, trabajo de guardia. Últimamente no he podido encontrar un empleo fijo. Mi única credencial es la honradez *(honesty)* y no me dan oportunidad de probarla.

—¿Cuida casas vacías *(empty)*?... ¿Qué se siente al vivir en una casa vacía?

—Se sienten muchas cosas, claro esto depende del tipo de casa. Las casas grandes, por ejemplo, nunca parecen del todo vacías. Las casas pequeñas resultan acogedoras *(quaint)* al principio, pero luego lo llenan a uno de inquietudes incómodas, para recordarle que no es su sitio, es sólo un extraño entre las paredes.

He hablado mucho. Ése es el problema de los silenciosos. Se les pide una opinión y se exceden. Sin embargo, veo en sus caras una cordialidad que no había antes, los gestos de estos dos señores se han suavizado.

¿Qué te parecen los trabajos de Juan Manuel?

¿Has cuidado una casa o arreglado jardines alguna vez?

¿Cómo describes este tipo de trabajo?

¿Qué piensas de la importancia de la honradez que menciona Juan Manuel? ¿Cuáles son otras cualidades importantes en la vida profesional? ¿Cómo podemos percibir la soledad de Juan Manuel?

Cuando una carrera no es suficiente...

Rubén Blades: Músico, abogado, actor del cine, político y mucho más...

Cuando Rubén Blades nació en Panamá en 1948, hijo de un policia y una actriz, ¿quién habría pensado que este hombre talentoso tendría éxitos extraordinarios en campos tan diversos como la música, la ley, el cine y la política, y todo eso antes de cumplir cincuenta años? Cómo músico, Rubén es el rey de la salsa afro-cubano. Compositor de más de diez álbums, el artista ha colobrado con cantantes famosos como Linda Ronstadt y autores de mucho renombre como Gabriel García Márquez. Cuando su carrera musical florecía en los años 80, Rubén nos mostró que tenía otros talentos y ambiciones cuando sacó un masters de Harvard en derecho internacional. Para muchos, esto habría sido suficiente. Pero para Rubén, apenas había comenzado a desarrollar su carrera. Siempre le había fascinado el cine y en 1985 tuvo el papel prinicpal en «Crossover Dreams», una película que promocionó la salsa en las discotecas norteamericanas. Desde entonces tambíen ha aparecido en «Waiting for Salazar», «The Milagro Beanfield War», «Mo'Better Blues» y «The Two Jakes». Cuando formó un partido político en 1992 dedicado a la justicia social, nadie dubaba la capacidad de este superhombre de gobernar el país. Aunque perdió su campaña presidencial en 1994, no hemos llegado al último capítulo de este hombre ejemplar.

¿Cómo será?

Imagina cómo será la oficina de una persona tan existosa como Rubén Blades. Como el arquitecto personal de Rubén, haz una descripción detallada del espacio profesional que propones para él con el vocabulario del Capítulo 11. Debes tener en cuenta todas las necesidades de un hombre tan original como tu jefe.

Un día con Rubén...

Imagina que eres el (la) asistente personal de Rubén. Describe un día típico trabajando para él. Intenta usar cinco de los siguientes verbos en tu descripción: **contestar, despedir, entregar, escribir a máquina, firmar, llamar por teléfono, imprimir, reunirse.**

13

El mundo del espectáculo: Perú y Ecuador

Communicative goals

In this chapter you will learn how to . . .

- Talk about television and other forms of popular culture
- Use the subjunctive to make statements of purpose and to express anticipated actions
- Talk about the arts and the vocations of artists
- Talk about unplanned or accidental occurrences
- Describe completed actions and resulting conditions with past participles

Grammar

- The present subjunctive in purpose and time clauses
- The no-fault **se**
- The past participle as adjective

Cultural information

- La cinematografía en Latinoamérica
- Oswaldo Guayasamín

La Plaza Independencia, Quito, Ecuador

CARTELERA DE PROGRAMACIÓN In this section you will learn to talk about television and movies.

el anuncio *commercial*	**la película**	**la película**
el canal *channel (TV)*	**de acción** *action film*	**extranjera** *foreign film*
el cine *movies; movie theater*	**de arte** *art film*	**romántica** *romantic film*
	de horror *horror film*	**el programa deportivo** *sports program*
la película *movie, film*	**de intriga (misterio)** *mystery film*	**el pronóstico del tiempo** *weather report (forecast)*
clásica *classic film*		

Verbos

aburrir *to bore*	**molestar** *to bother*
apreciar *to appreciate*	**poner** *to turn on (TV); to show (a movie)*
dejar *to leave; to let, to allow*	

¡A practicar!

A. PELÍCULAS Y PROGRAMAS La siguiente lista contiene títulos de películas y programas producidos en los Estados Unidos que ahora se pasan en la televisión. Indica el tipo de cada película o programa y luego, di si te gusta o no te gusta. Sigue el modelo.

MODELO: «X Files: The Movie»
Es una película de ciencia ficción y me gusta muchísimo. ¡Fox Mulder es fabuloso!

Título de película o programa:

1. «NYPD Blue»
2. «Tarzán»
3. «The Simpsons»
4. «Buffy, The Vampire Slayer»
5. «Cristina»[1]
6. «The Matrix»
7. «The Young and the Restless»
8. «Who Wants to Be a Millionaire?»
9. «Friends»
10. «Oprah»
11. «Monday Night Football»
12. «Evita»[2]
13. «The Weather Update»
14. «Buena Vista Social Club»[3]

B. **¡ADIVINA!** Éstos son los títulos de algunos programas y películas estadounidenses traducidos al español. Adivina qué programas son en inglés. Si no sabes, pregúntaselo a tu profesor(a). Después, decide qué tipo de película o programa es.

PELÍCULAS

1. «Lo que el viento se llevó»
2. «El mago de Oz»
3. «Hércules»
4. «La guerra de las galaxias»
5. «Un tranvía llamado deseo»

PROGRAMAS DE TELEVISIÓN

6. «La dama del oeste»
7. «La rueda de la fortuna»
8. «Doctor en Alaska»
9. «El expediente X»
10. «Sensación de vivir»

En voz alta

C. **MIS PROGRAMAS PREFERIDOS** Completa las siguientes oraciones con información relevante y luego explica tus preferencias a la clase.

1. Uno de mis programas de televisión preferidos es «_____» porque...
2. Un programa que quiero ver otra vez se llama «_____». Creo que es un programa muy _____ porque...
3. Un programa que me aburre es «_____» porque...
4. Cuando era niño(a), mis padres me dejaban ver «_____» pero no me dejaban ver «_____».
5. Me molestan los programas de _____ porque...
6. Un programa de televisión que no les recomiendo ver se llama «_____». No les recomiendo que lo vean porque...

D. **LOS PREMIOS** Uds. son críticos que van a seleccionar los mejores programas y películas para un premio prestigioso. Trabajando en grupos, decidan cuál es el mejor ejemplo en cada categoría. Después, anuncien los resultados a la clase y justifiquen sus selecciones.

MODELO: programa de entrevistas
En la categoría de mejor programa de entrevistas, le damos el premio a «El Show de Cristina» porque Cristina es muy talentosa y los panelistas siempre son interesantes.

CATEGORÍAS

dibujo animado
telenovela
película de horror
película romántica

documental
programa de entrevistas
película de acción

programa de concursos
programa deportivo
película de intriga

---

[1] "Cristina" is a popular talk show in Spanish from the United States. The host, Cristina Saralegui, is from a family of Cuban exiles and has enjoyed many years of success with her program.
[2] "Evita" is a musical play by Andrew Lloyd Weber and Tim Rice based on the life of Eva Perón (1919–1952), wife of Argentine dictator Juan Perón. It was made into a movie in 1996 by Alan Parker, starring Madonna as Evita and Antonio Banderas as Che Guevara.
[3] "Buena Vista Social Club" is a documentary directed by Ry Cooder. It was released in 1999 and is based on the rediscovery of a group of aging Cuban musicians who were forgotten after the Cuban Revolution.

¿NOS ENTENDEMOS?

Spanish speakers use **el televisor** for *television set* and **la televisión** for *television programming*. The same applies to **el radio** (the radio itself) and **la radio** (what you listen to), which is short for **la radiodifusión**.

E. **ENTREVISTA** Hazle a otro(a) estudiante las siguientes preguntas sobre la televisión y el cine.

LA TELEVISIÓN

1. ¿Cuántos televisores tienes en casa? ¿Con qué frecuencia miras la televisión?
2. ¿Cuál es tu programa favorito? ¿Por qué te gusta tanto?
3. Para ti, ¿qué programa de televisión es ridículo? ¿Por qué crees eso?
4. ¿Te molesta que haya tanta violencia en la televisión?
5. ¿Te quejas de la cantidad de anuncios que hay en la televisión?

EL CINE

1. ¿Con qué frecuencia vas al cine?
2. Si tienes un cine favorito, ¿cuál es?
3. Normalmente, ¿con quién vas al cine?
4. ¿Quién es tu actor favorito y por qué lo aprecias? ¿Quién es tu actriz favorita y por qué la aprecias?
5. ¿Viste una película buena recientemente? ¿Cuál fue?

F. **ENCUENTRA A ALGUIEN QUE...** Encuentra a alguien para quien sean verdaderas las siguientes frases. Después de encontrar a cada persona, pídele que firme tu papel. Al final, cuenta a la clase lo que has aprendido.

MODELO: Miro la tele más de dos horas por día.
           E1: *¿Helen, miras la televisión más de dos horas por día?*
           E2: *¡Dios mío! ¡No tengo tanto tiempo libre!* (look for someone else)
      o: E2: *Sí, miro tres telenovelas por día.* (ask Helen to sign your paper)
Al final: E1: *Helen mira más de dos horas de televisión por día. Jason nunca va al cine. Michelle prefiere la radio a la tele...*

1. Miro la tele más de dos horas por día.
2. No tengo televisor.
3. Nunca voy al cine.
4. Voy al cine cada semana.
5. Conozco a un(a) actor (actriz).
6. Soy actor (actriz).
7. Sigo una telenovela. Se llama «_____».
8. Prefiero la radio a la tele.
9. Siempre miro las noticias.
10. A mí me gusta mucho escuchar la radio pública (NPR).

¿NOS ENTENDEMOS?

You have already learned the difference between **la televisión** and **el televisor.** You will notice in everyday speech that it is common to use **la tele** when talking about watching TV. For example, **Voy a mirar la tele** is similar to an English speaker saying *I'm going to watch TV* or *I'm going to watch the tube,* as opposed to saying *I'm going to watch television,* which sounds a little more formal.

EN CONTEXTO

Lima, Perú. Son las 9:30 de una noche de febrero. Un grupo de artistas limeños *(from Lima)* están esperando el anuncio del ganador de la exposición de arte en La Galería Miraflores.

—Señoras y señores, ahora hemos llegado al momento culminante de esta magnífica exposición de arte limeño. Les pido unos segundos de silencio para que todos podamos celebrar este momento triunfante para uno o una de nuestros artistas. En este sobre *(envelope)* que tengo en la mano está el nombre del ganador *(winner)* o la ganadora de esta exposición. Señoras y señores... este año la ganadora es una pintora. Se llama... ¡Rosario María Ramos!

—Muchas gracias. Quiero darles las gracias a todos los organizadores de la exposición, al público, a mis amigos y especialmente a mi familia. No puedo pintar a menos que tenga el apoyo *(support)* y la inspiración de mis padres y mis hermanos. Éste es un gran honor para mí y para mi familia. Muchas gracias a todos.

—Rosario, ¿nos puede explicar algo sobre su estilo? En su obra *(work)* a veces notamos una organización muy abierta, muy espontánea. En otros cuadros *(paintings)* las imágenes están más cerradas, más controladas.

—Bueno, en cuanto a *(in regard to)* las obras espontáneas, confieso que a veces ocurren cosas inesperadas, aun accidentales. Por ejemplo, en mi obra «Manchas de café» yo tomaba un café antes de empezar un cuadro y de repente se me cayó la taza *(the cup fell)*. Y ¡voilá!, tenía justo lo que buscaba para crear una escena de la vida cotidiana *(daily)*.

—Antes de que revele todos sus secretos, Rosario, ¿nos diría *(would you tell)* cuál es su obra favorita?

—Pues sí, es otro de mis cuadros «accidentales». El cuadro se llama «Espacio en blanco». Es una obra posmodernista que invita al espectador *(viewer)* a terminar la obra. Después de pintarla media hora, se me acabó *(I ran out of)* la pintura, y decidí dejarla como era. Requiere la colaboración del espectador para completarla.

G. ¿COMPRENDISTE? Indica si las siguientes oraciones son ciertas o falsas. Si una es falsa, corrígela.

1. La exposición solamente incluye pintores.
2. Son artistas de todo el mundo.
3. La familia es importante a la producción artística de Rosario.
4. Rosario pinta solamente obras «accidentales».
5. Generalmente, Rosario pinta dentro del estilo clásico.
6. Algunos de sus cuadros requieren la participación del espectador.

ENCUENTRO *cultural*

La cinematografía en Latinoamérica

Aunque pasan muchísimas películas norteamericanas en los cines del mundo hispánico, los propios países de habla hispana han desarrollado una industria cinematográfica de importancia internacional. En el mundo hispánico los líderes de producción de películas son España, México, Cuba y Argentina. El director español Pedro Almodóvar es conocido mundialmente por sus películas cómicas. De México, una película muy famosa y exitosa es «Como agua para chocolate». Está basada en la novela del mismo nombre. «Fresa y chocolate», de Cuba, ha ganado premios internacionales en festivales de cine. La industria cinematográfica de Argentina es conocida por crear películas que tratan muchos problemas sociales.

Perú también tiene una larga historia cinematográfica. La primera película peruana de ficción fue «Negocio al agua», estrenada el 14 de abril de 1913 en el Cinema Teatro de Lima. Desde aquel entonces, los peruanos han tenido un amor especial por el cine.

Entre los directores más famosos de Perú está el Grupo Chaski que hizo filmes como «Gregorio» (1983–1984), «Juliana» (1988–1989) y «Anda, corre, vuela» (1994). Estas tres películas forman una trilogía llamada la «Trilogía peruana».

Para pensar: ¿Qué tipo de película te interesa más a ti? Explica por qué. ¿Vas al cine muy a menudo *(often)*? Describe una de tus películas favoritas. ¿Quiénes son tus actores favoritos? ¿directores favoritos? ¿Has visto una película en español alguna vez? ¿Cuál? ¿Dónde? ¿Pudiste comprenderla?

H. PREGUNTAS Contesta las siguientes preguntas a base de la lectura.

1. Nombra al director español que es conocido en todo el mundo.
2. ¿Cómo se llama la película mexicana mencionada? ¿la cubana?
3. ¿Qué pasó en Lima el 14 de abril de 1913?
4. ¿Quién es el Grupo Chaski? Nombra las tres partes de su trilogía famosa.

GRAMÁTICA I: *Using the subjunctive with purpose and time clauses*

In this section you will learn about using the present subjunctive with purpose and time clauses. Up until now you have been focusing on the word **que** to link the main and dependent clauses. In this section you will be introduced to other conjunctions that have the same function. Although most of the verbs in the dependent clauses will be in the present subjunctive, you will learn about cases in which the present indicative must be used.

A conjunction is a word that links words or groups of words, such as an independent clause and a dependent clause. Conjunctions of purpose and of time are listed below along with explanations and examples of how to use them.

Conjunctions of purpose

a fin de que *so that*	**a menos que** *unless*
sin que *without*	**con tal (de) que** *provided (that)*
para que *so (that)*	**en caso (de) que** *in case (of)*

1. Always use the subjunctive after the six conjunctions listed above.

Independent clause	Conjunction	Dependent clause
↓	↓	↓
Voy al cine	con tal (de) que	vayas conmigo.
I'm going to the cinema	*provided (that)*	*you go with me.*

2. When expressing an idea with the conjunction **aunque** *(although, even though)*, follow it with the indicative to state certainty, and the subjunctive to imply uncertainty.

certainty (indicative)

Aunque el concierto **es** en abril, no puedo ir.	***Although*** *the concert **is** in April, I can't go.*

uncertainty (subjunctive)

Aunque el concierto **sea** en abril, no puedo ir.	***Although*** *the concert **may be** in April, I can't go.*

Conjunctions of time

antes (de) que *before*	**tan pronto como** *as soon as*
después (de) que *after*	**cuando** *when*
en cuanto *as soon as*	**hasta que** *until*

1. The six conjunctions listed above may be followed by a verb in either the subjunctive or the indicative mood (see the one exception that follows). When an action, condition, or event has not yet taken place, use the subjunctive in the dependent clause. But when referring to habitual or completed actions, use the indicative in the dependent clause.

pending action (subjunctive)

Los músicos van a aplaudir **cuando llegue** el director.

*The musicians are going to applaud **when** the conductor **arrives**.*

habitual action (indicative)

Los músicos siempre aplauden **cuando llega** el director.

*The musicians always applaud **when** the conductor **arrives**.*

completed action (indicative)

Los músicos aplaudieron **cuando llegó** el director.

*The musicians applauded **when** the conductor **arrived**.*

2. One exception: Always use the subjunctive after **antes (de) que.**

Los invitados van a la recepción **antes de que lleguen** los artistas.

*The guests go to the reception **before** the artists **arrive**.*

¡A practicar!

I. **EL DOCUMENTAL** Completa la siguiente descripción de la producción de un documental sobre la vivienda peruana usando la forma correcta de cada verbo.

Es preferible que la entrevista (tiene / tenga) lugar en la casa de las personas con quienes estamos trabajando, a menos que su casa (es / sea) muy pequeña. En ese caso, la entrevista (va a ser / sea) en nuestro estudio. El día antes de que (comenzamos / comencemos), los dueños de la casa normalmente (decoran / decoren) la casa para que (está / esté) muy bonita. Al día siguiente (llegan / lleguen) temprano los técnicos para preparar el sitio y asegurar que todo está bien antes de que (viene / venga) el director. Normalmente, en cuanto (llega / llegue) la entrevistadora, ella (empieza / empiece) a preparar a los dueños de la casa para las preguntas que ella (va / vaya) a hacerles durante la entrevista. Después de que (termina / termine) la fase preparatoria, todo (está / esté) listo. Generalmente, cuando (llega / llegue) el director, el equipo (puede / pueda) comenzar. Después de que (termina / termine) con la filmación, el equipo (pasa / pase) un rato charlando con los dueños de la casa antes de volver al estudio.

J. **MALAS NOTICIAS PARA MATEO** Completa la siguiente conversación entre dos actores de la telenovela «¡No puedo más!». Usa las conjunciones apropiadas de la lista.

aunque   a menos que   después de que   cuando   antes de que   con tal de que

—Oye, Mateo. Tengo malas noticias _____ no vas a creerme.
—¿Malas noticias? Por Dios, ¿qué pasó, Laura?
—_____ te lo diga, tienes que prometerme que no vas a estar enojado conmigo.
—No, mujer. Dime, ¿qué pasó?
—¿Recuerdas a María Cristina, la cantante peruana?
—Claro. La conocí en Lima _____ llegamos al hotel Bolívar.

—Sí, sí. Pues, ella se va a casar el próximo mes.
—¡No me digas! Pero... ¿cón quién?
—Te lo digo _____ te calmes, Mateo.
—Estoy calmado. Dime más.
—Bueno, María Cristina va a casarse con Gregorio Vega, su novio, el que viste en Lima. Le dije a mi amiga Clara: _____ le diga a Mateo que María Cristina se casa en abril, va a estar triste.
—Pues, sí, pero no puedo hacer nada _____ los novios decidan no casarse.
—Es verdad, no puedes hacer nada.

K. **OTRA ESCENA DE «¡NO PUEDO MÁS!»** ¿Qué sugerencias le dio Clara a su amigo Gregorio antes de la boda? Conjuga los verbos subrayados en el presente del subjuntivo o del indicativo.

MODELO: Compra una casa tan pronto como ser posible.
              Compra una casa tan pronto como *sea* posible.

1. Antes de que tú y María Cristina casarse, piénsalo bien.
2. No compres nada muy caro sin que tu esposa lo saber.
3. Cuando ella estar enferma, haz todo lo posible para ayudarla.
4. No le des consejos a tu esposa a menos que ella te los pedir.
5. Habla frecuentemente con tu esposa para que Uds. comprenderse.
6. En caso de que tú tener algún problema serio, llámame, por favor.
7. Vengan a visitarme después de que Uds. volver de su luna de miel.
8. No tomes ninguna decisión económica hasta que tú consultar con ella.

En voz alta

L.   **UN SECRETO DE MATEO** Mateo está secretamente enamorado de María Cristina, la novia de Gregorio. Él no quiere que ellos se casen. ¿Qué le dice a María Cristina para que no se case con Gregorio?

1. Voy a hablar con María Cristina inmediatamente para que...
2. Ella siempre quiere saber la verdad cuando...
3. Tengo que verla antes de que...
4. Debo buscarla ahora en caso de que...
5. No puedo permitir que se case sin que...
6. Tengo que decirle la verdad aunque...
7. Es posible que no se case cuando...
8. No puedo estar tranquilo hasta que...

M. **PLANES PARA EL FIN DE SEMANA** Trabajando con un(a) compañero(a) de clase, terminen las siguientes oraciones de una manera relevante para Uds.

MODELO: No voy al cine a menos que...
              No voy al cine a menos que *tú me pagues la entrada.*
     o: No voy al cine a menos que *haya alguna película interesante.*

1. Voy a ver una película este fin de semana con tal de que...
2. (No) Voy a mirar un programa deportivo a menos que...
3. Espero ver _____ con tal que...
4. Mis amigos y yo no podemos ver _____ sin que...
5. Quiero ver _____ después de que...

N. **ENTREVISTA** Hazle a otro(a) estudiante las siguientes preguntas sobre el futuro.

1. ¿Qué vas a hacer cuando termines tus estudios?
2. ¿Qué tienes que hacer antes de terminarlos?
3. ¿Piensas casarte algún día? (¿Sí? ¿Cuándo piensas casarte? ¿Con quién?)
   (¿No? ¿Prefieres vivir solo[a] o con otra persona?)
4. ¿Qué vas a hacer tan pronto como consigas un trabajo bueno?
5. ¿Vas a tener una familia grande con tal de que la puedas mantener?
6. ¿Hasta qué edad piensas trabajar? ¿Qué vas a hacer después de que te jubiles?

VOCABULARIO: *Las artes*

ESCENAS DEL FESTIVAL INTERNACIONAL DE TEATRO EN MANTA, ECUADOR[1] In this
section you will learn how to talk about performing and visual arts and literature.

la arquitectura *architecture*	**la música** *music*	**la pintura** *painting*
el concierto *concert*	**la obra (de arte)** *work (of*	**la poesía** *poetry*
la escultura *sculpture*	*art)*	**el teatro** *theater*
la fotografía *photography*	**la ópera** *opera*	
la literatura *literature*	**el papel** *role*	

Los artistas   *Artists*

el (la) arquitecto(a)	**el (la) escritor(a)** *writer*	**el (la) fotógrafo(a)**
architect	**el (la) escultor(a)** *sculptor*	*photographer*
el (la) autor(a) *author*		**el (la) poeta** *poet*

⏩

---

[1] The cities of Manta, Quito, Guayaquil, and Cuenca represent the hubs of professional and semiprofes-
sional theatrical and artistic activity in Ecuador. For the past eight years Manta has hosted the **Festival
Internacional de Teatro.** Malayerba and La Trinchera, among the national groups that participate in
this gathering, have established a significant following.

Verbos

dirigir *to direct* **esculpir** *to sculpt* **interpretar** *to play a role*

Adjetivos

clásico(a) *classical* **moderno(a)** *modern* **popular** *popular*
folklórico(a) *folkloric*

Palabras útiles

el escenario *stage* el guión *script* la obra maestra *masterpiece*

¡A practicar!

O. ASOCIACIONES Da una o dos palabras de la lista de vocabulario que se relaciona(n) con las siguientes vocaciones. Luego intenta formar una oración con las palabras.

MODELO: el dramaturgo
el drama, el director, dirigir
El dramaturgo escribió el drama que el director está dirigiendo.

1. el poeta
2. la bailarina
3. el pintor
4. la cantante
5. el compositor
6. el músico
7. la actriz
8. el escultor

P. OBRAS FAMOSAS En grupos de cuatro personas, indiquen qué tipo de arte representan las siguientes obras y den cualquier información que tengan sobre cada una. Pregúntenle al (a la) profesor(a) o busquen en el Internet si no saben.

1. los retratos *(portraits)* de Frida Kahlo
2. «La Traviata»
3. *Cien años de soledad*
4. *The Bald Soprano*
5. la obra de Rubén Darío
6. «Guernica»
7. *Don Quijote de la Mancha*
8. las estatuas de Botero

Q. ¿EN QUÉ MEDIO TRABAJAN? Abajo hay una lista de artistas de todos tipos. En grupos de tres o cuatro personas, intenten averiguar qué tipo de arte hace cada uno. Si no saben, pidan ayuda a su profesor(a).

1. Wilfredo Lam
2. Frida Kahlo
3. Ricky Martin
4. Federico García Lorca
5. Jimmy Smits
6. Pedro Almodóvar
7. Oswaldo Guayasamín
8. Antonio Gaudí
9. Miguel de Cervantes
10. Salma Hayek

R. MIS SUEÑOS En los siguientes cuatro párrafos, cuatro jóvenes hablan de sus esperanzas profesionales y artísticas. Completa sus historias con las siguientes palabras.

ballet escritora poesía papel pintura canción cuadros
concierto escultura música músico director danza drama
ópera obra de arte

Carlos Manuel: Yo soy Carlos y quiero ser _____ en una orquesta grande algún día. Me fascina la idea de tocar en un _____ muy importante. Prefiero la música moderna, pero también me gusta la _____ clásica, sobre todo la _____. Mi _____ favorita es «El majo» del compositor español Enrique Granados.

Micaela: Yo soy una persona muy dramática. El _____ para mí es el mejor arte para explorar la condición humana. El _____ de la nueva obra teatral «Arte» va a darme el _____ principal —¡estoy muy contenta! La _____ de «Arte» es una mujer muy talentosa. Ella es dramaturga, pero también es poeta —escribe _____ en su tiempo libre.

José Eduardo: Hola, yo soy José y me encanta pintar. Tengo una colección de _____ que pinté yo mismo. Como no soy muy buen escultor, no quiero hacer _____. Mi medio preferido es la _____. Mi _____ favorita es «La jungla» de Wilfredo Lam.[1]

Tere Carmen: Yo me llamo Tere, y me encanta bailar. Yo creo que la _____ es la mejor manera de expresar las emociones con el cuerpo. Aunque me gusta la danza moderna, prefiero el _____ porque requiere mucha disciplina.

En voz alta

S. ACTIVIDADES ARTÍSTICAS ¿Eres artista? Escoge cuatro de las siguientes actividades artísticas que son importantes para ti y luego explícaselas a un(a) compañero(a) de clase. Debes mencionar con qué frecuencia las haces y si tienes un papel en la producción de un proyecto específico.

MODELO: la poesía
Escribo poesía de vez en cuando. El semestre pasado escribí cinco poemas sobre mis experiencias en Bolivia. Voy a publicarlos en la revista escolar.

1. el teatro
2. el baile
3. la pintura
4. la música
5. la escultura
6. la fotografía
7. la televisión
8. la arquitectura
9. ¿ ?

T. REACCIONES Forma preguntas para hacer a dos compañeros(as) de clase sobre sus reacciones a los siguientes medios artísticos y oportunidades. Usa los verbos de la lista para formar tus preguntas.

apreciar aburrir gustar preferir encantar interesar molestar fascinar

MODELO: ir a un museo de arte moderno
E1: *¿Les interesa ir a un museo de arte moderno?*
E2: *No. A mí no me gusta el arte moderno.*
E3: *Sí. Prefiero el arte moderno. Me encantan los cuadros de Picasso.*

1. ver programas de la televisión pública
2. ir a una galería de escultura
3. asistir a funciones teatrales
4. hablar con artistas sobre su obra
5. aprender sobre las obras maestras de la pintura clásica
6. ver un espectáculo de baile folklórico
7. ir a un ballet clásico
8. visitar el taller de un(a) artista
9. escuchar música clásica
10. ver una ópera

U. MI ARTISTA FAVORITO Con un(a) compañero(a) de clase, hagan una lista de preguntas para entrevistar a su artista favorito. Las preguntas pueden tratar

---

[1] Wilfredo Lam (1902–1982) was a Cuban-born artist who spent many years of his career between Madrid, Paris, and Cuba. "La jungla" is a famous painting of his, and it caused great scandal upon being viewed for the first time.

de su arte, sus inspiraciones, sus sueños o cualquier tema que les interese sobre esta persona. Después de hacer la lista de preguntas, un(a) estudiante toma el papel del artista y el otro le hace las preguntas.

MODELO: *Carlos Santana*
E1: *Carlos, ¿cuándo empezó Ud. a tener interés en la música?*
E2: *Empecé a tener interés en la música desde muy joven.*
E1: *¿Quién para Ud. es un modelo importante en su música?*
E2: *La música de B.B. King me influyó mucho.*

V. ENTREVISTA Hazle las siguientes preguntas a un(a) compañero(a) de clase.

1. ¿Eres una persona artística? ¿Por qué (no) es importante el arte en tu vida? ¿Has hecho algo artístico recientemente? ¿Quieres ser artista algún día? ¿Has hablado con un(a) artista profesional? ¿Es famosa esta persona?

2. ¿Te identificas con un(a) artista en particular? ¿Por qué te atrae *(attract)* el estilo o la obra de esa persona? ¿Piensas que es difícil ser artista? ¿Tiene que sufrir el artista para que produzca una obra buena?

3. ¿Qué piensas del arte popular? En tu opinión, ¿tiene algún mérito o importancia? ¿Es demasiado comercializado el arte de hoy? ¿Qué efecto va a tener la tecnología sobre el arte en el futuro?

ENCUENTRO *cultural*

Oswaldo Guayasamín

Éstas son unas nuevas palabras para la lectura:

deslumbrar   *to dazzle*
la raíz   *root*
los desamparados   *defenseless people*
el retrato al óleo   *oil painting*

Para pensar: ¿Conoces a un pintor de tu país con quién se podría comparar a Guayasamín? Pensando en lo que Guayasamín ha pintado, ¿crees que se puede hablar de una ideología predominante en su obra?

El pintor ecuatoriano Oswaldo Guayasamín (1919–1999) dibujó y pintó desde los siete años, y a los 12 años **deslumbró** a maestros y compañeros por su capacidad creativa y su vocación de trabajo. Su primera exposición individual la realizó antes de graduarse. Luego se dedicó a la búsqueda de la identidad del continente americano y trataba de encontrar las **raíces** que diferenciaban a los anglosajones de los aborígenes y mestizos que vivían en las tierras desde el Río Bravo hasta la Patagonia —su tierra.

Este artista ecuatoriano es uno de los más representativos del continente sudamericano. Todas sus obras constituyen un monumento dedicado a la humanidad, a los que sufren, a **los desamparados** y a los inocentes. Guayasamín pintó una variedad de temas antes de crear su primera gran obra, «El camino del Llanto». Los cuadros que pertenecen a esa época constituyen la selección denominada «Retrospectiva». Su técnica era impresionante. Hay **retratos al óleo** hechos en solamente 20 minutos; tienen la misma calidad que las obras que Guayasamín tardaba hasta tres horas en hacer.

En las últimas décadas, Guayasamín ha pintado retratos de figuras públicas como Rigoberta Menchú, Fidel Castro y Danielle Mittérand. En particular, le interesa pintar a las personas conocidas por su lucha por los derechos humanos.

1. ¿Quién era Guayasamín?
2. ¿A quién le dedicaba Guayasamín sus obras?
3. Mira la foto de la obra de Guayasamín. ¿Qué emociones te hace sentir?

GRAMÁTICA II: *No-fault se*

Using the no-fault *se* to describe unplanned or accidental events

In addition to using **se** for reflexive constructions, impersonal expressions, and reciprocal actions, Spanish speakers also use **se** to mark events in which a person is subjected to an occurrence outside of his or her control. Rather than assign responsibility for, say, losing keys, Spanish speakers may portray a person as the victim of an action. Consider the following:

Responsible for action

Yo perdí las llaves de mi casa.   *I lost the keys to my house.*

Victim of action

Se me perdieron las llaves de   *The keys to my house were (got)*
mi casa.   *lost.*

Forming the no-fault *se* construction

1. In order to portray someone as a victim of circumstance, an indirect object **(me, te, le, nos, os, les)** is used to identify the person(s) to whom the event occurred. The indirect object pronoun immediately follows the **se** that begins all constructions of this type.

a + *noun* or *pronoun*	**se**	*indirect object pronoun*	*verb*	*subject*
A Juan	se	le	cayó	el vaso.
A mí	se	me	olvidaron	las gafas.
A nosotros	se	nos	acabó	el tiempo.

2. The verb is always conjugated in either the third-person singular or third-person plural and normally in the preterite tense, although the verb can occur in other tenses as well. In the examples above, **el vaso, las gafas,** and **el tiempo** serve as the grammatical subjects of the sentences and require third-person conjugations of the verbs.[1] It may be helpful to think of these verbs as functioning like the verbs **gustar, molestar,** and **encantar.** The only difference is that an extra **se** is added before the indirect object pronoun to stress the accidental or unintentional nature of the event. In effect, **se** makes the verb passive.

Verbs commonly used in no-fault **se** constructions are:

acabar	*to finish, to run out*	**perder (ie)**	*to lose*
caer	*to fall*	**quedar**	*to remain, to be left*
escapar	*to escape*	**romper**	*to break*
olvidar	*to forget*		

---

[1] With the verb **olvidar**, it is also possible to use an infinitive as the grammatical subject: **Se me olvidó entregar la tarea.** *(I forgot to hand in the homework.)* When negating these constructions, place the **no** before the se: **No se me olvidó entregar la tarea.** *(I didn't forget to hand in the homework.)*

¡A practicar!

X. EN EL TALLER DEL MAESTRO OSWALDO Beto es un asistente incompetente que trabaja en el taller *(workshop)* del famoso artista de Quito, Oswaldo Guayasamín. Convierte las siguientes oraciones a construcciones con el *no-fault* **se,** según el modelo.

MODELO: Beto perdió las llaves del taller. (perder)
A Beto se le perdieron las llaves del taller.

1. Beto no recordó llamar a los clientes. (olvidar)
2. Beto no compró la pintura suficiente para el proyecto. (olvidar)
3. Beto dejó caer *(dropped)* los pinceles *(brushes).* (caer)
4. Beto rompió las jarras *(jars)* que pintaba el maestro. (romper)
5. Beto no puede encontrar los atriles *(easels).* (perder)
6. Beto dejó escapar el gato favorito del maestro. (escapar)

Y. ¡YO TAMBIÉN QUIERO SER ASISTENTE! Carmela busca un trabajo nuevo. Quiere trabajar en el taller del maestro Guayasamín. Ella sabe que su asistente Beto tiene muchos problemas en el taller y que ella podría *(she could)* hacer su trabajo mucho mejor que Beto. Termina su historia con el *no-fault* **se. ¡Ojo!** Es necesario usar verbos en el presente y en el pasado.

Yo soy Carmela, y quiero ser asistente del gran maestro Oswaldo. A mí nunca _____ (caer) la pintura por el suelo, y nunca _____ (romper) las cosas frágiles; yo siempre tengo mucho cuidado. Cuando era niña yo tenía un gato que _____ (escapar) de la casa, pero ahora soy más responsable que antes. Tengo muy buena memoria. A mí nunca _____ (olvidar) las fechas importantes. Siempre sé dónde está todo —tampoco _____ (perder) las cosas importantes, como las llaves del taller. Ay, ¡caramba! Quería dejarle al maestro mi currículum, pero _____ (quedar) en casa. Tengo que irme, porque tengo una cita en cinco minutos; _____ (acabar) el tiempo. ¡Hasta luego!

En voz alta

Z. UN DÍA DESASTROSO PARA EL MAESTRO El maestro Oswaldo acaba de tener un día difícil. Forma una oración de tipo *no-fault* **se** para explicar los eventos desafortunados que se les ocurrieron a él y a su asistente.

AA. ¡A MÍ NUNCA! Tú quieres convencer a tu compañero(a) de clase que eres una persona muy responsable, pero claro, ¡todos somos humanos y cometemos errores de vez en cuando! Habla con él o ella de las siguientes preguntas, contestándolas de una manera honesta.

1. ¿**Se te perdió** algo alguna vez?
2. ¿**Se te olvidó** alguna vez una cita importante?
3. ¿A ti nunca **se te rompió** una cerámica o algo frágil?
4. ¿**Se te perdió** alguna vez algo de mucho valor?
5. ¿Nunca **se te cayó** un florero *(vase)* o algo parecido?
6. ¿**Se te acabó** alguna vez el dinero en una situación importante?

ASÍ SE DICE: *Using the past participle to describe completed actions or resulting conditions*

In **Capítulo 10** you learned how to form the past participle of verbs in order to generate the present perfect tense. The past participle can also be used as an adjective to modify a noun. When used as an adjective, the past participle must agree in number and in gender with the noun that it modifies.

Voy a escuchar **canciones escritas** en español.
*I'm going to listen to **songs written** in Spanish.*

Ramón tiene dos **cuadros pintados** en Ecuador.
*Ramón has two **paintings painted** in Ecuador.*

The past participle is also frequently used with the verbs **estar** and **ser.** When used with the verb **estar,** the emphasis is placed on the result of an action of the verb, as opposed to the action itself. When a past participle is used with the verb **ser,** the emphasis is placed on the action rather than the result of the action; Spanish speakers often use the preposition **por** with this agent of the action. Compare the following examples:

Result of an action
La puerta **está cerrada.**   *The door **is closed.***

Emphasis on the action itself
La puerta **fue cerrada por el dueño**   *The door **was closed by the owner**
  de la casa.   of the house.*

Remember that the following verbs have irregular past participle forms:

abrir **abierto**	escribir **escrito**	resolver **resuelto**
cubrir **cubierto**	hacer **hecho**	romper **roto**
decir **dicho**	morir **muerto**	ver **visto**
descubrir **descubierto**	poner **puesto**	volver **vuelto**

¡A practicar!

BB. ¿CÓMO ESTÁ LA CLASE? Indica si las siguientes oraciones son ciertas o falsas para tu clase en este momento.

1. Las ventanas están abiertas.
2. Todos los libros de los estudiantes están cerrados.

3. Las luces están apagadas.
4. El (La) profesor(a) está sentado(a).
5. Hay algunas palabras escritas en la pizarra.
6. Todos los estudiantes tienen los zapatos puestos.
7. Algo en la clase está roto.
8. Las persianas *(blinds)* están cerradas.
9. Los estudiantes están muertos de hambre.
10. Mi tarea para hoy ya está hecha.

CC. **¿QUIÉN LO HIZO?** Convierte las siguientes oraciones en frases que contienen el verbo **ser** + el participio pasado y también indica quién hizo las siguientes acciones con **por** + agente.

MODELO: Julia puso la mochila del instructor debajo de la mesa.
La mochila del instructor fue puesta debajo de la mesa por Julia.

1. Cindy resolvió los problemas con la luz.
2. Anne descubrió el secreto de un artista famoso.
3. Tim vio los cuadros en la exposición antes de clase.
4. Un ladrón *(theif)* rompió las ventanas del taller.
5. Keith puso los pinceles en el escritorio del instructor.
6. Tony hizo un anuncio a la clase.
7. Silvia dijo la verdad sobre unos cuadros misteriosos.
8. Antes de salir del taller, el instructor cubrió los cuadros.
9. Un estudiante rompió la computadora.

DD. **¿FUE HECHO POR QUIÉN?** Contesta las siguientes preguntas usando la construcción **ser** + participio pasado.

MODELO: ¿Quién escribió *Don Quijote de la Mancha*? (Cervantes)
Don Quijote *fue escrito por Cervantes.*

1. ¿Quién pintó el cuadro «Les demoiselles d'Avignon»? (Picasso)
2. ¿Quién escribió el poema «Las alturas de Machu Picchu»? (Pablo Neruda)[1]
3. ¿Quién abrió el museo La Reina Sofía en Madrid? (La Reina Sofía)
4. ¿Quién dirigió la película «Todo sobre mi madre»? (Pedro Almodóvar)
5. ¿Quién hizo el papel de Selena en la película sobre su vida? (Jennifer López)

En voz alta

EE. **PREGUNTAS DEL MAESTRO** Imagínate que eres Beto, el asistente del maestro Oswaldo. Contesta las siguientes preguntas indicando que todo su trabajo ya está hecho. Si hubo algún accidente, échale la culpa al gato del maestro utilizando **ser** + participio pasado.

MODELOS: ¿Has cerrado las ventanas del taller?
Sí, profesor. Todas las ventanas están cerradas.

¿Comiste la manzana que dejé en la mesa?
No, la manzana fue comida por el gato.

---

[1] Although the Chilean poet and Nobel Prize winner Pablo Neruda is not Peruvian, one of his most famous works exalts the beauty of Peru's Machu Picchu.

1. ¿Vendiste los dos cuadros?
2. ¿Has sacado la basura?
3. ¿Rompiste este pincel?
4. ¿Devolviste todos los recibos *(receipts)* del mes al banco?
5. ¿Has escrito todas las cartas?
6. ¿Descubriste aquel ratón *(mouse)* que está debajo de mi escritorio?
7. ¿Abriste tú la ventana aunque hace tanto frío?
8. ¿Cubriste los cuadros que terminé ayer con las sábanas *(sheets)*?
9. ¿Preparaste las pinturas para hoy?
10. ¿Pusiste el periódico encima de las pinturas?

FF. **ACCIDENTES MEMORABLES E INVENTADOS** Cuéntale a un(a) compañero(a) de clase tres accidentes memorables. Primero describe la situación antes de que ocurriera el accidente y luego indica lo que pasó.

MODELO: *Una taza de café estaba puesta encima de algunos libros en mi escritorio. Luego se me cayó la taza sobre mi proyecto final para la clase de español.*

Síntesis

¡A ver!

El **Capítulo 13** se centra en el tema del espectáculo incluyendo el baile, la música, la canción y el arte. También abarca *(includes)* el mundo de la televisión, la radio, el teatro y el cine. Nuestro presentador de los segmentos de video se llama Carlos y él es dueño de un bar-salón de espectáculos en Cuzco, Perú. Carlos nos va a hablar del mundo del espectáculo en los países hispanos, especialmente en Perú.

ACTIVIDAD 1   **Pre-viewing task (Segmento 1 del video)**

Paso 1: En el primer segmento del video, vas a ver una serie de ocho clips cortos, cada uno enfocado en un aspecto del mundo del espectáculo. Para cada clip, apunta en la siguiente tabla la información que identifica el tipo de espectáculo que es.

MODELO: *grupo de dos cantantes y tres músicos; guitarra; música tradicional; en un restaurante*

Los espectáculos
1.
2.
3.
4.
5.
6.
7.
8.

Paso 2: Con un(a) compañero(a) de clase, haz una descripción de cada uno de los clips de video utilizando la información que tienes en la tabla. Tu compañero(a) puede decir si está de acuerdo o no con tu descripción.

ACTIVIDAD 2   Pre-viewing task (Segmento 2 del video)

Paso 1: ¿Te gustaría trabajar en la televisión? Si tu respuesta es positiva, ¿qué te gustaría hacer en la televisión? Si tu respuesta es negativa, ¿por qué no te gustaría trabajar en la televisión? Apunta tus ideas en un papel.

Paso 2: Intercambia tus ideas con un(a) compañero(a) de clase. ¿Tienes las cualidades necesarias, tanto educativas como personales y profesionales, para poder trabajar en la televisión? Si no tienes esas cualidades, es posible que tengas que prepararte antes de entrar en la televisión. Utilizando palabras y expresiones como **a menos que, con tal de que, sin que, para que, aunque, antes de que, hasta que** y **tan pronto como** (ver **Gramática I** de este capítulo), explica a tu compañero(a) lo que tienes que hacer para prepararte antes de empezar una carrera en la televisión.

MODELO: *No tengo la educación necesaria para entrar en la televisión a menos que haga un Master's en producción de televisión.*

ACTIVIDAD 3   Viewing task (Segmento 2 del video)

En el segundo segmento del video, vas a conocer a Fernando Cuña. Fernando trabaja en la televisión chilena. Actualmente ocupa los cargos de productor de televisión y director ejecutivo y socio *(business partner)* de una productora independiente *(independent production company)* de televisión chilena.

Paso 1: En la primera parte de este segmento del video, Fernando relata su carrera en el mundo de la televisión hasta sus cargos actuales. Completa la tabla con los cinco puestos de trabajo que faltan.

La carrera de Fernando Cuña
1. Ayudante en un programa de concursos que se llamaba «Sábado gigante»
2.
3.
4.
5.
6.
7 . Socio en la compañía Nueva Imagen

Paso 2: En la próxima parte de la entrevista, Fernando habla de sus éxitos profesionales. Mira la lista de compañías estadounidenses, todas relacionadas con el mundo del espectáculo, e identifica (a) cuáles son mencionadas por Fernando, y (b) por qué son mencionadas.

Billboard	MTV		ESPN
		NBC	
Discovery Channel			Travel Channel
Disney Channel		Time	HBO

ACTIVIDAD 4 **Post-viewing task (Segmento 2 del video)**

Paso 1: Compara la información que tienes sobre Fernando Cuña con la de un(a) compañero(a) de clase.

Paso 2: Con tu compañero(a) de clase, escriban un texto corto con el siguiente título: ¿Quién es Fernando Cuña? Pueden utilizar el siguiente esquema *(outline)* para estructurar su texto:

- pequeña introducción con datos personales sobre Fernando
- posición actual que ocupa
- trabajos que ha tenido durante su carrera en la televisión
- algunos de los éxitos profesionales que ha tenido
- pequeña conclusión

¡A leer!

Following a chronology

Diaries, anecdotes, and short stories usually contain a series of interrelated actions and events, including the writer's opinions. These kinds of narrative descriptions require the reader to follow a chronology. The central questions implicit in most narrations are:

- What happened?
- Where, when, and how did it happen?
- To whom did it occur, why, and for how long?
- What else was going on at the same time?

Paso 1: Lee el cuento que sigue. Luego, contesta las tres preguntas.

1. ¿Qué tipo de literatura es el cuento?
2. ¿Cree el autor que la chancha encantada realmente existe?
3. ¿En qué orden ocurrió cada evento en el cuento? Escribe los números 1 a 4 en los espacios apropiados.

_____ The tremendous pig became furious and began to attack.
_____ The master plumber was hired to do a water installation.
_____ The plumber drove his pickax into the pig.
_____ The plumber and his assistant were walking home at 3:00 in the morning.

4. ¿Cómo se termina el cuento?

La literatura oral o mágica comprende los mitos _(myths)_, los cuentos y las leyendas _(legends)_. Nació antes de la literatura escrita y se ha trasmitido de padres a hijos desde tiempos muy remotos. Toda la comunidad toma parte en su creación y su transmisión a través de las generaciones. El propósito de esta literatura popular es enseñar el origen de los antepasados _(ancestors)_, morales, hechos heroicos, etcétera. El siguiente cuento nos presenta una leyenda popular de Pacasmayo, una ciudad en el norte de Perú.

La chancha encantada°

El siguiente relato° no es producto de mentes° infantiles ni alucinación de gentes enfermizas, ¡Es la vivencia de personas serias y bien ilustradas°!

La primera vez que oí hablar de la misteriosa chancha fue de boca del profesor Alberto. Me dio fechas y lugares donde había tenido encuentros con dicho animal. En cierta ocasión varios amigos tuvieron la osadía° de tirarle lazo logrando° tenerla por unos momentos en la soga,° pero la soga se rompió y el animal se largó...° Los lugares que con frecuencia aparece es por la primera cuadra de Larco Herrera y 2 de Mayo.

Lo que sigue es el relato de un maestro gasfitero° quien vivió en carne propia° una inolvidable° experiencia con la misteriosa chancha.

«...Hace ya varios años cuando tuve un mal encuentro con la chancha, sucedió así: El señor Arana solicitó mis servicios para hacerle una instalación de agua. Como el trabajo no se podía hacer en el día, arreglé para trabajar en la noche, porque a esa hora cortaban el agua y así se podía trabajar con tranquilidad. Me demoré° en el trabajo más de lo que pensé hacerlo. Sería cerca de las 3:00 de la mañana que regresábamos a casa yo y mi ayudante.° Estábamos por la calle Leoncio Prado para dar la vuelta a° la calle Ayacucho cuando nos encontramos con una tremenda chanchaza. Al verse perturbada, muy furiosa se venía a atacarnos. No pudimos correr —los pies se paralizaron. Ni articulamos palabra alguna.° Lo único que atiné° era a defenderme con mi barretilla° que traía al hombro. Cuando la chancha me atacó, le clavé° mi barretilla prendida en su cuerpo, y oí que un poco más allá cayó al suelo. Nosotros nos quedamos como plantados en el mismo sitio donde nos había sorprendido. Cuando volvimos en sí,° fui a recoger mi barretilla. ¡Cuánto no sería mi sorpresa! La punta que había entrado en el cuerpo del animal estaba convertida en... »

The haunted pig

cuento / _minds_
learned, knowledgeable

audacity, daring / succeeding
rope / got away

master plumber /
in the flesh / unforgettable

I was delayed

assistant / to turn onto

Nor could we say a word. /
The only thing I could
do. / pickax / I stuck, drove

When we came back to our
senses

Paso 2: Lee el cuento una vez más y contesta las preguntas que siguen.

1. ¿Cuál es el tema principal del cuento?
2. ¿Cuál es tu interpretación de la última frase?
3. ¿Conoces algún cuento o leyenda de la cultura estadounidense que tenga semejanzas con «La chancha encantada»?

¡A escribir!

Writing a critical essay

Paso 1: Every day we evaluate many conditions, situations, and people. Occasionally, we write down our comments and opinions about them. In this section you will write a critical essay related to one or more of the topics you discussed in this chapter. When beginning to write a critical essay, the following guidelines will help you get started:

1. Choose a subject or topic that interests you.
2. Write a brief introduction about the subject you choose.
3. List three or four things that you like about your subject.
4. Think of one or two things that could be done realistically to improve your subject. Write these ideas down.
5. Come to a conclusion about your subject.

Paso 2: For example, consider the following essay a student wrote about the art and history museum in her city. Note how she includes the information described in the above guidelines.

El Museo de Historia y Arte de mi ciudad es muy interesante. Me gustan las exposiciones de arte por artistas locales. Cada martes a las 12:15 de la tarde, hay un evento especial en el museo. Por ejemplo, la semana pasada un señor presentó una charla interesante sobre el arte de Egipto. En verano el museo tiene conciertos de música clásica. Me gusta comer un sándwich y escuchar la música. No cuesta nada entrar en el museo. ¡Eso me gusta mucho! Pero también hay algo que no me gusta mucho: no cambia con suficiente frecuencia algunas de las exposiciones, que duran por tres o cuatro meses.

En general, me gusta mucho el Museo de Historia y Arte. Aprendo mucho allí y me divierto al mismo tiempo.

Functions: Writing an essay; Writing an introduction; Writing a conclusion; Expressing an opinion
Vocabulary: Arts; Poetry; Prose; Musical instruments
Grammar: Verbs: subjunctive

Paso 3: Ahora te toca a ti. Escribe un ensayo crítico en español, teniendo en cuenta *(taking into account)* las ideas descritas en la sección anterior. Elige un tema para tu ensayo de la siguiente lista de ideas:

- una pintura famosa
- un poema
- un cuento corto
- una novela
- una película
- un programa de televisión
- un museo de arte en tu cuidad

¡A conversar!

Paso 1: Hoy día, muchas personas consideran que la televisión es el medio de comunicación más popular. Teniendo en cuenta el papel de la televisión en nuestra sociedad, pregúntale a un(a) compañero(a) de clase acerca de sus preferencias y sus hábitos con la tele. Por ejemplo:

- ¿Ve él (ella) la televisión con frecuencia?
- ¿Cuántas horas a la semana pasa tu compañero(a) frente al televisor aproximadamente?
- ¿Qué tipo de programa prefiere: las comedias, las películas, los deportes, las noticias, las telenovelas, los concursos, los videos musicales, etcétera?

Paso 2: Luego, cambien de papel. Para finalizar, presenta a la clase un informe sobre las respuestas de tu compañero(a).

Programas y películas *Programs and movies*

el anuncio *commercial*
el canal *channel (TV)*
el cine *movies; movie theater*
la comedia *comedy*
el dibujo animado *cartoon*
el documental *documentary*
la función musical *musical (play)*

las noticias *news*
la película *movie, film*
 clásica *classic film*
 de acción *action film*
 de arte *art film*
 de ciencia ficción *science fiction film*
 de horror *horror film*

de intriga (misterio) *mystery film*
del oeste *western film*
extranjera *foreign film*
romántica *romantic film*
el programa de concursos *game show*
el programa de entrevistas *talk show*

el programa deportivo *sports program*
el pronóstico del tiempo *weather report (forecast)*
la telenovela *soap opera*

Verbos

aburrir *to bore*
apreciar *to appreciate*

dejar *to leave; to let, to allow*

molestar *to bother*

poner *to turn on (TV); to show (a movie)*

Las artes *The arts*

la arquitectura *architecture*
el ballet *ballet*
la danza *dance*
el drama *drama, play*
la canción *song*

el concierto *concert*
el cuadro *painting*
la escultura *sculpture*
la fotografía *photography*
la literatura *literature*

la música *music*
la obra (de arte) *work (of art)*
la ópera *opera*
el papel *role*

la pintura *painting*
la poesía *poetry*
el teatro *theater*

Los artistas *Artists*

el actor *actor*
la actriz *actress*
el (la) arquitecto(a) *architect*
el (la) autor(a) *author*
el bailarín *dancer*

la bailarina *dancer*
el (la) cantante *singer*
el (la) compositor(a) *composer*
el (la) director(a) *director*

el (la) dramaturgo(a) *playwright*
el (la) escritor(a) *writer*
el (la) escultor(a) *sculptor*

el (la) fotógrafo(a) *photographer*
el (la) músico *musician*
el (la) pintor(a) *painter*
el (la) poeta *poet*

Verbos

dirigir *to direct*

esculpir *to sculpt*

interpretar *to play a role*

Adjetivos

clásico(a) *classical*

folklórico(a) *folkloric*

moderno(a) *modern*

popular *popular*

Conjunciones *Conjunctions*

a fin de que *so that*
a menos que *unless*
antes (de) que *before*
aunque *although, even though*

con tal (de) que *provided (that)*
cuando *when*
después (de) que *after*
en caso (de) que *in case (of)*

en cuanto *as soon as*
hasta que *until*
para que *so (that)*

tan pronto como *as soon as*
sin que *without*

14

CAPÍTULO

La vida pública:
Chile

Communicative goals

In this chapter you will learn how to . . .

- Talk about politics and elections
- Use the simple future tense to talk about future events
- Talk about political issues and the media
- Express conjecture or probability with the future tense and the conditional
- Use the present perfect in the subjunctive mood

Grammar

- The simple future tense
- The conditional
- Present perfect subjunctive

Cultural information

- El gobierno de Chile
- La libertad de la prensa

La Plaza de la Constitución, Santiago, Chile

EL PROCESO POLÍTICO EN LA PLAZA DE ARMAS[1] In this section you will learn how to talk about politics and elections.

el congreso *congress*	**la dictadura** *dictatorship*	**el poder** *power*
el debate *debate*	**el ejército** *army*	**el (la) presidente**
el deber *duty*	**el gobierno** *government*	*president*
la democracia *democracy*	**la ley** *law*	**la reforma** *reform*
el (la) dictador(a) *dictator*	**la paz** *peace*	

Verbos

apoyar *to support*	**discutir** *to discuss*	**oponer** *to oppose*
aprobar (ue) *to approve;*	**elegir (i, i)** *to elect*	**votar** *to vote*
to pass	**firmar** *to sign*	
defender (ie) *to defend*	**gobernar (ie)** *to govern*	

Adjetivos

conservador *conservative*	**liberal** *liberal*	**republicano** *republican*
demócrata *democratic*		

Palabras útiles

el (la) alcalde(sa) *mayor*	**la cámara de representantes (diputados)** *house of representatives*	**la constitución** *constitution* **el (la) diputado(a)** *representative*

➡ **Palabras útiles** are for recognition only; you will not be tested on these words. However, you might find some of these words useful for talking about politics.

⏩

---

[1] The **Plaza de Armas** is the most important public commons of Santiago, Chile. The main cathedral of the city as well as the **Museo Histórico Nacional** and the central post office are located around the plaza.

el (la) gobernador(a) *governor*
los grupos paramilitares *paramilitary groups*
los guerrilleros *guerrillas*
la ideología *ideology*
el (la) ministro *minister*
la monarquía *monarchy*
el senado *senate*
el (la) senador(a) *senator*

¡A practicar!

A. **DEFINICIONES** Empareja las palabras a la izquierda con la definición correcta a la derecha.

1. _____ aprobar
2. _____ el congreso
3. _____ la dictadura
4. _____ el gobierno
5. _____ los políticos
6. _____ el ejército
7. _____ las elecciones
8. _____ democrático

a. el cuerpo político que controla un país o un estado
b. un tipo de gobierno conservador que cuenta con el apoyo del ejército
c. un cuerpo armado que defiende el país
d. el proceso en el cual se determina quién va a gobernar en el futuro
e. una división del gobierno
f. una orientación política que refleja el apoyo y los intereses de los ciudadanos
g. permitir que algo se realice
h. las personas que gobiernan el país

B. **LA VIDA DE SALVADOR ALLENDE GOSSENS[1]** Pon los siguientes eventos en un orden lógico para organizar la historia de este líder chileno.

_____ Dio algunos discursos radicales mientras asistía a la escuela de medicina en la Universidad de Chile.
_____ Organizó el partido socialista de Chile y fue apoyado por el proletario de Chile.
_____ Los ciudadanos que le apoyaban dijeron que fue asesinado.
_____ Firmó varias leyes para la reforma de tierras.
_____ Nació el 26 de julio de 1908.
_____ El gobierno de Allende defendió los derechos *(rights)* de los mineros.
_____ En 1973 perdió el control del gobierno a Augusto Pinochet, un general conservador que tenía el apoyo del ejército.
_____ Fue elegido presidente de Chile en 1970.

C. **EL LARGO CAMINO HACIA LA PRESIDENCIA** Completa la historia abajo con las palabras de la lista.

discutir   debates   republicano   reformas   deber   liberal   campaña

1. Ricardo Lagos hizo una _____ para la presidencia en Chile en el año 1999. Ganó las elecciones de enero 2000.
2. Antes de las elecciones, muchas veces hay _____ para dar a los candidatos la oportunidad de _____ sus ideas.
3. El opuesto de un conservador en la política es generalmente un _____.
4. En los Estados Unidos, el partido _____ es el partido más conservador.
5. Votar en las elecciones es el _____ de los ciudadanos.
6. Muchos políticos nuevos proponen _____ para mejorar una situación mala.

---

[1] Salvador Allende was president in Chile until the coup d'état in 1973 by Augusto Pinochet. Allende was a socialist president, and many of his followers were persecuted during the ensuing dictatorship. In January 2000, Ricardo Lagos was elected president of Chile. Lagos is the first socialist president that Chile has had since Pinochet seized power in 1973.

D. ORACIONES Forma seis oraciones completas combinando los elementos de las tres columnas.

MODELO: *El dictador aprobó el uso del poder militar para controlar el país.*

los partidos políticos	apoyar	el candidato
el presidente	elegir	el poder
el ejército	firmar	las leyes
el ciudadano	votar	las elecciones
el gobierno	gobernar	la reforma
el dictador	defender	la paz
el grupo conservador	aprobar	la dictadura

En voz alta

E. IDEAS Y REACCIONES Después de leer las siguientes opiniones, formula una respuesta empezando con las frases de abajo. ¡Ten cuidado con el subjuntivo!

MODELO: Sin un ejército, un país no puede tener poder internacional.
No es evidente que sin un ejército un país no pueda tener poder internacional. Costa Rica tiene mucho poder internacional sin un ejército.

(No) Estoy de acuerdo en que...	(No) Es evidente que...	Es (im)posible que...
(No) Dudo que...	Es una lástima que...	Es bueno (malo) que...

1. A veces hay que defender la paz con el ejército.
2. Los ciudadanos generalmente no apoyan las dictaduras.
3. Los políticos siempre mienten (*lie*).
4. Nuestro gobierno es demasiado conservador.
5. Nuestros partidos políticos representan las opiniones de todos los ciudadanos.
6. El congreso y el senado mantienen el equilibrio de poder en este país.
7. Los ciudadanos participan en las elecciones.
8. Los candidatos tienen plataformas llenas de promesas.
9. No hay corrupción en la política.
10. Los jóvenes son muy activos políticamente.

F. ¿ERES ACTIVO(A) EN LA POLÍTICA? Completa la siguiente encuesta. Después, en grupos de cuatro personas, comparen sus respuestas. Hablen de por qué participan (o no participan) en la política.

casi nunca = 0   a veces = 1   frecuentemente = 2   siempre = 3

____ Voto.
____ Participo en discusiones políticas.
____ Miro los debates entre los candidatos en la tele.
____ Escribo cartas a un(a) político(a).
____ Me identifico con un partido político.
____ Hago un esfuerzo para informarme sobre los candidatos antes de las elecciones.
____ Trabajo para un(a) candidato(a) o para un(a) político(a).
____ Las acciones del presidente de este país me afectan.
____ Sé lo que está pasando en otros países con respecto a la política.

INTERPRETACIONES
0–7   Debes matricularte en una clase de ciencias políticas.
8–15   Debes aprender más sobre el proceso político.
16–21   Tienes mucho conocimiento político.
22–27   Vas a tener un puesto político algún día.

G. OPINIONES POLÍTICAS Con un(a) compañero(a) de clase, tomen turnos haciéndose las siguientes preguntas el uno al otro para determinar sus preferencias políticas.

1. ¿Votaste en las últimas elecciones? ¿Ganó el (la) candidato(a) que apoyabas? ¿Qué opinas de las elecciones? ¿Piensas que siempre gana el (la) mejor candidato(a)? ¿Qué partido político mejor corresponde a tus ideas y necesidades?
2. ¿Cuáles son las ventajas (*advantages*) y desventajas de una democracia? ¿Es siempre la democracia el mejor sistema de gobierno? ¿Cuántas dictaduras hay en el mundo hoy en día? ¿Puedes nombrar algunos dictadores del siglo XX del mundo hispánico?
3. ¿Por qué no hemos tenido una mujer presidente en este país? En tu opinion, ¿pueden gobernar las mujeres igual o mejor que los hombres? ¿Quiénes son algunas mujeres que han sido elegidas para gobernar una nación? ¿Han tenido éxito?

H. ¡AHORA ES TU TURNO! Tú y un(a) compañero(a) son candidatos(as) para la presidencia. Uno de Uds. (Estudiante 1) es liberal, el (la) otro(a) (Estudiante 2), conservador(a). Sigan la plataforma abajo y hablen de sus diferentes puntos de vista según la información.

> **¿NOS ENTENDEMOS?**
>
> The idea of it being your turn to do something is also expressed by the phrase **te toca a ti.** To indicate this idea for other people, simply substitute the appropriate indirect object pronoun: **me toca a mí, les toca a ellos,** etc.

ESTUDIANTE 1: LIBERAL
1. La educación en las universidades debe ser gratis.
2. Cuidar a los pobres es el deber del gobierno.
3. Debemos pagar más impuestos (*taxes*) y tener seguro médico del gobierno.
4. Es importante controlar la industria y sus efectos en el medio ambiente. Tenemos que conservar la naturaleza.

ESTUDIANTE 2: CONSERVADOR(A)
1. La universidad es un privilegio. El gobierno no debe pagar los estudios.
2. Los pobres deben buscar trabajo si quieren casa y comida.
3. El seguro médico es un negocio y el gobierno no debe pagarlo para la gente. No debemos pagar más impuestos; ya pagamos bastantes.
4. El gobierno no tiene nada que ver con la industria y el medio ambiente. Todos tenemos que ser responsables con la tierra sin leyes del gobierno.

EN CONTEXTO

Son las 3:00 de la tarde en la Plaza de las Armas en Santiago, Chile. Allí, Marina, una estudiante ecuatoriana, reconoce a un chico que vio en la recepción de su hotel en la mañana.

MARINA: Perdona. Creo que te vi esta mañana en el Hotel Imperial.
ÓSCAR: ¡Sí, es cierto! Soy Óscar.
MARINA: Mucho gusto, Óscar. Soy Marina.
ÓSCAR: Encantado. Espero que hayas venido (*have come*) para la manifestación (*demonstration*).
MARINA: ¡Ah! Por eso hay tanta gente aquí. Bueno, la verdad es que quería sacar unas fotos de la plaza, pero aprovecharé (*I will take advantage*) de la ocasión y sacaré (*I will take*) unas fotos de la manifestación.
ÓSCAR: Mira, no es un espectáculo (*show*). Protestaremos la violación de los derechos humanos en nuestro país. Estamos aquí por razones bien serias.
MARINA: Lo siento, Óscar. No sabía que sería (*it would be*) algo tan importante.
ÓSCAR: Está bien. No eres de aquí, ¿verdad?
MARINA: Soy de Ecuador, de Quito. Vine aquí para una conferencia sobre filosofía y para hacer algo de turismo.

ÓSCAR: ¿Filosofía? Me interesaría si no estuviera tan metido *(It would interest me if I weren't so involved)* en los asuntos actuales *(current)* de nuestro país.

MARINA: Si la estudiaras *(If you were to study it)*, entenderías que tiene mucho que ver con *(it has a lot to do with)* la política. Pero, yo tengo que confesarte que no estoy muy al día *(up to date)* con lo que pasará en las próximas elecciones ni aquí ni en mi propio país.

ÓSCAR: Tú tienes que informarte, Marina. Es tu deber cívico. ¿Qué tal si yo estudio la filosofía y tú tomas una clase de la política contemporánea?

MARINA: ¡Trato hecho! *(It's a deal!)*

ÓSCAR: Es bueno que nosotros nos hayamos conocido. ¡Así los dos aprenderemos algo nuevo!

I. **¿COMPRENDISTE?** Contesta las siguientes preguntas en oraciones completas.

1. ¿Por qué vino Marina a la Plaza de las Armas?
2. ¿Por qué está Óscar en la plaza?
3. ¿Por qué se pone enojado Óscar?
4. ¿Son los dos estudiantes o profesionales? ¿Cuál es la especialidad de Marina? ¿de Óscar?
5. ¿De dónde son los dos y qué planes tienen para el futuro?

¿NOS ENTENDEMOS?

To express the idea of *How about (if) . . . ?* Spanish speakers use the expression **¿Qué tal si...?** followed by the appropriate phrase. For example, to say, *How about going to the movies on Saturday?*, one would say **¿Qué tal si vamos al cine el sábado?**

ENCUENTRO *cultural*

El gobierno de Chile

Éstas son unas nuevas palabras para la lectura:

enmendar *to amend*
el mando popular *popular rule*
derrocar *to overthrow*

el golpe de estado *coup d'état*
la redada *raid*
el encarcelamiento *imprisonment*

Chile es una democracia con una constitución que estipula una rama ejecutiva y una legislatura bicameral. Aprobada por un referéndum y luego **enmendada** en 1989, la constitución fue escrita y establecida con límites institucionales por **mando popular.**

En 1973, el comandante en jefe del ejército, el general Augusto Pinochet, violentamente **derrocó** al presidente Salvador Allende, que había sido elegido constitucionalmente por el pueblo. Eso marcó el principio de 17 años de dirigencia militar en Chile. Este **golpe de estado** y sus inesperadas repercusiones pusieron fin a un largo período de dirigencia constitucional en Chile, y puso en marcha un régimen de facto autoritario que sería sostenido por fuerza hasta 1990.

Desde 1973 hasta 1990, y particularmente al principio del régimen militar, hubo muchas violaciones de los derechos humanos. Éstos incluyeron arrestos arbitrarios, **redadas** en hogares privados, **encarcelamiento,** torturas, relegación y exilio.

A fines del año de 1998, Augusto Pinochet fue detenido en Gran Bretaña, donde se encontraba recuperándose de una cirugía. España y muchos grupos de defensa de los derechos humanos lucharon por conseguir la extradición del ex dictador. Sin embargo, debido a su estado de salud, Inglaterra negó la extradición y Pinochet regresó a Chile.

Para pensar: ¿Quién es el comandante en jefe en los Estados Unidos? ¿Sabes si en la historia de los EE.UU. ha habido redadas? ¿Sabes qué tipo de gobierno hay en tu país? ¿Sabes algo del golpe de estado que ocurrió en Chile?

PREGUNTAS Contesta las siguientes preguntas a base de la lectura.

1. ¿Qué tipo de gobierno había en Chile antes del golpe de estado de Pinochet?
2. ¿Qué tipos de violaciones de los derechos humanos sucedieron en Chile durante la dirigencia militar?
3. ¿Por qué celebraron grupos de derechos humanos en el año 1998?

GRAMÁTICA I: *The future tense*

In **Capítulo 3,** you learned to use the present indicative forms of **ir a** + infinitive to express actions, conditions, and events that are going to take place, for example, **Voy a viajar a Chile este verano.** *(I'm going to travel to Chile this summer.)* Spanish speakers use this construction frequently in everyday conversation. Another way to express these ideas in Spanish is to use the future tense.

Formation of the future tense

To form the future tense for most verbs, add these personal endings to the infinitive: **é, ás, á, emos, éis, án.**

viajar	volver	vivir	irse
viajar**é**	volver**é**	vivir**é**	me ir**é**
viajar**ás**	volver**ás**	vivir**ás**	te ir**ás**
viajar**á**	volver**á**	vivir**á**	se ir**á**
viajar**emos**	volver**emos**	vivir**emos**	nos ir**emos**
viajar**éis**	volver**éis**	vivir**éis**	os ir**éis**
viajar**án**	volver**án**	vivir**án**	se ir**án**

Several verbs have a different future stem from the infinitive form.

Verb	Stem	Ending
decir	**dir-**	
hacer	**har-**	é
poder	**podr-**	ás
poner	**pondr-**	á
querer	**querr-**	emos
saber	**sabr-**	éis
salir	**saldr-**	án
tener	**tendr-**	
venir	**vendr-**	

Note: The future tense of **hay** is **habrá** *(there will be).*

—¿**Habrá** una elección este año?	***Will there be** an election this year?*
—Sí. **Tendremos** una para nuestro club de estudiantes internacionales en marzo.	*Yes. **We'll have** one for our international students' club in March.*
—¿Qué **harán** los candidatos?	*What **will** the candidates **do**?*

—**Darán** un discurso de diez minutos.	***They'll give** a ten-minute speech.*
—¿**Podremos** hacerles preguntas?	***Will we be able** to ask questions?*
—Cómo no. ¿**Vendrás**?	*Of course. **Will you come?***

Using the future tense

Spanish speakers use the future tense to express actions, conditions, and events that will take place in the future.

Los candidatos **llegarán** a Santiago a las 11:00 de la mañana el 24 de julio. Al día siguiente, **subirán** el autobús y **saldrán** para las otras ciudades.	*The candidates **will arrive** in Santiago at 11:00 in the morning July 24th. The next day, **they will get on** the bus and **they will leave** for the other cities.*

Spanish speakers also use the future tense to speculate about actions, conditions, and events that are probably taking place at the moment or will most likely occur sometime in the future. If the future of probability is expressed in a question, it carries the meaning of *I wonder* in English; if it is expressed in a statement, it means *probably*.

—¿Qué tiempo **hará** en Santiago?	***I wonder how** the weather **is** in Santiago?*
—**Estará** a 35 grados.	***It's probably** 35 degrees (centigrade).*
—Siempre hace calor allí.	*It's always hot there.*
—**Será** por la humedad.	***It's probably** due to the humidity.*

¡A practicar!

K. **PLANES PARA EL FUTURO** ¿Qué harán las siguientes personas el próximo año?

MODELO: Marina: volver a Ecuador / tomar una clase de ciencias políticas
Volverá a Ecuador. Tomará una clase de ciencias políticas.

1. Marina: terminar sus estudios universitarios / poder encontrar un buen trabajo / casarse con su novio / ir a Florida para su luna de miel / vivir en un apartamento en Quito / estar muy contenta / mirar sus fotos de Chile / recordar sus experiencias con Óscar / escribirles a sus amigos chilenos / mandarles unas tarjetas postales
2. Óscar: cumplir 21 años / comenzar a estudiar filosofía / leer sobre los grandes filósofos / trabajar para una compañía de negocios / poder salir frecuentemente con sus amigos / hacer un viaje a Ecuador para visitar a Marina y a su esposo / darles un regalo de boda / decirles «¡Felicidades!»
3. Óscar y su novia: casarse en Santiago / vivir en Valparaíso / tener un niño guapo / dar una fiesta grande / hacer muchos amigos / ahorrar su dinero / comprar un velero / visitar a sus amigos en Tierra del Fuego / pescar en el mar
4. nosotros: poder ir a Santiago / visitar la Chascona[1] / viajar a Punta Arenas[2] / ver una manifestación política en la Plaza Italia de Santiago
5. tú: terminar los estudios / salir del país / conocer al jefe del grupo ecologista *Greenpeace* / participar en una campaña mundial para mejorar el medio ambiente
6. yo: terminar la carrera / mudarme a una ciudad grande / comprar un apartamento / presentarme como candidato(a) para alcalde(sa) *(mayor)* de la ciudad

---

[1] La Chascona, a Chilean word meaning *messy-haired woman*, is also the name of a famous house in the artsy neighborhood of Bella Vista. The house La Chascona was built by 1973 Nobel Prize for Literature winner Pablo Neruda.
[2] Punta Arenas is located in the far south of Chile. It is the southernmost city of importance in that country.

L. ¿QUÉ PASARÁ? Completa las siguientes oraciones, usando los verbos indicados.

1. ¿Qué harán Marina y Óscar después de participar en la manifestación en Santiago?

   Ellos ＿＿＿＿＿＿＿ (salir) de la plaza y ＿＿＿＿＿＿＿ (volver) al hotel donde ＿＿＿＿＿＿＿ (hacer) las maletas. ＿＿＿＿＿＿＿ (Ir) a la recepción donde ＿＿＿＿＿＿＿ (pagar) las cuentas de sus cuartos. Después, Marina ＿＿＿＿＿＿＿ (llamar) un taxi por teléfono. ＿＿＿＿＿＿＿ (Haber) mucha lluvia. Óscar ＿＿＿＿＿＿＿ (tener) que subir al autobús para la estación de tren. Ellos se ＿＿＿＿＿＿＿ (decir) «Adiós» en frente del hotel.

2. ¿Qué piensa Marina mientras espera en el aeropuerto?

   querer   saber   poner   venir   haber   votar   explicar

   Cuando yo llegue a Quito, ＿＿＿＿＿＿＿ llamar a Marcos para recogerme del aeropuerto. Le ＿＿＿＿＿＿＿ todo lo que he aprendido aquí en Santiago. La próxima vez, Marcos ＿＿＿＿＿＿＿ conmigo. En Quito, nosotros ＿＿＿＿＿＿＿ todo sobre los candidatos para las próximas elecciones. ＿＿＿＿＿＿＿ elecciones en noviembre. ¡En noviembre los dos ＿＿＿＿＿＿＿ por el mejor candidato! Finalmente yo ＿＿＿＿＿＿＿ la foto de Óscar sobre mi escritorio como recuerdo de mi conciencia política.

M. CINCO PREDICCIONES Escribe cinco acciones, condiciones o eventos interesantes que pasarán en tu vida dentro de los próximos cinco años. Luego comparte tus predicciones con otro(a) estudiante.

MODELOS: *Compraré un auto nuevo.*
Me casaré y viviré en Chile.
Viajaré a Europa con una amiga.

En voz alta

N. ¿QUÉ SERÁN? Mira las fotos, y luego contesta las preguntas con un(a) compañero(a) de clase. Después, hagan sus propias preguntas.

MODELO: *Este hombre será un político. Será una persona muy importante. Estará con los ciudadanos y los periodistas. Dará un discurso político.*

¿Quién será este hombre? ¿Qué tipo de trabajo hará? ¿Será simpático o antipático, y por qué? ¿Quiénes serán las otras personas en la foto?

¿Quiénes serán estas personas? ¿De dónde serán? ¿Dónde vivirán ahora? ¿Qué harán allí? ¿Qué lenguas hablarán? ¿Cómo se divertirán? ¿Qué problemas tendrán?

O. **¿QUÉ HAREMOS?** Forma un grupo pequeño con otros tres o cuatro estudiantes. Una persona comienza, diciendo una actividad que hará en el futuro. Entonces, otro(a) estudiante repite lo que dijo la primera persona y luego dice lo que él o ella hará en el futuro. Continúen de la misma forma.

MODELO: E1: *Buscaré otro trabajo.*
E2: *Pete buscará otro trabajo y yo daré una fiesta.*
E3: *Pete buscará otro trabajo, Camilla dará una fiesta y yo haré un viaje.*

P. **PLAN DE VACACIONES** Usando las frases de abajo, piensa en un plan para tus próximas vacaciones. Luego, con un(a) compañero(a) de clase, háganse preguntas sobre sus planes.

MODELO: E1: *¿Adónde irás para tus vacaciones?*
E2: *Iré a Valparaíso. Y tú, ¿adónde irás?*
E1: *Mi esposa y yo iremos a Viña del Mar.*

1. adónde vas a ir
2. por qué quieres ir allá
3. cuánto tiempo vas a estar
4. quién va a ir contigo
5. en qué día vas a irte
6. a qué hora vas a salir
7. dónde vas a quedar
8. qué vas a hacer allá
9. cuánto va a costar el viaje
10. qué vas a comprar en el viaje
11. cómo vas a pagarlo
12. cuándo vas a volver

VOCABULARIO: *Las preocupaciones cívicas y los medios de comunicación*

UNA MANIFESTACIÓN EN LA PLAZA ITALIA[1]

[1] **La Plaza Italia** is a public place where many political protests take place. It lies just off the Alameda, a road that runs from one end of Santiago de Chile to the other.

Las preocupaciones cívicas

el aborto *abortion*
el (an)alfabetismo *(il)literacy*
la defensa *defense*
los derechos humanos (civiles) *human (civil) rights*
la (des)igualdad *(in)equality*
la huelga *strike*

la inflación *inflation*
la inmigración *immigration*
la libertad de la prensa *freedom of the press*
la política internacional *international policy*

Los medios de comunicación

el Internet *Internet*
el noticiero *newscast*
el periódico *newspaper*

la prensa *press*
el reportaje *report*
la revista *magazine*

Verbos

aumentar *to increase*
eliminar *to eliminate*
informar *to inform*

investigar *to investigate*
protestar *to protest*
reducir *to reduce*

¡A practicar!

Q. DEFINICIONES Empareja cada palabra o frase abajo con su definición.

1. _____ el terrorismo
2. _____ la inflación
3. _____ los impuestos
4. _____ la desigualdad
5. _____ el aborto
6. _____ la libertad de la prensa
7. _____ el desempleo
8. _____ la guerra
9. _____ el analfabetismo
10. _____ la huelga

a. una pelea *(fight)* entre dos fuerzas armadas
b. la terminación de un embarazo *(pregnancy)*
c. una protesta de los trabajadores
d. actos violentos de protesta
e. injusticias entre gente o grupos de gente
f. la subida de precios y la disminución del valor del dinero
g. la incapacidad de leer o escribir
h. la falta de trabajo para todos
i. la falta de la censura *(censorship)*
j. el dinero que los ciudadanos pagan al gobierno

R. LOS MEDIOS DE COMUNICACIÓN Escoge la palabra apropiada de la lista de abajo para completar las siguientes oraciones.

Internet   periódico   reportaje   libertad de prensa   revista   noticiero

1. Yo soy Mario, y escribo para una _____ que sale cada mes.
2. Emilio y Maruja son reporteros para un programa de noticias de Valparaíso. Esta noche en el _____ ellos van a hacer un _____ sobre la manifestación en la Plaza Italia.
3. *La Prensa* es el nombre de un _____ que sale cada mañana en Santiago de Chile.
4. Yupi.com es una compañía que tiene información, tiempo y deportes sobre el mundo latino en el _____.
5. Para los escritores y periodistas, la _____ es muy importante.

S. ¿QUÉ HARÁ ESTA GENTE PARA MEJORAR EL MUNDO? Todas las siguientes personas harán su parte para mejorar *(to improve)* el mundo. Completa las oraciones con el futuro del verbo para especular *(to speculate)* sobre sus posibles planes.

MODELO: el congreso / eliminar / el crimen en el país
          El congreso eliminará el crimen en el país.

1. el nuevo candidato / eliminar / el desempleo
2. los periodistas / investigar / la corrupción en el gobierno
3. ellos / informar / al público sobre los problemas en la política internacional
4. el Ministro de Defensa / aumentar / el presupuesto de la defensa nacional
5. nosotros, los estudiantes, / protestar el alto costo de la vivienda / en una manifestación en la Plaza Italia
6. el grupo Amnistía Internacional / proteger / los derechos humanos en todo el mundo
7. la guardia civil / reducir / el crimen
8. la educación sobre la salud / reducir / la drogadicción entre los jóvenes del país
9. el Ministro del Interior / crear nuevas leyes / de inmigración al país
10. los senadores / trabajar / para eliminar el crimen en las ciudades

En voz alta

T. **¿CUESTIÓN NACIONAL O INTERNACIONAL?** Ahora, vuelve a los temas de la **Actividad Q.** Imagínate que eres un(a) asesor(a) del presidente y que tienes que decidir si las siguientes cuestiones tienen más relevancia al nivel nacional, internacional o los dos. Para cada tema, explica tu decisión. En grupos de tres, comparen sus respuestas.

MODELO: los derechos humanos
Es un asunto internacional. Ahora no tenemos problemas con esta cuestión en los Estados Unidos, pero sí es un problema en otros países.

U. **ENTREVISTA CON EL (LA) PRESIDENTE** Imagínate que eres presidente de un país y que tu compañero(a) de clase es un(a) reportero(a) que quiere hacerte algunas preguntas sobre tu política. El (La) periodista puede usar las siguientes preguntas y luego inventar cinco más.

1. ¿Qué ha hecho recientemente para controlar el terrorismo en este país? ¿Hay mejor seguridad en los aeropuertos y en las fronteras *(borders)*? ¿Qué podemos hacer para reducir el riesgo *(risk)* en las escuelas?
2. ¿Piensa Ud. que necesitamos controlar mejor el Internet para los menores de 18 años? ¿Sería una cuestión de la libertad de la prensa?
3. Para Ud., ¿cuál es el problema más grave que tenemos ahora en este país? ¿Qué hará para resolverlo?
4. Algunos de sus críticos dicen que Ud. debe prestar más atención a los problemas internos en vez de los asuntos internacionales. ¿Qué ha hecho Ud. recientemente con respecto a cuestiones como la vivienda para los pobres y el seguro médico *(medical insurance)* para los ancianos?

V. **UN DEBATE** Trabajando con otro(a) estudiante, preparen argumentos para un debate político. Una persona debe representar una perspectiva liberal y la otra, una posición conservadora. Cada persona tendrá dos minutos para presentar sus ideas sobre cada tema. Luego la otra persona puede reaccionar a las ideas del (de la) otro(a) candidato(a). Intenten usar el vocabulario de esta sección.

MODELO: la inmigración ilegal a los Estados Unidos
E1: *Yo creo que el gobierno de los Estados Unidos es demasiado duro con los inmigrantes ilegales. Estos inmigrantes son trabajadores muy importantes para nuestra economía. Además, sus hijos tienen derecho a una educación en las escuelas públicas, y todos deben recibir atención médica si la necesitan.*

¿NOS ENTENDEMOS?

To refer to the elderly, Spanish speakers use the term **ancianos** without conveying the literal translation of *the ancient ones.* It is also common to refer to seniors as **personas de la tercera edad.**

E2: *Yo no estoy de acuerdo contigo. Yo pienso que el gobierno de los Estados Unidos necesita limitar el número de inmigrantes en este país. Los inmigrantes que vienen aquí hacen que aumente el crimen, y no deben tener derecho a la asistencia pública. Además, ellos toman los trabajos de la gente de este país. Es un problema grave.*

TEMAS

1. los impuestos
2. el aborto
3. la educación
4. la defensa
5. las relaciones con los países hispánicos
6. la inflación
7. las huelgas de los trabajadores insatisfechos *(unsatisfied)*
8. la libertad de la prensa

ENCUENTRO *cultural*

La libertad de la prensa

Éstas son unas nuevas palabras para la lectura:

la enmienda *amendment*
reinar *to rule*
vigente *existing*
interpelar *to question*
demandar *to sue*
el desafío *challenge*

La libertad de prensa es uno de los elementos más importantes en la democracia. Tal como en los Estados Unidos, la primera **enmienda** establece la libertad de expresión y de prensa en Chile. En otros países latinoamericanos sus constituciones garantizan derechos similares.

Bajo los regímenes autoritarios del pasado, **reinaba** la censura gubernamental. Esos gobiernos anteriores aprobaron leyes que efectivamente quitaron la libertad de prensa. Todavía siguen **vigentes** algunas de esas leyes y siguen siendo usadas para controlar la prensa. En 1998, una periodista chilena, Paula Codou, y un presentador de televisión, Rafael Gumucio, fueron **interpelados** por denunciar a un juez de la Corte Suprema chilena. La periodista hizo una entrevista humorística con Rafael Gumucio, en la cual se dijo que el juez era «bastante feo». El juez invocó una vieja ley sobre la seguridad del estado que protege a políticos, magistrados y militares, para **demandarlos** por difamación.

En junio de 1998 se reunieron muchas organizaciones periodísticas en Antigua, Guatemala, para hablar del estado de la libertad de prensa. Entre los participantes estaban la Organización de Estados Americanos (OEA), la Sociedad Interamericana de Prensa (SIP) y el Centro Latinoamericano de Periodismo (CELAP). Los temas discutidos abarcaron todo lo que tuviera que ver con la libertad de prensa, incluyendo los **desafíos** legales.

Para pensar: ¿Crees tú en la libertad de prensa? ¿Crees que hay alguna ocasión en que sea necesario que el gobierno utilice la censura? ¿Piensas que hay una fuerza que controla la prensa en los EE.UU.?

W. PREGUNTAS Contesta las siguientes preguntas basándote en la lectura.

1. ¿Cuál es la semejanza entre el gobierno estadounidense, el gobierno chileno y los de otros países latinoamericanos frente a la libertad de prensa?
2. ¿Por qué fueron interpelados Paula Codou y Rafael Gumucio?
3. Explica qué temas se discutieron en junio 1998 en la reunión en Guatemala.

GRAMÁTICA II: *The conditional*

In English, we express hypothetical ideas using the word *would* with a verb (e.g., *I would travel if I had the time and money).* Spanish speakers also express these ideas by using the conditional, which you have already used in the expression **me gustaría: Me gustaría viajar a Latinoamérica.** *(I would like to travel to Latin America.)*

Forming the conditional

For most verbs, add these personal endings to the infinitive: **ía, ías, ía, íamos, íais, ían.**

viajar	volver	vivir	irse
viajaría	volvería	viviría	me iría
viajarías	volverías	vivirías	te irías
viajaría	volvería	viviría	se iría
viajaríamos	volveríamos	viviríamos	nos iríamos
viajaríais	volveríais	viviríais	os iríais
viajarían	volverían	vivirían	se irían

Add the conditional endings to the irregular stems of these verbs. These are the identical stems you used to form the future tense.

Verb	Stem	Ending
decir	**dir-**	
hacer	**har-**	ía
poder	**podr-**	ías
poner	**pondr-**	ía
querer	**querr-**	íamos
saber	**sabr-**	íais
salir	**saldr-**	ían
tener	**tendr-**	
venir	**vendr-**	

Note: The conditional of **hay** is **habría** *(there would be).*

—¿A qué hora dijo Marina que **saldría** para Quito?	*What time did Marina say she **would leave** for Quito?*
—Dijo que lo **sabría** después de llamar al aeropuerto.	*She said that **she would know** after calling the airport.*

Using the conditional

Spanish speakers use the conditional to express what would happen in a particular situation, given a particular set of circumstances.

—¿Qué **harías** con $1.000?	What **would you do** with $1,000?
—Yo **viajaría** a Latinoamérica.	*I would travel to Latin America.*

Spanish speakers use the conditional tense with the past subjunctive (presented in the next chapter) to express hypothetical or contrary-to-fact statements about what would happen in a particular circumstance or under certain conditions.

Si tuviéramos el dinero, **iríamos** a Santiago.[1]
If we had the money, we would go to Santiago.

The conditional is also used to soften a request or to express politeness and/or respect.

¿Podrías ayudarme con la lectura para mañana?	**Could you** help me with the reading for tomorrow?
¿Querría Ud. ir con nosotros al museo?	**Would you like** to go to the museum with us?
Ud. **debería** votar en las próximas elecciones.	**You should** vote in the next elections.

Similar to what you just learned about the future tense, Spanish speakers also use the conditional to speculate about actions, conditions, and events that probably took place *in the past*. As in the case of the future for speculation about the present, the conditional of probability also carries the meaning of *I wonder* in English; if it is expressed in a statement, it means *probably*.

—¿Qué tiempo **haría** en Santiago ayer?	*I wonder how* the weather *was* in Santiago yesterday.
—**Estaría** a 35 grados.	*It was probably 35 degrees (centigrade).*
—Siempre hacía calor allí.	*It was always hot there.*
—**Sería** por la humedad.	*It was probably due to the humidity.*

¡A practicar!

X.   ¡SEÑORA CANDIDATA, POR FAVOR! Tú y tus amigos están asistiendo a un discurso de Ángela Montero. Uds. quieren hacerle preguntas, pero con amabilidad. Usa el condicional para formar tus preguntas.

MODELO: decir a la gente que es necesario respetar a los jóvenes
¿Diría Ud. a la gente que es necesario respetar a los jóvenes?

1. decir a la policía que necesitamos más libertad en las manifestaciones
2. poner más énfasis en la educación pública
3. haber la posibilidad de darnos mejor empleo después de la universidad

---

[1] In the example above, the *if* clause (**Si tuviéramos el dinero**) states a hypothesis, and the conditional clause (**iríamos a Santiago**) states the probable result if that hypothesis were true. You will learn more about forming *if* clauses with the past subjunctive in the next chapter.

4. (a sus asistentes) salir a los pueblos para animar a la gente a participar en las elecciones

5. querer eliminar el crimen en las ciudades

6. hacer un esfuerzo para comunicarse con la prensa

Y. ¿QUÉ HARÍA ESA GENTE ANOCHE? Tú no sabes qué hacía esa gente anoche. Un amigo te pregunta y tú tienes que contestar con el condicional del verbo entre paréntesis para especular sobre qué hacía.

MODELO: ¿Qué haría Ángela Montero anoche? (trabajar en su campaña para la presidencia)
Ángela Montero trabajaría en su campaña para la presidencia anoche.

1. ¿Qué haría el presidente anoche? (prepararse para un debate contra Ángela Montero)

2. ¿Qué harían los estudiantes anoche? (hacer una manifestación en la Plaza Italia)

3. ¿Qué harían los senadores anoche? (ponerse ropa elegante para una cena del congreso)

4. ¿Qué haríamos nosotros anoche? (decir a nuestros amigos que es necesario votar en las próximas elecciones)

5. ¿Qué haría yo anoche? (estudiar para tu examen de ciencia política)

Z. PROMESAS DE UNA CANDIDATA Termina las oraciones de Ángela Montero, una mujer que quiere ser la próxima presidente de Chile, conjugando los infinitivos en el condicional.

MODELO: Como presidente del país / pagar más a los profesores
Como presidente del país, yo pagaría más a los profesores.

1. con una lluvia fuerte / todos los pobres tener paraguas

2. con mucho sol / yo les dar sombreros

3. con una mujer como presidente / haber menos guerras *(wars)*

4. con un dictador en el poder / los ciudadanos protestar

5. con mejores escuelas / nuestros hijos poder recibir trabajos buenos

6. sin tanta violencia en las ciudades / venir más turistas

7. como presidente / yo saber cómo reducir la inflación

8. yo como presidente / eliminar el alto nivel de desempleo en el país

AA. MÁS PROMESAS Termina el discurso de Ángela Montero conjugando los verbos entre paréntesis o en el futuro o el condicional.

Si yo fuera *(If I were)* su presidente, yo _____ (reducir) los impuestos por un diez por ciento. También yo _____ (aumentar) los salarios de los empleados públicos. La semana que viene, el presidente actual y yo _____ (hablar) de los abusos de los derechos humanos de los prisioneros políticos de este país. Yo personalmente _____ (investigar) los casos para asegurar que ellos reciban un trato humano. Si todos nosotros protestáramos, nosotros _____ (poder) cambiar esta injusticia. Si yo fuera presidente, también _____ (hablar) a otras naciones sobre lo que está ocurriendo en nuestras cortes y cárceles *(prisons)* para atraer la atención internacional a este asunto. Trabajando juntos, nosotros _____ (eliminar) toda la corrupción que hemos sufrido en los últimos años.

En voz alta

BB. **¿QUÉ HARÍAS TÚ?** ¿Qué harías durante una visita de un mes a Chile? Con un(a) compañero(a) de clase, hablen de las siguientes ideas y respondan según sus gustos.

MODELO: E1: ¿Irías a Santiago o a una ciudad más pequeña?
E2: *Iría a Santiago.*
o: E2: *Iría a una ciudad pequeña en la costa.*

1. ¿Viajarías por avión o en barco?
2. ¿Comprarías muchos recuerdos?
3. ¿Participarías en una manifestación política?
4. ¿Escucharías los discursos de los candidatos?
5. ¿Qué ropa llevarías?
6. ¿Qué dirían tus padres sobre tus planes?
7. ¿Sería fácil volver a los Estados Unidos?

CC. **¡DINERO PARA TODOS!** Indica lo que estas personas harían con un premio grande de la lotería.

MODELO: Matt
Matt compraría un coche nuevo e iría a la playa.

1. yo
2. nosotros
3. el (la) profesor(a)
4. mi compañero(a) de cuarto
5. mi novio(a)
6. mis padres
7. los estudiantes de la clase de español
8. el presidente del país

DD. **¿ERES UNA PERSONA TOLERANTE?** Dile a un(a) compañero(a) de clase lo que tú harías en las siguientes situaciones y por qué.

MODELO: Después de clase, tú vuelves a tu cuarto y tu compañero(a) ha dejado el cuarto desarreglado *(messy).*
No haría ni diría nada porque mi cuarto siempre está desarreglado.
o: *Yo limpiaría el cuarto porque no querría molestar a mi compañero(a) de cuarto.*

1. Vuelves a la biblioteca y alguien se sienta en el lugar donde estudias.
2. A la 1:00 de la mañana, dos personas en otro cuarto comienzan a hablar tan fuerte que tú te despiertas.
3. Tú estás duchándote en tu cuarto cuando suena el teléfono.
4. Tú estás nadando en una piscina cuando un niño te echa agua.
5. Tú miras la cuenta en un restaurante y ves que no está correcta.

EE. **EXPRESIONES DE CORTESÍA** Forma una oración con el condicional para hacer una pregunta a un(a) compañero(a) de clase para las siguientes situaciones.

MODELO: Necesitas $10 para el fin de semana.
¿Podrías prestarme $10 para el fin de semana?
o: *¿Me prestarías $10 para el fin de semana?*

1. Necesitas ayuda para un examen de matemáticas.
2. Quieres que tu amigo(a) vaya contigo al cine.
3. Quieres que tú y tu amigo(a) compartan *(share)* la cuenta en un restaurante.
4. Necesitas que tu amigo(a) te llame esta noche.

5. Quieres que tú y tu compañero(a) limpien el cuarto.

6. Quieres que un grupo de estudiantes participe en las elecciones universitarias.

FF. **PRESIDENTE POR UN DÍA** Imagina que eres candidato(a) para presidente del país. ¿Qué cambios recomendarías a los ciudadanos? Explica a otro(a) estudiante los cambios que harías con respecto a los temas siguientes.

MODELO: la medicina
           Yo daría más dinero para la investigación y el trato del cáncer.

1. el medio ambiente
2. las relaciones internacionales
3. la educación
4. la economía

5. la pobreza *(poverty)*
6. el crimen en las ciudades grandes
7. el desempleo

GRAMÁTICA III: *Using the present perfect in the subjunctive mood*

The present perfect subjunctive is formed with the present subjunctive of the verb **haber** plus the past participle. The present perfect subjunctive is used in every situation in which the present subjunctive is used. Although it generally expresses the idea of *having done* something, it can also mean *did* something. Consider the following examples.

Es bueno que **hayas venido.**	It's good that you **have come (came).**
No creo que ella **haya hecho** la tarea.	I don' t believe (that) she **has done (did)** the homework.
Me alegro que mi mamá me **haya escrito.**	I'm happy that my mother **has written (wrote)** me.
Tenemos que salir antes de que **hayas terminado.**	We'll have to leave before you **have finished (finish).**

¡A practicar!

GG. **EN OTRAS PALABRAS** Convierte los verbos subrayados al presente perfecto del subjuntivo.

MODELO: Tulia está contenta que <u>vengas</u> con nosotros.
           Tulia está contenta que hayas venido con nosotros.

1. Óscar se alegra de que Marina <u>estudie</u> ciencias políticas.
2. No creo que todos <u>digan</u> la verdad.
3. Es bueno que <u>tengan</u> la oportunidad de informar a los ciudadanos sobre sus ideas.
4. Es mejor que <u>votemos</u> temprano.
5. Dudo que el presidente <u>pueda gobernar</u> bien.
6. Es interesante que el senador <u>asista</u> a esta conferencia.
7. Me encanta que tú <u>vengas</u> con nosotros a la manifestación.
8. Es imposible que la candidata <u>tenga</u> suficiente dinero para la campaña.

HH. APOYAR A UNA CANDIDATA Claudia está trabajando en la campaña de Ángela Montero. Ella habla de la campaña con su amiga Pía que ha venido a un discurso de Montero. Termina el párrafo con el presente perfecto del subjuntivo.

¡Hola Pía! Me alegro mucho que tú _____ (venir). Es una lástima que las otras chicas no _____ (poder) asistir al discurso con nosotras. Me entristece que yo no les _____ (convencer) de la importancia de esta reunión. Estoy buscando a Ángela Montero ahora. Espero que ella _____ (llegar). Muchas veces ella viene tarde a estos eventos. Es bueno que nosotros _____ (empezar) a ayudarla con la campaña porque ahora está más organizada. ¡Ven! Tenemos que buscar dónde sentarnos. ¡Ojalá el discurso no _____ (comenzar) sin nosotras!

Ahora, Pía y Claudia están escuchando el discurso de Ángela Montero. Completa el párrafo con el presente perfecto del indicativo o del subjuntivo.

Yo _____ (conocer) a todos los otros candidatos y no hay ninguno que _____ (tener) tanta experiencia como yo. Mis asistentes y yo _____ (contestar) francamente a todas las preguntas. Nadie duda que nosotros _____ (ser) honestos con la gente. Yo espero que _____ (poder) comunicar claramente mis ideas. Los discursos que nosotros _____ (escuchar) en los últimos días fueron muy ambiguos. Mi padre siempre _____ (decir) «vamos al grano *(let's get to the point)*». Creo que estas palabras me _____ (servir) bastante bien durante esta elección. Si la gente me _____ (elegir) es porque yo les _____ (decir) la verdad.

En voz alta

II. ¡MENTIROSO! Tu amigo Guzmán puede exagerar a veces cuando está hablando con sus amigos. Indica cuáles de las siguientes afirmaciones de él son dudosas, respondiendo con una de las expresiones de la primera columna. Si lo crees, responde con una expresión de la segunda columna.

MODELO: Yo he hablado con el presidente de los Estados Unidos.
Es dudoso que hayas hablado con el presidente de los Estados Unidos.

No creo que...	No niego *(deny)* que...
Es imposible...	Estoy seguro(a) que...
Dudo que...	Es verdad...
Es dudoso que...	No hay duda...
Es improbable...	

1. Mis padres me han comprado una bicicleta nueva.
2. He visto una película de horror.
3. Mis amigos y yo hemos conocido a un extraterrestre *(alien)*.
4. Mi hermano ha bailado con Madonna.
5. Yo he jugado en un partido profesional de baloncesto.
6. Mi padre ha corrido un maratón.
7. Mi hermano ha comprado un coche nuevo.
8. He estado en el Caribe cinco veces en el último año.
9. He comido pizza esta tarde.
10. Mis amigos me han dicho que soy mentiroso *(a liar)*.

JJ. LOS EVENTOS POLÍTICOS EN TU VIDA Piensa en la política y cómo la política ha afectado tu vida últimamente. Forma oraciones para expresar tus opiniones sobre lo que ha pasado usando un elemento de cada columna a continuación. Usa el subjuntivo del presente perfecto cuando sea necesario. Después, explica tus opiniones a un(a) compañero(a).

MODELO: *Pienso que la nueva presidente ha ayudado a los pobres porque hay menos gente viviendo en la calle hoy.*

     o: *Dudo que los ciudadanos de mi país hayan participado en la política. Sólo un 40 por ciento de mi ciudad votó el mes pasado. ¡Qué lástima!*

Me alegro que...	la nueva presidente	eliminar el desempleo
Estoy triste/contento(a) que...	los ciudadanos de mi país	dar muchos discursos
Pienso que...	los senadores	participar en la política
Dudo que...	la policía	ayudar a los pobres
Es probable que...	nosotros los estudiantes	disminuir el crimen
Es una lástima que...	los liberales	prohibir el aborto
Es bueno/malo que...	los conservadores	limpiar el medio ambiente
Es posible que...	el (la) candidato(a) X	controlar la corrupción

Síntesis

¡A ver!

El **Capítulo 14** tiene como tema principal la política y los medios informativos que reportan sobre la actividad política. La presentadora de este capítulo se llama Ana María y es periodista para un diario importante de la República de Chile. Ana María nos hablará del tema de la política, enfocándose para el primer segmento en una serie de imágenes tanto de Chile como de Argentina, todas relacionadas con la actualidad política en estos dos países. Y el segundo segmento nos presentará al jefe de relaciones públicas del congreso de Chile.

ACTIVIDAD 1   Pre-viewing task (Segmento 1 del video)

Paso 1: En el primer segmento del video, verás una serie de fotos y clips cortos, todos relacionados con la política de dos países del sur de Latinoamérica: Chile y Argentina. Apunta en una frase corta la relación que tiene cada foto o clip corto con la política de estos dos países. Si no estás muy seguro(a) de la relación, adivínala.

MODELO: *Podría ser el presidente de Argentina.*

Paso 2: Compara tus respuestas con las de un(a) compañero(a) de clase.

ACTIVIDAD 2   Pre-viewing task (Segmento 2 del video)

Paso 1: ¿Qué significa para ti que un país sea (a) una república; (b) una democracia; (c) una dictadura? O sea, ¿qué es lo que define una república, una democracia y una dictadura? ¿Qué países se consideran repúblicas, democracias o dictaduras? Apunta en un papel una lista de ideas sobre tus definiciones.

Paso 2: Comparte con dos compañeros(as) de clase tu lista. Entre los tres, lleguen a un acuerdo de una definición de una república, una democracia y una dictadura y preséntenlas a toda la clase, con ejemplos.

ACTIVIDAD 3   Viewing task (Segmento 2 del video)

En el segundo segmento del video, vas a conocer a Rodrigo de la Fuente, jefe de Relaciones Públicas y Protocolo del Senado de la República de Chile. Rodrigo nos explicará cómo está organizado el gobierno de la República de Chile. Antes de ver el video, mira el organigrama *(flow chart)* que describe la estructura del gobierno de Chile. A continuación, rellena el organigrama con la información necesaria, basándote en lo que nos explica Rodrigo de la Fuente.

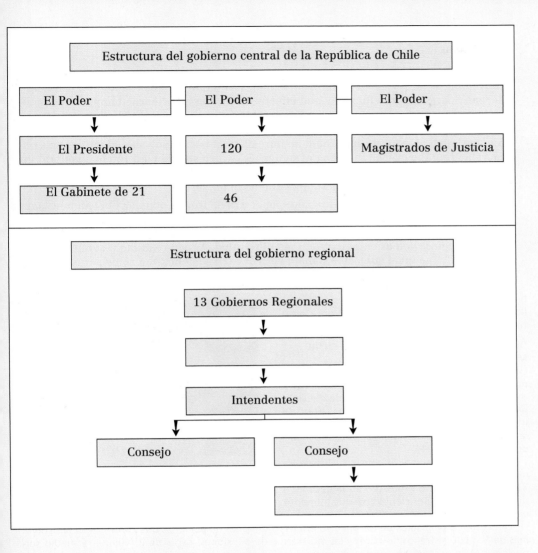

Estructura del gobierno central de la República de Chile

El Poder	El Poder	El Poder
↓	↓	↓
El Presidente	120	Magistrados de Justicia
↓	↓	
El Gabinete de 21	46	

Estructura del gobierno regional

13 Gobiernos Regionales

↓

↓

Intendentes

↓   ↓

Consejo   Consejo

↓

ACTIVIDAD 4   Post-viewing task (Segmento 2 del video)

Paso 1: Compara tus respuestas en la Actividad 3 con las de un(a) compañero(a) de clase.

Paso 2: Con tu compañero(a) de clase, utiliza la información en el organigrama de la **Actividad 3** para hacer una descripción oral de la organización del gobierno de la República de Chile. Terminen su descripción con una comparación con la organización del gobierno de este país.

¡A leer!

Reading complex sentences

Determining what is essential and what is nonessential in complex sentences will help you read Spanish more efficiently and effectively. As you have learned in previous reading strategies, it is not essential to understand the meaning of every single word you come across when reading in Spanish; in fact, as a learner of Spanish as a foreign language, such an expectation would be unrealistic. Instead, you should try to focus on understanding the overall meaning of sentences, which should lead you to a general understanding of the passage as a whole. When dealing with a complex sentence, the core of its meaning will come from its subject and its main verb.

Paso 1: As you turn to the following newspaper article from a popular Chilean newspaper, start by reading the title, subtitles, and first three paragraphs. Underline the subject and the main verb in each sentence. This will help you get an idea about the main point(s) of the article before you attempt to read the entire thing. As you read the rest of the article, try to identify the main subject and main verb of each sentence you come across.

En la última década del siglo XX, los salarios del llamado sexo débil crecieron° el 70,3 por ciento frente al 46,5 por ciento de los hombres.

grew

DISMINUYE DIFERENCIA DE SUELDOS ENTRE MUJERES Y HOMBRES

La tradicional disparidad entre los sueldos de las mujeres y de los hombres comenzó lentamente a quedar atrás durante la última década del siglo pasado. Al menos así lo confirman las cifras° de ingreso promedio, según estadísticas oficiales de la Superintendencia de Administradoras de Fondos de Pensiones (AFP).

figures, numbers

Las cifras también indican que el sueldo de las mujeres que trabajan bajo contrato creció un 70,3 por ciento como promedio en la década, a diferencia del 46,5 por ciento real que aumentó el sueldo de los hombres en el mismo período.

La brecha° a principios de los años 90 era de más de $63.000 entre los hombres y las mujeres, obviamente en desmedro° de éstas, mientras que hasta octubre de 1999 la diferencia se redujo a poco menos de $45.000 en promedio al mes.

gap, difference

impairment

Aunque la relación sigue siendo perjudicial para las trabajadoras, la tasa de crecimiento del ingreso femenino ha sido constante. De hecho, de representar el sueldo de la mujer el 70,2 por ciento del ingreso promedio de los hombres en 1990 pasó a ser equivalente al 79,6 por ciento del mismo en 1995, hasta terminar la década representando el 85,1 por ciento del salario de los varones.

to support, to back up

Esto equivale a decir que el sueldo de un hombre es equivalente a 1,17 sueldos de una mujer.

Así, los registros previstos son un reflejo de la incorporación de la mujer al trabajo. De los casi 6 millones de personas que contribuyen al sistema de pensiones, cerca de 2 millones y medio son mujeres.

Según cifras de la superintendencia, la mitad de las mujeres que trabajan en forma dependiente tienen entre 25 y 40 años de edad, y se espera que su participación en el espectro laboral siga en aumento con la llegada de nuevas generaciones.

El incremento de los sueldos femeninos en la última década parece respaldar° que las mujeres están mejorando su situación dentro del mercado laboral, y que la tan rechazada discriminación pueda ser una cosa del pasado.

Paso 2: Ahora, lee el resto del artículo y contesta las siguientes preguntas.

1. ¿Cuál es el tema del artículo? ¿Qué tipo de información contiene?
2. ¿Qué cambios han tenido lugar en la última década en cuanto a la situación de los salarios de las mujeres en el mercado laboral chileno?
3. ¿Cómo ha cambiado la brecha entre los sueldos de los hombres y las mujeres en Chile en la última década?
4. Hoy día, ¿cómo se comparan los ingresos de los hombres y las mujeres en Chile? Sé específico(a).
5. Según el artículo, ¿qué edades tienen las mujeres que trabajan en el mercado laboral chileno?

Paso 3: Piensa ahora en la situación de la mujer en el mercado laboral estadounidense y contesta las siguientes preguntas.

1. ¿Crees que en el campo laboral la mujer estadounidense tiene las mismas oportunidades que el hombre? ¿Por qué sí o no?
2. ¿A qué problemas se enfrenta *(does she face)* la mujer estadounidense en el trabajo hoy en día?
3. ¿Crees que la situación de la mujer en el mercado laboral estadounidense ha mejorado en la última década frente a la de los hombres? Explica tu respuesta.

¡A escribir!

Writing from diagrams

In this section you will write a brief composition based on information in diagrams. Diagrams present charts, tables, and graphs of specific information that can be readily understood and remembered.

El Internet es un medio de comunicación que ha crecido mucho en los años recientes. Tiene la capacidad de facilitar la transmisión de información a una cantidad enorme de ciudadanos a través del mundo. Sin embargo, no todos disfrutan igual de los beneficios del Internet. Los siguientes gráficos presentan algunas estadísticas acerca del acceso al Internet que tienen diferentes sectores de la población de España. Vamos a ver que no todas las personas tienen el mismo acceso a este medio de comunicación.

Paso 1: Estudia los tres gráficos que siguen. Nota los títulos, los colores y las categorías que aparecen en cada uno.

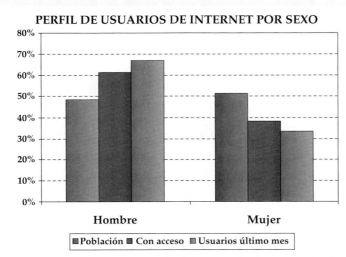

PERFIL DE USUARIOS DE INTERNET POR SEXO

Functions: Comparing and contrasting; Comparing and distinguishing
Vocabulary: Computers
Grammar: Comparisons

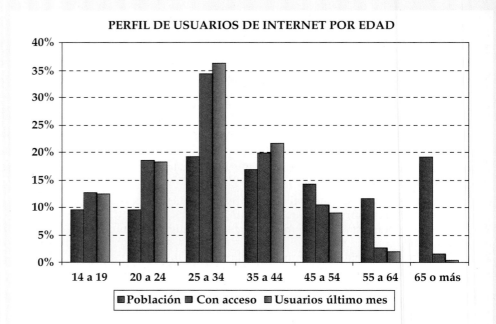

PERFIL DE USUARIOS DE INTERNET POR EDAD

■ Población ■ Con acceso ■ Usuarios último mes

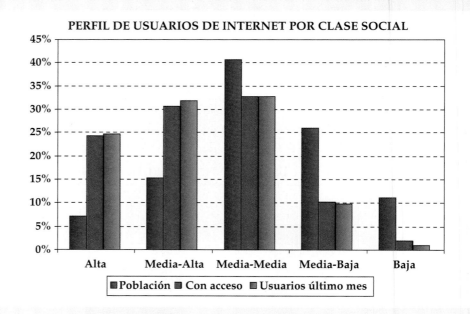

PERFIL DE USUARIOS DE INTERNET POR CLASE SOCIAL

■ Población ■ Con acceso ■ Usuarios último mes

Paso 2: Basándote en la información presentada en los gráficos, contesta las preguntas que siguen.

1. ¿Cuáles son los tres factores sociales considerados en los gráficos?
2. ¿Quién tiene más acceso al Internet, los hombres o las mujeres?
3. ¿Cuáles son las edades de las personas que tienen el mayor acceso?
4. ¿Cuál de las clases sociales tiene el mayor acceso?

Paso 3: ¿Hay desigualdad en el acceso al Internet? ¿Por qué sí o no? Escribe un párrafo en el cual respondes a estas preguntas. Debes hacer lo siguiente:

- escribir una frase principal para indicar tu respuesta a la pregunta
- considerar los tres factores sociales
- mencionar algunas estadísticas específicas para apoyar tu posición
- explicar por qué hay desigualdad o no en el acceso al Internet

¡A conversar!

Paso 1: La siguiente lista presenta algunas preocupaciones cívicas a las que se enfrenta nuestra sociedad hoy en día. Lee la lista y escoge las tres preocupaciones que son más graves en tu opinión. Debes pensar en algunas razones para apoyar tu posición. ¿Por qué son estas tres preocupaciones más graves que las otras? ¿Cómo afectan a la sociedad?

- el terrorismo
- la inflación
- los impuestos
- la desigualdad
- el aborto
- la libertad de la prensa
- el desempleo
- la guerra
- el analfabetismo
- las huelgas

Paso 2: Habla con un(a) compañero(a) de clase acerca de las tres preocupaciones cívicas que has escogido. Si tu compañero(a) de clase no está de acuerdo en que éstas son las más graves, trata de convencerlo(la) explicándole las razones que apoyan tu opinión. Luego, preséntale a la clase un informe sobre sus opiniones.

La política y el voto

la campaña *campaign*	**el deber** *duty*	**las elecciones** *elections*	**el poder** *power*
el (la) candidato(a) *candidate*	**la democracia** *democracy*	**el gobierno** *government*	**el (la) político** *politician*
el (la) ciudadano(a) *citizen*	**el (la) dictador(a)** *dictator*	**la ley** *law*	**el (la) presidente** *president*
el congreso *congress*	**la dictadura** *dictatorship*	**el partido político** *political party*	**la reforma** *reform*
el debate *debate*	**el discurso** *speech*	**la paz** *peace*	**el voto** *vote*
	el ejército *army*		

Verbos

apoyar *to support*	**defender (ie)** *to defend*	**elegir (i, i)** *to elect*	**gobernar (ie)** *to govern*
aprobar (ue) *to approve; to pass*	**discutir** *to discuss*	**firmar** *to sign*	**oponer** *to oppose*
			votar *to vote*

Adjetivos

conservador *conservative*	**demócrata** *democratic*	**liberal** *liberal*	**republicano** *republican*

Las preocupaciones cívicas

el aborto *abortion*	**el (des)empleo** *(un)employment*	**la huelga** *strike*	**la manifestación** *demonstration*
el (an)alfabetismo *(il)literacy*	**la (des)igualdad** *(in)equality*	**los impuestos** *taxes*	**la política internacional** *international policy*
la corrupción *corruption*	**la drogadicción** *drug addiction*	**la inflación** *inflation*	**el terrorismo** *terrorism*
el crimen *crime*	**la educación** *education*	**la inmigración** *immigration*	**la vivienda** *housing*
la defensa *defense*	**la guerra** *war*	**la libertad de la prensa** *freedom of the press*	
los derechos humanos (civiles) *human (civil) rights*			

Los medios de comunicación

el Internet *Internet*	**el periódico** *newspaper*	**el reportaje** *report*
el noticiero *newscast*	**la prensa** *the press*	**la revista** *magazine*

Verbos

aumentar *to increase*	**informar** *to inform*	**protestar** *to protest*
eliminar *to eliminate*	**investigar** *to investigate*	**reducir** *to reduce*

Los avances tecnológicos: Uruguay

Communicative goals

In this chapter you will learn how to . . .

- Talk about home electronics
- Make statements in the past with the subjunctive mood
- Talk about hypothetical situations
- Talk about computer-related activities and accessories
- Review expressions and constructions with the subjunctive mood

Grammar

- Past (imperfect) subjunctive
- *If* clauses
- Indicative and subjunctive uses (summary)
- Infinitive and subjunctive uses (summary)

Cultural information

- Las telecomunicaciones en Uruguay
- Los cafés cibernéticos

Plaza Independencia, Montevideo, Uruguay

UNA CASA DEL SIGLO XXI In this section you will learn about technological innovations that we use in our homes. How many of the items pictured below are in your house?

la alarma *alarm*	**la cámara (digital)** *(digital) camera*	**el equipo** *equipment*
		el satélite *satellite*

Verbos

apagar *to turn off*	**(des)enchufar** *to plug in (to unplug)*	**grabar** *to record*
(des)conectar *to (dis)connect*	**funcionar** *to function (to work)*	**prender** *to turn on*

Adjetivos

apagado(a) *off*	**encendido(a)** *on*	**enchufado(a)** *plugged in*

¡A practicar!

A. UNA VIDA TECNOLÓGICA La abuela Adelaida habla de la vida de su nieta, Minia. Minia es joven y tiene muchas invenciones de tecnología. Su abuela comenta sobre qué vida más fácil tiene su nieta. Completa su historia usando las palabras de la siguiente lista y conjugando los verbos a la forma apropiada.

prender   equipo   apagado(a)   desenchufar   encendido(a)   enchufado(a)
funcionar   alarma   apagar   desconectar   control remoto

Mi nieta tiene una vida tan fácil, a veces no me lo creo. Le encanta ver la tele. Todos los días, cuando se levanta, la _____ y la deja _____ todo el día. A veces yo la _____, pero después de unos minutos está _____ de nuevo. Minia tiene tanto _____ tecnológico que tuvo que instalar una _____ para nuestra seguridad. ¡Caramba! Cuando mira la tele, se sienta en el sillón con el _____ en las manos. Un día, yo quiero _____ todo. Voy a _____ todas sus máquinas. Ojalá que deje todo _____ para darme un poco de silencio. Pero nunca va a pasar. Ahora, toda su tecnología _____ muy bien y yo tengo que aguantarlo *(to put up with it)*.

B. TIPOS DE TECNOLOGÍA Indica dos o tres aparatos domésticos que corresponden a cada una de las siguientes categorías.

MODELO: la seguridad personal
la alarma, el teléfono celular

1. la diversión
2. las comunicaciones
3. la música
4. el trabajo profesional
5. los recuerdos

En voz alta

C. ¿PARA QUÉ SE USA? Imagínate que tienes que describir la función de los siguientes elementos a una persona del siglo XIX (un[a] compañero[a] de clase). Explica para qué se usa cada cosa y luego cómo usarla. En algunos casos, tendrás mucho que explicarle a tu compañero(a).

1. la videocámara
2. el disco compacto
3. la antena parabólica
4. el estéreo
5. la alarma
6. el control remoto
7. el satélite
8. el teléfono celular

D. ANTES DE QUE SALGAS DE LA CASA Trabajando con otro(a) estudiante, forma siete oraciones con las palabras de abajo para formar algunas sugerencias que darías a una persona que va a cuidar tu casa mientras que estés de vacaciones. Usa mandatos informales para tus sugerencias. La otra persona debe responder de una manera lógica.

MODELO: la alarma
E1: *Antes de entrar en la casa, asegúrate de que esté apagada la alarma.*
E2: *Gracias. ¿Puedes darme el código* (code) *para apagarla?*

VERBOS	SUSTANTIVOS	ADJETIVOS
(des)conectar	la alarma	apagado(a)
prender	el estéreo	encendido(a)
apagar	el contestador automático	enchufado(a)
grabar	el teléfono celular	abierto(a)
(des)enchufar	el control remoto	
llamar		
usar		
asegurar		

E. **OPINIONES** Hazle las siguientes preguntas a un(a) compañero(a) de clase. ¿Tienen Uds. algo en común con respecto a la tecnología?

1. ¿Dependes mucho de la tecnología en tu casa? ¿Qué aparatos usas con frecuencia? ¿Qué aparatos usaste hoy y para qué? ¿Qué aparato te gustaría tener que no tienes ahora? ¿Por qué sería útil para ti?

2. ¿Cuáles son algunos aparatos que no usaban tus padres cuando eran jóvenes? Para ellos, ¿cuáles son los aparatos más útiles? ¿Qué aparato usas tú que no usan ellos? ¿Tienen ellos el mismo entusiasmo que tú por la tecnología? ¿Por qué sí o por qué no?

3. ¿Es la tecnología algo positivo o negativo para nuestra civilización? ¿Cuáles son algunos ejemplos de los beneficios o los efectos negativos de la tecnología? ¿Cuáles son los avances tecnológicos más importantes del siglo XX (el avión, la computadora, los satélites, el Internet, la clonación genética, los avances en la medicina)?

4. ¿Cómo serán nuestras casas en el año 2050? ¿Habrá cambios radicales o inovaciones menores? ¿Cómo serían nuestras vidas sin los avances tecnológicos mencionados en esta sección? Si pudieras inventar una máquina nueva, ¿qué sería? ¿En qué sentido mejoraría nuestras vidas?

EN CONTEXTO

Federico y Alejandra, una pareja uruguaya, están estableciendo una tienda de computadoras en Montevideo, Uruguay, donde viven los padres de Alejandra. Ahora están hablando de sus planes para el primer día de su negocio nuevo.

—¡Ay! No sé, Federico. ¿Y si no viene mucha gente?

—No te preocupes, mi amor. No habríamos establecido la tienda si no hubiera habido *(if there had not been)* tanta demanda. La gente vendrá.

—¿Y si no podemos pagarles a mis padres el dinero que nos prestaron?

—Tranquila. Estoy seguro de que podremos pagarles dentro de dos meses. No hay problema.

—Pero Federico, solamente tenemos la mitad *(half)* de las computadoras que pedimos. Y las impresoras no han llegado todavía.

—Espero que no sigas así, mi amor. Tenemos que ser optimistas. Si tuviéramos *(If we had)* todo en orden, no habría aventura. Tenemos que arriesgarnos *(to take a risk)* un poco.

—Para ti es fácil decir eso. No piensas en los detalles.

—Al contrario. Según mi amigo Paco, no hay mejor momento para nuestra tienda. Con tantas personas navegando la red *(surfing the Internet)*, con los nuevos negocios electrónicos... , la tecnología digital...

— Tu amigo vive en los Estados Unidos. No creo que sea exactamente lo mismo aquí.

—Bueno, lo sabremos muy pronto, ¿eh?

F. **¿COMPRENDISTE?** Indica si las siguientes oraciones son ciertas o falsas. Si la oración es falsa, ¡corrígela!

1. Alejandra tiene miedo de que la tienda no vaya a tener éxito.
2. Federico ha investigado la demanda para computadoras en Montevideo.
3. La pareja tiene todos los productos que pidieron para la tienda.
4. Federico es un poco conservador.
5. Alejandra es más realista que Federico.

ENCUENTRO *cultural*

Las telecomunicaciones en Uruguay

Éstas son unas palabras nuevas para la lectura:

creciente *growing*
carecer de *to lack*
el abonado *subscriber*

MERCOSUR Mercado Común del Sur *(an area of free trade similar to NAFTA in North America)*

La tecnología tiene un papel muy importante en el **creciente** mercado global. Para integrarse económicamente es esencial poder comunicarse. Por eso, el rol de las telecomunicaciones es cada vez más importante para la globalización. Es increíble pensar en la cantidad de telecomunicaciones en Uruguay si uno tiene en cuenta la realidad latinoamericana. Históricamente, los países latinoamericanos **han carecido de** una infraestructura que pudiera apoyar las nuevas tecnologías. Durante muchos años se creía que era peligroso invertir dinero en Uruguay y otros países latinoamericanos precisamente por las malas comunicaciones, especialmente las comunicaciones internacionales.

Ese factor negativo ha desaparecido. Recientemente se observó que el 27 por ciento de los habitantes de Uruguay tiene teléfono en casa. La densidad en telefonía celular es de tres **abonados** cada cien habitantes, o sea, un nivel muy positivo para el país. El congestionamiento en las comunicaciones de telefonía móvil que se notó recientemente en las zonas de vacación durante el verano es un ejemplo del rápido crecimiento del uso de los teléfonos celulares en Uruguay.

Antel es una compañía que ofrece diferentes sistemas de telecomunicaciones y distintos tipos de servicios (instalaciones, mantenimiento y apoyo técnico) en Uruguay. Aparte existe un distribuidor de Ericsson, que vende aparatos de telefonía al público. Los uruguayos consideran Uruguay como el centro del **MERCOSUR**. Esta realidad convierte a Uruguay en un mercado de importancia estratégica.

Para pensar: ¿Tienes tú un teléfono celular? ¿Alguien de tu familia tiene uno? ¿Tus amigos? ¿Crees que es conveniente usar el teléfono móvil? ¿Cuáles son algunas desventajas de este modo de comunicación? ¿Cuáles son algunas ventajas?

G. PREGUNTAS Contesta las siguientes preguntas a base de la lectura.

1. ¿Por qué se consideró antes peligroso invertir dinero en Uruguay?
2. ¿Qué porcentaje de la población uruguaya tiene teléfono en casa? ¿Cuántas personas de cada 100 usan un teléfono móvil?

Spanish speakers use the past (imperfect) subjunctive to express wishes, emotions, opinions, uncertainty, and indefiniteness about the past.

Forming the past subjunctive

For all Spanish verbs, drop the -**ron** ending from the **Uds./ellos(as)** form of the preterite tense, then add the personal endings shown in boldface below.[1] Any irregularities in the third-person plural of the preterite will be maintained in the imperfect subjunctive (as demonstrated below with the verbs **venir** and **irse**).[2]

	hablar	**venir**	**irse**
Uds., ellos(as)	hablaron	vinieron	se fueron
	habla**ra**	vinie**ra**	me fue**ra**
	habla**ras**	vinie**ras**	te fue**ras**
	habla**ra**	vinie**ra**	se fue**ra**
	hablá**ramos**	vinié**ramos**	nos fué**ramos**
	habla**rais**	vinie**rais**	os fue**rais**
	habla**ran**	vinie**ran**	se fue**ran**

Uses of the past subjunctive

You have learned to use the present subjunctive to express actions, conditions, and situations that take place in the present or the future. Spanish speakers use the past subjunctive to communicate the same information about the past.

In noun clauses

• To express desires, preferences, suggestions, requests, and recommendations

Federico esperaba que a Alejandra **le gustara** la idea de abrir una tienda de computadoras.

*Federico hoped that Alejandra **would like** the idea of opening a computer store.*

• To express happiness, hope, likes, complaints, worries, regret, sorrow, surprise, fear, and other emotions

Federico y Alejandra se alegraron que su nueva tienda de computadoras **saliera** bien.

*Federico and Alejandra were glad that their new computer store **turned out** well.*

---

[1] The **nosotros(as)** form always has an accent mark because it is the only form in which the stress falls on the third-from-the-last syllable.
[2] The past subjunctive has alternate forms that use -**se** instead of -**ra** endings. For example: **hablase, hablases, hablase, hablásemos, hablaseis, hablasen** and **fuese, fueses, fuese, fuésemos, fueseis, fuesen.** These forms are sometimes used in Spain and in literary works or legal documents.

Federico esperaba que **hubiera** muchos clientes el primer día, pero Alejandra tenía miedo que nadie **viniera.**

*Federico hoped that **there would be** lots of customers the first day, but Alejandra was afraid that no one **would come.***

• To make impersonal expressions

Era bueno que **estuvieran** los padres de la pareja para la inauguración de la tienda.

*It was good that the couple's parents **were** there for the opening of the store.*

• To express doubt and uncertainty

Alejandra dudó que ellos **pudieran** pagar a muchos empleados al principio.

*Alejandra doubted that **they could** pay several employees at first.*

In adjective clauses

• To express nonexistent conditions

Para la tienda, Federico buscaba un sitio que **tuviera** mucho espacio.

*For the store, Federico looked for a site that **had** lots of space.*

In adverbial clauses

• To express purpose and future contingency

Los padres de Federico y Alejandra les prestaron el dinero con tal de que **pudieran** devolvérselo dentro de un año.

*Federico and Alejandra's parents lent them the money provided that **they could** pay it back to them within a year.*

In making polite requests or suggestions

• In addition to the conditional tense, Spanish speakers also use the past subjunctive of verbs such as **querer, deber,** and **poder** to soften requests, to make polite suggestions, and to persuade gently.

—¿**Quisieran** Uds. acompañarnos? *Would you like to accompany us?*

—Gracias, pero **debiéramos** volver. *Thank you, but **we should** return.*

—Quizás **pudiéramos** ir otra noche. *Maybe **we could** go another night.*

¡A practicar!

H. LOS RECUERDOS DE UN ABUELO El abuelo de Federico le indica cómo los tiempos han cambiado. Conjuga los verbos entre paréntesis en la forma correcta del imperfecto del subjuntivo.

1. Cuando yo era niño, no teníamos computadoras. Mis padres insistían que yo _____ (estudiar) mucho.

2. Ellos querían que mi hermano y yo _____ (sacar) una beca para asistir a la universidad de Montevideo.[1]

3. Mi padre, tu bisabuelo, trabajaba mucho para que la familia _____ (tener) las necesidades básicas. ¡No teníamos tiempo para jugar, y no teníamos juegos electrónicos!

4. En aquella época no era común que una esposa _____ (trabajar) fuera de la casa.

5. Por esa razón yo empecé a trabajar cuando tenía 15 años en caso de que no _____ (recibir) una beca para mis estudios universitarios.

6. Yo quería trabajar en la librería de mi tío. Más gente leía libros entonces, como no existía la televisión o el Internet. Le pedí que él me _____ (dar) un trabajo durante los fines de semana.

7. Mi madre no quería que nosotros _____ (estar) fuera de la casa los domingos, pero era el día más ocupado de la tienda.

8. En aquella época no teníamos el Internet, y era importante que los estudiantes _____ (tener) y _____ (leer) todos los libros para las clases.

I. RECUERDOS DE MI JUVENTUD Forma oraciones sobre tu juventud usando frases de cada grupo.

Cuando yo era joven...

1. mis padres insistían en que yo...
2. mi mejor amigo(a) quería que nosotros...
3. yo quería vivir en una casa que...
4. mi abuela me pedía que yo...
5. mi madre se alegraba de que la familia...

aprender a usar la computadora
estar cerca del mar / de las montañas
estudiar mucho
portarse bien *(to behave)* en la clase
no pasar demasiado tiempo en el teléfono
ir de vacaciones juntos
ser amigos para la vida
ser honesto(a)
estar en la ciudad / en el campo
no gastar todo mi dinero en discos compactos

J. PÁGINAS DE MI DIARIO Escribe dos párrafos sobre tu niñez y tu adolescencia y luego comparte tus experiencias con un(a) compañero(a) de clase.

MI NIÑEZ

Cuando era niño(a), era importante que yo...
Mi(s) (papá/mamá/padres) prohibía(n) que...
No me gustaba que mi(s) (papá/mamá/padres)... , pero sí me gustaba que (él/ella/ellos)...

MI ADOLESCENCIA

De adolescente, no estaba seguro(a) de que...
Por ejemplo, dudaba que...
A veces, sentía que... ; en otras ocasiones me alegraba de que...

En voz alta

K. ENTREVISTA Hazle las siguientes preguntas a un(a) compañero(a) de clase para saber un poco sobre su niñez.

---

[1] Montevideo is the capital of Uruguay. It has 1.5 million inhabitants, 44 percent of the country's entire population.

1. **La familia:** ¿Qué te gustaba que hicieran tus padres cuando eras niño(a)?
2. **La escuela:** ¿Qué te prohibían tus profesores en la escuela primaria? ¿y en la secundaria?
3. **Los pasatiempos:** ¿Qué deportes practicabas cuando eras niño(a)? ¿En qué deportes te prohibían tus padres que participaras? ¿Por qué?
4. **La tecnología:** ¿Tenías televisor en casa cuando eras niño(a)? ¿Qué programas permitían tus padres que vieras? ¿Qué programas te prohibían que vieras? ¿Por qué? ¿Tenías computadora e Internet en casa? ¿Qué te dejaban hacer con la computadora? ¿Qué te decían que no hicieras con la computadora?

L. ES MEJOR SER CORTÉS Imagínate que tú y un(a) compañero(a) de clase están de vacaciones en Uruguay. Uds. desean ser corteses con los uruguayos y por eso, usan el subjuntivo del pasado de los verbos **querer, deber** y **poder**. ¿Qué les dirían a las siguientes personas?

MODELO: Pides que alguien te saque una foto.
¿*Pudiera sacarnos una foto?*

1. Quieres que un amigo te muestre cómo usar la videocámara.
2. Un amigo uruguayo usa una palabra que no entiendes. Pídele que te la explique.
3. Estás en un hotel. Una mujer de limpieza toca a la puerta para ver si puede limpiar tu cuarto. Tú acabas de levantarte. Le pides que vuelva en una hora.
4. Llamas a un amigo por teléfono para persuadirle que vaya de compras contigo mañana.
5. No entiendes a un policía porque habla demasiado rápido.
6. Estás de paseo en Montevideo cuando tú y tu amigo conocen a una pareja joven. Los invitas a cenar.
7. Después de la cena, pides permiso para volver al hotel.

VOCABULARIO: *La computadora*

EN LA TIENDA DE FEDERICO Y ALEJANDRA In this section, you will learn how to talk about computers and their functions.

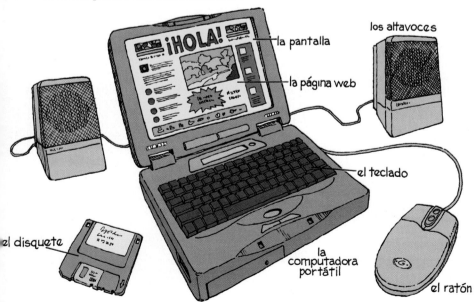

los altavoces
la pantalla
la página web
el teclado
el disquete
la computadora portátil
el ratón

el archivo *file*
el ciberespacio *cyberspace*
la conexión *connection*
el correo electrónico *e-mail*
el disco duro *hard drive*

el escáner *scanner*
la impresora *printer*
el Internet *Internet*
el mensaje *message*

el programa (de CD-ROM) *(CD-ROM) program*
el salón (la sala) de charla *chat room*

Verbos

abrir un documento (un programa) *to open a document (program)*
archivar (guardar) *to save*
estar conectado(a) (en línea) *to be online*

hacer click (sobre) *to click (on)*
imprimir *to print*
navegar la red *to surf the net*

programar *to program*
quitar el programa *to quit the program*
teletrabajar *to telecommute*

Palabras útiles

Localizador Uniforme de Recursos *URL*
el módem *modem*
la página de bienvenida (de entrada, de presentación, inicial, principal, de la red) *home page*

la plataforma de operación *operating platform (system)*
el proveedor de servicios Internet *Internet service provider*
el servidor *server*

¿NOS ENTENDEMOS?

Directions on a web page telling a cybernaut to "click" on an icon can be stated in at least three different ways: **hacer click, oprimir,** or **pulsar.**

¿NOS ENTENDEMOS?

With the emergence of the Internet, the Spanish language is quickly adopting and creating new vocabulary to talk about **el ciberespacio,** or *cyberspace.* Many of these words are cognates of their English counterparts. The web can be referred to as either **el Internet, la telaraña mundial,** or **la red.** One who navigates **la red** can be called **un(a) cibernauta** or **internauta.** To surf the web can be referred to as **navegar la red** or even **surfear.** One may visit a **salón (sala) de chat** to visit, or **chatear,** with friends around the world.

¡A practicar!

M. ¡SOCORRO! Es la segunda semana en la tienda de Federico y Alejandra. Hoy, muchos clientes llaman con problemas. Completa las frases con la palabra necesaria de la lista.

disquete   computadora portátil   hacer click   pantalla   ciberespacio   imprimir
página web   navegar la red   correo electrónico   altavoces   conexión
abrir   salón de charla   Internet   archivar   mensajes   escáner

1. El Sr. Ramírez:
¡Ayúdeme, por favor, Alejandra! Voy a hacer un viaje a Punta del Este[1] y necesito una computadora que pueda llevar conmigo. ¿Qué me recomienda Ud.?
   Alejandra: Cómprese una _____.
2. Judith:
Alejandra, necesito algo para archivar mis documentos. No quiero archivarlos en la computadora misma. ¿Qué puedo usar?
   Alejandra: Tú necesitas un _____.
3. Juan Pablo:
Alejandra, yo quisiera escuchar música del Internet con mi computadora. ¿Qué necesito?
   Alejandra: Ud. necesita unos _____.
4. La Sra. Marga:
Tengo un problema con la _____ de mi computadora. No puedo ver las imágenes.

---

[1] Punta del Este, Uruguay, is a city that lies on the coast, just 140 kilometers from Montevideo. It is a famous resort spot for the jet-set crowd from both Uruguay and Argentina. Many famous people own vacation homes there.

5. José Eduardo: Quiero navegar el _____. ¿Me podría mostrar cómo hacer una _____ con el Internet? Quisiera diseñar una _____ con fotos de El Rosedal en los Jardines Botánicos.[1]

Federico: Mire, José Eduardo, para poner sus fotos en el _____, va a necesitar un _____ si no tiene una cámera digital. También necesita tener una dirección de _____ para que la gente que ve su página web pueda mandarle _____.

6. Soledad: Alejandra, yo quiero conocer al hombre de mis sueños en el Internet. ¿Conoces tú algún _____ para solteros?

Alejandra: No sé, pero puedes mirar en el Internet. ¿Sabes _____?

7. Cordelia: No quiero perder mis documentos, ¡pero no sé cómo _____ en mi nueva computadora!

8. Maruja: Yo sé cerrar mis documentos, pero no sé cómo _____ los.

Alejandra: Para abrir tus documentos, necesitas _____ con el ratón en el ícono.

9. Eduardo Espina: ¿Para qué es esa impresora, para _____ mis documentos?

N. **¿QUÉ BUSCA ESTA GENTE?** Ahora Federico tiene descripciones de lo que sus clientes necesitan. Ayúdale a encontrar las cosas que necesitan.

1. _____ algo para imprimir documentos
2. _____ algo con muchas teclas y letras para escribir en la computadora
3. _____ el objeto que se usa para hacer click
4. _____ lo que se usa para escribir en la computadora
5. _____ la parte de la computadora que tiene memoria

a. el disco duro
b. el programa (de Word)
c. el teclado
d. la impresora
e. el ratón

O. **¿QUÉ NECESITAS?** Indica el equipo y los programas que necesitas para realizar las siguientes funciones en la computadora.

MODELO: producir una nueva versión de tu currículum
Necesito el disquete con la versión vieja, una computadora, un programa de Word y una impresora.

1. producir copias de unas fotos
2. escribir una carta
3. buscar información sobre el turismo en Uruguay
4. charlar con alguien con el teclado
5. escribir un trabajo para tu clase de inglés
6. tomar apuntes *(to take notes)* por computadora en la biblioteca o en clase
7. escuchar música del Internet en tu computadora
8. imprimir copias de tu trabajo de inglés para tus amigos

---

[1] The Botanical Gardens in Montevideo are located near the Parque del Prado on Washington Street. These gardens boast more than 1,000 species of indigenous plants. El Rosedal, or the Rose Garden, was once the meeting place for women from high society.

En voz alta

P. **¿CUÁNTO USAS LA TECNOLOGÍA?** Hazle las siguientes preguntas a un(a) compañero(a) de clase para determinar cuánto él o ella usa la tecnología.

nunca = 0   a veces = 1   frecuentemente = 2   todos los días = 3

_____ ¿Te escribes con amigos o familiares por el correo electrónico?
_____ ¿Usas la computadora para escribir trabajos escritos para tus clases?
_____ ¿Haces presentaciones con la computadora?
_____ ¿Escribes páginas que aparecen en el Internet?
_____ ¿Te comunicas con gente en las salas de charla?
_____ ¿Compras cosas de un vendedor en la telaraña mundial?
_____ ¿Navegas la red para diversión?
_____ ¿Usas un escáner para modificar fotos?
_____ ¿Imprimes cartas o tarjetas que creaste en la computadora?
_____ ¿Usas la computadora para programar?

INTERPRETACIONES

0–8   Debes comprarte una computadora.
9–17   Necesitas más práctica con la computadora.
18–24   ¿Quieres una entrevista con Microsoft?
25–30   Eres un(a) genio(a) con la computadora.

Q. **ENTREVISTA** Hazle las siguientes preguntas a otro(a) estudiante y luego discutan sus respuestas.

1. ¿Para qué actividades usas la computadora? ¿Usas la computadora más como un componente de tu trabajo o tus estudios o como una fuente de diversión? ¿Te ha simplificado la vida la computadora o es la causa de más estrés para ti?
2. ¿Es la computadora una tecnología privilegiada que se reserva solamente para los ricos? ¿Es un problema que los jóvenes sepan más que la gente mayor con respecto a la tecnología? ¿Será más fácil usar la computadora en el futuro o será tan complicado como ahora? ¿Cómo se puede asegurar que todos tengan acceso a la red y los servicios que ofrece?
3. ¿Hay suficiente control sobre el contenido de páginas web? ¿Qué harías si tuvieras un niño de diez años que quisiera navegar la red? ¿Qué papel debe tener el Internet en las escuelas públicas?
4. En tu opinión, ¿son la mayoría de los programas de CD-ROM educativos o solamente para diversión? ¿Cuáles son algunos programas que te gustaría usar que no has encontrado todavía en las tiendas?
5. ¿Son la computadora y el Internet novedades o representan el medio de comunicación dominante para el futuro? Explica tu respuesta.

ENCUENTRO *cultural*

Los cafés cibernéticos

Éstas son unas palabras nuevas para la lectura:

proveer   *to make available*
acceder   *to access*
cálido(a)   *warm*

Un café cibernético es una cafetería con computadoras donde se puede trabajar, jugar o entrar en el Internet y a la vez disfrutar de una variedad de cafés, sándwiches o la especialidad de la casa. Se puede navegar por la red, leer las noticias, revisar el correo electrónico o visitar lugares exóticos a través de la telaraña mundial.

El cibercafé en Uruguay ha dado un paso más adelante para **proveer** la posibilidad de servir como laboratorio para estudiantes, talleres para profesionales y también como centros de entretenimiento para juegos interactivos y la realidad virtual.

El primer café cibernético del Uruguay está en Pocitos. Tiene lo más reciente en cuanto a tecnología informática, a través de la cual se puede **acceder** a una biblioteca de software que incluye desde los entretenimientos más novedosos a los programas de diseño gráfico más avanzados. Ahora los montevideanos tienen un lugar donde además de disfrutar de un café pueden acceder el Internet e interactuar con amigos conectados a la red. Lo pueden hacer con otros cibernautas que navegan desde otros cibercafés del mundo a través del teclado o de videófonos.

Los cafés cibernéticos se conocen en Estados Unidos, Chile, Argentina, España, México, Ecuador y Brasil. Casi todos los cibercafés en Latinoamérica son del mismo estilo. El ambiente es muy familiar. La idea es que el café parezca ser una casa, con mesas y sillas de madera, y ser lo más **cálido** posible.

Para pensar: ¿Has visitado un cibercafé en los Estados Unidos? ¿Dónde? ¿Cuál fue tu impresión? Si tú pudieras, ¿dónde abrirías un cibercafé? ¿Por qué crees que es necesario abrirlo en ese lugar?

R. **PREGUNTAS** Contesta las siguientes preguntas a base de la lectura.

1. Nombra tres cosas que se puede hacer en un café cibernético.
2. ¿Dónde queda el primer cibercafé en Uruguay? ¿Cómo es?
3. ¿Cómo es el ambiente en la mayoría de los cibercafés en Latinoamerica?

GRAMÁTICA II: *Using the imperfect subjunctive to make hypothetical statements*

You have seen the conditional tense used with the past subjunctive to speculate about what would happen under certain conditions (**Si tuviéramos el dinero, iríamos al Ecuador**). Now you will learn how to form and use these hypothetical statements that are often called *if* clauses.

Forming and using *if* clauses

• To imply that a situation is contrary to fact or is unlikely to occur, use **si** *(if)* with a past subjunctive verb in the *if* (dependent) clause, and a conditional verb in the conclusion (independent clause).

Contrary to fact
Si tuvieras el dinero, **¿irías** a Uruguay?
*If you had the money, **would you go** to Uruguay?*

Unlikely to occur
Si yo pagara tu boleto, **¿irías** conmigo?
*If I payed for your ticket, **would you go** with me?*

• To imply that a situation is a fact or is likely to occur, however, use **si** with an indicative verb form in both the *if* clause and the conclusion.

Factual situation
—Ya he ahorrado más de 2.000 dólares para mis vacaciones.
I've already saved more than 2,000 dollars for my vacation.
—Si tienes tanto dinero, puedes visitar Uruguay.
If you have so much money, you can visit Uruguay.

Likely to occur
Si ahorro 200 dólares más, visitaré ese país.
If I save 200 dollars more, I will visit that country.

¡A practicar!

S. SI VIAJARA A URUGUAY... ¿A ti te gustaría viajar a Uruguay algún día? Haz oraciones completas para expresar tus ideas como en el modelo.

MODELO: si / viajar / Uruguay / ir / con...
Si viajara al Uruguay, iría con mi amigo Bob.

1.   si / planear un viaje / Uruguay / buscar información / el Internet
2.   si / viajar / Uruguay / día / ir / con...
3.   si / necesitar / una computadora portátil para el viaje / comprarla / en...
4.   si / tener / dinero / alojarme / en Plaza Victoria[1]
5.   si / tener / problemas / hotel / hablar / con...
6.   si / estar / mercado / comprar / un(a)...

T. VIVIR CON LA TECNOLOGÍA ¿Te simplifica la vida la tecnología? Completa por escrito las siguientes oraciones escogiendo entre el presente del indicativo o el imperfecto del subjuntivo para cada verbo indicado.

MODELO: Si yo *necesito* (necesitar) más información sobre alguna cosa, la busco en el Internet.

---

[1] Plaza Victoria is a hotel and conference center in the heart of the business district of Montevideo. It is near the largest shopping centers and is 25 minutes from the International Airport.

1. Si nosotros _____ (tener) problemas con un programa, pediríamos la ayuda de un amigo.
2. Si mi compañero(a) de cuarto no _____ (recordar) apagar el estéreo, lo apago yo.
3. Si mi madre _____ (aprender) un poco sobre la computadora, la usaría mucho.
4. Si los teléfonos celulares _____ (ser) más baratos, todo el mundo los tendría.
5. Si no _____ (haber) satélites, la comunicación internacional sería más difícil.
6. Si mis padres no _____ (pagar) la cuenta de mi teléfono celular, yo lo desconectaría.
7. Si mi abuela _____ (usar) el correo electrónico, hablaríamos con más frecuencia.
8. Si no _____ (tener) tiempo para mandar una carta normal, mando un mensaje de correo electrónico.
9. Si mis amigos _____ (venir) esta tarde, nosotros buscaremos información sobre Punta del Este en la red.
10. Si mi profesor _____ (comprar) una máquina de fax, yo le mandaría un fax con mi tarea.

En voz alta

U. OPORTUNIDADES Y DECISIONES Pregúntale a otro(a) estudiante sobre estas posibilidades fantásticas y las decisiones que él o ella tomaría.

1. Si tuvieras el dinero y el tiempo, ¿te gustaría comprar una computadora mejor? ¿Qué tipo comprarías? ¿Para qué la usarías?
2. ¿Harías una página web en el Internet si tuvieras la oportunidad? ¿Qué información pondrías? ¿Pondrías una foto tuya en esa página?
3. Si pudieras inventar una máquina, ¿qué inventarías? ¿Por qué inventarías esta cosa?
4. Si vivieras en otro siglo, ¿en qué época querrías vivir y por qué? ¿Qué objetos de la tecnología echarías de menos *(would you miss)*?
5. Si conocieras a una persona en un salón de chat, ¿qué le preguntarías?
6. Si tú y tus amigos descubrieran el secreto de la vida eterna, ¿qué harían con esta información?
7. ¿Querrías saber algo de tu vida si pudieras visitar el futuro?
8. ¿Qué haría tu mejor amigo(a) si ganara la lotería? ¿Compartiría el dinero contigo? ¿Te compraría él o ella un nuevo estéreo u otra cosa parecida?

V. ¿UN MUNDO IDEAL? Con un(a) compañero(a) de clase, discutan las consecuencias de las siguientes situaciones y decidan si el mundo realmente sería mejor.

¿Qué pasaría si...

1. todos se cuidaran bien?
2. no hubiera guerras?
3. nadie tuviera problemas emocionales?
4. fuera posible vivir 200 años?
5. no existieran diferencias de opinión?
6. cada persona se vistiera de la misma manera?

The following explanations and examples summarize how Spanish speakers use the indicative to describe factual information as well as habitual and completed actions and the subjunctive to express doubt and indefiniteness.

Use an indicative verb form . . .	Use a subjunctive verb form . . .
1. to refer to habitual actions and completed actions. Llevo mi mochila cuando **viajo** al extranjero. *I take my backpack when I travel abroad.* Llevé mi mochila cuando **viajé** a Uruguay. *I took my backpack when I traveled to Uruguay.*	1. to refer to a future action dependent on another action. Llevaré mi mochila cuando **viaje** a Uruguay. *I will take my backpack when I travel to Uruguay.*
2. to refer to a specific person, place, or thing. Tengo una maleta que **es** vieja. *I have a suitcase that is old.*	2. to refer to an unknown or non-existent person, place, or thing. Quiero una que **sea** más grande. *I want one that is larger.*
3. to express certainty. Estoy seguro de que **puedo** ir. *I am sure that I can go.*	3. to express uncertainty. No estoy seguro de que **pueda** ir. *I am not sure that I can go.*
4. in an *if* clause to imply that a situation is factual or will likely occur. Si **tienes** 1.000 dólares, **puedes** ir a Uruguay. *If you have 1,000 dollars, you can go to Uruguay.* Si **ahorro** 100 dólares más, **iré** allí. *If I save 100 dollars more, I will go there.*	4. in an *if* clause to imply that a situation is contrary to fact and will not likely occur. Si **tuvieras** 1.000 dólares, ¿**irías** a Uruguay? *If you had 1,000 dollars, would you go to Uruguay?* Si **ahorrara** el dinero esta semana, **iría** contigo. *If I saved the money this week, I would go with you.*

Uses of infinitives and subjunctive forms (summary)

The following explanations and examples summarize how Spanish speakers use infinitives and the subjunctive to express wants, preferences, intentions, advice, suggestions, and opinions.

Use an infinitive . . .	Use a subjunctive verb form . . .
1. after verbs of volition when there is only one subject in a sentence. Federico quiere **trabajar**. *Federico wants to work.*	1. after verbs of volition when there is a change of subject in a sentence. Federico quiere que Alejandra **trabaje**. *Federico wants Alejandra to work.*

2. after verbs of emotion when there is only one subject in a sentence.	2. after verbs of emotion when there is a change of subject in a sentence.
Federico espera **tener** éxito.	Federico espera que ellos **tengan** éxito.
*Federico hopes **to be** successful.*	*Federico hopes that **they will be** successful.*
3. after impersonal expressions when there is no personal subject in a sentence.	3. after impersonal expressions when there is a personal subject in a sentence.
Es bueno **viajar.** *It's good **to travel.***	Es bueno que Ud. **viaje.** *It's good that **you travel.***

¡A practicar!

W. ENTREVISTA CON ALEJANDRA Alejandra describe la primera semana de su nuevo negocio. Completa los siguientes párrafos, subrayando las formas correctas de los verbos entre paréntesis.

Mi marido y yo tuvimos una semana exitosa con el nuevo negocio. Federico quería (abrir/abrió/abriera) la tienda el domingo por la tarde, pero yo insistí en que (tener/tuvimos/tuviéramos) un día de descanso. Él siempre quiere (trabajar/trabaja/trabaje) más, pero yo le digo que es mejor que (descansar/descansamos/descansemos) por lo menos un día a la semana. Si (haber/había/hubiera) otra persona para cuidar la tienda ese día, sería otra cosa. Si las ventas siguen tal como son ahora, creo que (poder/podemos/podamos) emplear a un asistente.

Nuestros padres nos ayudaron mucho. Me alegro de que (estar/estuvieron/estuvieran) con nosotros. Si mi padre no estuviera jubilado, (querer/quisiera/querría) trabajar todos los días con nosotros. Es bueno que él (hacer/hace/haga) algo de vez en cuando. Después de (jubilarse/se jubiló/se jubilara) no conseguía mantenerse ocupado. Él nos dijo que podemos llamarlo cuando (necesitar/necesitamos/necesitemos) ayuda. De todas maneras él está contento de que todo (haber/ha/haya) salido bien la primera semana. Yo espero (tener/tengo/tenga) muchas semanas semejantes. No dudo que (ir/vamos/vayamos) a tener una de las mejores tiendas de Montevideo.

X. POBRECITO FEDERICO Completa esta conversación entre Federico y Alejandra usando los verbos de la lista.

es	vayas	sentirme	te sientas	fuera	traiga	descansar	te sientes

Federico:	Ay, me duele el estómago. Creo que _____ por el desayuno que comí esta mañana.
Alejandra:	Es posible que _____ la comida, pero francamente lo dudo. Pero espero que _____ mejor, Federico. ¿Quieres que te _____ algo para tomar... algún jugo?
Federico:	No, gracias, Alejandra. Ahora prefiero _____ un poco.
Alejandra:	Si _____ peor, sugiero que _____ a la clínica.
Federico:	Sí, pero espero _____ mejor esta tarde. ¡No podemos cerrar la tienda!
Alejandra:	Tú tranquilo. Llamaré a mi padre.

Y. EN LA CLÍNICA Por la tarde, Federico no se sintió mejor y fue a la clínica. Completa el diálogo que ocurrió allí con las formas correctas de los verbos entre paréntesis.

MODELO: Médico: ¿Cómo *está* (estar) Ud. hoy?

Médico:	¿Cómo _____ (sentirse) Ud., señor?
Federico:	No _____ (sentirse) bien, doctor. Creo que _____ (estar) muriéndome.
Médico:	¿Por qué _____ (creer) Ud. eso?
Federico:	Porque esta mañana cuando _____ (levantarse), _____ (tener) un dolor de cabeza muy fuerte y _____ (sentirse) mal. No _____ (dormir) bien anoche.
Médico:	¿Todavía le _____ (doler) la cabeza?
Federico:	Sí, mucho. Recientemente he _____ (sufrir) mucha tensión en mi trabajo. Mi esposa _____ (decir) que yo _____ (tener) que trabajar menos horas al día, pero necesito estar allí. Somos los dueños de una tienda.
Médico:	¿_____ (Poder) Ud. encontrar a otra persona que _____ (poder) ayudarles con la tienda?
Federico:	No sé, doctor. Me _____ (gustar) encontrar a una persona que _____ (querer) trabajar los fines de semana. _____ (Necesitar) el dinero. Ojalá _____ (poder) encontrar a alguien muy pronto.
Médico:	Ojalá, señor. Ahora yo _____ (ir) a darle unas pastillas. Yo _____ (querer) que Ud. _____ (tomar) una antes de acostarse.
Federico:	Sí, doctor. Muchas gracias.

En voz alta

Z. ¡A CONVERSAR! Escoge uno de los siguientes temas para discutir con un(a) compañero(a) de clase. Intenten usar construcciones con el subjuntivo.

1. sus consejos y recomendaciones para el uso de la tecnología en su universidad
2. sus opiniones sobre la tecnología en general
3. una descripción de una experiencia frustrante que tuviste recientemente con la tecnología
4. una descripción de la tecnología en el futuro

AA. ¡BUEN VIAJE! Usando las siguientes situaciones, conversa con otro(a) estudiante.

Estudiante A: Imagínate que a ti te gustaría hacer un viaje a Uruguay. Pregúntale a un(a) agente de viajes (otro[a] estudiante) sobre la siguiente información de aquel país: actividades de interés turístico, clima, ropa necesaria, alojamiento *(lodging)*, recuerdos típicos, etcétera. Trata de conseguir la mayor información que sea posible. Aquí tienes algunas frases para ayudarte:

Quisiera visitar...
¿Pudiera Ud. decirme... ?
Quiero un hotel que...

Me gustaría comprar...
Es importante que...
(No) Creo que...

Estudiante B: Imagínate que tú eres un(a) agente de viajes en Los Ángeles, California. Prepárate a contestar preguntas de uno(a) de sus clientes de habla española (otro[a] estudiante) sobre: (1) qué hacer en Montevideo, (2) el clima en ese lugar y (3) lo que una persona debe llevar en el viaje. Aquí tienes algunas frases para ayudarte:

¿Cuánto tiempo... ?   Espero que Ud....
Es mejor que Ud....   Pues, recomiendo (que)...
Es una lástima que Ud....   (No) Creo que...

Síntesis ◆◆◆

¡A ver!

El tema principal del **Capítulo 15** es el mundo tecnológico y el efecto que tiene en nuestra vida diaria, especialmente en el hogar. Nuestro presentador videográfico para este capítulo es Felipe, que da clases de informática en una escuela privada en Montevideo, la capital de Uruguay.

ACTIVIDAD 1 Pre-viewing task (Segmento 1 del video)

Paso 1: En el primer segmento del video, vas a ver una serie de fotos y clips cortos, cada uno enfocado en una tecnología que ya es bastante común en nuestras vidas en la actualidad. En la tabla, apunta el nombre de las diez tecnologías representadas en el video. Al lado de cada nombre, y en su columna correspondiente, apunta si tienes o no tienes tal tecnología en tu propia casa y si te parece de mucha o de poca utilidad.

Tecnología	Hay en mi casa	La considero de mucha utilidad	La considero de poca utilidad
1.			
2.			
3.			
4.			
5.			
6.			
7.			
8.			
9.			
10.			

Paso 2: En grupos de tres, averigüen qué tecnologías tiene cada persona del grupo y cuál es su opinión sobre su utilidad. En caso de no tener determinada tecnología, la persona tendrá que hablar en términos hipotéticos sobre su utilidad.

MODELO: *Si tuviera un teléfono celular, lo encontraría de mucha utilidad porque podría mantenerme en contacto todo el tiempo con mi abuela, que ya es bastante mayor y vive sola.*

ACTIVIDAD 2   Pre-viewing task (Segmento 2 del video)

Paso 1: ¿Tienes una computadora? ¿Para qué la utilizas? Si tienes una computadora, apunta en una lista las funciones que tiene en tu vida. Si no tienes computadora, apunta las funciones que tendría si tuvieras una.

Paso 2: Explícale a un(a) compañero(a) de clase las ideas que has apuntado en el **Paso 1**.

ACTIVIDAD 3   Viewing task (Segmento 2 del video)

En el segundo segmento del video, vas a conocer a tres personas que son estudiantes de la informática en una escuela en Buenos Aires, Argentina. Cada una de ellos habla de la utilidad que tiene la computadora en su vida personal y profesional. Identifica los usos que tiene la computadora para cada persona entrevistada.

¿Para qué utiliza la computadora?			

ACTIVIDAD 4   Post-viewing task (Segmento 2 del video)

En grupos de tres, hablen de cada una de las personas entrevistadas para la **Actividad 3**. Enfoca en los usos que tiene cada uno para la computadora en su vida personal y profesional.

¡A leer!

Integrating your reading strategies

In previous lessons, you have learned many strategies for becoming a more proficient reader of Spanish. In this section you will practice integrating several of these reading strategies.

Paso 1: Antes de leer: Comprende el tema del texto.

1. Mira el gráfico en la próxima página. ¿Cuál de las tecnologías del Internet es la más popular?
2. En tu opinión, ¿cuál es el tema que vas a encontrar en el texto?
3. Lee el título y el primer párrafo de la sección de abajo. ¿Tienes una idea más específica del tema del texto? ¿Cuál es?
4. Piensa en tu experiencia personal. ¿Qué ya sabes del tema?

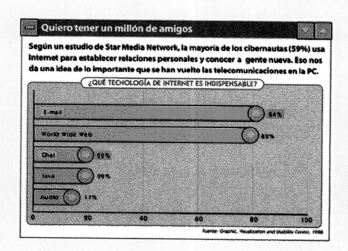

Quiero tener un millón de amigos

Según un estudio de Star Media Network, la mayoría de los cibernautas (59%) usa Internet para establecer relaciones personales y conocer a gente nueva. Eso nos da una idea de lo importante que se han vuelto las telecomunicaciones en la PC.

¿QUÉ TECNOLOGÍA DE INTERNET ES INDISPENSABLE?

E-mail	84%
World Wide Web	82%
Chat	22%
Java	09%
Audio	17%

0   20   40   60   80   100

Fuente: Graphic, Visualization and Usability Center, 1998.

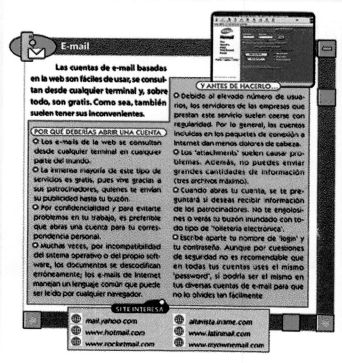

E-mail

Las cuentas de e-mail basadas en la web son fáciles de usar, se consultan desde cualquier terminal y, sobre todo, son gratis. Como sea, también suelen tener sus inconvenientes.

POR QUÉ DEBERÍAS ABRIR UNA CUENTA

○ Los e-mails de la web se consultan desde cualquier terminal en cualquier parte del mundo.

○ La inmensa mayoría de este tipo de servicios es gratis, pues vive gracias a sus patrocinadores, quienes te envían su publicidad hasta tu buzón.

○ Por confidencialidad y para evitarte problemas en tu trabajo, es preferible que abras una cuenta para tu correspondencia personal.

○ Muchas veces, por incompatibilidad del sistema operativo o del propio software, los documentos se descodifican erróneamente; los e-mails de Internet manejan un lenguaje común que puede ser leído por cualquier navegador.

Y ANTES DE HACERLO...

○ Debido al elevado número de usuarios, los servidores de las empresas que prestan este servicio suelen caerse con regularidad. Por lo general, las cuentas incluidas en los paquetes de conexión a Internet dan menos dolores de cabeza.

○ Los 'attachments' suelen causar problemas. Además, no puedes enviar grandes cantidades de información (tres archivos máximo).

○ Cuando abras tu cuenta, se te preguntará si deseas recibir información de los patrocinadores. No te engolosines o verás tu buzón inundado con todo tipo de 'voletería electrónica'.

○ Escribe aparte tu nombre de 'login' y tu contraseña. Aunque por cuestiones de seguridad no es recomendable que en todas tus cuentas uses el mismo 'password', sí podría ser el mismo en tus diversas cuentas de e-mail para que no lo olvides tan fácilmente.

SITE INTERESA

○ mail.yahoo.com   ○ altavista.iname.com
○ www.hotmail.com   ○ www.latinmail.com
○ www.rocketmail.com   ○ www.myownemail.com

Paso 2: Primera lectura: Comprender la idea general del texto

1. Lee rápidamente el texto para comprender la idea general de su contenido. Usa los cognados, los prefijos y los sufijos para ayudarte a comprender el significado de las palabras que no conozcas.
2. Subraya las ideas principales del texto.

Paso 3: Segunda lectura: Localizar información específica en el texto

Al leer rápidamente el texto otra vez, pon un círculo alrededor de los detalles que apoyan las ideas principales que has subrayado.

Paso 4: Tercera lectura: Verificar la comprensión total del texto

1. Contesta **sí** o **no** a las preguntas que siguen.
   - **a.** Las cuentas de e-mail basadas en la web son gratis.　　　　　Sí　　No
   - **b.** A veces hay problemas de compatibilidad con los e-mails del Internet.　Sí　　No
   - **c.** Los servidores de e-mail suelen *(tend to)* caerse con regularidad.　Sí　　No
   - **d.** Es posible enviar un número ilimitado de «attachments».　　Sí　　No
   - **e.** Es aconsejable que uses la misma contraseña *(password)* en tus　Sí　　No
     diversas cuentas de e-mail.
2. Escribe una respuesta breve a las preguntas que siguen.
   - **a.** ¿Cuáles son algunas ventajas de tener una cuenta de e-mail basada en la web?
   - **b.** ¿Cuáles son algunos problemas tecnológicos que pueden ocurrir cuando envías y recibes los e-mails del Internet?
   - **c.** Piensa en tu propia experiencia ahora. ¿Tienes una cuenta de e-mail? ¿Con qué frecuencia te comunicas por e-mail?

¡A escribir!

Speculating and hypothesizing

In this section, you are going to use what you have learned to write about a hypothetical situation. After deciding on a hypothetical situation to write about, you will then outline some of the positive and/or negative consequences of this situation. This will involve speculating about the future and imagining possible outcomes that may arise from the hypothetical situation you select.

For example, consider the following situation:

Ojalá yo tuviera una computadora portátil. De momento, no poseo ninguna computadora, y estoy harto de hacer la cola *(stand in line)* en los laboratorios de computadoras de la universidad. Si tuviera mi propia computadora portátil, podría navegar la red o mirar mi correo electrónico en cualquier momento. Tendría más tiempo para estudiar o pasar con mis amigos porque no tendría que hacer la cola en la universidad para usar una computadora. No importaría si estuviera en casa, en la universidad o en la casa de un amigo —siempre la tendría a mi lado. Sería mucho más fácil conectarme al Internet. También la podría llevar conmigo cuando estoy de vacaciones en casa de mis padres o en otro sitio.

Paso 1: Piensa en las siguientes situaciones hipotéticas. Luego, elige una de ellas o inventa tu propia situación.

- tener tu propio avión
- tener tu propio yate
- ser un(a) famoso(a) músico(a) o actor (actriz)
- ser presidente de los Estados Unidos
- descubrir una cura para el cáncer
- ¿ ?

Paso 2: Ahora que has elegido una situación hipotética, piensa en lo que pasaría en el contexto que has seleccionado. Piensa en las siguientes preguntas y escribe tus ideas en una hoja de papel.

- ¿Qué harías tú?
- ¿Qué reacción tendría tu familia? ¿tus amigos? ¿otros estudiantes en tu universidad?
- ¿Qué ventajas tendría esta situación? ¿Qué desventajas tendría?

Paso 3: Ahora, escribe una breve composición acerca de lo que pasaría en la situación hipotética que has elegido. Debes incluir la información que has usado en los **Pasos 1** y **2**. También, podrías usar el párrafo de arriba como un modelo.

Functions: Expressing a wish or desire; Expressing conditions; Hypothesizing

Vocabulary: Dreams & aspirations; Health: diseases & illnesses; Means of transportation; Working conditions

¡A conversar!

Piensa en los cambios que ha provocado el creciente nivel de tecnología en los Estados Unidos (en cuanto a las computadoras, el Internet, las comunicaciones, el transporte, la medicina, el mundo financiero, los negocios y el mercado laboral, etcétera). Habla con un(a) compañero(a) acerca de los efectos positivos y negativos de la tecnología en nuestra sociedad. Luego, preséntenles un resumen de sus ideas a sus compañeros de clase.

Los avances tecnológicos

la alarma *alarm*
la antena parabólica *satellite dish*
la cámara (digital) *(digital) camera*

el contestador automático *answering machine*
el control remoto *remote control*
el disco compacto *compact disc (CD)*

el equipo *equipment*
el estéreo *stereo*
el satélite *satellite*
el teléfono celular *celluar phone*

la videocámara *video camera*
el videocasete *videotape*
la videocasetera *VCR*

Verbos

apagar *to turn off*
(des)conectar *to (dis)connect*

(des)enchufar *to plug in (to unplug)*

funcionar *to function (to work)*

grabar *to record*
prender *to turn on*

Adjetivos

apagado(a) *off*

encendido(a) *on*

enchufado(a) *plugged in*

La computadora

los altavoces *speakers*
el archivo *file*
el ciberespacio *cyberspace*
la computadora portátil *laptop computer*
la conexión *connection*

el correo electrónico *e-mail*
el disco duro *hard drive*
el disquete *diskette*
el escáner *scanner*
la impresora *printer*
el Internet *Internet*

el mensaje *message*
la página web *web page*
la pantalla *screen*
el programa (de CD-ROM) *(CD-ROM) program*

el salón (la sala) de charla *chat room*
el teclado *keyboard*
el ratón *mouse (of computer)*

Verbos

abrir un documento (un programa) *to open a document (program)*
archivar (guardar) *to save*

estar conectado(a) (en línea) *to be online*
hacer click (sobre) *to click (on)*

imprimir *to print*
navegar la red *to surf the Net*
programar *to program*

salir del programa *to quit the program*
teletrabajar *to telecommute*

PLAZAS

BIENVENIDOS A *PLAZAS*, UNA PUBLICACIÓN QUE DESCRIBE EL PANORAMA DE LOS PAÍSES DE HABLA ESPAÑOLA.

El faro del sur: luces, cámara, acción

Fiebre del sábado por la noche

Pianista en miniatura

La fantasía en Perú, Chile y Uruguay te espera

Conquistadoras del nuevo milenio

En esta sección de Plazas, conocerás a varias personas de fama internacional de los países hispanos que nos ayudan a comprender mejor las particularidades de estos países. ¿Qué harías en tu tiempo libre si vivieras en uno de estos países? ¿Visitarías un museo? ¿Entrarías en discusiones sobre la política? ¿Verías películas en el cine o programas en la televisión?

EL FARO DEL SUR:
luces, cámara, acción

Cuando los padres de Meme mueren en un accidente automovilístico, ella se ocupa de cuidar a su hermana menor, Aneta. En esta película cargada de emoción, que cubre un período de siete u ocho años, las dos hermanas emprenden *(embark on)* un viaje tanto físico como espiritual para perderse y luego encontrarse en España, Uruguay y Argentina. El desenlace *(ending)* dramático, culminación de las altas y las bajas de Meme, depende del gran simbolismo del *Faro del Sur* para mostrar cómo estas dos chicas buscan la tranquilidad que se les fue robada en el accidente. El director argentino, el famoso Eduardo Mignogna *(Sol de otoño)*, depende de la actuación de la española Ingrid Rubio como Meme y de Jimena Barón (Aneta niña) / Florencia Bertotti (Aneta adolescente) para revelar las idiosincracias de sus relaciones con los amigos, Andy (Ricardo Darin), dueño del faro *(lighthouse)* y Dolores (Norma Aleandro), amiga de la madre de Meme y Aneta.

● ¿Cómo crees que termina la película?
● ¿Quiénes son algunos de tus directores de películas favoritos?
● ¿Qué tipo de película te gusta?
● ¿Con qué frecuencia vas al cine?
● Escribe una reseña *(review)* de tu película favorita.

Fiebre del sábado por la noche

SÁBADO GIGANTE

En la televisión latinoamericana, uno de los programas más exitosos ha sido "Sábado gigante", el cual se ha convertido en una sensación internacional tanto en Latinoamérica como en los Estados Unidos, donde actualmente tiene sus estudios de producción. La popularidad del programa se debe a la variedad de juegos, entrevistas, música, baile y, sobre todo, al carisma del animador. El animador y visionario del programa desde su inicio en 1962 es el chileno Mario Kreutzberg, mejor conocido como 'Don Francisco'. Además de "Sábado gigante", Mario Kruetzberg, hijo de inmigrantes alemanes que se instalaron en Talca (ciudad chilena sureña) durante la Segunda Guerra Mundial, concibió la idea de crear una teletón para ayudar a los niños. En 1978 se estrenó *(debuted)* la primera "Teletón" y hasta el momento, el programa ha recaudado *(raised)* fondos para construir institutos de rehabilitación y hospitales para miles de niños descapacitados y sus familias. La personalidad jovial de 'Don Francisco' contribuye su popularidad como animador, tanto en "Teletón" como en "Sábado gigante". Ahora, veamos un segmento de "Sábado gigante":

Don Francisco explica esta parte del programa. "Vamos a pasar al próximo juego de esta noche: 'Hazme reír'. Los dos participantes están aquí para contarnos un relato cómico para ver quién es el que más nos hace reír. El ganador del concurso cualificará para tomar clases de comedia en "Centro Cómico" aquí en Miami. Damas y caballeros, un aplauso para David Solano, de 27 años, peruano:

DAVID: El año pasado, fui a una exposición de arte moderno. Todas las pinturas consistían de cuadros verdes en diferentes posiciones, pero en realidad había pocas diferencias entre un cuadro y el otro. Les pedí a los guardias que me enseñaran la pintura que estaba en la portada *(cover)* del folleto que describía las pinturas. ¡Qué cómico! El guardia empezó a buscar, pero como todas se parecían tanto, era imposible que me dijera cuál pintura aparecía en la portada. Si él supiera... sólo le pregunté porque sabía que esa pintura en particular no estaba en la exposición; ¡sólo estaba en la portada como ejemplo del arte!

DON FRANCISCO: Gracias, David. Ahora escuchemos el siguiente relato. La segunda participante se llama Sara Otero, de Ecuador, y tiene 31 años.

SARA: Sabrán Uds. que mi jefe es muy serio y se enfoca mucho en su trabajo. Pues, un día, hablábamos en su oficina sobre unos clientes insolentes que querían un descuento por nuestro servicio de publicidad porque habían querido que nosotros le hubiéramos planificado mejor su campaña de publicidad. Entonces, mi jefe se enfadó *(got angry)* y gritó: "¡Ésta es la tercera vez que vienen con esta reclamación! ¿Creen que estoy sordo *(deaf)*? ¡Ya les expliqué que no íbamos a ofrecerles ningún descuento!" Cuando vi que estaba tan, pero tan enfadado, se me ocurrió que era el momento oportuno para inyectar un poco de comedia y empecé a hablar, pero sólo moviendo los labios y sin hacer sonido. Me dijo que lo repitiera e hice lo mismo hasta que él se dio cuenta del chiste y los dos empezamos a reírnos.

DON FRANCISCO: Un aplauso para los dos participantes. Ahora, veremos cuál de los dos participantes quieren ustedes que gane.

¿Has visto el programa "Sábado gigante"?

¿Cuál de las dos historias te parece más chistosa?

¿Qué hubieras hecho si trabajaras de guardia en el museo?

¿Te gusta hacer chistes como éstos?

Si fueras a participar en este concurso, ¿qué historia nos contarías?

¿Pianista en miniatura?

Isabel Allende (1942 –) nació en Lima, Perú de padres chilenos. Empezó su carrera como periodista antes de iniciar su carrera de novelista y cuentista. Su tío, Salvador Allende, fue presidente de Chile desde 1970 hasta 1973 cuando murió como resultado del golpe de estado (coup d'état), después del cual subió al poder el general Augusto Pinochet hasta 1990. Pasaron muchos años antes de que Isabel Allende se diera cuenta del impacto que su tío han tenido en su vida. Uno de los temas principales de su obra literaria es la disección de la familia en torno al conflicto político de la sociedad latinoamericana contemporánea. Otra característica que tienen en común sus obras es la presencia de una narradora o una protagonista femenina. En su colección *Los cuentos de Eva Luna* (1990), aparece "Tosca", cuento que narra las ironías en la vida de la protagonista, Maurizia Rugieri.

"Tosca"

Su padre la sentó al piano a los cinco años y a los diez Maurizia Rugieri dio su primer recital en el club Garibaldi, vestida de organza rosada y botines de charol *(patent leather ankle boots)*, ante un público benévolo, compuesto en su mayoría por miembros de la colonia italiana. Al término de la presentación pusieron varios ramos de flores a sus pies y el presidente del club le entregó una placa conmemorativa y una muñeca de loza *(china)*, adornada con cintas *(ribbons)* y encajes *(lace)*.

—Te saludamos, Maurizia Rugieri, como a un genio precoz, un nuevo Mozart. Los grandes escenarios del mundo te esperan—declamó.

La niña aguardó a que se callara el aplauso y, por encima del llanto orgulloso de su madre, hizo oír su voz con una altanería inesperada.

—Ésta es la última vez que toco el piano. Lo que quiero ser es cantante —anunció y salió de la sala arrastrando a la muñeca por un pie.

¿Qué opinas de los niños pródigos? ¿Trabajan bajo mucha presión o en algo que verdaderamente les apasiona?

¿Cómo muestra Allende el espíritu libre e independiente de Maurizia?

¿Tocas algún instrumento musical? Si no, ¿te gustaría? ¿Cuál instrumento?

¿Qué tipo de música te interesa? ¿Quién es tu cantante favorito?

¿Con qué frecuencia asistes a espectáculos de música: conciertos, sinfonías, óperas, etc.?

LA FANTASÍA EN PERÚ, CHILE Y URUGUAY TE ESPERA

Los editores de **Plazas** quieren reclutar un grupo de estudiantes de arte para participar en un programa de enriquicimiento cultural. El proyecto se trata de una visita a los museos principales de Lima, Santiago y Montevideo para apreciar el arte de estos países. Abajo aparece una descripción de algunos de los artistas del siglo XX cuyas obras te invitarán a explorar la fantasía artística, a veces abstracta, a veces basada en la realidad.

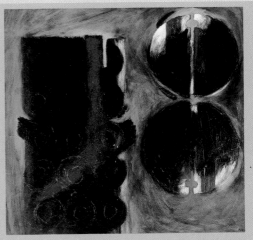

Considerado el fundador del arte abstracto peruano, Fernando de Szyszlo (1925–) buscaba la renovación en el arte contemporáneo. Es interesante que el mismo artista no se considera pintor abstracto porque dice que pinta lo que existe, dado significado después de un análisis profundo. Se inspiró en la poesía quechua para crear imágenes arquetípicas, evidente en su pintura "Puka Wamani" (1968), localizada en el Museo de Arte de Lima. Syszlo es colorista y depende del contraste entre colores para distinguir entre luz y sombra *(shadow)*.

Al llegar a Chile, visitarás el Museo Nacional de Bellas Artes en Santiago y verás las obras maestras de José Gil de Castro, Gonzalo Cienfuegos, entre otros. Uno de los artistas chilenos más influyentes de este siglo ha sido el surrealista Roberto Matta (1911–) quien incorpora varios elementos temáticos, por ejemplo en cuadros que captan una turbulencia caótica de la vida como "El día es un atenuado" *(transgression)*. Matta recibió fama internacional a través de sus viajes por varios países europeos y latinoamericanos, lo cual le accedió *(afforded)* la oportunidad de establecer amistades con algunos de los artistas predominantes de su época como Salvador Dalí.

En Montevideo, verás las obras de arte de uruguayos famosos como Pedro Figari (1861–1938). Los temas que este artista abarca incluyen los que son típicos de Latinoamerica como la clase burguesa y escenas literarias e históricas. También utiliza como modelo en algunos cuadros las escenas ritualistas con elementos africanos. Para este pintor, la función de la memoria es primordial y utiliza el paso del tiempo para evocar las impresiones del pasado. Por ejemplo, de la serie de cuadros "Cambacuá" (1923), el público puede observar los ritmos y el movimiento de la gente de descendencia africana.

¿Te gustaría participar en este viaje? Explica.

¿Cómo se refleja el contraste de luz y sombra en el cuadro de Szyszlo?

Da tu propia interpretación de "El día es un atenuado".

En "Cambacuá" de Figari, ¿cuál es la relación entre la claridad de la memoria y el retrato *(portrayal)* de las caras de sus sujetos?

Además de decorar las paredes de un museo, en tu opinión ¿en qué aspectos es importante el arte y la expresión artística?

Conquistadoras del nuevo milenio

En la edición anterior de *Plazas*, mencionamos la presidencia nicaragüense de Violeta Barrios de Chamorro. Ahora, en honor del servicio público de las mujeres en la vida política de Latinoamérica en el nuevo milenio, hemos decidido examinar más a fondo su influencia en la vida política de varios países. Su papel es muy variado pero lo que tienen en común es la dedicación a la gente que representan.

María Angélica Fuentes: La gobernadora provincial de Concepción, Chile[1], aboga por (*advocates*) mejores programas de la educación de los niños y también se ha mostrado tolerante de la situación de los mapuches, un *group* indígena que representa casi un millón de los habitantes de Chile. Como la industria marina representa una gran fuente de ingresos (*source of income*) para el área que representa, Fuentes enfatiza la importancia del apoyo para los negocios que dependen de su localización para sobrevivir y por lo tanto para combatir el desempleo.

Desde el 1 de septiembre de 1999, la presidenta de Panamá ha sido Mireya Moscoso de Arias, viuda de Arnulfo Arias que fue presidente de Panamá tres veces: de 1940 a 1941, de 1949 a 1951 y en octubre 1968. En la plataforma política de Moscoso de Arias, una de las primeras actividades políticas que llamó la atención internacional de esta presidencia fue la retirada total del Canal de Panamá de la presencia militar de los Estados Unidos que ha protegido el canal desde su construcción y apertura en 1914. La presidente ha prometido luchar en contra del desempleo y de la pobreza. Apoya la educación descentralizada y un papel más grande de las comunidades en el sistema educativo.

[1] Located in the south central area of Chile, Concepción is a major industrial city, with a population over 300,000. Due to heavy damage suffered as a result of numerous earthquakes, the rebuilding of this colonial city (founded in 1550) has beautified Concepción with a façade of a modern city.

 En San Juan, Puerto Rico, Sila Calderón de Krans sirve como alcaldesa *(mayor)* pero tiene aspiraciones a ser la primera gobernadora de la isla. Calderón representa el Partido Popular Democrático y las elecciones prometen ser muy reñidas *(hard-fought)*, sobre todo por la controversia que divide Puerto Rico: ¿debe Puerto Rico convertirse en estado, mantener su clasificación actual como estado libre asociado *(commonwealth)* o tener la independencia? A pesar de que los contrincantes de Calderón favorecen la estadidad *(statehood)* o la independencia, Calderón está convencida de que la mejor relación de Puerto Rico con los Estados Unidos sería una que de alguna forma mantuviera relaciones con los Estados Unidos sin convertirse en estado.

 Aunque Irene Saez perdió las elecciones presidenciales de Venezuela en 1999, en ese mismo año ganó las elecciones para la gobernación de Nueva Esparta, una combinación de tres islas caribeñas al norte del país. Uno de sus mayores intereses es la promoción de la estabilidad económica, la cultura y la educación. Un dato de interés sobre Saez es que fue coronada Miss Universo en 1981 y que fue alcadesa del municipio de Chacao, una ciudad al norte de Caracas.

¿Qué futuro ves para las mujeres en la política en nuestro país y en los países hispanos?

¿Votas en las elecciones? ¿Por qué sí o no?

De estas figuras políticas, ¿hay una cuya *(whose)* ideología o cuyos valores coincida con los tuyos? Explica.

Apéndices

QuickGuide to English Grammar

For more detailed explanations of these grammar points, consult the Index to find the pages where they are explained fully in the body of the textbook.

ACTIVE VOICE (La voz activa) A sentence written in the active voice identifies a subject that performs the action of the verb.

Juan	cantó	la canción.
Juan	*sang*	*the song.*
subject	**verb**	**direct object**

In the sentence above Juan is the performer of the verb **cantar**.
(*See also* **Passive voice.**)

ADJECTIVES (Los adjetivos) are words that modify or describe **nouns** or **pronouns** and agree in **number** and generally in **gender** with the nouns they modify.

Las casas **azules** son **bonitas**.
*The **blue** houses are **pretty**.*

Esas mujeres **mexicanas** son mis amigas **nuevas**.
*Those **Mexican** women are my **new** friends.*

Plazas es un libro **interesante** y **divertido**.
***Plazas** is an **interesting** and **fun** book.*

- **Demonstrative adjectives (Los adjetivos demostrativos)** point out persons, places or things relative to the position of the speaker. They always agree in **number** and **gender** with the **noun** they modify. The forms are: **este, esta, estos, estas / ese, esa, esos, esas / aquel, aquella, aquellos, aquellas**. There are also neuter forms that refer to generic ideas or things, and hence have no gender: **esto, eso, aquello.**

Este libro es fácil.	*This book is easy.*
Esos libros son difíciles.	*Those books are hard.*
Aquellos libros son pesados.	*Those books (over there) are boring.*

Demonstratives may also function as **pronouns**, replacing the **noun** but still agreeing with it in **number** and **gender**. **Demonstrative pronouns** carry an accent mark over the syllable that would be naturally stressed anyway:

Me gustan esas blusas verdes.	*I like those green blouses.*
¿Cuáles, **éstas**?	*Which ones, these?*
No. Me gustan **ésas**.	*No. I like those.*

- **Stressed possessive adjectives (Los adjetivos posesivos acentuados)** are used for emphasis and follow the noun that they modifiy. These adjectives may also function as pronouns and always agree in **number** and in **gender**. The forms are: **mío, tuyo, suyo, nuestro, vuestro, suyo.** Unless they are directly preceded by the verb **ser**, stressed possessives must be preceded by the **definite article.**

Ese perro pequeño es **mío**.	*That little dog is **mine**.*
Dame el **tuyo**; el **nuestro** no funciona.	*Give me **yours**; **ours** doesn't work.*

- **Unstressed possessive adjectives (Los adjetivos posesivos no acentuados)** demonstrate ownership and always precede the **noun** that they modify.

La señora Elman es **mi** profesora.	*Mrs. Elman is **my** professor.*
Debemos llevar **nuestros** libros a clase.	*We should take **our** books to class.*

ADVERBS (Los adverbios) are words that modify **verbs, adjectives** or other adverbs and, unlike **adjectives,** do not have **gender** or **number.** Here are examples of different classes of adverbs:

Practicamos **diariamente**.	*We practice **daily**.* (adverb of manner)
Ellos van a salir **pronto**.	*They will leave **soon**.* (adverb of time)
Jennifer está **afuera**.	*Jennifer is **outside**.* (adverb of place)
No quiero ir **tampoco**.	*I don't want to go **either**.* (adverb of negation)
Paco habla **demasiado**.	*Paco talks **too much**.* (adverb of quantity)

AGREEMENT (La concordancia) refers to the correspondence between parts of speech in terms of **number, gender,** and **person.** Subjects agree with their verbs; articles and adjectives agree with the nouns they modify, etc.

Tod**as** l**as** lengu**as** son interesant**es**.	*All languages are interesting.* (number)
Ella es bonit**a**.	*She is pretty.* (gender)
Nosotros somos de España.	*We are from Spain.* (person)

ARTICLES (Los artículos) precede nouns and indicate whether they are definite or indefinite persons, places or things.

- **Definite articles (Los artículos definidos)** refer to particular members of a group and are the equivalent of *the* in English. The definite articles are: **el, la, los, las.**

| **El** hombre guapo es mi padre. | *The handsome man is my father.* |
| **Las** mujeres de esta clase son inteligentes. | *The women in this class are intelligent.* |

- **Indefinite articles (Los artículos indefinidos)** refer to any unspecified member(s) of a group and are the equivalent of *a(n)* and *some.* The indefinite articles are: **un, una, unos, unas.**

| **Un** hombre vino a nuestra casa anoche. | *A man came to our house last night.* |
| **Unas** niñas jugaban en el parque. | *Some girls were playing in the park.* |

CLAUSES (Las cláusulas) are subject and verb combinations; for a sentence to be complete it must have at least one main clause.

- **Main clauses** (Independent clauses) **(Las cláusulas principales)** communicate a complete idea or thought.

| Mi hermana va al hospital. | *My sister goes to the hospital.* |

- **Subordinate clauses** (Dependent clauses) **(las cláusulas subordinadas)** depend upon a main clause for their meaning to be complete.

Mi hermana va al hospital	con tal que no llueva.
My sister goes to the hospital	*provided that it's not raining.*
main clause	**subordinate clause**

In the sentence above, *provided that it's not raining* is not a complete idea without the information supplied by the main clause.

COMMANDS (Los mandatos) (*See* **Imperatives.**)

COMPARISONS (Las formas comparativas) are statements that describe one person, place or thing relative to another in terms of quantity, quality, or manner.

- **Comparisons of equality (Las formas comparativas de igualdad)** demonstrate an equal share of a quantity or degree of a particular characteristic. These statements use a form of **tan(to)(ta)(s)** and **como.**

Ella tiene **tanto** dinero **como** Elena.	*She has as **much** money as Elena.*
Fernando trabaja **tanto como** Felipe.	*Fernando works **as much as** Felipe.*
Jim baila **tan** bien **como** Anne.	*Jim dances **as well as** Anne.*

- **Comparisons of inequality (Las formas comparativas de desigualdad)** indicate a difference in quantity, quality or manner between the compared subjects. These statements use **más/menos... que** or comparative **adjectives** such as **mejor/peor, mayor/menor.**

| España tiene **más** playas **que** México. | *Spain has **more** beaches **than** Mexico.* |
| Tú hablas español **mejor que** yo. | *You speak Spanish **better than** I.* |

(*See also* **Superlatives.**)

CONJUGATIONS (Las conjugaciones) represent the inflected form of the verb as it is used with a particular **subject** or **person.**

Yo **bailo** los sábados.	*I dance* on Saturdays. (1st-person singular)
Tú **bailas** los sábados.	*You dance* on Saturdays. (2nd-person singular)
Ella **baila** los sábados.	*She dances* on Saturdays. (3rd-person singular)
Nosotros **bailamos** los sábados.	*We dance* on Saturdays. (1st-person plural)
Vosotros **bailáis** los sábados.	*You dance* on Saturdays. (2nd-person plural)
Ellos **bailan** los sábados.	*They dance* on Saturdays. (3rd-person plural)

CONJUNCTIONS (Las conjunciones) are linking words that join two independent **clauses** together.

Fuimos al centro **y** mis amigos compraron muchas cosas.
*We went downtown **and** my friends bought a lot of things.*

Yo quiero ir a la fiesta, **pero** tengo que estudiar.
*I want to go to the party, **but** I have to study.*

CONTRACTIONS (Las contracciones) in Spanish are limited to preposition/article combinations, such as **de + el = del** and **a + el = al,** or preposition/pronoun combinations such as **con + mí = conmigo** and **con + ti = contigo.**

DIRECT OBJECTS (Los objetos directos) in sentences are the direct recipients of the action of the verb. Direct objects answer the questions *What?* or *Whom?*

¿Qué hizo?	*What did she do?*
Ella hizo **la tarea.**	*She did her **homework.***
Y luego llamó **a su amiga.**	*And then called **her friend.***

(*See also* **Pronoun, Indirect object, Personal a.**)

EXCLAMATIVE WORDS (Las palabras exclamativas) communicate surprise or strong emotion. Like interrogative words, exclamatives also carry accents.

¡**Qué** sorpresa!	*What a surprise!*
¡**Cómo** canta Miguel!	*How well Miguel sings!*

(*See also* **Interrogatives.**)

GENDER (El género) is a grammatical feature of Romance languages that classifies words as either masculine or feminine. The gender of the word is sometimes used to distinguish meaning (**la papa** = *the potato,* but **el Papa** = *the Pope;* **la policía** = *the police force,* but **el policía** = *the policeman*). It is important to memorize the gender of nouns when you learn the nouns.

GERUNDS (Los gerundios) are the Spanish equivalent of the *-ing* verb form in English. Regular gerunds are created by replacing the **infinitive** endings (**-ar, -er/-ir**) with **-ando** or **-iendo.** Gerunds are often used with the verb **estar** to form the present progessive tense. The present progressive tense places emphasis on the continuing or progressive nature of an action.

Miguel está **cantando** en la ducha.   *Miguel is **singing** in the shower.*

(*See also* **Present participle.**)

IDIOMATIC EXPRESSIONS (Las frases idiomáticas) are phrases in Spanish that do not have a literal English equivalent.

Hace mucho frío.   *It is very cold.* (Literally, *It makes a lot of cold.*)

IMPERATIVES (Los imperativos) represent the mood used to express requests or commands. It is more direct than the **subjunctive** mood. Imperatives are commonly called commands and fall into two categories: affirmative and negative. Spanish speakers must also choose between using formal commands and informal commands based upon whether one is addressed as **usted** (formal) or **tú** (informal).

Habla conmigo.	**Talk** to me. (informal, affirmative)
No me hables.	**Don't talk** to me. (informal, negative)
Hable con la policía.	**Talk** to the police. (formal, singular, affirmative)
No hable con la policía.	**Don't talk** to the police. (formal, singular, negative)
Hablen con la policía.	**Talk** to the police. (formal, plural, affirmative)
No hablen con la policía	**Don't talk** to the police. (formal, plural, negative)

(*See also* **Mood.**)

IMPERFECT (el imperfecto) The imperfect tense is used to make statements about the past when the speaker wants to convey the idea of 1) habitual or repeated action, 2) two actions in progress simultaneously, or 3) an event that was in progress when another action interrupted. The imperfect tense is also used to emphasize the ongoing nature of the middle of the event, as opposed to its beginning or end. Age and clock time are always expressed using the imperfect.

Cuando María **era** joven, ella **cantaba** en el coro.
*When María **was** young, she **used to sing** in the choir.*

Aquel día **llovía** mucho y el cielo **estaba** oscuro.
*That day **it was raining** a lot and the sky **was** dark.*

Juan **dormía** cuando sonó el teléfono.
*Juan **was sleeping** when the phone rang.*

(*See also* **Preterite**.)

IMPERSONAL EXPRESSIONS (Las expresiones impersonales) are statements that contain the impersonal subjects of *it* or *one*.

Es necesario estudiar.   *It is necessary* to study.
Se necesita estudiar.   *One needs to study.*

(*See also* **Passive**.)

INDEFINITE WORDS (Las palabras indefinidas) are **articles, adjectives, nouns** or **pronouns** that refer to unspecified members of a group.

Un hombre vino.   *A man came.* (indefinite article)
Alguien vino.   *Someone came.* (indefinite noun)
Algunas personas vinieron.   *Some people came.* (indefinite adjective)
Algunas vinieron.   *Some came.* (indefinite pronoun)

(*See also* **Articles**.)

INDICATIVE (El indicativo) The indicative is a mood, rather than a tense. The indicative is used to express ideas that are considered factual or certain and, therefore, not subject to speculation, doubt, or negation.

Josefina **es** española.   *Josefina is Spanish.*
(present indicative)

(*See also* **Mood**.)

INDIRECT OBJECTS (Los objetos indirectos) are the indirect recipients of an action in a sentence and answer the questions *To whom?* or *For whom?* In Spanish it is common to include an indirect object **pronoun** along with the indirect object.

Yo **le** di el libro **a Sofía**.   *I gave the book **to Sofia**.*
Sofía **les** guardó el libro **para sus padres**.   *Sofia kept the book **for her parents**.*

(*See also* **Direct objects** and **pronouns**.)

INFINITIVES (Los infinitivos) are verb forms that are uninflected or not **conjugated** according to a specific **person**. In English, infinitives are preceded by *to: to talk, to eat, to live.* Infinitives in Spanish end in **-ar (hablar), -er (comer)**, and **-ir (vivir)**.

INTERROGATIVES (Las formas interrogativas) are used to pose questions and carry accent marks to distinguish them from other uses. Basic interrogative words include: **quién(es), qué, cómo, cuánto(a)(s), cuándo, por qué, dónde.**

¿**Qué** quieres?   *What do you want?*
¿**Cuándo** llegó ella?   *When did she arrive?*
¿De **dónde** eres?   *Where are you from?*

(*See also* **Exclamatives**.)

MOOD (El modo) is like the word *mode*, meaning *manner* or *way*. It indicates the way in which the speaker views an action, or his/her attitude toward the action. Besides the **imperative** mood, which is simply giving commands, you learn two basic moods in Spanish: the **subjunctive** and the **indicative**. Basically, the subjunctive mood communicates an attitude of uncertainty or negation toward the action, while the indicative indicates that the action is certain or factual. Within each of these moods there are many **tenses.** Hence you have the present indicative and the present subjunctive, the present perfect indicative and the present perfect subjunctive, etc.

- **Indicative mood (El indicativo)** implies that what is stated or questioned is regarded as true.

Yo **quiero** ir a la fiesta.	*I want to go to the party.*
Quieres ir conmigo?	*Do you want to go with me?*

- **Subjunctive mood (El subjuntivo)** indicates a recommendation, a statement of doubt or negation, or a hypothetical situation.

Yo recomiendo que tú **vayas** a la fiesta.	*I recommend **that you go** to the party.*
Dudo que **vayas** a la fiesta.	*I doubt that **you'll go** to the party.*
No creo que **vayas** a la fiesta.	*I don't believe that **you'll go** to the party.*
Si **fueras** a la fiesta, te divertirías.	*If **you were to go** to the party, you would have a good time.*

- **Imperative mood (El imperativo)** is used to make a command or request.

¡**Ven** conmigo a la fiesta!	*Come with me to the party!*

(*See also* **Indicative, Imperative,** and **Subjunctive.**)

NEGATION (La negación) takes place when a negative word, such as **no,** is placed before an affirmative sentence. In Spanish, double negatives are common.

Yolando va a cantar esta noche.	*Yolando will sing tonight.* (affirmative)
Yolando **no** va a cantar esta noche.	*Yolanda will **not** sing tonight.* (negative)
Ramón quiere algo.	*Ramón wants something.* (affirmative)
Ramón **no** quiere **nada.**	*Ramón **doesn't** want **anything.*** (negative)

NOUNS (Los sustantivos) are persons, places, things or ideas. Names of people, countries, and cities are proper nouns and are capitalized.

Alberto	*Albert* (person)
el pueblo	*town* (place)
el diccionario	*dictionary* (thing)

ORTHOGRAPHY (La ortografía) refers to the spelling of a word or anything related to spelling such as accentuation.

PASSIVE VOICE (La voz pasiva), as compared to **active voice (la voz activa),** places emphasis on the action itself rather than the agent of the action (the person or thing that is indirectly responsible for committing the action). The passive **se** is used when there is no apparent agent of the action.

Luis vende los coches.	*Luis sells the cars.* (active voice)
Los coches **son vendidos por** Luis.	*The cars **are sold by** Luis.* (passive voice)
Se venden los coches.	*The cars **are sold.*** (passive voice)

(*See also* **Active voice.**)

PAST PARTICIPLES (El participio pasado) are verb forms used in compound tenses such as the **present perfect.** Regular past participles are formed by dropping the **-ar** or **-er/-ir** from the **infinitive** and adding **-ado** or **-ido.** Past participles are the equivalent of verbs ending in *-ed* in English. They may also be used as **adjectives,** in which case they agree in **number** and **gender** with their nouns. Irregular past participles include: **escrito, roto, dicho, hecho, puesto, vuelto, muerto, cubierto.**

Marta ha **subido** la montaña.	*Marta has **climbed** the mountain.*
Hemos **hablado** mucho por teléfono.	*We have **talked** a lot on the phone.*
La novela **publicada** en 1995 es su mejor novela.	*The novel **published** in 1995 is her best novel.*

PERFECT TENSES (Los tiempos perfectos) communicate the idea that an action has taken place before now (present perfect) or before a moment in the past (past perfect). The perfect tenses are compound tenses consisting of the verb **haber** plus the **past participle** of a second verb.

Yo **he comido.**	*I have eaten.* (present perfect indicative)
Antes de la fiesta, yo **había comido.**	*Before the party I had eaten.* (past perfect indicative)
Yo espero que **hayas comido.**	*I hope that **you have eaten.*** (present perfect subjunctive)
Yo esperaba que **hubieras comido.**	*I hoped that **you had eaten.*** (past perfect subjunctive)

PERSON (La persona) refers to changes in the subject pronouns that indicate if one is speaking (first person), if one is spoken to (second person), or if one is spoken about (third person).

Yo hablo.	*I speak*. (1st-person singular)
Tú hablas.	*You speak*. (2nd-person singular)
Ud./Él/Ella habla.	*You/He/She speaks*. (3rd-person singular)
Nosotros(as) hablamos.	*We speak*. (1st-person plural)
Vosotros(as) habláis.	*You speak*. (2nd-person plural)
Uds./Ellos/Ellas hablan.	*They speak*. (3rd-person plural)

PERSONAL A (La *a* personal) The personal **a** refers to the placement of the preposition **a** before the name of a person when that person is the **direct object** of the sentence.

Voy a llamar **a** María.	*I'm going to call María.*

PREPOSITIONS (Las preposiciones) are linking words indicating spatial or temporal relations between two words.

Ella nadaba **en** la piscina.	*She was swimming **in** the pool.*
Yo llamé **antes de** las nueve.	*I called **before** nine o'clock.*
El libro es **para** ti.	*The book is **for** you.*
Voy **a** la oficina.	*I'm going **to** the office.*
Jorge es **de** Paraguay.	*Jorge is **from** Paraguay.*

PRESENT PARTICIPLE (*See* **Gerunds.)**

PRETERITE (El pretérito) The preterite tense, as compared to the **imperfect tense,** is used to talk about past events with specific emphasis on the beginning or the end of the action, or emphasis on the completed nature of the action as a whole.

Anoche yo **empecé** a estudiar a las once y **terminé** a la una.
*Last night I **began** to study at eleven o'clock and **finished** at one o'clock.*

Esta mañana **me desperté** a las siete, **desayuné, me duché** y **vine** al campus para las ocho.
*This morning I **woke up** at seven, I **ate** breakfast, I **showered,** and I **came** to campus by eight.*

PRONOUNS (Los pronombres) are words that substitute for **nouns** in a sentence.

Yo quiero **éste.**	*I want **this one.*** (demonstrative—points out a specific person, place or thing)
¿Quién es tu amigo?	***Who** is your friend?* (interrogative—used to ask questions)
Yo voy a llamar**la.**	*I'm going to call **her.*** (direct object—replaces the direct object of the sentence)
Ella va a dar**le** el reloj.	*She is going to give **him** the watch.* (indirect object—replaces the indirect object of the sentence)
Juan **se** baña por la mañana.	*Juan bathes **himself** in the morning.* (reflexive—used with reflexive verbs to show that the agent of the action is also the recipient)
Es la mujer **que** conozco.	*She is the woman **that** I know.* (relative—used to introduce a clause that describes a noun)
Nosotros somos listos.	***We** are clever.* (subject—replaces the noun that performs the action or state of a verb)

SUBJECTS (Los sujetos) are the persons, places or things that perform the action or state of being of a verb. The **conjugated** verb always agrees with its subject.

Carlos siempre baila solo.	***Carlos** always dances alone.*
Colorado y **California** son mis estados preferidos.	***Colorado** and **California** are my favorite states.*
La cafetera produce el café.	*The **coffee pot** makes the coffee.*

(*See also* **Active voice.**)

SUBJUNCTIVE (El subjuntivo) The subjunctive mood is used to express speculative, doubtful, or hypothetical situations. It also communicates a degree of subjectivity or influence of the main clause over the subordinate clause.

No creo que **tengas** razón.
Si yo **fuera** el jefe, pagaría más a mis empleados.
Quiero que **estudies** más.

*I don't think that **you're right**.*
*If I **were** the boss, I would pay my employees more.*
*I want **you to study** more.*

(*See also* **Mood, Indicative.**)

SUPERLATIVE STATEMENTS (Las frases superlativas) are formed by adjectives or adverbs to make comparisons among three or more members of a group. To form superlatives, add a definite article **(el, la, los, las)** before the comparative form.

Juan es **el más alto** de los tres.
Este coche es **el más rápido** de todos.

*Juan is **the tallest** of the three.*
*This car is **the fastest** of them all.*

(*See also* **Comparisons.**)

TENSES (Los tiempos) refer to the manner in which time is expressed through the **verb** of a sentence.

Yo estudio.
Yo estoy estudiando.
Yo he estudiado.
Yo había estudiado.
Yo estudié.
Yo estudiaba.
Yo estudiaré

I study. (present tense)
I am studying. (present progressive)
I have studied. (present perfect)
I had studied. (past perfect)
I studied. (preterite tense)
I was studying. (imperfect tense)
I will study. (future tense)

VERBS (Los verbos) are the words in a sentence that communicate an action or state of being.

Helen **es** mi amiga y ella **lee** muchas novelas.
*Helen **is** my friend and she **reads** a lot of novels.*

Auxiliary verbs (Los verbos auxiliares) or helping verbs are verbs such as **estar** and **haber** used to form the present progressive and the present perfect, respectively.

Estamos estudiando mucho para el examen mañana.
*We **are** studying a lot for the exam tomorrow.*

Helen **ha** trabajado mucho en este proyecto.
*Helen **has** worked a lot on this project.*

Reflexive verbs (Los verbos reflexivos) use reflexive **pronouns** to indicate that the person initiating the action is also the recipient of the action.

Yo **me afeito** por la mañana.

*I **shave (myself)** in the morning.*

Stem-changing verbs (Los verbos con cambios de raíz) undergo a change in the main part of the verb when conjugated. To find the stem, drop the **-ar, -er,** or **-ir** from the **infinitive: dorm-, empez-, ped-.** There are three types of stem-changing verbs: **o** to **ue, e** to **ie** and **e** to **i.**

dormir: Yo d**ue**rmo en el parque.
empezar: Ella siempre emp**ie**za su trabajo temprano.
pedir: ¿Por qué no p**i**des ayuda?

I sleep in the park. (**o** to **ue**)
She always starts her work early. (**e** to **ie**)
Why don't you ask for help? (**e** to **i**)

APÉNDICE B: Los verbos regulares

Infinitive	Present Indicative	Imperfect	Preterite	Future	Conditional	Present Subjunctive	Past Subjunctive	Commands
hablar to speak	hablo hablas habla hablamos habláis hablan	hablaba hablabas hablaba hablábamos hablabais hablaban	hablé hablaste habló hablamos hablasteis hablaron	hablaré hablarás hablará hablaremos hablaréis hablarán	hablaría hablarías hablaría hablaríamos hablaríais hablarían	hable hables hable hablemos habléis hablen	hablara hablaras hablara habláramos hablarais hablaran	habla (no hables) hable hablad (no habléis) hablen
aprender to learn	aprendo aprendes aprende aprendemos aprendéis aprenden	aprendía aprendías aprendía aprendíamos aprendíais aprendían	aprendí aprendiste aprendió aprendimos aprendisteis aprendieron	aprenderé aprenderás aprenderá aprenderemos aprenderéis aprenderán	aprendería aprenderías aprendería aprenderíamos aprenderíais aprenderían	aprenda aprendas aprenda aprendamos aprendáis aprendan	aprendiera aprendieras aprendiera aprendiéramos aprendierais aprendieran	aprende (no aprendas) aprenda aprended (no aprendáis) aprendan
vivir to live	vivo vives vive vivimos vivís viven	vivía vivías vivía vivíamos vivíais vivían	viví viviste vivió vivimos vivisteis vivieron	viviré vivirás vivirá viviremos viviréis vivirán	viviría vivirías viviría viviríamos viviríais vivirían	viva vivas viva vivamos viváis vivan	viviera vivieras viviera viviéramos vivierais vivieran	vive (no vivas) viva vivid (no viváis) vivan

Compound tenses

Present progressive	estoy estás está estamos estáis están	hablando	aprendiendo	viviendo
Present perfect indicative	he has ha hemos habéis han	hablado	aprendido	vivido
Present perfect subjunctive	haya hayas haya hayamos hayáis hayan	hablado	aprendido	vivido
Past perfect indicative	había habías había habíamos habíais habían	hablado	aprendido	vivido

Infinitive / Present Participle / Past Participle	Present Indicative	Imperfect	Preterite	Future	Conditional	Present Subjunctive	Past Subjunctive	Commands
pensar / to think / **e → ie** / pensando / pensado	**pienso** / **piensas** / **piensa** / pensamos / pensáis / **piensan**	pensaba / pensabas / pensaba / pensábamos / pensabais / pensaban	pensé / pensaste / pensó / pensamos / pensasteis / pensaron	pensaré / pensarás / pensará / pensaremos / pensaréis / pensarán	pensaría / pensarías / pensaría / pensaríamos / pensaríais / pensarían	**piense** / **pienses** / **piense** / pensemos / penséis / **piensen**	pensara / pensaras / pensara / pensáramos / pensarais / pensaran	**piensa** (no **pienses**) / **piense** / pensad (no **penséis**) / **piensen**
acostarse / to go to bed / **o → ue** / acostándose / acostado	me **acuesto** / te **acuestas** / se **acuesta** / nos acostamos / os acostáis / se **acuestan**	me acostaba / te acostabas / se acostaba / nos acostábamos / os acostabais / se acostaban	me acosté / te acostaste / se acostó / nos acostamos / os acostasteis / se acostaron	me acostaré / te acostarás / se acostará / nos acostaremos / os acostaréis / se acostarán	me acostaría / te acostarías / se acostaría / nos acostaríamos / os acostaríais / se acostarían	me **acueste** / te **acuestes** / se **acueste** / nos acostemos / os acostéis / se **acuesten**	me acostara / te acostaras / se acostara / nos acostáramos / os acostarais / se acostaran	acuéstate (no te acuestes) / acuéstese / acostaos / (no os acostéis) / acuéstense
sentir / to feel / **e → ie, i** / **sintiendo** / sentido	**siento** / **sientes** / **siente** / sentimos / sentís / **sienten**	sentía / sentías / sentía / sentíamos / sentíais / sentían	sentí / sentiste / **sintió** / sentimos / sentisteis / **sintieron**	sentiré / sentirás / sentirá / sentiremos / sentiréis / sentirán	sentiría / sentirías / sentiría / sentiríamos / sentiríais / sentirían	**sienta** / **sientas** / **sienta** / **sintamos** / **sintáis** / **sientan**	**sintiera** / **sintieras** / **sintiera** / **sintiéramos** / **sintierais** / **sintieran**	siente (no sientas) / sienta / sentid (no sintáis) / sientan
pedir / to ask for / **e → i, i** / **pidiendo** / pedido	**pido** / **pides** / **pide** / pedimos / pedís / **piden**	pedía / pedías / pedía / pedíamos / pedíais / pedían	pedí / pediste / **pidió** / pedimos / pedisteis / **pidieron**	pediré / pedirás / pedirá / pediremos / pediréis / pedirán	pediría / pedirías / pediría / pediríamos / pediríais / pedirían	**pida** / **pidas** / **pida** / **pidamos** / **pidáis** / **pidan**	**pidiera** / **pidieras** / **pidiera** / **pidiéramos** / **pidierais** / **pidieran**	pide (no pidas) / pida / pedid (no pidáis) / pidan
dormir / to sleep / **o → ue, u** / **durmiendo** / dormido	**duermo** / **duermes** / **duerme** / dormimos / dormís / **duermen**	dormía / dormías / dormía / dormíamos / dormíais / dormían	dormí / dormiste / **durmió** / dormimos / dormisteis / **durmieron**	dormiré / dormirás / dormirá / dormiremos / dormiréis / dormirán	dormiría / dormirías / dormiría / dormiríamos / dormiríais / dormirían	**duerma** / **duermas** / **duerma** / **durmamos** / **durmáis** / **duerman**	**durmiera** / **durmieras** / **durmiera** / **durmiéramos** / **durmierais** / **durmieran**	duerme (no duermas) / duerma / dormid (no durmáis) / duerman

APÉNDICE D: Los verbos con cambios de ortografía

Infinitive / Present Participle / Past Participle	Present Indicative	Imperfect	Preterite	Future	Conditional	Present Subjunctive	Past Subjunctive	Commands
comenzar (e → ie) *to begin* **z → c before e** comenzando comenzado	comienzo	comenzaba	**comencé**	comenzaré	comenzaría	**comience**	comenzara	comienza (no **comiences**)
	comienzas	comenzabas	comenzaste	comenzarás	comenzarías	**comiences**	comenzaras	**comience**
	comienza	comenzaba	comenzó	comenzará	comenzaría	**comience**	comenzara	comencemos
	comenzamos	comenzábamos	comenzamos	comenzaremos	comenzaríamos	**comencemos**	comenzáramos	comenzad (no **comencéis**)
	comenzáis	comenzabais	comenzasteis	comenzaréis	comenzaríais	**comencéis**	comenzarais	**comiencen**
	comienzan	comenzaban	comenzaron	comenzarán	comenzarían	**comiencen**	comenzaran	
conocer *to know* **c → zc before a, o** conociendo conocido	**conozco**	conocía	conocí	conoceré	conocería	**conozca**	conociera	conoce (no **conozcas**)
	conoces	conocías	conociste	conocerás	conocerías	**conozcas**	conocieras	**conozca**
	conoce	conocía	conoció	conocerá	conocería	**conozca**	conociera	conozcamos
	conocemos	conocíamos	conocimos	conoceremos	conoceríamos	**conozcamos**	conociéramos	conoced (no **conozcáis**)
	conocéis	conocíais	conocisteis	conoceréis	conoceríais	**conozcáis**	conocierais	**conozcan**
	conocen	conocían	conocieron	conocerán	conocerían	**conozcan**	conocieran	
construir *to build* **i → y; y inserted before a, e, o** construyendo construido	**construyo**	construía	construí	construiré	construiría	**construya**	**construyera**	**construye** (no **construyas**)
	construyes	construías	construiste	construirás	construirías	**construyas**	**construyeras**	**construya**
	construye	construía	**construyó**	construirá	construiría	**construya**	**construyera**	**construya**
	construimos	construíamos	construimos	construiremos	construiríamos	**construyamos**	**construyéramos**	construyamos
	construís	construíais	construisteis	construiréis	construiríais	**construyáis**	**construyerais**	construid (no **construyáis**)
	construyen	construían	**construyeron**	construirán	construirían	**construyan**	**construyeran**	**construyan**
leer *to read* **i → y; stressed i → í** **leyendo** **leído**	leo	leía	leí	leeré	leería	lea	**leyera**	lee (no leas)
	lees	leías	leíste	leerás	leerías	leas	**leyeras**	lea
	lee	leía	**leyó**	leerá	leería	lea	**leyera**	leed (no leáis)
	leemos	leíamos	leímos	leeremos	leeríamos	leamos	**leyéramos**	lean
	leéis	leíais	leísteis	leeréis	leeríais	leáis	**leyerais**	
	leen	leían	**leyeron**	**leyeron**	leerían	lean	**leyeran**	

Infinitive / Present Participle / Past Participle	Present Indicative	Imperfect	Preterite	Future	Conditional	Present Subjunctive	Past Subjunctive	Commands
pagar *to pay* **g → gu before e** pagando pagado	pago pagas paga pagamos pagáis pagan	pagaba pagabas pagaba pagábamos pagabais pagaban	**pagué** pagaste pagó pagamos pagasteis pagaron	pagaré pagarás pagará pagaremos pagaréis pagarán	pagaría pagarías pagaría pagaríamos pagaríais pagarían	**pague** **pagues** **pague** **paguemos** **paguéis** **paguen**	pagara pagaras pagara pagáramos pagarais pagaran	paga (**no pagues**) **pague** pagad (**no paguéis**) **paguen**
seguir (e → i, i) *to follow* **gu → g before a, o** siguiendo seguido	**sigo** sigues sigue seguimos seguís siguen	seguía seguías seguía seguíamos seguíais seguían	seguí seguiste siguió seguimos seguisteis siguieron	seguiré seguirás seguirá seguiremos seguiréis seguirán	seguiría seguirías seguiría seguiríamos seguiríais seguirían	**siga** **sigas** **siga** **sigamos** **sigáis** **sigan**	siguiera siguieras siguiera siguiéramos siguierais siguieran	sigue (**no sigas**) **siga** seguid (**no sigáis**) **sigan**
tocar *to play, to touch* **c → qu before e** tocando tocado toco	tocas toca tocamos tocáis tocan	tocaba tocabas tocaba tocábamos tocabais tocaban	**toqué** tocaste tocó tocamos tocasteis tocaron	tocaré tocará tocarás tocaremos tocaréis tocarán	tocaría tocarías tocaría tocaríamos tocaríais tocarían	**toque** **toques** **toque** **toquemos** **toquéis** **toquen**	tocara tocaras tocara tocáramos tocarais tocaran	toca (**no toques**) **toque** tocad (**no toquéis**) **toquen**

APÉNDICE E: Los verbos irregulares

Infinitive / Present Participle / Past Participle	Present Indicative	Imperfect	Preterite	Future	Conditional	Present Subjunctive	Past Subjunctive	Commands
andar *to walk* andando andado	ando andas anda andamos andáis andan	andaba andabas andaba andábamos andabais andaban	anduve anduviste anduvo anduvimos anduvisteis anduvieron	andaré andarás andará andaremos andaréis andarán	andaría andarías andaría andaríamos andaríais andarían	ande andes ande andemos andéis anden	anduviera anduvieras anduviera anduviéramos anduvierais anduvieran	anda (no andes) ande andad (no andéis) anden
*caer *to fall* **cayendo** caído	**caigo** caes cae caemos caéis caen	caía caías caía caíamos caíais caían	caí caíste **cayó** caímos caísteis **cayeron**	caeré caerás caerá caeremos caeréis caerán	caería caerías caería caeríamos caeríais caerían	**caiga** **caigas** **caiga** **caigamos** **caigáis** **caigan**	cayera cayeras cayera cayéramos cayerais cayeran	cae (no caigas) **caiga** caed (no caigáis) **caigan**
*dar *to give* dando dado	**doy** das da damos dais dan	daba dabas daba dábamos dabais daban	**di** diste **dio** dimos disteis dieron	daré darás dará daremos daréis darán	daría darías daría daríamos daríais darían	**dé** des **dé** demos deis den	diera dieras diera diéramos dierais dieran	da (no des) **dé** dad (no deis) den
*decir *to say, tell* **diciendo** **dicho**	**digo** **dices** **dice** decimos decís **dicen**	decía decías decía decíamos decíais decían	**dije** **dijiste** **dijo** **dijimos** **dijisteis** **dijeron**	**diré** **dirás** **dirá** **diremos** **diréis** **dirán**	**diría** **dirías** **diría** **diríamos** **diríais** **dirían**	**diga** **digas** **diga** **digamos** **digáis** **digan**	**dijera** **dijeras** **dijera** **dijéramos** **dijerais** **dijeran**	**di (no digas)** diga decid (no digáis) digan
*estar *to be* estando estado	**estoy** **estás** **está** estamos estáis **están**	estaba estabas estaba estábamos estabais estaban	**estuve** **estuviste** **estuvo** **estuvimos** **estuvisteis** **estuvieron**	estaré estarás estará estaremos estaréis estarán	estaría estarías estaría estaríamos estaríais estarían	**esté** **estés** **esté** **estemos** **estéis** **estén**	**estuviera** **estuvieras** **estuviera** **estuviéramos** **estuvierais** **estuvieran**	**está (no estés)** **esté** estad (no estéis) **estén**

APÉNDICE E: Los verbos irregulares
(continued)

Infinitive / Present Participle / Past Participle	Present Indicative	Imperfect	Preterite	Future	Conditional	Present Subjunctive	Past Subjunctive	Commands
haber *to have* habiendo habido	he has ha [hay] hemos habéis han	había habías había habíamos habíais habían	hube hubiste hubo hubimos hubisteis hubieron	habré habrás habrá habremos habréis habrán	habría habrías habría habríamos habríais habrían	haya hayas haya hayamos hayáis hayan	hubiera hubieras hubiera hubiéramos hubierais hubieran	
*hacer *to make, to do* haciendo **hecho**	hago haces hace hacemos hacéis hacen	hacía hacías hacía hacíamos hacíais hacían	hice hiciste hizo hicimos hicisteis hicieron	haré harás hará haremos haréis harán	haría harías haría haríamos haríais harían	haga hagas haga hagamos hagáis hagan	hiciera hicieras hiciera hiciéramos hiciérais hicieran	haz (no hagas) haga haced (no hagáis) hagan
ir *to go* **yendo** ido	voy vas va vamos vais van	iba ibas iba íbamos ibais iban	fui fuiste fue fuimos fuisteis fueron	iré irás irá iremos iréis irán	iría irías iría iríamos iríais irían	vaya vayas vaya vayamos vayáis vayan	fuera fueras fuera fuéramos fuerais fueran	ve (no vayas) vaya id (no vayáis) vayan
*oír *to hear* **oyendo** **oído**	oigo oyes oye oímos oías oyen	oía oías oía oíamos oíais oían	oí oíste oyó oímos oísteis oyeron	oiré oirás oirá oiremos oiréis oirán	oiría oirías oiría oiríamos oiríais oirían	oiga oigas oiga oigamos oigáis oigan	oyera oyeras oyera oyéramos oyerais oyeran	oye (no oigas) oiga oíd (no oigáis) oigan

APÉNDICE E: Los verbos irregulares

(continued)

Infinitive / Present Participle / Past Participle	Present Indicative	Imperfect	Preterite	Future	Conditional	Present Subjunctive	Past Subjunctive	Commands
poder (o → ue) *can, to be able* **pudiendo** podido	**puedo** **puedes** **puede** podemos podéis **pueden**	podía podías podía podíamos podíais podían	**pude** **pudiste** **pudo** **pudimos** **pudisteis** **pudieron**	**podré** **podrás** **podrá** **podremos** **podréis** **podrán**	**podría** **podrías** **podría** **podríamos** **podríais** **podrían**	**pueda** **puedas** **pueda** podamos podáis **puedan**	pudiera pudieras pudiera pudiéramos pudierais pudieran	
*poner *to place, to put* poniendo **puesto**	**pongo** pones pone ponemos ponéis ponen	ponía ponías ponía poníamos poníais ponían	**puse** **pusiste** **puso** **pusimos** **pusisteis** **pusieron**	**pondré** **pondrás** **pondrá** **pondremos** **pondréis** **pondrán**	**pondría** **pondrías** **pondría** **pondríamos** **pondríais** **pondrían**	**ponga** **pongas** **ponga** **pongamos** **pongáis** **pongan**	pusiera pusieras pusiera pusiéramos pusierais pusieran	**pon (no pongas)** **ponga** poned (**no pongáis**) **pongan**
querer (e → ie) *to want, to wish* queriendo querido	**quiero** **quieres** **quiere** queremos queréis **quieren**	quería querías quería queríamos queríais querían	**quise** **quisiste** **quiso** **quisimos** **quisisteis** **quisieron**	**querré** **querrás** **querrá** **querremos** **querréis** **querrán**	**querría** **querrías** **querría** **querríamos** **querríais** **querrían**	**quiera** **quieras** **quiera** querramos querráis **quieran**	quisiera quisieras quisiera quisiéramos quisierais quisieran	**quiere (no quieras)** **quiera** quered (**no queráis**) **quieran**
reír (e → i) *to laugh* **riendo** **reído**	**río** **ríes** **ríe** **reímos** reís **ríen**	reía reías reía reíamos reíais reían	reí **reíste** **rio** **reímos** **reísteis** **rieron**	reiré reirás reirá reiremos reiréis reirán	reiría reirías reiría reiríamos reiríais reirían	**ría** **rías** **ría** **riamos** **riáis** **rían**	**riera** **rieras** **riera** **riéramos** **rierais** **rieran**	**ríe (no rías)** **ría** **reíd (no riáis)** **rían**

APÉNDICE E: Los verbos irregulares
(continued)

Infinitive / Present Participle / Past Participle	Present Indicative	Imperfect	Preterite	Future	Conditional	Present Subjunctive	Past Subjunctive	Commands
*saber *to know* sabiendo sabido	sé sabes sabe sabemos sabéis saben	sabía sabías sabía sabíamos sabíais sabían	supe supiste supo supimos supisteis supieron	sabré sabrás sabrá sabremos sabréis sabrán	sabría sabrías sabría sabríamos sabríais sabrían	sepa sepas sepa sepamos sepáis sepan	supiera supieras supiera supiéramos supierais supieran	sabe (no sepas) sepa sabed (no sepáis) sepan
*salir *to go out* saliendo salido	salgo sales sale salimos salís salen	salía salías salía salíamos salíais salían	salí saliste salió salimos salisteis salieron	saldré saldrás saldrá saldremos saldréis saldrán	saldría saldrías saldría saldríamos saldríais saldrían	salga salgas salga salgamos salgáis salgan	saliera salieras saliera saliéramos salierais salieran	sal (no salgas) salga salid (no salgáis) salgan
ser *to be* siendo sido	soy eres es somos sois son	era eras era éramos erais eran	fui fuiste fue fuimos fuisteis fueron	seré serás será seremos seréis serán	sería serías sería seríamos seríais serían	sea seas sea seamos seáis sean	fuera fueras fuera fuéramos fuerais fueran	sé (no seas) sea sed (no seáis) sean
*tener *to have* teniendo tenido	tengo tienes tiene tenemos tenéis tienen	tenía tenías tenía teníamos teníais tenían	tuve tuviste tuvo tuvimos tuvisteis tuvieron	tendré tendrás tendrá tendremos tendréis tendrán	tendría tendrías tendría tendríamos tendríais tendrían	tenga tengas tenga tengamos tengáis tengan	tuviera tuvieras tuviera tuviéramos tuvierais tuvieran	ten (no tengas) tenga tened (no tengáis) tengan

Infinitive Present Participle Past Participle	Present Indicative	Imperfect	Preterite	Future	Conditional	Present Subjunctive	Past Subjunctive	Commands
*traer	**traigo**	traía	**traje**	traeré	traería	**traiga**	**trajera**	trae (**no traigas**)
to bring	traes	traías	**trajiste**	traerás	traerías	**traigas**	**trajeras**	**traiga**
trayendo	trae	traía	**trajo**	traerá	traería	**traiga**	**trajera**	traed (**no**
traído	traemos	traíamos	**trajimos**	traeremos	traeríamos	**traigamos**	**trajéramos**	**traigáis)**
	traéis	traíais	**trajisteis**	traeréis	traeríais	**traigáis**	**trajerais**	**traigan**
	traen	traían	**trajeron**	traerán	traerían	**traigan**	**trajeran**	
*venir	**vengo**	venía	**vine**	**vendré**	**vendría**	**venga**	**viniera**	**ven (no vengas)**
to come	**vienes**	venías	**viniste**	**vendrás**	**vendrías**	**vengas**	**vinieras**	**venga**
viniendo	**viene**	venía	**vino**	**vendrá**	**vendría**	**venga**	**viniera**	venid (**no**
venido	venimos	veníamos	**vinimos**	**vendremos**	**vendríamos**	**vengamos**	**viniéramos**	**vengáis)**
	venís	veníais	**vinisteis**	**vendréis**	**vendríais**	**vengáis**	**vinierais**	**vengan**
	vienen	venían	**vinieron**	**vendrán**	**vendrían**	**vengan**	**vinieran**	
ver	**veo**	**veía**	**vi**	veré	vería	**vea**	viera	ve (**no veas**)
to see	ves	**veías**	**viste**	verás	verías	**veas**	vieras	**vea**
viendo	ve	**veía**	**vio**	verá	vería	**vea**	viera	ved (**no (veáis)**
visto	vemos	**veíamos**	**vimos**	veremos	veríamos	**veamos**	**viéramos**	**vean**
	veis	**veíais**	**visteis**	veréis	veríais	**veáis**	vierais	
	ven	**veían**	**vieron**	verán	verían	**vean**	vieran	

*Verbs with irregular **yo** forms in the present indicative

Glosario español-inglés

This Spanish-English Glossary includes all the words and expressions that appear in the text except verb forms, regular superlatives and diminutives, and most adverbs ending in **-mente**. Only meanings used in the text are given. Gender of nouns is indicated except for masculine nouns ending in **-o** and feminine nouns ending in **-a**. Feminine forms of adjectives are shown except for regular adjectives with masculine forms ending in **-o**. Verbs appear in the infinitive form. Stem changes and spelling changes are indicated in parentheses: e.g., **divertirse (ie, i)**; **buscar (qu)**. The number following each entry indicates the chapter in which the word with that particular meaning first appears; M indicates one of the magazine sections. The following abbreviations are used:

adj.	adjective	*m.*	masculine	*prep.*	preposition
adv.	adverb	*f.*	feminine	*pron.*	pronoun
conj.	conjunction	*pl.*	plural	*s.*	singular

A

a *prep.* at, to
  a la derecha de *prep.* to the right of, 9
  a la izquierda de *prep.* to the left of, 9
  a la luz de in light of, M3
  a menos que *conj.* unless, 13
  a primera vista at first sight, 10
  ¿A qué hora? At what time?, 1
  a tiempo on time, 1
  a última hora at the last minute, 8
  a veces *adv.* sometimes, 8
abajo *adv.* below, 3
abogado(a) lawyer, 11
abogar (ue) por to advocate, M5
abonado(a) subscriber, 15
abordar to board, 9
aborto abortion, 14
abrazar(se) to hug (each other), 10
abrigo overcoat, 7
abril April, 3
abrir to open, 2
abrochar el cinturón de seguridad to buckle the seat belt, 9
abuela grandmother, 2
abuelo grandfather, 2
aburrido *adj.* bored, 4
aburrir to bore, 13
acabar to run out, 12
  acabar de + infinitive to have just (done something), 5
acceder to access, 15; to afford, M5
accesorio accessory, 7
accionista *m./f.* stockbroker, 11
aceite *m.* oil, 6

acelerado *adj.* accelerated, 12
acercamiento encroachment, 12
acercar (qu) to approach, move closer, 12
acogedor *adj.* quaint, M4
acompañar(se) to accompany each other, 10
acostarse (ue) to go to bed, 5
acostumbrar to be in the habit of, 11
actor *m.* actor, 13
actriz *f.* actress, 13
Adiós. Good-bye. P
adivinanza riddle, 8
administración *(f.)* **de empresas** business administration, 1
¿Adónde? Where (to)?, 8
aduana customs, 9
aerolínea airline, 9
aeropuerto airport, 9
afán *m.* desire, 12
afeitarse to shave, 5
aficionado(a) fan (sports), 3
agarrar to catch, 10
agencia de viajes travel agency, 9
agente de viajes *m./f.* travel agent, 9
agosto August, 3
agregar to add, 6
agricultor(a) farmer, 12
agua *(f.)* **mineral con/sin gas** carbonated/noncarbonated mineral water, 6
aguacate *m.* avocado, 6
agudeza particular strong suit, sharpest sense, 12
ahijado(a) godchild, 2
ahora *adv.* now, 1
ahorrar to save, 11

aire *m.* air, 12
  aire acondicionado air-conditioning, 9
ajo garlic, 6
al día up to date, 14
  al lado de *prep.* next to, 9
alarido shriek, scream, cry, 12
alarma alarm, 15
alcalde(sa) mayor, 14
aldea village, town, 8
alemán *m.* German (language), 1
alemán(ana) *adj.* German, 2
alergia allergy, 5
alfabetismo literacy, 14
alfombra carpet, 4; rug, floor covering, 8
algo something, anything, 8
algodón *m.* cotton, 7
alguien somebody, someone, anybody, anyone, 8
algún, alguno(a/os/as) some, any, 8
allí *adv.* there P
alma soul, 8
  almas gemelas soul mates, 3
almorzar (ue) to have (eat) lunch, 4
almuerzo lunch, 6
alrededor de around, M2
altavoces *m.* speakers, 15
altiplano occidental western highlands, 8
alto *adj.* tall, 2
amable *adj.* friendly, 2
amar to love, 10
amarillo *adj.* yellow, 1
ambiente *(m.)* **ameno** pleasant atmosphere, M2
ambulancia ambulance, 5
amigo(a) friend, 1
amistad *f.* friendship, 10

amor *m.* love, 10
analfabetismo illiteracy, 14
analista de sistemas *m./f.* systems analyst, 11
anaranjado *adj.* orange, 1
andar en bicicleta to ride a bike, 3
anfitrión *m.* host, 8
anfitriona hostess, 8
angosto *adj.* narrow, 11
anillo ring, 9
animal *m.* animal, 12
anoche *adv.* last night, 6
anteayer *adv.* the day before yesterday, 6
antena parabólica satellite dish, 15
antes (de) que *conj.* before, 13
antibiótico antibiotic, 5
antigüedad *f.* antique, 7
antipático *adj.* unpleasant, 2
anuncio commercial, 13
año year, 3
apagado *adj.* off, 15
apagar (ue) to turn off, 15
aparador *m.* shop window, 13
apartamento apartment, 1
apellido last name, 2
aplaudir to applaud, 10
apoyar to support, 14
apoyo support, 13
apreciar to appreciate, 13
aprender to learn, 2
apretón *(m.)* **de manos** handshake, 11
aprobar (ue) to approve; to pass, 14
aprovechar to take advantage, 14
aquel (aquella) *adj.* that (over there), 6
aquí *adv.* here P

árbol *m.* tree, 3
archivar to save, 15
archivo file, 15
arete *m.* earring, 9
argentino *adj.* Argentine, 2
arma *m.* weapon, 12
armario wardrobe, armoire, closet, 4
arquitecto(a) architect, 11
arquitectura architecture, 1
arreglado *adj.* neat, tidy, 9
arriesgarse (ue) to take a risk, 15
arrogante *adj.* arrogant, 2
arroyo stream, 12
arroz *m.* rice, 6
arte *m./f.* art, 1
artesanía handicrafts, 7
articular to say, 13
artístico *adj.* artistic, 2
ascensor *m.* elevator, 4
Así así. So-so. P
  Así que... So . . . , 2
asiento seat, 9
asistente de vuelo *m./f.* flight attendant, 9
asistir a to attend, 2
aspiradora vacuum cleaner, 4
aspirina aspirin, 5
asustarse to be frightened, 8
aterrizar to land, 9
atinar to find 13
atlético *adj.* athletic, 2
atontado *adj.* dazed, stupefied, 12
aumentar to grow, 1; to increase, 14
aún *adv.* still, M2
aunque *conj.* although, even though, 12
autobús *m.* bus (*Spain*) P
automóvil *m.* car P
autor(a) author, 13
ave *m.* bird, 12
avión *m.* plane, 9
ayer *adv.* yesterday, 6
ayudante *m./f.* assistant, 13
ayudar(se) to help (each other), 1
azada hoe, 12
azul *adj.* blue, 1

B

babear to spew, M3
bachata type of dance, 9
bailar to dance, 1
bailarín *m.* dancer, 13
bailarina dancer, 13
baile *m.* dance, 1
bajar(se) (de) to get off, 9
bajo *adj.* short (height), 2
ballet *m.* ballet, 13

balneario beach resort, 8
baloncesto basketball, 3
banana banana, 6
banco bank, 3; bench, M3
banderín *m.* small flag, 6
banquero(a) banker, 11
banquete *m.* banquet, 10
bañarse to take a bath, 5
bañera bathtub, 4
barato *adj.* inexpensive, cheap, 7
bárbaro *adj.* awesome, M3
barrer el piso to sweep the floor, 4
barretilla pickaxe, 13
barrio neighborhood P
Bastante bien. Rather well. P
basura trash, 12
beber to drink, 2
bebida beverage, 6
béisbol *m.* baseball, 3
belleza beauty, M3
bello *adj.* beautiful, 12
beneficios benefits, 11
besar(se) to kiss (each other), 10
biblioteca library, 1
bibliotecario(a) librarian, 1
bicicleta bicycle, 3
bien *adv.* Well, fine
  Bastante bien. Mather well. P
  bien asado well done, 6
  Bien, gracias. Fine, thanks. P
  Muy bien. Very well. P
¡Bienvenido! Welcome!, 9
bilingüe *adj.* bilingual, 2
billete *m.* ticket
  billete de ida one-way ticket, 9
  billete de ida y vuelta round-trip ticket, 9
biología biology, 1
bistec *m.* steak, 6
blanco *adj.* white, 1
blusa blouse, 7
boca mouth, 5
boda wedding, 10
boleto ticket, 3
  boleto de ida one-way ticket, 9
  boleto de ida y vuelta round-trip ticket, 9
bolígrafo ballpoint pen, 1
boliviano *adj.* Bolivian, 2
bolsa purse, bag, 7
bombero(a) firefighter, 11
bonito *adj.* pretty, 2
borrador *m.* eraser, 1
bosque *m.* forest, 12
  bosque nuboso cloud forest, 12
bota boot, 7
botines de charol *m.* patent leather ankle boots, M5

brasileño *adj.* Brazilian, 2
brazo arm, 5
brecha gap, difference, 14
brindis *m.* toast, 8
broncearse to get a suntan, 8
bucear to scuba-dive, 8
¡Buen provecho! Enjoy your meal!, 6
¡Buen viaje! Have a nice trip!, 9
Buenas noches. Good evening (night). P
Buenas tardes. Good afternoon. P
bueno *adj.* good, 2
Buenos días. Good morning. P
buey *m.* ox, 12
bufanda scarf, 7
búho owl, 12
bullicioso *adj.* busy, 7
burlarse de to make fun of, 3
buscar (qu) to look for, 1
búsqueda de trabajo job hunt, 11

C

cabeza head, 5
cabina cabin, 9
cada *adv.* each, M1
  cada año each (every) year, 8
  cada día (semana, etc.) every day (week, etc.), 10
café *m.* café, 3; coffee, 6
cafetería cafeteria, 1
caimán *m.* alligator, 12
cajero automático ATM, 11
cajero(a) cashier, 11
cajón *m.* box, 12
calamares (fritos) *m.* (fried) squid, 6
calcetines *m. pl.* socks, 7
calculadora calculator, 1
calendario calendar, 1
cálido *adj.* warm, 15
caliente *adj.* hot (temperature), 6
calle *f.* street, 3
cama bed, 4
  cama sencilla (doble) single (double) bed, 9
cámara camera, 3
  cámara digital digital camera, 15
camarero(a) waiter (waitress), 6
camarones (fritos) *m.* (fried) shrimp, 6
cambiar to change, 7
camello camel, 12
cámera de representantes (diputados) house of representatives, 14

caminar to walk, 1
  caminar por las montañas to hike/walk in the mountains, 3
caminata walk, 7
camión *m.* bus (Mexico) P
camisa shirt, 7
camiseta T-shirt, 7
campaña campaign, 14
campesino(a) farm worker, peasant, 12
campo country, 8
  campo de fútbol (de golf) football field (golf course), 3
campus *m.* campus, 1
canadiense *adj.* Canadian, 2
canal *m.* channel (TV), 13
canción *f.* song, 13
candado lock, 4
candidato(a) candidate, applicant, 11
cansancio tiredness, 5
cantante *m./f.* singer, 13
cantar to sing, 1
capa de ozono ozone layer, 12
cara face, 5
carecer de to lack, 15
cariño affection, 10
carne (de res) *f.* meat (beef), 6
carnicería butcher shop, 3
caro *adj.* expensive, 7
carpintero(a) carpinter, 11
carrera major, field of study, 1
carreta wagon, cart, 12
carretera highway, 12
carro car P
cartera wallet, 7
cartón *m.* cardboard, 4
casa house, 4
casado *adj.* married, 2
casarse (con) to get married, to marry, 2
casi (siempre) *adv.* almost (always), 10
catarata waterfall, 12
catarro cold, 5
catorce fourteen P
catre *m.* cot, light bed, 12
caza chase, 7
cebolla onion, 6
cebra zebra, 12
cejas eyebrows, 5
celebración *f.* celebration, 8
celebrar to celebrate, 8
cena dinner, supper, 6
cenar to have (eat) supper (dinner), 6
centro downtown, 3
  centro comercial mall, 3
  centro estudiantil student center, 1

cepillarse los dientes to brush one's teeth, 5
cerca de *prep.* near, 9
cerebro brain, 5
cero zero P
cerrar (ie) to close, 4
cerveza beer, 6
césped *m.* lawn, 4
champiñón *m.* mushroom, 6
chancha pig, 13
chaqueta jacket, 7
Chau. *(informal)* Bye. P
cheque *m.* check, 7
¡Chévere! Cool!, 3
chileno *adj.* Chilean, 2
chillido screech, M3
chimenea fireplace, chimney, 4
chino Chinese (language), 1; *adj.* Chinese, 2
chipichipi *m.* thumbnail-size clam, 6
chocarse (qu) con to crash into, 8
chuleta (de cerdo) (pork) chop, 6
ciberespacio cyberspace, 15
ciclismo cycling, 3
cien/ciento one hundred, 2
ciencias science, 1
ciervo deer, 12
cifra figure, number, 14
cinco five P
   Cinco de Mayo Cinco de Mayo, 8
cincuenta fifty, 2
cine *m.* movie theater, 3; movies, 13
cinta ribbon, M5
cinturón *m.* belt
circo circus, 8
cita date (social), 10
ciudadano(a) citizen, 14
clásico *adj.* classical, 13
clavar (estacas) to stick, drive (stakes in the ground), 12
cobarde *adj.* cowardly, 2
coche *m.* car P
cocina kitchen, 4
cocinar to cook, 6
cocinero(a) cook, chef, 11
codo elbow, 5
cognado falso false cognate, 1
cohete *m.* rocket, 8
colina hill, 12
colombiano *adj.* Colombian, 2
color *m.* color, 1
comedia comedy, 13
comedor *m.* dining room, 4
comenzar (ie) to start, begin, 3
comer to eat, 2
comerciante *m./f.* merchant, 11
cómico *adj.* humorous, 2

comida food, meal, 6
¿Cómo? How? P
   ¿Cómo está usted? How are you? (formal) P
   ¿Cómo estás? How are you? (informal) P
   ¡Cómo no! Of course!, 6
   ¿Cómo se llama usted? What's your name? (formal) P
   ¿Cómo te llamas? What's your name? (informal) P
cómoda dresser, 4
comodidad *f.* comfort, M3
cómodo *adj.* comfortable, 9
compadre *m./f.* co-parent, 2
compañero(a) de clase classmate, 1
   compañero(a) de cuarto roommate, 1
compartir to share, M2
compositor(a) composer, 13
comprar to buy, 1
comprender to understand P
comprometido *adj.* engaged, 10
compromiso engagement, 10
computación *f.* computer science, 1
computadora computer, 1
   computadora portátil laptop computer, 15
con *prep.* with
   con destino a departing for, 9
   con permiso pardon me, excuse me P
   con respecto a with regard to, 11
con tal (de) que *conj.* provided (that), 13
concha shell, 6
concierto concert, 13
condimento condiment, 6
condominio condominium, 4
conectar to connect, 15
conexión *f.* connection, 15
congestionado *adj.* congested, 5
congreso congress, 14
conocer(se) to know (each other); to meet, 3
conseguir (i) to get, to obtain, 4
consejero(a) advisor, 1
conservación *f.* conservation, 12
conservador(a) *adj.* conservative, 2
conservar to conserve, 12
constitución *f.* constitution, 14
construir to construct, 12
contabilidad *f.* accounting, 1
contador(a) accountant, 11
contaminación *f.* pollution, 12

contaminado *adj.* polluted, 12
contaminar to pollute, 12
contar (ue) to count; to tell, 4
   contar con to count on, 3
contento *adj.* happy, 4
contestador automático *m.* answering machine, 15
contestar to answer P
contratar to hire, 11
control *m.* **remoto** remote control, 15
corazón *m.* heart, 5
corbata necktie, 7
coreano *adj.* Korean, 2
coronación *(f.)* **de una reina** crowning of a queen, 8
correo electrónico e-mail, 11
correr to run, 3
   correr las olas to surf, 8
corrupción *f.* corruption, 14
cortar el césped to mow the lawn, 4
corto *adj.* short (length), 2
coser to sew, M2
costa coast, 8
costar (ue) to cost, 4
costarricense *adj.* Costa Rican, 2
cotidiano *adj.* daily, 13
cotización *f.* exchange rate, M4
crear to create, M1
crecer to grow, 14
creciente *adj.* growing, 15
creer to believe, 2
crema bronceadora suntan lotion, 8
crimen *m.* crime, 14
crucero cruise liner, 9
cruzar to cross, 9
cuaderno notebook, 1
cuadra city block, 9
cuadro painting, 4
¿Cuál(es)? Which? P
   ¿Cuál es tu dirección? *(informal)* What's your address? *(informal)* P
   ¿Cuál es tu nombre? What's your name? *(informal)* P
   ¿Cuál es tu número de teléfono? What's your telephone number? *(informal)* P
cuando *conj.* when, 13
¿Cuándo? When? P
¿Cuánto(a)? How much?, 8
¿Cuántos(as)? How many? P
   ¿Cuánto le debo? How much do I owe you?, 7
   ¿Cuántos años tienes? How old are you? P
cuarenta forty, 2

cuarto room, 1
   cuarto de baño bathroom, 4
cuatro four P
cuatrocientos four hundred, 4
cubano *adj.* Cuban, 2
cuello neck
cuenta check, bill, 6; account, 11
   cuenta corriente checking account, 11
   cuenta de ahorros savings account, 11
   La cuenta, por favor. The check, please., 6
cuento story, 13
cuero leather, 7
cuerpo humano body, 5
cuidar(se) to take care (of oneself), 5
culebra snake, 12
cultivar to plant, 5; to cultivate; to grow (plants), 12
cumpleaños *m.* birthday, 8
cumplir años to have a birthday, 8
   cumplir con to honor, 10
cuñada sister-in-law, 2
cuñado brother-in-law, 2
currículum *m.* résumé, 11
curso course, 1

D

dado que since, due to, 1
danza dance, 1
dar to give, 3
   dar una fiesta to give a party, 8
   dar la vuelta a to turn onto, 13
   dar un paseo to go for a walk, 3
   darse cuenta to realize, M3
   darse la mano to shake hands, 10
de from, of
   de cuadros plaid, 7
   ¿De dónde eres tú? Where are you from? *(informal)* P
   ¿De dónde es usted? Where are you from? *(formal)* P
   ¿De dónde? From where? P
   de la (mañana, tarde, noche) in the (morning, afternoon/evening), 1
   de lujo deluxe, fancy, 11
   de lunares polka-dotted, 7
   ¿De quién(es)? Whose?, 8
   de rayas striped, 7
   de repente suddenly, 8
   de tiempo completo full-time, 11
   de tiempo parcial part-time, 11

debate *m.* debate, 14

deber (+ infinitive) should, must, ought (to do something), 2

deber *m. noun* duty, 14

debilidad *f.* weakness, 5

decano(a) dean, 1

decir (i) to say, to tell P

¡**No me digas más!** Say no more!, 11

dedo finger, 5

dedo de pie toe, 5

defender (ie) to defend, 14

defensa defense, 14

dejar to quit, 11; to leave; to let, to allow, 13

delante de *prep.* in front of, 9

delatar su presencia to give oneself away, 12

delgado *adj.* thin, 2

demandar to sue, 14

demás: los (las) demás others, 9

demasiado *adv.* too much, 9

democracia democracy, 14

demócrata *adj.* democratic, 14

demora delay, 9

demorarse to be delayed, 13

denso *adj.* dense, 12

dentista *m./f.* dentist, 11

departamento apartment, 4

dependiente *m./f.* salesclerk, 7

deporte *m.* sport, 3

depositar to deposit (money), 11

derecha: a la derecha de *prep.* to the right of, 9

derecho law, 1; straight, 9

derechos humanos (civiles) human (civil) rights, 14

derrocar (qu) to overthrow, 14

desafío challenge, 14

desamparado(a) defenseless person, 13

desarrollar to develop, 12

desarrollo development, 12

desastre *m.* disaster, 1

desatar to untie, 6

desayunar to have (eat) breakfast, 6

desayuno breakfast, 6

descansar (por una hora) to rest (for an hour), 1

desconectar to disconnect, 15

desconocido *adj.* unknown, M3

descuento discount, 7

desde *prep.* from, 1

desear to want, to wish, 1

desempleo unemployment, 14

desenchufar to unplug, 15

desenlace *m.* ending, M5

desigualdad *f.* inequality, 14

deslizarse to slip away, 12

deslumbrar to dazzle, 13

desmedro impairment, 14

desordenado *adj.* messy, 4

despacho personal office, 11

despedirse (i) to say good-bye P; to fire, 11

despegar to take off, 9

desperdicio waste, 12

despertador *m.* alarm clock, 4

despertarse (ie) to wake up, 5

despierto *adj.* lively, M1

después *adv.* afterward, 10

después (de) (que) *conj.* after, 13

destrucción *f.* destruction, 12

destruido *adj.* destroyed, 12

destruir to destroy, 12

detrás de *prep.* behind, 9

día *m.* day, 1

al día up to date, 14

Día de la Raza Columbus Day, 8

Día de los Muertos Day of the Dead, 8

Día de los Reyes Magos Day of the Magi (Three Kings), 8

Día de Todos los Santos All Saints' Day, 8

Día del santo saint's day, 8

día feriado *m.* holiday, 8

dibujar to draw, 1

dibujo animado cartoon, 13

diccionario dictionary, 1

diciembre December, 3

dictador(a) dictator, 14

dictadura dictatorship, 14

diecinueve nineteen P

dieciocho eighteen P

dieciséis sixteen P

diecisiete seventeen P

diente *m.* tooth, 5

diez ten P

dinero money, 1

diputado(a) representative, 14

director(a) director, 13

dirigir to direct, 13

disco compacto compact disc (CD), 15

disco duro hard drive, 15

disculpe pardon me P

discurso speech, 14

discutir to discuss, 14

disfraz *m.* costume, 8

disfrazarse to wear a costume, 8

disfrutar to enjoy, 9

disquete *m.* diskette, 15

divorciado *adj.* divorced, 2

divorciarse (de) to get divorced (from), 10

divorcio divorce, 10

doblar to turn, 9

doce twelve P

documental *m.* documentary, 13

doler (ue) (a alguien) to be painful (to someone), 5

dolor (de oídos, de cabeza) *m.* ache, pain (earache, headache), 5

domingo Sunday, 1

dominicano *adj.* Dominican (from the Dominican Republic), 2

donar to donate, 3

¿**Dónde?** Where? P

dormir (ue) to sleep, 4

dormirse (ue) to fall asleep, 5

dormitorio bedroom, 4

dos two P

doscientos(as) two hundred, 4

drama *m.* drama, play, 13

dramático *adj.* dramatic, 2

dramaturgo *m./f.* playwright, 13

drogadicción *f.* drug addiction, 14

ducha shower, 4

ducharse to take a shower, 5

dulce *adj.* sweet, M1

durante *prep.* throughout, M3

durar to last, 1

E

echar una ojeada alrededor to take a look around, 12

ecología ecology, 1

economía economics, 1

edificio building, 1

educación *f.* education, 1

efectivo cash, 7

egipcio *adj.* Egyptian, 2

ejército army, 14

él *pron.* he P

elecciones *f.* elections, 14

electricista *m./f.* electrician, 11

electrodomésticos electric appliance, 4

elefante *m.* elephant, 12

elegir (i, i) to elect, 14

elemento item, 3

eliminar to eliminate, 14

ella *pron.* she P

ellos(as) *pron.* they P

embarque *m.* shipping, 11

emigrar to emigrate, 1

emocionado *adj.* excited, 4

empezar (ie) to begin, 4

empleado(a) employee, 11

empleo employment, 14

emprender to embark on, M5

empresa corporation; business, 11

en in

en carne propia in the flesh, 13

en caso (de) que *conj.* in case (of), 13

en conclusión in conclusion, 12

en cuanto a in regard to, 13

en nuestra época in our time, 3

en peligro de extinción in danger of extinction, 12

en regla in order, 8

en sí misma in itself, 3

en vez de instead, M2

enamorarse (de) to fall in love (with), 10

encaje *m.* lace, M5

encantado *adj.* haunted, 13

Encantado(a). Nice to meet you. P

encarcelamiento imprisonment, 14

encendido *adj.* on, 15

enchufado *adj.* plugged in, 15

enchufar to plug in, 15

encontrar to find, 5

encontrarse to feel, 5

energía solar solar energy, 12

enero January, 3

enfermarse to get sick, 5

enfermedad *f.* illness, 5

enfermero(a) nurse, 5

enfermo *adj.* sick, 4

enfocarse (qu) to focus, M2

enfrente de *prep.* across from, 9

enmendar (ie) to amend, 14

enmienda amendment, 14

enojado *adj.* angry, 4

enorgullecerse to take pride in something, 3

ensalada salad, 6

enseñar to teach, 1

entender (ie) to understand, 4

enterarse de to find out about, to inform oneself about, 11

entonces *adv.* then; so, 10

entrar to enter, 1

entre *prep.* between, 9

entremés *m.* hors d'oeuvre, 8

entretener (ie) to entertain, 4

entrevista interview, 11

envilecido *adj.* underappreciated, M1

equipaje (de mano) *m.* (carry-on) baggage, luggage, 9
equipo equipment, 15
escalera stairs, 4
escáner *m.* scanner, 15
escasez *f.* lack, shortage, 12
escenario stage, M2
escoger to choose, 2
escribir to write, 2
escritor(a) writer, 13
escritorio desk, 1
escuchar (música) to listen (to music), 1
escuela school, 1
esculpir to sculpt, 13
escultor(a) sculptor, 13
escultura sculpture, 13
ese(a) *adj.* that, 6
esfuerzo físico physical exertion, 5
espacio abierto open space, 4
espalda back, 5
español *m.* Spanish (language), 1
español(a) *adj.* Spanish, 2
especialidad *(f.)* **de la casa** house specialty, 6
especialización *f.* major, 1
especies *f.* species, 12
espectador(a) viewer, 13
espejo mirror, 4
esperar to hope; to wait, 1
espeso *adj.* thick, M3
esposa wife, 2
esposo husband, 2
esquiar (en el agua) to (water) ski, 3
esquina corner, 4
esquís (acuáticos) *m.* (water) skis, 3
¡Está de última moda! It's the latest style!, 7
está nublado it's cloudy, 3
estación *f.* season, 3
estación de trenes *f.* train station, 9
estadidad *f.* statehood, M5
estadio stadium, 3
estado libre asociado free associated state, 1
estadounidense *adj.* from the United States, 2
estante *m.* bookshelf, 4
estar to be
  estar conectado(a) (en línea) to be online, 15
  estar de acuerdo to agree, 10
  estar enfermo(a) to be sick, 5
  estar sano(a) to be healthy, 5

este *m.* east, 9
éste *pron.* this one, 6
este(a) *adj.* this, 6
estéreo stereo, 15
estilo style, 7
estómago stomach, 5
estornudar to sneeze, 5
Estoy a dieta. I'm on a diet., 6
  Estoy satisfecho(a). I'm satisfied. I'm full., 6
estudiante *m. /f.* student, 1
estudiar to study, 1
estufa stove, 4
examen *m.* test, 5
examinar to examine, 5
explicar (qu) to explain, 9
explotación *f.* exploitation, 12
explotar to exploit, 12
extranjero *adj.* foreign, M2
extraviado *adj.* lost, M3
extrovertido *adj.* outgoing, 2

F
fábrica factory, 12
factura bill, 11
facturar el equipaje to check the luggage, 9
falda skirt, 7
falta lack, 11
farmacia pharmacy, 5
fax *m.* fax machine, 11
fe *f.* faith, M2
febrero February, 3
fecundo *adj.* fruitful, 6
¡Felicitaciones! Congratulations!, 8
felicitar to congratulate, 10
feo *adj.* ugly, 2
ferretería hardware store, 3
fiesta (de sorpresa) (surprise) party; holiday, 8
filosofía philosophy, 1
fin *(m.)* **de semana** weekend, 1
finalmente *adv.* at last, finally, 10
finca farm, 12
firmar to sign, 10
física physics, 1
flan (casero) *m.* (homemade) caramel custard, 6
flor *f.* flower, 10
folklórico *adj.* folkloric, 13
fotocopiadora photocopier, 11
fotografía photography, 13
fotógrafo(a) photographer, 11
francés *m.* French (language), 1
francés(esa) *adj.* French, 2
fresco *adj.* fresh, 6
frontera border, 12
fruta fruit, 6

frutería fruit store, 3
fuego de artificio firework, M1
fuente *f.* source, M1; fountain, M3
función *(f.)* **musical** musical (play), 13
funcionar to function (to work), 15
furioso *adj.* furious, 4
fútbol (americano) *m.* soccer (football), 3

G
gafas de sol sunglasses, 3
gallina hen, 12
gallinero henhouse, 12
ganador(a) winner, 13
ganar to win, 3
ganga: ¡Es una ganga! It's a bargain!, 7
garaje *m.* garage, 4
garganta throat, 5
gasolinera gas station, 3
gastar to spend (money), 7
gato cat, 2
generoso *adj.* generous, 2
¡Genial! Great!, 1
gente *f.* people P
geografía geography, 1
geología geology, 1
gerente *m./f.* manager, 11
gimnasio gymnasium, 1
gobernador(a) governor, 14
gobernar (ie) to govern, 14
gobierno government, 14
golf *m.* golf, 3
golpe de estado *m.* coup d'etat, 14
gordo *adj.* fat, 2
gorila *m.* gorilla, 12
grabar to record, 15
grande *adj.* big, large, 2
gratis *adj.* free, 1
greda ground, clay soil, 12
gritar to shout, 8
grupo paramilitar paramilitary group, 14
guagua bus *(Puerto Mico)* P
guante *m.* glove, 7
guapo *adj.* good-looking, 2
guardaparques *m./f.* park ranger, 12
guardar to save, 15
  guardar cama to stay in bed, 5
guatemalteco *adj.* Guatemalan, 2
guerra war, 14
guerrillero *m./f.* guerrilla, 14
güira percussion instrument scraped by a metal rod, 9

gustar to be pleasing (to someone), 3
  (no) me gusta + infinitive I (don't) like to (do something), 1
gusto: El gusto es mío. The pleasure is mine. P

H
hablar(se) to speak, to talk (with each other), 1
hace buen tiempo it's nice, 3
  hace calor it's hot, 3
  hace fresco it's cool, 3
  hace frío it's cold, 3
  hace sol it's sunny, 3
  hace viento it's windy, 3
hacer to do; to make, 3
  hacer (un picnic, planes, ejercicio) to go on a picnic, to make plans, to exercise, 3
  hacer camping to go camping, 8
  hacer click (sobre) to click (on), 15
  hacer escala (en) to make a stop (on a flight) (in), 9
  hacer esnórquel to snorkel, 8
  hacer juego con to match, 7
  hacer la cama to make one's bed, 4
  hacer la(s) maleta(s) to pack one's suitcase(s), 9
  hacer un brindis to make a toast, 8
  hacer una fiesta to give a party, 8
  hacer una parrillada to have a cookout, 8
  hacerse falta to need, M3
hacia *adv.* toward, 9
haitiano *adj.* Haitian, 2
hamburguesa hamburger, 6
harina de maíz corn flour, 6
hasta *adv.* up to, until, 9
  Hasta luego. See you later. P
  Hasta mañana. See you tomorrow. P
  Hasta pronto. See you soon. P
  hasta que *conj.* until, 13
hay there is, there are P
helado ice cream, 6
hembra female, 12
herencia heritage, 8
hermana sister, 2
hermanastra stepsister, 2
hermanastro stepbrother, 2
hermano brother, 2
herramientas tools, 12
hierba herb, 5; grass, M3
hierro iron, 5

hígado liver, 5
hija daughter, 2
hijo son, 2
hipopótamo hippopotamus, 12
hispanohablante *m./f.* native Spanish speaker
historia history, 1; story, 4
historial clínica *f.* medical history, 5
hogar *m.* home, 4
hoja leaf, 5
¡Hola! Hi! (informal) P
hombre *m.* man, 1
   hombre de negocios businessman, 11
hondureño *adj.* Honduran, 2
honesto *adj.* honest, 2
honradez *f.* honesty, M4
honrar to honor, 8
hora hour, time
   ¿A qué hora? At what time?, 1
   a última hora at the last minute, 8
horario schedule, 9
horno (de microondas) (microwave) oven, 4
hotel de cuatro estrellas *m.* four-star hotel, 9
hoy *adv.* today, 1
huelga strike, 14
huérfano(a) orphan, M3
hueso bone, 5
huevo duro hard-boiled egg, 6
huipil *m.* traditional women's tunic, 8
humanidades *f. pl.* humanities, 1
humilde *adj.* humble, 2
hundirse to sink into, 6

I

ideología ideology, 14
iglesia church, 3
igualdad *f.* equality, 14
ilustrado *adj.* learned, knowledgeable, 13
impermeable *m.* raincoat, 7
impresora printer, 11
imprimir to print, 11
impuestos taxes, 14
inagotable *adj.* endless, M1
indeciso *adj.* indecisive, 2
inflación *f.* inflation, 14
información *f.* information P
informar to inform, 14
informe *m.* report, 11
ingeniería engineering, 1
ingeniero(a) engineer, 11
inglés *m.* English (language), 1
inglés(esa) *adj.* English, 2

inmigración *f.* passport control, immigration, 9
inodoro toilet, 4
inolvidable *adj.* unforgettable, 13
insólito *adj.* unusual, unaccustomed, 12
intelectual *adj.* intellectual, 2
inteligente *adj.* intelligent, 2
Internet *m.* Internet, 14
interpelar to question, 14
interpretar to play a role, 13
intuitivo *adj.* intuitive, 2
investigar to investigate, 14
invierno winter, 3
invitado *m./f.* guest, 8
invitar: Te invito. It's on me (my treat)., 6
ir to go, 3
   ir a pie to go on foot, 9
   ir a un bar to go to a bar, 3
   ir a un club to go to a club, 3
   ir a un concierto to go to a concert, 3
   ir a una discoteca to go to a disco, 3
   ir a una fiesta to go to a party, 3
   ir al cine to go to the movies, 3
   ir de compras to go shopping, 3
   ir en autobús to go by bus, 9
   ir en avión to go by plane, 9
   ir en barco to go by boat, 9
   ir en bicicleta to go by bike, 9
   ir en coche to go by car, 9
   ir en metro to go by subway, 9
   ir en taxi to go by taxi, 9
   ir en tren to go by train, 9
irresponsable *adj.* irresponsible, 2
isla island, 9
italiano Italian (language), 1; *adj.* Italian, 2
izquierda: a la izquierda de *prep.* to the left of, 9

J

jadeo panting, 5
jamón *m.* ham, 6
japonés *m.* Japanese (language), 1
japonés(esa) *adj.* Japanese, 2
jarabe *m.* cough syrup, 5
jardín *m.* garden, 4
jeans *m. pl.* blue jeans, 7
jefe *m./f.* boss, 11
jerarquía hierarchy, 11
joven *adj.* young, 2
joya gem, M2
joyas jewelry, 7

joyería jewelry store, 3
jubilarse to retire, 11
juego game, 3
jueves *m.* Thursday, 1
juez *m./f.* judge, 10
jugador(a) player, 3
jugar (ue) to play, 4
   jugar al tenis to play tennis, 3
jugo de fruta fruit juice, 6
julio July, 3
junio June, 3

L

lago lake, 8
lámpara lamp, 4
lana wool, 7
langosta lobster, 6
lápiz *m.* pencil, 1
largarse to get away, 13
largo *adj.* long, 2
lavabo bathroom sink, 4
lavadora washing machine, 4
lavaplatos *m.* dishwasher, 4
lavar (los platos, la ropa, las ventanas) to wash (dishes, clothes, windows), 4
lavarse to wash up, 5
lección *f.* lesson, 1
leche *f.* milk, 6
lechuga lettuce, 6
leer to read, 2
lejos (de) *prep.* far (away) (from), 9
lengua language, 1; tongue, 5
   lenguas extranjeras foreign languages, 1
león *m.* lion, 12
levantar pesas to lift weights, 3
levantarse to get up, 5
ley *f.* law, 14
liberal *adj.* liberal, 2
libertad (f.) de la prensa freedom of the press, 14
librería bookstore, 1
libro (de texto) (text)book, 1
ligeramente *adv.* slightly, M2
ligero *adj.* light (meal, food), 6
limeño *adj.* from Lima, 13
limpiar la casa to clean the house, 4
limpio *adj.* clean, 4
linde *f.* edge, 12
listo *adj.* smart; ready, 2
literatura literature, 1
llamar to call, to phone, 1
   Me llamo... My name is . . . P
   llamar por teléfono to make a phone call, 11
llano plain, 12
llave *f.* key, 9
llegada arrival, 9
llegar to arrive, 1

llenar to fill out (a form), 11
llevar to wear, to carry, 7
   llevar a cabo to take place, 8
   llevar una vida tranquila to lead a peaceful life, 12
   llevarse bien (mal) (con) to get along well (poorly) (with) each other, 10
llorar to cry, 8
llover (ue) to rain, 4
lo que *pron.* what, 10
lobo wolf, 12
Localizador Uniforme de Recursos *m.* URL, 15
lograr to succeed, 13; to accomplish, M3
loza china, M5
luego *adv.* then, 10
lugar *m.* place, 1
lujoso *adj.* luxurious, 7
luna de miel honeymoon, 10
lunes *m.* Monday, 1
luz *f.* light, 1
   a la luz de in light of, M3

M

macho male, 12
madrastra stepmother, 2
madre *f.* mother, 2
maestro(a) teacher, 11
   maestro gasfitero master plumber, 13
maleta suitcase, 9
malo *adj.* bad, 2
mamá mother, 2
mamífero mammal, 12
mandar (cartas) to send (letters), 1
mando popular popular rule, 14
manifestación *f.* demonstration, 14
manjar *m.* delicacy, 6
mano *f.* hand, 5
manta blanket, 8
mantequilla butter, 6
manzana apple, 6
mañana *adv.* tomorrow, 1
mapa *m.* map, 1
maquillarse to put on makeup, 5
mar *m.* sea, 8
marcar (qu) to dial (the telephone), P
marcha passing, M1
mareado *adj.* dizzy, 5
mareo dizziness, 5
mariposa butterfly, 12
mariscos shellfish, seafood, 6
marítimo *adj.* having to do with the sea, 11
marrón *adj.* purple, 1

martes *m.* Tuesday, 1
marzo March, 3
Más o menos. So-so., P
  más... que more . . . than, 5
máscara mask, 8
mascota pet, 2
masticar (qu) to chew, 5
matemáticas math, 1
matrícula tuition, 1
matrimonio marriage, 10
mayo May, 3
mayor older P
  el mayor oldest, 6
mayoría majority, 1
mecánico(a) mechanic, 11
mechado shredded, 6
medianoche *f.* midnight, 1
medias stockings, 7
medicina medicine, 1
médico *m./f.* physician, doctor, 5; *adj.* medical, 5
medio ambiente environment, 12
mediodía *m.* noon, 1
medios de comunicación means of communication, 14
mejor better, 5
  el mejor best, 3
menor younger, 5
  el menor youngest, 6
menos... que less . . . than, 5
mensaje *m.* message, 15
mente mind, 13
menú *m.* menu, 6
mercado (al aire libre) (outdoor) market, 3
merengue *m.* type of dance and music, 9
mes *m.* month, 3
mesa table, 1
mesita coffee (side) table, 4
metrópolis *f.* metropolis, 12
mexicano *adj.* Mexican, 2
miembro de la familia member of the family, 2
miércoles *m.* Wednesday, 1
mil one thousand, 4
millón million, 4
ministro *m./f.* minister, 14
mío *adj.* my, mine, 7
mirar to watch, 1
  mirar la tele to watch television, 3
mirarse to look at each other, 10
mochila backpack, 1
módem *m.* modem, 15
moderno *adj.* modern, 2
molestar to bother, 13
molido *adj.* ground, 6
monarquía monarchy, 14
moneda currency, M4

mono monkey, 12
montar a caballo to go horseback riding, 3
morado *adj.* brown, 1
moreno *adj.* dark-haired, 2
morir (ue) to die, 4
mostrar (ue) to show, 7
Mucho gusto. Nice to meet you. P
muerto *adj.* dead, 4
mujer *f.* woman, 1
  mujer de negocios businesswoman, 11
muralla de piedra stone wall, 9
museo museum, 3
música music, 1
músico *m./f.* musician, 13

N
nacer to be born, 2
nacionalidad *f.* nationality, 2
nada nothing, not anything, at all, 8
nadar to swim, 3
nadie nobody, no one, 8
naranja orange, 6
nariz *f.* nose, 5
narrar to narrate, 4
natación *f.* swimming, 3
naturaleza nature, 12
naturalista *m./f.* naturalist, 12
navegar la red to surf the Net, 15
Navidad *f.* Christmas, 8
necesitar to need, 1
negocios business, 1
negro *adj.* black, 1
ni... ni neither . . . nor, 8
nicaragüense *adj.* Nicaraguan, 2
nieta granddaughter, 2
nieto grandson, 2
ningún, ninguno(a) none, not any, 8
Noche Vieja *f.* New Year's Eve, 8
Nochebuena Christmas Eve, 8
nombre *m.* first name, 2
  nombre compuesto compound name, 2
norte *m.* north, 9
norteamericano *adj.* North American, American, 2
nosotros(as) *pron.* we P
noticias news, 13
noticiero newscast, 14
novecientos nine hundred, 4
noventa ninety, 2
novia girlfriend, 1; bride, 10
noviazgo courtship, 10
noviembre November, 3
novio boyfriend, 1; groom, 10
nuera daughter-in-law, 2

nuestro *adj.* our, 7
nueve nine, P
nuevo *adj.* new, 2
número number, P; shoe size, 7
nunca *adv.* never, 8

O
o *conj.* or, 3
  o... o either . . . or, 8
objeto object, 1
obra (de arte) work (of art), 13
  obra maestra masterpiece
obrero(a) worker; laborer, 11
océano ocean, 8
ochenta eighty, 2
ocho eight, P
ochocientos eight hundred, 4
octubre October, 3
ocupado *adj.* busy, 4
oeste *m.* west, 9
oficina office, 1
  oficina de correos post office, 3
ofrecer (zc) to offer, 9
oído inner ear, 5
ojalá que I wish that, 12
ojo eye, 5
once eleven, P
ondulado *adj.* wavy, 4
ópera opera, 13
oponer to oppose, 14
oposición *f.* competitive examination for entrance into a school or job, 1
orar to pray, 8
ordenado *adj.* neat, 4
oreja (outer) ear, 5
orilla bank (of a lake), 8; shoreline, 9
orquesta band, 10
orquídea orchid, 12
osadía audacity, daring, 13
osezno bear cub, 12
oso bear, 12
otoño fall, 3
otra vez *adv.* again, 10

P
paciente *adj.* patient, 2; *noun m./f.* patient, 5
padrastro stepfather, 2
padre *m.* father, 2
padrina godmother, 2
padrino godfather, 2
pagar to pay, 1
  pagar a plazos to pay in installments, 11
  pagar en efectivo to pay in cash, 11
página de bienvenida (de entrada, de presentación,

inicial, principal, de la red) home page, 15
página web web page, 15
paisaje *m.* landscape, 12
pájaro bird, 2
palabra word, 1
pan (tostado) *m.* bread (toast), 6
panameño *adj.* Panamanian, 2
páncreas *m.* pancreas, 5
pantalla screen, 1
pantalones (cortos) *m.* pants (shorts), 7
pantera panther, 12
papá *m.* father, 2
papas (fritas) (french fried) potatoes, 6
papel *m.* paper, 1; role, 13
papelería stationery store, 3
para *prep.* for
  para colmo on top of that, 4
  para que *conj.* so that, 13
  ¿Para qué? For what purpose?, 8
parada stop, M3
paraguas *m.* umbrella, 7
paraguayo *adj.* Paraguayan, 2
parar(se) to stop, 9
parecer to appear, 1
parecido *adj.* similar, M1
pared *f.* wall, 4
pareja couple, 10
pariente *m./f.* relative, 2
parque *m.* park, 3
partido game, 3
  partido político political party, 14
pasado: (la semana, el mes, el año) pasado(a) last (week, month, year), 6
pasajero(a) passenger, 9
pasaporte *m.* passport, 9
pasar to spend (time); to pass, 1
  pasar la aspiradora to vacuum, 4
  pasar por to go through, 9
  pasarlo bien (mal) to have a good (bad) time, 8
pasatiempo pastime, 3
Pascua Easter, Passover, Christmas, 8
pasear en canoa/velero to go canoeing/sailing, 8
paseo stroll, 7
pasillo aisle, 9
paso step, 7
pastel *m.* cake, 8
pastilla pill, 5
pasto pasture, grazing land, 12
patinar (en línea) to (in-line) skate, 3

patines (en línea) *m.* (in-line) skates, 3
patio patio, 4
pato duck, 12
patrón *m.* pattern, 7
pavo turkey, 6
paz *f.* peace, 14
peatonal *adj.* pedestrian, M3
pedazo piece, M2
pedir (i) to ask for, P; to order (food), 6; to request, 9
  pedir prestado to borrow, 11
  pedir un aumento to ask for a raise, 11
peinarse to comb one's hair, 5
película movie, film, 13
  película clásica classic film, 13
  película de acción action film, 13
  película de arte art film, 13
  película de ciencia ficción science fiction film, 13
  película de horror horror film, 13
  película de intriga (misterio) mystery film, 13
  película del oeste western film, 13
  película extranjera foreign film, 13
  película romántica romantic film, 13
peligroso *adj.* dangerous, M3
pelo hair, 5
peluquería hair salon
peluquero(a) hairstylist, 11
pensar (ie) to think, 4
pensión *f.* boarding house
peor worse, 5
  el peor worst, 6
pequeño *adj.* small, 2
perder (ie) to lose; to miss (a function), 4
perdón pardon me, excuse me, P
perejil *m.* parsley, 6
perezoso *adj.* lazy, 2
perezoso con tres dedos three-toed sloth, 12
periódico newspaper, 14
periodismo journalism, 1
periodista *m./f.* journalist, 11
perjudicial *adj.* detrimental, harmful, 14
pero *conj.* but, 3
perro dog, 2
peruano *adj.* Peruvian, 2
pesado *adj.* heavy (meal, food), 6
pescado fish (dead), 6
pescar (qu) to fish, 8

pestañas eyelashes, 5
petróleo petroleum, 12
pez *m.* fish (live), 2
picar (qu) to eat appetizers, 6; to bite, 12
pico beak, 12
pie *m.* foot, 5
piedra stone, M3
piel *f.* skin, 5
pierna leg, 5
piloto *m./f.* pilot, 9
pimienta pepper, 6
pintarse to put on makeup, 5
pintor(a) painter, 13
pintura painting, 1
piscina pool, 3
piso floor, 4
pizarra chalkboard, 1
plancha iron, 4
planchar (la ropa) to iron (clothes), 4
plano *adj.* flat, M1
plataforma de operación operating platform (system), 15
plato principal main dish, 6
playa beach, 8
plaza plaza, 3
plomero(a) plumber, 11
pluma fountain pen, 1; feather, M2
pobre *adj.* poor, 2
poder (ue) to be able, 4
  No puedo más. I can't (eat) any more., 6
poder *m.* power, 14
poesía poetry, 13
poeta *m./f.* poet, 13
policía *m./f.* police officer, 11
politécnico technical school, 1
política internacional international policy, 14
político *m./f.* politician, 14
pollo (asado) (roast) chicken, 6
poner to put (on), 3; to turn on (TV); to show (a movie), 13
  poner la mesa to set the table, 4
ponerse + adjective to become, to get + adjective, 8
popular *adj.* popular, 13
por *prep.* for
  por ciento percent, 7
  por ejemplo for example, 12
  por eso therefore, 12
  por favor please, P
  por fin *adv.* finally, 10
  por la (mañana, tarde, noche) in the (morning, afternoon/evening), 1
  por otro lado on the other hand, 12

¿Por qué? Why?, P
  por supuesto of course, 2
portada cover, M5
portarse bien (mal) to behave well (poorly), 8
portugués *m.* Portuguese (language), 1
postre *m.* dessert, 6
pozo well, 12
practicar (qu) to practice, 1
precaverse de to be on one's guard against, 12
preferir (ie) to prefer, 4
pregunta question, P
preguntar to ask (a question), 1
prender to turn on, 15
prensa press, 14
preocupación *f.* concern, M2
preocupado *adj.* worried, 4
preparar to prepare, 6
presentación *f.* introduction, P
presidente de la universidad *m./f.* president of the university, 1
préstamo loan, 11
prestar to lend, 9
presupuesto budget, 11
primavera spring, 3
primero first, 10
primo(a) cousin, 2
privado *adj.* private, 9
probarse (ue) to try on, 7
problema *m.* problem, 5
procedente de arriving from, 9
procesión *f.* parade, 8
profesor(a) professor, 1
programa (de CD-ROM) *m.* (CD-ROM) program, 15
programa de concursos game show, 13
programa de entrevistas talk show, 13
programa deportivo sports program, 13
programador(a) programmer, 11
programar to program, 15
progresivo *adj.* progressive, 2
prometer to promise, 9
pronóstico del tiempo weather report (forecast), 13
proteger to protect, 12
protestar to protest, 14
proveedor *(m.)* **de servicios Internet** Internet service provider, 15
proveer to provide, make available, 11
proyecto project, 11
pueblo town, 3
puerta door, 4; gate, 9

puerto port, 9
puertorriqueño *adj.* Puerto Mican, 2
puesto job, position, 11
pulmones *m.* lungs, 5
puro *adj.* pure, 12

Q

que *pron.* that, which, who, 3
¿Qué? What? Which?, P
¡Qué bueno! Wonderful!, 2
¡Qué casualidad! What a coincidence!, P
¡Qué cursi! How corny!, 3
¿Qué hay? What's new? (informal), P
¿Qué hora es? What time is it?, 1
¿Qué tal? What's up? (informal), P
¿Qué te apetece? What would you like (to eat)?, 6
¿Qué te pasa? What's the matter with you?, 5
¿Qué tiene usted? What's the problem?, 5
quedarle (a uno) to fit (someone), 7
  ¿Cómo me queda? How does it look?, 7
quedarse to stay, 9
quehacer doméstico *m.* chore, 4
quejarse de to complain about, 9
quemar to burn, 8
querer (ie) to want; to love, 4
  Yo quisiera... I would like . . ., 6
queso cheese, 6
quetzal *m.* bird with long beautiful feathers found in Central America, 12
quien *pron.* who, 10
¿Quién(es)? Who?, P
química chemistry, 1
quince fifteen, P
quinientos five hundred, 4
quinqué *m.* oil lamp, M2
quitar la mesa to clear the table, 4
quitarse to take off, 5

R

raíz *f.* root, 13
ramo bouquet, 10
ranchero(a) rancher, 11
raras veces *adv.* rarely, infrequently, 8
rascacielos *m.* skyscraper, 12
rato: un buen rato a good time, 3

ratón *m.* mouse (of computer), 15

razón *f.* reason, 12

reaccionar to react, 8

rebaja sale (*Spain*), reduction (in price), 7

rebajar to reduce (in price), 7

rebelde *adj.* rebellious, 2

rebotar to bounce (a check), 11

recaudar to raise, M5

recepción *f.* front desk, 9

recepcionista *m./f.* receptionist, 9

receta prescription, 5

recibir to receive, 2

reciclar to recycle, 12

recién casados *m.* newlyweds, 10

recoger (j) to pick up; to claim, 9

recomendar (ie) to recommend, 6

recordar (ue) to remember, 8

recursos naturales natural resources, 12

redada raid, 14

redondez *f.* roundness, 4

reducir to reduce, 14

reforestar to reforest, 12

reforma reform, 14

refresco soft drink, 6

refrigerador *m.* refrigerator, 4

refugio natural wildlife preserve, 12

regalar to give (as a gift), 9

regalo gift, 8

regar (ie) las plantas to water the plants, 4; to irrigate, 12

registrarse to register, 9

regresar (a casa) to return (home), 1

reinar to rule, 14

reino kingdom, M2

relaciones sentimentales *f.* relationships, 10

relato story, 13

rellenar to stuff, 6

reloj *m.* clock, 1

remedio casero home remedy, 5

renunciar to resign, 11

reñido *adj.* hard-fought, M5

reportaje *m.* report, 14

reportero(a) reporter, 11

reposado *adj.* quiet, 6

republicano *adj.* republican, 14

reseña review, M2

reserva reservation, 9

reservado *adj.* reserved, 2

resfriado cold, 5

resfriarse to catch a cold, 5

residencia dormitory, 1

resolver (ue) to solve, resolve, 12

respaldar to support, to back up, 14

responder to respond, P

responsable *adj.* responsible, 2

restaurante *m.* restaurant, 3

retrato portrayal, M3

retrato al óleo oil painting, 13

reunión *f.* meeting, 11

reunirse con to get together with, 8

revista magazine, 14

rico *adj.* rich, 2; delicious, 6

rinoceronte *m.* rhinoceros, 12

riñones *m.* kidneys, 5

río river, 8

rodeado *adj.* surrounded, 9

rodear to surround, 11

rodilla knee, 5

rojo *adj.* red, 1

romper (con) to break up (with), 10

ropa clothing, 7

rostro face, M3

rubio *adj.* blonde, 2

rugir (j) to roar, M3

ruido noise, 12

ruidoso noisy, 9

ruso Russian (language), 1; *adj.* Russian, 2

S

sábado Saturday, 1

saber to know (how), 3

sabor *m.* flavor, 5

sacar (qu) to withdraw (money), 11

sacar fotos to take pictures, 3

sacar la basura to take out the garbage, 4

sagrado *adj.* sacred, 8

sal *f.* salt, 6

sala living room, 4

sala de clase classroom, 1

sala de conferencias conference room, 11

sala de emergencia emergency room, 5

sala de espera waiting room, 5

salario salary, 11

salida departure, 9

salida de emergencia emergency exit, 9

salir to leave, to go out, 3

salir del programa to quit the program, 15

salón (la sala) de charla *m.* chat room, 15

salsa sauce, 6

salud *f.* health, 5

¡Salud! Cheers!, 6

saludar(se) to greet (each other), P

salvadoreño *adj.* Salvadoran, 2

sandalia sandal, 7

sándwich *m.* sandwich, 6

santo(a) patron saint, 2

Semana Santa Holy Week, 8

satélite *m.* satellite, 15

secadora clothes dryer, 4

secarse (qu) to dry off, 5

sección de (no) fumar *f.* (non)smoking section, 9

secretario(a) secretary, 1

seda silk, 7

seguir (i) to pursue, to follow, 1; to continue, 4

seguir fielmente to follow faithfully, 3

seis six, P

seiscientos six hundred, 4

selva jungle, 12

semana week, 1

Semana Santa Holy Week, 8

sembrar (ie) to plant, 12

senado senate, 14

senador(a) senator, 14

sencillez *f.* simplicity, M2

sencillo *adj.* simple, M3

sentirse (bien/mal) to feel (good/bad), 5

señor (Sr.) Mr., sir, P

señora (Sra.) Mrs., ma'am, P

señorita (Srta.) Miss, P

separación *f.* separation, 10

separado *adj.* separated, 2

separarse (de) to separate (from), 10

septiembre September, 3

ser to be, P

servidor *m.* server, 15

servir (i) to serve, 4

sesenta sixty, 2

setecientos seven hundred, 4

setenta seventy, 2

sí yes, P

sicología psychology, 1

siempre always, 8

siete seven, P

silla chair, 1

sillón *m.* easy chair, arm chair, 4

simpático *adj.* nice, 2

sin *prep.* without

sin esfuerzo alguno effortless, 7

sin que *conj.* without, 13

sincero *adj.* sincere, 2

síntoma *m.* symptom, 5

sinvergüenza *m./f.* shameless person, 4

siquiatra *m./f.* psychiatrist, 11

sobrepoblación *f.* overpopulation, 12

sobrina niece, 2

sobrino nephew, 2

sociología sociology, 1

sofá *m.* sofa, couch, 4

soga rope, 13

solamente only, just, 10

soldado (la mujer soldado) soldier, 11

solicitar un puesto to apply for a job, 11

solicitud *f.* application (form), 11

sólo only, P

soltar to release, M2

soltero *adj.* single, 2

sombra shade, 3

sombreado *adj.* shaded, M2

sombrero hat, 7

sopa soup, 6

soportar: No suporto más! I can't take it anymore!, 4

sordo deaf, M5

sótano basement, 4

subida climb, 5

subir to climb, to go up, 5

subsiguiente subsequent, M2

sucio *adj.* dirty, 4

suegra mother-in-law, 2

suegro father-in-law, 2

sueldo salary, 11

suéter *m.* sweater, 7

sumar to add, M1

superficie plana *f.* flat surface, 4

supermercado supermarket, 3

sur *m.* south, 9

suyo *adj.* your, yours, his, her, hers, its, 7

T

tacaño *adj.* stingy, 2

tajada slice, 6

talar to cut down (trees), 12

talla size (clothing), 7

también *adv.* also, too, 8

tambora type of drum, 9

tampoco *adv.* neither, not either, 8

tan pronto como *conj.* as soon as, 13

tan... como as . . . as, 5

tanto(a)... como as much . . . as, 5

tantos(as)... como as many . . . as, 5

tarde *adv.* late, 1

tarea homework, 1

tarjeta de crédito credit card, 7

tasa rate, 14

té (helado) *m.* (iced) tea, 6
teatro theater, 1
techo roof, 4
teclado keyboard, 15
técnico *m./f.* technician, 11
tejido weaving, fabric, 8
tela fabric, 7
teléfono celular celluar phone, 15
telenovela soap opera, 3
teletrabajar to telecommute, 15
telón *m.* curtain, M2
temporada de deporte sports season, 3
temprano *adv.* early, 1
tener (ie) to have, P
tener calor to be hot, 3
tener celos to be jealous, 4
tener dolor de cabeza to have a headache, 5
tener escalofríos to have chills, 5
tener éxito to be successful, 2
tener fiebre to have a fever, 5
tener frío to be cold, 3
tener ganas de to feel like (doing something), 4
tener gripe to have a cold, 5
tener hambre to be hungry, 2
tener lugar to take place, 6
tener miedo (de) to be afraid (of something), 4
tener náuseas to be nauseous, 5
tener paciencia to be patient, 4
tener prisa to be in a hurry, 2
tener que to have to (do something), 3
tener razón to be right, 2
tener sed to be thirsty, 2
tener sueño to be tired, sleepy, 2
tener tos to have a cough, 5
terminal de autobuses *f.* bus station, 9
terminar to finish, end, 1
terraza terrace, 4
terrorismo terrorism, 14
testigo *m./f.* witness, 10
tía aunt, 2

tiempo weather, 3
tienda store, 3
tienda de antigüedades (de música [de discos], de ropa) antique (music, clothing) store, 3
tierra land, earth, 12
tigre *m.* tiger, 12
tímido *adj.* shy, timid, 2
tío uncle, 2
tirar to throw, 10
titubear to hesitate, 12
tiza chalk, 7
tobillo ankle, 5
tocador *m.* dresser, 4
tocar (qu) to touch; to play an instrument, 1
tocarse (qu) to touch each other, 10
todos all
todos los años (días, meses, etc.) every year (day, month, etc.), 10
todos los días every day, 1
tolerante *adj.* tolerant, 2
tomar (clases/exámenes) to take (classes/tests); to drink, 1
tomar el sol to sunbathe, 3
tomar turnos to take turns, 4
tomarle la temperatura (a alguien) to take (someone's) temperature, 5
tomate *m.* tomato, 6
tonto *adj.* silly, foolish, 2
tos *f.* cough, 5
toser to cough, 5
tostadora toaster, 4
trabajador(a) *adj.* hardworking, 2
trabajar (por la noche) to work (at night), 1
trabajo work, 11
traductor(a) translator, 11
traer to bring, 3
tráfico traffic, 12
traje *m.* suit, 7
traje de baño bathing suit, 3
tranquilo *adj.* tranquil, peaceful, 12
transporte *(m.)* **público** public transportation, 12
tratarse de to be about, M2
trato hecho it's a deal, 14

trece thirteen, P
treinta thirty, P
tres three, P
trescientos three hundred, 4
triste *adj.* sad, 4
tú *pron.* you, P
turismo tourism, 1
tuyo *adj.* your, yours, 7

U

ubicación *f.* location, M3
umbroso *adj.* shadowed, M2
una vez *adv.* once, 10
una vez al mes once a month, 8
universidad *f.* university, 1
uno one, P
uña fingernail, 5
uruguayo *adj.* Uruguayan, 2
usar to use, 1; to wear, 7
usted(es) *pron.* you, P

V

valiente *adj.* brave, 2
valle *m.* valley, 12
vamos a ver let's see, 6
vegetal *m.* vegetable, 6
veinte twenty, P
veintidós twenty-two, P
veintiséis twenty-six, P
veintitrés twenty-three, P
veintiuno twenty-one, P
vela candle, 8
vendedor(a) salesperson, 11
vender to sell, 2
venezolano *adj.* Venezuelan, 2
venir (ie) to come, 4
¡Venga! Come on!, 3
ventana window, 4
ventanilla window, 9
ver to see, 3
Nos vemos. See you later., P
ver una película to watch a movie, 3
verano summer, 3
verdad *f.* truth, 1
verde *adj.* green, 1
verdura vegetable, 6
vestido dress, 7
vestirse (i) to get dressed, 5
veterinario *m./f.* veterinarian, 11
vez time

dos (tres, etc.) veces twice (three times, etc.), 10
en vez de instead, M2
muchas veces often, 8
otra vez *adv.* again, 10
viajar to travel, 1
viaje *m.* trip, 9
viajero(a) traveler, 5
víbora de cascabel rattlesnake, 12
vida life, 10
vida nocturna night life, M3
videocámara video camera, 15
videocasete *m.* videotape, 15
videocasetera VCR, 15
viejo *adj.* old, 2
viernes *m.* Friday, 1
vigente *adj.* existing, 14
vinagre *m.* vinegar, 6
vino (blanco, tinto) (white, red) wine, 6
visitar to visit, 1
visitar un museo to visit a museum, 3
viuda widow, M2
viudo *adj.* widowed, 2; *noun* widower, M2
vivienda housing, 4
vivir to live, 2
volcán *m.* volcano, 12
vólibol *m.* volleyball, 3
volver (ue) to return, 4
vosotros(as) *pron.* you, P
votar to vote, 14
voto vote, 14
vuelo (sin escala) (nonstop) flight, 9
vuestro *adj.* your, yours, 7

Y

y and, 3
yate *m.* yacht, 9
yerno son-in-law, 2

Z

zapatería shoe store, 7
zapato shoe, 7
zapato de tenis (deportivo) tennis shoe (sneaker), 3
zoología zoology, 1
zorro fox, 12

Glosario inglés-español

bouquet ramo, 10
box cajón *m.*, 12
boyfriend novio, 1
brain cerebro, 5
brave valiente *adj.*, 2
Brazilian brasileño *adj.*, 2
bread (toast) pan (tostado) *m.*, 6
break up (with) romper (con), 10
breakfast desayuno, 6
bride novia, 10
bring traer, 3
brother hermano, 2
brother-in-law cuñado, 2
brown morado *adj.*, 1
brush one's teeth cepillarse los dientes, 5
buckle the seat belt abrochar el cinturón de seguridad, 9
budget presupuesto, 11
building edificio, 1
burn quemar, 8
bus autobús *m.* (*Spain*), P; camión *m.* (*Mexico*), P; guagua (*Puerto Mico*), P
bus station terminal de autobuses *f.*, 9
business negocios, 1; empresa, 11
business administration administración (*f.*) de empresas, 1
businessman hombre de negocios, 11
businesswoman mujer de negocios, 11
busy ocupado *adj.*, 4; bullicioso *adj.*, 7
but pero *conj.*, 3
butcher shop carnicería, 3
butter mantequilla, 6
butterfly mariposa, 12
buy comprar, 1
Bye. Chau. (*informal)*, P

C

cabin cabina, 9
café café *m.*, 3
cafeteria cafetería, 1
cake pastel *m.*, 8
calculator calculadora, 1
calendar calendario, 1
call llamar, 1
camel camello, 12
camera cámara, 3
campaign campaña, 14
campus campus *m.*, 1
Canadian canadiense *adj.*, 2
candidate candidato(a), 11
candle vela, 8
car automóvil *m.*, carro, coche *m.*, P
caramel custard (homemade) flan (casero) *m.*, 6
cardboard cartón *m.*, 4
carpenter carpintero(a), 11
carpet alfombra, 4
carry llevar, 7

cart carreta, 12
cartoon dibujo animado, 13
cash efectivo, 7
cashier cajero(a), 11
cat gato, 2
catch agarrar, 10
catch a cold resfriarse, 5
CD-ROM program programa de CD-ROM *m.*, 15
celebrate celebrar, 8
celebration celebración *f.*, 8
celluar phone teléfono celular, 15
chair silla, 1
chalk tiza, 1
chalkboard pizarra, 1
challenge desafío, 14
change cambiar, 7
channel (TV) canal *m.*, 13
chase caza, 7
chat room salón *m.* (la sala) de charla, 15
cheap barato *adj.*, 7
check cuenta, 6; cheque *m.*, 7
The check, please. La cuenta, por favor., 6
check the luggage facturar el equipaje, 9
checking account cuenta corriente, 11
Cheers! ¡Salud!, 6
cheese queso, 6
chef cocinero(a), 11
chemistry química, 1
chew masticar (qu), 5
chicken (roast) pollo (asado), 6
Chilean chileno *adj.*, 2
chimney chimenea, 4
china loza, M5
Chinese chino *adj.*, 2; (language) chino, 1
choose escoger, 2
chop (pork) chuleta (de cerdo), 6
chore quehacer doméstico *m.*, 4
Christmas Navidad *f.;* Pascua, 8
Christmas Eve Nochebuena, 8
church iglesia, 3
circus circo, 8
citizen ciudadano(a), 14
city block cuadra, 9
claim recoger (j), 9
clam (thumbnail-size) chipichipi *m.*, 6
classical clásico *adj.*, 13
classmate compañero(a) de clase, 1
classroom sala de clase, 1
clay soil greda, 12
clean limpio *adj.*, 4
clean the house limpiar la casa, 4
clear the table quitar la mesa, 4
click (on) hacer click (sobre), 15

climb subida, 5
climb subir, 5
clock reloj *m.*, 1
close cerrar (ie), 4
closet armario, 4
clothes dryer secadora, 4
clothing ropa, 7
cloud forest bosque nuboso, 12
cloudy: it's cloudy está nublado, 3
coast costa, 8
coffee café *m.*, 6
coffee (side) table mesita, 4
cold catarro, resfriado, 5
it's cold hace frío, 3
Colombian colombiano *adj.*, 2
color color *m.*, 1
Columbus Day Día (*m.*) de la Maza, 8
comb one's hair peinarse, 5
come venir (ie), 4
Come on! ¡Venga!, 3
comedy comedia, 13
comfort comodidad *f.*, M3
comfortable cómodo *adj.*, 9
commercial anuncio, 13
compact disc (CD) disco compacto, 15
competitive examination for entrance into a school or job oposición *f.*, 1
complain about quejarse de, 9
composer compositor(a), 13
compound name nombre compuesto, 2
computer computadora, ordenador, 1
computer science computación *f.*, 1
concern preocupación *f.*, M2
concert concierto, 13
condiment condimento, 6
condominium condominio, 4
conference room sala de conferencias, 11
congested congestionado *adj.*, 5
congratulate felicitar, 10
Congratulations! ¡Felicitaciones!, 8
congress congreso, 14
connect conectar, 15
connection conexión *f.*, 15
conservation conservación *f.*, 12
conservative conservador(a) *adj.*, 2
conserve conservar, 12
constitution constitución *f.*, 14
construct construir, 12
continue seguir (i), 4
cook cocinar, 6
cook cocinero(a), 11
Cool! ¡Chévere!, 3
it's cool hace fresco, 3
co-parent compadre *m./f.*, 2
corn flour harina de maíz, 6

corner esquina, 4
corporation empresa, 11
corruption corrupción *f.*, 14
cost costar (ue), 4
Costa Mican costarricense *adj.*, 2
costume disfraz *m.*, 8
cot, light bed catre *m.*, 12
cotton algodón *m.*, 7
couch sofá *m.*, 4
cough tos *f.*, 5
cough toser, 5
cough syrup jarabe *m.*, 5
count contar (ue), 4
count on contar con, 3
country campo, 8
coup d'etat golpe de estado *m.*, 14
couple pareja, 10
course curso, 1
courtship noviazgo, 10
cousin primo(a), 2
cover portada, M5
cowardly cobarde *adj.*, 2
crash into chocarse (qu) con, 8
create crear, M1
credit card tarjeta de crédito, 7
crime crimen *m.*, 14
cross cruzar, 9
crowning of a queen coronación (*f.*) de una reina, 8
cruise liner crucero, 9
cry alarido, 12
cry llorar, 8
Cuban cubano *adj.*, 2
cultivate cultivar, 12
currency moneda, M4
curtain telón *m.*, M2
customs aduana, 9
cut down (trees) talar, 12
cyberspace ciberespacio, 15
cycling ciclismo, 3

D

daily cotidiano *adj.*, 13
dance baile *m.*, danza, 1
dance bailar, 1
type of dance bachata, 9
type of dance and music merengue *m.*, 9
dancer bailarín(ina), 13
dangerous peligroso *adj.*, M3
daring osadía, 13
dark-haired moreno *adj.*, 2
date (social) cita, 10
daughter hija, 2
daughter-in-law nuera, 2
day día *m.*, 1
day before yesterday anteayer *adv.*, 6
Day of the Dead Día (*m.*) de los Muertos, 8
Day of the Magi (Three Kings) Día (*m.*) de los Meyes Magos, 8
dazed atontado *adj.*, 12
dazzle deslumbrar, 13

dead muerto *adj.*, 4
deaf sordo *adj.*, M5
deal: it's a deal trato hecho, 14
dean decano(a), 1
debate debate *m.*, 14
December diciembre, 3
deer ciervo, 12
defend defender (ie), 14
defense defensa, 14
defenseless person desamparado(a), 13
delay demora, 9
delicacy manjar *m.*, 6
delicious rico *adj.*, 6
deluxe de lujo, 11
democracy democracia, 14
democratic demócrata *adj.*, 14
demonstration manifestación *f.*, 14
dense denso *adj.*, 12
dentist dentista *m./f.*, 11
departing for con destino a, 9
departure salida, 9
deposit (money) depositar, 11
desire afán *m.*, 12
desk escritorio, 1
dessert postre *m.*, 6
destroy destruir, 12
destroyed destruido *adj.*, 12
destruction destrucción *f.*, 12
detrimental perjudicial *adj.*, 14
develop desarrollar, 12
development desarrollo, 12
dial (the telephone) marcar (qu), P
dictator dictador(a), 14
dictatorship dictadura, 14
dictionary diccionario, 1
die morir (ue), 4
difference brecha, 14
digital camera cámara digital, 15
dining room comedor *m.*, 4
dinner cena, 6
direct dirigir, 13
director director(a), 13
dirty sucio *adj.*, 4
disaster desastre *m.*, 1
disconnect desconectar, 15
discount descuento, 7
discuss discutir, 14
dishwasher lavaplatos *m.*, 4
diskette disquete *m.*, 15
divorce divorcio, 10
divorced divorciado *adj.*, 2
dizziness mareo, 5
dizzy mareado *adj.*, 5
do hacer, 3
doctor médico *m./f.*, 5
documentary documental *m.*, 13
dog perro, 2
Dominican (from the Dominican Republic) dominicano *adj.*, 2
donate donar, 3

door puerta, 4
dormitory residencia, 1
downtown centro, 3
drama drama *m.*, 13
dramatic dramático *adj.*, 2
draw dibujar, 1
dress vestido, 7
dresser cómoda, 4; tocador *m.*, 4
drink beber, 2
drive (stakes in the ground) clavar (estacas), 12
drug addiction drogadicción *f.*, 14
drum tambora, 9
dry off secarse (qu), 5
duck pato, 12
due to dado que, 1
duty deber *m.*, 14

E
each cada *adv.*, M1
    each/every day (week, etc.) cada día (semana, etc.), 10
    each/every year cada año, 8
ear (outer) oreja, 5
    inner ear oído, 5
earache dolor de oídos *m.*, 5
early temprano *adv.*, 1
earring arete *m.*, 9
earth tierra, 12
east este *m.*, 9
Easter Pascua, 8
easy chair sillón *m.*, 4
eat comer, 2
    eat appetizers picar (qu), 6
    eat breakfast desayunar, 6
    eat lunch almorzar (ue), 4
    eat supper (dinner) cenar, 6
ecology ecología, 1
economics economía, 1
edge linde *f.*, 12
education educación *f.*, 1
effortless sin esfuerzo alguno, 7
Egyptian egipcio *adj.*, 2
eight ocho, P
eight hundred ochocientos, 4
eighteen dieciocho, P
eighty ochenta, 2
either . . . or o... o, 8
elbow codo, 5
elect elegir (i, i), 14
elections elecciones *f.*, 14
electric appliance electrodomésticos, 4
electrician electricista *m./f.*, 11
elephant elefante *m.*, 12
elevator ascensor *m.*, 4
eleven once, P
eliminate eliminar, 14
e-mail correo electrónico, 11
embark on emprender, M5
emergency exit salida de emergencia, 9
emergency room sala de emergencia, 5
emigrate emigrar, 1

employee empleado(a), 11
employment empleo, 14
encroachment acercamiento, 12
end terminar, 1
ending desenlace *m.*, M5
endless inagotable *adj.*, M1
engaged comprometido *adj.*, 10
engagement compromiso, 10
engineer ingeniero(a), 11
engineering ingeniería, 1
English (language) inglés *m.*, 1; inglés(esa) *adj.*, 2
enjoy disfrutar, 9
    Enjoy your meal! ¡Buen provecho!, 6
enter entrar, 1
entertain entretener (ie), 4
environment medio ambiente, 12
equality igualdad *f.*, 14
equipment equipo, 15
eraser borrador *m.*, 1
even though aunque *conj.*, 12
every year (day, month, etc.) todos los años (días, meses, etc.), 10
examine examinar, 5
exchange rate cotización *f.*, M4
excited emocionado *adj.*, 4
excuse me con permiso, perdón, disculpe, P
exercise hacer ejercicio, 3
existing vigente *adj.*, 14
expensive caro *adj.*, 7
explain explicar (qu), 9
exploit explotar, 12
exploitation explotación *f.*, 12
eye ojo, 5
eyebrows cejas, 5
eyelashes pestañas, 5

F
fabric tela, 7; tejido, 8
face rostro, M3; cara, 5
factory fábrica, 12
faith fe *f.*, M2
fall (season) otoño, 3
fall asleep dormirse (ue), 5
    fall in love (with) enamorarse (de), 10
false cognate cognado falso, 1
fan (sports) aficionado(a), 3
fancy de lujo *adj.*, 11
far (away) (from) lejos (de) *prep.*, 9
farm finca, 12
farm worker campesino(a), 12
farmer agricultor(a), 12
fat gordo *adj.*, 2
father padre *m.*, papá *m.*, 2
    father-in-law suegro, 2
fax machine fax *m.*, 11
feather pluma, M2
February febrero, 3
feel encontrarse, 5
    feel (good/bad) sentirse (bien/mal), 5

feel like (doing something) tener ganas de, 4
female hembra, 12
fifteen quince, P
fifty cincuenta, 2
figure cifra, 14
file archivo, 15
fill out (a form) llenar, 11
film película, 13
    action film película de acción, 13
    art film película de arte, 13
    classic film película clásica, 13
    foreign film película extranjera, 13
    horror film película de horror, 13
    mystery film película de intriga (misterio), 13
    romantic film película romántica, 13
    science fiction film película de ciencia ficción, 13
    western film película del oeste, 13
finally por fin *adv.*, 10
find encontrar, 5; atinar, 13
    find out about enterarse de, 11
fine bien *adv.*, P
    Fine, thanks. Bien, gracias., P
finger dedo, 5
fingernail uña, 5
finish terminar, 1
fire despedirse (i), 11
firefighter bombero(a), 11
fireplace chimenea, 4
firework fuego de artificio, M1
first primero, 10
    first name nombre *m.*, 2
fish pescar (qu), 8
    fish (dead) pescado, 6; **(live)** pez *m.*, 2
fit (someone) quedarle (a uno), 7
five cinco, P
five hundred quinientos, 4
flag: small flag banderín *m.*, 6
flat plano *adj.*, M1
    flat surface superficie plana *f.*, 4
flavor sabor *m.*, 5
flight attendant asistente de vuelo *m./f.*, 9
    (nonstop) flight vuelo (sin escala), 9
floor piso, 4
    floor covering alfombra, 8
flower flor *f.*, 10
focus enfocarse (qu), M2
folkloric folklórico *adj.*, 13
follow seguir (i), 1
    follow faithfully seguir fielmente, 3
food comida, 6
foolish tonto *adj.*, 2
foot pie *m.*, 5

football field campo de fútbol, 3

for para, por *prep.*
  for example por ejemplo, 12
  For what purpose? ¿Para qué?, 8

foreign extranjero *adj.*, M2
  foreign languages lenguas extranjeras, 1

forest bosque *m.*, 12

forty cuarenta, 2

fountain fuente *f.*, M3

fountain pen pluma, 1

four cuatro, P

four hundred cuatrocientos, 4

four-star hotel hotel de cuatro estrellas *m.*, 9

fourteen catorce, P

fox zorro, 12

free gratis *adj.*, 1
  free associated state estado libre asociado, 1

freedom of the press libertad *(f.)* de la prensa, 14

French (language) francés *m.*, 1; francés(esa) *adj.*, 2

fresh fresco *adj.*, 6

Friday viernes *m.*, 1

friend amigo(a), 1

friendly amable *adj.*, 2

friendship amistad *f.*, 10

from desde *prep.*, 1
  From where? ¿De dónde?, P

front desk recepción *f.*, 9

fruit fruta, 6
  fruit juice jugo de fruta, 6
  fruit store frutería, 3

fruitful fecundo *adj.*, 6

full-time de tiempo completo, 11

function (to work) funcionar, 15

furious furioso *adj.*, 4

G

game juego, partido, 3
  game show programa de concursos, 13

gap brecha, 14

garage garaje *m.*, 4

garden jardín *m.*, 4

garlic ajo, 6

gas station gasolinera, 3

gate puerta, 9

gem joya, M2

generous generoso *adj.*, 2

geography geografía, 1

geology geología, 1

German (language) alemán *m.*, 1; alemán(ana) *adj.*, 2

get conseguir (i), 4
  get + adjective ponerse + adjective, 4
  get a suntan broncearse, 8
  get along well (poorly) (with) each other llevarse bien (mal) (con), 10
  get away largarse, 13

get divorced (from) divorciarse (de), 10

get dressed vestirse (i), 5

get married casarse (con), 2

get off bajar(se) (de), 9

get sick enfermarse, 5

get together with reunirse con, 8

get up levantarse, 5

gift regalo, 8

girlfriend novia, 1

give dar, 3 ; **(as a gift)** regalar, 9
  give a party dar/hacer una fiesta, 8
  give oneself away delatar su presencia, 12

glove guante *m.*, 7

go ir, 3
  go by bike (boat, bus, car, plane, subway, taxi, train) ir en bicicleta (barco, autobús, coche, avión, metro, taxi, tren), 9
  go camping hacer camping, 8
  go canoeing/sailing pasear en canoa/velero, 8
  go for a walk dar un paseo, 3
  go horseback riding montar a caballo, 3
  go on a picnic hacer un picnic, 3
  go on foot ir a pie, 9
  go out salir, 3
  go shopping ir de compras, 3
  go through pasar por, 9
  go to a bar (club, concert) ir a un bar (club, concierto), 3
  go to a disco (party) ir a una discoteca (fiesta), 3
  go to bed acostarse (ue), 5
  go to the movies ir al cine, 3
  go up subir, 5

godchild ahijado(a), 2

godfather padrino, 2

godmother padrina, 2

golf golf *m.*, 3
  golf course campo de golf, 3

good bueno *adj.*, 2
  Good afternoon. Buenas tardes., P
  Good evening (night). Buenas noches., P
  Good morning. Buenos días., P

Good-bye. Adiós., P

good-looking guapo *adj.*, 2

gorilla gorila *m.*, 12

govern gobernar (ie), 14

government gobierno, 14

governor gobernador(a), 14

granddaughter nieta, 2

grandfather abuelo, 2

grandmother abuela, 2

grandson nieto, 2

grass hierba, M3

Great! ¡Genial!, 1

green verde *adj.*, 1

greet (each other) saludar(se), P

groom novio, 10

ground molido *adj.*, 6
  ground greda, 12

grow aumentar, 1; crecer, 14; **(plants)** cultivar, 12

growing creciente *adj.*, 15

Guatemalan guatemalteco *adj.*, 2

guerrilla guerrillero *m./f.*, 14

guest invitado *m./f.*, 8

gymnasium gimnasio, 1

H

hair pelo, 5
  hair salon peluquería

hairstylist peluquero(a), 11

Haitian haitiano *adj.*, 2

ham jamón *m.*, 6

hamburger hamburguesa, 6

hand mano *f.*, 5

handicrafts artesanía, 7

handshake apretón *(m.)* de manos, 11

happy contento *adj.*, 4

hard drive disco duro, 15

hard-boiled egg huevo duro, 6

hard-fought reñido *adj.*, M5

hardware store ferretería, 3

hardworking trabajador(a) *adj.*, 2

harmful perjudicial *adj.*, 14

hat sombrero, 7

haunted encantado *adj.*, 13

have tener (ie), P
  have breakfast desayunar, 6
  have lunch almorzar (ue), 4
  have supper (dinner) cenar, 6
  have a birthday cumplir años, 8
  have a cold tener gripe, 5
  have a cookout hacer una parrillada, 8
  have a cough tener tos, 5
  have a fever tener fiebre, 5
  have a good (bad) time pasarlo bien (mal), 8
  have a headache tener dolor de cabeza, 5
  Have a nice trip! ¡Buen viaje!, 9
  have chills tener escalofríos, 5
  have just (done something) acabar de + infinitive, 5
  have to (do something) tener que, 3

he él *pron.*, P

head cabeza, 5

headache dolor de cabeza *m.*, 5

health salud *f.*, 5

heart corazón *m.*, 5

heavy (meal, food) pesado *adj.*, 6

help (each other) ayudar(se), 1

hen gallina, 12

henhouse gallinero, 12

her, hers suyo *adj.*, 7

herb hierba, 5

here aquí *adv.*, P

heritage herencia, 8

hesitate titubear, 12

Hi! ¡Hola! (informal) P

hierarchy jerarquía, 11

highway carretera, 12

hike/walk in the mountains caminar por las montañas, 3

hill colina, 12

hippopotamus hipopótamo, 12

hire contratar, 11

his suyo *adj.*, 7

history historia, 1

hoe azada, 12

holiday fiesta, día feriado *m.*, 8

Holy Week Semana Santa, 8

home hogar *m.*, 4
  home page página de bienvenida (de entrada, de presentación, inicial, principal, de la red), 15
  home remedy remedio casero, 5

homework tarea, 1

Honduran hondureño *adj.*, 2

honest honesto *adj.*, 2

honesty honradez *f.*, M4

honeymoon luna de miel, 10

honor honrar, 8; cumplir con, 10

hope esperar, 1

hors d'oeuvre entremés *m.*, 8

host anfitrión *m.*, 8

hostess anfitriona, 8

hot (temperature) caliente *adj.*, 6
  it's hot hace calor, 3

hour hora

house casa, 4
  house of representatives cámara de representantes (diputados), 14
  house specialty especialidad *(f.)* de la casa, 6

housing vivienda, 4

How? ¿Cómo?, P
  How are you? ¿Cómo está usted? (formal); ¿Cómo estás? (informal), P
  How corny! ¡Qué cursi!, 3
  How does it look? ¿Cómo me queda?, 7
  How many? ¿Cuántos(as)?, P
  How much do I owe you? ¿Cuánto le debo?, 7
  How old are you? ¿Cuántos años tienes?, P

hug (each other) abrazar(se), 10

human (civil) rights derechos humanos (civiles), 14

humanities humanidades *f. pl.*, 1
humble humilde *adj.*, 2
humorous cómico *adj.*, 2
husband esposo, 2

I

I yo *pron.*
I (don't) like to (do something) (no) me gusta + infinitive, 1
I can't (eat) any more. No puedo más., 6
I can't take it anymore! ¡No suporto más!, 4
I wish that ojalá que, 12
I would like . . . Yo quisiera..., 6
I'm on a diet. Estoy a dieta., 6
I'm satisfied. I'm full. Estoy satisfecho(a)., 6
ice cream helado, 6
ideology ideología, 14
illiteracy analfabetismo, 14
illness enfermedad *f.*, 5
immigration inmigración *f.*, 9
impairment desmedro, 14
imprisonment encarcelamiento, 14
in en
in case (of) en caso (de) que *conj.*, 13
in conclusion en conclusión, 12
in danger of extinction en peligro de extinción, 12
in front of delante de *prep.*, 9
in itself en sí misma, 3
in light of a la luz de, M3
in order en regla, 8
in our time en nuestra época, 3
in regard to en cuanto a, 13
in the (morning, afternoon/evening) de/por la (mañana, tarde, noche), 1
in the flesh en carne propia, 13
increase aumentar, 14
indecisive indeciso *adj.*, 2
inequality desigualdad *f.*, 14
inexpensive barato *adj.*, 7
inflation inflación *f.*, 14
inform informar, 14
inform oneself about enterarse de, 11
information información *f.*, P
infrequently raras veces *adv.*, 8
instead en vez de, M2
intellectual intelectual *adj.*, 2
intelligent inteligente *adj.*, 2
international policy política internacional, 14
Internet Internet *m.*, 14
Internet service provider proveedor *(m.)* de servicios Internet, 15

interview entrevista, 11
introduction presentación *f.*, P
intuitive intuitivo *adj.*, 2
investigate investigar, 14
iron plancha, 4; hierro, 5
iron (clothes) planchar (la ropa), 4
irresponsible irresponsable *adj.*, 2
irrigate regar (ie) las plantas, 12
island isla, 9
It's on me (my treat). Te invito., 6
Italian (language) italiano, 1; italiano *adj.*, 2
item elemento, 3
its suyo *adj.*, 7

J

jacket chaqueta, 7
January enero, 3
Japanese (language) japonés *m.*, 1; japonés(esa) *adj.*, 2
jewelry joyas, 7
jewelry store joyería, 3
job puesto, 11
job hunt búsqueda de trabajo, 11
journalism periodismo, 1
journalist periodista *m./f.*, 11
judge juez *m./f.*, 10
July julio, 3
June junio, 3
jungle selva, 12
just solamente, 10

K

key llave *f.*, 9
keyboard teclado, 15
kidneys riñones *m.*, 5
kingdom reino, M2
kiss (each other) besar(se), 10
kitchen cocina, 4
knee rodilla, 5
know (each other) conocer(se), 3; (how) saber, 3
knowledgeable ilustrado *adj.*, 13
Korean coreano *adj.*, 2

L

lace encaje *m.*, M5
lack falta, 11; escasez *f.*, 12
lack carecer de, 15
lake lago, 8
lamp lámpara, 4
land tierra, 12
land aterrizar, 9
landscape paisaje *m.*, 12
language lengua, 1
laptop computer computadora portátil, 15
large grande *adj.*, 2
last durar, 11
last (week, month, year) (la semana, el mes, el año) pasado(a), 6

last name apellido, 2
last night anoche *adv.*, 6
late tarde *adv.*, 1
law derecho, 1; ley *f.*, 14
lawn césped *m.*, 4
lawyer abogado(a), 11
lazy perezoso *adj.*, 2
lead a peaceful life llevar una vida tranquila, 12
leaf hoja, 5
learn aprender, 2
learned ilustrado *adj.*, 13
leather cuero, 7
leave salir, dejar, 3
left of a la izquierda de *prep.*, 9
leg pierna, 5
lend prestar, 9
less . . . than menos... que, 5
lesson lección *f.*, 1
let dejar, 13
let's see vamos a ver, 6
lettuce lechuga, 6
liberal liberal *adj.*, 2
librarian bibliotecario(a), 1
library biblioteca, 1
life vida, 10
lift weights levantar pesas, 3
light luz *f.*, 1
light (meal, food) ligero *adj.*, 6
Lima: from Lima limeño *adj.*, 13
lion león *m.*, 12
listen (to music) escuchar (música), 1
literacy alfabetismo, 14
literature literatura, 1
live vivir, 2
lively despierto *adj.*, M1
liver hígado, 5
living room sala, 4
loan préstamo, 11
lobster langosta, 6
location ubicación *f.*, M3
lock candado, 4
long largo *adj.*, 2
look at each other mirarse, 10
look for buscar (qu), 1
lose perder (ie), 4
lost extraviado *adj.*, M3
love amor *m.*, 10
love querer (ie), 4; amar, 10
luggage (carry-on) equipaje (de mano) *m.*, 9
lunch almuerzo, 6
lungs pulmones *m.*, 5
luxurious lujoso *adj.*, 7

M

ma'am señora (Sra.), P
magazine revista, 14
maid criado(a), 11
main dish plato principal, 6
major, field of study carrera; especialización *f.*, 1
majority mayoría, 1
make hacer, 3

make a phone call llamar por teléfono, 11
make a stop (on a flight) (in) hacer escala (en), 9
make a toast hacer un brindis, 8
make available proveer, 11
make fun of burlarse de, 3
make one's bed hacer la cama, 4
make plans hacer planes, 3
male macho, 12
mall centro comercial, 3
mammal mamífero, 12
man hombre *m.*, 1
manager gerente *m./f.*, 11
map mapa *m.*, 1
March marzo, 3
market (outdoor) mercado (al aire libre), 3
marriage matrimonio, 10
married casado *adj.*, 2
marry casarse (con), 2
mask máscara, 8
master plumber maestro gasfitero, 13
masterpiece obra maestra
match hacer juego con, 7
math matemáticas, 1
May mayo, 3
mayor alcalde(sa), 14
meal comida, 6
means of communication medios de comunicación, 14
meat (beef) carne (de res) *f.*, 6
mechanic mecánico(a), 11
medical médico *adj.*, 5
medical history historial clínica *f.*, 5
medicine medicina, 1
meet conocer(se), 3
meeting reunión *f.*, 11
member of the family miembro de la familia, 2
menu menú *m.*, 6
merchant comerciante *m./f.*, 11
message mensaje *m.*, 15
messy desordenado *adj.*, 4
metropolis metrópolis *f.*, 12
Mexican mexicano *adj.*, 2
midnight medianoche *f.*, 1
milk leche *f.*, 6
million millón, 4
mind mente, 13
mine mío *adj.*, 7
minister ministro *m./f.*, 14
mirror espejo, 4
Miss señorita (Srta.), P
miss (a function) perder (ie), 4
modem módem *m.*, 15
modern moderno *adj.*, 2
monarchy monarquía, 14
Monday lunes *m.*, 1
money dinero, 1
monkey mono, 12
month mes *m.*, 3

more . . . than más... que, 5
mother madre *f.*; mamá, 2
   mother-in-law suegra, 2
mouse (of computer) ratón *m.*, 15
mouth boca, 5
move closer acercar (qu), 12
movie película, 13
   movie theater cine *m.*, 3
   movies cine *m.*, 13
mow the lawn cortar el césped, 4
Mr. señor (Sr.), P
Mrs. señora (Sra.), P
museum museo, 3
mushroom champiñón *m.*, 6
music música, 1
musical (play) función *(f.)*, 13
musician músico *m./f.*, 13
must deber (+ infinitive), 2
my mío *adj.*, 7

N

name: My name is . . . Me llamo..., P
narrate narrar, 4
narrow angosto *adj.*, 11
nationality nacionalidad *f.*, 2
native Spanish speaker hispanohablante *m./f.*
natural resources recursos naturales, 12
naturalist naturalista *m./f.*, 12
nature naturaleza, 12
near cerca de *prep.*, 9
neat ordenado *adj.*, 4; arreglado *adj.*, 9
neck cuello
necktie corbata, 7
need necesitar, 1; hacerse falta, M3
neighborhood barrio, P
neither . . . nor ni... ni, 8
   neither, not either tampoco *adv.*, 8
nephew sobrino, 2
never nunca *adv.*, 8
new nuevo *adj.*, 2
New Year's Eve Noche Vieja *f.*, 8
newlyweds recién casados *m.*, 10
news noticias, 13
newscast noticiero, 14
newspaper periódico, 14
next to al lado de *prep.*, 9
Nicaraguan nicaragüense *adj.*, 2
nice simpático *adj.*, 2
   it's nice (weather) hace buen tiempo, 3
   Nice to meet you. Encantado(a). Mucho gusto., P
niece sobrina, 2
night life vida nocturna, M3
nine nueve, P
nine hundred novecientos, 4
nineteen diecinueve, P
ninety noventa, 2

nobody, no one nadie, 8
noise ruido, 12
noisy ruidoso, 9
none, not any ningún, ninguno(a), 8
nonsmoking section sección de no fumar *f.*, 9
noon mediodía *m.*, 1
north norte *m.*, 9
   North American, American norteamericano *adj.*, 2
nose nariz *f.*, 5
notebook cuaderno, 1
nothing, not anything, at all nada, 8
November noviembre, 3
now ahora *adv.*, 1
number número, P; cifra, 14
nurse enfermero(a), 5

O

object objeto, 1
obtain conseguir (i), 4
ocean océano, 8
October octubre, 3
of course por supuesto, 2; ¡Cómo no!, 6
off apagado *adj.*, 15
offer ofrecer (zc), 9
office oficina, 1
   personal office despacho, 11
often muchas veces, 8
oil aceite *m.*, 6
   oil lamp quinqué *m.*, M2
   oil painting retrato al óleo, 13
old viejo *adj.*, 2
older mayor, P
oldest el mayor, 6
on encendido *adj.*, 15
   on the other hand por otro lado, 12
   on time a tiempo, 1
   on top of that para colmo, 4
once una vez *adv.*, 10
   once a month una vez al mes, 8
one uno, P
one hundred cien/ciento, 2
one thousand mil, 4
one-way ticket billete/ boleto de ida, 9
onion cebolla, 6
only sólo, P; solamente, 10
open abrir, 2
   open space espacio abierto, 4
opera ópera, 13
operating platform (system) plataforma de operación, 15
oppose oponer, 14
or o *conj.*, 3
orange (color) anaranjado *adj.*, 1
orange (fruit) naranja, 6
orchid orquídea, 12
order (food) pedir (i), 6
orphan huérfano(a), M3
others los (las) demás, 9

ought deber (+ infinitive), 2
our nuestro *adj.*, 7
outgoing extrovertido *adj.*, 2
oven (microwave) horno (de microondas), 4
overcoat abrigo, 7
overpopulation sobre-población *f.*, 12
overthrow derrocar (qu), 14
owl búho, 12
ox buey *m.*, 12
ozone layer capa de ozono, 12

P

pack one's suitcase(s) hacer la(s) maleta(s), 9
pain dolor *m.*, 5
painter pintor(a), 13
painting pintura, 1; cuadro, 4
Panamanian panameño *adj.*, 2
pancreas páncreas *m.*, 5
panther pantera, 12
panting jadeo, 5
pants (shorts) pantalones (cortos) *m.*, 7
paper papel *m.*, 1
parade procesión *f.*, 8
Paraguayan paraguayo *adj.*, 2
paramilitary group grupo paramilitar, 14
pardon me con permiso, perdón, disculpe, P
park parque *m.*, 3
   park ranger guardaparques *m./f.*, 12
parsley perejil *m.*, 6
part-time de tiempo parcial, 11
party (surprise) fiesta (de sorpresa), 8
pass pasar, 1; aprobar (ue), 14
passenger pasajero(a), 9
passing marcha, M1
Passover pascua, 8
passport pasaporte *m.*, 9
   passport control inmigración *f.*, 9
pastime pasatiempo, 3
pasture, grazing land pasto, 12
patient paciente *adj.*, 2; paciente *m./f.*, 5
patio patio, 4
patron saint santo(a), 2
pattern patrón *m.*, 7
pay pagar, 1
   pay in cash pagar en efectivo, 11
   pay in installments pagar a plazos, 11
peace paz *f.*, 14
peaceful tranquilo *adj.*, 12
peasant campesino(a), 12
pedestrian peatonal *adj.*, M3
pencil lápiz *m.*, 1
people gente *f.*, P
pepper pimienta, 6
percent por ciento, 7

percussion instrument scraped by a metal rod güira, 9
Peruvian peruano *adj.*, 2
pet mascota, 2
petroleum petróleo, 12
pharmacy farmacia, 5
philosophy filosofía, 1
phone llamar, 1
photocopier fotocopiadora, 11
photographer fotógrafo(a), 11
photography fotografía, 13
physical exertion esfuerzo físico, 5
physician médico *m./f.*, 5
physics física, 1
pick up recoger (j), 9
pickaxe barretilla, 13
piece pedazo, M2
pig chancha, 13
pill pastilla, 5
pilot piloto *m./f.*, 9
place lugar *m.*, 1
plaid de cuadros *adj.*, 7
plain llano, 12
plane avión *m.*, 9
plant cultivar, 5; sembrar (ie), 12
play drama *m.*, 13
   play jugar (ue), 4
   play a role interpretar, 13
   play an instrument tocar (qu), 1
   play tennis jugar al tenis, 3
player jugador(a), 3
playwright dramaturgo *m./f.*, 13
plaza plaza, 3
please por favor, P
pleasure: The pleasure is mine. El gusto es mío., P
plug in enchufar, 15
plugged in enchufado *adj.*, 15
plumber plomero(a), 11
poet poeta *m./f.*, 13
poetry poesía, 13
police officer policía *m./f.*, 11
political party partido político, 14
politician político *m./f.*, 14
polka-dotted de lunares *adj.*, 7
pollute contaminar, 12
polluted contaminado *adj.*, 12
pollution contaminación *f.*, 12
pool piscina, 3
poor pobre *adj.*, 2
popular popular *adj.*, 13
   popular rule mando popular, 14
port puerto, 9
portrayal retrato, M3
Portuguese (language) portugués *m.*, 1
position puesto, 11
post office oficina de correos, 3
potatoes (french fried) papas (fritas), 6

power poder *m.*, 14
practice practicar (qu), 1
pray orar, 8
prefer preferir (ie), 4
prepare preparar, 6
prescription receta, 5
president of the university presidente de la universidad *m./f.*, 1
press prensa, 14
pretty bonito *adj.*, 2
print imprimir, 11
printer impresora, 11
private privado *adj.*, 9
problem problema *m.*, 5
professor profesor(a), 1
program programar, 15
programmer programador(a), 11
progressive progresivo *adj.*, 2
project proyecto, 11
promise prometer, 9
protect proteger, 12
protest protestar, 14
provide proveer, 11
provided (that) con tal (de) que *conj.*, 13
psychiatrist siquiatra *m./f.*, 11
psychology sicología, 1
public transportation transporte *(m.)* público, 12
Puerto Mican puertorriqueño *adj.*, 2
pure puro *adj.*, 12
purple marrón *adj.*, 1
purse bolsa, 7
pursue seguir (i), 1
put (on) poner, 3
   put on makeup maquillarse, pintarse, 5

Q
quaint acogedoro *adj.*, M4
question pregunta, P
  question interpelar, 14
quiet reposado *adj.*, 6
quit dejar, 11
  quit the program salir del programa, 15

R
raid redada, 14
rain llover (ue), 4
raincoat impermeable *m.*, 7
raise recaudar, M5
rancher ranchero(a), 11
rarely raras veces *adv.*, 8
rate tasa, 14
Rather well. Bastante bien., P
rattlesnake víbora de cascabel, 12
react reaccionar, 8
read leer, 2
ready listo *adj.*, 2
realize darse cuenta, M3
reason razón *f.*, 12
rebellious rebelde *adj.*, 2
receive recibir, 2

receptionist recepcionista *m./f.*, 9
recommend recomendar (ie), 6
record grabar, 15
recycle reciclar, 12
red rojo *adj.*, 1
reduce reducir, 14
  reduce (in price) rebajar, 7
  reduction (in price) rebaja, 7
reforest reforestar, 12
reform reforma, 14
refrigerator refrigerador *m.*, 4
register registrarse, 9
relationships relaciones sentimentales *f.*, 10
relative pariente *m./f.*, 2
release soltar, M2
remember recordar (ue), 8
remote control control remoto *m.*, 15
report informe *m.*, 11; reportaje *m.*, 14
reporter reportero(a), 11
representative diputado(a), 14
republican republicano *adj.*, 14
request pedir (i), 9
reservation reserva, 9
reserved reservado *adj.*, 2
resign renunciar, 11
resolve resolver (ue), 12
respond responder, P
responsible responsable *adj.*, 2
rest (for an hour) descansar (por una hora), 1
restaurant restaurante *m.*, 3
résumé currículum *m.*, 11
retire jubilarse, 11
return volver (ue), 4
  return (home) regresar (a casa), 1
review reseña, M2
rhinoceros rinoceronte *m.*, 12
ribbon cinta, M5
rice arroz *m.*, 6
rich rico *adj.*, 2
riddle adivinanza, 2
ride a bike andar en bicicleta, 3
right of a la derecha de *prep.*, 9
ring anillo, 9
river río, 8
roar rugir (j), M3
rocket cohete *m.*, 8
role papel *m.*, 13
roof techo, 4
room cuarto, 1
roommate compañero(a) de cuarto, 1
root raíz *f.*, 13
rope soga, 13
roundness redondez *f.*, 4
round-trip ticket billete/ boleto de ida y vuelta, 9
rug alfombra, 8
rule reinar, 14
run correr, 3

run out acabar, 12
Russian (language) ruso, 1; ruso *adj.*, 2

S
sacred sagrado *adj.*, 8
sad triste *adj.*, 4
saint's day Día (*m.*) del santo, 8
salad ensalada, 6
salary salario, sueldo, 11
sale rebaja (*Spain*), 7
salesclerk dependiente *m./f.*, 7
salesperson vendedor(a), 11
salt sal *f.*, 6
Salvadoran salvadoreño *adj.*, 2
sandal sandalia, 7
sandwich sándwich *m.*, 6
satellite satélite *m.*, 15
  satellite dish antena parabólica, 15
Saturday sábado, 1
sauce salsa, 6
save ahorrar, 11; archivar, guardar, 15
savings account cuenta de ahorros, 11
say decir (i), P; articular, 13
  say good-bye despedirse (i), P
  Say no more! ¡No me digas más!, 11
scanner escáner *m.*, 15
scarf bufanda, 7
schedule horario, 9
school escuela, 1
science sciencias, 1
scream alarido, 12
screech chillido, M3
screen pantalla, 1
scuba-dive bucear, 8
sculpt esculpir, 13
sculptor escultor(a), 13
sculpture escultura, 13
sea mar *m.*, 8
  having to do with the sea marítimo *adj.*, 11
seafood mariscos, 6
season estación *f.*, 3
seat asiento, 9
secretary secretario(a), 1
see ver, 2
  See you later. Hasta luego. Nos vemos., P
  See you soon. Hasta pronto., P
  See you tomorrow. Hasta mañana., P
sell vender, 2
senate senado, 14
senator senador(a), 14
send (letters) mandar (cartas), 1
separate (from) separarse (de), 10
separated separado *adj.*, 2
separation separación *f.*, 10
September septiembre, 3

servant criado(a), 11
serve servir (i), 4
server servidor *m.*, 15
set the table poner la mesa, 4
seven siete, P
seven hundred setecientos, 4
seventeen diecisiete, P
seventy setenta, 2
sew coser, M2
shade sombra, 3
shaded sombreado *adj.*, M2
shadowed umbroso *adj.*, M2
shake hands darse la mano, 10
shameless person sinvergüenza *m./f.*, 4
share compartir, M2
shave afeitarse, 5
she ella *pron.*, P
shell concha, 6
shellfish mariscos, 6
shipping embarque *m.*, 11
shirt camisa, 7
shoe zapato, 7
  shoe size número, 7
  shoe store zapatería, 7
shop window aparador *m.*, 13
shoreline orilla, 9
short (height) bajo *adj.*; (length) corto *adj.*, 2
shortage escasez *f.*, 12
should deber (+ infinitive), 2
shout gritar, 8
show mostrar (ue), 7
  show (a movie) poner, 13
shower ducha, 4
shredded mechado, 6
shriek alarido, 12
shrimp (fried) camarones (fritos) *m.*, 6
shy tímido *adj.*, 2
sick enfermo *adj.*, 4
sign firmar, 10
silk seda, 7
silly tonto *adj.*, 2
similar parecido *adj.*, M1
simple sencillo *adj.*, M3
simplicity sencillez *f.*, M2
since dado que, 1
sincere sincero *adj.*, 2
sing cantar, 1
singer cantante *m./f.*, 13
single soltero *adj.*, 2
single (double) bed cama sencilla (doble), 9
sink into hundirse, 6
sir señor (Sr.), P
sister hermana, 2
  sister-in-law cuñada, 2
six seis, P
six hundred seiscientos, 4
sixteen dieciséis, P
sixty sesenta, 2
size (clothing) talla, 7
skates (in-line) patines (en línea) *m.*, 3
skate (in-line) patinar (en línea), 3
ski (water) esquiar (en el agua), 3

skin piel *f.*, 5
skirt falda, 7
skis (water) esquís (acuáticos)
  m. (3
skyscraper rascacielos *m.*, 12
sleep dormir (ue), 4
slice tajada, 6
slightly ligeramente *adv.*, M2
slip away deslizarse, 12
small pequeño *adj.*, 2
smart listo *adj.*, 2
smoking section sección de
  fumar *f.*, 9
snake culebra, 12
sneeze estornudar, 5
snorkel hacer esnórquel, 8
so entonces *adv.*, 10
  So . . . Así que..., 2
  so that para que *conj.*, 13
soap opera telenovela, 3
soccer (football) fútbol (americano) *m.*, 3
sociology sociología, 1
socks calcetines *m. pl.*, 7
sofa sofá *m.*, 4
soft drink refresco, 6
solar energy energía solar, 12
soldier soldado (la mujer soldado), 11
solve resolver (ue), 12
some algún, alguno(a/os/as), 8
somebody alguien, 8
someone alguien, 8
something algo, 8
sometimes a veces *adv.*, 8
son hijo, 2
  son-in-law yerno, 2
song canción *f.*, 13
So-so. Así así. Más o menos., P
soul alma, 8
  soul mates almas gemelas, 3
soup sopa, 6
source fuente *f.*, M1
south sur *m.*, 9
Spanish (language) español
  m., 1; español(a) *adj.*, 2
speak hablar(se), 1
speakers altavoces *m.*, 15
species especies *f.*, 12
speech discurso, 14
spend (time) pasar, 1;
  (money) gastar, 7
spew babear, M3
sport deporte *m.*, 3
  sports program programa
    deportivo, 13
  sports season temporada de
    deporte, 3
spring primavera, 3
squid (fried) calamares
  (fritos) *m.*, 6
stadium estadio, 3
stage escenario, M2
stairs escalera, 4
start comenzar (ie), 3
statehood estadidad *f.*, M5
stationery store papelería, 3
stay quedarse, 9
  stay in bed guardar cama, 5

steak bistec *m.*, 6
step paso, 7
stepbrother hermanastro, 2
stepfather padrastro, 2
stepmother madrastra, 2
stepsister hermanastra, 2
stereo estéreo, 15
stick (stakes in the ground)
  clavar (estacas), 12
still aún *adv.*, M2
stingy tacaño *adj.*, 2
stockbroker accionista *m./f.*,
  11
stockings medias, 7
stomach estómago, 5
stone piedra, M3
  stone wall muralla de
    piedra, 9
stop parada, M3
  stop parar(se), 9
store tienda, 3
story historia, 4; cuento, relato, 13
stove estufa, 4
straight derecho, 9
stream arroyo, 12
street calle *f.*, 3
strike huelga, 14
striped de rayas, 7
stroll paseo, 7
strong suit, sharpest sense
  agudeza particular, 12
student estudiante *m. /f.*, 1
  student center centro estu-
    diantil, 1
study estudiar, 1
stuff rellenar, 6
stupefied atontado *adj.*, 12
style estilo, 7
  It's the latest style! ¡Está de
    última moda!, 7
subscriber abonado(a), 15
subsequent subsiguiente, M2
succeed lograr, 13
suddenly de repente, 8
sue demandar, 14
suit traje *m.*, 7
suitcase maleta, 9
summer verano, 3
sunbathe tomar el sol, 3
Sunday domingo, 1
sunglasses gafas de sol, 3
sunny: it's sunny hace sol, 3
suntan lotion crema bronceadora, 8
supermarket supermercado,
  3
supper cena, 6
support apoyo, 13
  support apoyar, respaldar,
    14
surf correr las olas, 8
  surf the Net navegar la red,
    15
surround rodear, 11
surrounded rodeado *adj.*, 9
sweater suéter *m.*, 7
sweep the floor barrer el
  piso, 4

sweet dulce *adj.*, M1
swim nadar, 3
swimming natación *f.*, 3
symptom síntoma *m.*, 5
systems analyst analista de
  sistemas *m./f.*, 11

T
table mesa, 4
take tomar
  take (classes/tests) tomar
    (clases/exámenes), 1
  **take (someone's) tempera-
    ture** tomarle la tempe-
    ratura (a alguien), 5
  take a bath bañarse, 5
  take a look around echar
    una ojeada alrededor, 12
  take a risk arriesgarse (ue),
    15
  take a shower ducharse, 5
  take advantage aprovechar,
    14
  take care (of oneself)
    cuidar(se), 5
  take off (clothing) quitarse,
    5; **(airplane)** despegar, 9
  take out the garbage sacar
    la basura, 4
  take pictures sacar fotos, 3
  take place tener lugar, 6;
    llevar a cabo, 8
  take pride in something
    enorgullecerse, 3
  take turns tomar turnos, 4
talk (with each other)
  hablar(se), 1
  talk show programa de en-
    trevistas, 13
tall alto *adj.*, 2
taxes impuestos, 14
tea (iced) té (helado) *m.*, 6
teach enseñar, 1
teacher maestro(a), 11
technical school politécnico, 1
technician técnico *m./f.*, 11
telecommute teletrabajar, 15
tell decir (i), P; contar (ue), 4
ten diez, P
tennis shoe (sneaker) zapato
  de tenis (deportivo), 3
terrace terraza, 4
terrorism terrorismo, 14
test examen *m.*, 1
that que *pron.*, 3; ese(a) *adj.*;
  (over there) aquel (aquella)
  adj., 6
theater teatro, 1
then luego, entonces *adv.*, 10
there allí *adv.*, P
there is, there are hay, P
therefore por eso, 12
they ellos(as) *pron.*, P
thick espeso *adj.*, M3
thin delgado *adj.*, 2
think pensar (ie), 4
thirteen trece P
thirty treinta P
this este(a) *adj.*, 6

this one éste *pron.*, 6
three tres P
three hundred trescientos, 4
three-toed sloth perezoso con
  tres dedos, 12
throat garganta, 5
throughout durante *prep.*, M3
throw tirar, 10
Thursday jueves *m.*, 1
ticket billete *m.*, boleto, 3
tidy arreglado *adj.*, 9
tiger tigre *m.*, 12
time hora; vez
  a good time un buen rato, 3
timid tímido *adj.*, 2
tiredness cansancio, 5
toast brindis *m.*, 8
toaster tostadora, 4
today hoy *adv.*, 1
toe dedo de pie, 5
toilet inodoro, 4
tolerant tolerante *adj.*, 2
tomato tomate *m.*, 6
tomorrow mañana *adv.*, 1
tongue lengua, 5
too también *adv.*, 8
  too much demasiado *adv.*, 9
tools herramientas, 12
tooth diente *m.*, 5
touch tocar (qu), 1
  touch each other tocarse
    (qu), 10
tourism turismo, 1
toward hacia *adv.*, 9
town pueblo, 3; aldea, 8
traditional women's tunic
  huipil *m.*, 8
traffic tráfico, 12
train station estación de
  trenes *f.*, 9
tranquil tranquilo *adj.*, 12
translator traductor(a), 11
trash basura, 12
travel viajar, 1
  travel agency agencia de
    viajes, 9
  travel agent agente de
    viajes *m./f.*, 9
traveler viajero(a), 5
tree árbol *m.*, 3
trip viaje *m.*, 9
truth verdad *f.*, 1
try on probarse (ue), 7
T-shirt camiseta, 7
Tuesday martes *m.*, 1
tuition matrícula, 1
turkey pavo, 6
turn doblar, 9
  turn off apagar (ue), 15
  turn on prender, 15; **(TV)**
    poner, 13
  turn onto (street) dar la
    vuelta a, 13
twelve doce, P
twenty veinte, P
twenty-one veintiuno, P
twenty-six veintiséis, P
twenty-three veintitrés, P
twenty-two veintidós, P

twice (three times, etc.) dos (tres, etc.) veces, 10
two dos, P
two hundred doscientos(as), 4

U

U.S.: from the United States estadounidense *adj.*, 2
ugly feo *adj.*, 2
umbrella paraguas *m.*, 7
unaccustomed insólito *adj.*, 12
uncle tío, 2
underappreciated envilecido *adj.*, M1
understand comprender, P; entender (ie), 4
unemployment desempleo, 14
unforgettable inolvidable *adj.*, 13
university universidad *f.*, 1
unknown desconocido *adj.*, M3
unless a menos que *conj.*, 13
unpleasant antipático *adj.*, 2
unplug desenchufar, 15
untie desatar, 6
until hasta *adv.*, 9; hasta que *conj.*, 13
unusual insólito *adj.*, 12
up to hasta *adv.*, 9
up to date al día, 14
URL Localizador Uniforme de Recursos *m.*, 15
Uruguayan uruguayo *adj.*, 2
use usar, 1

V

vacuum pasar la aspiradora, 4
vacuum cleaner aspiradora, 4
valley valle *m.*, 12
VCR videocasetera, 15
vegetable vegetal *m.*, verdura, 6
Venezuelan venezolano *adj.*, 2
Very well. Muy bien., P
veterinarian veterinario *m./f.*, 11
video camera videocámara, 15
videotape videocasete *m.*, 15
viewer espectador(a), 13
village aldea, 8
vinegar vinagre *m.*, 6
visit visitar, 1
visit a museum visitar un museo, 3
volcano volcán *m.*, 12

volleyball vólibol *m.*, 3
vote voto, 14
vote votar, 14

W

wagon carreta, 12
wait esperar, 1
waiter (waitress) camarero(a), 6
waiting room sala de espera, 5
wake up despertarse (ie), 5
walk caminata, 7
walk caminar, 1
wall pared *f.*, 4
wallet cartera, 7
want desear, 1; querer (ie), 4
war guerra, 14
wardrobe armario, 4
warm cálido *adj.*, 15
wash (dishes, clothes, windows) lavar (los platos, la ropa, las ventanas), 4
wash up lavarse, 5
washing machine lavadora, 4
waste desperdicio, 12
watch mirar, 1
watch a movie ver una película, 3
watch television mirar la tele, 3
water the plants regar (ie) las plantas, 4
water: carbonated/noncarbonated mineral water agua (*f.*) mineral con/sin gas, 6
waterfall catarata, 12
wavy ondulado *adj.*, 4
we nosotros(as) *pron.*, P
weakness debilidad *f.*, 5
weapon arma *m.*, 12
wear usar, llevar, 7
wear a costume disfrazarse, 8
weather tiempo, 3
weather report (forecast) pronóstico del tiempo, 13
weaving tejido, 8
web page página web, 15
wedding boda, 10
Wednesday miércoles *m.*, 1
week semana, 1
weekend fin (*m.*) de semana, 1
Welcome! ¡Bienvenido!, 9
well pozo, 12

well done bien asado, 6
west oeste *m.*, 9
western highlands altiplano occidental, 8
what lo que *pron.*, 10
What? Which? ¿Qué?, P
What a coincidence! ¡Qué casualidad!, P
What time is it? ¿Qué hora es?, 1
What would you like (to eat)? ¿Qué te apetece?, 6
What's new? ¿Qué hay? (informal), P
What's the matter with you? ¿Qué te pasa?, 5
What's the problem? ¿Qué tiene usted?, 5
What's up? ¿Qué tal? (informal), P
What's your address? ¿Cuál es tu dirección? (informal), P
What's your name? ¿Cómo se llama usted? (formal); ¿Cómo te llamas? (informal); ¿Cuál es tu nombre? (informal), P
What's your telephone number? ¿Cuál es tu número de teléfono? (informal), P
when cuando *conj.*, 13
When? ¿Cuándo?, P
Where? ¿Dónde?, P
Where (to)? ¿Adónde?, 8
Where are you from? ¿De dónde eres tú? (informal); ¿De dónde es usted? (formal), P
which que *pron.*, 3
Which? ¿Cuál(es)?, P
white blanco *adj.*, 1
who que *pron.*, 3; quien *pron.*, 10
Who? ¿Quién(es)?, P
Whose? ¿De quién(es)?, 8
Why? ¿Por qué?, P
widow viuda, M2
widowed viudo *adj.*, 2
widower viudo *adj. noun*, M2
wife esposa, 2
wildlife preserve refugio natural, 12
win ganar, 3
window ventana, 4; ventanilla, 9

windy: it's windy hace viento, 3
wine (white, red) vino (blanco, tinto), 6
winner ganador(a), 13
winter invierno, 3
wish desear, 1
with con *prep.*
with regard to con respecto a, 11
withdraw (money) sacar (qu), 11
without sin *prep.*; sin que *conj.*, 13
witness testigo *m./f.*, 10
wolf lobo, 12
woman mujer *f.*, 1
Wonderful! ¡Qué bueno!, 2
wool lana, 7
word palabra, 1
work trabajo, 11
work (at night) trabajar (por la noche), 1
work (of art) obra (de arte), 13
worker; laborer obrero(a), 11
worried preocupado *adj.*, 4
worse peor, 5
worst el peor, 6
write escribir, 2
writer escritor(a), 13

Y

yacht yate *m.*, 9
year año, 3
yellow amarillo *adj.*, 1
yes sí, P
yesterday ayer *adv.*, 6
you tú, usted(es), vosotros(as) *pron.*, P
young joven *adj.*, 2
younger menor, 5
youngest el menor, 6
your, yours tuyo, vuestro, suyo *adj.*, 7

Z

zebra cebra, 12
zero cero, P
zoology zoología, 1

Índice

Credits

Text Credits

Plaza 1: Reprinted by permission of Center for Latino Studies in the Americas http://www.usfca.edu/celasa/
El laberinto de la soledad **by Octavio Paz. México: Fondo de Cultura Económica, 1973.**
Capítulo 4: *70 m²* by Lourdes Vijande, photography by Amparo Garrido, reprinted from *EL PAÍS Semanal,* Madrid, España, No. 1.202. 10 octubre 1999.
Concepto urbano by Isabel Núñez, reprinted from *EL PAÍS Semanal,* Madrid, España, No. 1.176, 11 abril 1999.
Capítulo 5: *Los cinco mandamientos de la automedicación* by Juan Manuel Barberá, reprinted from *Quo,* Madrid, España, No. 14, noviembre 1996.
Capítulo 6: "Oda al tomate" from *Odas elementales* by Pablo Neruda. Reprinted by permission of Agencia Literaria Carmen Balcells. © 1954
La primavera la moda altera by Marisol Abejón, reprinted from *CNR,* Madrid, España, No. 25, marzo 1999.
Plaza 2: *La casa de Bernarda Alba* by Federico García Lorca from Obras Completas (Galaxia Gutenburg, 1996 edition) ©Heredos de Federico Garcia Lorca. All rights reserved. For information regarding rights and permissions for works by Federico Garcia Lorca, please contact William Peter Kosmas, Esq., 8 Franklin Square, London W14 9UU, England.
Capítulo 8: *Guía del Viajero: Guatemala* by Cristina Morató, reprinted from *Rutas del Mundo,* Barcelona, España, No. 33, noviembre 1992.
Capítulo 9: *Los mejores destinos - Noches calientes en La Habana* by Guillem Gayà reprinted from *CNR,* Madrid, España, No. 16, julio 1998.
La chancha encantada from http://rtpnet.org/~felipe/literatura.htm#Chancha, reprinted by permission of Octavio Polo Briceño, Pacasmayo, Perú.
Plaza 3: Excerpt from "Flores del volcán" from FLOWERS FROM THE VOLCANO, by Claribel Alegría, translated by Carolyn Forché. Reprinted by permission of the University of Pittsburgh Press. (c) 1982
Capítulo 10: *Correo de am*or reprinted from *El Mundo,* Madrid, España, 1–7 octubre 1987, p. 5.
Capítulo 11: *El Jefe* (fragment) by Dimas Lidio Pitty reprinted from http://www.geocities.com/Athens/Olympus/9427/pitty.html
Plaza 4: *Responso por el niño Juan Manuel* by Carmen Naranjo, reprinted by permission of Editorial Universitaria Centroamericana, San José, Costa Rica, 1991.
Capítulo 14: *Disminuye diferencia de sueldos entre mujeres y hombres* by Sandra Rojas W., reprinted from *La Tercera,* 9 enero 2000.
Capítulo 15: *Cartero electrónico (Quiero tener un millón de amigos, E-mail)* by Ruy Xoconostle Waye, reprinted from *Quo,* Madrid, España, no. 23, septiembre 1999.
Plaza 5: "Tosca" from *Cuentos de Eva Luna* by Isabel Allende. Barcelona: Plaza & Janes, 1991.

Photo Credits

Photos from Corbis Images:
1 HR009566 Window to Plaza Vieja by Jeremy Horner; **20** GM004764 ice Rink in Rockefeller Center by Gail Mooney; **25** MY006582 Spinning Ride at Fiesta Texas by Buddy Mays; **58** SY0012028 Family of Prospector in Mexico by Pablo Corral;

59 ZEJ12159570 Gloria Estefan dancing at concert; 72 PC002560 People dancing by Pablo Corral, PT011586 Families in Bogota's Plaza Bolivar by the Purcell Team; 76 TP004643 Soccer player Carlos Valderrama by Jean-Yves Ruszniewski; 100 IA001614 Octavio Pissaro by Anna Clopet; 102 HZ00121 Fernando Botero by Marianne Haas; 100 130 OF010085 Spectators gather to watch World... by Owen Franken; 134 TD001506 La Paz by Penny Tweedy ; 143 OF006721 Woman selling coca leaves by Owen Franken; 148 OF006821 Pouring Argentine Yerba Mate by Owen Franken; 158 PC001112 Plaza Bolivar in Caracas by Pablo Corral; 163 PC002459 Woman putting arepas on a grill by Pablo Corral; 180 UG001754 The tomato; 184 FA001447 Interior of palatial House by Fernando Alda; 185 BB003639 Inside a Monte Carlo Restaurant in Morton Beebe, S.F., 58839 Seafood dinner by Chandra Clarke; 187 (second from bottom) PC003043 Miss Venezuela Contestants; 193 HB 001062 Buenos Aires shopping arcade by Hubert Stadler; 202 LJ001142 Tango dancers performing Tango by Abilio Lope; 219 IH013993 Girls with banners in parade by Jan Butchofsky-Houser; PT011902 Busy Downtown San Salvador Street by The Purcell Team; 225 GR013874 Sunday market outside San Tomas by Galen Rowell; 232 ME003825 Musician and dancer in Fiesta parade by Macduff Everton; 242 MY005551 Painted Mayan mask by Buddy Mays; 244 WK0188370 Old San Juan Plaza de Armas by Wolfgang Kaehler; 249 TA005808 Dancing the Merengue by Tony Arruza; 261 DH007208; 271 DH10586 Students working in a library by David G. Houser; 273 TA001648 Santo Domingo Landmarks by Tony Arruza, BL001872 Hotel Inglaterra by Richard Bickel; 276 DH003800 Beach at Vina del Mar by David G. Houser; 277 PT011981 Tegucigalpa Plaza by The Purcell Team; 281 RR016682 A romantic dinner by Roger Rossmeyer; 289 PC004248 Couple at their wedding by Pablo Corral; 300 DY005757 French Monument in Plaza by Danny Lehman; 304 AL009607 Panama Canal by Paul Almasy; 330 OG001474 Basilica of Our Lady of the Angels by Martin Rogers; 335 BV006081 Braulio Carillo National Park by Brian Vikander; 342 MD003302 Red-bellied turtle on a rock by Joe McDonald; 355 WK016239 Paine Valley by Wolfang Kaehler; 356 HT009744; 358 TU001112 Portrait of Violeta Chamorro in Nicaragua; 360 FT0039461, CL003341 Ruben Blades in Concert; 361 PC003362 Visitors wartching Ecuadorian painter Oswaldo Guayasamin by Pablo Corral, NW011666 Plaza Independencia in Quito, Ecuador, by Nik Wheeler; 384 ME009614 Santiago, Plaza de la Constitución by Macduff Everton; 411 DH007392 Plaza in Downtown Montevideo by David G. Houser;

Photos from other sources:
97 © Fernando Botero, courtesy, Marlborough Gallery, New York; 104 The Viesti Collection; 108 Polly Phillips photographer; 118 Polly Phillips photographer; 121 (left) Scala/Art Resource, NY; (right) Art Resource, NY; 122 (top) Erich Lessing/Art Resource, NY; (bottom) John Bigelow Taylor/Art Resource, NY; 183 AP/Wide World Photos; 187 (top) AP/Wide World Photos; (second photo from top and last at bottom) Victor Engelbert; 188 " a.g.e. fotostock; 189 (top) Stuart Cohen/The Image Works; 255 Steve Ferry/Liason Agency; 275 Courtesy of The Curbstone Press; 276 (right) Jimmy Dorantes/latin Focus; 372 Victor Engelbert; 392 (left) Carlos Carrion/Corbis Sygma; (right) Victor Engelbert; 396 Despotovic Dusko/Corbis Sygma; 435, 437 Susan Greenwood/Liason Agency; 438 Fotex/Shooting Star; 439 (top only) Cornell Capa/Magnum Photos; (all others) Christie's Images; 440 (right) Ron Sachs/Corbis Sygma; 441 (left) AFP/Corbis; (right) John Van Hassel/Corbis Sygma

All the other photos are from the Heinle & Heinle Image Resource Bank.

MAR CANTÁBRICO

FRANCIA

Avilés · Gijón
La Coruña · Santander
· PRINCIPADO
Lugo · DE ASTÚRIAS · Oviedo CANTABRIA Bilbao San Sebastián
PAÍS PIRINEOS
GALICIA Cordillera Cantábrica León VASCO Pamplona ANDORRA
· Pontevedra COM. FORAL
Vigo Palencia · Burgos DE NAVARRA
Zamora LA RIOJA ARAGÓN CATALUÑA
CASTILLA Y LEÓN R. Duero Valladolid Ebro Zaragoza Lérida
Sistema Ibérico · Barcelona
· Braga Salamanca Tarragona
· Oporto Segovia MAR
Sierra de Guadarrama MADRID MEDITERRÁNEO
· Ávila · Madrid
MENORCA
PORTUGAL Toledo MALLORCA
Coimbra · Valencia ISLAS Palma de
Tajo CASTILLA-LA MANCHA BALEARES Mallorca
· Cáceres
EXTREMADURA Júcar EIVISSA (IBIZA)
Mérida Almadén · Ciudad Real Albacete COMUNIDAD
Lisboa · Badajoz R. Guadiana VALENCIANA FORMENTERA
Setúbal Sierra Morena Alicante
Linares
R. Guadalquivir · Córdoba Murcia
· Jaén REGIÓN
ANDALUCÍA DE MURCIA Cartagena
· Sevilla Granada
Huelva Sierra Nevada ISLAS CANARIAS LANZAROTE
Jerez de la Almería Arrecife
Frontera Málaga Santa Cruz
Cádiz de la Palma FUERTEVENTURA
LA PALMA · Tenerife
OCÉANO Algeciras SANTA Puerto
ATLÁNTICO Estrecho de Gibraltar GOMERA CRUZ Las Palmas del
Tánger Ceuta (Esp.) Rosario
GRAN CANARIA
Melilla (Esp.)
Malabo
MARRUECOS CAMERÚN
GUINEA
ECUATORIAL
0 50 100 150 millas ÁFRICA
0 50 100 150 250 kilómetros GABÓN

SPAIN ◆◆◆

Word stress and written accents

In Spanish the natural stress of words most commonly occurs on the second-to-the-last syllable, or the last syllable—more commonly on the former. Words that deviate from the norm must carry a written accent mark, known as the **acento ortográfico,** to indicate where the stress of the word falls. The following three principles describe where word stress occurs and when a written accent is necessary:

1. The pronunciation of words that end in a vowel or in the consonants **n** or **s** are stressed on the second-to-the-last syllable:

problem	pro-**ble**-ma	trabajo	tra-**ba**-jo
resumen	re-**su**-men	bailas	**bai**-las

2. Words that end in a consonant other than **n** or **s** are stressed on the last syllable:

bailar	bai-**lar**	similar	si-mi-**lar**
normal	nor-**mal**	reloj	re-**loj**

3. If a word does not follow one of the first principles described above, the word is an exception to the norm and must carry a written accent to indicate where the stress falls:

sofá	árbol	comerás	menú	función

Dividing syllables in a word

Dividing syllables in Spanish can be summarized in four principles for both consonants and vowels:

Consonants

1. Spanish is a language that favors the pronunciation of vowels over consonants. The simplest syllable is formed by the combination of a consonant and a vowel (rather than a vowel and a consonant):

mi	tu	la	su

2. If a consonant is found between two vowels, it is united with the second vowel:

baila	bai-**la**	oro	o-**ro**